Vietnam Order of Battle

Vietnam Order of Battle

by Shelby L. Stanton

U.S.News Books

Washington, D.C.

Vietnam Order of Battle
By Shelby L. Stanton

U.S.News Books

Editor/Publisher
Roy B. Pinchot

Editor
Herb Golden

Book Design
Roy A. Teller

Cover Design
Feldman McPherson Topin, Inc.

Director of Production
Harold F. Chevalier

Production Coordinator
Diane Breunig Freed

Production Assistant
Mary Ann Haas

Picture Coordination
Leah Bendavid-Val
Chandley McDonald

Art Staff
Raymond J. Ferry
David Riss
Gregory A. Johnson

Editorial Assistance
Ina Bloomberg
H. Samuel Willis

Copy Staff
Glenna Mickelson
Barbara M. Clark
Carol Bashara
Sharon Turner

Quality Control Director
Joseph Postilion

Director of Sales
James Brady

Business Manager
Robert Licht

U.S.News Books, a division of U.S.News & World Report, Inc.

Library of Congress Cataloging in Publication Data

Stanton, Shelby L., 1948-
  U.S. Army order of battle, Vietnam.

  Bibliography: p.
  Includes index.
    1. Vietnamese Conflict, 1961-1971 — United States.
2. United States.   Army — Organization.   I. Title.
DS558.2.S73   959.704'33'73   81-12929
ISBN 0-89193-700-5   AACR2

This book is dedicated to my wife, Kathryn

Contents

List of Maps

List of Tables

Foreword

A veteran of the war in Vietnam and a former captain in the United States Army Special Forces, Shelby Stanton has prepared a work of rare commemorative and historical value. It will go a long way toward preserving important facts about the U.S. Army's role in the war in Vietnam.

The author has provided, for example, brief but authoritative histories of all major units; their commanders, locations, and principal activities; dates of arrival and departure, including those of subordinate units; and myriad details on smaller units. There are descriptions of combat methods, of organization for combat, of weapons and equipment. There are numerous pages of photographs that graphically preserve a record of the Vietnam experience, detailed charts and 32 pages of color reproductions of unit insignia and badges.

The encyclopedic detail that the author has assembled is unequaled for any war in which the United States Army has engaged. For example, although the army has published a prodigious multivolume official history of World War II, there is no comparable order of battle. To find the kind of material on World War II that the author has put together in convenient and visually exciting form on Vietnam, a researcher would have to turn to a multitude of yellowing documents in various depositories, if indeed he could ever locate all the material at all.

By assuring that this kind of information about Vietnam is available for the veteran, the historian and others and that it will be preserved indefinitely, Shelby Stanton and U.S.NEWS BOOKS have made a major contribution to the history of a unique war and a troubled era.

WILLIAM C. WESTMORELAND
General — United States Army, Retired

Former Commander, United States Military Assistance Command, Vietnam

Former Chief of Staff, United States Army

Preface

Vietnam Order of Battle details the composition of the U.S. Army during the conflict from 1961 – 73 and is concerned primarily with ground forces and organization. Emphasis has been placed on listing units and their terms of service, locations, previous stations, authorized strengths and command relationships. Additionally, unit functions, organizations and missions have been highlighted. Only in the case of critical independent commands have brief historical narratives and the names of commanding officers been furnished. Though strictly speaking beyond the scope of a U.S. Army compendium, units of other services and allies have received mention because of the joint nature of the military effort within Vietnam and the resulting impact on U.S. Army operations.

Several topics were added because of their relationship to the overall theme of this work. The U.S. Army organization section was added to familiarize the reader with the army's structure and general mode of combat in Vietnam. A listing of selected major operations was included within that section to place unit terms of service in historical perspective. Photographs of army weapons, aircraft, vessels, vehicles, transport and engineer equipment are included to familiarize the reader with those items as they were used by their respective units. A section on Army Medal of Honor recipients has been included to illustrate the critical role of individual heroism in a war fought mainly at the small-unit level.

Though this author has enjoyed the assistance and cooperation of the Department of the Army's Chief of Military History and other military officials, it must be emphasized that this book is the effort of a private citizen. However, it contains no material not warranted by official records and documents, all of which are fully cited in the source notes at the end of this volume.

While the Office of the Chief of Military History is currently preparing an extensive history of the Vietnam war and has already compiled an advance series of Vietnam Studies, it has no plans to publish a convenient one-volume directory of the U.S. Army Order of Battle in Vietnam.

Finally, since this work is intended as an historical order of battle and record of service, it does not attempt to trace lineage or matters of unit heraldry.

Acknowledgments

Many individuals have contributed their time and expertise toward making this book possible and the author is indebted to them all. Special praise must go to Dr. Robert K. Wright and Mr. Charles B. MacDonald, whose diligence and insight were instrumental during all phases of research. Outstanding help was offered by members of the Army's Office of the Chief of Military History, particularly Colonel William F. Strobridge, Ms. Janice E. McKenney, Mr. John B. Wilson, Mr. Vincent H. Demma, Ms. Hannah M. Zeidlik, Dr. Young G. Chang, Mr. Jefferson Powell and Ms. Toni Bowie. All of these people provided guidance to critical documentation for this project. Dr. John H. Hatcher and Mr. Paul Taborn of the Adjutant General's office deserve credit for their professional help in gathering specific record requests.

Dr. O. P. Fitzgerald of the Naval Historical Center and Dr. Martin Gordon of the U.S. Marine Corps Historical Center both supplied important materials. In Australia Mr. Barry A. Crowell, J. P., of Lidcombe and Mr. A. M. Beveridge of the Australian Department of Defence provided the data on Australia's Vietnam effort. Colonel James F. Greene, Jr., and Mr. Clement V. Kelly, Jr., kindly permitted use of their extensive collections of military insignia. James W. Loop, Lieutenant Colonel, U.S. Army, Retired, and Frederick W. Crismon, Automotive Historian, kindly offered needed help and photographs. Thanks also to John F. Sloan, Lieutenant Colonel, U.S. Army, Retired, and Mr. Gordon Rottman for sharing their expertise. Finally, special thanks go to the author's parents, Samuel Shelton and Henrietta Stanton.

How to Use This Book

Scope of Book

The purpose of this book is to list every significant U.S. Army unit present in the Republic of Vietnam from 1961 and to detail its service while stationed there. The following basic format has been adopted.

All units within this book have a minimal data base. In all cases the unit designation and branch, its descriptive type, exact term of Vietnam service, station previous to Vietnam, and authorized in-country strengths have been given.

In general, more information is included for the larger organizations. Thus, major commands include detailed listings of commanding officers and component elements in addition to standard information and brief historical narratives. Combat battalions of the infantry, aviation, armor and cavalry branches have been detailed as to precise assignment on a monthly basis, composition and locational service. The functions of other battalions in both the combat support and service categories are explained and data is provided on major command and location changes. Companies are given a representative location.

To keep this work within manageable proportions, as a general rule it does not include details on U.S. Army offices, missions, elements, services, detachments, schools, installations, teams, centers, depots, facilities, agencies, activities or miscellaneous components. Usually these are directly subordinated to or an integral part of a unit already listed, and at that point most of the more important ones are mentioned. As an exception, a wealth of statistical data on all U.S. Special Forces detachments is provided to reflect their impact on the unique conflict in Vietnam.

Unit Designations

Unit designations are self-explanatory. Unit identification in the **Order of Battle** has been determined by its official title. In some rare instances this may conflict with how particular units were known in Vietnam. The most notable local instances were the American Division and the 11th Armored Cavalry Regiment, which officially were the 23d Infantry Division and the 11th Armored Cavalry respectively. Sometimes units in Vietnam existed under a completely unauthorized title (as Troop H, 16th Cavalry whose service is given under its correct designation, Troop F, 9th Cavalry). Such discrepancies are resolved in favor of official terminology. However, all units that actually existed in Vietnam, whether authorized or not, have been included to the extent that this author has been able to verify their existence. The word "provisional" has been added when a unit has been identified as such or found to be unauthorized but existing. Of course, provisional elements of negligible size, very transient nature, or of questionable authenticity have not been included.

The branch served by a unit in some cases may vary due to changes in army structure, especially in the support fields. Thus, units are listed either under the branch they served the longest or under the branch deemed most appropriate. Changes in branch assignment are usually noted.

A most careful effort has been made to resolve all unit service and designation discrepancies, but in a few cases the source material was itself contradictory. In such instances the discrepancies have been fully noted and explained. It must be remembered that many organizational changes were made within the army during the decade covered, both in Vietnam and worldwide, and these changes invariably led to complications both in branch assignments and numerical-titular alterations.

Unit Type

Type refers to a one-phrase basic description of unit function. Out of necessity, some of these are abbreviated on company level and complete explanations of the abbreviations are to be found in Appendix E. The type is not given when it is considered covered by the unit title.

Unit Arrival and Departure

Arrival and departure dates show when the unit was in and out of Vietnam, corresponding to the Vietnam Service category in the company listings. It must be realized that this is a standardized heading and is not intended to convey whether a unit was raised, activated, organized or inactivated as opposed to whether a unit actually arrived or departed Vietnam from or to some other station. A check of the Previous Station or the narrative should resolve questions about how the unit came to be in Vietnam.

Unit Previous Station

Previous Station is another standardized heading inserted for the sake of consistency. It denotes either the prior unit location outside of Vietnam or, if "Vietnam" has been inserted, that the unit was formed or raised in Vietnam.

Unit Location

Unit locations are exact for battalions or larger groups and representative on a company level. Typical locations are always marked as such. If applicable, the typical location given is as of January 1969 — the peak of U.S. troop involvement in Vietnam. Of course, if the unit was not in Vietnam at that time, a typical location is just that, a fairly representative duty station during Vietnam service.

Where detailed monthly location listings are given in the infantry and cavalry sections, it must be noted that these reflect brigade headquarters locations. All assignments in such lists are administrative and do not reflect the fact that the unit was often attached to or under the operational control of another brigade. Where dual locations appear on the same line separated by a dash, the first gives the brigade administrative headquarters and the second gives the brigade's forward field headquarters. Moreover, this location information is subject to a one-month time lag since the weekly updates of the Department of Defense Joint Chiefs of Staff were used to acquire most of this data. This same source was relied upon to give aviation-company service intervals within their respective higher commands and for the same reason may contain a margin of error of one month either way.

Unit Strength

Authorized strengths were decided upon as the most useful gauge of unit size. Actual strengths varied frequently and a complete list would require more space than this volume allowed. In some cases, especially in the U.S. Army Special Forces section, some exact personnel strengths are listed for specific time intervals. The authorized strength is not the army's Table of Organization and Equipment (TOE) figure but rather the size authorized through MACV modification in Vietnam. This varied quite widely from the standard TOE tables. For instance, while light infantry battalions (TOE 7-175 Test) ran 778 men, they were permitted 920 in Vietnam due to combat augmentation. Of course, some units were either increased or decreased on a local supplemental level (for example, the 23rd Infantry Division administration company personnel figure was apparently upgraded by the division from 545 to over 1,000), but no attempt has been made to reflect such purely local command-level temporary strength allocations. Such precise accounting would only invite infinite variation well beyond the scope of this **Order of Battle** and such detail should be properly sought within the individual unit records themselves.

Unit Illustrations

The illustrations accompanying certain units represent their distinctive insignia, which were manufactured in metal and enamel and worn on the uniform by all personnel of that outfit. These are not to be confused with unit cloth shoulder patches. Both actual patches and distinctive insignia are shown in the full-color section. Only battalions and larger organizations were authorized distinctive insignia based on elements of the design of the coat of arms or historic badge and reflecting that particular unit's lineage and battle honors. Serving as identifying devices, each is distinctive to the organization for which approved and is depicted as it appeared during the Vietnam conflict. Where no illustration is present, none had been approved at that time. Additionally, several unauthorized distinctive insignia were included because they were made and worn in Vietnam on a local basis with local unit approval. Such are always marked as "unauthorized."

During the Vietnam conflict distinctive insignia were often worn in the field on combat uniforms and were duplicated as cloth pocket patches on jungle fatigues. They were also painted on vehicles and aircraft as well as on large weapons and fire or support base structures.

The illustrations are reproduced courtesy by Colonel James F. Greene, Jr., who is President of the American Society of Military Insignia Collectors. The Institute of Heraldry, United States Army, also provided needed information.

Abbreviations and Acronyms

All abbreviations and acronyms used in the text and not explained where they appear are fully detailed in Appendix E. Emphasis has been placed on Vietnam usage and not official terminology. For example, USASTRATCOM is used in lieu of the official abbreviation USASCC for the U.S. Army Strategic Communications Command, because in Vietnam USASCC was used to signify the U.S. Army Support Command, Cam Ranh Bay, and USASTRATCOM identified the former.

Sources

Though all sources are listed at the back of this volume, it is appropriate at this point to make some comment regarding those used. In compiling the information for this book, several basic sources soon proved somewhat unreliable for determining Vietnam service. The army monthly station lists are computerized listings containing a large number of discrepancies which had to be painstakingly cross-checked for accuracy. Another seemingly valid basis for Vietnam service determination is the Department of the Army General Orders, which list campaign credit and decorations for Vietnam participation. However, these were found to contain errors (most commonly numerical misprints) and list units which were in supporting capacities in Okinawa, Hawaii and elsewhere as entitled to Vietnam awards. It must be stressed that only those units *actually located* in and on permanent orders to Vietnam are considered in this work. Therefore, if it appears a certain unit has been neglected, it is suggested that careful scrutiny be given unit records to determine its true status. The author used the unit records themselves as the final authority in all instances, though army and MACV/USARV station listings were relied upon for some of the location and command information. The division orders of battle are intended to cover the more important assigned and attached elements and serve merely as a key to further detailed data within the applicable individual unit sections.

With these explanations in mind it is hoped that readers find the information in this book both useful and accurate. If an ommission or error is discovered, moreover, the author would be most grateful for any corrections submitted for incorporation into future editions.

U.S. Army Organization in Vietnam

Chapter 1

General Army Structure

The Army of the United States during the Vietnam era consisted of the Regular Army (the permanent full-time professional force), the Army National Guard and the Army Reserve. While the terms of service differed for each of the three components, each had the military purpose of securing the United States and its commitments with allies. The conflict in Vietnam was primarily a "Regular Army war" because the great bulk of units serving in the combat zone were Regular Army. The Reserve and National Guard were represented by only 43 units, most of which were companies or detachments. All units appearing in this Order of Battle are Regular Army unless otherwise identified. However, it should be noted all army units fighting in Vietnam were properly part of the Active Army by definition; Active Army being those elements of the Army of the United States on full-time service. This included the Regular Army as well as those units drawn from Army National Guard or Army Reserve to serve one-year tours in Vietnam.

The Department of the Army itself was a component of the Department of Defense and colocated with the Departments of the Air Force and Navy at the Pentagon in Washington, D.C., under the Defense Department's command and control. The dominance of the Department of Defense led not only to the jointly planned and executed combined operations prevalent during the Vietnam era, but led also to complex and sometimes conflicting relationships at higher command levels, especially in Vietnam and the Pacific area.

The Department of the Army was headed by the Secretary of the Army. Cyrus R. Vance became Secretary of the Army on 21 May 1962. He was followed by Stephen Ailes on 20 January 1964, Stanley R. Resor on 17 June 1965, Robert F. Froehlke on 15 June 1971 and by Howard H. Callaway on 2 May 1973. The Secretary of the Army was responsible primarily for the affairs of the army establishment and was assisted by an intricate staffing system at Department of the Army level composed of three distinct staffs: the Chief of Staff and his office, the General Staff and the Special Staff. These staffs were instrumental in the actual functioning of

the army on a worldwide basis. With the exception of those assigned to this departmental staffing, all Active Army members were assigned to one of the army's thirteen major field commands. Some of these commands were placed under the operational control of the Secretary of Defense and thus became army components of unified joint service commands operated by the Defense Department via the Joint Chiefs of Staff. The Secretary of the Army remained responsible for the administrative and logistical support of the army elements within such unified commands.

During the Vietnam conflict the major army field commands remained fairly constant and were as follows:

U.S. Continental Army Command (USCONARC)

USCONARC contained the five U.S. armies located in the contiguous United States as well as the Military District of Washington. The five U.S. Armies were First Army, Third Army, Fourth Army, Fifth Army and Sixth Army. The Second Army was deactivated on 1 January 1966.

U.S. Army Combat Developments Command (USACDC)

USACDC was responsible for the development of doctrine, concepts and requirements within the army and, although located at Fort Belvoir, had agency representation in Vietnam directly as well as through Army service schools and the like.

U.S. Army Material Command (USAMC)

USAMC directed the development, testing, evaluation, procurement, distribution and maintenance of most army equipment. Headquartered in Washington, D.C., this agency had subordinate command elements in Vietnam.

U.S. Army Security Agency (USASA)

USASA had worldwide security responsibilities and sent several units into Vietnam. These are listed under the USASA heading in this book.

U.S. Army Strategic Communications Command (USASCC or USASTRATCOM)

USASTRATCOM managed the army's portion of the global Defense Communications System and fielded several units in its own right in the Vietnam theater of operations.

U.S. Army Intelligence Command (USAINTC)

USAINTC provided counterintelligence support inside the continental United States.

Military Traffic Management and Terminal Service (MTMTS)

MTMTS managed army transportation matters.

Additionally, several major army field commands were components of unified joint service commands and were as follows:

U.S. Army Air Defense Command (USARADCOM)

USARADCOM was part of the Continental Air Defense Command and responsible for anti air/missile protection of the continental United States.

U.S. Army Forces Strike Command (USARSTRIKE)

USARSTRIKE, part of the U.S. Strike Command (STRICOM), served as a strategic reserve to deploy army units to crisis points throughout the world. During the Vietnam conflict it committed elements in response to the 1968 Tet offensive.

U.S. Army, Alaska (USARAL)

USARAL was part of the U.S. Alaskan Command and contributed units to the Vietnam effort.

U.S. Army Forces, Southern Command (USARSOUTH)

USARSOUTH was part of the U.S. Southern Command located in the Canal Zone and was charged with responsibilities in the Caribbean area and South America.

U.S. Army, Europe (USAREUR)

USAREUR was part of the U.S. European Command (USEUCOM) and included the Seventh Army, V Corps and VII Corps in Germany as well as other European-based army formations.

U.S. Army, Pacific (USARPAC)

USARPAC was part of the U.S. Army Pacific Command (USAPACOM). Headquartered at Fort Shafter, Hawaii, USARPAC supervised all army components in the Pacific area, including the Eighth Army and I Corps in Korea, IX Corps in Okinawa, and those army components in U.S. Military Assistance Command, Vietnam (USMACV) as well as many other major army elements in Japan and Thailand. USMACV was also included under the unified USAPACOM since it was also a unified joint service command. However, U.S. Army, Vietnam (USARV) had a dual chain of command since USARV was not only the army component of USMACV and under its operational control but also under the command (without operational control) of USARPAC as an army component in the Pacific area. Thus, USARV was not considered a major army field command in its own right but rather was considered a part of USMACV under USARPAC, which explains the involvement of USARPAC in the Vietnam theater of operations.

Army units were organized by the branch which represented that particular unit's military specialty. Units were further grouped into "Arms" (those branches whose primary mission was to fight or directly support the fighting elements) and "Services" (those branches with a primary mission of combat service support and/or administration). Since in Vietnam some units had unique missions or missions in both fields, they are not arranged accord-

ing to the strict scheme assigned them by Department of the Army (Table 1-1).

Army designations were either by number or title. While in most cases the system is self-explanatory, one distinct concept was the Combat Arms Regimental System (CARS), under which the infantry, artillery and cavalry/armor units were organized. Before the adoption of CARS, there was no satisfactory means of maintaining the active life of the combat arms organizations. Whenever the nation entered periods of military retrenchment, units were invariably broken up, reorganized, consolidated or disbanded. During periods of mobilization, large numbers of new units were created. Changes in weapons and techniques of warfare produced new types of units to replace old ones. As a result, soldiers frequently served in organizations with little or no history, while units with long combat records remained inactive.

In the late 1950s requirements for maneuverable and flexible major tactical organizations demanded highly mobile divisions with greatly increased firepower. For this purpose the regiment was deemed too large and unwieldy and had to be broken up into smaller organizations. Most artillery and armored regiments had already been broken up for the same reasons during World War II. When the division was reorganized under the Pentomic struc-

TABLE 1–1
Comparison of Army Organization by Branch and Book Structure

DA Classification	Book Classification
Combat Arms	**Combat Units**
Armor/Cavalry	Armor
Artillery	Aviation
Infantry	Cavalry
	Infantry
Combat Support Arms	**Combat Support Units**
Corps of Engineers*	Engineers
Military Intelligence*	Military Police
Military Police Corps*	Signal
Signal Corps*	
Services	**Service Units †**
Adjutant General's Corps	Support Commands, Brigades, Groups
Corps of Engineers*	Adjutant General
Finance Corps ‡	Chemical
Quartermaster Corps	Composite Service
Army Medical Department	Maintenance
Ordnance Corps	Medical
Signal Corps*	Ordnance
Chemical Corps	Quartermaster
Military Police Corps*	Transportation
Transportation Corps	
Military Intelligence*	
NA	**Special Warfare**
—	Army Security Agency
	Military Intelligence
	Psychological Operations
	U.S. Army Special Forces

* Considered by Department of Army to be both a combat support arm and service.

† Listing does not include Judge Advocate General's Corps or Women's Army Corps, which did not form units in Vietnam.

‡ No finance units larger than detachment-level served in Vietnam and thus are not included in this Order of Battle.

ture in 1957, the traditional regimental structure was eliminated, thus raising questions as to what the new units were to be called, how they were to be numbered and what their relationship to former organizations was to be.

On 24 January 1957 the Secretary of the Army approved the CARS concept, which was designed to provide a flexible regimental structure that would permit perpetuation of unit history and tradition in the new tactical organization of divisions, without restricting the organizational trends of the future. Accordingly, the Army went into Vietnam under this system. Those regiments organized under the CARS concept during the Vietnam era are listed in Table 1-2. The parent regiments for use under CARS had been carefully selected according to age and honors accrued.

Under CARS, each company, battery or troop in the regiment (as originally organized) was reorganized as the headquarters

TABLE 1–2
Regiments Organized Under the Combat Arms Regimental System (CARS):

Armor/Cavalry

1st Cavalry*	15th Cavalry*	64th Armor
4th Cavalry*	16th Armor*†	66th Armor
5th Cavalry*	17th Cavalry*	67th Armor
7th Cavalry*	32d Armor	68th Armor
8th Cavalry*	33d Armor	69th Armor*
9th Cavalry*	34th Armor*	70th Armor
10th Cavalry*	35th Armor	72d Armor
12th Cavalry*	37th Armor	73d Armor
13th Armor	40th Armor	77th Armor*
	63d Armor	81st Armor

Infantry

1st Infantry*	21st Infantry*	52d Infantry*
2d Infantry*	22d Infantry*	54th Infantry*
3d Infantry*	23d Infantry*	58th Infantry*
4th Infantry	26th Infantry*	60th Infantry*
5th Infantry*	27th Infantry*	61st Infantry*
6th Infantry*	28th Infantry*	75th Infantry*
7th Infantry*	29th Infantry	87th Infantry*
8th Infantry*	30th Infantry	187th Infantry*
9th Infantry*	31st Infantry*	188th Infantry
10th Infantry	32d Infantry	325th Infantry
11th Infantry*	34th Infantry	327th Infantry*
12th Infantry*	35th Infantry*	501st Infantry*
13th Infantry	36th Infantry	502d Infantry*
14th Infantry*	38th Infantry	503d Infantry*
15th Infantry	39th Infantry*	504th Infantry
16th Infantry*	41st Infantry	505th Infantry*
17th Infantry*	46th Infantry*	506th Infantry*
18th Infantry*	47th Infantry*	508th Infantry*
19th Infantry	48th Infantry	509th Infantry
20th Infantry*	50th Infantry*	511th Infantry
	51st Infantry*	

National Guard Infantry

151st Infantry (Indiana)*

Special Forces

1st Special Forces*

Artillery §

1st Artillery	28th Artillery	62d Artillery
2d Artillery*	29th Artillery*	65th Artillery*
3d Artillery	30th Artillery*	67th Artillery
4th Artillery*	31st Artillery	68th Artillery
5th Artillery*	32d Artillery*	71st Artillery*
6th Artillery*	33d Artillery*	73d Artillery
7th Artillery*	34th Artillery*	75th Artillery

8th Artillery*	35th Artillery*	76th Artillery
9th Artillery*	36th Artillery	77th Artillery*
10th Artillery	37th Artillery	78th Artillery
11th Artillery*	38th Artillery	79th Artillery*
12th Artillery*	39th Artillery*	80th Artillery
13th Artillery*	40th Artillery*	81st Artillery
14th Artillery*	41st Artillery*	82d Artillery*
15th Artillery*	42d Artillery*	83d Artillery*
16th Artillery*	43d Artillery	84th Artillery*
17th Artillery*	44th Artillery*	92d Artillery*
18th Artillery*	51st Artillery	94th Artillery*
19th Artillery*	52d Artillery	319th Artillery*
20th Artillery*	55th Artillery*	320th Artillery*
21st Artillery*	56th Artillery*	321st Artillery*
22d Artillery*	57th Artillery	333d Artillery
25th Artillery*	59th Artillery	377th Artillery*
26th Artillery*	60th Artillery*	517th Artillery
27th Artillery*	61st Artillery	562d Artillery

National Guard Artillery

138th Artillery (KY)*   197th Artillery (NH)*

Note: Army Reserves are not listed in this chart because no Army Reserve regimental elements served in Vietnam.

* Vietnam service (National Guard unlisted unless in Vietnam).

† In addition the following Armored Cavalry retained their regimental structure and were not reorganized under CARS: 2d, 3d, 6th, 11th*, 14th Armored Cavalry.

‡ The 16th Armor was redesignated as the 16th Cavalry on 2 September 1969. Thus Troop C, 16th Cavalry served in Vietnam 1970–73, while Company D, 16th Armor, was in Vietnam 1965–68.

§ On 1 September 1971 the artillery regiments were designated either field artillery or air defense artillery. The following were still serving in Vietnam at that time and became properly air defense artillery: 1st Battalion, 44th Air Defense Artillery; 4th Battalion, 60th Air Defense Artillery; Battery G, 65th Air Defense Artillery; Battery D, 71st Air Defense Artillery.

and headquarters element of a battalion or squadron in the new regiment. The new battalion or squadron's organic elements, the lettered elements, were constituted and activated as new units. Each of the old companies, batteries or troops of the former regiment also had the capability of becoming a separate company, battery or troop in the new regiment. The regimental headquarters itself was transferred to Department of the Army control. This transformation under CARS is illustrated for a typical infantry regiment in Table 1-3.

It can be seen that "regiment" became an historic and heraldic term except for five armored cavalry regiments that were not reorganized under CARS and retained their regimental structure. Of these, the 11th Armored Cavalry served in Vietnam with its three fixed cavalry reconnaissance squadrons.

In a regiment not organized under CARS, there was a fixed number of organic elements organized into squadrons (or battalions if other than armor/cavalry). A brigade, however, could have several different kinds of units attached to it, such as three infantry battalions, a cavalry troop, an engineer company and other supporting units. In tactical structure, therefore, a brigade was very similar to the regimental combat team (RCT) of World War II and Korea. Since brigades were flexible, except for the headquarters and headquarters company, no two needed to be alike, whereas all regiments were fixed with organic elements provided for under basic tables of organization and equipment.

In organizing units within the army, each is formed under either a table of organization and equipment (TOE, which became modified under the combat conditions of Vietnam to MTOE), a table of distribution and allowances (TDA), or provisionally. Tables of organization and equipment (TOE) are issued by the Department of the Army and establish for each category of Army unit its title, the number and grades of its officers and men, its organic equipment and its interior organization. Tables of Distribution and Allowances (TDA) allow for temporary units (technically organizations) which have personnel levels and equipment approved formally by the Department of the Army. They are created only for a specific mission and discontinued after the mission need passes. Provisional units are created in the field by reallocation of existing resources, do not receive formal Department of the Army approval and are as a rule even less permanent than TDA organizations.

Except for the armored cavalry regiment, which contained a mix of units, the division was the main unit of combined arms and services. Although there were five types of combat divisions present during the Vietnam period (armored, mechanized, infantry, airmobile and airborne), only the latter three served as complete divisions in Vietnam. Nevertheless, a brigade task force from a mechanized infantry division (1st Brigade, 5th Infantry Division) was sent to Vietnam. Armored cavalry squadrons were detached from both armored divisions stationed at Fort Hood for Vietnam duty. The structure of the Army division in Vietnam is

better understood through a discussion of the ROAD concept under which divisions had been organized.

In December of 1960 the Army reevaluated the organization then in existence, and as a result a major Army-wide reorganization of divisions was recommended. Called ROAD (Reorganization Objective Army Divisions), this reorganization was approved by the Secretary of the Army in April 1961. The first ROAD units were organized in February 1962 under draft TOEs. By the end of June 1964 this reorganization was completed in both the Regular Army and the reserve components.

ROAD was specifically designed to fit into the national strategy of flexible response to handle situations short of nuclear war as well as the "massive retaliation" scheme that the former Pentomic plan of 1957-59 for divisions had envisioned. The single most important characteristic of the new system was its flexibility, since each division under ROAD had a fixed base common to all divisions, but the number and type of its infantry and armor elements varied according to its mission. By using different combinations of organic maneuver elements, divisions could be tailored to fit any environment or situation. Three brigades were established in each division to serve as an intermediary headquarters between the division commander and the battalion com-

TABLE 1–3

Typical Infantry Regiment Under Combat Arms Regimental System.   17th Infantry Illustrated:

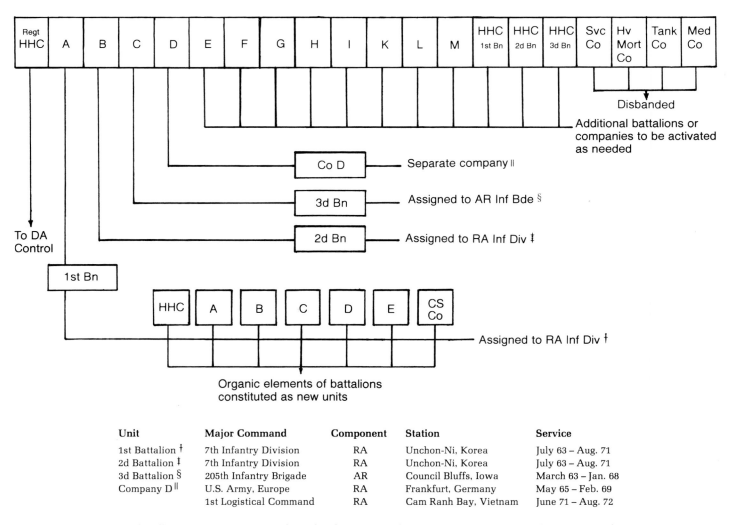

Unit	Major Command	Component	Station	Service
1st Battalion [†]	7th Infantry Division	RA	Unchon-Ni, Korea	July 63 – Aug. 71
2d Battalion [‡]	7th Infantry Division	RA	Unchon-Ni, Korea	July 63 – Aug. 71
3d Battalion [§]	205th Infantry Brigade	AR	Council Bluffs, Iowa	March 63 – Jan. 68
Company D [‖]	U.S. Army, Europe	RA	Frankfurt, Germany	May 65 – Feb. 69
	1st Logistical Command	RA	Cam Ranh Bay, Vietnam	June 71 – Aug. 72

As this illustration demonstrates, the 17th Infantry is entitled to Vietnam service credit because one of its elements, a separate company, was present in Vietnam during the conflict.

manders. The new brigades could control a variable number and type of units. Army divisions serving in Vietnam were of two basic types: infantry and airmobile (the 1st Cavalry Division and the 101st Airborne Division were organized as airmobile). Commanded by a major general, a division had three brigades, division artillery (usually consisting of four to five battalions), a reconnaissance cavalry squadron, standard division support command assets and aviation depending on requirement. Divisions usually had nine or ten battalions of infantry (1st Cavalry Division ground cavalry battalions were organized just like infantry), but the 23d Infantry Division (AMERICAL) had eleven battalions. Two divisions in Vietnam, the 4th and 25th, also had one tank battalion, whereas the 1st Infantry Division had left its two tank battalions stateside when deployed to Vietnam. Typical personnel strengths of a division are reflected in Table 1-4.

TABLE 1-4
Authorized Personnel in a Typical Infantry Division in Vietnam

23d Infantry Division (AMERICAL) Illustrated:

Subordinate Unit	Officers	Warrant Officers	Enlisted
Division Headquarters and Headquarters Company	61	—	109
11th Infantry Brigade	208	12	3,827
196th Infantry Brigade	165	10	2,952
198th Infantry Brigade	206	12	3,824
1st Squadron, 1st Cavalry (Armored)	50	36	963
Division Artillery*	330	49	4,295
Division Support Command†	148	23	2,153
16th Aviation Group (Combat)‡	206	312	2,268
26th Engineer Battalion	44	4	970
523d Signal Battalion	25	5	611
23d Military Police Company	9	2	178
Provisional Military Intelligence Detachment	18	5	73
Totals:	1,470	470	22,223
Aggregate for division:	24,163		

Source: *Americal Division Organization and Equipment Reference Data Book* circa 1969. Figures were compiled from the modified tables of equipment used in Vietnam. However, strengths authorized by "special letters of authorization" are not included. Actual strengths were probably much higher than this chart represents due to excess personnel in support and staffing functions.

* Division artillery included: HHB; 3/82, 3/16, 3/18, 1/82, 6/56, G/55, 1/14, and 6/11 Artillery; 251st and 252d Radar Detachments.

† Division Support Command included: HHC & Band, 23d S&T Bn, 23d Med Bn, 723d Maint Bn, 23d Admin Co, G/75 Infantry, 63d Infantry Platoon.

‡ 16th Aviation Group included: HHC; 123d, 14th Avn Bns; 132d, 178th, 71st, 174th, 176th Avn Cos; 335th Trans Co; F/8 Cav; numerous signal and medical detachments, etc.

A brigade, roughly equivalent to a group, was the next level below division. Commanded by a colonel, a brigade was a headquarters element only, providing command and control to attached or assigned units. Separate infantry brigades in Vietnam typically had assigned four infantry battalions, one artillery (105mm) battalion, one reconnaissance troop and a supporting battalion. One fixed regiment, the 11th Armored Cavalry, was

also present in Vietnam. The difference between this unit and the brigade formation concept has already been explained. Brigades within a division normally had three infantry battalions but were reinforced for mission purposes by a host of divisional elements.

The battalion in Vietnam was of two basic types: fixed and flexible. A fixed battalion had assigned lettered companies, usually four or five with a headquarters company. A flexible battalion controlled any number of attached separate companies and in itself consisted only of a headquarters detachment. The cavalry used the term squadron instead of battalion unless the cavalry was actually organized as an infantry battalion (as in the 1st Cavalry Division). In both cases the formation was commanded by a lieutenant colonel. Fixed battalions usually ran 500 to 920 personnel, but flexible battalions varied widely.

The company in Vietnam was either assigned to some battalion with a lettered designation within that battalion, or was separate and had its own number sequence or title. Companies were called batteries by the artillery and troops by the cavalry. Consisting of between 120 to 250 men, companies were commanded by captains in most instances.

The U.S. Army Special Forces had a unique organization which is fully discussed within that section.

Chapter 2

Combat Operations in General

The U.S. Army had six basic combat missions in Vietnam: (1) containing the enemy at the borders, (2) locating and destroying the enemy inside the Republic of Vietnam, (3) neutralizing enemy base areas, (4) supporting rural development, (5) opening and securing lines of communication, and (6) the security of key installations.

Missions typical of U.S. combat operations in Vietnam were centered about three operational tasks: (1) search and destroy (later termed offensive sweeps, reconnaissance in force, or spoiling attacks due to adverse political connotations at the time); (2) clear and secure, and (3) security. These missions entailed the conduct of offensive, defensive, reconnaissance, security and economy-of-force operations. In Vietnam, units were frequently assigned missions in various combinations simultaneously; for example, "perform search and destroy operations in assigned area of operations and secure a given route," or "conduct clear and secure operations in assigned area of operations and provide convoy escort to elements passing along a designated route." These missions were assigned to infantry, tank, mechanized infantry and armored cavalry or air cavalry units. Such tasks must be detailed before discussing the unit types themselves.

A list of selected major operations conducted by U.S. forces in Vietnam is displayed in Table 2-1.

Search and Destroy. These operations were designed to locate enemy installations, to destroy or evacuate supplies and equipment, and to destroy or capture enemy forces. Less importance was attached to seizing and holding critical terrain than to finding and finishing the enemy armed forces and political infrastructure. Ideally, search and destroy operations were planned so that forces physically searched zones within the area of operations with ultimate domination of enemy bases attempted. Operations were conducted so that the enemy would be attacked by a combination of maneuvering and blocking elements supported by both artillery and aerial fire.

Clear and Secure. These were offensive combat operations aimed at driving enemy units out of a populated area so that pacification efforts could proceed. U.S., ARVN and allied forces conducted clear and secure operations in selected areas in accordance with theater plans. These operations were usually initiated by search and destroy actions but differed from pure search and destroy in that they were sustained. Emphasis was placed on seizing and holding key population and communications centers.

Security. These operations included convoy, route, base and area security and became increasingly important as U.S. involvement in Vietnam drew down. Convoy security operations were prevalent throughout the conflict and were accomplished either by temporarily securing the route to be used or by accompanying the convoy with an appropriate mix of combat units. The time involved was limited to that required to complete the movement of the convoy. By their nature, other security missions were generally longer in duration and, like clear and secure operations, normally conducted in conjunction with some search and destroy actions. These security operations were designed for the purpose of seizing and holding routes, installations and facilities. In the immediate environs of their bases, U.S. units were specifically charged with securing key military installations and routes. Securing operations to safeguard such installations and areas undergoing pacification became of paramount concern from late 1968 on. On 12 November 1971, President Nixon announced that U.S. ground forces were now in a strictly defensive role and position and that all offensive operations would be conducted by the South Vietnamese. At that point Army ground troops were concerned with base defense and withdrawal matters.

Revolutionary Development. All missions assigned to U.S. units were designed to contribute to the goal of re-establishing South Vietnamese government control over the South Vietnamese people. In general, Revolutionary Development (RD) was conducted in phases: (1) U.S., ARVN or allied units conducted military operations within their designated areas of dubious or no government control (typically search and destroy followed by clear and secure operations); (2) ARVN units then assumed responsibility for securing the area and securing operations; (3) ARVN units then further secured the zone by establishing the necessary Regional Forces and Popular Forces (RF/PF) units from the local population; (4) South Vietnamese civil government officials and national and local police gradually assumed control from the ARVN, and (5) the ARVN units were released to conduct operations in other areas. U.S. units conducted civic action operations in conjunction with tactical operations, especially through medical assistance, engineer construction assistance and supply distribution.

TABLE 2–1
List of Selected Major Operations in Vietnam

After the introduction of significant U.S. forces into Vietnam in March 1965, several hundred major and thousands of smaller combat operations were conducted. The chronological listing that follows includes only those operations in which more than 500 known casualties * were inflicted on the NVA or VC. Although this list provides data primarily on U.S. forces ground operations, significant South Vietnamese and allied operations are also included.

Date and duration	Operation	Corps/MR
18 – 21 Aug. 65 *4 days*	STARLIGHT. U.S. Marine Corps operation against VC 1st Regiment south of Chu Lai in Quang Ngai Province. 700 known enemy casualties.	I
23 Oct. – 20 Nov. 65 *29 days*	SILVER BAYONET. 1st Cavalry Division (Airmobile) and ARVN units operation in Pleiku Province. Operation included the division's 3d Brigade battle of Ia Drang Valley. 1,771 known enemy casualties.	II
19 Jan. – 21 Feb. 66 *34 days*	VAN BUREN. 1st Brigade, 101st Airborne Division; Republic of Korea 2d Marine Brigade, and the ARVN 47th Regiment rice-security operation in Phu Yen Province. 679 known enemy casualties.	II
24 Jan. – 6 March 66 *42 days*	MASHER/WHITE WING/THANG PHONG II. Conducted by 1st Cavalry Division (Airmobile), ARVN and ROK forces in Binh Dinh Province. First large unit operation across corps boundaries when Marines on DOUBLE EAGLE crossed into Binh Dinh and linked up with soldiers of the 1st Cavalry Division. 2,389 known enemy casualties.	II
4 – 8 March 66 *5 days*	UTAH/LIEN KET 26. U.S. Marine Corps/ARVN operation in vicinity of Quang Ngai City against NVA and VC main force units. 632 known enemy casualties.	I
20 – 24 March 66 *5 days*	TEXAS/LIEN KET 28. U.S. Marine Corps/ARVN/Vietnamese Marine Corps reaction force operation to retake An Hoa outpost in Quang Ngai Province. 623 known enemy casualties.	I
10 May – 30 July 66 *82 days*	PAUL REVERE/THAN PHONG 14. 3d Brigade, U.S. 25th Infantry Division and ARVN forces border screening and area control operation in Pleiku Pronvince. 546 known enemy casualties.	II
2 – 21 June 66 *20 days*	HAWTHORNE/DAN TANG 61. 1st Brigade, 101st Airborne Division and ARVN units operation in Kontum Province. 531 known enemy casualties.	II
2 June – 13 July 66 *42 days*	EL PASO II. U.S. 1st Infantry Division and ARVN 5th Infantry Division against VC 9th Division in Binh Long Province. 855 known enemy casualties.	III
4 July – 27 Oct. 66 *116 days*	MACON. U.S. Marine Corps security operation for An Hoa industrial complex in Quang Nam Province. 507 known enemy casualties.	I
7 July – 3 Aug. 66 *28 days*	HASTINGS/DECKHOUSE II. U.S. Marine Corps/ARVN/Vietnamese Marine Corps operation in Quang Tri Province against NVA 324B Division in area of Demilitarized Zone. 882 known enemy casualties.	I
1 – 25 Aug. 66 *25 days*	PAUL REVERE II. 1st Cavalry Division (Airmobile) and ARVN operation in Pleiku Province. 809 known enemy casualties.	II
3 Aug. 66 – 31 Jan. 67 *182 days*	PRAIRIE. A continuing 3d Marine Division operation in Con Thien/Gio Linh areas of the Demilitarized Zone. Followed HASTINGS and was initiated by one battalion left behind from that operation to keep track of the NVA 324B Division. 1,397 known enemy casualties.	I
6 – 21 Aug. 66 *16 days*	COLORADO/LIEN KET 52. U.S. Marine Corps/ARVN operation in Quang Nan/Quang Tin Provinces. 674 known enemy casualties.	I
26 Aug. 66 – 20 Jan. 68 *513 days*	BYRD. 1st Cavalry Division (Airmobile) economy-of-force operation in Binh Thuan Province. Usually one or two battalions involved. 849 known enemy casualties.	II
14 Sept. – 24 Nov. 66 *72 days*	ATTLEBORO. In War Zone C (Tay Ninh Province). Initiated by 196th Infantry Brigade. No significant contact until 19 October when a sizable base area was uncovered. By early November the 1st Infantry Division; 3d Brigade, 4th Infantry Division; 173d Airborne Brigade, and several ARVN Battalions were involved. 1,106 known enemy casualties in largest U.S. operation to date.	III
23 Sept. – 9 Nov. 66 *48 days*	HAENG HO 6. Republic of Korea Capital Division operation in Binh Dinh Province. 1,161 known enemy casualties.	II

Date and duration	Operation	Corps/MR
2 – 24 Oct. 66 *23 days*	IRVING. 1st Cavalry Division (Airmobile), ARVN, and Republic of Korea units in Binh Dinh Province. 681 known enemy casualties.	II
18 Oct. – 30 Dec. 66 *74 days*	PAUL REVERE IV. Continuing operation near the Cambodian border of Pleiku Province. Conducted primarily by the newly arrived 4th Infantry Division along with elements of the 25th Infantry Division and 1st Cavalry Division (Airmobile). 977 known enemy casualties.	II
25 Oct. 66 – 12 Feb. 67 *111 days*	THAYER II. 1st Cavalry Division (Airmobile) operation in Binh Dinh Province. Followed THAYER I and was in turn followed by PERSHING in the rich northern coastal plain and Kim Son and Luoi Ci Valleys to the west. 1,757 known enemy casualties.	II
30 Nov. 66 – 14 Dec. 67 *380 days*	FAIRFAX. Started by three U.S. battalions, one each from 1st, 4th, and 25th Infantry Divisions, in and around Saigon and taken over by the 199th Infantry Brigade in January 1967. Emphasis was on joint U.S./ARVN operations. Upon withdrawal of the 199th, the area of operations was taken over by the ARVN 5th Ranger Group. 1,043 known enemy casualties.	III
1 Jan. – 5 Apr. 67 *95 days*	SAM HOUSTON. A continuation of the 4th and 25th Infantry Division border surveillance operations in Pleiku and Kontum Provinces. Followed by FRANCIS MARION. 733 known enemy casualties.	II
6 Jan. – 31 May 67 *146 days*	PALM BEACH. 9th Infantry Division operation in Dinh Tuong Province. 570 known enemy casualties.	IV
8 – 26 Jan. 67 *19 days*	CEDAR FALLS. 1st and 25th Infantry Divisions, 173d Airborne Brigade, 11th Armored Cavalry, and ARVN units undertook joint operation against VC Military Region 4 Headquarters in the Iron Triangle. 720 known enemy casualties.	III
1 Feb. – 18 March 67 *46 days*	PRAIRIE II. Continuation of the 3d Marine Division operations in the area of the Demilitarized Zone. 693 known enemy casualties.	I
11 Feb. 67 – 19 Jan. 68 *343 days*	PERSHING. 1st Cavalry Division (Airmobile) operation in Binh Dinh Province against elements of the NVA 610th Division and VC units. Followed by Pershing II in the same area when major elements of the 1st Cavalry Division (Airmobile) moved to I Corps. 5,401 known enemy casualties.	II
13 Feb. 67 – 11 March 68 *393 days*	ENTERPRISE. 9th Infantry Division operation combined with ARVN and Regional and Popular Forces in Long An Province. 2,107 known enemy casualties.	III
17 – 22 Feb. 67 *6 days*	LIEN KET 81. ARVN 2d Division operation in Quang Ngai Province. 813 known enemy casualties.	I
22 Feb. – 14 May 67 *83 days*	JUNCTION CITY. Largest operation in Vietnam to date: 22 U.S. battalions and four ARVN battalions. Elements of the U.S. 1st, 4th, and 25th Infantry Divisions, 196th Infantry Brigade, 11th Armored Cavalry and 173d Airborne Brigade. Conducted in War Zone C (Tay Ninh Province) and bordering provinces. 2,728 known enemy casualties.	III
7 March – 18 April 67 *43 days*	OH JAC KYO I. Largest Republic of Korea operation to date. Accomplished the linkup of the two Republic of Korea division areas of operations along the central coast of South Vietnam. 831 known enemy casualties.	II
5 April – 12 Oct. 67 *191 days*	FRANCIS MARION. 4th Infantry Division operation in western highlands of Pleiku Province. Followed SAM HOUSTON and upon termination combined forces with GREELEY to commence MAC ARTHUR. 1,203 known enemy casualties.	II
21 April – 17 May 67 *27 days*	UNION. 1st Marine Division operation against NVA forces in Quang Nam and Quang Tin Provinces. 865 known enemy casualties.	I
14 May – 7 Dec. 67 *208 days*	KOLE KOLE. 25th Infantry Division operation in Hau Nghia Province. 645 known enemy casualties.	III
25 May – 5 June 67 *12 days*	UNION II. 1st Marine Division operation against NVA forces in Quang Nam and Quang Tin Provinces. 701 known enemy casualties.	I
2 – 14 July 67 *13 days*	BUFFALO. Continuing 3d Marine Division operation in the Demilitarized Zone. Followed CIMARRON and was followed by HICKORY II. 1,281 known enemy casualties.	I
16 July – 31 Oct. 67 *108 days*	KINGFISHER. Continuing 3d Marine Division operation in the Demilitarized Zone. Followed HICKORY II and was followed by KENTUCKY and LANCASTER. 1,117 known enemy casualties.	I
4 – 15 Sept. 67 *12 days*	SWIFT. 1st Marine Division operation in Quang Nam and Quang Tin Provinces. 517 known enemy casualties.	I
5 Sept. – 30 Oct. 67 *57 days*	DRAGON FIRE. Elements of the Republic of Korea 2d Marine Brigade operations in Quang Ngai Province. 541 known enemy casualties.	I
19 Sept. 67 – 31 Jan. 69 *501 days*	BOLLING. Operations by elements of the 1st Cavalry Division (Airmobile) and 173d Airborne Brigade in Phu Yen Province. 715 known enemy casualties.	II

Date and duration	Operation	Corps/MR
27 Sept. – 19 Nov. 67 *54 days*	SHENANDOAH II. 1st Infantry Division operation in Binh Duong Province and extended to include the Loc Ninh area of Binh Long Province after enemy attacks on the district town. 956 known enemy casualties.	III
12 Oct. 67 – 31 Jan. 69 *478 days*	MAC ARTHUR. 4th Infantry Division continuing operations in the western highlands. 5,731 known enemy casualties.	II
1 Nov. 67 – 31 March 68 *152 days*	SCOTLAND. 3d Marine Division operation in the westernmost part of Quang Tri Province. Action centered on the Khe Sanh area. Terminated with the commencement of PEGASUS. 1,561 known enemy casualties.	I
1 Nov. 67 – 28 Feb. 69 *485 days*	KENTUCKY. 3d Marine Division continuing operations in the Con Thien area of the Demilitarized Zone. 3,921 known enemy casualties.	I
11 Nov. 67 – 11 Nov. 68 *367 days*	WHEELER/WALLOWA. 23d Infantry Division/AMERICAL operations by two of its brigades in Quang Nam and Quang Tin Provinces. 10,000 known enemy casualties.	I
8 Dec. 66 – 24 Feb. 68 *79 days*	YELLOWSTONE. 25th Infantry Division operation in War Zone C (Tay Ninh Province). 1,254 known enemy casualties.	III
8 Dec. 67 – 11 March 68 *95 days*	SARATOGA. A continuation of the 25th Infantry Division operations in the southern half of their area of operations west of Saigon and along the Cambodian border. Commenced at the same time as YELLOWSTONE in the northern half of the division area of operations. 3,862 known enemy casualties.	III
17 Dec. 67 – 8 March 68 *83 days*	UNIONTOWN. 199th Infantry Brigade operation in Bien Hoa Province. Included Tet offensive operations. 922 known enemy casualties.	III
17 Dec. 67 – 30 Jan. 68 *45 days*	MAENG HO 9. Republic of Korea Capital Division operation in Binh Dinh Province. 749 known enemy casualties.	II
19 Dec. 67 – 10 June 68 *175 days*	MUSCATINE. 23d Infantry Division (AMERICAL) operations by one brigade in Quang Ngai Province. 1,129 known enemy casualties.	I
20 Jan. 68 – 31 Jan. 69 *375 days*	McLAIN. 173d Airborne Brigade reconnaissance-in-force operation in support of pacification in Binh Thuan Province. 1,042 known enemy casualties.	II
21 Jan. – 23 Nov. 68 *308 days*	LANCASTER II. Elements of the 3d Marine Division conducted multibattalion search-and-clear operations. 1,801 known enemy casualties.	I
22 Jan. – 29 Feb. 68 *39 days*	PERSHING II. A continuation of the 1st Cavalry Division (Airmobile) operations in Binh Dinh Province after major division forces had deployed to I Corps. 614 known enemy casualties.	II
22 Jan. – 31 March 68 *70 days*	JEB STUART. 1st Cavalry Division (Airmobile) initial operation in northern I Corps following PERSHING operations in II Corps. 3,268 known enemy casualties.	I
31 Jan. – 25 Feb. 68 *26 days*	BATTLE OF HUE. ARVN and U.S. Marine Corps elements defended and drove the enemy out of Hue City during the Tet offensive. 5,113 known enemy casualties.	I
5 – 17 Feb. 68 *13 days*	TRAN HUNG DAO. South Vietnamese Joint General Staff conducted operation in the Saigon area with six Vietnamese marine, four ranger and five airborne battalions during the Tet offensive. 953 known enemy casualties.	III
16 Feb. – 1 March 68 *15 days*	MAENG HO 10. Republic of Korea Capital Division operation in Binh Dinh Province. 664 known enemy casualties.	II
17 Feb. – 8 March 68 *21 days*	TRAN HUNG DAO II. A continuation of the South Vietnamese Joint General Staff operation TRAN HUNG DAO in the Saigon area with slightly reduced forces. 713 known enemy casualties.	III
26 Feb. – 12 Sept. 68 *200 days*	HOUSTON. 1st Marine Division conducted operations in the Thua Thien and Quang Nam border region. 702 known enemy casualties.	I
29 Feb. – 9 Dec. 68 *285 days*	NAPOLEON/SALINE. U.S. Marine Corps operations along the Cua Viet River to keep this supply line of communications open to the port facility in the Dong Ha area of Quang Tri Province. 3,495 known enemy casualties.	I
1 March – 30 July 68 *152 days*	TRUONG CONG DINH. Operation by ARVN units and elements of the U.S. 9th Infantry Division in Dinh Tuong and Kien Tuong Provinces of the IV Corps Tactical Zone. On 21 May combined with Operation PEOPLE'S ROAD.	IV
11 March – 7 April 68 *28 days*	QUYET THANG (Resolve to Win). Largest operation to date. Conducted in the Saigon area and the five surrounding provinces. Elements of the U.S. 1st, 9th and 25th Infantry Divisions; ARVN 5th and 25th Divisions ARVN airborne battalions, and Vietnamese marine corps task forces. A total of 22 U.S. and 11 ARVN battalions were involved. 2,658 known enemy casualties.	III
17 March – 30 July 68 *136 days*	DUONG CUA DAN (People's Road). Operations by 9th Infantry Division to provide security for engineers working on Route 4. Combined with Operation TRUONG CONG DINH on 21 May. In the two operations, over 1,251 known enemy casualties.	IV
30 March 68 – 31 Jan. 69 *308 days*	COCHISE GREEN. 173d Airborne Brigade operation in Binh Dinh Province. 929 known enemy casualties.	

Date and duration	Operation	Corps/MR
1–15 April 68 *15 days*	PEGASUS/LAM SON 207. 1st Cavalry Division (Airmobile) with U.S. Marine and ARVN airborne battalions conducted operation to relieve the siege of Khe Sanh. 17 U.S. and four ARVN battalions involved. 1,044 known enemy casualties.	I
1 April – 17 May 68 *47 days*	CARENTAN II. 101st Airborne Division (Airmobile), and 3d Brigade, 82d Airborne Division in conjunction with ARVN 1st Division operations along the lowlands of Quang Tri and Thua Thien Provinces. 2,100 known enemy casualties.	I
8 April – 31 May 68 *54 days*	TOAN THANG (Complete Victory).† Largest operation to date. A combined III ARVN Corps and II Field Force, Vietnam, offensive to destroy VC and NVA forces within the Capital Military District. 42 U.S. and 37 Vietnamese battalions were involved for total of 79 battalions. 7,645 known enemy casualties.	III
8 April – 11 Nov. 68 *218 days*	BURLINGTON TRAIL. Combat sweep operation by the 198th Infantry Brigade of the 23d Infantry Division (AMERICAL) in Quang Tin Province along the Quang Nam Province border. 1,931 known enemy casualties.	I
15 April 68 – 28 Feb. 69 *320 days*	SCOTLAND II. Continuation of U.S. Marine Corps operations around Khe Sanh upon termination of PEGASUS. 3,311 known enemy casualties.	I
19 April – 17 May 68 *29 days*	DELAWARE/LAM SON 216. 1st Cavalry Division (Airmobile), 101st Airborne Division (Airmobile), and elements of 196th Infantry Brigade, plus ARVN 1st Division and ARVN Airborne Task Force Bravo, conduct operations into A Shau Valley to preempt enemy preparations for an attack on the Hue area. 869 known enemy casualties.	I
4 May – 24 Aug. 68 *113 days*	ALLEN BROOK. U.S. Marine Corps operation west of Hoi An City in southern Quang Nam Province. 1,017 known enemy casualties.	I
17 May – 3 Nov. 68 *171 days*	JEB STUART III. Continuation of the 1st Cavalry Division (Airmobile) operations along the border of Quang Tri and Thua Thien Provinces. 2,114 known enemy casualties.	I
17 May 68 – 28 Feb. 69 *288 days*	NEVADA EAGLE. Continuation of 101st Airborne Division (Airmobile) operations in central Thua Thien Province. 3,299 known enemy casualties.	I
18 May – 23 Oct. 68 *159 days*	MAMELUKE THRUST. U.S. 1st Marine Division operation in central Quang Nam Province. 2,728 known enemy casualties.	I
17 July 68 – 4 March 69 *231 days*	QUYET CHIEN. ARVN 7th, 9th and 21st Infantry Divisions and 44th Special Tactical Zone unit operations in IV Corps. 15,953 known enemy casualties.	IV
2 Aug. 68 – 24 April 69 *266 days*	LAM SON 245. Operation by ARVN 54th Regiment in Thua Thien Province. 636 known enemy casualties.	I
24 Aug. – 9 Sept. 68 *17 days*	TIEN BO. ARVN 23d Division operation in Quang Duc Province. 1,091 known enemy casualties.	II
11 Sept. 68 – 24 April 69 *226 days*	LAM SON 261. ARVN 1st Regiment operation in Thua Thien and Quang Tri Provinces. 724 known enemy casualties.	I
16 Oct. 68 – 24 April 69 *191 days*	LAM SON 271. ARVN 2d Regiment operation in Quang Tri Province. 603 known enemy casualties.	I
24 Oct. – 6 Dec. 68 *44 days*	HENDERSON HILL. U.S. 5th Marine Regiment conducted search-and-clear operation in north central Quang Nam Province. 700 known enemy casualties.	I
1 Dec. 68 – 31 May 69 *151 days*	SPEEDY EXPRESS. Operations by 9th Infantry Division throughout MR IV. 10,899 known enemy casualties.	IV
6 Dec. 68 – 7 March 69 *92 days*	TAYLOR COMMON. Operations by 1st Marine Division in Quang Nam Province. 1,299 known enemy casualties.	I
8 Dec. 68 – 10 Feb. 69 *65 days*	LE LOI I. ARVN 1st Ranger Group operation in Quang Nam Province. 695 known enemy casualties.	I
1 Jan. – 31 Dec. 69 *365 days*	QUYET THANG. Multidivision operation involving the ARVN 7th, 9th and 21st Infantry Divisions in IV Corps Tactical Zone. 37,874 known enemy casualties.	IV
1 Jan. – 31 Aug. 69 *243 days*	RICE FARMER. Operations conducted throughout the Delta by elements of 9th Infantry Division and 5th ARVN Regiment together with appropriate supporting forces. 1,860 known enemy casualties.	IV
22 Jan. – 18 March 69 *56 days*	DEWEY CANYON. Operation by U.S. 9th Marine Regiment (Reinforced) north of the A Shau Valley. 1,335 known enemy casualties.	I
24 Feb. – 10 March 69 *15 days*	QUYET THANG 22. ARVN 2d Division operation in Quang Ngai Province. 777 known enemy casualties.	I
27 Feb. – 20 June 69 *114 days*	QUANG NAM. ARVN 1st Ranger Group operation in Quang Nam Province. 688 known enemy casualties.	I
1 March – 29 May 69 *90 days*	OKLAHOMA HILLS. Operations by U.S. 7th and 26th Marine Regiments southwest of Da Nang in Quang Nam Province. 596 known enemy casualties.	I

Date and duration	Operation	Corps/MR
1 March – 14 April 69 *45 days*	WAYNE GREY. Operations by 4th Infantry Division in Kontum Province. 608 known enemy casualties.	II
20 – 31 March 69 *12 days*	QUYET THANG 25. ARVN 4th Regiment operation in Quang Ngai Province. 592 known enemy casualties.	I
15 April 69 – 1 Jan. 71 *627 days*	WASHINGTON GREEN. The 173d Airborne Brigade conducted a pacification operation in the An Lao Valley of Binh Dinh Province. 1,957 known enemy casualties.	II
18 April – 31 Dec. 69 *258 days*	DAN THANG 69. ARVN 22d Division operation in Binh Dinh Province. 507 known enemy casualties.	II
22 April – 20 June 69 *70 days*	LAM SON 277. ARVN 2d Regiment operation in Quang Tri Province. 541 known enemy casualties.	I
22 April – 22 Sept. 69 *154 days*	PUTNAM TIGER. Operations by 4th Infantry Division in Kontum and Pleiku Provinces. 563 known enemy casualties.	II
1 May – 16 July 69 *77 days*	VIRGINIA RIDGE. Operation by U.S. 9th Marine Regiment in northern Quang Tri Province along the Demilitarized Zone. 560 known enemy casualties.	II
10 May – 7 June 69 *29 days*	APACHE SNOW. Operation by U.S. 9th Marine Regiment and elements of 101st Airborne Division (Airmobile) in western Thua Thien Province. 977 known enemy casualties.	I
15 May – 7 June 69 *21 days*	DAN QUYEN 38-A (People's Rights). Operation by 42d ARVN Regiment and 22d ARVN Ranger Group in Ben Het – Dak To area. 945 known casualties.	II
16 May – 13 Aug. 69 *90 days*	LAMAR PLAIN. Operation southwest of Tam Ky in Quang Tin Province by elements of 23d Infantry and 101st Airborne Divisions. 524 known enemy casualties.	I
21 July – 25 Sept. 69 *77 days*	IDAHO CANYON. Operations by U.S. 3d Marine Regiment in Quang Tri Province. 565 known enemy casualties.	I
25 Aug. – 31 Dec. 69 *129 days*	LIEN KET 414. ARVN 4th Regiment operation in Quang Ngai Province. 710 known enemy casualties.	I
26 Aug. – 31 Dec. 69 *128 days*	LIEN KET 531. ARVN 5th Regiment operation in Quang Tin Province. 542 known enemy casualties.	I
29 Sept. – 31 Dec. 69 *94 days*	QUYET THANG 21/38. ARVN 32d Regiment operation in An Xuyen Province. 721 known enemy casualties.	IV
1 Nov. – 28 Dec. 69 *58 days*	DAN TIEN 33D. ARVN 23d Division operation in Quang Duc Province. 746 known enemy casualties.	II
12 Nov. – 28 Dec. 69 *47 days*	DAN TIEN 40. ARVN 23d Division operation in Quang Duc Province. 1,012 known enemy casualties.	II
7 Dec. 69 – 31 March 70 *115 days*	RANDOLPH GLEN. The 101st Airborne Division (Airmobile), in coordination with the ARVN 1st Infantry Division, was committed to provide a shield of security on the periphery of the populated lowlands of Thua Thien Province. 670 known enemy casualties.	I
1 April – 5 Sept. 70 *158 days*	TEXAS STAR. This operation exploited the successes of Operation RANDOLPH GLEN by incorporating the lessons learned during that operation and continuing the cooperation developed among all allied elements in the province. The significant difference between the operations was that only one brigade of the 101st Airborne Division (Airmobile) had the responsibility for pacification and development support throughout the province, while the other two brigades conducted offensive operations against enemy units in the western portions of Quang Tri and Thua Thien Provinces. 1,782 known enemy casualties.	I
29 April – 30 June 70 *63 days*	OPERATIONS IN CAMBODIA. Allied forces began a military incursion into the Cambodian sanctuaries on 29 April 70; 13 major combat operations were conducted in the two months that followed. Only two of these operations involved U.S. ground combat units, but U.S. advisors accompanied all ARVN operations and U.S. air assets supported all operations as required until 30 June 70. U.S. ground forces and U.S. advisors confined their operations to a depth of 30 km. The success of the Cambodian incursion of 1970 was measured in part by the capture of individual weapons sufficient to equip 55 full strength VC infantry battalions, sufficient crew-served weapons to equip 82 to 90 VC battalions, and enough small arms ammunition to provide a basic load for 52,000 soldiers. Although strategic results of the cross-border operations were difficult to define, it was evident that the operations successfully forestalled an immediate counteroffensive by the NVA/VC against the Lon Nol government. In addition to promoting Vietnamization, the most significant result was the exacerbation of the enemy's logistical, tactical, and psychological problems within an expanded area of conflict. Over 10,000 known enemy casualties.	III

Date and duration	Operation	Corps/MR
5 Sept. 70 – 8 Oct. 71 *399 days*	JEFFERSON GLENN/OP ORD 13-70 ‡. The operation was initiated by the 101st Airborne Division (Airmobile) in coordination with the ARVN 1st Infantry Division and government officials in the Thua Thien Province. 2,026 known enemy casualties.	I
30 Jan. – 6 April 71 *67 days*	LAM SON 719. Conceived as a large-scale offensive operation against the enemy's lines of communications in Laos. The area of operations was in that part of Laos immediately adjacent to the two northern provinces of RVN. The South Vietnamese would provide and command the ground forces operating against the NVA forces, while the U.S. forces, which were specifically enjoined from a ground role in Laos, would furnish aviation, airlift and the majority of the supporting firepower. The organization of U.S. Army aviation assets was unique in that the 101st Airborne Division (Airmobile) commanded all U.S. Army aviation units in direct support of the operation. Phase I of the operation (30 Jan. – 7 Feb. 71), renamed Operation DEWEY CANYON II, was primarily a U.S. operation. It was initiated on 30 Jan. 71 as lead elements of the 1st Brigade, 5th Infantry Division (Mechanized), attacked with an armored cavalry/engineer task force on two axes from Vandegrift base camp toward Khe Sanh. Meanwhile, the ARVN made final preparations and moved administratively into position for the attack across the Laotian border. On 8 Feb. 71 Phase II began with a helicopter assault of six ARVN combat infantry battalions and an ARVN armored brigade task force thrust along Route 9 into Laos. 19,360 known enemy casualties for the entire operation.	I

Sources: General W. C. Westmoreland, "Report on Operations in South Vietnam," in *Report on the War in Vietnam*, U.S. Government Printing Office (Washington, D.C., 1968), Appendix L, pp. 281-89 and MACV Command History Reports (1968 – 71).

* Known casualties include only reported enemy KIA.

† Friendly-initiated operations in I, II and IV Corps tended to revolve around individually named operations conducted by specific units for a prescribed time in a relatively limited area of operations. Operations in III CTZ were considered a part of Operation TOAN THANG II, III, IV which had been initiated 1 June 68 as a follow up to Operation TOAN THANG I.

‡ JEFFERSON GLENN was the last major operation in which U.S. ground forces participated. On 12 November 1971, President Nixon stated that "American troops are now in a defensive position . . . in a defensive role. The offensive activities of search and destroy are now being undertaken entirely by the South Vietnamese."

TABLE 2–2
The Official Army Campaign Designations in Vietnam

Sequence Number	Campaign*	Inclusive Dates
1	Advisory	15 March 62 – 7 March 65
2	Defense	8 March 65 – 24 Dec. 65
3	Counteroffensive	25 Dec. 65 – 30 June 66
4	Counteroffensive, Phase II	1 July 66 – 31 May 67
5	Counteroffensive, Phase III	1 June 67 – 29 Jan. 68
6	Tet Counteroffensive	30 Jan. 68 – 1 April 68
7	Counteroffensive, Phase IV	2 April 68 – 30 June 68
8	Counteroffensive, Phase V	1 July 68 – 1 Nov. 68
9	Counteroffensive, Phase VI	2 Nov. 68 – 22 Feb. 69
10	Tet 69 Counteroffensive	23 Feb. 69 – 8 June 69
11	Summer – Fall 1969	9 June 69 – 31 Oct. 69
12	Winter – Spring 1970	1 Nov. 69 – 30 April 70
13	Sanctuary Counteroffensive	1 May 70 – 30 June 70
14	Counteroffensive, Phase VII	1 July 70 – 30 June 71
15	Consolidation I	1 July 71 – 30 Nov. 71
16	Consolidation II	1 Dec. 71 – 29 March 72
17	Cease – Fire	30 March 72 – 28 Jan. 73

* For purposes of the Vietnam Service Medal, the cutoff award date was 28 March 1973.

The central element of the Department of the Army Plaque is a Roman cuirass, a symbol of strength and defense. The United States Flag, of a design used in the formative years of the Nation, and the United States Army flag emphasize the role of the Army in the establishment of and the protection of the Nation.

The sword, esponton (a type of half-pike formerly used by subordinate officers), musket, bayonet, cannon, cannon balls, mortar and mortar bombs are representative of traditional army implements. The date "1775" refers to the year of the Army's establishment.

The drum and drumsticks are symbols of public notification of the army's purpose and intent to serve the Nation and its people.

The Phrygian cap (often called the Cap of Liberty) supported on the point of the unsheathed sword and the motto "This We'll Defend" on a scroll held by the rattlesnake signify the Army's constant readiness to defend and preserve the United States.

The colors of the design elements are traditionally associated with the ideals of the United States and of the Army. The flags are in proper colors. Blue is symbolic of loyalty, vigilance, perseverance and truth. Red denotes courage, zeal and fortitude. White alludes to deeds worthy of remembrance. Black is indicative of determination and constancy. Gold represents achievement, dignity and honor.

Source: Department of the Army

Army Badges and Insignia in Vietnam

Various ornamentation were worn on the army uniform during the Vietnam conflict, usually in subdued colors on the field utility jungle fatigues, but also in metal or fully colored cloth on the army green, khaki, and other formal uniforms. Sometimes unit differentiation was highlighted by the use of solid color or camouflaged baseball caps and berets to supplement the basic uniform, often with only local approval. Uniform insignia identified the wearer's status and denoted rank and grade, branch, capacity, duty assignment and prior army service. These consisted of brassards, branch scarfs, combat leaders' identification cloth loops, distinctive unit insignia (worn on shoulder straps, appropriate headgear, and jungle fatigue pockets, and often called "crests"), combat and special skill badges, insignia of branch, insignia of rank, special military police appurtenances, organizational shoulder sleeve insignia, pocket badges and tabs signifying extra skills or missions, and even cloth tapes or plastic tags displaying the individual's name and "U.S. Army" as the nationality and armed force. In Vietnam such material was sometimes embroidered directly onto the tunic.

Personal awards for valor, achievement or service were given in the form of decorations, service medals and special badges. Foreign decorations received from friendly nations were popular and often embellished army uniforms, especially in Vietnam, where close advisory and combat support fostered much inter-allied cooperation. Although the United States Constitution requires the consent of Congress for a person to accept such a foreign award, soldiers routinely added them in the field without formal approval. Likewise, various army uniform badges and insignia used in Vietnam were strictly unauthorized and produced and worn locally.

This color section illustrates those items directly connected with and worn in Vietnam whether officially sanctioned or not. However, those not authorized by the Department of the Army are marked (UA) for Unauthorized. Some patches have been reduced in size to accommodate printing.

Note: *The Air Assault Badge* was awarded only to members of the 11th Air Assault Division, and then for only a limited time before airmobile proficiency became an accepted army tactic. Though rare, recipients wore them in Vietnam. Most were transferred into the 1st Cavalry Division. The badge was unauthorized during the Vietnam era, but was authorized by the Department of the Army in 1979.

1st Armored Division insignia was authorized for wear by members of the 1st Squadron, 1st Cavalry (Armored).

2d Armored Division insignia was authorized for wear by members of the 2d Squadron, 1st Cavalry (Armored).

38th Infantry Division insignia was authorized for wear by members of Company D, 151st Infantry (Long-Range Patrol).

Unless otherwise identified, all badges and insignia are from the collection of Clement V. Kelly, Jr.

Branch Insignia and Aides-de-Camp

Army personnel, except most general officers who wore only their rank, wore the following branch insignia either on the left shirt collar or, if a uniform coat, on both lapels. Enlisted men had their branch symbols contained in circular discs while warrant officers wore the warrant officer device shown.

General officers and certain high officials were authorized personal officer aides, or Aides-de-Camp. This was considered a very honored position and such officers wore special aide insignia instead of their normal branch insignia.

Infantry

Special Forces (UA)

Field Artillery

Air Defense Artillery

Armor

Cavalry

Corps of Engineers

Signal Corps

Transportation Corps

Ordnance Corps

Adjutant General's Corps

Quartermaster Corps

Military Police Corps

**Judge Advocate
General's Corps**

Chemical Corps

**Vietnam Army
Instructor Parachutist**

Vietnam Ranger Beret Badge

**Vietnam Ranger
Qualification Badge**

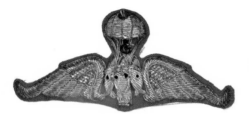

Thai Army Basic Parachutist

**Thai Honorary Parachutist
(non-airborne)**

**Thai Border Patrol Police
(BPP) Basic Parachutist**

Laotian Parachutist

Laotian Instructor Parachutist

**Laotian Cloth
Parachutist Patch**

**Thai Parachutist
cloth patch**

Authorized Army Organizational Shoulder Sleeve Insignia

These DA approved shoulder sleeve insignia are the ones authorized during the Vietnam conflict for wear on the left uniform shoulder sleeve by assigned personnel of that unit. On the normal duty service army green uniform, these insignia were in full color as shown. However in Vietnam they were also issued in subdued colors (shown by the samples illustrated) for combat jungle fatigues and other field utility tunics. This was officially extended army-wide on 1 July 1970. Though most of the patches displayed feature merrow or over-edge stitching for chart consistency, this process was not in use prior to 1968.

All patches in this section are from the author's collection except MAAG-VIETNAM, courtesy of Clement V. Kelly, Jr., and Capital Military Assistance Command, courtesy of Colonel James F. Greene, Jr.

MAAG-Vietnam (Military Assistance Advisory Group, Vietnam)

MACV (United States Military Assistance Command, Vietnam)

USARPAC (U. S. Army, Pacific)

USARV (U. S. Army, Vietnam)

I Field Force, Vietnam

II Field Force, Vietnam

Capital Military Assistance Command

XXIV Corps

1st Cavalry Division

1st Armored Division (see opening notes, this section)

2d Armored Division (see opening notes, this section)

1st Infantry Division

4th Infantry Division

5th Infantry Division

9th Infantry Division

23d Infantry Division (AMERICAL)

25th Infantry Division

38th Infantry Division (see opening notes, this section)

82d Airborne Division

101st Airborne Division

11th Armored Cavalry Regiment

11th Infantry Brigade (Light)

173d Airborne Brigade

196th Infantry Brigade (Light)

198th Infantry Brigade (Light)

199th Infantry Brigade (Light)

1st Special Forces

U. S. Army Security Agency

1st Aviation Brigade

U. S. Army Engineer Command, Vietnam

18th Engineer Brigade

20th Engineer Brigade

18th Military Police Brigade

1st Signal Brigade

USASTRATCOM (U.S. Army Strategic Communications Command)

1st Medical Brigade

U.S. Army Health Services Command

1st Logistical Command

15th Support Brigade

4th Transportation Command

5th Transportation Command

124th Transportation Command

125th Transportation Command

U.S. Army Combat Developments Command

U.S. Army Material Command

U.S. Army Criminal Investigation Command

U.S. Army Military Traffic Management and Terminal Service

Examples of Unauthorized Insignia

Many U.S. Army units procured locally-made patches, usually hand-sewn, either to substitute for unavailable authorized insignia or to feature special unit capabilities or informal titles and designs. The following sampling were all made in South Vietnam during the war. While the wearing of such insignia became commonplace and even unofficially accepted, it was still not permissible to wear them on regulation uniforms outside the combat zone.

**Subdued Insignia,
1st Cavalry Division**

**Subdued Insignia,
U. S. Army, Vietnam**

**Subdued Insignia,
173d Airborne Brigade**

**Subdued Insignia,
199th Infantry Brigade**

**Command and Control North,
MACV-SOG (UA)**

**Command and Control
Central, MACV-SOG (UA)**

**Command and Control South,
MACV-SOG (UA)**

**MACV Airborne unit. Worn by
MACV Advisory Team 162
(advising ARVN Airborne).**

**I Field Force, Vietnam para-
chutist-qualified component.**

**II Field Force, Vietnam para-
chutist-qualified component.**

**1st Aviation Brigade para-
chutist-qualified component.**

**U. S. Army Engineer Com-
mand, Vietnam, Provisional.
Untrimmed variant. (UA)**

**USARV UITG/FANK Training
Command (UA)**

**USARV Special Missions
Advisor Group. (UA)**

**U. S. Army Combined Material
Exploitation Center, Vietnam
(Military Intelligence). (UA)**

**23d Military Police
Company (UA)**

**605th Transportation
Company (Aircraft Direct
Support) (UA)**

**261st Maintenance
Detachment (UA)**

**Battery A, 4th Battalion,
77th Artillery (UA)**

**Company A, 5th Battalion,
60th Infantry (UA)**

95th Evacuation Hospital (UA)

**11th Aviation Group
Medical Evacuation (UA)**

**Task Force Ivory Coast
(Son Tay Commando Raid)**

**Recon Team Asp, CCN,
MACV-SOG (UA)**

**Recon Team Kansas, CCN,
MACV-SOG (UA)**

**Recon Team Arizona, CCC,
MACV-SOG (UA)**

**Recon Team Alaska, CCN,
MACV-SOG (UA)**

**Recon Team Anaconda, CCN,
MACV-SOG (UA)**

**Recon Team Arkansas, CCC,
MACV-SOG (UA)**

**Recon Team Intruder, CCN,
MACV-SOG (UA)**

Examples of Elite Foreign Cloth Insignia Worn by U.S. Army Special Forces Advisors

These insignia were worn most often as pocket patches. It is interesting to note the red casket, candles and joss sticks on MACV-SOG's indigenous Command and Control South insignia used to represent the extreme danger of their missions. Note also how Recon Team Hunter's traditional emblem was adopted by its Cambodian counterpart, the 537th *Bac Chen.*

RVN Special Forces (LLDB) Old Style 1959-1963 (UA)

RVN Special Forces (LLDB) New Style 1963-1975 (UA)

II Mobile Strike Force Command (B-20) (UA)

IV Mobile Strike Force Command (B-40) (UA)

RVN Airborne Jump Status designator (UA)

Indigenous Command and Control South, MACV-SOG (UA)

IV CTZ Recon Reaction Force (UA)

B-55 Liaison (UA)

CIDG early war variant Reconnaissance (UA)

Provincial Reconnaissance Unit, Project PHOENIX (UA)

Cambodian Mercenary Force (UA)

Cambodian Army Airborne Recon (UA)

Cambodian Army Forward Recon (UA)

Recon Team Hunter, MACV-SOG (UA)

537th BAC CHEN (Cambodian Shock) Attack team (UA)

Examples of Cloth Shoulder Tabs

Long Range Reconnaissance
Patrol (UA)

Explosive Ordnance
Disposal Team (UA)

Kit Carson Scout (Vietnamese
with U.S. unit) (UA)

U.S. Special Forces advisor,
"Suicide" LLDB (South
Vietnamese Special
Forces) team (UA)

U.S. advisor, ARVN
Ranger Command (UA)

U.S. advisor, ARVN
1st Ranger Group (UA)

U.S. advisor, ARVN
51st Ranger Battalion (UA)

Combat Tracker Team, 1st
Brigade, 101st Airborne
Division (UA)

42d Scout Dog Platoon (UA)

Combat Tracker Team, 1st
Brigade, 5th Infantry Division
(UA)

Sniper Expert, 2d Battalion,
502d Infantry (Airborne) (UA)

Long Range Patrol,
Company F, 58th Infantry (UA)

Long Range Patrol,
101st Airborne Division (UA)

Long Range Patrol,
Company E, 51st Infantry (UA)

Hunter Killer Team, Troop F,
4th Cavalry (UA)

74th Infantry
Detachment (UA)

Company C, 75th Infantry
(UA)

Company H, 75th Infantry
(UA)

Company M, 75th Infantry
(UA)

Company N, 75th Infantry
(UA)

Examples of Beret Flashes and Pocket Identification Emblems

5th Special Forces Group, (Airborne), 1st Special Forces Beret Flash

5th Special Forces Group, (Airborne), 1st Special Forces Beret Flash (UA)

5th Special Forces Group Captain, team commander Beret Flash (UA)

5th Special Forces Group "Bright Light" Team Beret Flash (UA)

75th Ranger Infantry Beret Flash (UA)

U.S. Special Forces, Vietnam Pocket Emblem

II Field Force, Vietnam Pocket Emblem

1st Cavalry Division Pocket Emblem

1st Infantry Division Pocket Emblem

9th Infantry Division Pocket Emblem

23d Infantry Division (AMERICAL) Pocket Emblem

44th Medical Brigade Pocket Emblem

199th Infantry Brigade Pocket Emblem

1st Logistical Command Pocket Emblem

Free World Forces, Vietnam Pocket Emblem

Distinctive Insignia

Illustrated in this section are the distinctive insignia worn by battalion and larger units while serving in Vietnam. Dates shown are the dates on which the earliest samples were approved by the U.S. Army. An (A) following the date indicates the date of authorization of the insignia. In many cases the illustrated insignia were made locally in Vietnam. These local pieces were painted rather than enamelled on thin sheet brass and came to be known as "beercans" by the soldiers. In a few cases the word "Unauthorized" (UA) is used, indicating there is no approved design for the unit.

Collection courtesy of Colonel James F. Greene, Jr.

MACV Studies & Observation Group (MACV-SOG)

I Field Force, Vietnam (I FFV)
4 October 1968 (A)

II Field Force, Vietnam (II FFV)
27 November 1968 (A)

XXIV Corps
6 February 1969 (A)

1st Cavalry Division
25 August 1965

1st Infantry Division
9 October 1930

4th Infantry Division
16 November 1965

5th Infantry Division
27 September 1965

9th Infantry Division
2 January 1966

3d Brigade, 9th Infantry Division (UA)

23d Infantry Division (AMERICAL)
14 December 1967 (A)

25th Infantry Division
21 April 1965

2d Brigade, 25th Infantry Division (UA)

82d Airborne Division
23 October 1942

101st Airborne Division
22 December 1942

11th Infantry Brigade
16 August 1967

173d Airborne Brigade
10 August 1967

196th Infantry Brigade
1 March 1966

198th Infantry Brigade
20 October 1967

199th Infantry Brigade
27 June 1966

16th Armor
20 April 1950

34th Armor
10 December 1941

69th Armor
7 September 1942

77th Armor
26 June 1942

XXIV Corps Artillery (UA)

23d Artillery Group
29 November 1968

41st Artillery Group
9 July 1924

52d Artillery Group
25 May 1971 (A)

54th Artillery Group
14 November 1968 (A)

97th Artillery Group
28 July 1952

108th Artillery Group
1 November 1968

2d Artillery
8 July 1959

4th Artillery
21 April 1959

5th Artillery
24 February 1960

6th Artillery
15 May 1959

7th Artillery
1 March 1960

8th Artillery
24 April 1924

9th Artillery
21 October 1927

11th Artillery
16 June 1924

12th Artillery
28 September 1923

13th Artillery
3 November 1927

14th Artillery
28 November 1923

15th Artillery
5 July 1929

16th Artillery
16 March 1923

17th Artillery
9 June 1925

18th Artillery
14 August 1923

19th Artillery
14 April 1935

20th Artillery
25 May 1933

21st Artillery
16 February 1940

22d Artillery
22 August 1941

25th Artillery
7 August 1925

26th Artillery
11 September 1941

27th Artillery
8 July 1935

29th Artillery
5 November 1953

30th Artillery
6 March 1952

32d Artillery
21 August 1941

33d Artillery
8 July 1938

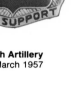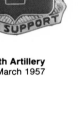

34th Artillery
6 March 1957

35th Artillery
29 June 1935

39th Artillery
17 October 1941

40th Artillery
5 December 1967

41st Artillery
16 September 1952

42d Artillery
4 November 1942

44th Artillery
16 April 1937

55th Artillery
5 January 1923

56th Artillery
21 February 1938

60th Artillery
22 Sept 1924

65th Artillery
21 September 1925

71st Artillery
3 August 1959

77th Artillery
27 September 1937

184th Ordnance Battalion
28 August 1970

191st Ordnance Battalion
29 May 1967

336th Ordnance Battalion
23 July 1969 (A)

64th Quartermaster Battalion
23 August 1966 (A)

240th Quartermaster Battalion
17 March 1967

259th Quartermaster Battalion
29 January 1969

262d Quartermaster Battalion
16 August 1967

5th Transportation Command
(UA)

8th Transportation Group
19 June 1972

48th Transportation Group
2 December 1968 (A)

500th Transportation Group
23 May 1969 (A)

507th Transportation Group
3 October 1969

1st Transportation Battalion
14 December 1966

5th Transportation Battalion
14 July 1969 (A)

6th Transportation Battalion
18 April 1967

7th Transportation Battalion
4 June 1968 (A)

10th Transportation Battalion
2 March 1967

11th Transportation Battalion
2 June 1939

14th Transportation Battalion
12 April 1967 (A)

15th Transportation Battalion
24 February 1964

24th Transportation Battalion
22 April 1966 (A)

27th Transportation Battalion
15 October 1951

36th Transportation Battalion
16 October 1967

39th Transportation Battalion
26 December 1968

54th Transportation Battalion
29 March 1967 (A)

57th Transportation Battalion
21 October 1971

58th Transportation Battalion
12 December 1966 (A)

71st Transportation Battalion
5 June 1967

124th Transportation Battalion
15 June 1967 (A)

159th Transportation Battalion
10 June 1954

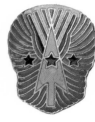

394th Transportation Battalion
19 September 1966

520th Transportation Battalion
29 September 1966 (A)

765th Transportation Battalion
19 May 1967

Transportation Battalion, Saigon (UA)

U.S. Army Security Agency
7 July 1969

224th Army Security Agency Battalion
2 August 1967 (A)

303d U.S. Army Security Agency Battalion
1 April 1964

313th U.S. Army Security Agency Battalion
20 March 1958

525th Military Intelligence Group
5 February 1971

1st Military Intelligence Battalion
1 May 1962

519th Military Intelligence Battalion
19 July 1967

4th Psychological Operations Group
12 August 1969

7th Psychological Operations Group
5 November 1969

6th Psychological Operations Battalion
8 February 1968

7th Psychological Operations Battalion
10 June 1969

8th Psychological Operations Battalion
27 October 1969

10th Psychological Operations Battalion
25 November 1968 (A)

1st Special Forces (Airborne)
17 June 1965

Nung Security Guards MACV-SOG (UA)

5th Special Forces Group Mobile Strike Force Command (UA)

Chapter 3

Combat Units in Vietnam

Combat units will be detailed within this separate section due to their overall importance to the Vietnam effort, for combat troop units were placed into the conflict at the expense of the logistical base. Although this was a planning decision initially seen as a short term expedient, the policy never really changed. While the lack of adequate logistical support led to a host of problems beyond the scope of this work, the emphasis in Vietnam was on combat units—armor/cavalry, aviation, artillery and infantry. This is reflected in this section accordingly. Combat support, service and special warfare units are briefly discussed as to mission and organization under their particular headings.

Armor. Only a few tank units served in Vietnam due to army reluctance to field them in the light of terrain and psychological considerations which later proved unfounded. By that time, however, the matrix of reinforcing units had been fixed. Though each army division sent to Vietnam had one or two tank battalions authorized, only the 4th and 25th Infantry Divisions brought a tank battalion into Vietnam with them. The third army tank battalion present in Vietnam was brought over by the 1st Brigade, 5th Infantry Division (Mechanized). All were outfitted with M48 90mm combat tanks. The only other tanks in Vietnam were provided by those organic to the 11th Armored Cavalry, brigade and divisional armored cavalry squadrons, and the armor company of the 173d Airborne Brigade. In January 1969 the first M551 armored reconnaissance assault vehicle, Sheridans, arrived in Vietnam to replace the M48 in armored cavalry organizations, and were first assigned to the 3d Squadron of the 4th Cavalry and the 1st Squadron of the 11th Armored Cavalry.

Armor doctrine developed contrary to tradition. Organizationally, the important ramifications stemming from this led to extensive and undisciplined modification of tables of organization and equipment so that no two armored units in Vietnam were organized alike. Extreme fragmentation of armor battalions throughout the war was caused by parceling out tank companies to various commands due to the deficiency of armor assets sent to Vietnam. Armored units were used to bust through jungle and fix the enemy while airmobile infantry became the encircling maneuver element. Another main mission for armor in Vietnam became route security and convoy escort where the daily clearing of mines and protecting logistical resupply routes and farm-to-market roads became a necessity.

Armor battalion organization in Vietnam is displayed in Table 3-1. A typical armored cavalry squadron is displayed in Table 3-2.

Aviation. Airmobile operations dominated the Vietnam battlefield during the U.S. involvement. All maneuver battalions became skilled in the use of the helicopter for tactical transportation to attempt to surprise and outmaneuver the enemy. The technique of shifting light and medium artillery pieces by helicopter to provide continuous fire support to units involved in rapidly changing engagements was perfected. The helicopter proved to be a rugged vehicle and the inordinate losses that had been predicted failed to materialize. The ability of the helicopter to survive in a combat environment was proven. Army aviation organizations were divided into two categories; divisional and nondivisional aviation. The missions, capabilities and limitations of the army aviation units were directly related to the types and number of aircraft authorized.

The division aviation battalion was organic to every division serving in Vietnam, but it had a very austere strength and often relied on separate aviation companies or divisional air cavalry troops to supplement it. The aviation battalion was employed to increase the supported commander's advantage in command and control, intelligence, mobility and firepower. The battalion usually consisted of a headquarters and headquarters company. The airmobile company (Table 3-3) was normally held in general support of the division and placed under the operational control of a unit for the period of time required to accomplish a specific

TABLE 3–1
Typical Armor Battalion as Modified in Vietnam (1st Battalion, 69th Armor in 1968)

	Officers	Warrant Officers	Enlisted	Tank, 90mm Gun, M48	M106 Carrier, 4.2-inch Mortar	M113 Carrier, personnel	Armored Vehicle Launched Bridge, Scissor, M48	M-88 Recovery Vehicle	5-ton Wrecker Truck	5-ton Truck	2½-ton Truck	¾-ton Truck	¼-ton Utility Truck	Individual Weapons *
Headquarters and HQ Company	16	1	139	3	4	9	—	—	—	—	5	—	12	174
Company A	5	—	87	17	—	1	—	1	—	—	1	1	3	127
Company B	5	—	87	17	—	1	—	1	—	—	1	1	3	127
Company C	5	—	87	17	—	1	—	1	—	—	1	1	3	127
Company D (Service)	6	2	152	—	—	2	2	2	2	20	10	5	12	160

Note: M48 Tank had 90mm main gun with coaxial 7.62mm machinegun as well as .50-cal machinegun mounted in cupola on top of turret. Each tank company had nine of its tanks equipped with xenon searchlights capable of illuminating targets at 900 meters.

* Includes M16 rifles, M3 submachineguns, M79 grenade launchers, pistols. Does not include crew-served weapons which were mounted on the vehicles themselves.

Source: MTOE 17-35E

TABLE 3–2
Typical Armored Cavalry Squadron in Vietnam   (1st Squadron, 1st Cavalry Illustrated):

	Officers	Warrant Officers	Enlisted	Tank, 90mm Gun M48	M125 Carrier, 81mm Mortar	M113 Carrier, Personnel	M132 Carrier, Flamethrower	M577 Carrier, Command Post	M88 Recovery Vehicle	6-ton Cargo Carrier	5-ton Wrecker Truck	5-ton Truck	2½-ton Truck	¾-ton Truck	¼-ton Utility Truck	40mm M79 Grenade Launcher	.50-cal Machinegun	7.62mm M60 Machinegun	5.56 M16 Rifle	.45-cal Pistol	.38-cal Revolver	AH-1G Helicopter*	OH-6A Helicopter*	UH-1B Helicopter*	UH-1D Helicopter*
Headquarters and HQ Troop	21	3	240	—	—	10	4	6	2	10	3	10	15	7	18	8	22	16	209	55	—	—	—	—	—
Troop A	5	—	192	9	3	21	—	—	1	—	—	—	1	1	3	29	1	42	123	74	—	—	—	—	—
Troop B	5	—	192	9	3	21	—	—	1	—	—	—	1	1	3	29	1	42	123	74	—	—	—	—	—
Troop C	5	—	192	9	3	21	—	—	1	—	—	—	1	1	3	29	1	42	123	74	—	—	—	—	—
Troop D	14	33	147	—	—	—	—	—	—	—	—	—	8	6	3	—	7	4	101	15	78	9	9	2	6

* With armament subsystems, includes a total of six door-mounted 7.62mm machineguns, seven 40mm helicopter-mounted grenade launchers, nine dual 40mm/7.62mm combinations, eighteen 7.62mm machinegun pods, four SS-11 guided-missile launchers, forty-six 2.75-inch rocket launchers.

Source: MTOE 17-106G, MTOE 17-107G, MTOE 17-78G

---

mission. There were many variations of this company in Vietnam. Often it was augmented with an armed platoon of UH-1B/1C helicopters, or there may have been only two airlift platoons with an armed helicopter platoon. In the general support company the general support platoon was the flying unit of the company. The utility support section was habitually utilized as command-and-control helicopters. The tactical support section provided the responsive armed helicopter support for escort of the airmobile company and aerial fire support and armed reconnaissance.

The separate aviation battalion was usually a headquarters unit to which subordinate aviation companies were assigned or temporarily attached. The mix of aviation companies consisted of any combination of airmobile (light), general support, medium helicopter, heavy helicopter and/or fixed-wing companies. The primary mission of a separate aviation battalion was to pool aircraft so that aviation support could be rendered to army units without aviation, or to reinforce units with organic aviation. A typical aviation battalion of this type consisted of a headquarters and headquarters company and any number of aerial weapons companies, airmobile (light) companies, and several aviation medium helicopter companies. The aerial weapons company had the mission of destroying enemy forces by aerial firepower, providing security for airmobile forces and participating in offensive, defensive and delaying actions as part of the highly mobile combined arms team. The aerial weapons company consisted of a company headquarters, three weapons platoons and a service platoon. Each weapons platoon initially possessed two armed UH-1C helicopters, but after 1 September 1967 these were gradually replaced

TABLE 3–3
Typical Airmobile/Assault Helicopter Company as Modified in Vietnam:

	Officers	Warrant Officers	Enlisted	UH-1C Utility Helicopter	UH-1D Utility Helicopter	2½-ton Truck, Fuel Servicing	2½-ton Truck, Crane	2½-ton Truck, Shop Van	2½-ton Truck	¾-ton Truck	¼-ton Truck	Forklift	7.62mm M60 Machinegun	5.56mm M16 Rifle	.38-cal Revolver	Helicopter Armament Subsystem, 7.62mm door-mounted Machinegun	Helicopter Armament Subsystem, 7.62mm MG/2.75" Rocket Launcher	Helicopter Armament Subsystem, 40mm Grenade Launcher
Company	19	20	219	8	23	6	1	1	6	12	1	1	2	219	68	23	6	2

Source: MTOE 1-77G

by the AH-1G Cobra attack helicopter. The aviation medium helicopter company (displayed in Table 3-4) provided tactical airlift with its larger CH-47 Chinook helicopters, which proved such an invaluable aircraft for artillery movement and heavy logistics that it was seldom used as an assault troop carrier. Heavy helicopter companies contained the CH-54 Tahre (flying crane) helicopter.

Airmobile divisions had an aerial rocket artillery battalion consisting of some 39 or more helicopters armed with 2.75-inch aerial rockets. In Vietnam, this battalion provided fire support directly, particularly when the division's 105mm artillery battalions were being displaced.

Cavalry. The army's cavalry formations were either ground or aerial reconnaissance units. Armored cavalry was used much like standard armor in Vietnam. It was in the air that cavalry played such a unique role. Separate air cavalry squadrons were deployed to Vietnam as early as practical. These units, with the great mobility and extensive communications provided by their organic aircraft, ranged throughout the country on both combat and reconnaissance missions. They proved to be especially useful in locating the enemy and developing the initial combat situation so that larger and heavier forces could be more effectively employed in reaction and exploitation roles. For example, in the 1st Cavalry Division practically every major engagement was started with a contact by its 1st Squadron, 9th Cavalry. This type of formation proved especially adept at screening missions, such as were conducted during the Cambodian invasion of May-June 1970.

The air cavalry troop (displayed typically in Table 3-2 as Troop D of the sample armored cavalry squadron) provided divisions, separate brigades and the 11th Armored Cavalry with a highly versatile reconnaissance capability. Consisting of a troop headquarters, aero scout platoon (equipped primarily with OH-6A observation helicopters), aero rifle platoon with five helicopters carrying an infantry-type element, and an aero weapons section with gunships, this organization proved highly successful.

Artillery. Artillery was so critical in Vietnam that 70 battalions of it served there (as compared to 81 infantry battalions). The primary characteristic was its massive firepower, allowing massed fires to be placed rapidly within a large area under all conditions of visibility, weather and terrain. One innovation prompted by the basic fluidity of the area battlefield was the system of interlocking fire support bases and improved night defensive positions developed to provide continuous all-around defense. This system was not unlike the all-around defense practiced during the American Indian wars. Major emphasis was put on fire support. Artillery was positioned so that any point in the area of operations could be reached by fire from at least one and usually two batteries or more. The batteries were mutually supporting in that they could fire in support of one another in case of attack. The great range of 175mm guns made it possible to deliver a heavy concentration of accurate fire to positions and patrols within 20 miles of the gun position regardless of weather.

TABLE 3–4
Typical Medium Helicopter Company/Assault Support Helicopter Company as Modified in Vietnam:

	Officers	Warrant Officers	Enlisted	CH-47 Cargo Helicopter*	OH-6A Observation Helicopter	5-ton Wrecker	5-ton Tractor	2½-ton Truck	2½-ton Truck, Van	¾-ton Truck	½-ton Platform Truck	¼-ton Truck	Forklift	40mm M79 Grenade Launcher	7.62mm M60 Machinegun	5.56mm M16 Rifle	.45-cal Pistol	.38-cal Revolver
Company	15	26	228	16	2	1	2	12	2	6	3	6	2	18	4	227	2	39

* Equipped with armament subsystem, 7.62mm machinegun.
Source: MTOE 1-258G

The division artillery in Vietnam contained a division artillery headquarters and headquarters battery, one 155mm towed/8-inch self-propelled howitzer (general support) battalion, and three 105mm towed (direct support) artillery battalions. Each separate infantry brigade in Vietnam had its own 105mm howitzer battalion present, except the 1st Brigade, 5th Infantry Division which brought its 155mm self-propelled M109 howitzers.

The 105mm towed howitzer most often served in the direct fire support role. Its light weight, dependability and high rate of fire made it an ideal weapon for moving with light infantry forces and responding quickly with high volumes of close-in fire. Units were initially equipped with the M101A1 howitzer, virtually the same 105mm howitzer that had been used to support U.S. forces since World War II. In 1966 the first M102s, a new towed 105mm howitzer, were received in Vietnam and the weapon was issued to the 1st Battalion, 21st Artillery in March. Replacement of the old howitzers continued steadily over the next four years throughout Vietnam. A typical 105mm howitzer battalion (towed) is displayed in Table 3-5.

Certain field force artillery battalions were equipped with the M108, a 105mm self-propelled weapon which was obsolescent but still in the army inventory. The M108 was too heavy to be lifted by helicopter, so its support of highly mobile forces in Vietnam was restricted. Still, it was employed effectively in area support roles and, if the terrain permitted, in support of ground operations. Only two of these battalions served.

The next larger caliber artillery weapons were the 155mm howitzers. Firing units were equipped with either the towed M114A1 or the self-propelled M109. Both weapons normally provided area coverage or augmented direct support. An exception was the 1st Brigade, 5th Infantry Division (Mechanized) where the 155mm self-propelled howitzers were used in direct support of maneuver elements. Like the M108, however, the towed M114A1 was considered obsolescent since it was no match for the 155mm self-propelled weapon for supporting conventional ground operations against a highly mobile, armor-heavy enemy. In Vietnam on the other hand, the M114A1 proved invaluable because it was light enough to be displaced by helicopter and so could provide medium artillery support to infantry forces even where roads were nonexistent. With a range over 3,000 meters greater than that of the 105mm howitzer, and a 95-pound projectile three times the weight of the 105mm projectile, the 155mm howitzers provided a welcome additional punch to existing direct support weapons. Typical 155mm howitzer battalions are shown in Tables 3-6 and 3-7.

The M107 self-propelled 175mm gun and the M110 8-inch howit-

TABLE 3–5
Typical 105mm Towed Howitzer Battalion as Modified in Vietnam:

	Officers	Warrant Officers	Enlisted	5-ton Wrecker	5-ton Truck	2½-ton Truck	¾-ton Truck	¼-ton Truck	105mm Howitzer, Towed	40mm M79 Grenade Launcher	7.62mm M60 Machinegun	5.56mm M16 Rifle	45-cal Pistol
Service and Battery HQ	20	3	158	1	1	16	20	20	—	8	8	154	27
Battery A	8	—	107	—	—	13	4	5	6	5	8	108	7
Battery B	8	—	107	—	—	13	4	5	6	5	8	108	7
Battery C	8	—	107	—	—	13	4	5	6	5	8	108	7
Battery D	8	—	107	—	—	13	4	5	6	5	8	108	7

Source: MTOE 6-156G, MTOE 6-157G

TABLE 3-6
Typical 155mm Towed Howitzer/8-inch Self-Propelled Howitzer Battalion as Modified in Vietnam:

	Officers	Warrant Officers	Enlisted	Cargo Carrier, Ammunition	Carrier, Command Post Light	5-ton Wrecker	5-ton Truck	2½-ton Truck	¾-ton Truck	¼-ton Truck	155mm Howitzer, Towed	8-inch Howitzer, Self-Propelled	40mm M79 Grenade Launcher	7.62mm M60 Machinegun	5.56mm M16 Rifle	45-cal Pistol
Service and Battery HQ	17	2	144	—	—	1	12	9	15	14	—	—	5	9	141	24
Battery A	4	—	109	—	—	—	9	3	2	2	6	—	5	8	101	7
Battery B	4	—	109	—	—	—	9	3	2	2	6	—	5	8	101	7
Battery C	4	—	109	—	—	—	9	3	2	2	6	—	5	8	101	7
Battery D	4	—	110	4	2	—	6	5	3	2	—	4	5	8	108	7

Source: MTOE 6-166G, MTOE 6-167G, MTOE 6-358G

TABLE 3-7
Typical 155mm Towed Howitzer Artillery Battalion as Modified in Vietnam:

	Officers	Warrant Officers	Enlisted	5-ton Wrecker	5-ton Truck	2½-ton Truck	¾-ton Truck	¼-ton Truck	155mm Howitzer, M114 Towed	40mm M79 Grenade Launcher	7.62mm M60 Machinegun	7.62mm M14 Rifle	5.56mm M16 Rifle	.45-cal Pistol	.38-cal Revolver
Headquarters and HQ Battery	17	3	113	—	—	7	20	10	—	6	—	—	114	17	2
Battery A	6	—	119	—	10	3	4	5	6	8	8	8	100	9	—
Battery B	6	—	119	—	10	3	4	5	6	8	8	8	100	9	—
Battery C	6	—	119	—	10	3	4	5	6	8	8	8	100	9	—
Service Battery	2	3	85	1	10	9	3	3	—	8	7	—	82	8	—

Source: MTOE 6-426G, MTOE 6-427G, MTOE 6-429G

TABLE 3-8
Typical 175mm Gun/8-inch Howitzer Battalion as Modified in Vietnam:

	Officers	Warrant Officers	Enlisted	6-ton Cargo Carrier	M578 Recovery Vehicle	M577 Command Post Carrier	5-ton Truck	5-ton Wrecker	2½-ton Truck	¾-ton Truck	¼-ton Truck	175mm Gun, M107 Self-Propelled	8-inch Howitzer, M110 Self-Propelled	7.62mm M60 Machinegun	40mm M79 Grenade Launcher	5.56mm M16 Rifle	.45-cal Pistol
Headquarters and HQ Battery	17	3	115	—	—	—	—	—	7	21	10	—	—	6	4	111	22
Battery A	6	—	112	4	—	1	4	—	5	4	6	2	2	7	3	113	5
Battery B	6	—	112	4	—	1	4	—	5	4	6	2	2	7	3	113	5
Battery C	6	—	112	4	—	1	4	—	5	4	6	2	2	7	3	113	5
Service Battery	2	3	71	—	1	—	8	1	8	3	3	—	—	4	4	70	8

Source: MTOE 6-436G, MTOE 6-437G, MTOE 6-439G

zer had identical carriages but different tubes. The 175mm gun fired a 174-pound projectile almost 33 kilometers, which proved of tremendous value in providing an umbrella of protection over large areas. The 8-inch howitzer fired a 200-pound projectile almost 17 kilometers and was the most accurate weapon in the field artillery. Since the weapons had identical carriages, the common practice in field force artillery units was to install those tubes that best fit the current tactical needs, so that one day a battery might be 175mm and a few days later it might be half 175mm and half 8-inch. A typical 175mm gun/8-inch howitzer battalion is displayed in Table 3-8.

Aerial rocket artillery, also discussed in aviation, proved to be extremely effective in augmenting and extending the range of the cannon artillery of the airmobile divisions. Aerial rocket artillery units were equipped first with UH-1B or UH-1C (Huey) helicopters but by early 1968 the improved AH-1G Cobra was outfitted in this mode, carrying a larger payload of 76 rockets. In early 1970 the designation of aerial rocket artillery was changed to aerial field artillery, but the former title is retained for consistency throughout this work.

Two HAWK missile battalions were sent to Vietnam, though three were planned (see Appendix A: Deployments), and these were designed to cope with low and medium altitude targets with special capabilities to counter aircraft which attacked at low altitude to escape radar detection by taking advantage of "ground clutter." The HAWK system continuous-wave radars and semiactive homing guidance were not seriously degraded by "ground clutter." A typical HAWK missile artillery battalion is displayed in Table 3-9.

Artillery in Vietnam was also represented by specialized batteries of .50-caliber quad machineguns and searchlights. The machinegun batteries supplemented those air defense battalions equipped with 40mm Duster M42 antiaircraft guns, but their employment in Vietnam consisted of providing convoy security, combat assault support and perimeter defense. Searchlight batteries provided target acquisition and battlefield illumination with

125,000,000 candlepower, 23-inch xenon searchlights. They also provided navigation aids. A typical machinegun battery is displayed in Table 3-10.

Infantry. When the build-up of U.S. troops began in 1965, infantry units in general were organized under 1963 ROAD tables and shortly thereafter a new series of new infantry TOEs was published. Standard and mechanized infantry tables were dated 31 March 1966, while the airborne infantry had two sets of tables, dated 30 June 1965 and 30 June 1966. Test TOEs were prepared for two new infantry unit types, the airmobile battalion organic to the airmobile division and a special infantry battalion which was to be assigned to light infantry divisions and separate light infantry brigades. With authorized strengths of 769 men, these units were smaller than the regular infantry battalion of 849 men. All infantry types retained the ROAD structure of a headquarters and headquarters company and three rifle companies.

Vietnam changed this multitude of types in the interest of combat standardization. Since personnel who would normally man the heavier infantry weapons were frequently used instead to make up a small fourth rifle company within the battalion as a command post security force and emergency reserve, official permission was soon granted to organize such units on a permanent basis in Vietnam. This was reflected in MTOEs which also allowed Vietnam-stationed or -bound infantry battalions a separate combat support company. Gradually all infantry battalions in Vietnam, with the exception of mechanized and riverine units, were reorganized under modifications of the light infantry TOE with a headquarters and headquarters company, four rifle companies, a combat support company and a total authorized strength of 920; this transition was completed by the end of 1968. Such a typical infantry battalion is displayed in Table 3-11.

Airmobility introduced a new dimension in flexibility so all-encompassing that the infantry and helicopter combination soon dominated the army tactical doctrine used in Vietnam. The helicopter was relied upon for transportation, medical evacuation, artillery spotting, fire support, insertion into and extraction out of combat, supply, command and control and communications relay. All infantry in Vietnam became proficient in airmobile tactics to the point that the only real distinction between airmobile infantry and regular infantry became whether or not aviation assets were organically assigned to the division.

Air support, close artillery fire support and gunships were used in massive quantities whenever the enemy was contacted, and became a mainstay of infantry. In fact, the available ordnance on call was so profuse that most infantry elements found it unnecessary to carry anything into the field heavier than machineguns, claymore mines and LAWS (expendable light antitank weapons used for bunker suppression if encountered)—they left their heavier authorized weapons behind.

Although few mechanized infantry units were sent to Vietnam, those that served there were remarkably effective, since their

TABLE 3–9
Typical HAWK Missile Artillery Battalion as Modified in Vietnam:

	Officers	Warrant Officers	Enlisted	Sentry Dog	5-ton Wrecker	5-ton Truck	2 ½-ton Truck	¾-ton Truck	¼-ton Truck	Launcher, Guided Missile (HAWK)	3.5-inch Rocket Launcher	7.62mm M60 Machinegun	5.56mm M16 Rifle	.45-cal Pistol
Headquarters and HQ Battery	20	7	255	4	—	—	18	10	15	—	6	4	171	12
Battery A	5	2	137	4	1	—	31	4	4	6	6	6	131	4
Battery B	5	2	137	4	1	—	31	4	4	6	6	6	131	4
Battery C	5	2	137	4	1	—	31	4	4	6	6	6	131	4
Battery D	5	2	137	4	1	—	31	4	4	6	6	6	131	4

Source: MTOE 44-236 D, MTOE 44-237D

TABLE 3–10
Typical .50-caliber Machinegun (Quad M55) Battery in Vietnam:

	Officers	Warrant Officers	Enlisted	2 ½-ton Truck	¾-ton Truck	¼-ton Truck	M55 Quad .50-cal Machinegun, Trailer-Mounted	40mm M79 Grenade Launcher	7.62mm M60 Machinegun	5.56mm M16 Rifle
Battery	2	—	140	25	1	1	24	24	26	141

Source: MTOE 44-58G

TABLE 3–11
Standard Infantry Battalion as Modified in Vietnam:

	Officers	Warrant Officers	Enlisted	2 ½-ton Truck	¾-ton Truck	¼-ton Truck	7.62mm Machinegun	40mm M79 Grenade Launcher	.45-cal Pistol	5.56mm M16 Rifle	4.2-inch Mortar	81mm Mortar	90mm Recoilless Rifle	Portable Flamethrower
Headquarters and HQ Company	15	2	147	9	4	9	2	8	15	149	—	—	—	—
Company A	6	—	158	—	—	5	6	24	9	149	—	3	3	—
Company B	6	—	158	—	—	5	6	24	9	149	—	3	3	—
Company C	6	—	158	—	—	5	6	24	9	149	—	3	3	—
Company D	6	—	158	—	—	5	6	24	9	149	—	3	3	—
Company E*	4	—	96	—	4	4	—	6	4	96	4	—	—	12

* Combat Support Company

Source: MTOE 176, MTOE 177, and MTOE 178 (all Test)

Organization of the standard U.S. infantry company (MTOE 7-177 Test used in Vietnam): The rifle company headquarters consisted of two officers and ten men, with three rifle platoons (one officer, 41 enlisted each) and one mortar platoon (one officer, 25 enlisted). Each rifle platoon had a platoon headquarters (one officer, two enlisted), three rifle squads (ten enlisted with M79 and M16 weapons) and one weapons squad (nine enlisted with M16 rifles and two M60 machineguns, and one 90mm recoilless rifle, the latter almost always left at base camp). The mortar platoon contained a headquarters of one officer and seven enlisted and three mortar squads (six enlisted with one M79, one 81mm mortar, and M16 rifles). Usually the 81mm mortars were also left at base and the squads used as rifle infantry.

TABLE 3–12
Typical Ranger Infantry Company in Vietnam   (Company G, 75th Infantry Illustrated):

	Officers	Warrant Officers	Enlisted	¼-ton Truck	40mm M79 Grenade Launcher	5.56mm M16 Rifle	.45-cal Pistol
Company*	3	—	115	9	32	116	2

* The company was broken down into two platoons, each platoon containing a platoon headquarters (one officer, one enlisted) and eight six-man patrols. The company headquarters itself contained one officer and 17 enlisted.

Source: MTOE 7-157E

M113 armored personnel carriers were up-gunned and armored as "armored cavalry assault vehicles" and used in a tanklike shock role. The mechanized battalion was modified to include a smaller fourth rifle company, but a separate combat support company was not authorized.

Due to the fragmented and mobile nature of the conflict waged against an enemy who could be highly elusive if he desired to be, a premium was soon placed on intelligence gathering to locate enemy forces, which in turn led to a profusion of both special and regular infantry patrolling formations. These included long range patrols (LRPs) and long range reconnaissance patrols (LRRPs) and by late 1967 an LRP company was attached to each division in Vietnam and eventually to each separate brigade. The number of companies continued to increase, and by the end of 1968 about half of all separate companies in the Active Army were long-range patrol units. They were elements of various regiments and had no common numerical designation or historical connection with each other until 1 January 1969. On that day the 75th Infantry, the famous "Merrill's Marauders" of World War II, was reorganized under CARS and became the parent regiment for LRP units. At the same time the parenthetical designation of the companies was changed from LRP to Ranger, although their long-range patrol mission remained unchanged. A typical ranger company is illustrated in Table 3-12.

Other small infantry units in Vietnam were outfitted with trained scout and sentry dogs, highly intelligent and loyal, which served in a variety of assignments. As sentinels, the dogs strengthened the security and perimeter defenses of bases. Operating as scouts with tactical units they provided early warning of the enemy's approach or presence. They could detect the enemy's entry into a prepared ambush and were particularly useful in spotting booby traps, locating enemy tunnels and bunkers as well as caches of weapons, supplies and food. Combat Tracker Teams were also formed. These five-man teams used dogs chosen for endurance, color, stability and good nature rather than ferocity. The dog's sense of smell and the soldier's specialized scouting skills formed a powerful combination. By mid-1968 some 1,500 dogs would be used throughout Vietnam. Thirty-six were killed in action and 153 wounded by this time.

Airmobile units were capable of such swift and direct movement to their objectives regardless of terrain obstacles and enemy troop concentrations that the airborne assault techniques developed in World War II became unnecessary. Airborne-qualified infantry in Vietnam served merely as elite foot soldiers and were retained because of their *esprit de corps* (though several parachutist battalions in the 1st Cavalry and 101st Airborne Divisions were discontinued in jump proficiency as the war progressed). The few parachute assaults made in Vietnam are shown in Table 3-13.

One type of infantry which was truly unique was the mobile riverine infantry, an amphibious force operating entirely afloat and organized in Vietnam for the first time since the U.S. Civil War, when similar Union Army forces operated on the Mississip-

pi, Cumberland and other rivers. Part of the 9th Infantry Division, the troops lived on barracks ships docked at the Mobile Riverine Base anchorage and were transported along the network of waterways in the Mekong River Delta by navy armored troop carrier boats and monitors, which also provided close-in fire support. Riverine artillery, army 105mm howitzers mounted on barges, could augment this firepower when needed.

Despite the overall impression of combat in Vietnam as one of air assault, perimeter defense and "fire base psychosis," violent and traditional combat flared up between maneuvering elements on both sides with infantry digging in and taking stubborn strongpoints by fire and movement. Near Duc Pho in July 1967, for example, Company C, 1st Battalion, 35th Infantry (25th Infantry Division) decided one particular standoff by conducting a classic rifle charge against fortified positions. Though brigade and battalion operations resulted in some pitched battles such as the Ia Drang Valley and city fighting such as in Saigon and Hue, the general pattern of the Vietnam war centered around small-unit actions which were not only typical but decisive in most instances. As the war stalemated, U.S. Army infantry became increasingly engaged in support of pacification, base security and protecting lines of communication. The loss of momentum, undue political restrictions on engaging the enemy in combat, general dissatisfaction with the war—especially within the drafted ranks—and lack of meaningful objectives all took their toll on morale and combat effectiveness. This culminated in November 1971 when a Presidential announcement that American troops were strictly in a defensive posture forbade further offensive activities.

TABLE 3–13
U.S. Army Combat Parachute Assaults Vietnam

Defined as those directed by U.S. commands; thus several parachute assaults conducted by ARVN airborne battalions, even if they included a handful of MACV advisors, are not included.

Unit	Date	Aircraft	U.S. Paratroopers	Indigenous Paratroopers	Location
173d Abn Bde elements: HHC, 173d Abn Bde (partial) 2d Bn, 503d Inf (Airborne) Battery A, 3d Bn, 319th Arty	22 Feb. 67	C-130	845	—	War Zone C, north of Katum, Tay Ninh Provinces
5th Special Forces Group	2 April 67	C-123	39	314 *	Bunard, III CTZ
5th Special Forces Group	13 May 67	C-130	20	374 *	Dropzone Blackjack, south of Nui Gai, IV CTZ
5th Special Forces Group	5 Oct. 67	C-130	25†	355 ‡	Bu Prang, II CTZ
5th Special Forces Group	17 Nov. 68	C-130	25†	495 *	Seven Mountains Region, IV CTZ

* Mobile Strike Force composed of Civilian Irregular Defense Group (CIDG) parachutists.

† American number is included in paratrooper total in next column. U.S. participation figures are only approximate.

‡ 296 MIKE force and 59 member pathfinder contingent.

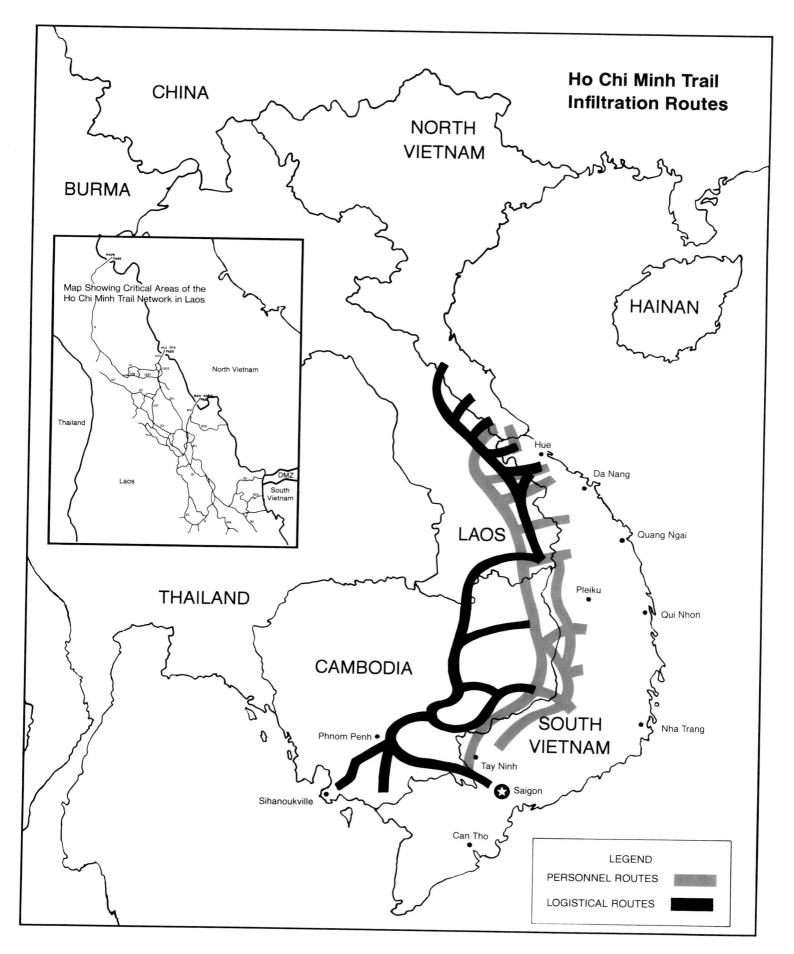

**Ho Chi Minh Trail
Infiltration Routes**

CHINA

NORTH
VIETNAM

BURMA

HAINAN

Map Showing Critical Areas of the
Ho Chi Minh Trail Network in Laos

NAPE
PASS

MU GIA
PASS

North Vietnam

BAN KARAI
PASS

Thailand

Laos

DMZ

South
Vietnam

LAOS

Hue

Da Nang

Quang Ngai

Pleiku

THAILAND

Qui Nhon

CAMBODIA

Phnom Penh

SOUTH
VIETNAM

Nha Trang

Tay Ninh

Saigon

Sihanoukville

Can Tho

LEGEND

PERSONNEL ROUTES

LOGISTICAL ROUTES

55

Major Commands

Chapter 4

Army and Advisory Level Commands

Military Assistance Advisory Group, Indochina (MAAG – Indochina)

No Insignia Authorized

Arrived Vietnam: 17 September 1950
Departed Vietnam: 31 October 1955
Location: Saigon – Cholon
Mission: Advisor support for Laos, Vietnam, Cambodia

Commanders

Brigadier General Francis G. Brink	Oct. 50
Major General Thomas J. H. Trapnell	Aug. 52
Lieutenant General John W. O'Daniel	April 54

Military Assistance Advisory Group, Vietnam (MAAG – Vietnam)

No Insignia Authorized

Arrived Vietnam: 1 November 1955
Departed Vietnam: 15 May 1964
Location: Saigon
Authorized Strength: 1,606* (1961)

Commanders

Lieutenant General Samuel T. Williams	Nov. 55
Lieutenant General Lionel C. McGarr	Sept. 60
Major General Charles J. Timmes	July 62

* U.S. Army element only.

The Military Assistance Advisory Group, Vietnam was formed from the Military Assistance Advisory Group, Indochina and concentrated on joint services support for the South Vietnamese Army as well as combat arms training to include field advisors at expanding rates. It existed for two years after MACV was established in order to avoid disrupting the institutional expertise it had gained, as well as to enable a smooth transition in field advisor relationships. During this group's service the authorized number of U.S. military advisors was increased from 746 in the beginning of 1961 to over 3,400 at the beginning of 1963. For further discussion of U.S. Army advisors in Vietnam, see section on the MACV Field Advisory Element.

U.S. Military Assistance Command, Vietnam (MACV)

No Insignia Authorized

Arrived Vietnam: 8 February 1962
Reorganized: 15 May 1964
Departed Vietnam: 29 March 1973
Location: Saigon, Tan Son Nhut

Authorized Strength	1966	1968	1971	1972
U.S. Army Element	1,488	6,407	13,095	6,681

Commanders

General Paul D. Harkins	Feb. 62
General William C. Westmoreland	June 64
General Creighton W. Abrams	July 68
General Frederick C. Weyand	June 72

Deputy Commanders

Lieutenant General William C. Westmoreland	Jan. 64
Lieutenant General John L. Throckmorton	Aug. 64

Lieutenant General John A. Heintges	Nov. 65
General Creighton W. Abrams	June 67
General Andrew J. Goodpaster	July 68
General William B. Rosson	May 69
General Frederick C. Weyand	April 70
General John W. Vogt, Jr. USAF	May 72

The U.S. Military Assistance Command, Vietnam (MACV) was established as a unified command subordinated to the Commander-in-chief, Pacific, in order to provide a joint headquarters for the expanding United States military effort in Vietnam. The Commander had responsibility for and authority over all U.S. military activities in Vietnam. In May 1964 it was reorganized and greatly enlarged when it absorbed the Military Assistance Advisory Group, Vietnam. MACV had control over USARV, Naval Forces Vietnam, Seventh Air Force, III Marine Amphibious Force as well as the I and II Field Forces Vietnam, XXIV Corps, the 5th Special Forces Group, and a host of internal MACV projects and matters such as the advisory activities and Civil Operations and Rural Development Support (CORDS).

Field Advisory Element, MACV

Authorized Strength	1964	1966	1968	1971
Field Advisory Element	4,741	5,394	9,430	1,486

Senior U.S. Army Advisors in the Corps Tactical Zones (CTZ) June 1966 – March 1973:

I Corps Tactical Zone

Brigadier General A. L. Hamblen, Jr.	June 66
Colonel John J. Beeson III	July 67
Brigadier General Salve H. Matheson	Jan. 68
Colonel John J. Beeson III	April 68
Colonel Roland H. Renwanz	Aug. 68
Brigadier General Henry J. Muller, Jr.	Sept. 69
Brigadier General Charles A. Jackson	July 70
Lieutenant General James W. Sutherland, Jr.*	Oct. 70
Lieutenant General Welborn G. Dolvin*	July 71
Major General Frederick J. Kroesen, Jr.*	April 72
Major General Howard H. Cooksey*	June 72

II Corps Tactical Zone

Brigadier General James S. Timothy	June 66
Major General Richard M. Lee	Aug. 66
Colonel Charles A. Cannon	Nov. 66
Major General John W. Barnes	Nov. 67
Colonel Robert M. Piper	Jan. 68
Brigadier General Gordon J. Duquemin	Dec. 69
Brigadier General Jack MacFarlane	July 70
Lieutenant General Arthur S. Collins, Jr.†	Oct. 70
Major General Charles P. Brown †	Jan. 71
Mr. John Paul Vann ‡	May 71
Major General Michael D. Healy †	June 72

III Corps Tactical Zone

Colonel Arndt L. Mueller	June 66
Colonel Gus S. Peters	Nov. 67
Brigadier General Donald D. Dunlop	June 68
Brigadier General Carleton Preer, Jr.	May 69

Brigadier General Dennis P. McAuliffe	Jan. 70
Lieutenant General Michael S. Davison §	Oct. 70
Major General Jack J. Wagstaff §	May 71
Major General James F. Hollingsworth §	Jan. 72
Major General Marshall B. Garth §	Sept. 72

IV Corps Tactical Zone ‖

Colonel George A. Barton	June 64
Colonel Leroy B. Wilson	June 66
Brigadier General William R. Desobry	Aug. 66
Major General George S. Eckhardt	Jan. 67
Major General Roderick Wetherill	June 69
Major General Hal D. McCown #	Jan. 70
Major General John H. Cushman**	May 71
Brigadier General Frank E. Blazey**	Feb. 72
Major General Thomas M. Tarpley**	March 72

* The senior general in Military Region 1 was considered the senior U.S. army advisor.

† The senior general in Military Region 2 was considered the senior U.S. army advisor.

‡ Mr. John Paul Vann, a legendary advisor throughout the Vietnam war, was killed in a helicopter crash 9 June 1972 while in charge of Military Region 2.

§ The senior general in Military Region 3 was considered the senior U.S. army advisor.

‖ The IV Corps Tactical Zone was redesignated as the Delta Military Assistance Command (DMAC) 8 April 1968 and later Military Region 4 in October 1970.

Assumed command of Military Region 4 and as such performed also as the senior U.S. army advisor in the region.

** The senior general in the area was considered the senior U.S. army advisor. These generals commanded the Delta Regional Assistance Command (DRAC).

The Field Advisory Element, MACV initially had only enough assets to field army advisors on sector (province) and regimental levels. They assisted the South Vietnamese military in combat planning and operations, training, intelligence, pyschological warfare, communications, civil affairs, logistics and medical areas. This advisory effort was expanded in April and May of 1964 when subsector (district) advisory teams were deployed to the 13 districts in the Saigon vicinity. On a tactical level, such teams were also directly assigned to selected battalions. Of these, 169 subsector teams were fielded by December 1965. In addition, all 43 sectors had advisors assigned to them. Beginning in 1968 some 354 new advisory teams were specifically created to provide assistance to the Regional and Popular Forces (RF/PF) so that the South Vietnamese territorial military would be covered as well. Starting in 1969 the mobile advisory teams were assigned to Vietnam directly from the United States for one-year tours instead of being raised in Vietnam from available officers and sergeants. From 1968 through 1972 the advisory effort was emphasized following the Vietnamization doctrine implemented to upgrade and modernize the South Vietnamese Army. The U.S. Army advisors served with great distinction in the dangerous and hostile circumstances to which they were constantly exposed. Despite political adversity and the lack of all command authority, the army advisors insured liaison with needed U.S. fire support and airpower and often rallied their South Vietnamese units, saving them from destruction on the battlefield.

U.S. Army, Vietnam (USARV)

No Insignia
Authorized

Arrived Vietnam: 20 July 1965
Departed Vietnam: 15 May 1972
Location: Long Binh

Authorized Strength Headquarters	1966	1968	1970	1972
USARV	808	1,329	1,521	559

Commanders

General William C. Westmoreland	July 65
General Creighton W. Abrams	July 68

Deputy Commanders

Major General John Norton	July 65
Lieutenant General Jean E. Engler	Jan. 66
Lieutenant General Bruce Palmer, Jr.	July 67
Lieutenant General Frank T. Mildren	June 68
Lieutenant General William J. McCaffrey	July 70
Major General Morgan G. Roseborough*	Sept. 72

* Became Commanding General of USARV/MACV Support Command in October 1972 and the position of Deputy Commander, USARV ceased to exist.

The U.S. Army, Vietnam (USARV) was created on 20 July 1965, but reflected an outgrowth of U.S. Army involvement in Vietnam going back to the late 1950s. The first complete combat units of American forces arrived in December 1961 after the Republic of Vietnam had declared a state of national emergency on 18 October 1961, together with a support team from the 9th Logistical Command on Okinawa. This small team formed the nucleus from which USARV evolved. As the army units in the country increased, the U.S. Army Ryukyu Support Group (Provisional) took over logistics control of U.S. units in Vietnam. Further increases in U.S. troops necessitated the support command be changed to U.S. Army Support Group, Vietnam. During 1965 the increase of U.S. forces was rapid and, with the arrival of the additional combat units, the U.S. Army Support Command, Vietnam was redesignated U.S. Army, Vietnam (USARV) to control all logistical and administrative units of the U.S. Army in Vietnam. The Commander of MACV was also the Commander of USARV; this led to some confusion and duplication but reflected the close association of USARV to the MACV effort. The Deputy Commanding Generals are thus listed, for the actual functioning of USARV fell upon their shoulders in light of the great responsibility that MACV already placed upon the latter's Commanding Generals. On 15 May 1972 USARV was converted into the Headquarters of the combined U.S. Army Vietnam/Military Assistance Command Vietnam (USARV/MACV) Support Command. The following major elements were contained within the USARV area of responsibility:

1st Logistical Command
1st Aviation Brigade
34th General Support Group
U.S. Army Security Agency Group
U.S. Army Engineer Command (Provisional)
18th Military Police Brigade
525th Military Intelligence Group
U.S.A. Headquarters Area Command (USAHAC)
All U.S. Army support commands until the 1st Logistical Command took them over

Additionally, the formations that USARV controlled directly are listed in the following USARV Order of Battle:

U.S. Army Vietnam (USARV) Assigned and Attached Components

Components	USARV Service	Authorized Strength		
		1966	1968	1971
Headquarters, Special Troops	15 Feb. 66 – 15 May 72	130	135	170
Headquarters, Support Troops	27 July 65 – 28 March 73 *	218	25	?
Headquarters, U.S. Army Area Command	1 April 66 – 15 May 72	472	472	218
USARV Individual Training Group	1 March 71 – 29 June 72 *	—	—	?
USARV Training Advisory Group	1 March 71 – 29 April 72	—	—	666
USARV Special Missions Advisory Group	1 March 71 – 19 April 72	—	—	136

* Complete Vietnam service, extended beyond the life of USARV proper.

USARV Components

Capital Military Assistance Command, Saigon
Delta Military Assistance Command (Provisional), Can Tho
Department of the Army Audit Agency Elements
Department of the Army Armed Forces Courier Station
Department of the Army Combat Development Command Liaison Field Office
Department of the Army Edgewood Arsenal Headquarters Office, Saigon
Department of the Army Special Security Groups (multiple locations)
GOCO Generator & Electrical Distribution Facility
GOCO Tuy Hoa High Voltage Facility
Regional Support Activity (RSA), Military Region 2
U.S. Army Material Command Communications System, Saigon
U.S. Army Material Command Customer Assistance Agency
U.S. Army Material Command Damage Assessment Reporting Team

U.S. Army Material Command Electronics Command Field Service Activity
U.S. Army Material Command Logistics Assistance Office, Long Binh
U.S. Army Material Command Logistics Area Communications System Office
U.S. Army Material Command Logistics Office, Special Foreign Activity
U.S. Army Material Command Logistics Office, Unified Strategic Communications
U.S. Army Material Command Field Service Activity
U.S. Army Material Command Office of Procurement & Material, Army Area
U.S. Army Material Command Weapons Command, Vietnam
U.S. Army Material Command Wounds-Munitions Effects Team, Vietnam
U.S. Army China Beach Rest & Recuperation Center, Da Nang
U.S. Army Class IV Equipment Pool, Long Binh

U.S. Army Concept Team Activity

U.S. Army Engineer Command, Vietnam

U.S. Army Engineer Construction Agency

U.S. Army Forces, Military Region 2

U.S. Army Headquarters Area Command (USAHAC)

U.S. Army Element Vietnam Army-Air Force Regional Exchange, USAHAC

U.S. Army Highway Traffic Center

U.S. Army Medical Command, Vietnam

U.S. Army Philco-Ford Parts Facility, Saigon

U.S. Army Postal Group, Vietnam

U.S. Army Procurement Agency

U.S. Army Service Support Element, Long Binh

U.S. Army Support Command, Cam Ranh Bay (see separate Order of Battle)

U.S. Army Support Command, Da Nang (see separate Order of Battle)

U.S. Army Support Command, Saigon (see separate Order of Battle)

U.S. Army Support Element, Military Region 1 (see First Regional Assistance Command Order of Battle)

U.S. Army Support Element, Military Region 2 (see Second Regional Assistance Command Order of Battle)

U.S. Army Support Element, Military Region 3 (see Third Regional Assistance Command Order of Battle)

U.S. Army Support Element, Military Region 4 (see Delta Regional Assistance Command Order of Battle)

U.S. Army Vietnam Advisor School

U.S. Army Vietnam Inventory Control Center

U.S. Army Vietnam Security Forces

U.S. Army Vietnam Special Troops, to include:

Adjutant General Data Service Center

Engineer Hydro Survey Detachment

Finance Central Security Accounting Office

Property Disposal Agency, Vietnam

Religious Retreat Center, Cam Ranh Bay

Women's Army Corps (WAC) Detachment

U.S. Army Central Civilian Personnel Office

U.S. Army Drug Control Support Facility, Long Binh

U.S. Army Element, Vietnam Regional Exchange

U.S. Army Finance & Accounting Office, Vietnam

U.S. Army Marine Maintenance Activity

U.S. Army Support Company, Long Binh

U.S. Army Vietnam Administration Company

U.S. Army Vietnam Dog Training Detachment

U.S. Army Vietnam Security Guard Company

U.S. Army Vietnam Special Services Agency

U.S. Army Vietnam Transportation Company

U.S. Army Vietnam Support Troops

U.S. Army Vietnam Training Support Headquarters, to include:

U.S. Army Individual Training Group (see separate Order of Battle)

U.S. Army Special Missions Advisor Group, Nha Trang

U.S. Army Training Advisor Group

Vietnam Open Mess Agency

Vinnell Preserving Facility, Saigon

USARV Supply Organization

1st Logistical Command

Inventory Control Center, Vietnam*

U.S. Army Support Command, Saigon and Army Depot

U.S. Army Support Command, Cam Ranh Bay and Army Depot

U.S. Army Support Command, Qui Nhon and Army Depot

U.S. Army Support Command, Da Nang and Field Depot

1. General Supply System (less aviation, avionics, medical, cryptographic and missile-peculiar items)
    a. Class II: clothing and other "housekeeping" materials
    b. Class IV: construction materials
    c. Class VII: major end items
    d. Class IX: repair parts
2. Ammunition Supply System (Class V)
3. POL Supply System (Class III Petroleum, Oil, Lubricants)
4. Subsistence Supply System (Class I)

44th Medical Brigade

32d Medical Depot†

5. Medical Supply System (Class VIII)

34th General Support Group

Aviation Material Management Center‡

Aviation Depot, Qui Nhon

Aviation Depot, Saigon

6. Aviation Supply System (Class II, VII and IX aviation-peculiar items only)

---

* Formed as the 14th Inventory Control Center on 9 January 1966 to provide continuous and up-to-date inventory accounting of all depot stocks within Vietnam. In late 1967, a fully automated center with a complex control system involving the large-scale use of electronic computers was established at Long Binh.

† Established 4 October 1965 with its base depot at Cam Ranh Bay and subordinated advanced medical depots located at Phu Bai, Chu Lai, Qui Nhon and Long Binh. It managed in-country inventory for all medical material and provided technical assistance and medical supply support for the U.S. and allied forces in Vietnam. Upon arrival it was assigned to the 1st Logistical Command but on 1 May 1966 was assigned to the 44th Medical Brigade.

‡ Established in November 1965 as a provisional aviation material inventory control center providing centralized accountability for depot stocks. It initially used assets of the Aviation Supply Point and resources from the 14th and 765th Transportation Battalions. The center was formalized and expanded in July 1966 when the 58th Transportation Battalion assumed operational control and was used to manage it. In February 1968 the Aviation Material Management Center was officially approved on a TDA basis, relieving the 58th Transportation Battalion of this assignment.

USARV/MACV
Support Command

No Insignia
Authorized

Arrived Vietnam: 15 May 1972
Departed Vietnam: 28 March 1973
Previous Station: Vietnam
Authorized Strength: 425 (1972)

The U.S. Army, Vietnam/Military Assistance Command, Vietnam (USARV/MACV) Support Command was a redesignation of the USARV headquarters when the two major commands were consolidated due to the downgrading of the U.S. military effort in Vietnam. The following elements constituted its headquarters:

Headquarters, USARV/MACV Support Command

U.S. Army, Vietnam, Special Troops

HHC, The Support Troops, USARV/MACV Support Command *

* 7 November 1972 – 28 March 1973 only.

The following components served USARV/MACV Support Command:

Class III Qui Nhon Terminal Complex
GOCO Element, U.S. Advisor, Da Nang
GOCO Generator & Electrical Distribution Facility
GOCO Machine Shop, Cat Lai
GOCO Pacific Architects & Engineers Communication Vehicle Parts
 Facility
GOCO Pacific Architects & Engineers High Voltage Facility
GOCO Pacific Architects & Engineers Repair & Utilities Facility
GOCO Philco-Ford Facility
GOCO Tire Repair & Retread Facility
GOCO Tuy Hoa High Voltage Facility
GOCO Vinnell Corporation
Property Disposal Agency, Vietnam
Regional Support Activity (RSA), Military Region 2
U.S. Army Area Command, Vung Tau
U.S. Army Material Command Logistics Assistance Office
U.S. Army Contract Administration Agency, Vietnam
U.S. Army Depot, Long Binh
U.S. Army Engineer Group, Vietnam
U.S. Army Mortuary, Saigon
U.S. Army Non-Appropriated Fund Agency
U.S. Army Postal Group, Vietnam
U.S. Army Procurement Agency
U.S. Army Support Element, Military Region 1 (Da Nang)
U.S. Army Support Element, Military Region 2 (Pleiku)
U.S. Army Support Element, Military Region 3 (Long Binh)
U.S. Support Element, Military Region 4 (Can Tho)
U.S. Army Movement Control Center, 3d Traffic Region
U.S. Army Vietnam Inventory Control Center
U.S. Army Vietnam Support Troops
Vietnam Regional Exchange, Long Binh

Capital Military Assistance Command, Vietnam

No Insignia Authorized

Arrived Vietnam: 4 June 1968 (Provisional)
          1 January 1969 (Non-provisional)
Departed Vietnam: 19 March 1973
Location: Saigon

Authorized Strength	1968	1971
Headquarters	359	378

Commanders

Major General John H. Hay, Jr.*	May 68
Major General Fillmore K. Mearns	Aug. 68
Major General Walter B. Richardson	April 69
Brigadier General Charles J. Girard	Nov. 69
Brigadier General Herbert E. Wolf	March 70

* In command of both "Hurricane Forward" Headquarters from II FFV and Task Force HAY before it was redesignated the Capital Military Assistance Command, Vietnam.

Capital Military Assistance Command, Vietnam (CMAC) was originally the provisional "Hurricane Forward" Headquarters sent from II Field Force, Vietnam to Saigon to counter the Tet

offensive of 1968 around and in the city. Since it was led by Major General Hay it was known as Task Force HAY. In June it was redesignated the Capital Military Assistance Command (Provisional), with the qualifier dropped six months later. The command served the Saigon vicinity until folded down in March 1973.

First Regional Assistance Command (FRAC)

No Insignia Authorized

Arrived Vietnam: 19 March 1972
Departed Vietnam: March 1973
Location: Da Nang

Authorized Strength	1972
Advisors	560
CORDS *	868

* Civil Operations and Revolutionary Development Support, MACV

Commanders

Major General Frederick J. Kroesen, Jr.	March 72
Major General Howard H. Cooksey	June 72

The First Regional Assistance Command (FRAC) was formed out of the assets of the XXIV Corps in Military Region 1.

U.S. Army Support Elements, Military Region 1:

U.S. Army Da Nang Installation
U.S. Army Liaison Office National Security, Da Nang
U.S. Army Liaison Office National Security, Phu Bai
U.S. Army Phu Bai Installation
U.S. Army Movement Control Center, 1st Traffic Region

Second Regional Assistance Command (SRAC)

No Insignia Authorized

Arrived Vietnam: 30 April 1971
Departed Vietnam: March 1973
Locations: Nha Trang, Pleiku

Authorized Strength	1972
Advisors	566
CORDS*	920

* Civil Operations and Revolutionary Development Support, MACV.

Commanders

Major General Charles P. Brown	April 71
Brigadier General Dewitt C. Armstrong	May 71
Brigadier General George E. Wear †	Nov. 71
Brigadier General John G. Hill †	May 72
Brigadier General Michael D. Healy	June 72

† Commander of U.S. Army Forces, Military Region 2.

The Second Regional Assistance Command (SRAC) was formed at Nha Trang from the assets of I Field Force, Vietnam. The command was redesignated as a group 16 May 1971 – 31 October 1971, at which time it was merged with U.S. Army Forces, Military Region 2, remaining under the latter designation until 10 June 1972 when SRAC was re-established. In 1972 it was located at Pleiku.

U.S. Army Forces/Support Elements, Military Region 2:

GOCO Center, Navigation & Transportation
U.S. Army Liaison Office National Security, Nha Trang
U.S. Army Liaison Office National Security, Pleiku
U.S. Army Liaison Office National Security, Qui Nhon
U.S. Army Logistics Assistance Team, Nha Trang
U.S. Army Nha Trang Installation
U.S. Army Pleiku Installation
U.S. Army Qui Nhon Installation
U.S. Army Movement Control Center, 2d Traffic Region

Third Regional Assistance Command (TRAC)

No Insignia Authorized

Arrived Vietnam: 30 April 1971
Departed Vietnam: March 1973
Location: Long Binh

Authorized Strength	1972
Advisors	952
CORDS *	966

* Civil Operations and Revolutionary Development Support, MACV.

Commanders

Major General Jack J. Wagstaff	May 71
Major General James F. Hollingsworth	Jan. 72
Major General Marshall B. Garth	Sept. 72

The Third Regional Assistance Command (TRAC) was formed at Long Binh using assets from the II Field Force, Vietnam.

U.S. Army Support Elements, Military Region 3:

U.S. Army Command, Vung Tau
U.S. Army Bien Hoa Installation
U.S. Army Long Binh Installation:
    U.S. Army Central Civilian Personnel Office
    U.S. Army Central Finance & Accounting Office, Vietnam
    U.S. Army Liaison Security Office, Long Binh
    U.S. Army Marine Maintenance Activity
    U.S. Army Rehabilitation Center, Long Binh
    U.S. Army Security Guard Detachment, Long Binh
    U.S. Army Special Troops, Long Binh
    U.S. Army Vietnam Special Services Agency
U.S. Army Long Thanh Installation

Delta Regional Assistance Command (DRAC)

No Insignia Authorized

Arrived Vietnam: 30 April 1971
Departed Vietnam: March 1973
Location: Can Tho

Authorized Strength	1972
Advisors	1,008
CORDS *	1,992

* Civil Operations and Revolutionary Development Support, MACV.

Commanders

Major General John H. Cushman	May 71
Brigadier General John E. Blazey (acting)	Feb. 72
Major General Thomas M. Tarpley	March 72

The Delta Regional Assistance Command (DRAC) was established utilizing the assets contained within Military Region 4.

U.S. Army Support Elements, Military Region 4:

U.S. Army Can Tho Installation
U.S. Army Liaison Office National Security, Can Tho

U.S. Army Support Command, Vietnam

No Insignia Authorized

Arrived Vietnam: 1 March 1964
Departed Vietnam: 20 July 1965
Location: Saigon
Authorized Strength: 508 (1965)

Commanders

Brigadier General Joseph W. Stilwell	March 64
Brigadier General Delk M. Oden	July 64
Brigadier General John Norton	April 65

The U.S. Army Support Command, Vietnam was created by expanding the U.S. Army Support Group, Vietnam. In July 1965 it was relieved of assignment to the U.S. Army, Ryukyu Islands and assigned to the U.S. Army, Pacific and redesignated as the Headquarters of U.S. Army, Vietnam (USARV).

U.S. Army Support Group, Vietnam

No Insignia Authorized

Arrived Vietnam: 1 June 1962
Departed Vietnam: 1 March 1964
Location: Saigon – Cholon
Authorized Strength: 462 (1963)

Commanders

Colonel Marvin H. Merchant	April 62
Brigadier General Joseph W. Stilwell	Aug. 62

The U.S. Army Support Group, Vietnam was under the command of the U.S. Army, Ryukyu Islands, but under the operational control of the U.S. Military Assistance Command, Vietnam. In March 1964 it was redesignated the U.S. Army Support Command, Vietnam.

Joint Operations and Evaluation Group, Vietnam

No Insignia Authorized

Arrived Vietnam: 1 August 1962
Departed Vietnam: 23 April 1964
Location: Saigon

The Joint Operations and Evaluation Group, Vietnam was responsible for the development of counterinsurgency tactics and doctrine under the Military Assistance Advisory Group, Vietnam. In February 1964 it was placed under the Joint Research and Test Activity (JRATA) along with several other previously separate research and development agencies: Department of Defense Advanced Research Projects Agency Research-and-Development Field Unit, U.S. Army Concept Team, Vietnam and the Air Force Test Unit, Vietnam. The JRATA performed then as a single unified organization under the Joint Chiefs of Staff directing research, development, testing, and evaluation and combat development activities inside Vietnam. With the reorganization of MACV headquarters the JRATA acted as a joint agency under the operational control of the MACV Commander.

MACV Studies & Observation Group (MACV-SOG)

See Special Warfare Section.

Chapter 5

Corps Level Commands

Field Force, Vietnam (FFV)

No Insignia Authorized

Arrived Vietnam: 15 November 1965
Departed Vietnam: 15 March 1966
Location: Nha Trang

Authorized Strength	1966
Headquarters	265

Commander

Major General Stanley R. Larsen   Sept. 65

Increased roles of U.S. combat units in field operations spurred creation of a provisional field force headquarters in the II Corps Tactical Zone on 1 August 1965, Task Force ALPHA (Provisional). Field Force, Vietnam was created from this basis and was redesignated I Field Force, Vietnam 15 March 1966. The field force concept was adopted instead of a normal corps headquarters for three basic reasons: First, since the headquarters was to operate within an existing South Vietnamese corps zone, it would be confusing to introduce another corps designation within the same zone; second, unlike a corps headquarters, which has only tactical functions, the field force was to have additional responsibilities, such as supply, pacification and an advisory role to the South Vietnamese; third, the field force organization was more flexible, making it possible to add additional subordinate units if required, even including one or more subordinate corps headquarters.

I Field Force, Vietnam (I FFV)

Arrived Vietnam: 15 March 1966
Departed Vietnam: 30 April 1971
Location: Nha Trang

Authorized Strength	1966	1968	1971
Headquarters	340	432	263

Commanders

Lieutenant General Stanley R. Larsen	March 66
Lieutenant General William R. Peers	March 68
Lieutenant General Charles A. Corcoran	March 69
Lieutenant General Arthur S. Collins, Jr.	March 70
Major General Charles P. Brown	Jan. 71

I Field Force, Vietnam had the mission of exercising operational control over the U.S. and allied forces in the II Corps Tactical Zone as well as providing combat assistance to the Vietnamese units in the area. I Field Force, Vietnam was used as a basis for the Second Regional Assistance Command (SRAC) on 30 April 1971 and U.S. Army Forces, Military Region 2.

Major U.S. forces under I Field Force, Vietnam included:

1st Cavalry Division	4th Infantry Division
3d Brigade, 25th Infantry Division	173d Airborne Brigade
1st Brigade, 101st Airborne Division	Task Force SOUTH *

* Task Force SOUTH was organized 24 July 1968 to increase pressure on enemy forces operating in the four southern provinces of II CTZ, composed of elements of the 4th Inf Div, 173d Abn Bde, and 101st Abn Div. Its command post was colocated with the Light Infantry Command Post of the ARVN 23d Infantry Division to ensure coordinated operations in the region. It was headquartered at Dalat and had an authorized strength of 40.

II Field Force, Vietnam (II FFV)

Arrived Vietnam: 15 March 1966
Departed Vietnam: 2 May 1971
Locations: Bien Hoa, Long Binh

Authorized Strength	1966	1968	1970
Headquarters	284	360	?

Commanders

Major General Jonathan O. Seaman	March 66
Lieutenant General Bruce Palmer, Jr.	March 67
Major General Frederick C. Weyand	July 67
Major General Walter T. Kerwin, Jr.	Aug. 68
Lieutenant General Julian J. Ewell	April 69
Lieutenant General Michael S. Davison	April 70

II Field Force, Vietnam (II FFV) became the largest army combat command in Vietnam. Prior to arriving in Vietnam from Fort Hood, Texas, the II FFV had been activated in January 1966 as a redesignation of the XXII Corps, which had seen action in the Rhineland and various Central European campaigns during World War II. The II FFV had the mission of exercising operational control over U.S. and allied forces in the III Corps Tactical Zone, as well as rendering assistance as directed to the South Vietnamese forces there. It became the nucleus of the Third Regional Assistance Command (TRAC) on 30 April 1971.

Major U.S. forces under II Field Force, Vietnam included:

1st Infantry Division	1st Cavalry Division
3d Brigade, 4th Infantry Division	9th Infantry Division
3d Brigade, 82d Airborne Division	25th Infantry Division
11th Armored Cavalry (Regiment)	101st Airborne Division
196th Infantry Brigade	173d Airborne Brigade
199th Infantry Brigade	

XXIV Corps

Arrived Vietnam: 15 August 1968
Departed Vietnam: 30 June 1972
Location: Phu Bai, Da Nang
Authorized Strength: HHC – 367 (1968)

Commanders

Lieutenant General William B. Rosson *	Feb. 68
Lieutenant General Richard G. Stilwell †	July 68
Lieutenant General Melvin Zais	June 69
Lieutenant General James W. Sutherland, Jr.	June 70
Lieutenant General Welborn G. Dolvin	June 71

* Commanding General of MACV Forward and later the Provisional Corps, Vietnam.

† Commanding General of Provisional Corps, Vietnam as well.

XXIV Corps was activated in Vietnam 15 August 1968 and consolidated with the Provisional Corps, Vietnam, which had been organized 10 March 1968, using the assets of MACV Forward. MACV Forward was established 9 February 1968 to assist in stemming the tide of the North Vietnamese Army Tet offensive in early 1968. The XXIV Corps was placed under the operational control of the III Marine Amphibious Force, its brother-in-arms of 24 years earlier in the Pacific. XXIV Corps was first activated at Fort Shafter, Hawaii, on 8 April 1944 and remained at Hawaii until 11 September 1944, first seeing combat near Dulag on Leyte in the Philippines 20 October 1944. At that time the 7th and 96th Infantry Divisions were the major components of the Corps, later to be joined by the 77th Infantry Division. From the Philippines the corps moved to Okinawa and in September 1945 moved into Korea, being deactivated 25 January 1949. On 15 August 1968 the XXIV Corps was recalled to the colors at Phu Bai, controlling combat elements in the I Corps Tactical Zone. It moved to Da Nang on 9 March 1970. The XXIV Corps was inactivated 30 June 1972 and its assets integrated into the First Regional Assistance Command (FRAC).

The following major U.S. Army units served under the control of XXIV Corps:

23d Infantry (AMERICAL) Division	1st Cavalry Division
1st Bde, 5th Infantry Division [Mechanized]	101st Airborne Division (Airmobile)
3d Bde, 82d Airborne Division	196th Infantry Brigade (separate)

Divisions and Separate Infantry Brigades

Chapter 6

Divisions and Task Force OREGON

1st Cavalry Division (Airmobile)

Arrived Vietnam: 11 September 1965
from Fort Benning
Departed Vietnam: 29 April 1971
to Fort Hood

Commanders

Major General Harry W. B. Kinnard	July 65
Major General John Norton	May 66
Major General John J. Tolson III	April 67
Major General George I. Forsythe	July 68
Major General Elvy B. Roberts	May 69
Major General George W. Casey *	May 70
Brigadier General Jonathan R. Burton (acting)	July 70
Major General George W. Putnam, Jr.	July 70

* Killed in helicopter crash 7 July 70.

The 1st Cavalry Division ("The First Team") was activated 13 September 1921 at Fort Bliss and dismounted in 1943 prior to being sent overseas 23 May 1943 to the Pacific in World War II. It fought first in the Admiralty Islands in February 1944 and landed at Leyte in the Philippines 20 October 1944 and became the first to enter Manila, sending another flying column 100 miles inland to liberate allied prisoners. It left Luzon for occupation duty in Japan and was the first U.S. division into Tokyo, arriving there 8 September 1945. The division remained there until rushed into Korea, where it carried out the first amphibious invasion at Pohangdong and was the first U.S. division to enter the North Korean capital of Pyongyang. In December 1951 it was moved back to Japan (service in Korea was 18 July 1950 – 22 December 1951). In 1957 it redeployed to Korea. At Fort Benning the 11th Air Assault Divi-

sion (Test) was raised in 1963 and thoroughly tested in airmobile tactics during 1964. In June 1965 the colors of the 1st Cavalry Division were flown to Fort Benning and the 11th Air Assault Division's assets transferred to the 1st Cavalry Division, which was then sent to Vietnam as the first full division of the U.S. Army to arrive. During October – November 1965 the 1st Cavalry Division fought the enemy to a standstill in the bitter battle of Ia Drang Valley in Pleiku Province, winning a Presidential Unit Citation. For the next 13 months members of "The First Team" met and defeated strong enemy forces throughout the II Corps Tactical Zone. In the spring of 1966, the 1st Cavalry Division fought to clear Binh Dinh Province in a series of operations known as MASHER/WHITE WING/THANG PHONG II which became the first large unit operations across corps boundaries when the U.S. Marines crossed into Binh Dinh to link up with the 1st Cavalry Division. In August 1966 the division went into Pleiku Province in Operation PAUL REVERE II. Battalion-sized elements of the division's Skytroopers were also battling in Binh Thuan Province from August 1966 through January 1968. In October 1966 the division teamed up with the Republic of Korea and South Vietnamese forces in Binh Dinh Province in Operation IRVING. From the end of October into February of 1967 the 1st Cavalry Division continued to clear Binh Dinh Province in Operation THAYER II, which was in turn followed by Operation PERSHING in the rich northern coastal plain as well as the Kim Son and Luoi Ci Valleys to the west. Throughout the remainder of 1967 the division combated the North Vietnamese Army's 610th Division and Viet Cong units in the II Corps Tactical Zone. In January 1968 the division was ordered to I Corps Tactical Zone, arriving in time to blunt the enemy's Tet offensive. Elements in II Corps continued the fight for Binh Dinh Province in Operation PERSHING II in February 1968, but because of events the larger part of the division was committed to the contest near Hue. Then the 1st Cavalry Division moved swiftly to relieve the embattled U.S. Marine base at Khe Sanh in April 1968, along with other U.S. Marine and South

Vietnamese airborne battalions. During the Tet offensive the division performed well, clearing Quang Tri City and crushing resistance on the northwest and southwest walls of the Imperial city of Hue outside the Citadel. In April and May the division was rushed into the A Shau Valley to preempt enemy preparations for another attack in the Hue vicinity; the balance of the year was spent on sustained operations along the border of Quang Tri and Thua Thien Provinces. In October 1968 the 1st Cavalry Division was needed in III Corps Tactical Zone to thwart a potential enemy threat north of Saigon. While thrusting against enemy positions along the Cambodian border northwest of the capital, some elements of the division moved further south into IV Corps Tactical Zone, working with U.S. Naval forces in an operation called NAV-CAV. Thus the 1st Cavalry Division became the first American division to have fought in all four tactical zones in the Republic of Vietnam. During the summer of 1969 the enemy made frequent attacks attempting to overrun division firebases, actions which were costly to both sides. During May and June of 1970 the 1st Cavalry Division invaded Cambodia although strategic success was somewhat hampered by a restriction of 30-kilometer advance. The 1st Cavalry Division had recorded an unparalleled series of firsts as well as demonstrating the effectiveness of airmobile warfare. As part of the Phase VI Redeployment Increment, the bulk of the division was withdrawn from Vietnam during the spring of 1971. The division headquarters was credited with 2,056 days overseas. The 1st Cavalry Division left behind a brigade task force centered around the 3d Brigade.

1st Cavalry Division (Airmobile) Order of Battle: Assigned and Attached Units

Cavalry Battalions (Airmobile Infantry)

1st Battalion, 5th Cavalry
2d Battalion, 5th Cavalry
1st Battalion, 7th Cavalry
2d Battalion, 7th Cavalry
5th Battalion, 7th Cavalry
1st Battalion, 8th Cavalry
2d Battalion, 8th Cavalry
1st Battalion, 12th Cavalry
2d Battalion, 12th Cavalry

Division Aviation

11th Aviation Group
227th Aviation Battalion (Assault Helicopter)
228th Aviation Battalion (Assault Support Helicopter)
229th Aviation Battalion (Assault Helicopter)
11th Aviation Company (General Support)
17th Aviation Company (Fixed Wing Transport)
478th Aviation Company (Heavy Helicopter)

Other Aviation Assets*

110th Aviation Company (Aerial Weapons)
131st Aviation Company (Aerial Weapons)
132d Aviation Company (Assault Support Helicopter)
133d Aviation Company (Assault Support Helicopter)
194th Aviation Company (Assault Helicopter)
202d Aviation Company (Assault Helicopter)
Company A, 4th Aviation Battalion (Assault Helicopter)
Company A, 5th Aviation Battalion (Assault Helicopter)
Aviation Company, 6th Special Forces Group (Assault Helicopter)
Aviation Company, 7th Special Forces Group (Assault Helicopter)

Division Artillery

2d Battalion, 17th Artillery (105mm)
2d Battalion, 19th Artillery (105mm)
2d Battalion, 20th Artillery (Aerial Rocket)
1st Battalion, 21st Artillery (105mm)
1st Battalion, 30th Artillery (155mm)
1st Battalion, 77th Artillery (105mm)
Battery E, 82d Artillery (Aviation)

Division Reconnaissance

1st Squadron, 9th Cavalry (Air)
11th Pathfinder Company (Provisional)
Company E, 52d Infantry (Long Range Recon)
Company H, 75th Infantry (Ranger)

Division Support

1st Personnel Service Battalion (Provisional)
8th Engineer Battalion
13th Signal Battalion
15th Medical Battalion
15th Supply & Service Battalion
15th Transportation Battalion (Aircraft Maintenance)
27th Maintenance Battalion
15th Administrative Company
371st Army Security Agency Company
545th Military Police Company

Other Units on Temporary Assignment

1st Battalion, 50th Infantry (Mechanized)
2d Battalion, 2d Infantry (Mechanized)
1st Squadron, 11th Armored Cavalry
2d Squadron 11th Armored Cavalry
3d Squadron, 11th Armored Cavalry

* Assets of these aviation companies were utilized to build the 11 aviation companies of the 227th, 228th and 229th Aviation Battalions of the division, since at the deployment date only Company A of the 227th Aviation Battalion had complete equipment and personnel required. Though officially these were never part of the division's aviation force, many early documents and official records in the September – November 1965 time frame still carry the above companies by name in lieu of the proper aviation battalion lettered companies.

1st Cavalry Division (Airmobile)

Elements

	Vietnam Service	1966	Authorized Strength 1968	1970	1972
Division Headquarters and HQ Company	11 Sept. 65 – 29 April 71	167	195	195	—
1st Brigade Headquarters and HQ Company	12 Sept. 65 – 29 April 71	223	223	223	—
2d Brigade Headquarters and HQ Company	12 Sept. 65 – 26 March 71	223	223	223	—
3d Brigade Headquarters and HQ Company*	12 Sept. 65 – 26 June 72	223	223	223	346
Division Artillery Headquarters and HQ Battery	12 Sept. 65 – 29 April 71	162	162	162	—
Support Command Headquarters and HQ Company	12 Sept. 65 – 29 April 71	163	163	163	—

Division Headquarters Locations in Vietnam

An Khe	Sept. 65 – June 67
An Khe/Bong Son	July 67 – Jan. 68
An Khe/Hue	Feb. 68
An Khe/Phong Dien	March 68 – April 68
An Khe/Quang Tri	May 68
An Khe/Phong Dien	June 68 – Oct. 68
An Khe/Phuoc Vinh	Nov. 68 – April 69
Bien Hoa/Phuoc Vinh †	May 69 – April 71

* Also considered in this book as a separate command, which see.

† Cambodian invasion May – June 1970.

3d Brigade, 1st Cavalry Division (Separate)

Arrived Vietnam: 30 April 1971*
Departed Vietnam: 26 June 1972
Location: Bien Hoa
Authorized Strength: HHC – 346 (1971)

Commanders

Brigadier General Jonathan R. Burton	April 71
Brigadier General James F. Hamlet	Dec. 71

The 3d Brigade of the 1st Cavalry Division was a separate command created after the bulk of the division departed Vietnam. It served in the III Corps Tactical Zone until redeployed from Vietnam, being in turn reduced to Task Force GARRY OWEN, built around the 1st Battalion, 7th Cavalry and minor supporting units formed in July 1972.

* Date after the division departed Vietnam and the 3d Brigade became separate in Vietnam. The brigade first arrived 12 September 1965 with the rest of the division.

3d Brigade, 1st Cavalry Division (Separate) Order of Battle: Assigned and Attached Units

Cavalry Battalions (Airmobile Infantry)

2d Battalion, 5th Cavalry
1st Battalion, 7th Cavalry
2d Battalion, 8th Cavalry
1st Battalion, 12th Cavalry

Brigade Aviation

229th Aviation Battalion (Assault Helicopter)
362d Aviation Company (Assault Helicopter)
Troop F, 9th Cavalry (Air)

Other Units on Temporary Duty

2d Squadron, 11th Armored Cavalry

Brigade Artillery

1st Battalion, 21st Artillery (105mm)
Battery F, 26th Artillery (105mm), Provisional
Battery F, 77th Artillery (Aviation)
Battery F, 79th Artillery (Aerial Rocket)

Brigade Support

215th Support Battalion
501st Engineer Company
525th Signal Company

1st Infantry Division

Arrived Vietnam: 2 October 1965
from Fort Riley
Departed Vietnam: 15 April 1970
to Fort Riley
(3d Brigade to Germany)

Commanders

Major General Jonathan O. Seaman	Oct. 65
Major General William E. DePuy	March 66
Major General John H. Hay, Jr.	Feb. 67
Major General Keith L. Ware*	March 68
Major General Orwin C. Talbott	Sept. 68
Major General Albert E. Milloy	Aug. 69
Brigadier General John Q. Herrion	March 70

* Killed in helicopter crash 13 September 1968.

The 1st Infantry Division ("The Big Red One") was originally formed as the First Expeditionary Division, going overseas in World War I on 22 December 1917. It was the first division to go overseas, land in France, meet the enemy (participating in the major offensives of Aisne–Marne, St. Mihiel, Meuse–Argonne and Montidier–Noyons), and enter Germany. After its return to the United States in September 1919 its units were scattered along the Eastern Seaboard. In August 1942 the division was sent across the Atlantic again, landing at Oran in North Africa in November and securing Tunisia by May 1943. After assaulting Sicily in July 1943 the division went to England, and on D-Day (6 June 1944) the 1st Infantry Division stormed Omaha Beach in particularly costly combat. Following the breakout at St. Lô the division drove across Northern France and laid siege to Aachen, taking the fortress-city by direct assault 21 October 1944. After combat in the Hurtgen Forest the division was rushed up to stem the German counteroffensive in the Ardennes. Next it breached the Siegfried Line and crossed the Rhine River at Remagen Bridge, closed the Ruhr Pocket, and drove across Central Europe into Czechoslovakia, where it was when World War II ended. The 1st Infantry Division then served ten years on occupation duty in Germany before returning to the U.S. at Fort Riley, the previous station of the 10th Infantry Division. The 1st Infantry Division was alerted for Vietnam in 1965 and its 2d Brigade under Colonel James E. Simmons became the first element of an infantry division to arrive there. The 1st Infantry Division served in the III Corps Tactical Zone and by mid-1966 the division was fighting in Binh Long Province against the 9th Viet Cong Division. That fall the division invaded War Zone C of Tay Ninh Province in the largest operation to date in the Vietnam war, Operation ATTLEBORO (14 September – 24 November 1966). Despite these efforts, the division was called upon again to quash enemy strength in War Zone C in Operation JUNCTION CITY during the period February – May 1967, along with the 4th and 25th Infantry Divisions and three separate brigades. In the fall of 1967 the division operated against the enemy in Binh Duong Province and extended the scope of combat to include Loc Ninh areas of Binh Long Province after enemy attacks on the district town. During the Tet offensive of 1968 and later the division fought in the Saigon vicinity. The division then moved to Lai Khe in March 1968 and remained there to perform pacification activities. In July 1969 the Big Red One soldiers began a coordinated war effort between their division and the South Vietnamese 5th Division called "Dong Tien" (Progress Together) in an attempt to train the ARVN soldiers in combat operations. The division moved to Di An shortly before deployment back to the United States as Increment III of the withdrawal. The 1st Infantry Division served 1,656 days in Vietnam.

1st Infantry Division

Elements	Vietnam Service	Authorized Strength 1966	Authorized Strength 1968
Division Headquarters and HQ Company	2 Oct. 65 – 15 April 70	153	170
1st Brigade Headquarters and HQ Company	6 Oct. 65 – 15 April 70	122	128
2d Brigade Headquarters and HQ Company	11 July 65 – 15 April 70	122	128
3d Brigade Headquarters and HQ Company	2 Oct. 65 – 15 April 70	122	128
Division Artillery Headquarters and HQ Battery	17 Oct. 65 – 15 April 70	205	213
Division Support Command Headquarters and HQ Co	2 Oct. 65 – 15 April 70	97	103

Division Headquarters Locations in Vietnam

Bien Hoa	Oct. 65 – Jan. 66
Di An	Feb. 66 – Jan. 67
Di An/Lai Khe	Feb. 67 – Sept. 67
Lai Khe	Oct. 67 – Oct. 69
Di An	Nov. 69 – April 70

1st Infantry Division Order of Battle: Assigned and Attached Units

Infantry Battalions

1st Battalion, 2d Infantry
2d Battalion, 2d Infantry (Mechanized)
1st Battalion, 16th Infantry (Mechanized)
2d Battalion, 16th Infantry
1st Battalion, 18th Infantry
2d Battalion, 18th Infantry
1st Battalion, 26th Infantry
1st Battalion, 28th Infantry
2d Battalion, 28th Infantry

Division Artillery

1st Battalion, 5th Artillery (105mm)
8th Battalion, 6th Artillery (155mm)
1st Battalion, 7th Artillery (105mm)
6th Battalion, 15th Artillery (105mm)
2d Battalion, 33d Artillery (105mm)
Battery D, 25th Artillery (Target Acquisition)

1st Infantry Division

Division Aviation

1st Aviation Battalion (Airmobile)
162d Aviation Company (Airmobile)
173d Aviation Company (Airmobile)
Troop C, 16th Cavalry (Air)

Other Units on Temporary Assignment

3d Squadron, 11th Armored Cavalry
5th Battalion, 60th Infantry (Mechanized)

Division Reconnaisance

1st Squadron, 4th Cavalry (Armored)
Company F, 52d Infantry (Long Range Patrol)
Company I, 75th Infantry (Ranger)

Division Support

1st Engineer Battalion
1st Medical Battalion
1st Supply & Transport Battalion
121st Signal Battalion
1st Administration Company
701st Maintenance Battalion
1st Military Police Company
337th Army Security Agency Company

4th Infantry Division

Arrived Vietnam: 25 September 1966
from Fort Lewis
Departed Vietnam: 7 December 1970
to Fort Carson

Commanders

Brigadier General David O. Byars	Aug. 66
Major General Arthur S. Collins, Jr.	Sept. 66
Major General William R. Peers	Jan. 67
Major General Charles P. Stone	Jan. 68
Major General Donn R. Pepke	Dec. 68
Major General Glenn D. Walker	Nov. 69
Major General William A. Burke	July 70
Brigadier General Maurice K. Kendall (acting)	Dec. 70

The 4th Infantry Division ("Ivy Division") was organized in December 1917 at Camp Green, North Carolina, and sent overseas to France 5 June 1918, fighting in the Aisne – Marne, St. Mihiel and Meuse – Argonne during World War I, cracking the Hindenburg Line and stopping the Kaiser's all-out drive to Paris. After seven months on occupation duty in Germany the division returned to the U.S. and was inactivated 1 August 1919. In June 1940 it was re-raised at Fort Benning and sent to England 18 January 1944 for training for the invasion of France. The 4th Infantry Division landed at Utah Beach on D-Day, 6 June 1944, relieved the 82d Airborne Division isolated in the St. Mere Eglise marshes and spearheaded the drive to Cherbourg. After clearing the Cotentin Peninsula it turned south to break through the German Army's flank in France and was the first U.S. division to liberate Paris.

The division continued its drive through Belgium and fought in the Hurtgen Forest until it met the German counteroffensive in the Ardennes head on. After severe combat the division went over to the offensive and crossed the Rhine at Worms, becoming the first Allied division to set foot on German soil in World War II. Inactivated at Camp Butner, North Carolina, it was reraised as a training division in July 1947 at Fort Ord, converted into a combat division, and sent to Germany in 1951. In September 1956 the division returned to the U.S. at Fort Lewis where it was serving when alerted for Vietnam. The bulk of the 4th Infantry Division went to the II Corps Tactical Zone, but a brigade reinforced with the divisional armor battalion was sent into the III Corps Tactical Zone. In August 1967 the elements of the 3d Brigade, including the armor, were officially turned over to the 25th Infantry Division in exchange for the elements of its own 3d Brigade, which was in the II Corps area. This constituted the only major element switch between divisions during the Vietnam war—transferral of the 3d Brigade Headquarters of the 4th Infantry Division to the operational control of Task Force OREGON and relocation into the I Corps Tactical Zone at Duc Pho. The 4th Infantry Division entered combat as soon as it arrived in Vietnam, sending a brigade into War Zone C of Tay Ninh Province as part of Operation ATTLEBORO (14 September – 24 November 1966). When the bulk of the division arrived it immediately conducted a major operation near the Cambodian border in Pleiku Province, which lasted through December 1966. In 1967 the division continued border surveillance operations in Pleiku and Kontum Provinces, while its 3d Brigade was participating in Operation JUNCTION CITY February – May 1967, again in War Zone C. Throughout 1968 and into 1969 the division continued operations in the western Highlands, seeing fierce action in the border regions. In June 1970 the 4th Infantry Division thrust into Cambodia to punish the North Vietnamese Army sanctuaries there. The 3d Brigade of the division pulled out of Vietnam first in Increment III of the U.S. Army withdrawal and was inactivated at Fort Lewis. When the division was sent back to the U.S. in Increment V to Fort Carson, its former 3d Brigade joined it from the 25th Infantry Division, which had returned to Hawaii. The 4th Infantry Division served 1,534 days in Vietnam.

4th Infantry Division

Elements	Vietnam Service	Authorized Strength 1966	Authorized Strength 1968
Division Headquarters and HQ Company	25 Sept. 66 – 7 Dec. 70	—	170
1st Brigade Headquarters and HQ Company	4 Oct. 66 – 7 Dec. 70	—	128
2d Brigade Headquarters and HQ Company	10 Aug. 66 – 7 Dec. 70	130	128
3d Brigade Headquarters and HQ Company	9 Oct. 66 – 15 April 70	—	128
Division Artillery Headquarters and HQ Battery	4 Oct. 66 – 7 Dec. 70	—	213
Division Support Command Headquarters and HQ Co	4 Oct. 66 – 7 Dec.70	—	103

Division Headquarters Locations in Vietnam

Pleiku	Sept. 66 – Feb. 68
Dak To	March 68
Pleiku	April 68 – Feb. 70
An Khe/Pleiku	March 70
An Khe	April 70 – Dec. 70

4th Infantry Division Order of Battle: Assigned and Attached Units

Infantry Battalions

1st Battalion, 8th Infantry
2d Battalion, 8th Infantry (Mechanized)
3d Battalion, 8th Infantry
1st Battalion, 12th Infantry
2d Battalion, 12th Infantry †
3d Battalion, 12th Infantry
1st Battalion, 14th Infantry *
1st Battalion, 22d Infantry
2d Battalion, 22d Infantry †
3d Battalion, 22d Infantry †
1st Battalion, 35th Infantry *
2d Battalion, 35th Infantry *

Division Support

4th Engineer Battalion
4th Medical Battalion
4th Supply & Transport Battalion
124th Signal Battalion
704th Maintenance Battalion
4th Administration Company
4th Military Police Company
374th Army Security Agency Company

Artillery Battalions

2d Battalion, 9th Artillery (105mm) *
5th Battalion, 16th Artillery (155mm)
6th Battalion, 29th Artillery (105mm)
4th Battalion, 42d Artillery (105mm)
2d Battalion, 77th Artillery (105mm) †

Armor Battalions

2d Battalion, 34th Armor †
1st Battalion, 69th Armor*

Division Reconnaissance

1st Squadron, 10th Cavalry (Armored)
Company E, 20th Infantry (Long Range Patrol)
Company E, 58th Infantry (Long Range Patrol)
Company K, 75th Infantry (Ranger)

Division

4th Aviation Battalion

Other Units on Temporary Assignment

8th Psychological Operations Battalion
2d Squadron, 1st Cavalry (Armored)
3d Battalion, 506th Infantry (Airmobile)
1st Battalion, 50th Infantry (Mechanized)

* Arrived from the 25th Infantry Division in August 1967.
† Transferred to the 25th Infantry Division in August 1967.

1st Brigade, 5th Infantry Division (Mechanized)

Arrived Vietnam: 25 July 1968
Departed Vietnam: 27 August 1971
Location: Quang Tri
Authorized Strength: HHC – 316 (1968)

Commanders

Colonel Richard J. Glikes	July 68
Colonel James M. Gibson	Oct. 68
Colonel John L. Osteen, Jr.	June 69
Brigadier General William A. Burke	April 70
Brigadier General John G. Hill, Jr.	July 70
Brigadier General Harold H. Dunwoody	May 71

The 1st Brigade of the 5th Infantry Division was reorganized at Fort Carson in March 1968 into a unique combination of heavy firepower and mechanized mobility for Vietnam deployment and was posted to the I Corps Tactical Zone. The brigade moved a few miles south of the DMZ to the Quang Tri area for search and clear, cordon and sweep operations. From time to time it became involved in 3d Marine Division operations on the Khe Sanh plains and up to the vicinity of the DMZ with the U.S. Marines. In January 1971 it initiated an attack toward Laos with an armored cavalry/engineer task force on two axes from the Vandegrift Base Camp toward Khe Sanh, allowing a South Vietnamese attack across the Laotian border in Operation LAM SON 719. The brigade was withdrawn from Vietnam in August of that year and rejoined its parent division at Fort Carson.

1st Brigade, 5th Infantry Division (Mechanized) Order of Battle:

Assigned and Attached Units

Brigade Armor

1st Battalion, 77th Armor

Brigade Infantry

1st Battalion, 11th Infantry
1st Battalion, 61st Infantry (Mechanized)

Brigade Reconnaissance

Troop A, 4th Squadron, 12th Cavalry
Company P, 75th Infantry (Ranger)

Brigade Artillery

5th Battalion, 4th Artillery (155mm SP)

Brigade Support

75th Support Battalion
Company A, 7th Eng Bn
298th Signal Company

Other Units on Temporary Assignment

3d Squadron, 5th Cavalry
3d Battalion, 187th Infantry (Airmobile)

9th Infantry Division

Arrived Vietnam: 16 December 1966 from Fort Riley
Departed Vietnam: 27 August 1969 to Fort Lewis

Commanders

Major General George S. Eckhardt	Dec. 66
Major General George G. O'Connor	June 67
Major General Julian J. Ewell	Feb. 68
Major General Harris W. Hollis	April 69

The 9th Infantry Division ("Old Reliables") was constituted 1 August 1940 at Fort Bragg and deployed overseas 11 December 1942 to invade North Africa, where advanced elements of the division landed 8 November 1942. It pushed through Tunisia into Bizerte, which fell 7 May 1943. The division then landed at Palermo in Sicily that August and was later sent to England for the impending cross-channel invasion of France. The 9th Infantry Division landed in Normandy 10 June 1944, cutting off the Cotentin Peninsula and assisting in the capture of fortified Cherbourg. In July the division participated in the breakthrough at St.-Lô and swept across northern France. It held defensive positions near the Roer River from December 1944 through January 1945, then crossed the Rhine at Remagen Bridge 7 March 1945, pushing into the German Harz Mountains. The division was inactivated, but reactivated 15 July 1947 at Fort Dix, serving some 15 years before being inactivated once more. On 1 February 1966, however, the division was reraised at Fort Riley and sent to the III Corps Tactical Zone of Vietnam. The division swept through Dinh Tuong Province 6 January – 31 May 1967 in Operation PALM BEACH, spending February and March with South Vietnamese forces combating the enemy in Long An Province. Meanwhile, one of its brigades was selected to fulfill the concept of a Mobile Riverine Force, created in 1967 and integrated with a Navy task force at each level of the brigade's command. For the first time since the American Civil War, when Union Army forces operated on the Mississippi, Cumberland and other rivers, the U.S. Army was utilizing an amphibious force operating entirely afloat. The force was a complete package, independent of fixed support bases and with all of its normal fire support embarked or in tow. The troops lived on barrack ships docked at the mobile riverine base anchorage. On tactical operations Navy armored troop carrier boats, preceded by minesweeping craft and escorted by armored boats ("monitors"), transported the soldiers along the vast network of waterways in the Delta. The first element of the Mobile Riverine Force (2d Brigade) arrived in Vietnam in January 1967 and after shakedown training in the Rung Sat swamps, moved to its base near My Tho, which was named Dong Tam — a base on a 600-acre island created among inundated rice paddies by dredging earth from the bottom of the Mekong River. The mobile riverine force often operated with other specialized units such as Navy SEAL teams, South Vietnamese Marines, units of the ARVN 7th Division and River Assault Groups on reconnaissance, blocking and pursuit operations. In 1968 the 9th Infantry Division engaged in bitter fighting in the Saigon area, and in 1969 operated throughout the IV Corps Tactical Zone. The division was redeployed to Hawaii as part of the first increment of the U.S. withdrawal, but it left the 3d Brigade in Vietnam. The 9th Infantry Division served 985 days in Vietnam.

9th Infantry Division	Elements	Vietnam Service	Authorized Strength 1968
	Division Headquarters and HQ Company	16 Dec. 66 – 27 Aug. 69	170
	1st Brigade Headquarters and HQ Company	3 Jan. 67 – 12 Aug. 69	199
	2d Brigade Headquarters and HQ Company *	28 Jan. 67 – 28 July 69	199
	3d Brigade Headquarters and HQ Company †	16 Dec. 66 – 11 Oct. 70	128
	Division Artillery Headquarters and HQ Battery	19 Dec. 66 – 18 Aug. 69	213
	Division Support Command Headquarters and HQ Co	19 Dec. 66 – 27 Aug. 69	103

Division Headquarters Locations in Vietnam

Bear Cat	Dec. 66 – July 68
Dong Tam	Aug. 68 – Aug. 69

* Mobile Riverine Force
† Also considered in this book as a separate Command, which see.

**9th Infantry Division Order of Battle:
Assigned and Attached Units**

Division Infantry

6th Battalion, 31st Infantry
2d Battalion, 39th Infantry
3d Battalion, 39th Infantry
4th Battalion, 39th Infantry
2d Battalion, 47th Infantry (Mechanized)
3d Battalion, 47th Infantry (Riverine)
4th Battalion, 47th Infantry (Riverine)
2d Battalion, 60th Infantry
3d Battalion, 60th Infantry (Riverine)
5th Battalion, 60th Infantry (Mechanized)

Division Reconnaissance

3d Squadron, 5th Cavalry (Armored)
Company E, 50th Infantry (Long Range Patrol)
Company E, 75th Infantry (Ranger)

Division Aviation

9th Aviation Battalion

Division Artillery

2d Battalion, 4th Artillery (105mm)
1st Battalion, 11th Artillery (105mm)
3d Battalion, 34th Artillery (105mm) (Riverine)
1st Battalion, 84th Artillery (155mm)
Battery H, 29th Artillery (Searchlight)

Division Support

9th Medical Battalion
9th Signal Battalion
9th Supply and Transport Battalion
15th Engineer Battalion
709th Maintenance Battalion
9th Administration Company
9th Military Police Company
335th Army Security Company

Other Units on Temporary Assignment

1st Battalion, 16th Infantry

Unauthorized

3d Brigade, 9th Infantry Division (Separate)

Arrived Vietnam: 26 July 1969 *
Departed Vietnam: 11 October 1970
Location: Tan An
Authorized Strength: HHC – 316 (1970)

Commanders

Colonel Andrew J. Gatsis	Sept. 69
Colonel Walworth F. Williams	March 70

The 3d Brigade (separate) of the 9th Infantry Division served under the command of the 25th Infantry Division performing operations in the southern III Corps Tactical Zone from July 1969 until it departed Vietnam. Its base camp of Tan An was located in the extreme southern portion of the III Corps. The major portion of the 9th Infantry Division departed Vietnam in September 1969, leaving the 3d Brigade the sole remaining element of the division in Vietnam from that time forward, and thus the brigade commanders are listed from that point only above. The 3d Brigade left

Vietnam as part of Increment IV of the U.S. Army withdrawal and was sent to Fort Lewis.

* Date the 3d Brigade was separated from the 9th Infantry Division and placed under the operational control of the 25th Infantry Division. The brigade first arrived in Vietnam December 1966.

**3d Brigade, 9th Infantry Division Order of Battle:
Assigned and Attached Units**

Brigade Infantry

6th Battalion, 31st Infantry
2d Battalion, 47th Infantry (Mechanized)
2d Battalion, 60th Infantry
5th Battalion, 60th Infantry

Brigade Reconnaissance

Troop D, 3d Squadron, 5th Cavalry (Air)
Company E, 75th Infantry (Ranger)

Brigade Artillery

2d Battalion, 4th Artillery (105mm)

Brigade Special Unit

39th Cavalry Platoon (Air Cushion Vehicle)

Brigade Support

99th Support Battalion
571st Engineer Company
56th Signal Company

23d Infantry Division (AMERICAL)

Arrived Vietnam: 25 September 1967
organized in Vietnam
Departed Vietnam: 29 November 1971
to Fort Lewis*

Commanders

Major General Samuel W. Koster	Oct. 67
Major General Charles M. Gettys	June 68
Major General Lloyd B. Ramsey †	June 69
Major General Albert E. Milloy	March 70
Major General James L. Baldwin	Nov. 70
Major General Frederick J. Kroesen, Jr.	July 71

* Colors only went back to the United States. Actual division assets folded down in Vietnam.

† Seriously wounded in helicopter crash 18 March 1970.

In May 1942, General Douglas MacArthur, commander of allied forces in the Southwest Pacific, activated the AMERICAL Division using American troops already on New Caledonia, thus the name AMERICAL. The division landed on Guadalcanal on 12 October 1942 and relieved the 1st Marine Division, becoming the first U.S. Army unit to conduct an offensive operation against the enemy in that war. After bitter combat on Guadalcanal the division left in February 1943 for extensive training in the Fiji Islands and struck next at Bougainville Island 25 December 1943 where it fought until November 1944. At that time the division was sent into the southern Philippines, where it served through June 1945. It took part in the initial occupation of Japan and was inactivated 12 December 1945. It was reactivated on 1 December 1954, officially redesignated the 23d Infantry Division (AMERICAL) and served for almost a year and a half till 10 April 1956 with headquarters in the Canal Zone. It was reactivated again when Gen. William C. Westmoreland, needing an infantry division in Vietnam but aware that none would be arriving from the United States for some time, and conscious of the AMERICAL Division's relationship with the 1st Marine Division in World War II, decided to reraise the army division to operate in the northern coastal sector adjacent to the Marines. He first established a headquarters known as Task Force OREGON and, as additional troops arrived, transformed the task force into the AMERICAL Division. Because Department of the Army policy required that divisions be numbered, the division was known officially as the 23d Infantry Division (AMERICAL) and was reactivated as such in Vietnam on 25 September 1967. MACV, however, preferred the name AMERICAL, listed it as such in numerous official orders, called it "the Army's only named division on active service," and used the vehicle bumper abbreviation AMCAL. The rugged terrain of southern I Corps Tactical Zone, where the division made its home at Chu Lai, ran the gamut from marshy, coastal lowlands to triple-canopy jungle on steep mountain slopes. The AMERICAL Division battled the strong enemy influence in both Quang Nam and Quang Tri Provinces 11 November 1967 – 11 November 1968 in Operation WHEELER/WALLOWA with two of its brigades. Another brigade was sent to Quang Ngai Province in early 1968. During 1969 and 1970 the division continued to fight in the Duc Pho, Chu Lai and Tam Ky areas along the coast. In November 1971 the division was inactivated and the 196th Infantry Brigade became separate. The 23d Infantry Division (AMERICAL) served a total of 1,526 days in Vietnam.

23d Infantry Division (AMERICAL)

Elements	Vietnam Service	Authorized Strength 1968	1971
Division Headquarters and HQ Company	25 Sept. 67 – 29 Nov. 71	170	247
11th Infantry Brigade Headquarters and HQ Company *	19 Dec. 67 – 13 Nov. 71	188	128
196th Infantry Brigade Headquarters and HQ Company *	26 Aug. 66 – 29 June 72	188	128
198th Infantry Brigade Headquarters and HQ Company *	21 Oct. 67 – 13 Nov. 71	188	128
Division Artillery Headquarters and HQ Battery	25 Sept. 67 – 29 Nov. 71	213	213
Division Support Command Headquarters and HQ Co	25 Sept. 67 – 29 Nov. 71	97	?

Division Headquarters Location in Vietnam

Chu Lai	Sept. 67 – Nov. 71

* Also considered as separate commands in this work. Entire brigade Vietnam service has been listed above.

**23d Infantry Division (AMERICAL) Order of Battle:
Assigned and Attached Units**

Division Infantry

2d Battalion, 1st Infantry
3d Battalion, 1st Infantry
4th Battalion, 3d Infantry
1st Battalion, 6th Infantry
1st Battalion, 20th Infantry
3d Battalion, 21st Infantry
4th Battalion, 21st Infantry
4th Battalion, 31st Infantry
1st Battalion, 46th Infantry
5th Battalion, 46th Infantry
1st Battalion, 52d Infantry

Division Reconnaissance

Troop F, 8th Cavalry (Air)
Troop E, 1st Cavalry (Armored)
Troop F, 17th Cavalry (Armored)
Company E, 51st Infantry (Long Range Patrol)
Company G, 75th Infantry (Ranger)
AMERICAL Scout Infantry Company (Provisional)

Other Unit on Temporary Assignment

1st Squadron, 1st Cavalry (Armored)

Division Artillery

6th Battalion, 11th Artillery (105mm)
1st Battalion, 14th Artillery (105mm)
3d Battalion, 16th Artillery (155mm)
3d Battalion, 18th Artillery (175mm/8" SP)
1st Battalion, 82d Artillery (155mm)
3d Battalion, 82d Artillery (105mm)
Battery G, 55th Artillery (.50-cal MG)

Division Aviation

16th Aviation Group
14th Aviation Battalion (Combat)
123d Aviation Battalion (Airmobile)
212th Aviation Battalion (Combat)

Division Support

23d Medical Battalion
23d Supply & Transport Battalion
26th Engineer Battalion
523d Signal Battalion
723d Maintenance Battalion
23d Administration Company
23d Military Police Company
328th Army Security Agency Company

23d Infantry Division (AMERICAL) Formation Assets

Components	Assets Derived From:
23d Infantry Division Support Command	15th Support Brigade
23d Administration Company	Company A, 6th Support Battalion
23d Supply & Transport Battalion	94th Supply & Service Battalion
723d Maintenance Battalion	188th Maintenance Battalion (bulk)
26th Engineer Battalion:	
Company A	175th Engineer Company
Company B	155th Engineer Company
Company C	6th Engineer Company
Company D	Company B, 39th Engineer Battalion
Company E (Float Bridge)	554th Engineer Company
523d Signal Battalion	509th Signal Battalion
Company E, 51st Infantry (Long Range Patrol)	Detachment A (Long Range Patrol) *
123d Aviation Battalion	161st Aviation Company

* Provisional long-range patrol unit formed from the provisional long-range patrol detachment of the 196th Infantry
Brigade and from men with long-range patrol experience from the 11th and 198th Infantry Brigades.

25th Infantry Division

Arrived Vietnam: 28 March 1966
from Hawaii
Departed Vietnam: 8 December 1970
to Hawaii

Commanders

Major General Frederick C. Weyand	Jan. 66
Major General John C. F. Tillson III	March 67
Major General Fillmore K. Mearns	Aug. 67
Major General Ellis W. Williamson	Aug. 68
Major General Harris W. Hollis	Sept. 69
Major General Edward Bautz, Jr.	April 70

The 25th Infantry Division ("Tropic Lightning") was formed on Hawaii 10 October 1941 and was machinegunned at Schofield Barracks during the Japanese attack on Pearl Harbor, 7 December 1941. The division moved onto Guadalcanal 17 December 1942 and entered combat, relieving the U.S. Marines there. It continued fighting in the Solomon Islands on New Georgia, Vella Lavella, Arundel Island and Kolombangara, moving back to New Zealand in December 1944 for rest and training. On 11 January 1945 the division landed on Luzon in the Philippines to help liberate the country. It saw intense combat in the Caraballo Mountains. After five years of occupation duty in Japan, the division was transferred into combat in Korea 18 July 1950. At first forced onto the defensive, the division later drove north with the U.N. counterof-fensive. When the Communist Chinese Army entered the war, the 25th Infantry Division was hard-hit, but by March 1951, was counterattacking to retake Seoul. After 1953 the division was posted back to Hawaii. In January 1963 the division was providing soldiers for combat duty in Vietnam, and its 3d Brigade was sent there in December 1965, being posted to the Highlands at Pleiku. Later the brigade elements were transferred to the 4th Infantry Division, also operating in the same II Corps Tactical Zone area in exchange for the elements of the 4th Infantry Division's brigade fighting in the III Corps Tactical Zone. When the remainder of the 25th Infantry Division arrived in early 1966, it was sent into the III Corps area in action against the enemy near the Cambodian border and in the Saigon vicinity. In January 1967 the division pushed into the Viet Cong Military Region 4 headquarters in the fortified "Iron Triangle." Next it was sent into War Zone C, Tay Ninh Province, along with several other major U.S. Army units during Operation JUNCTION CITY, 22 February – 14 May 1967. The rest of the year was spent largely in trying to clear Hau Nghia Province. The division again drove into War Zone C on 8 December 1967, continuing operations there until 24 February 1968. It was also involved in operations in the southern half of III Corps west of Saigon, and along the Cambodian border region. During the Tet counteroffensive of 1968 the division saw combat in the immediate Saigon area. The division then continued its primary operations around Cu Chi, and in the spring of 1970 sent elements into Cambodia seeking the North Vietnamese Army sanctuaries. In December 1970 the bulk of the division was withdrawn from Vietnam as part of Increment V of the U.S. withdrawal, but a separate brigade was left behind. The 25th Infantry Division served some 1,716 days in Vietnam.

25th Infantry Division

Elements	Vietnam Service	Authorized Strength 1968	1970
Division Headquarters and HQ Company	28 March 66 – 8 Dec. 70	152	170
1st Brigade Headquarters and HQ Company	29 April 66 – 8 Dec. 70	125	128
2d Brigade Headquarters and HQ Company*	20 Jan. 66 – 30 April 71	125	128
3d Brigade Headquarters and HQ Company	28 Dec. 65 – 8 Dec. 70	125	128
Division Artillery Headquarters and HQ Battery	4 April 66 – 8 Dec. 70	217	213
Division Support Command Headquarters and HQ Co	4 April 66 – 8 Dec. 70	97	103

Division Headquarters Location in Vietnam

Cu Chi	March 66 – Dec. 70

* Also considered as a separate command in this work. Entire Vietnam service listed above.

**25th Infantry Division Order of Battle:
Assigned and Attached Units**

Division Infantry

1st Battalion, 5th Infantry (Mechanized)
4th Battalion, 9th Infantry
2d Battalion, 12th Infantry*
1st Battalion, 14th Infantry †
2d Battalion, 14th Infantry
2d Battalion, 22d Infantry* (Mechanized)
3d Battalion, 22d Infantry*
4th Battalion, 23d Infantry (Mechanized)
1st Battalion, 27th Infantry
2d Battalion, 27th Infantry
1st Battalion, 35th Infantry †
2d Battalion, 35th Infantry †

Division Armor

2d Battalion, 34th Armor *
1st Battalion, 69th Armor †

Division Reconnaissance

3d Squadron, 4th Cavalry (Armored)
Company F, 50th Infantry (Long Range Patrol)
Company F, 75th Infantry (Ranger)

Division Aviation

25th Aviation Battalion

* Arrived from the 4th Infantry Division in August 1967.

† Transferred to the 4th Infantry Division in August 1967.

Division Artillery

1st Battalion, 8th Artillery (105mm)
2d Battalion, 9th Artillery (105mm) †
7th Battalion, 11th Artillery (105mm)
3d Battalion, 13th Artillery (155mm)
2d Battalion, 77th Artillery (105mm)*
6th Battalion, 77th Artillery (105mm)

Division Support

1st Support Battalion (Provisional)
2d Support Battalion (Provisional)
3d Support Battalion (Provisional)
25th Medical Battalion
25th Supply & Transport Battalion
65th Engineer Battalion
125th Signal Battalion
725th Maintenance Battalion
25th Administration Company
25th Military Police Company
372d Army Security Agency Company

Other Units on Temporary Assignment

3d Brigade, 9th Infantry Division
1st and 3d Squadrons, 11th Armored Cavalry

Unauthorized

**2d Brigade,
25th Infantry Division
(Separate)**

Arrived Vietnam: 8 December 1970*
Departed Vietnam: 30 April 1971
Locations: Long Binh, Xuan Loc
Authorized Strength: HHC – 128 (1971)

Commanders

Colonel Joseph R. Ulatoski   Dec. 70

The 2d Brigade of the 25th Infantry Division constituted a separate command after the bulk of the division departed Vietnam in December 1970. It served under the operational control of II Field Force, Vietnam and was based in III Corps Tactical Zone. It was redeployed to Hawaii as part of Increment VI of the U.S. Army withdrawal.

* Date division left Vietnam and the brigade became separate; the brigade first arrived in Vietnam 20 January 1966.

2d Brigade, 25th Infantry Division (Separate) Order of Battle: Assigned and Attached Units

Brigade Infantry

1st Battalion, 5th Infantry (Mechanized)
2d Battalion, 12th Infantry
3d Battalion, 22d Infantry
1st Battalion, 27th Infantry

Brigade Support

225th Support Battalion
54th Engineer Company
532d Signal Company

Brigade Artillery

1st Battalion, 8th Artillery (105mm)

Brigade Reconnaissance

Troop F, 4th Cavalry (Air)
Company F, 75th Infantry (Ranger)

3d Brigade,
82d Airborne Division

Arrived Vietnam: 18 February 1968
from Fort Bragg
Departed Vietnam: 11 December 1969
to Fort Bragg
Locations: Hue – Phu Bai
Phu Loi – Saigon
Authorized Strength: HHC – 203 (1968)

Commanders

Colonel Alex R. Bolling, Jr.	Feb. 68
Brigadier General George W. Dickerson	Dec. 68

When the brigade's paratroopers jumped in a training exercise in Florida on 22 January 1968, little did they realize the brigade would be fighting in Vietnam less than one month later. But on 13 February 1968 the advance party departed Pope Air Force Base for the Republic of Vietnam. On the afternoon of Valentine's Day the huge airlift began, an operation which was to require 135 C-141 and six C-133 aircraft before it was over. Landing at Chu Lai, the brigade had just begun to muster from its deployment when it was moved again. The brigade was attached to the 101st Airborne Division (Airmobile) and given the mission of protecting the ancient capital of Hue in the I Corps Tactical Zone. In September 1968 it moved south, switched to counter enemy forces around Saigon and came under the control of the Capital Military Assistance Command, securing the western approaches and preventing ground and rocket attacks against the Saigon – Tan Son Nhut complex. Sent to Vietnam as part of the emergency response to the enemy 1968 Tet offensive, the brigade rejoined the division at Fort Bragg as soon as possible as part of Increment II of the U.S. Army withdrawal, since its parent division was the United States Army strategic reserve on a worldwide basis. At one time it was contemplated committing the entire 82d Airborne Division to Vietnam, but this never materialized.

3d Brigade, 82d Airborne Division Order of Battle:
Assigned and Attached Units

Brigade Infantry

1st Battalion, 505th Infantry (Airborne)
2d Battalion, 505th Infantry (Airborne)
1st Battalion, 508th Infantry (Airborne)

Brigade Reconnaissance

82d Support Battalion
58th Signal Company
Company C, 307th Engineer Battalion (Airborne)

Brigade Artillery

2d Battalion, 321st Artillery (105mm) (Airborne)

Brigade Reconnaissance

Troop B, 1st Squadron, 17th Cavalry (Armored)
Company O, 75th Infantry (Ranger)

Brigade Aviation

Company A, 82d Aviation Battalion

101st Airborne Division
(Airmobile)

Arrived Vietnam: 19 November 1967
from Fort Campbell
Departed Vietnam: 10 March 1972
to Fort Campbell

Commanders

Major General Olinto M. Barsanti	Dec. 67
Major General Melvin Zais	July 68
Major General John M. Wright, Jr.	May 69
Major General John J. Hennessey	May 70
Major General Thomas M. Tarpley	Jan. 71

The 101st Division ("The Screaming Eagles") was only partially organized in World War I, demobilized in December 1918 and reorganized June 1921 in Wisconsin. In the carefully conceived plans for the invasion of Nazi-held Europe, it became evident that a large force of hard-hitting, superbly trained airborne troops would be needed to nullify coastal defenses and cut enemy lines. Thus, on 15 August 1942, the 101st Airborne Division was activated at Camp Claiborne and sent overseas 5 September 1943. After months of arduous training, drills and practice jumps, two parachute infantry regiments and two glider regiments landed in England for the future invasion of France. On D-Day, 6 June 1944, the division parachuted behind enemy lines in the Utah Beach area of Normandy, France, and took key objectives despite fierce resistance. Afterward the division returned to England to prepare for future air assaults, and on 17 September 1944 the division landed in Holland and seized two vital bridges as part of the heavy fighting in nearby towns, most notably St. Oedenrode and Eindhoven. In December the 101st Airborne Division thrust into the Ardennes to blunt the German counterattack there and was surrounded at Bastogne. Holding its perimeter against violent enemy attacks, the acting Commander, Brigadier General Anthony C. McAuliffe, earned the division immortality with the reply "Nuts" to the German invitation to surrender. It had been cut off since 22 December 1944, and the 4th Armored Division broke through to the beleaguered division 17 January 1945. The division went on to cross the Moder River and moved into the Ruhr pocket, reaching Hitler's retreat home at Berchtesgaden at the end of the war. After World War II, the division was inactivated and reactivated as a training division three times in 11 years. It later served as part of the U.S. Strike Command at Fort Campbell as a full-fledged Airborne Division once more, and sent its first element, the 1st Brigade, to Vietnam in July 1965. The entire division came over to Vietnam in November 1967 and was initially committed in the III Corps Tactical Zone, although its 1st Brigade continued to operate out of Phan Rang in II Corps. In April and May of 1968 the division participated in operations along the lowlands of Quang Tri and Thua Thien Provinces, having been shifted north into I Corps Tactical Zone in March. It was also engaged at Hue. The 101st Airborne Division was converted into a fully airmobile status from its former parachutist mode by August 1968. The division continued its far-ranging operations by sending its 3d Brigade into the Dak To Highlands in mid-1968. (In August this brigade would move down to reinforce the 25th Infantry Division's elements around Saigon.) The remainder of the division swept central Thua Thien Province to the north under XXIV Corps. In September 1968 the 3d Brigade redeployed to the northern area of Vietnam at Phong Dien, just a short distance from the rest of the division which was at Phu Bai. The division remained in I Corps protecting the populated regions of Thua Thien Province. Most of 1970 was spent on Operation TEXAS STAR, where one brigade had pacification responsibilities and the other two brigades conducted offensive sweeps against the enemy in the western portions of Quang Tri and Thua Thien. The division participated in the last major offensive operation in which U.S. ground troops were involved, Operation JEFFERSON GLENN, along with the ARVN 1st Infantry Division. JEFFERSON GLENN became the last such mission, for on 12 November 1971 President Nixon announced all American troops would be in a purely defensive mode thereafter. (Operation JEFFERSON GLENN took place 5 September 1970 – 8 October 1971.) However, the war was not yet over for the 101st Airborne Division (Airmobile), since its aviation assets and command structure were actively involved in Operation LAM SON 719, in which the South Vietnamese Army struck across the Laotian border with mixed results. During this time the commanding general of the division commanded all U.S. Army aviation in direct support of the operation. From 1 December 1971 – 31 January 1972 the bulk of the division was redeployed as part of Increment X of the U.S. Army withdrawal from Vietnam. The 101st Airborne Division (Airmobile) had served in Vietnam as a full division for 1,573 days.

101st Airborne Division (Airmobile)

Elements	Vietnam Service	Authorized Strength 1968	1970
Division Headquarters and HQ Company	19 Nov. 67 – 10 March 72	195	201
1st Brigade Headquarters and HQ Company*	29 July 65 – 19 Jan. 72	223	230
2d Brigade Headquarters and HQ Company	18 Nov. 67 – 14 Feb. 72	223	230
3d Brigade Headquarters and HQ Company	18 Nov. 67 – 21 Dec. 71	223	230
Division Artillery Headquarters and HQ Battery	18 Nov. 67 – 17 Jan. 72	162	162
Division Support Command Headquarters and HQ Co	18 Nov. 67 – 17 Jan. 72	163	163

Division Headquarters Locations in Vietnam

Bien Hoa	Nov. 67 – Jan. 68
Hue	Feb. 68 – May 68
Bien Hoa/Phu Bai	June 68 – April 69
Bien Hoa/Gia Le	May 69 – Sept. 69
Bien Hoa/Hue/Phu Bai	Oct. 69 – Nov. 69
Hue/Phu Bai	Dec. 69 – March 72

* Also considered as a separate command in this work. Entire Vietnam service is listed above.

101st Airborne Division (Airmobile) Order of Battle: Assigned and Attached Units

Division Infantry

3d Battalion, 187th Infantry (Airmobile)
1st Battalion, 327th Infantry (Airmobile)
2d Battalion, 327th Infantry (Airmobile)
1st Battalion, 501st Infantry (Airmobile)
2d Battalion, 501st Infantry (Airmobile)
1st Battalion, 502d Infantry (Airmobile)
2d Battalion, 502d Infantry (Airmobile)
1st Battalion, 506th Infantry (Airmobile)
2d Battalion, 506th Infantry (Airmobile)
3d Battalion, 506th Infantry (Airmobile)

Division Reconnaissance

Company F, 58th Infantry (Long Range Patrol)
Company L, 75th Infantry (Ranger)
2d Squadron, 17th Cavalry (Armored; later Air)*

Division Aviation

101st Aviation Group (formerly 160th Avn Gp)
101st Aviation Battalion (Airmobile)
158th Aviation Battalion (Assault Helicopter)
159th Aviation Battalion (Assault Helicopter)
163d Aviation Company (General Support)
478th Aviation Company (Heavy Helicopter)

Division Artillery

2d Battalion, 11th Artillery (155mm)
1st Battalion, 39th Artillery (155mm)
4th Battalion, 77th Artillery (Aerial Rocket)
2d Battalion, 319th Artillery (105mm)
2d Battalion, 320th Artillery (105mm)
1st Battalion, 321st Artillery (105mm)
Battery A, 377th Artillery (Aviation)

Division Support

5th Transportation Battalion (Aircraft Maintenance)
326th Medical Battalion
326th Engineer Battalion
426th Supply & Service Battalion
501st Signal Battalion
801st Maintenance Battalion
101st Administration Company
265th Army Security Agency Company

Other Units on Temporary Assignment

11th Infantry Brigade
1st Squadron, 1st Cavalry (Armored)
3d Squadron, 5th Cavalry (Armored)

* Officially regarded as air cavalry commencing 1 July 1969.

Unauthorized

1st Brigade, 101st Airborne Division (Separate)

Arrived Vietnam: 29 July 1965
Departed Vietnam: 18 November 1967
rejoined division

Locations:

Bien Hoa/Vung Tau	July 65 – Sept. 65
Cam Ranh Bay	Oct. 65
Ma Ca	Nov. 65
Phan Rang	Dec. 65 – May 67
Duc Pho	June 67
Phan Rang/Duc Pho	July 67 – Nov. 67

Authorized Strength: HHC – 146 (1966)

Commanders

Colonel Joseph D. Mitchell	Aug. 65
Brigadier General James S. Timothy	Sept. 65
Brigadier General Willard Pearson	Jan. 66
Brigadier General Salve H. Matheson	Feb. 67

The 1st Brigade of the 101st Airborne Division deployed to the II Corps Tactical Zone in Vietnam from Fort Campbell. In early 1966 the brigade helped to clear Phu Yen Province and in June moved into action near Kontum. In May 1967 the brigade became a part of Task Force OREGON, with which it served until it later rejoined the 101st Airborne Division when it arrived from the United States in November 1967.

1st Brigade, 101st Airborne Division Order of Battle:
Assigned and Attached Units

Brigade Infantry

1st Battalion, 327th Infantry (Airborne)
2d Battalion, 327th Infantry (Airborne)
2d Battalion, 502d Infantry (Airborne)

Brigade Reconnaissance

Troop A, 2d Squadron, 17th Cavalry (Armored)

Brigade Artillery

2d Battalion, 320th Artillery (105mm) (Airborne)

Brigade Support

101st Support Battalion (Provisional)
Company A, 326th Engineer Battalion (Airborne)
Company D, 326th Medical Battalion (Airborne)
Company B, 501st Signal Battalion (Airborne)

Unauthorized

Task Force OREGON

Arrived Vietnam: 12 April 1967
Departed Vietnam: 22 September 1967
Location: Chu Lai

Commanders

Major General William B. Rosson	April 67
Major General Richard T. Knowles	June 67

Task Force OREGON was a provisional division-sized organization established and deployed to Quang Ngai and the southern part of Quang Tin Province, where unabated enemy activity threatened security of that sector of Vietnam. The arrival of the task force permitted the U.S. Marines in Quang Ngai Province to move units further north to reinforce the DMZ vicinity. The presence of this large force in the north also hastened the northward extension of 1st Cavalry Division support operations in the coastal area of Binh Dinh Province and the opening of Highway 1 to Da Nang. Task Force OREGON was headquartered at Chu Lai with a provisional headquarters, division support troops borrowed from various units and three combat brigades taken from areas where they could be spared at minimum risk: the 3d Brigade, 25th Infantry Division; the 1st Brigade, 101st Airborne Division, and the 196th Infantry Brigade (Light). In September 1967 the task force was replaced by the 23d Infantry Division (AMERICAL). With the impending arrival of two other brigades, the 11th Infantry Brigade and the 198th Infantry Brigade, the division was able to release the two brigades borrowed from other commands. This left the 196th Infantry Brigade as the only brigade to serve both the task force and its descendant, the AMERICAL Division.

Task Force OREGON (Provisional) Order of Battle:
Assigned and Attached Units

Task Force Infantry

2d Battalion, 3d Infantry
1st Battalion, 14th Infantry
3d Battalion, 21st Infantry
4th Battalion, 31st Infantry
1st Battalion, 35th Infantry
2d Battalion, 35th Infantry
1st Battalion, 327th Infantry
2d Battalion, 327th Infantry
2d Battalion, 502d Infantry

Task Force Support

15th Support Brigade HHC
39th Engineer Battalion
94th Supply & Service Battalion
188th Maintenance Battalion
509th Signal Battalion

Task Force Artillery

2d Battalion, 9th Artillery (105mm)
3d Battalion, 16th Artillery (155mm)
3d Battalion, 18th Artillery (175mm)
3d Battalion, 82d Artillery (105mm)
2d Battalion, 320th Artillery (105mm)

Task Force Reconnaissance

1st Squadron, 1st Cavalry (Armored)
2d Squadron, 11th Armored Cavalry
Troop A, 2d Squadron, 17th Cavalry (Armored)
Troop C, 1st Squadron, 9th Cavalry (Air)
Troop D, 17th Cavalry (Armored)

Chapter 7

Infantry and Airborne Brigades

11th Infantry Brigade (Light)

Arrived Vietnam: 19 December 1967
Departed Vietnam: 13 November 1971
Locations: Duc Pho   Dec. 67 – June 71
           The Loi   July 71 – Nov. 71

Authorized Strength	**1968**	**1971**
HHC	188	128

Commanders

Brigadier General Andy A. Lipscomb	Dec. 67
Colonel Oran K. Henderson	March 68
Colonel John W. Donalson	Oct. 68
Colonel Jack L. Treadwell	Apr. 69
Colonel Hugh F. T. Hoffman	Sept. 69
Colonel Kendrick B. Barlow	March 70
Colonel John L. Insani	Sept. 70
Colonel Warner S. Goodwin	March 68

The 11th Infantry Brigade arrived in Vietnam as an emergency deployment from Schofield Barracks, Hawaii, where it was serving in a Strategic Armed Forces role replacing the 25th Infantry Division, which had already been sent to Vietnam. (The 11th Infantry Brigade was in turn replaced by the 29th Infantry Brigade, Hawaii National Guard, which closed into its mobilization station 13 May 1968.) The 11th Infantry Brigade was officially combined with the newly formed 23d Infantry Division (AMERICAL) on 15 February 1969 and operated in Quang Ngai and Quang Tin Provinces along the coastal lower portions of the I Corps Tactical Zone. It departed Vietnam as part as of Increment IX of the U.S. Army withdrawal along with the bulk of the AMERICAL Division and was folded up at Fort Lewis.

11th Infantry Brigade (Light) Order of Battle: Assigned and Attached Units

Brigade Infantry

3d Battalion, 1st Infantry
4th Battalion, 3d Infantry
1st Battalion, 20th Infantry
4th Battalion, 21st Infantry

Brigade Support

6th Support Battalion
6th Engineer Company

Brigade Artillery

6th Battalion, 11th Artillery (105mm)

Brigade Reconnaissance

Troop E, 1st Cavalry (Armored)

173d Airborne Brigade

Arrived Vietnam: 7 May 1965
Departed Vietnam: 25 August 1971
Locations:

Bien Hoa	May 65 – Oct. 67
An Khe	Nov. 67 – April 69
Bong Son	May 69 – Aug. 71

Authorized Strength	**1966**	**1968**
HHC	265	312

Commanders

Brigadier General Ellis W. Williamson	May 65
Brigadier General Paul F. Smith	Feb. 66
Brigadier General John R. Deane, Jr.	Dec. 66
Brigadier General Leo H. Schweiter	Aug. 67
Brigadier General Richard J. Allen	April 68
Brigadier General John W. Barnes	Dec. 68
Brigadier General Hubert S. Cunningham	Aug. 69
Brigadier General Elmer R. Ochs	Aug. 70
Brigadier General Jack MacFarlane	Jan. 71

Formed in May 1963, the 173d Airborne Brigade ("Sky Soldiers") began training for the type of warfare it would encounter in Vietnam and was sent to Vietnam from Okinawa as the first major U.S. Army ground combat unit. When committed to combat, the brigade represented the sole U.S. Pacific Command (USAPACOM) quick-reaction reserve and was to be on temporary duty only until it could be replaced by an airborne brigade from the United States. Despite these optimistic withdrawal intentions the brigade remained in Vietnam for almost the duration of the U.S. effort. A particularly elite unit, it also operated with an Australian battalion during the early part of its service. The brigade became famous at the Battle of Dak To in November 1967 when it fought an entrenched North Vietnamese Army regiment on Hill 875 and, in some of the most bitter fighting of the war, captured the hill on Thanksgiving Day, earning the Presidential Unit Citation. It was also noted for its combat parachute jump during Operation JUNCTION CITY 22 February 1967 in War Zone C of Tay Ninh Province. It had been initially sent to Vietnam to provide infantry security for the Bien Hoa airbase complex but launched into a series of intensely fought offensive operations including striking into War Zone C during September – November 1966 in Operation ATTLEBORO. The brigade struck this same location again early in 1967. Throughout 1968 the brigade fought in Binh Thuan and Binh Dinh Provinces. By 1969 the brigade was engaged in extensive pacification efforts and route security (securing portions of QL 1, Vietnam's only major north-south highway) in the An Lao Valley of Binh Dinh Province. The following years were spent in similar operations within the II Corps Tactical Zone.

173d Airborne Brigade Order of Battle:
Assigned and Attached Units

Brigade Infantry

1st Battalion, 503d Infantry (Abn)
2d Battalion, 503d Infantry (Abn)
3d Battalion, 503d Infantry (Abn)
4th Battalion, 503d Infantry (Abn)

Brigade Reconnaissance

Company D, 16th Armor
Troop E, 17th Cavalry (Armored)

Attached Allied Battalion

1st Battalion, Royal Australian
Regiment

Attached Unit on Temporary Assignment

3d Battalion, 506th Infantry (Airmobile)

Brigade Artillery

3d Battalion, 319th Artillery
(105mm) (Airborne)

Brigade Aviation

335th Aviation Company
(Airmobile)

Brigade Support

173d Support Battalion (Abn)
173d Engineer Company
534th Signal Company
173d Signal Company (Prov)

196th Infantry Brigade (Light)

Arrived Vietnam: 26 August 1966
Departed Vietnam: 29 June 1972
Locations:

Tay Ninh	Aug. 66 – May 67
Chu Lai	June 67 – Oct. 67
Tam Ky	Nov. 67 – March 68
Phong Dien	April 68 – May 68
Hoi An	June 68 – June 68
Chu Lai	July 68 – March 71
Da Nang	April 71 – June 72

Authorized Strength	1966	1968	1971
HHC	285	188	128

Commanders

Colonel Francis Conaty	Aug. 66
Brigadier General Edward H. deSaussure	Sept. 66
Colonel Francis Conaty	Sept. 66

Brigadier General Richard T. Knowles	Nov. 66
Brigadier General Frank H. Linnell	May 67
Colonel Louis Gelling	Nov. 67
Colonel Frederick J. Kroesen, Jr.	June 68
Colonel Thomas H. Tackaberry	May 69
Colonel James M. Lee	Nov. 69
Colonel Edwin L. Kennedy	April 70
Colonel William S. Hathaway	Nov. 70
Colonel Rutland D. Beard, Jr.	June 71
Brigadier General Joseph P. McDonough	Nov. 71

The 196th Infantry Brigade was raised at Fort Devens and originally scheduled to be sent to the Dominican Republic in mid-1966 but was rushed to Vietnam instead and posted in the western portion of the III Corps Tactical Zone. It initiated the operation into War Zone C of Tay Ninh Province, which developed into a major action after a large enemy base camp was uncovered 19 October 1966. In April 1967 the brigade was selected, along with the 1st Brigade, 101st Airborne Division and the 3d Brigade, 25th Infantry Division, to form a provisional division-sized unit called Task Force OREGON and then moved to the I Corps Tactical Zone. The brigade stayed with this command, which was converted into the 23d Infantry Division (AMERICAL) 25 September 1967. The 196th Infantry Brigade officially joined this division 15 February 1969. It operated throughout northern Vietnam, and after the division was closed out of Vietnam 29 November 1971, the 196th Infantry Brigade was reconstituted as a separate (provisional) brigade-sized element to safeguard the same area of operations. In April 1971 the brigade was relocated to Da Nang for major port security duties. It finally departed Vietnam as the last U.S. Army combat brigade to leave in Increment XII of the U.S. Army withdrawal.

196th Infantry Brigade (Light) Order of Battle:
Assigned and Attached Units

Brigade Infantry

2d Battalion, 1st Infantry
1st Battalion, 6th Infantry*
3d Battalion, 21st Infantry
4th Battalion, 31st Infantry
1st Battalion, 46th Infantry †

Brigade Reconnaissance

Troop F, 8th Cavalry (Air) †
Troop F, 17th Cavalry (Armored)

Brigade Artillery

3d Battalion, 82d Artillery (105mm)

Brigade Support

8th Support Battalion
175th Engineer Company
587th Signal Company †

* During November 1971 only.

† Only during the brigade service August 1971 – June 1972, after the 23d Infantry Division (AMERICAL) had departed. F/8 Cavalry joined the brigade in November 1971.

198th Infantry Brigade (Light)

Arrived Vietnam: 21 October 1967
Departed Vietnam: 13 November 1971
Locations:

Duc Pho	Oct. 67 – Nov. 67
Chu Lai	Dec. 67 – Nov. 71

Authorized Strength	1968	1971
HHC	188	128

Commanders

Colonel J. R. Waldie	Oct. 67
Colonel Charles B. Thomas	June 68
Colonel Robert B. Tully	Dec. 68
Colonel Jere D. Whittington	May 69

Colonel Joseph G. Clemons	Nov. 69
Colonel William R. Richardson	July 70
Colonel Charles R. Smith	Mar. 71

The 198th Infantry Brigade was raised at Fort Hood and scheduled for deployment to Vietnam as the "Practice Nine Barrier Brigade" in 1968. The barrier was to be a highly developed "Maginot Line" along the DMZ separating North and South Vietnam at the time. Parts of it were actually constructed in 1967. However, the planned fortifications never materialized, and the brigade was rushed to Vietnam to join Task Force OREGON, which in the meantime had become the basis of the 23d Infantry Division (AMERICAL). The 198th Infantry Brigade thus remained with this division throughout its service in Vietnam defending the I Corps Tactical Zone area. It departed with Increment IX of the U.S. Army withdrawal, along with the bulk of the AMERICAL Division.

198th Infantry Brigade (Light) Order of Battle: Assigned and Attached Units

Brigade Infantry

1st Battalion, 6th Infantry
1st Battalion, 46th Infantry
5th Battalion, 46th Infantry
1st Battalion, 52d Infantry

Brigade Reconnaissance

Troop H, 17th Cavalry (Armored)

Brigade Artillery

1st Battalion, 14th Artillery (105mm)

Brigade Support

9th Support Battalion
555th Engineer Company

199th Infantry Brigade (Light)

Arrived Vietnam: 10 December 1966
Departed Vietnam: 11 October 1970
Locations:

Song Be	Dec. 66 – Feb. 67
Long Binh	March 67
Bien Hoa	April 67 – June 67
Long Binh	July 67 – Feb. 68
Gao Ho Nai	March 68 – June 68
Long Binh	July 68 – Oct. 70

Authorized Strength: HHC – 203 (1968)

Commanders

Brigadier General Charles W. Ryder, Jr.	Dec. 66
Brigadier General John F. Freund	March 67
Brigadier General Robert C. Forbes	Sept. 67
Brigadier General Franklin M. Davis, Jr.	May 68
Colonel Frederic E. Davison	Aug. 68
Brigadier General Warren K. Bennett	May 69
Brigadier General William R. Bond *	Dec. 69
Colonel Joseph E. Collins	July 70
Lieutenant Colonel George E. Williams	Sept. 70

* Killed in action by enemy automatic-rifle fire.

The 199th Infantry Brigade was formed at Fort Benning and rushed to Vietnam to assist in safeguarding vital areas in the III Corps Tactical Zone, remaining in that region throughout its service in Vietnam. With emphasis on joint U.S. – South Vietnamese Army operations, the brigade swept around the Saigon area through 1967, moving into Bien Hoa Province in Operation UNIONTOWN in December. The 1968 Tet offensive began on 31 January 1968 with a 3 A.M. rocket attack against the II Field Force Vietnam Headquarters, Long Binh Post and Bien Hoa Air Base. The brigade was soon defending itself in fierce combat against

the 275th Viet Cong Regiment smashing against the 199th – II Field Force, Vietnam perimeter. During the 31 January 1968 Long Binh attacks, the brigade's 3d Battalion, 7th Infantry was helicoptered into Saigon to retake the Phu Tho Racetrack from enemy forces who had infiltrated the capital and were using the racetrack as a command post. The track was taken within eight hours and for the next grim two days the battalion engaged in house-to-house fighting in the Cholon sector of Saigon. The brigade next found only light and sporadic contact with enemy forces during numerous reconnaissance-in-force operations around the Xuan Loc – Long Binh area for the remainder of the year. In 1969 the brigade concentrated on security toward the north and east of Saigon. It departed Vietnam as part of Increment IV of the U.S. Army withdrawal and was inactivated at Fort Benning 15 October 1970.

199th Infantry Brigade (Light) Order of Battle: Assigned and Attached Units

Brigade Infantry

2d Battalion, 3d Infantry
3d Battalion, 7th Infantry
4th Battalion, 12th Infantry
5th Battalion, 12th Infantry

Brigade Reconnaissance

Troop D, 17th Cavalry (Armored)
Company F, 51st Infantry (Long Range Patrol)
Company M, 75th Infantry (Ranger)

Brigade Artillery

2d Battalion, 40th Artillery (105mm)

Brigade Support

7th Support Battalion

87th Engineer Company
313th Signal Company

Other Units on Temporary Duty

3d Squadron, 11th Armored Cavalry

Combat Units

Chapter 8

Armor

Company D, 16th Armor
(Airborne Antitank)

Arrived Vietnam: 6 May 1965
Departed Vietnam: 25 August 1968
Previous Station: Okinawa
Authorized Strength: 101 (1966)

Company D, 16th Armor was equipped with M56 self-propelled 90mm antitank "Scorpion" guns. The company was assigned to the 173d Airborne Brigade in Vietnam until August 1968. It should be noted that on 2 September 1969, after the unit had already departed Vietnam, it became Troop D of the 16th Cavalry.

2d Battalion, 34th Armor
(Division Armor)

Arrived Vietnam: 12 September 1966
Departed Vietnam: 15 December 1970
Previous Station: Fort Irwin

Authorized Strength	1966	1968	1970
Battalion	571	614	614

The 2d Battalion, 34th Armor was part of the 4th Infantry Division upon arrival in Vietnam and was equipped with M48A3 90mm-gun tanks. However, the battalion was attached to the II Field Force, Vietnam in the III Corps Tactical Zone to replace the 1st Battalion, 69th Armor, which had moved to the II Corps area.

Company B was detached almost immediately to the 1st Infantry Division at Phu Loi, Company A was detached to the 25th Infantry Division at Cu Chi and Company C was sent north to I Corps Tactical Zone. The constant parceling out of its tank companies seldom left the battalion with more than one company under its own control. At some points it controlled none of its organic companies. On 1 August 1967 the battalion was relieved of assignment to the 4th Infantry Division and reassigned to the 25th Infantry Division, but the battalion continued to serve in scattered locations throughout Vietnam.

1st Battalion, 69th Armor
(Division Armor)

Arrived Vietnam: 13 March 1966
Departed Vietnam: 10 April 1970
Previous Station: Hawaii

Authorized Strength	1966	1968
Battalion	571	614

The 1st Battalion, 69th Armor was initially part of the 25th Infantry Division and was refitted in Okinawa before arrival in Vietnam. Equipped with M48A3 90mm-gun tanks, it was constantly engaged throughout II Corps Tactical Zone, and on 1 August 1967 was officially reassigned to the 4th Infantry Division. The battalion had the distinction of being the only U.S. Army unit in tank-to-tank combat during the Vietnam war when, on 3 March 1969, North Vietnamese Army PT-76 76mm-gun light amphibious tanks of their 16th Company, 4th Battalion, 202d Armor Regiment attacked dug-in M48A3 tanks of Company B.

1st Battalion, 77th Armor (Division Armor)

Arrived Vietnam: 27 July 1968
Departed Vietnam: 23 July 1971
Previous Station: Fort Carson

Authorized Strength	1968	1970
Battalion	614	615

The 1st Battalion, 77th Armor was part of the 1st Brigade Task Force of the 5th Infantry Division (Mechanized) and served in the Quang Tri area of Vietnam. It was equipped with M48A3 90mm-gun tanks.

Tuy Hoa Armor Company, Provisional

No Insignia
Authorized

Arrived Vietnam: 10 May 1969
Departed Vietnam: 1 November 1969
Previous Station: Vietnam
Authorized Strength: Unknown

The Tuy Hoa Armor Company (Provisional) was established by the 173d Airborne Brigade to provide reaction firepower during pacification efforts in Binh Dinh Province, where primary emphasis was given hamlet and village protection in order to enable South Vietnamese territorial forces to conduct searches behind a protective shield of U.S. and regular Vietnamese units.

Chapter 9

Artillery

I Field Force
Vietnam Artillery

Arrived Vietnam: 16 November 1965*
Departed Vietnam: 21 June 1972
Previous Station: Fort Sill

Authorized Strength	1966	1968
HHB	195	194

* Arrived in Vietnam as XXX Corps Artillery. I Field Force, Vietnam was established 15 March 1966 and at this point it became I FFV Artillery.

I Field Force Vietnam Artillery was redesignated from the XXX Corps Artillery serving Task Force ALPHA, which had been organized 12 August 1965 at Fort Sill, going to Vietnam to coordinate and control U.S. artillery units in both the II and III Corps Tactical Zones. I Field Force Vietnam Artillery was stationed at Nha Trang and provided control for artillery in the II Corps Tactical Zone (CTZ). A provisional I FFV Artillery (Forward) task force was formed at Qui Nhon 26 December 1966 – 28 April 1967. In December 1970 it detached a Provisional I Field Force Artillery Group to Dalat, but this should not be confused with the I Field Force Vietnam Artillery itself. In April 1971 assets were used to create the Second Army Regional Command (SRAC) Artillery, and in June 1971 this became the U.S. Army Artillery Force, Military Region 2 (USARMYF, MR 2 Artillery). During the Vietnam conflict, the following artillery units served at one time or another with I Field Force Artillery:

41st Artillery Group	3d Battalion, 18th Artillery
52d Artillery Group	5th Battalion, 22d Artillery
8th Battalion, 4th Artillery	5th Battalion, 27th Artillery
3d Battalion, 6th Artillery	1st Battalion, 30th Artillery
7th Battalion, 8th Artillery	6th Battalion, 32d Artillery
7th Battalion, 13th Artillery	6th Battalion, 33d Artillery
6th Battalion, 14th Artillery	1st Battalion, 39th Artillery

7th Battalion, 15th Artillery	1st Battalion, 44th Artillery
5th Battalion, 16th Artillery	4th Battalion, 60th Artillery
2d Battalion, 17th Artillery	6th Battalion, 84th Artillery

II Field Force
Vietnam Artillery

Arrived Vietnam: 8 March 1966
Departed Vietnam: 2 May 1971
Previous Station: Fort Sill

Authorized Strength	1966	1968	1970
HHB	195	194	186

II Field Force Vietnam Artillery was formed as a controlling headquarters for U.S. artillery in the III Corps Tactical Zone (CTZ), and this mission was later expanded to include IV CTZ. It was first stationed at Bien Hoa, but in July 1968 moved to Long Binh. During the Vietnam conflict the following artillery units served at one time or another under II Field Force Artillery control:

23d Artillery Group	3d Battalion, 16th Artillery
54th Artillery Group	1st Battalion, 27th Artillery
5th Battalion, 2d Artillery	6th Battalion, 27th Artillery
3d Battalion, 6th Artillery	2d Battalion, 32d Artillery
1st Battalion, 8th Artillery	2d Battalion, 35th Artillery
7th Battalion, 8th Artillery	5th Battalion, 42d Artillery
7th Battalion, 9th Artillery	6th Battalion, 77th Artillery
2d Battalion, 11th Artillery	1st Battalion, 83d Artillery
2d Battalion, 12th Artillery	1st Battalion, 92d Artillery
2d Battalion, 13th Artillery	2d Battalion, 94th Artillery
6th Battalion, 15th Artillery	3d Battalion, 197th Artillery
7th Battalion, 15th Artillery	

Unauthorized

XXIV Corps Artillery

Arrived Vietnam: 20 February 1969
Departed Vietnam: 16 November 1971
Previous Station: Vietnam
Authorized Strength: HHB – 139 (1971)

XXIV Corps Artillery was redesignated from Provisional Corps Vietnam Artillery, which had been formed to control U.S. artillery units in the I Corps Tactical Zone on 15 August 1968. XXIV Corps Artillery was stationed at Phu Bai and in April 1970 relocated to Da Nang. During the Vietnam conflict the following artillery units served at one time or another with XXIV Corps Artillery:

108th Artillery Group	1st Battalion, 44th Artillery
8th Battalion, 4th Artillery	1st Battalion, 83d Artillery
6th Battalion, 33d Artillery	2d Battalion, 94th Artillery
1st Battalion, 40th Artillery	2d Battalion, 138th Artillery

XXX Corps Artillery

No Insignia
Authorized

Arrived Vietnam: 16 November 1965
Departed Vietnam: 15 March 1966
Previous Station: Fort Sill
Authorized Strength: 48

XXX Corps Artillery arrived at Nha Trang and provided the artillery control for Field Forces, Vietnam. It was later redesignated I Field Force Vietnam Artillery.

Provisional Corps Vietnam Artillery

No Insignia
Authorized

Arrived Vietnam: 15 August 1968
Departed Vietnam: 20 February 1969
Previous Station: Vietnam
Authorized Strength: Unknown

Provisional Corps Vietnam Artillery was formed at Phu Bai to control U.S. artillery units in the I Corps Tactical Zone and on 20 February 1969 was redesignated XXIV Corps Artillery.

23d Artillery Group (Field Artillery)

Arrived Vietnam: 16 November 1965
Departed Vietnam: 28 January 1972
Previous Station: Fort Lewis

Authorized Strength	1966	1968	1970
HHB	114	114	141

The 23d Artillery Group was part of II Field Force Vietnam Artillery and served at Phu Loi until May 1971 when it was moved to Long Binh. The following artillery battalions served at one time or another under 23d Artillery Group control:

5th Battalion, 2d Artillery	1st Battalion, 27th Artillery
7th Battalion, 8th Artillery	6th Battalion, 27th Artillery
7th Battalion, 9th Artilelry	2d Battalion, 32d Artillery
2d Battalion, 11th Artillery	2d Battalion, 35th Artillery
2d Battalion, 12th Artillery	5th Battalion, 42d Artillery
2d Battalion, 13th Artillery	3d Battalion, 197th Artillery
6th Battalion, 15th Artillery	

41st Artillery Group (Field Artillery)

Arrived Vietnam: 29 April 1967
Departed Vietnam: 15 November 1969
Previous Station: Fort Sill
Authorized Strength: HHB – 114

The 41st Artillery Group was part of I Field Force Vietnam Artillery responsible for the central coastal region of II CTZ and served at Phu Cat during its service in Vietnam. The following artillery battalions served at one time or another under 41st Artillery Group control:

7th Battalion, 13th Artillery	5th Battalion, 27th Artillery
7th Battalion, 15th Artillery	1st Battalion, 30th Artillery
2d Battalion, 17th Artillery	6th Battalion, 32d Artillery
3d Battalion, 18th Artillery	4th Battalion, 60th Artillery
5th Battalion, 22d Artillery	6th Battalion, 84th Artillery

52d Artillery Group (Field Artillery)

Arrived Vietnam: 17 June 1966
Departed Vietnam: 30 June 1971
Previous Station: Fort Sill

Authorized Strength	1966	1968	1970
HHB	106	106	109

The 52d Artillery Group was part of I Field Force Vietnam Artillery responsible for support of the western II CTZ highlands and served at Pleiku throughout its service in Vietnam. The following artillery battalions served at one time or another under 52d Artillery Group control:

3d Battalion, 6th Artillery	5th Battalion, 22d Artillery
7th Battalion, 13th Artillery	1st Battalion, 30th Artillery
6th Battalion, 14th Artillery	6th Battalion, 84th Artillery
7th Battalion, 15th Artillery	1st Battalion, 92d Artillery
2d Battalion, 17th Artillery	

54th Artillery Group (Field Artillery)

Arrived Vietnam: 1 October 1966
Departed Vietnam: 7 November 1969
Previous Station: Fort Bragg
Authorized Strength: HHB – 106

The 54th Artillery Group provided general support to II Field Force Vietnam Artillery and served at Xuan Loc, moving in late 1968 to Bien Hoa. The following artillery battalions served at one time or another under 54th Artillery Group control:

7th Battalion, 8th Artillery	5th Battalion, 42d Artillery
7th Battalion, 9th Artillery	6th Battalion, 77th Artillery
3d Battalion, 16th Artillery	1st Battalion, 83d Artillery
2d Battalion, 35th Artillery	

97th Artillery Group (Air Defense Artillery)

Arrived Vietnam: 30 September 1965
Departed Vietnam: 25 October 1968
Previous Station: Fort Bliss

Authorized Strength	1966	1968
HHB	47	130

The 97th Artillery Group was stationed at Tan Son Nhut and controlled the two artillery battalions containing HAWK missiles:

6th Battalion, 56th Artillery	6th Battalion, 71st Artillery

108th Artillery Group
(Field Artillery)

Arrived Vietnam: 28 October 1967
Departed Vietnam: 23 November 1971
Previous Station: Fort Riley

Authorized Strength	1968	1970
HHB	114	134

The 108th Artillery Group served under XXIV Corps. It was initially stationed at Dong Ha and moved in December 1970 to the Hue – Phu Bai vicinity. The following artillery battalions served at one time or another under 108th Artillery Group control:

8th Battalion, 4th Artillery	1st Battalion, 44th Artillery
6th Battalion, 33d Artillery	1st Battalion, 83d Artillery
1st Battalion, 39th Artillery	2d Battalion, 94th Artillery
1st Battalion, 40th Artillery	

5th Battalion, 2d Artillery
(Automatic Weapon, Self-propelled)

Arrived Vietnam: November 1966
Departed Vietnam: 22 June 1971
Previous Station: Fort Bliss

Authorized Strength	1966	1968	1971
Battalion	698	692	607

The 5th Battalion of the 2d Artillery was a self-propelled automatic weapons battalion consisting of M42A1 dual 40mm antiaircraft guns mustered from Reserve and National Guard assets to be utilized in a ground support role. The battalion, serving with II Field Force Vietnam Artillery, arrived at Qui Nhon and located to Long Binh. It was augmented with a battery of .50-cal quad machineguns, Battery D, 71st Artillery.

2d Battalion, 4th Artillery
(105mm Howitzer, Towed)

Arrived Vietnam: 28 January 1967
Departed Vietnam: 11 October 1970
Previous Station: Fort Riley
Authorized Strength: 468 (1968)

The 2d Battalion of the 4th Artillery was a towed 105mm howitzer battalion assigned to the 9th Infantry Division and initially in direct support of its 2d Brigade. It was located at Tan An. When the 9th Infantry Division departed Vietnam, the battalion continued in direct support of the separate 3d Brigade which remained at Tan An under the operational control of the 25th Infantry Division. The battalion then departed Vietnam along with the rest of the 3d Brigade.

5th Battalion, 4th Artillery
(155mm Howitzer, Self-propelled)

Arrived Vietnam: 29 July 1968
Departed Vietnam: 13 August 1971
Previous Station: Fort Carson

Authorized Strength	1968	1971
Battalion	663	658

The 5th Battalion of the 4th Artillery was an organic element of the 1st Brigade Task Force, 5th Infantry Division (Mechanized). It contained M109 155mm self-propelled howitzers and was located primarily at Quang Tri.

8th Battalion, 4th Artillery
(175mm Gun, Self-propelled)
(175mm Gun/8-inch Howitzer)

Arrived Vietnam: 13 August 1967
Departed Vietnam: 1 September 1971
Previous Station: Fort Sill
Authorized Strength: 565

The 8th Battalion of the 4th Artillery was originally a self-propelled M107 175mm gun battalion serving with I Field Force Vietnam Artillery at Dong Ha. It remained at Dong Ha as part of the 108th Artillery Group during its entire service in Vietnam. It converted to the dual 8-inch howitzer and 175mm self-propelled gun configuration in early 1969. It primarily provided reinforcing artillery support to the U.S. Marines.

1st Battalion, 5th Artillery
(105mm Howitzer, Towed)

Arrived Vietnam: 10 October 1965
Departed Vietnam: 15 April 1970
Previous Station: Fort Riley

Authorized Strength	1966	1968
Battalion	490	526

The 1st Battalion of the 5th Artillery, known as the "Alexander Hamilton Battery" because of its distinguished lineage, was a towed 105mm howitzer battalion serving the 1st Infantry Division and initially in direct support of the division's 1st Brigade. Its geographical locations included service at Bien Hoa through the end of 1965, Phuoc Vinh in 1966-67, Lai Khe and later Quan Loi in 1968, and finally Dau Tieng, where it was posted from August 1969 until its departure from Vietnam.

3d Battalion, 6th Artillery
(105mm Howitzer, Self-Propelled)

Arrived Vietnam: 17 June 1966
Departed Vietnam: 10 April 1970
Previous Station: Fort Sill

Authorized Strength	1966	1968
Battalion	509	505

The 3d Battalion of the 6th Artillery ("Centaurs") was composed of M108 105mm self-propelled howitzers. It was assigned initially to II Field Force Vietnam Artillery but soon transferred to the 52d Artillery Group. The battalion served at Pleiku throughout its service in Vietnam.

8th Battalion, 6th Artillery
(155mm Towed/8-inch Howitzer, Self-Propelled)

Arrived Vietnam: 20 October 1965
Departed Vietnam: 15 April 1970
Previous Station: Fort Riley

Authorized Strength	1966	1968
Battalion	598	612

The 8th Battalion of the 6th Artillery ("Centaurs") rendered the general artillery support for the 1st Infantry Division and was a dual 155mm towed howitzer and 8-inch self-propelled M110 howitzer battalion. It served at Bien Hoa, Phu Lai and at Lai Khe.

1st Battalion, 7th Artillery
(105mm Howitzer, Towed)

Arrived Vietnam: 10 October 1965
Departed Vietnam: 15 April 1970
Previous Station: Fort Riley

Authorized Strength	1968	1970
Battalion	490	526

The 1st Battalion of the 7th Artillery (which used the unofficial title of "Pheons") was a towed 105mm howitzer battalion used for direct artillery support to the 1st Infantry Division's 2d Brigade. It served at Bien Hoa until 1967 and then at Di An until it departed Vietnam.

1st Battalion, 8th Artillery
(105mm Howitzer, Towed)

Arrived Vietnam: 20 January 1966
Departed Vietnam: 30 April 1971
Previous Station: Hawaii

Authorized Strength	1966	1968	1970
Battalion	490	526	641

The 1st Battalion of the 8th Artillery ("Automatic Eighth") was a towed 105mm howitzer battalion assigned to the 25th Infantry Division and in direct support of its 2d Brigade. The battalion spent the majority of its service at Cu Chi.

7th Battalion, 8th Artillery
(8-inch Howitzer,
Self-Propelled)
(175mm Gun/8-inch Howitzer)

Arrived Vietnam: 29 June 1967
Departed Vietnam: 27 July 1971
Previous Station: Fort Sill
Authorized Strength: 565

The 7th Battalion of the 8th Artillery ("Automatic Eighth") was originally an 8-inch self-propelled M110 howitzer battalion but was later converted in early 1969. It was located at Bear Cat with the 54th Artillery Group but moved to Bien Hoa on 14 October 1967, where it remained until departure from Vietnam. However, the battalion was transferred to the control of II Field Force Vietnam Artillery on 17 October 1969 and served the 23d Artillery Group from May 1971 until redeployment.

2d Battalion, 9th Artillery
(105mm Howitzer, Towed)

Arrived Vietnam: 28 December 1965
Departed Vietnam: 10 April 1970
Previous Station: Hawaii

Authorized Strength	1966	1968
Battalion	490	526

The 2d Battalion of the 9th Artillery ("The Mighty Ninth") was a towed 105mm howitzer battalion which served in the Pleiku vicinity throughout its duty in Vietnam. It arrived as the direct support artillery to the 25th Infantry Division's 3d Brigade but was reassigned as the direct support artillery of the 4th Infantry Division's 3d Brigade on 1 August 1967.

7th Battalion, 9th Artillery
(105mm Howitzer, Towed)

Arrived Vietnam: 23 October 1966
Departed Vietnam: 1 April 1970
Previous Station: Fort Riley
Authorized Strength: 529 (1968)

The 7th Battalion of the 9th Artillery ("The Mighty Ninth") was a towed 105mm howitzer battalion under control of the 54th Artillery Group of II Field Force, Vietnam during the majority of its Vietnam service. It arrived at Phu Loi and moved on 13 November 1966 to Bear Cat, where it remained until being relocated to Tay Ninh on 15 August 1969, and came under the 23d Artillery Group's control there until departure from Vietnam.

1st Battalion, 11th Artillery
(105mm Howitzer, Towed)

Arrived Vietnam: 1 January 1967
Departed Vietnam: 14 August 1969
Previous Station: Fort Riley
Authorized Strength: 468 (1968)

The 1st Battalion of the 11th Artillery ("Dragon Regiment") was a towed 105mm howitzer battalion providing direct artillery support for the 9th Infantry Division. It was first stationed with the 2d Brigade at Bear Cat and in 1968 was located to Dong Tam.

2d Battalion, 11th Artillery
(155mm Howitzer, Towed)

Arrived Vietnam: 13 December 1966
Departed Vietnam: 1 January 1972
Previous Station: Fort Campbell
Authorized Strength: 598

The 2d Battalion of the 11th Artillery ("Dragon Regiment") was a towed 155mm howitzer battalion at Dau Tieng which saw service first as part of II Field Force Vietnam Artillery and later with Task Force OREGON. It was deployed to Duc Pho on 19 April 1967, Bien Hoa in January 1968 and on 8 March 1968 to I CTZ and 23rd Artillery Group's control at Gia Le. On 10 June 1968 it was assigned to the 101st Airborne Division.

6th Battalion, 11th Artillery
(105mm Howitzer, Towed)

Arrived Vietnam: 20 December 1967
Departed Vietnam: 19 September 1971
Previous Station: Hawaii

Authorized Strength	1968	1970
Battalion	526	641

The 6th Battalion of the 11th Artillery ("The Dragon Regiment") was a towed 105mm howitzer battalion, part of the 11th Infantry Brigade (Light) and later of the 23d Infantry Division (AMERICAL). It was stationed at Duc Pho.

7th Battalion, 11th Artillery
(105mm Howitzer, Towed)

Arrived Vietnam: 29 April 1966
Departed Vietnam: 8 December 1970
Previous Station: Hawaii

Authorized Strength	1968	1970
Battalion	490	526

The 7th Battalion of the 11th Artillery ("The Dragon Regiment") was a 105mm towed howitzer battalion providing direct artillery support to the 25th Infantry Division's 1st Brigade during its service in Vietnam. It served at both Cu Chi and Tay Ninh while it was in Vietnam.

2d Battalion, 12th Artillery
(155mm Howitzer, Towed)

Arrived Vietnam: 13 September 1969
Departed Vietnam: 29 August 1971
Previous Station: Fort Lewis
Authorized Strength: 598

The 2d Battalion of the 12th Artillery was activated in 1969 using the assets of the New Hampshire National Guard's 3d Battalion, 197th Artillery when the latter unit left Vietnam. It was composed of towed 155mm howitzers and was stationed at Phu Loi, assigned to the 23d Artillery Group. It rendered support for the 1st Cavalry Division.

2d Battalion, 13th Artillery
(105mm Howitzer, Towed)

Arrived Vietnam: 30 October 1965
Departed Vietnam: 16 March 1970
Previous Station: Fort Sill

Authorized Strength	1966	1968
Battalion	523	529

The 2d Battalion of the 13th Artillery ("The Clan") was assigned to the 23d Artillery Group of II Field Force, Vietnam and composed of towed 105mm howitzers. It arrived at Tan Son Nhut and was posted to Phu Loi on 11 December 1965. On 6 January 1967 it relocated to Tay Ninh, but in December was posted to Saigon. It then returned to Phu Loi. This battalion formed a "Jungle Battery" (Battery D) composed of mixed 105/155mm howitzers from the assets of its Battery A, with 155mm weapons out of Battery B, 3d Battalion, 197th Artillery.

3d Battalion, 13th Artillery
(155mm Towed/8-inch Howitzer, Self-Propelled)

Arrived Vietnam: 2 April 1966
Departed Vietnam: 8 December 1970
Previous Station: Hawaii

Authorized Strength	1966	1968
Battalion	592	612

The 3d Battalion of the 13th Artillery ("The Clan") rendered the general artillery support for the 25th Infantry Division and was a dual 155mm towed howitzer and 8-inch self-propelled M110 howitzer battalion. It was stationed at Cu Chi while in Vietnam.

7th Battalion, 13th Artillery
(105mm Howitzer, Towed)

Arrived Vietnam: 28 October 1966
Departed Vietnam: 12 October 1970
Previous Station: Fort Irwin
Authorized Strength: 529

The 7th Battalion of the 13th Artillery ("The Clan") was a towed 105mm howitzer battalion attached to the 41st Artillery Group of I Field Force, Vietnam. First stationed at Phu Cat, it moved in April 1967 to Qui Nhon and then Bong Son. In October 1969 it returned to Phu Cat. On 15 November 1969 the battalion was detached from the 41st Artillery Group and became part of I Field Force Vietnam Artillery directly.

1st Battalion, 14th Artillery
(105mm Howitzer, Towed)

Arrived Vietnam: 23 October 1967
Departed Vietnam: 18 November 1971
Previous Station: Fort Hood

Authorized Strength	1968	1970
Battalion	526	641

The 1st Battalion ("Battle Kings") of the 14th Artillery ("Warbonnets") was a towed 105mm howitzer battalion and part of the 198th Infantry Brigade (Light), later part of the 23d Infantry Division (AMERICAL). The battalion served between Chu Lai and Duc Pho while in Vietnam.

6th Battalion, 14th Artillery
(175mm Gun, Self-Propelled)
(175mm Gun/8-inch Howitzer)

Arrived Vietnam: 29 October 1965
Departed Vietnam: 2 December 1970
Previous Station: Fort Sill

Authorized Strength	1966	1968
Battalion	554	565

The 6th Battalion of the 14th Artillery ("Warbonnets") was originally an M107 self-propelled 175mm gun battalion and in fall 1966 was converted to the dual M110 self-propelled 8-inch howitzer and M107 self-propelled 175mm gun configuration. Initially part of Field Forces, Vietnam it served at Qui Nhon and on 20 July 1966 was attached to the 52d Artillery Group of I Field Force, Vietnam. It moved to Pleiku where it remained until leaving Vietnam.

6th Battalion, 15th Artillery
(105mm Howitzer, Towed)

Arrived Vietnam: 22 May 1967
Departed Vietnam: 22 November 1969
Previous Station: Fort Sill
Authorized Strength: 529

The 6th Battalion of the 15th Artillery ("Indianheads") was a towed 105mm howitzer battalion initially placed at Lai Khe and attached to the 1st Infantry Division there. On 15 July 1968 the battalion was transferred to the 23d Artillery Group and posted to Tan Son Nhut and then to Tay Ninh. On 15 August 1969, with the 54th Artillery Group, it was located to Long Thanh. It was assigned directly to II Field Force Vietnam Artillery on 21 October 1969.

7th Battalion, 15th Artillery (8-inch Howitzer, Self-Propelled) (175mm Gun/8-inch Howitzer)

Arrived Vietnam: 1 July 1967
Departed Vietnam: 28 November 1971
Previous Station: Fort Bragg

Authorized Strength	1968	1970
Battalion	565	560

The 7th Battalion of the 15th Artillery ("Indianheads") was originally an 8-inch self-propelled M110 howitzer battalion but was converted in early 1969 to the dual 8-inch howitzer and 175mm self-propelled M107 gun configuration. It served at Phu Cat with the 41st Artillery Group and while at Phu Cat it became part of I Field Force Vietnam Artillery. It was relocated to An Khe in January 1970. In late 1970 the battalion was transferred to the 52d Artillery Group and returned to Phu Cat, where it served until leaving Vietnam.

3d Battalion, 16th Artillery (155mm Howitzer, Towed)

Arrived Vietnam: 9 June 1967
Departed Vietnam: 1 October 1971
Previous Station: Fort Bragg
Authorized Strength: 598

The 3d Battalion of the 16th Artillery was a towed 155mm howitzer battalion which arrived in Chu Lai to be attached to Task Force OREGON and was part of the 54th Artillery Group of II Field Force, Vietnam. In August 1968 it was attached to the 23d Infantry Division (AMERICAL), providing general artillery support along with the division's 1st Battalion of the 82d Artillery, which had arrived that July. The 3d Battalion of the 16th Artillery remained stationed at Chu Lai.

5th Battalion, 16th Artillery (155mm Towed/8-inch Howitzer, Self-Propelled)

Arrived Vietnam: 4 October 1966
Departed Vietnam: 26 April 1971
Previous Station: Fort Lewis
Authorized Strength: 612

The 5th Battalion of the 16th Artillery rendered the general artillery support for the 4th Infantry Division and was a dual 155mm towed howitzer and 8-inch self-propelled M110 howitzer battalion. It served at Pleiku, and when the division left Vietnam the battalion was attached to I Field Force Vietnam Artillery and moved to Phu Cat in January 1971, where it remained until its withdrawal from Vietnam.

Battery C, 6th Howitzer Battalion, 16th Artillery (155mm Howitzer, Towed)

Arrived Vietnam: 17 June 1966
Departed Vietnam: 26 August 1968
Previous Station: Fort Sill

Authorized Strength	1966	1968
Battalion	120	125

Battery C of the 6th Howitzer Battalion, 16th Artillery was composed of 155mm towed howitzers and served with the 1st Cavalry Division at An Khe. It was stationed in 1967 at Qui Nhon under 41st Artillery Group control but was attached to the 1st Cavalry Division. On 15 April 1968 it was moved to I CTZ and its assets were transferred to Battery F of the 16th Artillery.

Battery F, 16th Artillery (155mm Howitzer, Towed)

Arrived Vietnam: 26 August 1968
Departed Vietnam: 1 April 1970
Previous Station: Fort Sill
Authorized Strength: 125

Battery F of the 16th Artillery was a redesignation of Headquarters and Headquarters Battery, 6th Howitzer Battalion, 16th Artillery. Formed from the assets of Battery C, 6th Howitzer Battalion, 16th Artillery, it served with the 1st Cavalry Division until October 1968 when it was transferred to the 108th Artillery Group at Phu Bai. Later that year it became part of the 23d Artillery Group of II Field Force, Vietnam and was posted to Quan Loi. In October 1969, while still at Quan Loi, it was attached directly to II Field Force Vietnam Artillery and in January 1970 the battery was located to Phu Loi, where it remained until leaving Vietnam.

2d Battalion, 17th Artillery (105mm Howitzer, Towed)

Arrived Vietnam: 12 September 1965
Departed Vietnam: 26 April 1971
Previous Station: Fort Sill

Authorized Strength	1966	1968	1970
Battalion	516	529	528

The 2d Battalion ("The Persuaders") of the 17th Artillery was a towed 105mm howitzer battalion stationed at An Khe as part of Field Forces, Vietnam and later I Field Force, Vietnam, while working closely with the 1st Cavalry Division through 1968. Still at An Khe, the battalion was placed under the 41st Artillery Group's control in 1969. In February 1970 it was relocated to Ban Me Thuot as part of the 52d Artillery Group until departing Vietnam.

3d Battalion, 18th Artillery (8-inch Howitzer, Self-Propelled) (175mm Gun/8-inch Howitzer)

Arrived Vietnam: 29 October 1965
Departed Vietnam: 7 October 1971
Previous Station: Fort Lewis

Authorized Strength	1966	1968	1970
Battalion	583	565	565

The 3d Battalion of the 18th Artillery was originally an 8-inch self-propelled M110 howitzer battalion but was converted in fall 1966 to the dual 8-inch howitzer self-propelled and 175mm self-propelled M107 gun configuration. Initially attached to the 1st Cavalry Division and Field Forces, Vietnam, it was located at An Khe. In April 1967 the battalion moved to Chu Lai with the mission of general support of Task Force OREGON. In February 1968 the battalion was attached to the 23d Infantry Division (AMERICAL) at Chu Lai, where it remained.

2d Battalion, 19th Artillery (105mm Howitzer, Towed)

Arrived Vietnam: 14 September 1965
Departed Vietnam: 2 April 1971
Previous Station: Fort Benning

Authorized Strength	1966	1968	1971
Battalion	407	426	334

The 2d Battalion of the 19th Artillery was a towed 105mm howitzer battalion assigned to the 1st Cavalry Division during the Vietnam conflict. It was in direct support of the division's 1st Brigade and had the distinctive title of the "Eagles" and the added qualification of being airborne initially. It saw extensive service throughout South Vietnam, being located at An Khe until it moved to Tay Ninh and Phong Dien in 1968, Bu Dop in 1969, and back to Tay Ninh and Song Be in 1970. In late 1970 the battalion was posted to Bien Hoa, where it remained until departing Vietnam.

2d Battalion, 20th Artillery (Aerial Rocket)

Arrived Vietnam: 13 September 1965
Departed Vietnam: 10 April 1971
Previous Station: Fort Benning

Authorized Strength	1966	1968	1971
Battalion	415	415	329

The 2d Battalion ("Armed Falcons," "Blue Max," "Bobcats") of the 20th Artillery was an aerial rocket artillery battalion equipped with armed helicopters and assigned to the 1st Cavalry Division. The battalion served continuously with division and was colocated with it during its service in Vietnam. The battalion was headquartered at An Khe until the division moved north. From 1968 until departure it was headquartered at Phuoc Vinh.

1st Battalion, 21st Artillery (105mm Howitzer, Towed)

Arrived Vietnam: 11 September 1965
Departed Vietnam: 29 June 1972
Previous Station: Fort Benning

Authorized Strength	1966	1968	1971
Battalion	407	436	536

The 1st Battalion of the 21st Artillery was a towed 105mm howitzer battalion assigned to the 1st Cavalry Division's 3d Brigade at An Khe until 1968 when it was moved to Quan Loi. It was at Quan Loi and later at Gia Ray. In April 1971 it was selected to remain in Vietnam as the artillery support of the separate 3d Brigade, 1st Cavalry Division and it was reinforced accordingly and posted to Bien Hoa.

5th Battalion, 22d Artillery (175mm Gun, Self-Propelled) (175mm Gun/8-inch Howitzer)

Arrived Vietnam: 24 December 1967
Departed Vietnam: 3 December 1970
Previous Station: Fort Irwin
Authorized Strength: 565

The 5th Battalion of the 22d Artillery was originally a self-propelled M107 175mm gun battalion serving with the 41st Artillery Group of I Field Force, Vietnam. It was converted in early 1969 to the dual 8-inch self-propelled M110 howitzer and 175mm self-propelled gun configuration. Having arrived at Nha Trang, it immediately moved to An Khe. The battalion was transferred to 52d Artillery Group Control in March 1969 while at that location. In 1969 it was relocated to Ban Me Thuot and in January 1970 was attached directly to I Field Force Vietnam Artillery and moved to Phan Rang. It remained there until departing Vietnam.

Battery D, 25th Artillery (Target Acquisition)

Arrived Vietnam: 25 September 1969
Departed Vietnam: 1 August 1970
Previous Station: Vietnam
Authorized Strength: 162

This battery was stationed in Saigon with the Capital Military Assistance Command, Vietnam until 27 March 1970 when it was transferred to Chau Hiep with II Field Force Vietnam Artillery.

Headquarters Battery, 8th Battalion, 25th Artillery (Target Acquisition)

Arrived Vietnam: 2 August 1966
Departed Vietnam: 27 January 1971
Previous Station: Fort Bragg

Authorized Strength	1966	1968
Battery	136	135

Headquarters Battery of the 8th Battalion, 25th Artillery was a target acquisition battery with II Field Force Vietnam Artillery. The battery was located at Long Binh during its Vietnam service.

Battery C, 2d Battalion, 26th Artillery (Target Acquisition)

Arrived Vietnam: 17 October 1967
Departed Vietnam: 12 February 1968
Previous Station: Fort Bragg
Authorized Strength: 188

Battery C of the 2d Battalion, 26th Artillery was a target acquisition battery on 90–180 days temporary duty from Fort Bragg and attached to the 108th Artillery Group. Its assets were used to form Battery F, 26th Artillery.

Battery F, 26th Artillery (Target Acquisition)

Arrived Vietnam: 5 February 1968
Departed Vietnam: 31 July 1971
Previous Station: Fort Sill

Authorized Strength	1968	1970
Battery	253	250

During its service in Vietnam Battery F of the 26th Artillery was a target acquisition battery serving with the 108th Artillery Group at Dong Ha as well as XXIV Corps Artillery.

Battery F, 26th Artillery, Provisional (105mm Howitzer, Towed)

Arrived Vietnam: June 1972
Departed Vietnam: September 1972
Previous Station: Vietnam
Authorized Strength: 162

Battery F of the 26th Artillery (Provisional) was a towed 105mm howitzer battery provisionally formed from the assets of the 1st Battalion, 21st Artillery when the latter departed Vietnam. It was assigned to the 3d Brigade, 1st Cavalry Division and later Task Force GARY OWEN at Bien Hoa.

Headquarters Battery, 8th Battalion, 26th Artillery (Target Acquisition)

Arrived Vietnam: 20 January 1967
Departed Vietnam: 27 April 1971
Previous Station: Fort Sill
Authorized Strength: 192

Headquarters Battery of the 8th Battalion, 26th Artillery was a target acquisition battery attached to the 41st Artillery Group for II CTZ support. Stationed at Qui Nhon and attached to I FFV Artillery on 17 February 1968, it was moved to An Khe in 1969 as part of I Field Force Vietnam Artillery.

1st Battalion, 27th Artillery (155mm Howitzer, Self-Propelled)

Arrived Vietnam: 14 April 1967
Departed Vietnam: 4 December 1970
Previous Station: Fort Sill
Authorized Strength: 537

The 1st Battalion of the 27th Artillery was a 155mm self-propelled M109 howitzer battalion attached to the 23d Artillery Group of II Field Force, Vietnam. The battalion served at Phu Loi until November 1967 when it was moved to Dau Tieng. On 7 February 1970 the unit left Dau Tieng and located to Cu Chi, where it remained until departing Vietnam. It primarily reinforced the 25th Infantry Division.

5th Battalion, 27th Artillery (105mm Howitzer, Towed)

Arrived Vietnam: 3 November 1965
Departed Vietnam: 30 August 1971
Previous Station: Fort Lewis

Authorized Strength	1966	1968	1970
Battalion	516	529	528

The 5th Battalion of the 27th Artillery was a towed 105mm howitzer battalion initially stationed at Nha Trang through 1965. In January 1966 it was placed under the 1st Brigade, 101st Airborne Division at Phan Rang and in 1967 was posted to Tuy Hoa with I Field Force Vietnam Artillery. Transferred to the 41st Artillery Group in May 1967, the battalion returned to I Field Force Vietnam Artillery control in December 1967 at Phan Rang with a forward command post at Phan Thiet.

6th Battalion, 27th Artillery (8-inch Howitzer, Self-Propelled) (175mm Gun/8-inch Howitzer)

Arrived Vietnam: 3 November 1965
Departed Vietnam: 25 September 1971
Previous Station: Fort Bliss

Authorized Strength	1966	1968	1970
Battalion	583	565	565

The 6th Battalion of the 27th Artillery was originally an 8-inch self-propelled M110 howitzer battalion but was converted to the dual 8-inch self-propelled howitzer and 175mm self-propelled M107 gun configuration. It arrived at Bien Hoa and became part of the 23d Artillery Group at Phuoc Vinh in November 1965, and was posted to Saigon in June 1966. The battalion went back to Phuoc Vinh and on to Quan Loi in January 1968. While at Quan Loi it became part of the II Field Force Vietnam Artillery on 21 October 1969. In March 1970 the battalion was posted to Phu Loi and there in April 1971 was reattached to the 23d Artillery Group. It primarily reinforced the 1st Infantry Division while in Vietnam.

Battery B, 29th Artillery (Searchlight)

Arrived Vietnam: 30 October 1965
Departed Vietnam: 22 June 1972
Previous Station: Fort Sill

Authorized Strength	1966	1968	1970
Battery	151	150	150

Battery B of the 29th Artillery was a searchlight battery attached to the 41st Artillery Group of I Field Force, Vietnam. The battery served at Qui Nhon and An Khe as part of I Field Force Vietnam Artillery. In 1971 it went to Tuy Hoa and in 1972 was posted to Cam Ranh Bay as part of the Cam Ranh Bay Support Command.

6th Battalion, 29th Artillery (105mm Howitzer, Towed)

Arrived Vietnam: 4 October 1966
Departed Vietnam: 14 December 1970
Previous Station: Fort Lewis
Authorized Strength: 526

The 6th Battalion of the 29th Artillery was a towed 105mm howitzer battalion assigned to the 4th Infantry Division, where it provided direct fire support for the 1st Brigade. The battalion primarily served at Pleiku until departing Vietnam.

Battery G, 29th Artillery (Searchlight)

Arrived Vietnam: 21 March 1967
Departed Vietnam: 1 October 1971
Previous Station: Fort Sill
Authorized Strength: 150

Battery G of the 29th Artillery was a searchlight battery located at Dong Ha and Da Nang during its service in Vietnam. It was variously attached to the 1st Battalion, 44th Artillery; 108th Artillery Group; and XXIV Corps.

Battery G, 29th Artillery, Provisional (105mm Howitzer, Towed)

Arrived Vietnam: June 1972
Departed Vietnam: September 1972
Previous Station: Vietnam
Authorized Strength: 138

Battery G of the 29th Artillery (Provisional) was formed from assets of the 3d Battalion, 82d Artillery when the latter unit departed Vietnam. It was a towed 105mm howitzer battery attached to the independent 3d Battalion, 21st Infantry at Da Nang.

Battery H, 29th Artillery (Searchlight)

Arrived Vietnam: 24 March 1967
Departed Vietnam: 31 March 1972
Previous Station: Fort Sill

Authorized Strength	1968	1970
Battery	150	151

Battery H of the 29th Artillery was a searchlight battery stationed at Can Tho. There it served with the 9th Infantry Division until it was assigned to the II Field Force, Vietnam in October 1967. The battery was later attached to the 164th Aviation Group at Can Tho and remained there until leaving Vietnam.

Battery I, 29th Artillery (Searchlight)

Arrived Vietnam: 24 March 1967
Departed Vietnam: 30 April 1971
Previous Station: Fort Sill
Authorized Strength: 150

Battery I of the 29th Artillery was a searchlight battery stationed at Long Binh where it served with the 5th Battalion, 2d Artillery. Later the battery came under the direct control of II Field Force Vietnam Artillery.

1st Battalion, 30th Artillery (155mm Howitzer, Towed)

Arrived Vietnam: 28 November 1965
Departed Vietnam: 7 April 1971

Authorized Strength	1966	1968	1970
Battalion	600	598	598

The 1st Battalion of the 30th Artillery was a towed 155mm howitzer battalion first stationed at Qui Nhon as part of the 52d Artillery Group and in April 1967 was transferred to the 41st Artillery Group at Bong Son. On 10 February 1968 the unit was attached to the 1st Cavalry Division (assigned 1 June 1968) and sent to Hue – Phu Bai, where it remained until departing Vietnam.

2d Battalion, 32d Artillery (175mm Gun, Self-Propelled) (175mm Gun/8-inch Howitzer)

Arrived Vietnam: 3 November 1965
Departed Vietnam: 22 January 1972
Previous Station: Fort Sill

Authorized Strength	1966	1968	1970
Battalion	555	565	565

The 2d Battalion of the 32d Artillery was originally a self-propelled M107 175mm gun battalion located at Cu Chi. The battalion was part of the 23d Artillery Group of II Field Force, Vietnam and relocated to Tay Ninh in April 1967. In early 1969 it was converted to the dual 8-inch self-propelled M110 howitzer and 175mm self-propelled gun configuration. On 21 October 1969 it was made part of II Field Force Vietnam Artillery and posted to Cu Chi and Phu Loi under the 23d Artillery Group, where it would remain until departure from Vietnam. It primarily reinforced the 25th Infantry Division.

6th Battalion, 32d Artillery (8-inch Howitzer, Self-Propelled) (175mm Gun/8-inch Howitzer)

Arrived Vietnam: 21 March 1967
Departed Vietnam: 2 November 1971
Previous Station: Fort Lewis
Authorized Strength: 565

The 6th Battalion of the 32d Artillery was originally an 8-inch M110 self-propelled howitzer battalion but was converted in early 1969 to the dual self-propelled 8-inch howitzer and 175mm self-propelled gun configuration. Assigned to the 41st Artillery Group of I Field Force, Vietnam it was at Tuy Hoa and on 21 January 1968 transferred to I Field Force Vietnam Artillery. The battalion was sent to Phu Hiep where it stayed until leaving Vietnam. It primarily supported the two Korean divisions in Vietnam.

2d Battalion, 33d Artillery (105mm Howitzer, Towed)

Arrived Vietnam: 2 October 1965
Departed Vietnam: 15 April 1970
Previous Station: Fort Riley

Authorized Strength	1966	1968
Battalion	490	526

The 2d Battalion of the 33d Artillery was a towed 105mm howitzer battalion providing direct artillery support to the 1st Infantry Division's 3d Brigade. Stationed at Bien Hoa, it was at Ben Cat in 1966 and moved to Lai Khe in July 1967, where it remained.

6th Battalion, 33d Artillery (105mm Howitzer, Towed)

Arrived Vietnam: 20 February 1968
Departed Vietnam: 27 February 1970
Previous Station: Fort Carson
Authorized Strength: 529

The 6th Battalion of the 33d Artillery was a towed 105mm howitzer battalion assigned to the 108th Artillery Group. The battalion served at Quang Tri until late November 1968 when it was relocated to Phu Bai and in 1969 was sent to its final Vietnam location at Dong Ha. It provided reinforcing artillery support for the 101st Airborne Division (Airmobile).

3d Battalion, 34th Artillery (105mm Howitzer, Towed, Riverine)

Arrived Vietnam: 19 December 1966
Departed Vietnam: 26 July 1969
Previous Station: Fort Riley
Authorized Strength: 468

The 3d Battalion of the 34th Artillery was a towed 105mm howitzer battalion assigned to the 9th Infantry Division. This battalion was unique in that it was placed on barge firing platforms to provide direct artillery support for the division's mobile riverine operations. It was administratively stationed at Dong Tam, arriving in Vietnam as direct support artillery for the division's 3d Brigade before its riverine role was undertaken.

2d Battalion, 35th Artillery (155mm Howitzer, Self-Propelled)

Arrived Vietnam: 17 June 1966
Departed Vietnam: 13 March 1971
Previous Station: Fort Carson

Authorized Strength	1966	1968	1970
Battalion	575	537	537

The 2d Battalion of the 35th Artillery was a self-propelled M109 155mm howitzer battalion and was first stationed at Xuan Loc

with the 23d Artillery Group. While at Xuan Loc, the battalion was placed under the 54th Artillery Group and in April 1970 was moved to Long Binh, where it remained until leaving Vietnam.

1st Battalion, 39th Artillery (155mm Howitzer, Self-Propelled) (175mm Gun/8-inch Howitzer)

Arrived Vietnam: 10 October 1969
Departed Vietnam: 21 December 1971
Previous Station: Vietnam
Authorized Strength: 537

The 1st Battalion of the 39th Artillery was formed from the assets of the Kentucky National Guard's 2d Battalion, 138th Artillery and thus at first retained its 155mm self-propelled M109 howitzers. However, the battalion later received new weapons and converted to the dual M110 8-inch self-propelled howitzer and M107 175mm self-propelled gun configuration. The battalion was under the control of the XXIV Corps Artillery and located at Phu Bai and Gia Le. On 1 March 1970 it was attached to the 108th Artillery Group and relocated to Fire Support Base Nancy, outside Phu Bai, where it was under the operational control of the 101st Airborne Division (Airmobile) during much of the time.

1st Battalion, 40th Artillery (105mm Howitzer, Self-Propelled)

Arrived Vietnam: 18 October 1966
Departed Vietnam: 20 November 1969
Previous Station: Fort Sill
Authorized Strength: 505

The 1st Battalion of the 40th Artillery was composed of M108 self-propelled 105mm howitzers and originally scheduled to serve at Cu Chi. Upon arrival it was diverted to I CTZ and later served under the 108th Artillery Group. It served in the Dong Ha area.

2d Battalion, 40th Artillery (105mm Howitzer, Towed)

Arrived Vietnam: 12 December 1966
Departed Vietnam: 15 October 1970
Previous Station: Fort Benning
Authorized Strength: 641

The 2d Battalion ("Redcatchers") of the 40th Artillery was a 105mm towed howitzer battalion and part of the 199th Infantry Brigade (Light). It thus was colocated with the brigade throughout its service in Vietnam, being stationed at Song Be, Long Binh, Xuan Loc and Gia Ray while in Vietnam.

Battery E, 41st Artillery
(.50-caliber Machinegun)

Arrived Vietnam: March 1967
Departed Vietnam: 26 December 1971
Previous Station: Fort Bliss
Authorized Strength: 142

Battery E of the 41st Artillery was equipped with quad .50-caliber M55 machineguns and assigned to the 41st Artillery Group of I Field Force, Vietnam. The battery was located at An Khe and Tuy Hoa. It was with the 4th Battalion, 60th Artillery.

4th Battalion, 42d Artillery
(105mm Howitzer, Towed)

Arrived Vietnam: 10 August 1966
Departed Vietnam: 7 December 1970
Previous Station: Fort Lewis

Authorized Strength	1966	1968
Battalion	493	526

The 4th Battalion of the 42d Artillery ("Straight Arrows") was a towed 105mm howitzer battalion assigned to the 4th Infantry Division to render direct artillery support to its 2d Brigade. The battalion remained in the Pleiku vicinity throughout its Vietnam service.

5th Battalion, 42d Artillery
(155mm Howitzer, Towed)

Arrived Vietnam: 2 April 1968
Departed Vietnam: 1 April 1972
Previous Station: Fort Bragg
Authorized Strength: 598

The 5th Battalion of the 42d Artillery ("Straight Arrows") was a towed 105mm howitzer battalion assigned to the 54th Artillery Group and then to the 23d Artillery Group within II Field Force, Vietnam. Stationed at Bear Cat in 1968, it was at Long Thanh in 1969 and Long Binh in 1970.

1st Battalion, 44th Artillery
(Automatic Weapon,
Self-Propelled)

Arrived Vietnam: 7 November 1966
Departed Vietnam: 30 December 1971
Previous Station: Fort Bliss

Authorized Strength	1966	1968	1970
Battalion	698	692	698

The 1st Battalion of the 44th Artillery was a self-propelled automatic weapons battalion consisting of M42 dual antiaircraft guns mustered from Reserve and National Guard assets to be utilized in a ground support role. Assigned to I Field Force Vietnam Artillery, the battalion was located at Dong Ha, where in 1968 it was attached to the 108th Artillery Group. It was made part of XXIV Corps Artillery and posted to Da Nang in 1970, where it remained, later coming under control of the Da Nang Support Command just prior to departure from Vietnam. It was augmented with a battery of quad .50-caliber machineguns—Battery G, 65th Artillery.

Battery G, 55th Artillery
(.50-caliber Machinegun)

Arrived Vietnam: 26 February 1968
Departed Vietnam: 31 July 1971
Previous Station: Fort Bliss

Authorized Strength	1968	1970
Battery	142	114

Battery G of the 55th Artillery was a quad M55 mounted .50-caliber machinegun battery stationed at Chu Lai and was attached to the 23d Infantry Division (AMERICAL) after 13 April 1968. It provided convoy security, combat assault support and perimeter defense.

6th Battalion, 56th Artillery
(HAWK Missile)

Arrived Vietnam: 30 September 1965
Departed Vietnam: 2 August 1969
Previous Station: Fort Bliss

Authorized Strength	1966	1968	1969
Battalion	858	751	714

The 6th Battalion of the 56th Artillery was a mobile HAWK missile battalion under control of the 97th Artillery Group stationed at Tan Son Nhut and Long Binh. In 1968 it was posted to Chu Lai, where it was attached to the AMERICAL Division. Battery C of the battalion was inactivated in Vietnam on 5 June 1969.

4th Battalion, 60th Artillery
(Automatic Weapon,
Self-Propelled)

Arrived Vietnam: 11 March 1967
Departed Vietnam: 21 December 1971
Previous Station: Fort Bliss

Authorized Strength	1968	1970
Battalion	692	698

The 4th Battalion of the 60th Artillery was a self-propelled automatic weapons battalion composed of 40mm M42 dual "Duster" antiaircraft guns. Part of the 41st Artillery Group of I Field Force, Vietnam, it served at Qui Nhon. On 17 February 1968 it was attached to I FFV Artillery and moved to An Khe on 28 June 1968. It went to Tuy Hoa in late 1970. The battalion was augmented with a battery of quad M55 .50-caliber machineguns—Battery E, 41st Artillery.

Battery G, 65th Artillery
(.50-caliber Machinegun)

Arrived Vietnam: 20 October 1966
Departed Vietnam: 26 December 1971
Previous Station: Fort Bliss

Authorized Strength	1968	1970
Battery	142	114

Battery G of the 65th Artillery was a quad-mounted M55 .50-caliber machinegun battery serving under the 1st Battalion, 44th Artillery at Dong Ha until attached to the 108th Artillery Group at that location in 1968. In 1970 the battery was sent to Da Nang as part of XXIV Corps Artillery and remained there.

Battery D, 71st Artillery
(.50-caliber Machinegun)

1st Tour:
Arrived Vietnam: 29 November 1966
Departed Vietnam: 25 June 1971
2nd Tour:
Arrived Vietnam: 15 September 1971
Departed Vietnam: 20 March 1972
Previous Station: Fort Bliss
Authorized Strength: 142

Battery D of the 71st Artillery was a quad-mounted M55 .50-caliber machinegun battery stationed on its first tour in Vietnam at Long Binh with the 5th Battalion, 2d Artillery and later II Field Force, Vietnam. On its second tour in Vietnam, the battery was attached to XXIV Corps and stationed at Da Nang.

6th Battalion, 71st Artillery
(HAWK Missile)

Arrived Vietnam: 29 September 1965
Departed Vietnam: 22 September 1968
Previous Station: Fort Bliss
Authorized Strength: 873

The 6th Battalion of the 71st Artillery was a mobile HAWK missile battalion located first at Qui Nhon. In 1966, as part of the 97th Artillery Group, the battalion was relocated to Cam Ranh Bay, where it remained until departing Vietnam.

1st Battalion, 77th Artillery
(105mm Howitzer, Towed)

Arrived Vietnam: 12 September 1965
Departed Vietnam: 28 March 1971
Previous Station: Fort Benning

Authorized Strength	1966	1968	1970
Battalion	407	436	436

The 1st Battalion of the 77th Artillery was a towed 105mm howitzer battalion and was initially in direct support of the 1st Cavalry Division's 2d Brigade. It served variously at An Khe, Dau Tieng, Quan Loi, Lai Khe and Song Be.

2d Battalion, 77th Artillery
(105mm Howitzer, Towed)

Arrived Vietnam: 9 October 1966
Departed Vietnam: 7 December 1970
Previous Station: Fort Lewis
Authorized Strength: 526

The 2d Battalion of the 77th Artillery was a towed 105mm howitzer battalion and arrived in Vietnam as part of the 4th Infantry Division where it was in direct support of the 3d Brigade at Dau Tieng and on 1 August 1967 was transferred to the 25th Infantry Division's 3d Brigade. In 1969 the battalion was relocated to Cu Chi where it remained until departure from Vietnam.

4th Battalion, 77th Artillery
(Aerial Rocket)

Arrived Vietnam: 17 October 1968
Departed Vietnam: 4 January 1972
Previous Station: Fort Sill

Authorized Strength	1968	1970
Battalion	515	575

The 4th Battalion of the 77th Artillery was an aerial rocket artillery battalion employing armed helicopters. It was assigned to the 101st Airborne Division (Airmobile) and colocated with divisional headquarters at Gia Le.

6th Battalion, 77th Artillery
(105mm Howitzer, Towed)

Arrived Vietnam: 22 May 1967
Departed Vietnam: 1 June 1969
Previous Station: Fort Irwin
Authorized Strength: 529

The 6th Battalion of the 77th Artillery was a towed 105mm howitzer battalion assigned to II Field Force, Vietnam at Cu Chi and attached to the 25th Infantry Division. In 1968 it joined the 54th Artillery Group at Quang Tri and on 20 July 1968 was attached to the 9th Infantry Division at Can Tho where it remained until departing Vietnam.

Battery F, 77th Artillery
(Aerial Rocket)

Arrived Vietnam: 30 April 1971
Departed Vietnam: 12 August 1971
Previous Station: Vietnam
Authorized Strength: 133

Battery F of the 77th Artillery was an aerial rocket artillery battery employing armed helicopters and was formed to render support to the 3d Brigade, 1st Cavalry Division. The battery was thus located at Bien Hoa. Battery F was a redesignation of Headquarters and Headquarters Battery, 6th Battalion, 77th Artillery (administratively redesignated 30 April 1971, the date of its activation). See also 6th Battalion, 77th Artillery.

Battery F, 79th Artillery
(Aerial Rocket)

Arrived Vietnam: 30 June 1971
Departed Vietnam: 22 August 1972
Previous Station: Vietnam
Authorized Strength: 161

Battery F of the 79th Artillery was an aerial rocket artillery battery employing armed helicopters and was raised to provide additional support to the 3d Brigade, 1st Cavalry Division. It was stationed at Bien Hoa. In 1972 the battery went to Long Thanh and was placed under control of the 1st Aviation Brigade there.

1st Battalion, 82d Artillery (155mm Howitzer, Towed/ 8-inch Howitzer, Self-Propelled)

Arrived Vietnam: 31 July 1968
Departed Vietnam: 8 November 1971
Previous Station: Fort Lewis
Authorized Strength: 616

The 1st Battalion of the 82d Artillery provided general artillery support for the 23d Infantry Division (AMERICAL) and was a dual 155mm towed howitzer and 8-inch self-propelled M110 howitzer battalion. It served with the division at Chu Lai.

3d Battalion, 82d Artillery (105mm Howitzer, Towed)

Arrived Vietnam: 15 August 1966
Departed Vietnam: 29 June 1972
Previous Station: Fort Devens

Authorized Strength	1966	1968	1970
Battalion	474	526	526

The 3d Battalion of the 82d Artillery was a towed 105mm howitzer battalion assigned to the 196th Infantry Brigade (Light) and landed at Vung Tau. It was immediately airlifted to Tay Ninh where the first base camp was constructed. It became part of the 23d Infantry Division (AMERICAL) in February 1969 while at Chu Lai and located to Tam Ky. It stayed at that location until April 1971 when it moved to Da Nang. In November 1971 the battalion was placed back under the control of the 196th Infantry Brigade there. Upon its departure its assets were used to form a 105mm howitzer battery, Battery G (Provisional), 29th Artillery.

Battery E, 82d Artillery (Aviation)

Arrived Vietnam: 30 October 1965
Departed Vietnam: 10 April 1971
Previous Station: Fort Benning

Authorized Strength	1966	1968	1970
Battery	104	104	108

Battery E of the 82d Artillery was an aviation artillery battery employing observation helicopters assigned to the 1st Cavalry Division. As such, it was colocated with the divisional headquarters while in Vietnam.

1st Battalion, 83d Artillery (8-inch Howitzer, Self-Propelled) (175mm Gun/8-inch Howitzer)

Arrived Vietnam: 30 October 1966
Departed Vietnam: 7 June 1971
Previous Station: Fort Sill
Authorized Strength: 565

The 1st Battalion of the 83d Artillery was originally an 8-inch M110 self-propelled howitzer battalion but was converted in December 1966 to the dual self-propelled 8-inch howitzer and 175mm

self-propelled gun configuration. As part of II Field Force, Vietnam (54th Artillery Group), it was located at Nui Dat and Xuan Loc. On 19 March 1968 it moved to Phu Bai under the 108th Artillery Group of XXIV Corps. The battalion later moved to Gia Le, where it remained.

1st Battalion, 84th Artillery (155mm Howitzer, Towed/ 8-inch Howitzer, Self-Propelled)

Arrived Vietnam: 2 February 1967
Departed Vietnam: 16 August 1969
Previous Station: Fort Riley
Authorized Strength: 616

The 1st Battalion of the 84th Artillery supplied general artillery support for the 9th Infantry Division at Bear Cat and later Dong Tam. It was a dual 155mm towed howitzer and 8-inch self-propelled M110 howitzer battalion.

6th Battalion, 84th Artillery (155mm Howitzer, Towed)

Arrived Vietnam: 24 March 1968
Departed Vietnam: 7 August 1969
Previous Station: Fort Irwin
Authorized Strength: 598

The 6th Battalion of the 84th Artillery was a towed 155mm howitzer battalion assigned to I Field Force Vietnam Artillery at An Khe. It remained at An Khe under the 41st Artillery Group. It was a "mobile artillery task force" reserve for II Corps Tactical Zone.

1st Battalion, 92d Artillery (155mm Howitzer, Towed)

Arrived Vietnam: 11 March 1967
Departed Vietnam: 3 November 1971
Previous Station: Fort Bragg

Authorized Strength	1968	1970
Battalion	598	586

The 1st Battalion of the 92d Artillery was a towed 155mm howitzer battalion assigned to the II Field Force, Vietnam and was transferred to the 52d Artillery Group. The battalion served in the Pleiku vicinity, where it supported the 4th Infantry Division and 173d Airborne Brigade in the central highlands area.

2d Battalion, 94th Artillery (175mm Gun, Self-Propelled) (175mm Gun/8-inch Howitzer)

Arrived Vietnam: 18 October 1966
Departed Vietnam: 21 April 1972
Previous Station: Fort Sill
Authorized Strength: 565

The 2d Battalion of the 94th Artillery was originally a self-propelled M107 175mm gun battalion located at Dong Ha. In early 1969 it was converted to the dual 8-inch self-propelled M110 howitzer and 175mm self-propelled gun configuration. Under I Field Force, Vietnam it was transferred to the 108th Artillery

Group on 31 March 1968 and was removed from operational control of the III Marine Amphibious Force. Later it was moved to Quang Tri, to Camp Evans on 28 November 1969 and then back to Dong Ha in 1970. In 1971 the battalion was transferred to Da Nang and XXIV Corps Artillery. Later that year it was sent to Phu Bai where it became closely connected with supporting the 101st Airborne Division (Airmobile).

2d Battalion, 138th Artillery (155mm Howitzer, Self-Propelled)

Arrived Vietnam: 30 October 1968
Departed Vietnam: 10 October 1969
Previous Station: Louisville via Fort Hood
Authorized Strength: 537

The 2d Battalion of the 138th Artillery was a Kentucky National Guard self-propelled M109 155mm howitzer battalion. It served in Vietnam as part of the Provisional Corps Vietnam Artillery (later XXIV Corps Artillery), at Phu Bai and Gia Le.

3d Battalion, 197th Artillery (155mm Howitzer, Towed)

Arrived Vietnam: 20 September 1968
Departed Vietnam: 3 September 1969
Previous Station: Portsmouth via Fort Bragg
Authorized Strength: 598

The 3d Battalion of the 197th Artillery was a New Hampshire National Guard towed 155mm howitzer battalion. It served with the 23d Artillery Group of II Field Force, Vietnam at Phu Loi.

2d Battalion, 319th Artillery (105mm Howitzer, Towed)

Arrived Vietnam: 19 November 1967
Departed Vietnam: 20 December 1971
Previous Station: Fort Campbell
Authorized Strength: 436

The 2d Battalion of the 319th Artillery was a towed 105mm howitzer battalion assigned to the 101st Airborne Division (Airmobile) and in direct support of the division's 3d Brigade. It was stationed at Bien Hoa, Phuoc Vinh, Gia Le and Camp Evans while in Vietnam.

3d Battalion, 319th Artillery (105mm Howitzer, Towed) (Airborne)

Arrived Vietnam: 13 May 1965
Departed Vietnam: 23 July 1971
Previous Station: Okinawa

Authorized Strength	1966	1968	1970
Battalion	458	591	484

The 3d Battalion of the 319th Artillery was a towed 105mm howitzer battalion and was part of the 173d Airborne Brigade. It

was the first artillery battalion sent to Vietnam and its Battery C fired the first artillery round in South Vietnam by the U.S. Army. On 22 February 1967 Battery A parachuted into Katum. The battalion served with the brigade at Bien Hoa, An Khe, Dong Tam and Bong Son.

2d Battalion, 320th Artillery (105mm Howitzer, Towed) (Airborne)

Arrived Vietnam: 29 July 1965
Departed Vietnam: 9 December 1971
Previous Station: Fort Campbell

Authorized Strength	1966	1968	1970
Battalion	469	436	532

The 2d Battalion of the 320th Artillery was a towed 105mm howitzer battalion which served with the 1st Brigade, 101st Airborne Division (Airmobile). It was stationed variously in Vietnam at Phan Rang, Gia Le, Phan Thiet, Kontum, and Phu Bai.

1st Battalion, 321st Artillery (105mm Howitzer, Towed)

Arrived Vietnam: 19 November 1967
Departed Vietnam: 16 February 1972
Previous Station: Fort Campbell
Authorized Strength: 436

The 1st Battalion of the 321st Artillery was a towed 105mm howitzer battalion providing direct artillery support to the 101st Airborne Division (Airmobile) 2d Brigade. Stationed first at Bien Hoa and Cu Chi, it moved to I CTZ on 18 February 1968 and then served in the Gia Le – Phu Bai area.

2d Battalion, 321st Artillery (105mm Howitzer, Towed) (Airborne)

Arrived Vietnam: 16 February 1968
Departed Vietnam: 11 December 1969
Previous Station: Fort Bragg
Authorized Strength: 526

The 2d Battalion of the 321st Artillery was a towed 105mm howitzer battalion assigned to the 3d Brigade Task Force of the 82d Airborne Division and served with the brigade at Phu Bai and Phu Loi.

Battery A, 377th Artillery (Aviation)

Arrived Vietnam: 20 December 1968
Departed Vietnam: 12 January 1972
Previous Station: Vietnam
Authorized Strength: 166

Battery A of the 377th Artillery was an aviation artillery battery employing observation helicopters. It was assigned to the 101st Airborne Division (Airmobile) and colocated with that division during its service in Vietnam at Gia Le.

Chapter 10

Aviation

1st Aviation Brigade

Arrived Vietnam: 25 May 1966
Departed Vietnam: 28 March 1973
Previous Station: Vietnam

Authorized Strength	1966	1968	1970
HHC		118	118	529

Commanders

Brigadier General George P. Seneff	May 66
Major General Robert R. Williams	Nov. 67
Brigadier General Allen M. Burdett, Jr.	April 69
Brigadier General George W. Putnam, Jr.	Jan. 70
Colonel Samuel G. Cockerham (acting)	Aug. 70
Brigadier General Jack W. Hemingway	Aug. 70
Brigadier General Robert N. Mackinnon	Sept. 71
Brigadier General Jack V. Mackmull	Sept. 72

The 1st Aviation Brigade was activated 25 May 1966 in Vietnam using the assets of a provisional unit organized 1 March 1966 and eventually became one of the largest commands in Vietnam. Possessing, at the height of its involvement, some 641 fixed-wing aircraft, 441 Cobra AH-1G attack helicopters, 311 CH-47 cargo helicopters, 635 OH-6A observation helicopters and 2,202 UH-1 utility helicopters, the brigade had complete airmobile dominion of the skies. Flying in support of U.S. and allied forces, the brigade conducted missions as varied as tactical combat assaults, direct fire support, aerial reconnaissance, medical evacuation (medevac), troop lift, cargo hauling and evacuation and relocation of Vietnamese civilians in support of the Rural Development Program. The brigade was headquartered at Tan Son Nhut until December 1967, when it relocated to Long Binh. In December 1972 the brigade was moved to Tan Son Nhut once more, remaining there until it departed Vietnam. The following units directly served with the brigade at one time or another:

Aviation Groups

11th, 12th, 16th, 17th, 160th, 164th, 165th.

Aviation Battalions

10th, 11th, 13th, 14th, 52d, 58th, 145th, 210th, 212th, 214th, 222d, 223d, 268th, 269th, 307th, 308th, PHANTOM (Prov), DELTA (Prov), CAPITAL (Prov), I Corps (Prov).

Air Cavalry Squadrons

7th Squadron, 1st Cavalry; 1st Squadron, 9th Cavalry; 3d Squadron, 17th Cavalry; 7th Squadron, 17th Cavalry.

Selected Aviation Companies or Detachments Under Direct Brigade Control

Company or Detachment	Type	Brigade Service/Remarks
I Corps (Prov) †	CAC	March 68 – March 69 Discontinued
5 Avn Det	CAC	Dec. 67 – March 68 Transferred to 58th Avn Bn
5 Avn Det*	CAC	Oct. 69 – Feb. 73 Inactivated in Vietnam 7 Feb. 73
176 Avn Co	AML	Feb. 67 – June 67 Transferred to 14th Avn Bn
205 Avn Co	MH	May 67 – July 67 Transferred to 268th Avn Bn

* Indicates second tour of service within the brigade. In January 1968 the 5th Aviation Detachment also served briefly with the 223d Aviation Battalion.

† This I Corps provisional aviation company is different from the one under 17th Aviation Group.

11th Aviation Group

Arrived Vietnam: August 1965
Departed Vietnam: 14 March 1973
Previous Station: Fort Benning

Authorized Strength	1966	1968	1971
HHC		223	223	93

The 11th Aviation Group was organic to the 1st Cavalry Division (Airmobile) where it primarily controlled the 227th, 228th and 229th Aviation Battalions. More information on the initial composition of this group may be found in the 1st Cavalry Division order of battle section. It was colocated with the division in Vietnam until the division departed, at which time the group was attached to the 1st Aviation Brigade and moved to Da Nang.

Troop or Company	Type	Group Service/Remarks
11th Avn Co	GS	Aug. 65 – April 71/ Departed Vietnam
17th Avn Co	FWT	Sept. 65 – Jan. 67/ CV–2 Caribou unit inactivated; assets to USAF
48th Avn Co	AHC	April 72 – Aug. 72/ Departed Vietnam
62d Avn Co	CAC	Dec. 71 – March 73/ Departed Vietnam
178th Avn Co	ASH	Dec. 71 – March 72/ Departed Vietnam
203d Avn Co	ASH	Dec. 71 – April 72/ Departed Vietnam
478th Avn Co	HH	Sept. 65 – Aug. 70/ Transferred to 164th Avn Gp
478th Avn Co*	HH	March 72 – May 72/ Transferred to 12th Avn Gp
Tp F, 4th Cav	Air Cav	May 72 – Feb. 73/ Departed Vietnam
Tp F, 8th Cav	Air Cav	Sept. 72 – Feb. 73/ Departed Vietnam
Tp D, 17th Cav†	Air Cav	May 72 – Feb. 73/ Departed Vietnam

* Indicates second tour of service with the group.

† Assets of Troop D, 1st Squadron, 1st Cavalry used in Troop D, 17th Cavalry.

12th Aviation Group

Arrived Vietnam: 28 August 1965
Departed Vietnam: 16 March 1973
Previous Station: Fort Benning

Authorized Strength	1966	1968	1971
HHC		75	75	93

The 12th Aviation Group was located at Tan Son Nhut until 29 June 1966 when it moved to Long Binh. Before January 1968 the group provided aviation support to both III and IV CTZ under II FFV. Afterward, it supported III CTZ. The 11th, 13th, 145th, 210th, 214th, 222d, 269th and 308th Aviation Battalions as well as the 3d Squadron, 17th Cavalry served with this group.

Troop or Company	Type	Group Service/Remarks
Command (Prov)	CAC	May 72 – March 73/ Departed Vietnam
54th Avn Co	FWT	Aug. 65 – Aug. 66/ Transferred to 222d Avn Bn

59th Avn Co	CAC	Sept. 72 – March 73/ Departed Vietnam
61st Avn Co	FWT	Aug. 65 – Dec. 66/ CV–2 Caribou unit inactivated 1 Jan. 67; assets to USAF
73d Avn Co	Surv	Aug.65 – Aug. 66/ Transferred to 222d Avn Bn
120th Avn Co	AHC	May 72 – Oct. 72/ Departed Vietnam
135th Avn Co	AHC	Sept. 71 – Feb. 72/ Departed Vietnam
273d Avn Co	HH	Dec. 71 – Feb. 72/ Departed Vietnam
334th Avn Co	AWC	July 71 – March 72/ Departed Vietnam
478th Avn Co	HH	May 72 – Oct. 72/ Departed Vietnam
Tp F, 4th Cav	Air Cav	Feb. 71 – May 72/ Transferred to 11th Avn Gp

16th Aviation Group

Arrived Vietnam: 20 December 1967
Departed Vietnam: 13 November 1971
Previous Station: Vietnam

Authorized Strength	1968	1970
HHC		85	93

The 16th Aviation Group was activated from assets of the provisional FALCON Aviation Group which had been established in September 1967 at An Son. The 16th Aviation Group was organized at Da Nang. In March 1969 the group was attached to the 23d Infantry Division (AMERICAL) at Chu Lai and remained with the division through November 1971. In addition to the 14th and 212th Aviation Battalions, the group also controlled the aviation staff resources of the division.

17th Aviation Group

Arrived Vietnam: 15 December 1965
Departed Vietnam: 16 March 1973
Previous Station: Vietnam

Authorized Strength	1966	1968	1970
HHC		85	85	93

The 17th Aviation Group was activated at Nha Trang, moved to Tuy Hoa in November 1970 and then to Pleiku in January 1972. The group had the mission of commanding and controlling all nondivisional aviation assets in II CTZ, under I FFV. The 10th, 14th, 52d, 223d and 268th Aviation Battalions as well as the 7th Squadron, 17th Cavalry served with the group.

Troop or Company/Detach	Type	Group Service/Remarks
I Corps (Prov)		Dec. 65 – July 66/ Expanded into the I Corps Avn Bn (Prov)
57th Avn Co	AHC	April 72 – March 73/ Departed Vietnam
58th Avn Det		Oct. 68 – Jan. 72/ Departed Vietnam
60th Avn Co	AHC	Jan. 72 – March 73/ Departed Vietnam

129th Avn Co	AHC	April 72 – March 73/ Departed Vietnam
180th Avn Co	ASH	Jan. 72 – Feb. 72/ Transferred to 7th Sqdn, 17th Cav
180th Avn Co*	ASH	April 72 – Feb. 73/ Departed Vietnam
220th Avn Co	Surv L	Dec. 65 – Aug. 66/ Transferred to I Corps Avn Bn (Prov)
361st Avn Co	AWC	April 72 – Aug. 72/ Departed Vietnam
Tp H, 10th Cav †	Air Cav	April 72 – Feb. 73/ Departed Vietnam
Tp H, 17th Cav ‡	Air Cav	April 72 – Feb. 73/ Departed Vietnam
Tp K, 17th Cav §	Air Cav	Oct. 70 – Dec. 70/ Departed Vietnam
Tp A, 7th Sqdn, 17th Cav	Air Cav	Jan. 72 – April 72/ Departed Vietnam

* Indicates second tour of service under direct group control.

† Utilized assets of Troop C, 7th Squadron, 17th Cavalry.

‡ Utilized assets of Troop B, 7th Squadron, 17th Cavalry.

§ Utilized assets of Troop D, 7th Squadron, 17th Cavalry.

101st Aviation Group

Arrived Vietnam: 25 June 1969
Departed Vietnam: 19 January 1972
Previous Station: Vietnam
Authorized Strength: HHC – 221 (1971)

The 101st Aviation Group was originally designated the 160th Aviation Group, created to give an airmobile capability to 101st Airborne Division operations. Becoming the division's aviation group, it was headquartered at Phu Bai. As part of the LAM SON 719 incursion into Laos in February – April 1971, the 101st Aviation Group saw intense aerial combat, becoming the command and control organization for all aviation assets involved in the operation. During this time frame the group was heavily reinforced by the 1st Aviation Brigade. The 101st Aviation Group normally commanded only the 101st, 158th, 159th Aviation Battalions and the 2d Squadron, 17th Cavalry (Air) in its role as division aviation headquarters.

160th Aviation Group

No Insignia
Authorized

Arrived Vietnam: 1 July 1968
Departed Vietnam: 25 June 1969
Previous Station: Vietnam
Authorized Strength: HHC – 223 (1968)

The 160th Aviation Group was created to convert the 101st Airborne Division to an airmobile configuration and was stationed between Bien Hoa and Phu Bai. During this time one of the division's major elements, the 2d Squadron, 17th Cavalry, was converted from a ground cavalry role (in which it had originally deployed in December 1967) to an air cavalry function from

December 1968 through June 1969. In June 1969, with three aviation battalions, the 101st, 158th and 159th as well as the newly reorganized 2d Squadron, 17th Cavalry, the group was redesignated as the 101st Aviation Group.

164th Aviation Group

Arrived Vietnam: 20 December 1967
Departed Vietnam: 14 March 1973
Previous Station: Vietnam

Authorized Strength	1968	1971
HHC	85	93

The 164th Aviation Group was activated in Vietnam from assets of the DELTA Provisional Aviation Group in the IV Corps Tactical Zone and was located at Can Tho throughout its service in Vietnam. The group included the 13th, 214th and 307th Aviation Battalions as well as the 7th Squadron, 1st Cavalry. The units that fell under direct group control are listed below.

Troop or Company	Type	Group Service/Remarks
18th Avn Co	CAC	Aug. 71 – March 73/ Departed Vietnam
163d Avn Co	GS	July 68 – Jan. 72/ Departed Vietnam
478th Avn Co	HH	Aug. 70 – July 71/ Transferred to 223d Avn Bn
Tp D, 3d Sqdn, 5th Cav	Air Cav	Nov. 71 only/ Departed Vietnam
Tp C, 16th Cav	Air Cav	March 72 – Feb. 73/ Departed Vietnam

165th Aviation Group

Arrived Vietnam: 17 February 1969
Departed Vietnam: 30 January 1972
Previous Station: Vietnam
Authorized Strength: HHC – 87 (1971)

The 165th Aviation Group was stationed at Long Binh and took over the functions of the 58th Aviation Battalion as an aviation control center. It had the following aviation or signal units under its direct control.

Detachment or Company	Type	Group Service/Remarks
Command (Prov)	CAC	Oct. 69 – Jan. 72/ Transferred to 223d Avn Bn
5th Avn Det	Command	Feb. 69 – Oct. 69/ Transferred to 1st Avn Bde
16th Sig Co	DECCA	Feb. 69 – April 69/ Departed Vietnam
73d Avn Co	SAC	July 71 – Jan. 72/ Transferred to 223d Avn Bn
120th Avn Co	AHC	Oct. 69 – Jan. 72/ Transferred to 223d Avn Bn
125th Avn Co	ATC	Feb. 69 – Sept. 71/ Departed Vietnam

1st Aviation Battalion (Divisional)

Arrived Vietnam: 16 October 1965
Departed Vietnam: 15 April 1970
Previous Station: Fort Riley

Authorized Strength	1966	1968
Battalion	383	387

The 1st Aviation Battalion was part of the 1st Infantry Division in Vietnam and was colocated with division headquarters. The following aviation units served with the battalion in Vietnam.

Troop or Company	Type	Battalion Service/Remarks
Co A	AM	Oct. 65 – April 70/ Departed Vietnam
Co B	AM	Oct. 65 – April 70/ Departed Vietnam
Co A, 82d Avn Bn	AM	Oct. 65 – Aug. 66/ Transferred to 145th Avn Bn
162d Avn Co	AM	March 66 – Aug. 66/ Transferred to 11th Avn Bn
173d Avn Co	AM	March 66 – April 70/ Attached from 11th Avn Bn
Tp D, 1st Sqdn, 4th Cav	Air Cav	Oct. 65 – Feb. 70/ Departed Vietnam; assets used by Tp C, 16th Cav
Tp C, 16th Cav	Air Cav	March 70 – April 70/ Transferred to 7th Sqdn, 1st Cav

4th Aviation Battalion (Divisional)

Arrived Vietnam: 25 April 1966
Departed Vietnam: 1 December 1970
Previous Station: Fort Lewis

Authorized Strength	1966	1968
Battalion	391	427

The 4th Aviation Battalion was part of the 4th Infantry Division in Vietnam. Company A, however, arrived in Vietnam on 11 September 1965 and served with the 1st Cavalry Division until 25 April 1966 when it returned to the battalion's control. The following aviation units served with the battalion in Vietnam.

Troop or Company	Type	Battalion Service/Remarks
Co A	AM	April 66 – Dec. 70/ Departed Vietnam
Co B	AM	April 66 – Dec. 70/ Departed Vietnam
Tp D, 1st Sqdn, 10th Cav	Air Cav	April 66 – Dec. 70/ Rejoined 1st Sqdn, 10th Cav

9th Aviation Battalion (Divisional)

Arrived Vietnam: 30 January 1967
Departed Vietnam: 23 August 1969
Previous Station: Fort Riley
Authorized Strength: 427 (1968)

The 9th Aviation Battalion was part of the 9th Infantry Division in Vietnam and was colocated with division headquarters. The following units served under the battalion while in Vietnam.

Troop or Company	Type	Battalion Service/Remarks
Co A	AM	Jan. 67 – Aug. 69/ Departed Vietnam
Co B	AM	Jan. 67 – Aug. 69/ Departed Vietnam
Tp D, 3d Sqdn, 5th Cav	Air Cav	Jan. 67 – Aug. 69/ Rejoined 3d Sqdn, 5th Cav

10th Aviation Battalion (Combat)

Arrived Vietnam: 29 October 1965
Departed Vietnam: 30 January 1972
Previous Station: Fort Benning

Authorized Strength	1966	1968	1970
HQ and HQ Det	109	109	108

The 10th Aviation Battalion ("Vagabonds of Vietnam") served with the 12th Aviation Group until assigned to the 17th Aviation Group on 1 March 1966. It was primarily located at Dong Ba Thin and responsible for general aviation support in the South coastal region of II CTZ. The following units served with the battalion in Vietnam.

Troop or Company	Type	Battalion Service/Remarks
48th Avn Co	AML	Nov. 65 – Sept. 67/ Transferred to 268th Avn Bn
48th Avn Co*	AML/ AHC	Aug. 68 – July 71/ Transferred to 223d Avn Bn
59th Avn Co †	AHC	Aug. 71 – Nov. 71/ Departed Vietnam
60th Avn Co	AHC	Aug. 71 – Jan. 72/ Transferred to 17th Avn Bn
61st Avn Co	AML	Nov. 67 – Aug. 68/ Transferred to 268th Avn Bn
92d Avn Co	AML/ AHC	Nov. 67 – Jan. 72/ Inactivated 1 Jan. 72
117th Avn Co	AML	Oct. 65 – Jan. 68/ Transferred to 145th Avn Bn
129th Avn Co	AML	Oct. 65 – Sept. 67/ Transferred to 268th Avn Bn
155th Avn Co	AML	Oct. 65 – Aug. 66/ Transferred to 52d Avn Bn
155th Avn Co*	AML/ AHC	Aug. 68 – March 71/ Inactivated 15 March 71
178th Avn Co	MH	March 66 – Aug. 66/ Transferred to 11th Avn Bn
179th Avn Co	MH	June 66 – Dec. 66/ Transferred to 52d Avn Bn
180th Avn Co	MH	Nov. 66 – Dec. 67/ Transferred to 268th Avn Bn
183d Avn Co	RAC	July 71 – Nov. 71/ Departed Vietnam
192d Avn Co	AML/ AHC	Feb. 68 – Jan. 71/ Inactivated 20 Jan. 71
196th Avn Co	MH	Dec. 67 – Aug. 68/ Transferred to 268th Avn Bn
205th Avn Co	MH	Aug. 67 – Sept. 67/ Transferred to 11th Avn Bn

Co D, 227th Avn Bn	AM	July 71 – Aug. 71/ Inactivated 30 Aug. 71; assets used as explained in footnote
243d Avn Co	MH	Oct. 67 – Sept. 71/ Departed Vietnam
244th Avn Co†	AHC	Aug. 71 – Dec. 71/ Inactivated 26 Dec. 71
281st Avn Co	AML/ AHC	June 66 – Dec. 70/ Departed Vietnam
Tp A, 7th Sqdn, 17th Cav	Air Cav	July 71 – Jan. 72/ Transferred to 17th Avn Gp

* Indicates second tour of service with the battalion.

† Companies B, C and D, 227th Aviation Battalion contributed assets to the formation of the 59th and 244th Aviation Companies.

11th Aviation Battalion (Combat)

Arrived Vietnam: 3 November 1965
Departed Vietnam: 1 March 1972
Previous Station: Fort Benning

Authorized Strength	1966	1968	1970
HQ and HQ Det	109	109	108

The 11th Aviation Battalion was attached to the 12th Aviation Group and was stationed at Phu Loi during most of its Vietnam service. It supported the 1st Infantry Division and other II FFV units. The following companies served with the battalion while in Vietnam.

Troop or Company	Type	Battalion Service/Remarks
74th Avn Co	RAC	July 71 – March 72/ Departed Vietnam
116th Avn Co	AML	Nov. 65 – April 67/ Tranferred to 269th Avn Bn
128th Avn Co	AML/ AHC	Nov. 65 – Jan. 72/ Departed Vietnam
135th Avn Co	AHC	July 71 – Sept. 71/ Transferred to 12th Avn Gp
147th Avn Co	MH	Nov. 65 – Aug. 66/ Transferred to 145th Avn Bn
147th Avn Co*	MH	Dec. 66 – April 67/ Transferred to 222d Avn Bn
162d Avn Co	AML	Aug. 66 – March 69/ Transferred to 214th Avn Bn
173d Avn Co	AML/ AHC	Dec. 66 – July 71/ Transferred to 223d Avn Bn; company was attached to 1st Avn Bn until April 70 time period
174th Avn Co	AML	April 66 – Aug. 66/ Transferred to 14th Avn Bn
178th Avn Co	MH	Aug. 66 – Sept. 67/ Transferred to 14th Avn Bn
184th Avn Co	Surv L	June 67 – Feb. 68/ Transferred to 210th Avn Bn
187th Avn Co	AHC	April 71 – Feb. 72/ Inactivated 14 Feb. 72
205th Avn Co	MH	Sept. 67 – April 68/ Transferred to 222d Avn Bn

205th Avn Co*	MH	March 69 – Sept. 70/ To joint training with South Vietnamese Air Force; de- parted Vietnam April 71
213th Avn Co	MH	June 67 – July 71/ Transferred to 145th Avn Bn

* Indicates second tour of service with the battalion.

13th Aviation Battalion (Combat)

Arrived Vietnam: 30 September 1964
Departed Vietnam: 1 April 1972
Previous Station: Vietnam

Authorized Strength	1966	1968	1970
HHD		111	109	108

The 13th Aviation Battalion ("Guardian") used assets from the DELTA Provisional Aviation Battalion and served with the 12th Aviation Group at Can Tho. On 30 July 1966 the battalion was placed under direct 1st Aviation Brigade control. In December 1967 it became part of the DELTA Provisional Aviation Group and on 20 December 1967 became part of the 164th Aviation Group. The group was located at Can Tho and Soc Trang and provided army aviation to allied forces in IV Corps Tactical Zone. The following units served under the battalion.

Troop or Company	Type	Battalion Service/Remarks
73d Avn Co	SAC	June 71 – July 71/ Transferred to 165th Avn Gp
Co A, 101st Avn Bn	AM	May 65 only/Assets transferred to 336th Avn Co
114th Avn Co	AML	Sept. 64 – Oct. 69/ Transferred to 214th Avn Bn
121st Avn Co	AML/ AHC	Sept. 64 – Oct. 70/ To joint training with South Vietnamese Air Force; departed Vietnam Dec. 30
134th Avn Co	FWT	Dec. 65 – Jan. 67/ CV-2 Caribou unit inactivated 1 Jan. 67; assets to USAF
147th Avn Co	AHC	June 71 – March 72/ Departed Vietnam
162d Avn Co	AHC	Oct. 69 – April 72/ Departed Vietnam
175th Avn Co	AML	Nov. 66 – Oct. 69/ Transferred to 214th Avn Bn
191st Avn Co	AHC	Oct. 69 – Oct. 71/ Departed Vietnam
199th Avn Co	Surv L	July 67 – Sept. 67/ Transferred to Prov Avn Bn (see 307th Avn Bn)
221st Avn Co	Surv L	July 65 – Sept. 67/ Transferred to Prov Avn Bn (see 307th Avn Bn)
221st Avn Co*	Surv L	March 69 – July 71/ Transferred to 214th Avn Bn
235th Avn Co	AWC	June 71 – Aug. 71/ Departed Vietnam
244th Avn Co	Surv	July 67 – Sept. 67/ Transferred to Prov Avn Bn (see 307th Avn Bn)

271st Avn Co	MH	April 68 – March 69/ Transferred to 307th Avn Bn
271st Avn Co*	ASH	June 71 – Sept. 71/ Departed Vietnam
336th Avn Co	AML/ AHC	Nov. 66 – March 71/ Inactivated 15 March 71
Co A, 502d Avn Bn	AM	Dec. 64 – Sept. 66/ Assets transferred to 175th Avn Co
Tp C, 16th Cav	Air Cav	Dec. 70 – Jan. 71/ To joint training with South Vietnamese Air Force; trans- ferred May 72 to 164th Avn Gp

* Indicates second tour of service with the battalion.

14th Aviation Battalion (Combat)

Arrived Vietnam: October 1964
Departed Vietnam: 27 October 1971
Previous Station: Fort Benning

Authorized Strength	1966	1968	1971
HHD	87	79	108

The 14th Aviation Battalion was responsible for aviation support in the northern coastal region of II CTZ and initially was located at Nha Trang, moving to Qui Nhon on March 1966 as part of the 17th Aviation Group. On 22 April 1967 the battalion was moved to Chu Lai as part of Task Force OREGON. In September 1967 it became part of the FALCON Aviation Group (Provisional) and became part of the 16th Aviation Group in January 1968. It then served with the 23d Infantry Division (AMERICAL) under that group.

Troop or Company	Type	Battalion Service/Remarks
18th Avn Co	FWT	Oct. 64 – Aug. 66/ Transferred to 223d Avn Bn
71st Avn Co	AML/ AHC	Sept. 67 – Oct. 71/ Departed Vietnam
92d Avn Co	FWT	Oct. 65 – Jan. 67/ CV-2 Caribou unit inactivated 1 Jan. 67; assets to USAF
116th Avn Co	AHC	April 71 – Oct. 71/ Transferred to 212th Avn Bn
132d Avn Co	MH	Aug. 68 – Nov. 71/ Departed Vietnam
135th Avn Co	FWT	Jan. 66 – Jan. 67/ CV-2 Caribou unit inactivated 1 Jan. 67; assets to USAF
161st Avn Co	AML	Aug. 66 – Dec. 67/ Assets transferred to Co A, 123d Avn Bn
174th Avn Co	AML/ AHC	Aug. 66 – Oct. 71/ Departed Vietnam 8 Nov. 71
176th Avn Co	AML/ AHC	June 67 – Oct. 71/ Departed Vietnam 10 Nov. 71
178th Avn Co	MH	Sept. 67 – Oct. 71/ Transferred to 212th Avn Bn
196th Avn Co	MH	June 67 – Sept. 67/ Transferred to 223d Avn Bn
282d Avn Co	AML	Aug. 66 – Sept. 67/ Transferred to 212th Avn Bn

25th Aviation Battalion (Divisional)

Arrived Vietnam: 30 April 1966
Departed Vietnam: 7 December 1970
Previous Station: Hawaii

Authorized Strength	1966	1968
Battalion	313	313

The 25th Aviation Battalion was part of the 25th Infantry Division in Vietnam. The following units served under this battalion.

Troop or Company	Type	Battalion Service/Remarks
Co A	AM	April 66 – Dec. 70/ Departed Vietnam
Co B	AM	April 66 – Dec. 70/ Departed Vietnam
Tp D, 3d Sqdn, 4th Cav	Air Cav	April 66 – Dec. 70/ Assets used to assist formation of Troop F 4th Cav raised 10 Feb. 71 (see 12th Avn Gp)

52d Aviation Battalion (Combat)

Arrived Vietnam: 19 March 1963
Departed Vietnam: 28 April 1972
Previous Station: Vietnam

Authorized Strength	1964	1966	1968	1970
HQ & HQ Det	137	111	111	108

The 52d Aviation Battalion ("Flying Dragons") was stationed at Pleiku as part of the 17th Aviation Group, to which it was assigned on 1 March 1966. It operated in the II CTZ northern highlands, primarily with the 4th Infantry Division.

Troop or Company	Type	Battalion Service/Remarks
3d Avn Co	AHC	Sept. 71 – March 72/ Inactivated 20 March 72
57th Avn Co	AML/ AHC	Oct. 67 – April 72/ Transferred to 17th Avn Gp
68th Avn Co	ASH	Sept. 71 – March 72/ Departed Vietnam
117th Avn Co	AML	Aug. 65 – Oct. 65/ Transferred to 10th Avn Bn
119th Avn Co	AML/ AHC	June 63 – Dec. 70/ Departed Vietnam
155th Avn Co	AML	Aug. 66 – Aug. 68/ Transferred to 10th Avn Bn
161st Avn Co	AML	Dec. 65 – Aug. 66/ Transferred to 14th Avn Bn
170th Avn Co	AML/ AHC	Dec. 65 – April 71/ Departed Vietnam
179th Avn Co	MH	Dec. 66 – July 71/ Transferred to 223d Avn Bn
189th Avn Co	AML/ AHC	May 67 – March 71/ Inactivated 15 March 71
196th Avn Co	MH	Jan. 67 – June 67/ Transferred to 14th Avn Bn
219th Avn Co	Surv L	June 65 – Aug. 66/ Transferred to 223d Avn Bn
219th Avn Co*	RAC	July 71 – Dec. 71/ Departed Vietnam
238th Avn Co	Escort	March 69 – Oct. 69/ Transferred to 268th Avn Bn
282d Avn Co	AML	June 66 – Aug. 66/ Transferred to 14th Avn Bn

355th Avn Co	HH	Jan. 68 – March 69/
		Transferred to 268th Avn Bn
361st Avn Co	Escort	Aug. 68 – April 72/
		Transferred to 17th Avn Gp
Tp B, 7th Sqdn,	Air Cav	July 71 – April 72/
		See 17th Avn Gp; assets to Tp H,
		17th Cav
Tp D, 7th Sqdn,	Air Cav	July 71 – April 72/
17th Cav		Departed Vietnam

* Indicates second tour of service with the battalion.

58th Aviation Battalion (Airfield Operations Command)

Arrived Vietnam: 1 March 1968
Departed Vietnam: 17 February 1969
Previous Station: Vietnam
Authorized Strength: HHC – 88 (1968)

The 58th Aviation Battalion was directly under the 1st Aviation Brigade and located in the vicinity of the Long Binh – Tan Son Nhut complex during its service in Vietnam. On 12 September 1968 it was reclassified as the 58th Aviation Group (FFM) (Provisional) by 1st Aviation Brigade. The battalion was inactivated and its personnel integrated into the 165th Aviation Group.

Detachment or Company	Type	Battalion Service/Remarks
5th Avn Det	CAC	March 68 – Feb. 69/
		Transferred to 165th Avn Gp
16th Sig Co	DECCA	March 68 – Feb. 69/
		Transferred to 165th Avn Gp
125th Avn Co	ATC	March 68 – Feb. 69/
		Transferred to 165th Avn Gp

101st Aviation Battalion (Divisional)

Arrived Vietnam: December 1967
Departed Vietnam: 5 February 1972
Previous Station: Fort Campbell

Authorized Strength	1968	1971
Battalion	580	824

The 101st Aviation Battalion was organic to the 101st Airborne Division (Airmobile) and was colocated with the division headquarters. It was placed under the 160th Aviation Group in July 1968 and later the 101st Aviation Group. The following companies were part of the battalion in Vietnam.

Company	Type	Battalion Service/Remarks
Co A*	AM	Dec. 67 – Feb. 72/
		Departed Vietnam
Co B	AM	Dec. 67 – Feb. 72/
		Departed Vietnam
Co C	AM	Dec. 68 – Feb. 72/
		Departed Vietnam. Co arrived in Vietnam 20 Dec. 68.
Co D	AWC	Dec. 68 – Feb. 72/
		Departed Vietnam. Co arrived in Vietnam 20 Dec. 68.

* Company A served a previous tour in Vietnam 1 May 1965 – 1 September 1966 (see 13th Aviation Battalion).

123d Aviation Battalion (Divisional)

Arrived Vietnam: 8 December 1967
Departed Vietnam: 7 November 1971
Previous Station: Vietnam

Authorized Strength	1968	1970
Battalion	367	370

The 123d Aviation Battalion was created to fulfill the division-level normal aviation requirements of the 23d Infantry Division (AMERICAL) and was stationed at Chu Lai. The following companies were part of this battalion.

Company	Type	Battalion Service/Remarks
Co A	AM	Dec. 67 – Nov. 71/
		Departed Vietnam
Co B	AM	Dec. 67 – Nov. 71/
		Departed Vietnam
Co C	AM	Dec. 67 – Nov. 71/
		Departed Vietnam
Tp F, 8th Cav	Air Cav	June 71 – Nov. 71/
		Transferred to 196th Inf Bde

145th Aviation Battalion (Combat)

Arrived Vietnam: 24 September 1963
Departed Vietnam: 2 April 1972
Previous Station: Vietnam

Authorized Strength	1964	1966	1968	1970
HQ & HQ Det	171	111	111	108

The 145th Aviation Battalion was located at Tan Son Nhut and later moved to Bien Hoa with the 12th Aviation Group in 1966. Its mission for the majority of its Vietnam service was augmenting II Field Force Vietnam aviation in III Corps Tactical Zone. In May 1971 it relocated to Long Binh.

Company	Type	Battalion Service/Remarks
25th Avn Co	CAC	July 71 – March 72/
		Departed Vietnam
68th Avn Co	AML	Aug. 64 – March 65/
		Departed Vietnam
68th Avn Co*	AML/ AHC	Nov. 65 – Feb. 71/
		To joint training with South Vietnamese Air Force; departed Vietnam April 71
71st Avn Co	AML	Sept. 66 – Sept. 67/
		Transferred to 14th Avn Bn
74th Avn Co	Surv L	March 65 – Feb. 68/
		Transferred to 210th Avn Bn
Co A, 82d Avn Bn	AML	Aug. 66 – Sept. 66/
		Departed Vietnam and assets used in the 335th Avn Co
117th Avn Co	AML	Sept. 63 – Aug. 65/
		Transferred to 52d Avn Bn
117th Avn Co*	AML	Jan. 68 – April 68/
		Transferred to 214th Avn Bn
117th Avn Co*	AHC	Dec. 71 – March 72/
		Departed Vietnam
118th Avn Co	AML/ AHC	Sept. 63 – Aug. 71/
		Departed Vietnam

120th Avn Co	AML	Sept. 63 – July 66/	
		Transferred to Capital Avn Bn	
135th Avn Co	AML	April 68 – March 69/	
		Transferred to 222d Avn Bn	
147th Avn Co †	AML/MH	Aug. 66 – Dec. 66/	
		Transferred to 11th Avn Bn	
184th Avn Co	Surv L	Aug. 66 – June 67/	
		Transferred to 11th Avn Bn	
190th Avn Co ‡	AML/	Oct. 67 – Sept. 70/	
	AHC	To joint training with South	
		Vietnamese Air Force;	
		departed Vietnam 10 Dec. 70	
197th Avn Co	AML	March 65 – Sept. 66/	
		Departed Vietnam	
213th Avn Co	ASH	July 71 – March 72/	
		Inactivated 31 March 72	
242d Avn Co	ASH	April 71 – Oct. 71/	
		Departed Vietnam	
334th Avn Co §	AML/	Nov. 66 – July 71/	
	Escort	Transferred to 12th Avn Gp	
335th Avn Co	AML	Nov. 66 – Dec. 66/	
		Transferred to 173d Abn Bde	
335th Avn Co*	AML	March 67 – Jan. 68/	
		Arrived from 173d Abn Bde;	
		transferred to 268th Avn Bn	
Co A, 501st Avn Bn	AML	March 65 – Sept. 66/	
		Inactivated 1 Sept. 66;	
		assets to 71st Avn Co	

* Additional tour with battalion.

† Converted to medium helicopter mode October 1966.

‡ On duty with U.S. Marine Corps.

§ Converted to armed escort mode October 1968. Transferred to Thailand 24 November 1967 on temporary duty.

158th Aviation Battalion (Assault Helicopter)

Arrived Vietnam: 23 February 1969
Departed Vietnam: 24 December 1971
Previous Station: Fort Carson
Authorized Strength: 824 (1970)

The 158th Aviation Battalion was used to provide organic aviation assets to the 160th Aviation Group of the 101st Airborne Division (Airmobile) and was colocated with division headquarters. Later the 160th Aviation Group became the 101st Aviation Group. The following companies served under the battalion:

Company	Type	Battalion Service	Remarks
Co A	AHC	Feb. 69 – Dec. 71	Departed Vietnam
Co B	AHC	Feb. 69 – Dec. 71	Departed Vietnam
Co C	AHC	Feb. 69 – Dec. 71	Departed Vietnam
Co D	AWC	Feb. 69 – Dec. 71	Departed Vietnam

159th Aviation Battalion (Assault Helicopter)

Arrived Vietnam: 1 July 1968
Departed Vietnam: 8 February 1972
Previous Station: Vietnam

Authorized Strength	1968	1970
Battalion	542	797

The 159th Aviation Battalion was activated in Vietnam from assets of the 308th Aviation Battalion in order to furnish a third

helicopter battalion to the 160th Aviation Group (later the 101st) of the 101st Airborne Division (Airmobile). The battalion consisted of the following companies:

Company	Type	Battalion Service	Remarks
Co A	AHC	July 68 – Feb. 72	Departed Vietnam
Co B	AHC	July 68 – Feb. 72	Departed Vietnam
Co C	AHC	July 68 – Feb. 72	Departed Vietnam

210th Aviation Battalion (Combat)

Arrived Vietnam: 2 April 1967
Departed Vietnam: 31 August 1971
Previous Station: Fort Bragg

	1968	1970
Authorized Strength		
HQ and HQ Det	109	107

The 210th Aviation Battalion was partially formed from the assets of the provisional CAPITAL Aviation Battalion at Tan Son Nhut and served with the 1st Aviation Brigade. On 15 January 1968 the battalion was assigned to the 12th Aviation Group and moved to Long Thanh. In July 1971 the unit was transferred to the 165th Aviation Group. It provided fixed-wing aircraft support to III and IV CTZ.

Detachment or Company	Type	Battalion Service/Remarks
USARV Flight Det	(Prov)	April 67 – May 68/
		Transferred to USARV
Command Avn Co	(Prov)	April 68 – Oct. 68/
		Discontinued
5th Avn Det		April 67 – Dec. 67/
		Transferred to 17th Avn Gp
16th Sig Co	DECCA	Dec. 67 – March 68/
		Transferred to 58th Avn Bn
25th Avn Co	CAC	Feb. 68 – July 71/
		Transferred to 145th Avn Bn
54th Avn Co	FWU	Feb. 68 – March 71/
		Departed Vietnam
73d Avn Co	Surv	Feb. 68 – June 70/
		Transferred to 307th Avn Bn
74th Avn Co	Surv L	Feb. 68 – July 71/
		Transferred to 11th Avn Bn
120th Avn Co	AML	April 67 – Oct. 69/
		Transferred to 165th Avn Gp
125th Avn Co	ATC	April 67 – March 68/
		Transferred to 58th Avn Bn
184th Avn Co	Surv L	Feb. 68 – July 71/
		Departed Vietnam

212th Aviation Battalion (Combat)

Arrived Vietnam: 30 July 1967
Departed Vietnam: 23 December 1971
Previous Station: Fort Campbell

	1968	1970
Authorized Strength		
HQ and HQ Det	109	108

The 212th Aviation Battalion was initially part of the provisional FALCON Aviation Group at Da Nang, became part of the 16th

Aviation Group in January 1968 and transferred to the 11th Aviation Group in July 1971. It provided fixed-wing aviation support to the I CTZ area.

Company	Type	Battalion Service/Remarks
Corps Avn Co	(Prov)	April 68 – March 69/ Assets transferred to 62d Avn Co
21st Avn Co	Surv L/RAC	Feb. 68 – Nov. 71/ Departed Vietnam
62d Avn Co	CAC	March 69 – Dec. 71/ Transferred to 11th Avn Gp
116th Avn Co	AHC	Oct. 71 – Dec. 71/ Departed Vietnam
131st Avn Co	Surv	Sept. 67 – July 71/ Departed Vietnam
178th Avn Co	ASH	Oct. 71 – Dec. 71/ Transferred to 11th Avn Gp
203d Avn Co	ASH	Aug. 71 – Dec. 71/ Transferred to 11th Avn Gp
220th Avn Co	Surv L/RAC	Sept. 67 – Dec. 71/ Departed Vietnam
Co A, 228th Avn Bn	ASH	June 71 only/ Assets transferred to 203d Avn Co
245th Avn Co	Surv/SAC	Oct. 67 – Oct. 70/ Departed Vietnam
282d Avn Co	AML/AHC	Sept. 67 – Jan. 71/ To joint training with South Vietnamese Air Force; departed Vietnam Jan. 72

214th Aviation Battalion (Combat)

Arrived Vietnam: 19 April 1967
Departed Vietnam: 3 January 1972
Previous Station: Fort Campbell

Authorized Strength	1968	1970
HQ and HQ Det	109	108

The 214th Aviation Battalion ("Cougars") was partially formed from the assets of the BUFFALO Aviation Battalion (Provisional) which was formed at Bear Cat on 15 January 1967. The battalion was initially stationed at Bear Cat as part of the 12th Aviation Group. On 15 November 1968 the battalion relocated to Dong Tam to support the 9th Infantry Division and moved on to Vinh Long in September 1969 to support the 7th and 9th ARVN Divisions. There it joined the 164th Aviation Group in November, becoming part of the Delta Regional Aviation Command in 1971.

Company	Type	Battalion Service/Remarks
17th Avn Co	AML	Sept. 67 – April 68/ Transferred to 308th Avn Bn
21st Avn Co	Surv L	Aug. 67 – Sept. 67/ Transferred to 269th Avn Bn
114th Avn Co	AHC	Oct. 69 – Feb. 72/ Departed Vietnam
117th Avn Co	AML	April 68 – March 69/ Transferred to 222d Avn Bn
135th Avn Co	AML	Jan. 68 – April 68/ Transferred to 145th Avn Bn

Company	Type	Battalion Service/Remarks
135th Avn Co*	AHC	Oct. 69 – July 71/ Transferred to 11th Avn Bn
147th Avn Co	MH	March 69 – Oct. 69/ Transferred to 307th Avn Bn
162d Avn Co	AML	March 69 – Oct. 69/ Transferred to 13th Avn Bn
175th Avn Co	AHC	Oct. 69 – Feb. 72/ Departed Vietnam
187th Avn Co	AML	April 67 – June 67/ Transferred to 269th Avn Bn
190th Avn Co	AML	Sept. 67 – Oct. 67/ Transferred to 145th Avn Bn
191st Avn Co	AML	May 67 – Oct. 69/ Transferred to 13th Avn Bn
195th Avn Co	AML	Nov. 67 – March 69/ Transferred to 222d Avn Bn
199th Avn Co	RAC	Oct. 69 – Oct. 70/ Departed Vietnam
200th Avn Co	MH	April 67 – April 68/ Transferred to 308th Avn Bn
221st Avn Co	RAC	July 71 – Nov. 71/ Departed Vietnam
240th Avn Co	AML	May 67 – March 69/ Transferred to 222d Avn Bn
335th Avn Co	AHC	Oct. 69 – Nov. 71/ Departed Vietnam

* Indicates second tour of service with the battalion.

222d Aviation Battalion (Combat Support)

Arrived Vietnam: 25 May 1966
Departed Vietnam: 15 December 1971
Previous Station: Vietnam

Authorized Strength	1966	1968	1970
HQ and HQ Det	91	91	108

The 222d Aviation Battalion was part of the 12th Aviation Group throughout its service in Vietnam rendering aviation support to U.S. and allied forces in III and IV CTZ. It was located at Vung Tau until December 1968 when the battalion moved to Bear Cat.

Company	Type	Battalion Service/Remarks
54th Avn Co	FWU	Aug. 66 – Feb. 68/ Transferred to 210th Avn Bn
73d Avn Co	Surv	Aug. 66 – Feb. 68/ Transferred to 210th Avn Bn
117th Avn Co	AML/AHC	March 69 – Dec. 71/ Transferred to 145th Avn Bn
135th Avn Co	AML	Oct. 67 – Jan. 68/ Transferred to 214th Avn Bn

135th Avn Co*	AML	March 69 – Oct. 69/ Transferred to 214th Avn Bn
147th Avn Co	MH	April 67 – March 69/ Transferred to 214th Avn Bn
195th Avn Co	AML/AHC	March 69 – Dec. 70/ Departed Vietnam
205th Avn Co	MH	April 68 – March 69/ Transferred to 11th Avn Bn
213th Avn Co	MH	Jan. 67 – April 67/ Transferred to 269th Avn Bn
240th Avn Co	AML/AHC	March 69 – Dec. 71/ Departed Vietnam
273d Avn Co	HH	Dec. 67 – Dec. 71/ Transferred to 12th Avn Gp

* Indicates second tour of service with the battalion.

223d Aviation Battalion (Combat Support)

Arrived Vietnam: 15 May 1966
Departed Vietnam: 1 April 1972
Previous Station: Vietnam

Authorized Strength	1966	1968	1970
HQ and HQ Det	109	109	107

The 223d Aviation Battalion was activated as part of the 17th Aviation Group and was stationed at Qui Nhon providing aviation support in II Corps Tactical Zone. It transferred in September to the FALCON Aviation Group and returned to the 17th Aviation Group that December. In March 1971 it moved to Dong Ha and became part of the 11th Aviation Group in July 1971.

Detachment or Company	Type	Battalion Service/Remarks
Command Avn Co		Jan. 72 – April 72/ Transferred to 12th Avn Gp
5th Avn Det		Jan. 68 – Feb. 68/ Transferred to 1st Avn Bde
18th Avn Co	FWU	Aug. 66 – April 71/ Departed Vietnam
48th Avn Co	AHC	July 71 – April 72/ Transferred to 11th Avn Gp
58th Avn Det		April 68 – Oct. 68/ Transferred to 17th Avn Gp
73d Avn Co	SAC	Jan. 72 – April 72/ Departed Vietnam
120th Avn Co	AHC	Jan. 72 – May 72/ Transferred to 12th Avn Gp
131st Avn Co	Surv	Dec. 66 – Sept. 67/ Transferred to 212th Avn Bn
173d Avn Co	AHC	July 71 – March 72/ Departed Vietnam
179th Avn Co	AHC	July 71 – Aug. 71/ Departed Vietnam

183d Avn Co*	Surv L/Surv	June 66 – July 71/ Transferred to 10th Avn Bn
185th Avn Co	Surv L/RAC	June 67 – Oct. 70/ Departed Vietnam
196th Avn Co	MH	Sept. 67 – Oct. 67/ Transferred to 268th Avn Bn
203d Avn Co	Surv L/RAC	Oct. 67 – April 71/ Departed Vietnam
219th Avn Co	Surv L/RAC	Aug. 66 – July 71/ Transferred to 52d Avn Bn
220th Avn Co	Surv L	Dec. 66 – Sept. 67/ Transferred to 212th Avn Bn
225th Avn Co	Surv/SAC	May 67 – July 71/ Transferred to 268th Avn Bn
478th Avn Co	HH	July 71 – March 72/ Transferred to 11th Avn Gp

* Converted to surveillance aircraft company from light surveillance February 1967.

224th "Aviation" Battalion (Army Security Agency)

See Army Security Agency section for coverage of this unit. It was referred to as an aviation battalion in Vietnam for security reasons only. Reference DA letter 29 November 1966, subject: HHD 224th Aviation Battalion, addressed to commanding general, USASA, stating that effective 1 June 1966 the 224th Battalion was activated as a U.S. Army Security Agency unit.

227th Aviation Battalion (Assault Helicopter)

Arrived Vietnam: 11 September 1965
Departed Vietnam: 25 July 1971
Previous Station: Fort Benning

Authorized Strength	1966	1968
Battalion	580	580

The 227th Aviation Battalion was part of the 1st Cavalry Division (Airmobile) in Vietnam and served the division's 11th Aviation Group. It was colocated with the group headquarters. When the division left Vietnam in April 1971, the battalion, then at Phuoc Vinh, for a short time was under 1st Aviation Brigade, standing down and transferring assets. Details of asset switches can be found in the notes and remarks for the 10th and 52d Aviation Battalions.

Company	Type	Battalion Service/Remarks
Co A	AHC	Sept. 65 – June 71/ Assets to 3d Avn Co (see 52d Avn Bn)
Co B	AHC	Sept. 65 – June 71/ Departed Vietnam
Co C	AHC	Sept. 65 – June 71/ Departed Vietnam
Co D	AWC	Sept. 65 – July 71/ Transferred to 10th Avn Bn

228th Aviation Battalion
(Assault Support Helicopter)

Arrived Vietnam: 11 September 1965
Departed Vietnam: 13 June 1971
Previous Station: Fort Benning

Authorized Strength	1966	1968
Battalion	542	542

The 228th Aviation Battalion was a component of the 1st Cavalry Division's 11th Aviation Group and was colocated with the latter's headquarters. The battalion moved with the group in May 1971 (after the division left Vietnam) to Da Nang, where it was involved in standing down and switching assets to the 52d and 212th Aviation Battalions. (For details see those unit entries.)

Company	Type	Battalion Service/Remarks
Co A	AHC	Sept. 65 – June 71/ Transferred to 212th Avn Bn
Co B	AHC	Sept. 65 – June 71/ Departed Vietnam
Co C	AHC	Sept. 65 – June 71/ Transferred assets to 68th Avn Co (see 52d Avn Bn)

229th Aviation Battalion
(Assault Helicopter)

Arrived Vietnam: 13 September 1965
Departed Vietnam: 12 August 1972
Previous Station: Fort Benning

Authorized Strength	1966	1968	1971
Battalion	580	580	630

The 229th Aviation Battalion was part of the 11th Aviation Group of the 1st Cavalry Division (Airmobile). After the group departed Vietnam with the bulk of the division, the 229th Aviation Battalion remained and rendered aviation support to the 3d Brigade, 1st Cavalry Division at Bien Hoa in June 1971. The following units served the battalion in Vietnam:

Troop or Company	Type	Battalion Service/Remarks
Co A	AHC	Sept. 65 – Aug. 72/ Departed Vietnam
Co B	AHC	Sept. 65 – Aug. 72/ Departed Vietnam
Co C	AHC	Sept. 65 – Aug. 72/ Departed Vietnam
Co D	AWC	Sept. 65 – March 72/ Departed Vietnam
362d Avn Co	ASH	June 71 – Aug. 72/ Departed Vietnam
Tp F, 9th Cav*	Air Cav	June 71 – Aug. 72/ Transferred to 12th Avn Gp

* Troop F, 9th Cavalry was formed in Vietnam as Troop H, 16th Cavalry, a designation never approved by the Department of the Army. Properly Troop F, 9th Cavalry, its true designation was not used in Vietnam until the May 1972 time frame. Many records of the period June 1971 – May 1972 show this particular unit under its unauthorized designation.

268th Aviation Battalion
(Combat)

Arrived Vietnam: 4 May 1967
Departed Vietnam: 21 January 1972
Previous Station: Fort Hood

Authorized Strength	1968	1970
HQ and HQ Det	109	108

The 268th Aviation Battalion, part of the 17th Aviation Group in Vietnam, was stationed at Phu Hiep. It provided aviation support for the northern coastal region of II Corps Tactical Zone. The battalion relocated to Tuy Hoa in September 1970.

Company	Type	Battalion Service/Remarks
21st Avn Co	Surv L	June 67 – Aug. 67/ Transferred to 214th Avn Bn
48th Avn Co	AML	Sept. 67 – Aug. 68/ Transferred to 10th Avn Bn
61st Avn Co	AML/AHC	Aug. 68 – July 71/ Transferred to 7th Sqdn, 17th Cav
129th Avn Co	AML/AHC	Sept. 67 – July 71/ Transferred to 7th Sqdn, 17th Cav
134th Avn Co	AML/AHC	Nov. 67 – Dec. 71/ Departed Vietnam
180th Avn Co	MH	Dec. 67 – Jan. 72/ Transferred to 17th Avn Gp
190th Avn Co	AML	Aug. 67 – Sept. 67/ Transferred to 214th Avn Bn
192d Avn Co	AML	Oct. 67 – Feb. 68/ Transferred to 10th Avn Bn
196th Avn Co	MH	Oct. 67 – Dec. 67/ Transferred to 10th Avn Bn
196th Avn Co*	MH	Aug. 68 – Dec. 70/ Departed Vietnam
205th Avn Co	MH	July 67 – Aug. 67/ Transferred to 10th Avn Bn
225th Avn Co	SAC	July 71 – Dec. 71/ Departed Vietnam
238th Avn Co	AWC	Oct. 69 – Dec. 71/ Departed Vietnam
242d Avn Co	MH	Aug. 67 – Sept. 67/ Transferred to 269th Avn Bn
335th Avn Co	AML	Jan. 68 – Oct. 69/ Transferred to 214th Avn Bn
355th Avn Co	HH	March 69 – Dec. 70/ Departed Vietnam

* Indicates second tour of service with the battalion.

269th Aviation Battalion (Combat)

Arrived Vietnam: 28 January 1967
Departed Vietnam: 15 April 1971
Previous Station: Fort Bragg
Authorized Strength: HHD – 109 (1968)

The 269th Aviation Battalion ("The Black Barons") was part of the 12th Aviation Group during its service in Vietnam and was located at Cu Chi. It reinforced the aviation assets of 25th Infantry Division and other units in western III CTZ.

Company	Type	Battalion Service/Remarks
21st Avn Co	Surv	Sept. 67 – Feb. 68/ Transferred to 212th Avn Bn
116th Avn Co	AML/AHC	April 67 – April 71/ Transferred to 14th Avn Bn
132d Avn Co	MH	July 68 – Aug. 68/ Transferred to 14th Avn Bn
187th Avn Co	AML/AHC	June 67 – April 71/ Transferred to 11th Avn Bn
188th Avn Co	AML	May 67 – April 68/ Transferred to 308th Avn Bn
213th Avn Co	MH	April 67 – June 67/ Transferred to 11th Avn Bn
242d Avn Co	MH	Sept. 67 – April 71/ Transferred to 145th Avn Bn
272d Avn Co	MH	May 68 – June 68/ Transferred to 308th Avn Bn
361st Avn Co	Escort	March 68 – July 68/ Transferred to 52d Avn Bn

307th Aviation Battalion (Combat)

Arrived Vietnam: 20 December 1967
Departed Vietnam: 30 June 1971
Previous Station: Vietnam
Authorized Strength: HHD – 109 (1968)

The 307th Aviation Battalion was formed using in part the assets of the provisional PHANTOM Aviation Battalion which had been formed 20 September 1967. The 307th Aviation Battalion was located at Can Tho. It later became an air traffic control battalion. The following companies served both the PHANTOM Aviation Battalion and the 307th Aviation Battalion (the latter being under 164th Aviation Group):

Company	Type	Battalion Service/Remarks
73d Avn Co	SAC	June 70 – June 71/ Transferred to 13th Avn Bn
147th Avn Co	ASH	Oct. 69 – June 71/ Transferred to 13th Avn Bn
199th Avn Co	Surv L	Sept. 67 – Oct. 69/ Includes PHANTOM Avn Bn svc; transferred to 214th Avn Bn
221st Avn Co	Surv L	Sept. 67 – March 69/ Includes PHANTOM Avn Bn svc; transferred to 13th Avn Bn
235th Avn Co*	AML/Escort	Nov. 67 – June 71/ Includes PHANTOM Avn Bn svc; transferred to 13th Avn Bn
244th Avn Co	Surv/SAC	Sept. 67 – Nov. 70/ Includes PHANTOM Avn Bn svc; departed Vietnam
271st Avn Co	MH	Feb. 68 – April 68/ Transferred to 13th Avn Bn
271st Avn Co †	MH	Feb. 68 – June 71/ Transferred to 13th Avn Bn

* Converted into armed escort helicopter mode in October 1968.

† Indicates second tour of service with the battalion.

Unauthorized

308th Aviation Battalion (Combat)

Arrived Vietnam: 20 December 1967
Departed Vietnam: 1 July 1968
Previous Station: Fort Campbell
Authorized Strength: HHD – 109 (1968)

The 308th Aviation Battalion was part of the 12th Aviation Group and was stationed at Bien Hoa before becoming attached to the 16th Aviation Group on 16 March 1968. From March – April 1968 it moved to I CTZ, and was in Hue – Phu Bai by 12 April 1968. Under the operational control of the 101st Airborne Division (Airmobile), its assets were utilized to assist in building the 159th Aviation Battalion. The following companies served with the 308th Aviation Battalion in Vietnam:

Company	Type	Battalion Service/Remarks
17th Avn Co	AML	April 68 – July 68/ Inactivated 1 July 1968; assets used by 160th Avn Gp
132d Avn Co	MH	May 68 – July 68/ Transferred to 269th Avn Bn
188th Avn Co	AML	April 68 – July 68/ Inactivated 1 July 1968; assets used by 160th Avn Gp
200th Avn Co	MH	April 68 – July 68/ Inactivated 1 July 1968; assets used by 160th Avn Gp
272d Avn Co	MH	June 68 – July 68/ Inactivated 1 July 1968; assets used by 160th Avn Gp

I Corps Aviation Battalion, Provisional

No Insignia
Authorized

Arrived Vietnam: June 1966
Departed Vietnam: December 1966
Previous Station: Vietnam
Authorized Strength: Unknown

The I Corps Aviation Battalion (Provisional) was established to provide reconnaissance to the I Corps Tactical Zone in mid-1966. Its assets were used in late 1966 to assist the 223d Aviation Battalion. The following companies served with this battalion.

Company	Type	Battalion Service/Remarks
131st Avn Co	Surv	June 66 – Dec. 66/ Transferred to 223d Avn Bn
220th Avn Co	Surv L	Aug. 66 – Dec. 66/ Transferred to 223d Avn Bn

CAPITAL Aviation Battalion, Provisional

Arrived Vietnam: 1 July 1966
Departed Vietnam: 2 April 1967
Previous Station: Vietnam
Authorized Strength: Unknown

Unauthorized

The CAPITAL Aviation Battalion (Provisional) was located at Saigon under the 1st Aviation Brigade; its assets were transferred to the 210th Aviation Battalion during the spring of 1967. The following units were part of this battalion in Vietnam:

Detachment or Company	Type	Battalion Service/Remarks
USARV Flight Det		July 66 – April 67/ Transferred to 210th Avn Bn
5th Avn Det		July 66 – April 67/ Transferred to 210th Avn Bn
120th Avn Co	AML	July 66 – April 67/ Transferred to 210th Avn Bn
125th Avn Co	ATC	July 66 – April 67/ Transferred to 210th Avn Bn

Unauthorized

DELTA Aviation Battalion, Provisional

Arrived Vietnam: 5 May 1963 (or 4 July 1963)
Departed Vietnam: 30 September 1964
Previous Station: Vietnam
Authorized Strength: HHC – 210 (1963)

The DELTA Aviation Battalion (Provisional) was formed in 1963 and discontinued on either 30 September 1964 or 3 October 1964 (conflicting sources). Its assets were transferred to the Headquarters & Headquarters Detachment, 13th Aviation Battalion. The following companies served the provisional battalion:

Company	Type	Battalion Service/Remarks
114th Avn Co	AML	May 63 – Sept. 64/ Transferred to 13th Avn Bn
121st Avn Co	AML	July 63 – Sept. 64/ Transferred to 13th Avn Bn

---

Aviation Companies in Vietnam (see also transportation section for other aircraft companies)

Company	Type(s)	Callsign*	Previous Station	Vietnam Service	Typical Location	1964	1966	1968	1970
1st Avn	Light FWT		Thailand	31 Dec. 62 – 9 Dec. 63	Vung Tau	158 (Oct. 63)			
	See Army Security Agency Section								
3d Avn	AHC		Vietnam	2 Dec. 64 – 14 Dec. 64	Unknown	?	—	—	—
3d Avn †	AHC		Vietnam	31 Aug. 71 – 20 March 72	Pleiku				
11th Avn	GS	Speedy Jaguars	Benning	30 July 65 – 19 April 71	Phuoc Vinh	—	202	202	202
17th Avn	FWT (CV-2)		Benning	15 Sept. 65 – 1 Jan. 67	An Khe	—	158	219	—
17th Avn †	AML		Riley	25 Sept. 67 – 1 July 68	Long Binh				
18th Avn	FWT	Otters	Riley	7 Feb. 62 – 16 April 71	Qui Nhon	177	174	174	174
18th Avn †	CAC		Vietnam	15 Aug. 71 – 27 March 73	Can Tho				
21st Avn	Surv L	Black Aces, Cats Bird Dogs	Lewis	29 June 67 – 8 Nov. 71	Chu Lai	—	—	128	123
25th Avn	CAC	Red Carpet	Hood	25 Oct. 67 – 26 March 72	Long Binh	—	—	115	127
48th Avn	AML, AHC	Blue Stars	Benning	6 Nov. 65 – 23 Aug. 72	Ninh Hoa	—	195	219	288
54th Avn	FWT	Big Daddy	Ord	30 Aug. 65 – 15 March 71	Vung Tau	—	158	158	158
	Utility Acft	Otter Air Service							
57th Avn	FWT (CV-2)	Gray Tigers	Sill	31 Dec. 65 – 1 Jan. 67	Vung Tau	—	189	219	288
57th Avn †	AML, AHC	Gladiators	Bragg	24 Oct. 67 – 13 March 73	Kontum				
59th Avn	AHC		Vietnam	31 Aug. 71 – 29 Nov. 71	Unknown	—	—	—	—
59th Avn †	CAC		Vietnam	30 Sept. 72 – 13 March 73	Tan Son Nhut				
60th Avn	AHC	Ghost Riders	Vietnam	31 Aug. 71 – 13 March 73	Ninh Hoa	—	—	—	—
61st Avn	FWT (CV-2)	Lucky Stars	Campbell	27 June 63 – 1 Jan. 67	Vung Tau	200	189	219	288
61st Avn †	AML, AHC	Star Blazers	Vietnam	21 Nov. 67 – 20 March 72	An Son				
62d Avn	AML	Royal Coachmen	Benning	3 Oct. 64 – 14 Dec. 64	Unknown	272	—	—	145
62d Avn †	CAC		Vietnam	4 March 69 – 27 March 73	Phu Bai				
68th Avn	ASH	Top Tigers	Benning	15 Aug. 64 – 1 March 65	Bien Hoa	168	195	219	209
68th Avn †	AML	Raiders	Vietnam	28 Nov. 65 – 1 April 71	Bien Hoa				
68th Avn ‡	AHC		Vietnam	31 Aug. 71 – 20 March 72	Pleiku				
71st Avn	AML, AHC	Fire Birds Rattlers	Vietnam	2 Sept. 66 – 1 Oct. 71	Chu Lai	—	195	219	288

Aviation Companies in Vietnam (see also transportation section for other aircraft companies)

Company	Type(s)	Callsign*	Previous Station	Vietnam Service	Typical Location	1964	1966	1968	1970
73d Avn	Surv, SAC	The Warriors, Uptight	Vietnam	31 May 63 – 29 April 72	Vung Tau	164	292	292	331
74th Avn	Surv L RAC	Aloft	Vietnam	26 March 65 – 20 March 72	Phu Loi	—	124	124	146
92d Avn	FWT (CV-2)	Stallions	Carson	15 Jan. 64 – 1 Jan. 67	Qui Nhon	158	189	219	288
92d Avn †	AML, AHC	Side Kicks	Vietnam	27 Nov. 67 – 1 Jan. 72	Dong Ba Thin				
114th Avn	AML, AHC	Knights of the Air	Knox	10 May 63 – 29 Feb. 72	Vinh Long	272	195	219	288
116th Avn	AML, AHC	Hornets, Stingers	Bragg	20 Oct. 65 – 26 Dec. 71	Cu Chi	—	195	219	288
117th Avn §	AML, AHC	Warlords Sidewinders	Vietnam	25 June 63 – 26 March 72	Long Binh	273	195	219	288
118th Avn	AML, AHC	Thunderbirds Bandits, Choppers	Vietnam	25 June 63 – 31 Aug. 71	Bien Hoa	245	195	219	167
119th Avn	AML, AHC	Gators, Crocodiles	Vietnam	25 June 63 – 14 Dec. 70	Pleiku	239	195	219	219
120th Avn	AML, AHC	The Deans, Snoopys	Vietnam	25 June 63 – Oct. 72	Long Binh	230	195	195	310
121st Avn ‖	AML, AHC	Soc Trang Tigers	Vietnam	25 June 63 – 10 Dec. 70	Soc Trang	245	195	219	219
125th Avn	Air Traffic Control	Traffic-Minder	Benning	5 Nov. 65 – 20 Sept. 71	Bien Hoa	—	357	343	343
128th Avn	AML, AHC	Tomahawks	Campbell	20 Oct. 65 – 30 Jan. 72	Phu Loi	—	195	219	288
129th Avn	AML, AHC	Bulldogs	Campbell	21 Oct. 65 – 8 March 73	An Son	—	195	219	288
131st Avn	Surv, SAC	Nighthawks	Riley	1 June 66 – 1 July 71	Hue – Phu Bai	—	292	292	292
132d Avn	MH	Hercules	Benning	Aug. 65 – 25 April 66	An Khe	—	170	181	268
132d Avn †	ASH		Vietnam	23 May 68 – 8 Nov. 71	Chu Lai				
134th Avn	FWT (CV-2)	Demons, Devils	Benning	31 Dec. 65 – 1 Jan. 67	Can Tho	—	189	219	288
134th Avn †	AML, AHC		Bragg	22 Nov. 67 – 29 Dec. 71	Phu Hiep				
135th Avn	FWT (CV-2)	Emus, Taipans	Benning	31 Dec. 65 – 1 Jan. 67	Dong Ba Thin	—	189	219	288
135th Avn †	AML, AHC		Hood	3 Oct. 67 – 14 Feb. 72	Vung Tau				
138th Avn	See Army Security Agency Section								
144th Avn	See Army Security Agency Section								
146th Avn	See Army Security Agency Section								
147th Avn	MH AML, AHC	Hill-Climbers	Benning	28 Nov. 65 – 17 March 72	Vung Tau	—	173	189	268
155th Avn	AML, AHC	Falcons Stage Coach	Korea	7 Oct. 65 – 15 March 71	Ban Me Thuot	—	195	219	288
156th Avn	See Army Security Agency Section								
161st Avn	AML		Benning	23 Dec. 65 – 8 Dec. 67	Qui Nhon	—	195	—	—
162d Avn	AML, AHC	Vultures Copperheads	Benning	7 March 66 – 3 April 72	Dong Tam	—	195	219	288
163d Avn	GS, AML	Woodstock	Vietnam	1 July 68 – 18 Jan. 72	Gia Le	—	—	202	203
170th Avn	AML, AHC	Bikinis Buccaneer	Benning	23 Dec. 65 – 30 April 71	Pleiku	—	195	219	288
171st Avn #	Airlift		Alaska	25 Oct. 65 – 20 Aug. 66	Saigon	—	121	—	—
172d Avn #	Airlift		Alaska	25 Oct. 65 – 20 Aug. 66	Saigon	—	121	—	—
173d Avn	AML, AHC	Robin Hood	Benning	10 March 66 – 31 March 72	Lai Khe	—	195	219	288
174th Avn	AML, AHC	Sharks, Dolphins	Benning	7 April 66 – 8 Nov. 71	Duc Pho	—	195	219	288
175th Avn	AML, AHC	Outlaws	Benning	11 April 66 – 5 May 66	Unknown	—	195	219	288
175th Avn †			Vietnam	10 Nov. 66 – 20 Feb. 72	Vinh Long				
176th Avn	AML, AHC	Minute Men	Benning	20 Feb. 67 – 10 Nov. 71	Chu Lai	—	—	219	288
178th Avn	MH, ASH	Boxcars	Benning	6 March 66 – 5 March 72	Chu Lai	—	173	186	268
179th Avn	MH	Shrimpboats, Hooks	Benning	25 June 66 – 23 Aug. 71	Pleiku	—	170	170	170
180th Avn	MH, ASH	Big Windy	Benning	10 Nov. 66 – 29 March 73	Phu Hiep	—	—	186	268
183d Avn	Surv L RAC	Sea Horses	Hood	30 June 66 – 30 Nov. 71	Dong Ba Thin	—	128	128	123
184th Avn	Surv L RAC	Non-Stops	Sill	13 Aug. 66 – 31 July 71	Phu Loi	—	128	128	123
185th Avn	Surv L RAC		Knox	30 June 67 – 1 Oct. 70	Ban Me Thuot	—	—	128	123
187th Avn	AML, AHC	Blackhawks Crusaders	Bragg	15 March 67 – 14 Feb. 72	Tay Ninh	—	—	219	288
188th Avn	AML, AHC	Black Widows	Campbell	4 May 67 – 1 July 68	Bien Hoa	—	—	219	—
189th Avn	AML, AHC	Ghostriders Avengers	Carson	7 May 67 – 15 March 71	Pleiku	—	—	219	288
190th Avn	AML, AHC	Gladiators	Campbell	12 Aug. 67 – 10 Dec. 70	Bien Hoa	—	—	219	288
191st Avn	AML, AHC	Boomerangs Bounty Hunters	Bragg	25 May 67 – 1 Oct. 71	Dong Tam	—	—	219	288
192d Avn	AML, AHC	Lonesome Polecats	Riley	30 Oct. 67 – 20 Jan. 71	Phan Thiet	—	—	219	288
195th Avn	AML, AHC	Skychiefs	Carson	1 Nov. 67 – 14 Dec. 70	Long Binh	—	—	219	288
196th Avn	MH		Sill	21 Jan. 67 – 23 Dec. 70	An Son	—	—	186	268

Aviation Companies in Vietnam (see also transportation section for other aircraft companies)

Company	Type(s)	Callsign*	Previous Station	Vietnam Service	Typical Location	1964	1966	1968	1970
						Authorized Strength			
197th Avn	AML, AHC	Gunbusters Playboys	Vietnam	1 March 65 – 1 Sept. 66	Bien Hoa	—	194	—	—
199th Avn	Surv L RAC	Maddogs, Swamp Fox	Hood	18 July 67 – 14 Oct. 70	Vinh Long	—	—	128	123
200th Avn	MH	Pachyderms	Benning	15 March 67 – 1 July 68	Bear Cat	—	—	181	—
201st Avn	CAC	Red Barons	Bragg	26 Oct. 67 – 13 March 73	Nha Trang	—	—	115	115
203d Avn	Surv L	Hawkeye	Sill	20 Oct. 67 – 15 April 71	Phu Hiep	—	—	128	123
203d Avn †	ASH	Wildcats	Vietnam	31 Aug. 71 – 30 April 72	Da Nang				
205th Avn	MH, ASH	Geronimos	Sill	30 May 67 – 15 April 71	Phu Loi	—	—	181	268
213th Avn	MH, ASH		Benning	13 Jan. 67 – 31 March 72	Phu Loi	—	—	186	268
219th Avn	Surv L RAC	Headhunters	Hood	25 June 65 – 26 Dec. 71	Pleiku	—	156	156	146
220th Avn	Surv L RAC	Catkillers	Lewis	3 July 65 – 26 Dec. 71	Hue – Phu Bai	—	156	156	146
221st Avn	Surv L RAC	Shotgun	Bragg	5 July 65 – 10 Nov. 71	Soc Trang	—	156	156	146
225th Avn	Surv, SAC	Phantom Hawks	Lewis	3 May 67 – 26 Dec. 71	Phu Hiep	—	—	273	331
235th Avn	AML, AWC	Delta Devils	Benning	1 Nov. 67 – 31 Aug. 71	Can Tho	—	—	189	154
238th Avn	Escort, AWC	Gun Runners	Riley	20 March 69 – 23 Dec. 71	An Khe	—	—	—	154
240th Avn	AML, AHC	Death-on-Call Grayhounds	Hood	25 May 67 – 26 Dec. 71	Bear Cat	—	—	219	288
242d Avn	MH, ASH	Muleskinners	Benning	12 Aug. 67 – 1 Oct. 71	Cu Chi	—	—	181	268
243d Avn	MH, ASH	Freight Train	Sill	30 Oct. 67 – 24 Sept. 71	Dong Ba Thin	—	—	181	268
244th Avn	Surv	Delta Hawks	Lewis	29 July 67 – 26 Nov. 70	Can Tho	—	—	273	331
244th Avn †	AHC		Vietnam	31 Aug. 71 – 26 Dec. 71	Bear Cat				
245th Avn	Surv		Lewis	8 Oct. 67 – 1 Oct. 70	Da Nang	—	—	273	273
271st Avn	ASH, MH	Innkeeper	Benning	26 Feb. 68 – 26 Sept. 71	Can Tho	—	—	181	268
272d Avn	MH		Sill	21 May 68 – 1 July 68	Unknown	—	—	181	—
273d Avn	HH	Skycranes	Sill	22 Dec. 67 – 29 Feb. 72	Long Binh	—	—	129	160
281st Avn	AML, AHC	Intruders, Wolfpack	Benning	30 June 66 – 10 Dec. 70	Nha Trang	—	195	219	288
282d Avn	AML, AHC	Black Cats	Benning	11 June 66 – 31 Jan. 72	Da Nang	—	195	219	288
334th Avn	AML, AWC	Dragons, Peacemakers	Vietnam	10 Nov. 66 – 1 March 72	Bien Hoa	—	194	194	254
335th Avn	AML, AHC	Cowboys, Falcons	Bragg	10 Nov. 66 – 18 Nov. 71	Phu Hiep	—	195	219	288
336th Avn	AML, AHC	T-Birds, Warriors	Campbell	10 Nov. 66 – 15 March 71	Soc Trang	—	195	219	288
355th Avn	HH		Sill	18 Jan. 68 – 28 Dec. 70	Phu Hiep	—	—	129	160
361st Avn	Escort, AWC	Pink Panthers	Vietnam	31 March 68 – 20 Aug. 72	Pleiku	—	—	93	236
362d Avn	ASH		Vietnam	30 June 71 – 20 Aug. 72	Bien Hoa	—	—	—	236
478th Avn	HH	Hurricane	Benning	15 Sept. 65 – 12 Oct. 72	Gia Le	—	107	107	187
Command Avn**	CAC – USARV	Long Trip	Vietnam	1 July 66 – 28 March 73	Tan Son Nhut	—	94	94	115
UTT Avn ††	Escort		Vietnam	19 April 63 – 15 Aug. 64	Tan Son Nhut	144	—	—	—
UTT Avn	Test Escort		Vietnam	16 Oct. 62 – 15 March 63	Tan Son Nhut	191 (Feb. 63)	—	—	—

Organic Battalion Aviation Companies Serving Separately From Their Parent Units ‡‡

Company			Previous Station	Vietnam Service	Typical Location	1964	1966	1968	1970
Company A, 5th Avn Bn			Benning	11 Sept. 65 – 25 April 66	An Khe	—	113	—	—
Company A, 82d Avn Bn			Bragg	1 May 65 – 1 Sept. 66	Vung Tau	—	196	—	—
Company A, 82d Avn Bn†			Bragg	13 Feb. 68 – 11 Dec. 69	Phu Bai	—	—	219	—
Company A, 501st Avn Bn			Hood	14 Dec. 64 – 1 Sept. 66	Bien Hoa	—	196	—	—
Company A, 502d Avn Bn			Hood	14 Dec. 64 – 1 Sept. 66	Vinh Long	—	196	—	—

* This list is admittedly an incomplete compilation of aviation callsigns encountered during the book's research. It represents aviation callsigns used in Vietnam that were associated with either the specific unit or its component gunship platoon.

† Indicates second tour in Vietnam.

‡ Indicates third tour in Vietnam.

§ Formed from assets of 8th Transportation Company.

‖ Formed from assets of 57th Transportation Company.

Both of these companies had only their 2d Platoons serving in Vietnam, but since "platoon" strength was in reality over 100 men they are nevertheless included in this tabulation.

** Command Aircraft Company formed from the USARV Flight Detachment on 25 September 69.

†† Assets used to form the 68th Aviation Company upon close-out of the Utility-Tactical Transport Aviation Company.

‡‡ Lists only those not mentioned in aviation battalion text of book. See also 1st Cavalry Division aviation assets (in assigned and attached units portion of its order of battle) as well as divisional aviation battalions (such as the 4th Aviation Battalion).

Chapter 11

Cavalry

1st Squadron, 1st Cavalry (Armored Cavalry)

Arrived Vietnam: 29 August 1967
Departed Vietnam: 10 May 1972
Previous Station: Fort Hood

Authorized Strength	1968	1970
Squadron	1,027	1,050

The 1st Squadron, 1st Cavalry was detached from the 1st Armored Division and sent to Vietnam as a separate armored cavalry squadron attached to the U.S. Army, Pacific (USARPAC). Traditionally, it was part of the "1st Regiment of Dragoons." The squadron consisted of three ground cavalry troops and one air cavalry troop, Troop D, which was deployed in July 1968 and attached to the 101st Airborne Division (Airmobile) until 1969, when it rejoined the squadron. Troop D's assets were later used in the reactivation of Troop D, 17th Cavalry when the latter unit was activated in Vietnam on 30 April 1972. Squadron personnel were entitled to wear the shoulder sleeve insignia of the 1st Armored Division.

Location	Service	Major Command
Chu Lai	Sept. 67 – Oct. 67	Task Force OREGON
Chu Lai	Nov. 67 – Nov. 68	23d Infantry Division (AMERICAL)
Da Nang	Dec. 68 – Jan. 69	23d Infantry Division (AMERICAL)
Da Nang – Tam Ky	Feb. 69 – Sept. 69	23d Infantry Division (AMERICAL)
Chu Lai	Nov. 69 – March 70	23d Infantry Division (AMERICAL)
Chu Lai – Mo Duc	April 70 – July 70	23d Infantry Division (AMERICAL)
Chu Lai – Tam Ky	Aug. 70	23d Infantry Division (AMERICAL)
Tam Ky	Sept. 70	23d Infantry Division (AMERICAL)
Thach Khe	Oct. 70	23d Infantry Division (AMERICAL)
Chu Lai – Tam Ky	Nov. 70 – March 71	23d Infantry Division (AMERICAL)
Chu Lai – Tam Ky	April 71	11th Infantry Brigade
Tam Ky – Phu Bai	May 71	101st Airborne Division (Airmobile)
Tam Ky – Phu Bai	June 71	23d Infantry Division (AMERICAL)
Tam Ky – Ai Nghia	July 71 – Nov. 71	23d Army of the Republic of Vietnam Infantry Division
Tam Ky – Ai Nghia	Dec. 71 – May 72	196th Infantry Brigade

2d Squadron, 1st Cavalry (Armored Cavalry)

Arrived Vietnam: 30 August 1967
Departed Vietnam: 11 October 1970
Previous Station: Fort Hood

Authorized Strength	1968	1970
Squadron	1,027	784

The 2d Squadron, 1st Cavalry ("1st Regiment of Dragoons") was a separate armored cavalry squadron attached to U.S. Army, Pacif-

ic (USARPAC) from the 2d Armored Division. Squadron personnel were entitled to wear the shoulder sleeve insignia of the 2d Armored Division.

Location	Service	Major Command
Pleiku	Aug. 67	4th Infantry Division
Pleiku	Sept. 67	Task Force OREGON
Pleiku	Oct. 67 – Feb. 68	4th Infantry Division
Dak To	March 68 – May 68	4th Infantry Division
Pleiku	June 68 – Nov. 68	4th Infantry Division
Suoi Doi	Dec. 68 – March 69	4th Infantry Division
An Khe	April 69	4th Infantry Division
Phan Thiet	May 69	Task Force SOUTH, I Field Force, Vietnam
Song Mao	June 69 – May 70	Task Force SOUTH, I Field Force, Vietnam
Phan Rang	June 70 – Sept. 70	Task Force SOUTH, I Field Force, Vietnam
Cam Ranh Bay	Oct. 70	U.S. Army, Vietnam (USARV)

Troop E, 1st Cavalry (Reconnaissance)

Arrived Vietnam: 19 December 1967
Departed Vietnam: 18 October 1971
Previous Station: Hawaii

Authorized Strength	1968	1970
Troop	198	210

Troop E, 1st Cavalry ("1st Regiment of Dragoons") was raised 1 July 1966 to serve as the brigade ground reconnaissance element in the 11th Infantry Brigade (Light). The troop was colocated with brigade headquarters in Vietnam.

7th Squadron, 1st Cavalry (Air Cavalry)

Arrived Vietnam: 26 February 1968
Departed Vietnam: 7 April 1972
Previous Station: Fort Knox

Authorized Strength	1968	1971
Squadron	850	1,037

The 7th Squadron, 1st Cavalry ("1st Regiment of Dragoons") was first attached to the 12th Aviation Group at Di An. On 3 June 1968 the squadron went to Vinh Long and became part of the 164th Aviation Group. The squadron contained the following troops while in Vietnam:

Troop	Type	Squadron Service/Remarks
Tp A	Air Cav	Feb. 68 – April 72/ Departed Vietnam
Tp B	Air Cav	Feb. 68 – April 72/ Departed Vietnam
Tp C	Air Cav	Feb. 68 – April 72/ Departed Vietnam
Tp D	Ground	Feb. 68 – April 72/ Departed Vietnam

Tp C, 16th Cav	Air Cav	March 70 – Dec. 70/ Transferred to 13th Avn Bn
Tp D, 3d Sqdn, 5th Cav	Air Cav	April 70 – Jan. 71/ Rejoined 3d Sqdn, 5th Cav
Tp C, 3d Sqdn, 17th Cav	Air Cav	Jan. 71 – April 72/ Departed Vietnam

1st Squadron, 4th Cavalry (Division Reconnaissance)

Arrived Vietnam: 20 October 1965
Departed Vietnam: 5 February 1970
Previous Station: Fort Riley

Authorized Strength	1966	1968
Squadron	870	870

The 1st Squadron, 4th Cavalry was the divisional ground reconnaissance squadron of the 1st Infantry Division in Vietnam and was colocated with the division headquarters although its troops were often parceled out to render brigade support. Troop D, an air cavalry troop, was often under the control of the division's 1st Aviation Battalion.

3d Squadron, 4th Cavalry (Division Reconnaissance)

Arrived Vietnam: 24 March 1966
Departed Vietnam: 8 December 1970
Previous Station: Hawaii

Authorized Strength	1966	1968	1970
Squadron	856	852	784

The 3d Squadron, 4th Cavalry was the divisional ground reconnaissance squadron of the 25th Infantry Division in Vietnam. The squadron was one of the first units to prove armor effectiveness in II Corps Tactical Zone and thereafter engaged in contested route and convoy security along Highway 1. In January 1969 it became the first division squadron to receive the new M551 Sheridan assault vehicles. Troop D, an air cavalry troop, served mostly with the division's 25th Aviation Battalion. After the squadron departed Vietnam, assets of this air troop continued to serve the division's separate 2d Brigade and later II Field Force, Vietnam. Finally these assets became the basis of Troop F, 4th Cavalry.

Troop F, 4th Cavalry (Air Cavalry)

Arrived Vietnam: 10 February 1971
Departed Vietnam: 26 February 1973
Previous Station: Vietnam
Authorized Strength: 266 (1971)

Troop F, 4th Cavalry was organized in Vietnam from assets of Troop D, 3d Squadron, 4th Cavalry, which had been serving II Field Force, Vietnam on a provisional basis in the Long Binh – Xuan Loc area during January 1971. Troop F served with both the 11th and 12th Aviation Groups during its service in Vietnam and was located at Lai Khe (later Long Binh). It located in late 1972 at Da Nang and in 1973 at Tan My.

1st Battalion, 5th Cavalry (Airmobile Infantry)

Arrived Vietnam: 15 September 1965
Departed Vietnam: 9 April 1971
Previous Station: Fort Benning

Authorized Strength	1966	1968
Battalion	767	920

The 1st Battalion, 5th Cavalry ("Black Knights") served as airmobile infantry with the 1st Cavalry Division in Vietnam.

Location	Service	Major Command
An Khe	Sept. 65 – June 67	2d Brigade, 1st Cavalry Division
An Khe – Bong Son	July 67 – Feb. 68	2d Brigade, 1st Cavalry Division
An Khe – Phong Dien	March 68 – April 68	2d Brigade, 1st Cavalry Division
An Khe – Dong Ha	May 68	2d Brigade, 1st Cavalry Division
An Khe – Phong Dien	June 68 – Nov. 68	2d Brigade, 1st Cavalry Division
An Khe – An Loc	Dec. 68	2d Brigade, 1st Cavalry Division
An Khe	Jan. 69	2d Brigade, 1st Cavalry Division
An Khe – An Loc	Feb. 69	2d Brigade, 1st Cavalry Division
An Khe – Tay Ninh	March 69	1st Brigade, 1st Cavalry Division
An Khe – Quan Loi	April 69	1st Brigade, 1st Cavalry Division
Bien Hoa – Tay Ninh	May 69 – Dec. 69	1st Brigade, 1st Cavalry Division
Tay Ninh	Jan. 70	1st Brigade, 1st Cavalry Division
Quan Loi	Feb. 70 – March 70	3d Brigade, 1st Cavalry Division
Quan Loi – An Loc	April 70 – May 70	3d Brigade, 1st Cavalry Division
Quan Loi – Cambodia	June 70 – July 70	3d Brigade, 1st Cavalry Division*
Quan Loi – An Loc	Aug. 70	3d Brigade, 1st Cavalry Division
Gia Ray	Sept. 70 – April 71	3d Brigade, 1st Cavalry Division

* In Cambodia during June 1970.

2d Battalion, 5th Cavalry (Airmobile Infantry)

Arrived Vietnam: 15 September 1965
Departed Vietnam: 1 April 1972
Previous Station: Fort Benning

Authorized Strength	1966	1968	1971
Battalion	767	920	884

The 2d Battalion, 5th Cavalry ("Black Knights") served as airmobile infantry with the 1st Cavalry Division (Airmobile) in Vietnam.

Location	Service	Major Command
An Khe	Sept. 65 – June 67	2d Brigade, 1st Cavalry Division

An Khe – Bong Son	July 67 – Feb. 68	2d Brigade, 1st Cavalry Division
An Khe – Phong Dien	March 68 – April 68	2d Brigade, 1st Cavalry Division
An Khe – Dong Ha	May 68	2d Brigade, 1st Cavalry Division
An Khe – Phong Dien	June 68 – July 68	2d Brigade, 1st Cavalry Division
An Khe – Phong Dien	Aug. 68 – Oct. 68	1st Brigade, 1st Cavalry Division
An Khe – Tay Ninh	Nov. 68 – Dec. 68	1st Brigade, 1st Cavalry Division
An Khe – Cu Chi	Jan. 69	1st Brigade, 1st Cavalry Division
An Khe – Tay Ninh	Feb. 69	1st Brigade, 1st Cavalry Division
An Khe – An Loc	March 69	2d Brigade, 1st Cavalry Division
An Khe – Lai Khe	April 69 – May 69	2d Brigade, 1st Cavalry Division
Bien Hoa – Lai Khe	June 69 – Dec. 69	2d Brigade, 1st Cavalry Division
Bien Hoa – Phuoc Vinh	Jan. 70	2d Brigade, 1st Cavalry Division
Tay Ninh	Feb. 70 – March 70	1st Brigade, 1st Cavalry Division
Tay Ninh – Katum	April 70 – May 70	1st Brigade, 1st Cavalry Division
Cambodia	June 70	1st Brigade, 1st Cavalry Division
Bien Hoa	July 70 – March 71	1st Brigade, 1st Cavalry Division
Gia Ray	April 71	3d Brigade, 1st Cavalry Division
Bien Hoa – Gia Ray	May 71	3d Brigade, 1st Cavalry Division
Bien Hoa	June 71 – May 72	3d Brigade, 1st Cavalry Division

3d Squadron, 5th Cavalry (Division Reconnaissance)

Arrived Vietnam: 2 February 1967
Departed Vietnam: 8 November 1971
Previous Station: Fort Riley

Authorized Strength	1968	1971
Squadron	952	1,114

The 3d Squadron, 5th Cavalry ("Black Knights") was initially the divisional ground reconnaissance squadron of the 9th Infantry Division in Vietnam. On 26 February 1968 the majority of the squadron was deployed to I CTZ and attached to the 1st Cavalry Division. In June 1969, with the 9th Infantry Division's departure from Vietnam imminent, the squadron (less Troop D, its air cavalry troop, which remained with the division's separate 3d Brigade until October 1970) was attached to the 1st Brigade of the 5th Infantry Division (Mechanized). In September 1969 the squadron moved under the control of the 101st Airborne Division (Airmobile) in the A Shau Valley along the Laotian border, where it remained until January 1970. The unit then returned to the 1st Brigade, 5th Infantry Division (Mechanized) that February. In July 1971 the squadron was posted once more to the control of the 101st Airborne Division (Airmobile) where it remained until it departed Vietnam. Troop D, which had served with the 9th Infantry Division's 9th Aviation Battalion until that battalion left in August 1969, next served the division's separate 3d Brigade and came under the control of the 7th Squadron, 1st Cavalry about

April 1970. In January 1971 the troop rejoined the rest of the 3d Squadron, 5th Cavalry. When the squadron closed out of Vietnam, the air troop was scheduled for further duty with the 164th Aviation Group but this never really materialized and Troop D was with this group for only a few days before departing Vietnam with the remainder of the squadron (although its assets remained in the 164th Aviation Group).

1st Battalion, 7th Cavalry (Airmobile Infantry)

Arrived Vietnam: 15 September 1965
Departed Vietnam: 22 August 1972
Previous Station: Fort Benning

Authorized Strength	1966	1968	1971
Battalion	767	920	884

The 1st Battalion, 7th Cavalry served as airmobile infantry with the 1st Cavalry Division (Airmobile) in Vietnam.

Location	Service	Major Command
An Khe	Sept. 65 – June 67	3d Brigade, 1st Cavalry Division
An Khe – Bong Son	July 67 – Sept. 67	3d Brigade, 1st Cavalry Division
An Khe – Chu Lai	Oct. 67 – Jan. 68	3d Brigade, 1st Cavalry Division
An Khe – Phong Dien	Feb. 68 – April 68	3d Brigade, 1st Cavalry Division
An Khe – A Luoi	May 68	3d Brigade, 1st Cavalry Division
An Khe – Phong Dien	June 68 – Oct. 68	3d Brigade, 1st Cavalry Division
An Khe – Quan Loi	Nov. 68	3d Brigade, 1st Cavalry Division
An Khe – An Loc	Dec. 68 – Jan. 69	3d Brigade, 1st Cavalry Division
An Khe – Bien Hoa	Feb. 69	3d Brigade, 1st Cavalry Division
An Khe – Phuoc Vinh	March 69	1st Cavalry Division direct control
An Khe – Quan Loi	April 69	3d Brigade, 1st Cavalry Division
Bien Hoa – Courtenay	May 69	3d Brigade, 1st Cavalry Division
Bien Hoa – Quan Loi	June 69 – Nov. 69	3d Brigade, 1st Cavalry Division
Bien Hoa – Phuoc Long	Dec. 69	3d Brigade, 1st Cavalry Division
Quan Loi	Jan. 70 – March 70	3d Brigade, 1st Cavalry Division
Quan Loi – An Loc	April 70 – May 70	3d Brigade, 1st Cavalry Division
Cambodia	June 70	3d Brigade, 1st Cavalry Division
Quan Loi	July 70	3d Brigade, 1st Cavalry Division
Quan Loi – An Loc	Aug. 70	3d Brigade, 1st Cavalry Division
Gia Ray	Sept. 70 – April 71	3d Brigade, 1st Cavalry Division
Bien Hoa – Gia Ray	May 71	3d Brigade, 1st Cavalry Division
Bien Hoa	June 71 – June 72	3d Brigade, 1st Cavalry Division
Bien Hoa	July 72 – Aug. 72	Task Force GARRY OWEN

2d Battalion, 7th Cavalry (Airmobile Infantry)

Arrived Vietnam: 15 September 1965
Departed Vietnam: 5 May 1971
Previous Station: Fort Benning

Authorized Strength	1966	1968
Battalion	767	920

The 2d Battalion, 7th Cavalry served as airmobile infantry with the 1st Cavalry Division (Airmobile) in Vietnam.

Location	Service	Major Command
An Khe	Sept. 65 – June 67	3d Brigade, 1st Cavalry Division
An Khe – Bong Son	July 67 – Sept. 67	3d Brigade, 1st Cavalry Division
An Khe – Chu Lai	Oct. 67 – Jan. 68	3d Brigade, 1st Cavalry Division
An Khe – Phong Dien	Feb. 68 – April 68	3d Brigade, 1st Cavalry Division
An Khe – A Luoi	May 68	3d Brigade, 1st Cavalry Division
An Khe – Phong Dien	June 68 – July 68	3d Brigade, 1st Cavalry Division
An Khe – Phong Dien	Aug. 68 – Nov. 68	2d Brigade, 1st Cavalry Division
An Khe – An Loc	Dec. 68	2d Brigade, 1st Cavalry Division
An Khe	Jan. 69	2d Brigade, 1st Cavalry Division
An Khe – An Loc	Feb. 69	2d Brigade, 1st Cavalry Division
An Khe – Bien Hoa	March 69	3d Brigade, 1st Cavalry Division
An Khe – Quan Loi	April 69	3d Brigade, 1st Cavalry Division
Bien Hoa – Courtenay	May 69	3d Brigade, 1st Cavalry Division
Bien Hoa – Quan Loi	June 69 – Nov. 69	3d Brigade, 1st Cavalry Division
Bien Hoa – Phuoc Long	Dec. 69	3d Brigade, 1st Cavalry Division
Quan Loi	Jan. 70	3d Brigade, 1st Cavalry Division
Tay Ninh	Feb. 70 – March 70	1st Brigade, 1st Cavalry Division
Tay Ninh – Katum	April 70 – May 70	1st Brigade, 1st Cavalry Division
Cambodia	June 70	1st Brigade, 1st Cavalry Division
Bien Hoa	July 70 – May 71	1st Brigade, 1st Cavalry Division

5th Battalion, 7th Cavalry (Airmobile Infantry)

Arrived Vietnam: 20 August 1966
Departed Vietnam: 28 March 1971
Previous Station: Fort Carson

Authorized Strength	1966	1968
Battalion	767	920

The 5th Battalion, 7th Cavalry was activated 1 April 1966 at Fort Carson to provide a ninth maneuver airmobile infantry battalion to the 1st Cavalry Division (Airmobile) in Vietnam.

Location	Service	Major Command
An Khe	Aug. 66 – June 67	3d Brigade, 1st Cavalry Division
An Khe – Bong Son	July 67 – Sept. 67	3d Brigade, 1st Cavalry Division
An Khe – Bong Son	Oct. 67 – Feb. 68	2d Brigade, 1st Cavalry Division
An Khe – Phong Dien	March 68 – April 68	2d Brigade, 1st Cavalry Division
An Khe – Dong Ha	May 68	2d Brigade, 1st Cavalry Division
An Khe – Phong Dien	June 68 – July 68	2d Brigade, 1st Cavalry Division
An Khe – Phong Dien	Aug. 68 – Oct. 68	3d Brigade, 1st Cavalry Division
An Khe – Quan Loi	Nov. 68	3d Brigade, 1st Cavalry Division
An Khe – An Loc	Dec. 68 – Jan. 69	3d Brigade, 1st Cavalry Division
An Khe – Bien Hoa	Feb. 69	3d Brigade, 1st Cavalry Division
An Khe – An Loc	March 69	2d Brigade, 1st Cavalry Division
An Khe – Lai Khe	April 69 – May 69	2d Brigade, 1st Cavalry Division
Bien Hoa – Lai Khe	June 69 – Dec. 69	2d Brigade, 1st Cavalry Division
Bien Hoa – Phuoc Vinh	Jan. 70 – March 70	2d Brigade, 1st Cavalry Division
Bien Hoa – Song Be	April 70 – Aug. 70	2d Brigade, 1st Cavalry Division
Bien Hoa – Phuoc Long	Sept. 70 – Nov. 70	2d Brigade, 1st Cavalry Division
Song Be	Dec. 70 – March 71	2d Brigade, 1st Cavalry Division

1st Battalion, 8th Cavalry (Airborne Infantry) (Airmobile Infantry)

Arrived Vietnam: 15 September 1965
Departed Vietnam: 28 March 1971
Previous Station: Fort Benning

Authorized Strength	1966	1968
Battalion	767	920

The 1st Battalion, 8th Cavalry was initially airborne infantry fully parachutist-qualified serving the 1st Cavalry Division (Airmobile). In November 1966 the battalion reverted to normal airmobile infantry, its usual capacity, after the possibility of airborne operational utilization became too remote to justify their continued paratrooper qualification.

Location	Service	Major Command
An Khe	Sept. 65 – June 67	1st Brigade, 1st Cavalry Division
An Khe – Bong Son	July 67 – Jan. 68	1st Brigade, 1st Cavalry Division
An Khe – Phong Dien	Feb. 68 – April 68	1st Brigade, 1st Cavalry Division
An Khe – A Luoi	May 68	1st Brigade, 1st Cavalry Division
An Khe – Phong Dien	June 68 – Oct. 68	1st Brigade, 1st Cavalry Division
An Khe – Tay Ninh	Nov. 68 – Dec. 68	1st Brigade, 1st Cavalry Division

Location	Service	Major Command
An Khe – Cu Chi	Jan. 69	1st Brigade, 1st Cavalry Division
An Khe – Tay Ninh	Feb. 69 – March 69	1st Brigade, 1st Cavalry Division
An Khe – Quan Loi	April 69	1st Brigade, 1st Cavalry Division
Bien Hoa – Tay Ninh	May 69 – Dec. 69	1st Brigade, 1st Cavalry Division
Tay Ninh	Jan. 70	1st Brigade, 1st Cavalry Division
Quan Loi	Feb. 70 – March 70	3d Brigade, 1st Cavalry Division
Quan Loi – An Loc	April 70 – May 70	3d Brigade, 1st Cavalry Division
Quan Loi – Bo Duc	June 70	3d Brigade, 1st Cavalry Division
Quan Loi	July 70	3d Brigade, 1st Cavalry Division
Quan Loi – An Loc	Aug. 70	3d Brigade, 1st Cavalry Division
Gia Ray	Sept. 70 – March 71	3d Brigade, 1st Cavalry Division

2d Battalion, 8th Cavalry (Airborne Infantry) (Airmobile Infantry)

Arrived Vietnam: 15 September 1965
Departed Vietnam: 28 June 1972
Previous Station: Fort Benning

Authorized Strength	1966	1968	1971
Battalion	767	920	884

The 2d Battalion, 8th Cavalry was initially fully parachutist-qualified airborne infantry serving with the 1st Cavalry Division (Airmobile). In November 1966 the battalion reverted to normal airmobile infantry, its usual capacity, after the possibility of airborne operational utilization became too remote to justify continued paratrooper qualification.

Location	Service	Major Command
An Khe	Sept. 65 – June 67	1st Brigade, 1st Cavalry Division
An Khe – Bong Son	July 67 – Jan. 68	1st Brigade, 1st Cavalry Division
An Khe – Phong Dien	Feb. 68 – April 68	1st Brigade, 1st Cavalry Division
An Khe – A Luoi	May 68	1st Brigade, 1st Cavalry Division
An Khe – Phong Dien	June 68 – July 68	1st Brigade, 1st Cavalry Division
An Khe – Phong Dien	Aug. 68 – Nov. 68	2d Brigade, 1st Cavalry Division
An Khe – An Loc	Dec. 68	2d Brigade, 1st Cavalry Division
An Khe	Jan. 69	2d Brigade, 1st Cavalry Division
An Khe – An Loc	Feb. 69	2d Brigade, 1st Cavalry Division
An Khe – Tay Ninh	March 69	1st Brigade, 1st Cavalry Division
An Khe – Quan Loi	April 69	1st Brigade, 1st Cavalry Division
Bien Hoa – Tay Ninh	May 69 – Dec. 69	1st Brigade, 1st Cavalry Division
Tay Ninh	Jan. 70 – March 70	1st Brigade, 1st Cavalry Division

Tay Ninh – Katum	April 70 – May 70	1st Brigade, 1st Cavalry Division
Cambodia	June 70	1st Brigade, 1st Cavalry Division
Bien Hoa	July 70 – March 71	1st Brigade, 1st Cavalry Division
Gia Ray	April 71	3d Brigade, 1st Cavalry Division
Bien Hoa – Gia Ray	May 71	3d Brigade, 1st Cavalry Division
Bien Hoa	June 71 – June 72	3d Brigade, 1st Cavalry Division

Troop F, 8th Cavalry
(Air Cavalry)

Arrived Vietnam: 1 April 1968
Departed Vietnam: 26 February 1973
Previous Station: Vietnam

Authorized Strength	**1968**	**1971**
Troop	170	266

Troop F, 8th Cavalry was a separate air cavalry troop raised from assets of Troop C, 7th Squadron, 17th Cavalry to provide aerial reconnaissance for the 23d Infantry Division (AMERICAL). After the division's 123d Aviation Battalion departed Vietnam, the troop became part of the 196th Infantry Brigade in December 1971. When the brigade left in July 1972 the troop was attached to the 11th Aviation Group at Da Nang. In 1973 it was posted to Bien Hoa under the 12th Aviation Group.

1st Squadron, 9th Cavalry
(Aerial Reconnaissance)

Arrived Vietnam: 15 September 1965
Departed Vietnam: 28 June 1971
Previous Station: Fort Benning

Authorized Strength	**1966**	**1968**	**1971**
Squadron	792	792	851

The 1st Squadron, 9th Cavalry served as the reconnaissance cavalry squadron of the 1st Cavalry Division (Airmobile). It possessed three air cavalry troops, each with an aero-scout ("white") platoon, an aero-weapons ("red") platoon and an aero-rifle ("blue") platoon. The squadron also had a ground cavalry element, D Troop. On 10 April 1971 the assets of this squadron were turned over to the 1st Aviation Brigade prior to the division's departure from Vietnam.

Troop	Type	Squadron Service/Remarks
Tp A	Air Cav	Sept. 65 – June 71 Departed Vietnam
Tp B	Air Cav	Sept. 65 – June 71 Departed Vietnam
Tp C	Air Cav	Sept. 65 – June 71 Departed Vietnam
Tp D	Ground	Sept. 65 – June 71 Departed Vietnam
Tp E (Prov)	Air Cav	Aug. 70 – June 71 Inactivated
Tp F (Prov)	Air Cav	Aug. 70 – June 71 Inactivated

Troop F, 9th Cavalry
(Air Cavalry)

Arrived Vietnam: 30 June 1971
Departed Vietnam: 26 February 1973
Previous Station: Vietnam
Authorized Strength: 260 (1971)

Troop F, 9th Cavalry was an air cavalry troop raised to provide reconnaissance for the separate 3d Brigade, 1st Cavalry Division (Airmobile) after the bulk of the division departed Vietnam. It served under the aviation battalion then with the brigade, the 229th; in 1973 the troop was inactivated. It should be noted that Troop F was formed unofficially as Troop H, 16th Cavalry, a designation never approved by the Department of the Army, and remained known by this unauthorized title in Vietnam until about May 1972.

1st Squadron, 10th Cavalry
(Division Reconnaissance)

Arrived Vietnam: 4 October 1966
Departed Vietnam: 8 November 1971
Previous Station: Fort Lewis

Authorized Strength	**1966**	**1968**	**1971**
Squadron	184*	934	1,050

* Troop B only.

The 1st Squadron, 10th Cavalry was the divisional ground reconnaissance squadron of the 4th Infantry Division in Vietnam. It spent most of its service securing the road net in the Pleiku area. When the division departed in December 1970 the squadron was transferred to the control of I Field Force, Vietnam. In January 1971 it was attached to the 173d Airborne Brigade. In August 1971, when the brigade left, the squadron became part of Military Region 2. Troop D, its air cavalry troop, was transferred to the 7th Squadron, 17th Cavalry in July 1971.

Troop H, 10th Cavalry
(Air Cavalry)

Arrived Vietnam: 30 April 1972
Departed Vietnam: 26 February 1973
Previous Station: Hawaii
Authorized Strength: 206

Troop H, 10th Cavalry was an air cavalry troop raised from the assets of Troop C, 7th Squadron, 17th Cavalry. The troop served with the 17th Aviation Group at An Son while in Vietnam.

11th Armored Cavalry
(Armored Cavalry Regiment)

Arrived Vietnam: 8 September 1966
Departed Vietnam: 5 March 1971
Previous Station: Fort Meade

Authorized Strength	**1966**	**1968**	**1970**
Regiment	3,672	3,689	3,891

Commanders

Colonel William W. Cobb	Sept. 66
Colonel Roy W. Farley	May 67

Colonel Jack MacFarlane	Dec. 67
Colonel Leonard D. Holder*	March 68
Colonel Charles R. Gorder	March 68
Colonel George S. Patton	July 68
Colonel James H. Leach	April 69
Colonel Donn A. Starry	Dec. 69
Colonel John L. Gerrity	June 70
Colonel Wallace H. Nutting	Dec. 70

* Killed in helicopter accident 21 March 1968.

The 11th Armored Cavalry ("The Blackhorse Regiment") was constituted 2 February 1901 in the Regular Army as 11th Cavalry and organized 11 March 1901 at Fort Myer, Virginia. Its campaign participation credits include the Philippine Insurrection, Mexican Expedition, Normandy, northern France, Rhineland, Ardennes – Alsace and Central Europe of World War II. In 1957 the CARS (Combat Arms Regimental System) plan reorganizing most combat-type units was approved. However, the 11th Armored Cavalry was not reorganized under CARS and retained its regimental structure. Under the 1963 reorganization of the armored cavalry regiment, its organic elements reverted to the traditional cavalry designations of squadrons and troops, and an aviation company was added, to be replaced by an air cavalry troop in 1965. When the 11th Armored Cavalry arrived in Vietnam it had 51 M48A3

90mm-gun tanks, 296 M113 personnel carriers, 18 self-propelled howitzers (each of its three squadrons had an organic 155mm self-propelled howitzer battery), 9 M132 flamethrower vehicles and 48 helicopters. This constituted a change from its stateside mode tailored for the Vietnam theater. Also attached were an engineer and medical companies. It was committed to the III Corps Tactical Zone to provide mobile-shock mechanized support in the favorable terrain there and was engaged in all principal operations. It fought consistently in War Zone C of Tay Ninh Province. Often, however, the demands of road clearance and route security scattered the unit's assets to the point that the commander only controlled the regimental air cavalry troop. The M551 armored reconnaissance assault vehicle, Sheridans, first appeared with the 11th Armored Cavalry in January 1969. From April 1969 through June 1970 the regiment, without the detached 3d Squadron, was under the operational control of the 1st Cavalry Division and participated in the sweep across the Cambodian frontier. The 3d Squadron rejoined the unit for that mission. After further service with II Field Force, Vietnam the 11th Armored Cavalry, minus the 2d Squadron, became attached to the 25th Infantry Division from October – November 1970. "The Blackhorse Regiment" left Vietnam as part of Increment VI of the U.S. Army withdrawal, leaving its 2d Squadron behind to rejoin it in April 1972. It should be noted that while the unit was often designated the 11th Armored Cavalry Regiment in Vietnam, the use of the word Regiment as part of the title is completely unauthorized.

Elements	Vietnam Service	Authorized Strengths		
		1966	1968	1970
11th Armored Cavalry Headquarters & HQ Troop	8 Sept. 66 – 5 March 71	201	201	223
1st Squadron, 11th Armored Cavalry	8 Sept. 66 – 5 March 71	1,104	1,104	1,146
2d Squadron, 11th Armored Cavalry	8 Sept. 66 – 6 April 72	1,104	1,104	1,165 (1971)
3d Squadron, 11th Armored Cavalry	12 Aug. 66 – 5 March 71	1,104	1,104	1,146
Air Cavalry Troop, 11th Armored Cavalry	3 Dec. 66 – 20 March 72	159	176	211

11th Armored Cavalry Headquarters Locations in Vietnam

Bien Hoa	Sept. 66 – Nov. 66
Long Binh	Dec. 66 – Feb. 67
Xuan Loc	March 67 – Jan. 69
Lai Khe	Feb. 69
Long Giao	March 69 – Sept. 69
Bien Hoa	Oct. 69 – June 70
Di An	July 70 – March 71

Units Attached to the 11th Armored Cavalry

919th Engineer Company
37th Medical Company

11th Armored Cavalry Internal Organization

Unit	Type
HHT, 11th Arm Cav	HQ
HHT, 1st Squadron	HQ
Tp A	Arm Cav
Tp B	Arm Cav
Tp C	Arm Cav
Tp D	Tank
Howitzer Battery	Artillery
HHT, 2d Squadron	HQ
Tp E	Arm Cav
Tp F	Arm Cav
Tp G	Arm Cav
Tp H	Tank
Howitzer Battery	Artillery
HHT, 3d Squadron	HQ
Tp I	Arm Cav
Tp K	Arm Cav
Tp L	Arm Cav
Tp M	Tank
Howitzer Battery	Artillery
11th Arm Cav – Air Cav Tp	Air Cav

Detailed Service of the 1st Squadron, 11th Armored Cavalry

Location	Service	Major Command
Bien Hoa	Sept. 66 – Nov. 66	11th Arm Cav
Long Binh	Dec. 66 – Feb. 67	11th Arm Cav
Xuan Loc	March 67 – Jan. 68	11th Arm Cav
Xuan Loc – Bien Hoa	Feb. 68	11th Arm Cav
Xuan Loc – Bear Cat	March 68 – May 68	11th Arm Cav
Xuan Loc – Ben Luc	June 68	11th Arm Cav
Xuan Loc – Long Binh	July 68 – Oct. 68	11th Arm Cav
Xuan Loc – Bien Hoa	Nov. 68 – Jan. 69	11th Arm Cav
Lai Khe – Bien Hoa	Feb. 69	11th Arm Cav
Long Giao – Bien Hoa	March 69	11th Arm Cav
Long Giao – Bien Hoa	April 69	1st Cav Div
Long Giao – Courtenay	May 69	1st Cav Div
Long Giao – An Loc	June 69	1st Cav Div
Long Giao – Quan Loi	July 69 – Sept. 69	1st Cav Div
Bien Hoa – An Khe	Oct. 69 – Nov. 69	1st Cav Div
Bien Hoa	Dec. 69	1st Cav Div
Bien Hoa – Quan Loi	Jan. 70 – May 70	1st Cav Div
Cambodia	June 70	1st Cav Div
Di An	July 70 – Aug. 70	II Field Force, Vietnam
Di An	Sept. 70	11th Arm Cav
Di An	Oct. 70 – Nov. 70	25th Inf Div
Di An	Dec. 70 – March 71	II Field Force, Vietnam

Detailed Service of the 2d Squadron, 11th Armored Cavalry

Location	Service	Major Command
Bien Hoa	Sept. 66 – Nov. 66	11th Armored Cavalry
Long Binh	Dec. 66 – Feb. 67	11th Armored Cavalry
Xuan Loc	March 67 – April 67	11th Armored Cavalry
Chu Lai	May 67 – Aug. 67	11th Armored Cavalry*
Xuan Loc	Sept. 67	Task Force OREGON
Xuan Loc	Oct. 67 – Dec. 67	11th Armored Cavalry
Xuan Loc – Bo Duc	Jan. 68	11th Armored Cavalry
Xuan Loc – Bien Hoa	Feb. 68	11th Armored Cavalry
Xuan Loc – Bear Cat	March 68 – May 68	11th Armored Cavalry
Xuan Loc – Ben Luc	June 68	11th Armored Cavalry
Xuan Loc – Long Binh	July 68 – Oct. 68	11th Armored Cavalry
Xuan Loc – Bien Hoa	Nov. 68 – Jan. 69	11th Armored Cavalry
Lai Khe – Bien Hoa	Feb. 69	11th Armored Cavalry
Long Giao – Bien Hoa	March 69	11th Armored Cavalry
Long Giao – Bien Hoa	April 69	1st Cavalry Division
Long Giao – Courtenay	May 69	1st Cavalry Division
Long Giao – An Loc	June 69	1st Cavalry Division
Long Giao – Quan Loi	July 69 – Sept. 69	1st Cavalry Division
Bien Hoa – An Khe	Oct. 69 – Nov. 69	1st Cavalry Division
Bien Hoa	Dec. 69	1st Cavalry Division
Bien Hoa – Quan Loi	Jan. 70 – May 70	1st Cavalry Division
Cambodia	June 70	1st Cavalry Division
Di An	July 70 – Aug. 70	1st Cavalry Division
Di An	Sept. 70	11th Armored Cavalry
Di An	Oct. 70 – Feb. 71	1st Cavalry Division
Ap Dai Mai	March 71 – April 71	1st Cavalry Division
Long Binh – Rung Cay	May 71	Third Regional Assistance Command (TRAC)
Long Binh – Rung Cay	June 71 – Sept. 71	Hau Nghia Province Command
Long Binh – Rung Cay	Oct. 71 – Dec. 71	25th Army of the Republic of Vietnam Infantry Division
Long Binh – Rung Cay	Jan. 72 – April 72	3d Brigade, 1st Cavalry Division

* Squadron on duty with Task Force OREGON.

Detailed Service of the 3d Squadron, 11th Armored Cavalry

Location	Service	Major Command
Bien Hoa	Aug. 66 – Nov. 66	11th Armored Cavalry
Long Binh	Dec. 66 – Feb. 67	11th Armored Cavalry
Xuan Loc	March 67 – Jan. 68	11th Armored Cavalry
Xuan Loc – Bien Hoa	Feb. 68	11th Armored Cavalry
Xuan Loc – Bear Cat	March 68 – May 68	11th Armored Cavalry
Xuan Loc – Ben Luc	June 68	11th Armored Cavalry
Xuan Loc – Long Binh	July 68 – Oct. 68	11th Armored Cavalry
Xuan Loc – Bien Hoa	Nov. 68 – Jan. 69	11th Armored Cavalry
Lai Khe – Bien Hoa	Feb. 69	11th Armored Cavalry
Long Giao – Bien Hoa	March 69	11th Armored Cavalry
Long Giao – Lai Khe	April 69 – June 69	1st Infantry Division
Long Giao – Courtenay	July 69 – Aug. 69	199th Infantry Brigade
Lai Khe	Sept. 69	1st Infantry Division
Bien Hoa – An Loc	Oct. 69 – Nov. 69	1st Infantry Division
Bien Hoa	Dec. 69	1st Infantry Division
Bien Hoa – Quan Loi	Jan. 70 – May 70	1st Cavalry Division
Cambodia	June 70	1st Cavalry Division
Di An	July 70 – Aug. 70	II Field Force, Vietnam
Di An	Sept. 70	11th Armored Cavalry
Di An	Oct. 70 – Nov. 70	25th Infantry Division
Di An	Dec. 70 – March 71	II Field Force, Vietnam

1st Battalion, 12th Cavalry (Airborne Infantry) (Airmobile Infantry)

Arrived Vietnam: 15 September 1965
Departed Vietnam: 26 June 1972
Previous Station: Fort Benning

Authorized Strength	1966	1968	1971
Battalion		767	920	884

The 1st Battalion, 12th Cavalry was initially airborne infantry, fully parachutist-qualified, serving the 1st Cavalry Division (Airmobile). In November 1966 the battalion reverted to normal airmobile infantry, its usual capacity, after the possibility of airborne operational utilization became too remote to justify their continued paratrooper qualification.

Location	Service	Major Command
An Khe	Sept. 65 – June 67	1st Brigade, 1st Cavalry Division
An Khe – Bong Son	July 67 – Jan. 68	1st Brigade, 1st Cavalry Division
An Khe – Phong Dien	Feb. 68 – April 68	1st Brigade, 1st Cavalry Division
An Khe – A Luoi	May 68	1st Brigade, 1st Cavalry Division
An Khe – Phong Dien	June 68 – Oct. 68	1st Brigade, 1st Cavalry Division
An Khe – Tay Ninh	Nov. 68 – Dec. 68	1st Brigade, 1st Cavalry Division
An Khe – Cu Chi	Jan. 69	1st Brigade, 1st Cavalry Division
An Khe – Tay Ninh	Feb. 69	1st Brigade, 1st Cavalry Division
An Khe – Bien Hoa	March 69	3d Brigade, 1st Cavalry Division
An Khe – Quan Loi	April 69	3d Brigade, 1st Cavalry Division
Bien Hoa – Courtenay	May 69	3d Brigade, 1st Cavalry Division
Bien Hoa – Quan Loi	June 69 – Nov. 69	3d Brigade, 1st Cavalry Division

Bien Hoa – Phuoc Long	Dec. 69	3d Brigade, 1st Cavalry Division
Quan Loi	Jan. 70	3d Brigade, 1st Cavalry Division
Bien Hoa – Phuoc Vinh	Feb. 70 – March 70	2d Brigade 1st Cavalry Division
Bien Hoa – Song Be	April 70 – May 70	2d Brigade, 1st Cavalry Division
Cambodia	June 70	2d Brigade 1st Cavalry Division
Bien Hoa – Song Be	July 70 – Aug. 70	2d Brigade, 1st Cavalry Division
Bien Hoa – Phuoc Long	Sept. 70 – Nov. 70	2d Brigade, 1st Cavalry Division
Song Be	Dec. 70 – March 71	2d Brigade, 1st Cavalry Division
Gia Ray	April 71	3d Brigade, 1st Cavalry Division
Bien Hoa – Gia Ray	May 71	3d Brigade, 1st Cavalry Division
Bien Hoa	June 71 – June 72	3d Brigade, 1st Cavalry Division

2d Battalion, 12th Cavalry (Airmobile Infantry)

Arrived Vietnam: 15 September 1965
Departed Vietnam: 27 March 1971
Previous Station: Fort Benning

Authorized Strength	1966	1968
Battalion	767	920

The 2d Battalion, 12th Cavalry served the 1st Cavalry Division (Airmobile) as airmobile infantry in Vietnam.

Location	Service	Major Command
An Khe	Sept. 65 – June 67	2d Brigade, 1st Cavalry Division
An Khe – Bong Son	July 67 – Sept. 67	2d Brigade, 1st Cavalry Division
An Khe – Chu Lai	Oct. 67 – Jan. 68	3d Brigade, 1st Cavalry Division
An Khe – Phong Dien	Feb. 68 – April 68	3d Brigade, 1st Cavalry Division
An Khe – A Luoi	May 68	3d Brigade, 1st Cavalry Division
An Khe – Phong Dien	June 68 – Oct. 68	3d Brigade, 1st Cavalry Division
An Khe – Quan Loi	Nov. 68	3d Brigade, 1st Cavalry Division
An Khe – An Loc	Dec. 68 – Jan. 69	3d Brigade, 1st Cavalry Division
An Khe – Bien Hoa	Feb. 69	3d Brigade, 1st Cavalry Division
An Khe – Tay Ninh	March 69	1st Brigade, 1st Cavalry Division
An Khe – Quan Loi	April 69	1st Brigade, 1st Cavalry Division
Bien Hoa – Tay Ninh	May 69 – Dec. 69	1st Brigade, 1st Cavalry Division
Tay Ninh	Jan. 70	1st Brigade, 1st Cavalry Division
Bien Hoa – Phuoc Vinh	Feb. 70 – March 70	2d Brigade, 1st Cavalry Division
Bien Hoa – Song Be	April 70 – May 70	2d Brigade, 1st Cavalry Division

Cambodia	June 70	2d Brigade, 1st Cavalry Division
Bien Hoa – Song Be	July 70 – Aug. 70	2d Brigade, 1st Cavalry Division
Bien Hoa – Phuoc Long	Sept. 70 – Nov. 70	2d Brigade, 1st Cavalry Division
Song Be	Dec. 70 – Feb. 71	2d Brigade, 1st Cavalry Division
Gia Ray	March 71	3d Brigade, 1st Cavalry Division

Troop A, 4th Squadron, 12th Cavalry (Reconnaissance)

Arrived Vietnam: 27 July 1968
Departed Vietnam: 30 November 1971
Previous Station: Fort Carson
Authorized Strength: 214

Troop A, 4th Squadron, 12th Cavalry served as the ground cavalry reconnaissance troop assigned to the 1st Brigade, 5th Infantry Division (Mechanized) in Vietnam at Quang Tri. When the brigade departed in August 1971 the troop was attached to the 3d Squadron, 5th Cavalry at Hue – Phu Bai with the 101st Airborne Division (Airmobile).

Troop G, 15th Cavalry (Armored Cavalry)

Arrived Vietnam: 15 December 1971
Departed Vietnam: 1 January 1972
Previous Station: Vietnam
Authorized Strength: 166 (1971)

Troop G, 15th Cavalry was a security force equipped with M551 Sheridan assault vehicles.

Troop C, 16th Cavalry (Air Cavalry)

Arrived Vietnam: 20 March 1970
Departed Vietnam: 26 February 1973
Previous Station: Vietnam
Authorized Strength: 266 (1971)

Troop C, 16th Cavalry was an air cavalry troop raised from the assets of Troop D, 1st Squadron, 4th Cavalry in the 1st Aviation Battalion. The troop later served the 7th Squadron, 1st Cavalry; the 13th Aviation Battalion; and the 164th Aviation Group at Can Tho.

Troop B, 1st Squadron, 17th Cavalry (Reconnaissance)

Arrived Vietnam: 18 February 1968
Departed Vietnam: 11 December 1969
Previous Station: Fort Bragg
Authorized Strength: 201 (1968)

Troop B, 1st Squadron, 17th Cavalry was the ground reconnaissance element of the 3d Brigade Task Force, 82d Airborne Division in Vietnam.

2d Squadron, 17th Cavalry
(Division Reconnaissance)
(Aerial Reconnaissance)

Arrived Vietnam: 12 December 1967
Departed Vietnam: 8 February 1972
Previous Station: Fort Campbell

Authorized Strength	1966	1968	1971
Squadron	151 *	318	1,022

* Troop A only.

The 2d Squadron, 17th Cavalry was originally deployed to Vietnam as the ground cavalry squadron of the 101st Airborne Division, but as the division changed to an airmobile mode the squadron was converted to an air cavalry status during the period December 1968 – June 1969. Troops A, B and C (airmobile aviation) thus joined the squadron in March 1969 to complete the conversion. It should be noted that the previous Troop A (ground reconnaissance) had been serving the 1st Brigade of the division since 29 July 1965. The entire squadron was involved in intense aerial combat during the Operation LAM SON 719 excursion into Laos, when the helicopters supported the South Vietnamese Army's drive and retreat directly. This action took place between February and April 1971. In 1970 – 71 the squadron raised provisional air cavalry Troops E and F.

3d Squadron, 17th Cavalry
(Air Cavalry)

Arrived Vietnam: 30 October 1967
Departed Vietnam: 30 April 1972
Previous Station: Fort Knox

Authorized Strength	1968	1971
Squadron	850	1,037

The 3d Squadron, 17th Cavalry was part of the 12th Aviation Group during its service in Vietnam, primarily stationed at Di An. It was responsible for air cavalry support in the western part of III Corps Tactical Zone. On 20 July 1970 it was placed under the control of II Field Force, Vietnam. In January 1971 Troop C was transferred to the 7th Squadron, 1st Cavalry. Troops A, B and D departed Vietnam together in April 1972 and Troop C rejoined them for the redeployment. In late 1970 the squadron was placed under the operational control of the 1st Cavalry Division and, when combined with the division's 1st Squadron, 9th Cavalry, enabled the 1st Cavalry Division to form an ad hoc air cavalry brigade — a highly successful organizational innovation.

Troop	Type	Squadron Service/Remarks
Tp A	Air Cav	Oct. 67 – April 72 Departed Vietnam
Tp B	Air Cav	Oct. 67 – April 72 Departed Vietnam
Tp C	Air Cav	Oct. 67 – Dec. 70 Transferred to 7th Squadron, 1st Cavalry
Tp D	Ground	Oct. 67 – April 72 Departed Vietnam

Troop D, 17th Cavalry
(Reconnaissance)
(Air Cavalry)

First Tour:
Arrived Vietnam: 13 December 1966
Departed Vietnam: 12 October 1970
Previous Station: Fort Benning

Second Tour:
Arrived Vietnam: 15 December 1971
Departed Vietnam: 20 March 1972
Previous Station: Vietnam

Third Tour:
Arrived Vietnam: 30 April 1972
Departed Vietnam: 26 February 1973
Previous Station: Vietnam

Authorized Strength	1968	1971
Troop	195	210

Troop D, 17th Cavalry was initially in Vietnam as the ground reconnaissance element of the 199th Infantry Brigade (Light). The troop was raised again as an air cavalry troop from assets of Troop D, 3d Squadron, 5th Cavalry to support the 101st Airborne Division (Airmobile). Finally, Troop D, 17th Cavalry was activated in Vietnam using assets of Troop D, 1st Squadron, 1st Cavalry to serve the 11th Aviation Group at Da Nang.

Troop E, 17th Cavalry
(Reconnaissance)

Arrived Vietnam: 6 May 1965
Departed Vietnam: 14 August 1971
Previous Station: Okinawa

Authorized Strength	1966	1968	1970
Troop	171	201	210

Troop E, 17th Cavalry was the ground reconnaissance element assigned to the 173d Airborne Brigade when it entered Vietnam. The troop was colocated with the brigade throughout its service in Vietnam.

Troop F, 17th Cavalry
(Reconnaissance)

Arrived Vietnam: 26 August 1966
Departed Vietnam: 31 March 1972
Previous Station: Fort Devens

Authorized Strength	1966	1968	1970
Troop	151	195	210

Troop F, 17th Cavalry was the ground reconnaissance element of the 196th Infantry Brigade (Light) and was colocated with the brigade throughout its service in Vietnam.

7th Squadron, 17th Cavalry
(Air Cavalry)

Arrived Vietnam: 28 October 1967
Departed Vietnam: 18 April 1972
Previous Station: Fort Knox

Authorized Strength	1968	1971
Squadron	850	1,037

The 7th Squadron, 17th Cavalry was attached to the 17th Aviation Group at Pleiku. It moved to Dak To in March 1968 and in May went back to Pleiku. In September 1969 the squadron relocated to Kontum, moved to Dragon Mountain in November and in January 1970 returned to Pleiku. In March 1971 it went to Qui Nhon and in late 1971 was posted to An Son. The following troops and companies served with the squadron at one time or another during its service in Vietnam:

Troop or Company	Type	Squadron Service/Remarks
Tp A	Air Cav	Oct. 67 – July 71/ Transferred to 10th Avn Bn
Tp B	Air Cav	Oct. 67 – July 71/ Transferred to 52d Avn Bn
Tp C	Air Cav	July 68 – April 72/ Assets transferred to Tp H, 10th Cav
Tp D	Ground	Oct. 67 – July 71/ Transferred to 52d Avn Bn
61st Avn Co	AHC	July 71 – March 72/ Departed Vietnam
129th Avn Co	AHC	July 71 – April 72/ Transferred to 17th Avn Gp
180th Avn Co	ASH	March 72 – April 72/ Transferred to 17th Avn Gp
Tp H, 10th Cav	Air Cav	April 72/ Transferred to 17th Avn Gp
Tp D, 1st Sqdn, 10th Cav	Air Cav	July 71 – Feb. 72/ Departed Vietnam

Troop K, 17th Cavalry
(Air Cavalry)

Arrived Vietnam: 1 October 1970
Departed Vietnam: December 1970
Previous Station: Vietnam
Authorized Strength: 266 (1970)

Troop K, 17th Cavalry served with the 17th Aviation Group at Nha Trang.

Unauthorized

39th Cavalry Platoon
(Air Cushion Vehicle)

Arrived Vietnam: 1 May 1970
Departed Vietnam: September 1970
Previous Station: Vietnam
Authorized Strength: 35 (1970)

The 39th Cavalry Platoon was activated 1 May 1970 using assets from a provisional air-cushion-vehicle unit called the "Airboat Platoon" that had been operating in the Delta since May 1968. It served with the 3d Brigade, 9th Infantry Division.

Troop H, 17th Cavalry
(Reconnaissance)
(Air Cavalry)

First Tour:
Arrived Vietnam: 22 October 1967
Departed Vietnam: 1 October 1971
Previous Station: Fort Hood

Second Tour:
Arrived Vietnam: 30 April 1972
Departed Vietnam: 26 February 1973
Previous Station: Vietnam

Authorized Strength	1968	1970
Troop	198	210

Troop H, 17th Cavalry was initially the ground reconnaissance element of the 198th Infantry Brigade (Light). It was reraised in Vietnam from assets of Troop B, 7th Squadron, 17th Cavalry and served the 17th Aviation Group at Pleiku.

Air Cavalry Aviation Callsigns in Vietnam

Unit	Callsign*
Tp D, 1st Sqdn, 1st Cav	Saber Shackers
HHT, 7th Sqdn, 1st Cav	Black Hawk
Tp A, 7th Sqdn, 1st Cav	Apaches
Tp B, 7th Sqdn, 1st Cav	Dutchmasters
Tp C, 7th Sqdn, 1st Cav	Commanches, Flying Circus
Tp D, 1st Sqdn, 4th Cav	Mustangs, Low-Level Hell
Tp D, 3d Sqdn, 4th Cav	Centaurs
Tp F, 4th Cav	Skeeters
Tp D, 3d Sqdn, 5th Cav	The Long Knives
Tp F, 8th Cav	Blue Ghost
HHT, 1st Sqdn, 9th Cav	Light Horse
Tp A, 1st Sqdn, 9th Cav	Brave Apaches, Apache Headhunters
Tp B, 1st Sqdn, 9th Cav	Flashing Sabres
Tp C, 1st Sqdn, 9th Cav	Dashing Cavaliers, Blue Annihilators
Tp F, 9th Cav (also known as Tp H, 16th Cav)	Scouts, Sabre, Scouts Kill
Tp D, 1st Sqdn, 10th Cav	Shamrock
Tp H, 10th Cav	
Air Cav Tp, 11th Arm Cav	Thunderhorse, Scalphunter, Eyes With Teeth
Tp C, 16th Cav	Darkhorse, The Four Horsemen
HHT, 2d Sqdn, 17th Cav	
Tp A, 2d Sqdn, 17th Cav	Assaulters
Tp B, 2d Sqdn, 17th Cav	Banshees
Tp C, 2d Sqdn, 17th Cav	Condors
HHT, 3d Sqdn, 17th Cav	Red Horse
Tp A, 3d Sqdn, 17th Cav	Silver Spur
Tp B, 3d Sqdn, 17th Cav	Burning Stogie
Tp C, 3d Sqdn, 17th Cav	Charlie Horse, Crusaders
Tp D, 17th Cav	

HHT, 7th Sqdn, 17th Cav   Ruthless Riders
   Tp A, 7th Sqdn, 17th Cav   Ruthless Alpha
   Tp B, 7th Sqdn, 17th Cav   Ruthless Bravo
   Tp C, 7th Sqdn, 17th Cav   Ruthless Charlie, Yellow Scarf
Tp H, 17th Cav
Tp K, 17th Cav

* This list is admittedly an incomplete compilation of aviation
callsigns encountered during the research for this book. It
represents aviation callsigns used in Vietnam that were associated with either the specific unit or its component gunship
platoon.

Chapter 12

Infantry

2d Battalion, 1st Infantry (Light Infantry)

Arrived Vietnam: 26 August 1966
Departed Vietnam: 29 June 1972
Previous Station: Fort Devens

Authorized Strength	1966	1968	1970
Battalion	778	920	920

The 2d Battalion, 1st Infantry, was part of the 196th Infantry Brigade (Light) in Vietnam and was one of the last infantry battalions to depart Vietnam. It was assigned to the 23d Infantry Division (AMERICAL) 15 February 1969 – 1 November 1971.

Location	Service	Major Command
Tay Ninh	Aug. 66 – April 67	196th Infantry Brigade
Chu Lai	May 67 – Aug. 67	196th Infantry Brigade*
Chu Lai	Sept. 67 – Feb. 68	196th Infantry Brigade
Tam Ky	March 68 – April 68	196th Infantry Brigade
Phong Dien	May 68	196th Infantry Brigade
Hoi An	June 68 – July 68	196th Infantry Brigade
Chu Lai/Tam Ky	Aug. 68 – Nov. 68	196th Infantry Brigade
Chu Lai/Xuyen Tay	Dec. 68 – Jan. 69	196th Infantry Brigade
Chu Lai/Xuyen Tay	Feb. 69 – July 69	23d Infantry Division (AMERICAL)
Chu Lai/Nuong Xuan	Aug. 69	23d Infantry Division (AMERICAL)
Chu Lai/Thang Binh	Sept. 69 – Dec. 69	23d Infantry Division (AMERICAL)
Chu Lai/Tuang Dong	Jan. 70 – July 70	23d Infantry Division (AMERICAL)
Chu Lai/Tam Ky	Aug. 70	23d Infantry Division (AMERICAL)
Tam Ky	Sept. 70 – April 71	23d Infantry Division (AMERICAL)
Da Nang	May 71 – Nov. 71	23d Infantry Division (AMERICAL)
Da Nang	Dec. 71 – June 72	196th Infantry Brigade

* With duty in Task Force OREGON.

3d Battalion, 1st Infantry (Light Infantry)

Arrived Vietnam: 19 December 1967
Departed Vietnam: 29 October 1971
Previous Station: Hawaii
Authorized Strength: 920

The 3d Battalion, 1st Infantry was part of the 11th Infantry Brigade (Light) and on 15 February 1969 was transferred to the 23d Infantry Division (AMERICAL).

Location	Service	Major Command
Duc Pho	Dec. 67 – Feb. 69	11th Infantry Brigade
Duc Pho	Feb. 69 – March 71	23d Infantry Division (AMERICAL)
Duc Pho/Dong Ha	April 71	23d Infantry Division (AMERICAL)*
Duc Pho	May 71 – June 71	23d Infantry Division (AMERICAL)
Chu Lai/The Loi	July 71	23d Infantry Division (AMERICAL)
The Loi	Aug. 71 – Oct. 71	23d Infantry Division (AMERICAL)

* Under operational control of 101st Airborne Division (Airmobile).

1st Battalion, 2d Infantry
(Infantry)

Arrived Vietnam: 17 October 1965
Departed Vietnam: 7 April 1970
Previous Station: Fort Devens

Authorized Strength	1966	1968	1970
Battalion	829	971	920

The 1st Battalion, 2d Infantry was assigned to the 1st Infantry Division in Vietnam.

Location	Service	Major Command
Bien Hoa	Oct. 65 – Nov. 65	3d Brigade, 1st Infantry Division
Ben Cat	Dec. 65 – Jan. 66	3d Brigade, 1st Infantry Division
Lai Khe	Feb. 66 – Nov. 66	3d Brigade, 1st Infantry Division
Phuoc Vinh	Dec. 66 – June 67	1st Brigade, 1st Infantry Division
Phuoc Vinh/Lai Khe	July 67 – Feb. 68	1st Brigade, 1st Infantry Division
Quan Loi/An Loc	March 68 – May 68	1st Brigade, 1st Infantry Division
Quan Loi	June 68 – Oct. 68	1st Brigade, 1st Infantry Division
Quan Loi/Loc Ninh	Nov. 68	1st Brigade, 1st Infantry Division
Quan Loi/Lai Khe	Dec. 68 – March 69	1st Brigade, 1st Infantry Division
Quan Loi	April 69	1st Brigade, 1st Infantry Division
Quan Loi/Song Be	May 69 – June 69	1st Brigade, 1st Infantry Division
Quan Loi/Dau Tieng	July 69 – Aug. 69	1st Brigade, 1st Infantry Division
Dau Tieng/Ben Cat	Sept. 69 – Nov. 69	1st Brigade, 1st Infantry Division
Phuoc Vinh	Dec. 69	1st Brigade, 1st Infantry Division
Dau Tieng	Jan. 70 – Feb. 70	1st Brigade, 1st Infantry Division
Lai Khe	March 70	1st Brigade, 1st Infantry Division
Di An	April 70	1st Brigade, 1st Infantry Division

2d Battalion, 2d Infantry
(Mechanized Infantry)

Arrived Vietnam: 17 October 1965
Departed Vietnam: 8 April 1970
Previous Station: Fort Devens

Authorized Strength	1966	1968	1970
Battalion	920	920	907

The 2d Battalion, 2d Infantry deployed to Vietnam as light infantry with the 1st Infantry Division and became fully mechanized by January 1967.

Location	Service	Major Command
Bien Hoa	Oct. 65 – Nov. 65	3d Brigade, 1st Infantry Division*

Ben Cat	Dec. 65 – Jan. 66	3d Brigade, 1st Infantry Division*
Lai Khe	Feb. 66 – May 67	3d Brigade, 1st Infantry Division*
Ben Cat	June 67	3d Brigade, 1st Infantry Division
Lai Khe	July 67 – March 68	3d Brigade, 1st Infantry Division
Lai Khe/Hoc Mon	April 68 – May 68	3d Brigade, 1st Infantry Division
Lai Khe	June 68 – Feb. 69	3d Brigade, 1st Infantry Division
Lai Khe	March 69	1st Cavalry Division (Airmobile)
Lai Khe	April 69 – Aug. 69	3d Brigade, 1st Infantry Division
Lai Khe/Chon Thanh	Sept. 69	3d Brigade, 1st Infantry Division
Lai Khe/Ben Cat	Oct. 69 – Nov. 69	3d Brigade, 1st Infantry Division
Lai Khe	Dec. 69 – Jan. 70	3d Brigade, 1st Infantry Division
Dau Tieng	Feb. 70	1st Brigade, 1st Infantry Division
Lai Khe	March 70	1st Brigade, 1st Infantry Division
Di An	April 70	1st Brigade, 1st Infantry Division

* Dismounted until November 1966 – January 1967 time frame.

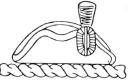

2d Battalion, 3d Infantry
(Light Infantry)

Arrived Vietnam: 10 December 1966
Departed Vietnam: 12 October 1970
Previous Station: Fort Benning
Authorized Strength: 920

The 2d Battalion, 3d Infantry ("The Old Guard") was part of the separate 199th Infantry Brigade (Light) during its service in Vietnam.

Location	Service	Major Command
Song Be	Dec. 66 – Feb. 67	199th Infantry Brigade
Long Binh	March 67	199th Infantry Brigade
Bien Hoa	April 67 – June 67	199th Infantry Brigade
Long Binh/Cat Lai	July 67 – Sept. 67	199th Infantry Brigade
Long Binh/Phu My	Oct. 67 – Jan. 68	199th Infantry Brigade
Long Binh/Saigon	Feb. 68	199th Infantry Brigade
Gao Ho Nai/Bien Hoa	March 68	199th Infantry Brigade
Gao Ho Nai	April 68 – June 68	199th Infantry Brigade
Long Binh	July 68 – Oct. 68	199th Infantry Brigade
Long Binh/Saigon	Nov. 68 – June 69	199th Infantry Brigade
Long Binh/Courtenay	July 69 – Aug. 69	199th Infantry Brigade
Long Binh/Xuan Loc	Sept. 69 – July 70	199th Infantry Brigade
Long Binh/Gia Ray	Aug. 70 – Sept. 70	199th Infantry Brigade
Long Binh	Oct. 70	199th Infantry Brigade

4th Battalion, 3d Infantry
(Light Infantry)

Arrived Vietnam: 20 December 1967
Departed Vietnam: 5 November 1971
Previous Station: Hawaii
Authorized Strength: 920

The 4th Battalion, 3d Infantry ("The Old Guard") was part of the 11th Infantry Brigade, transferring to the command of the 23d

Infantry Division (AMERICAL) on 15 February 1969. While in the division, the battalion was switched from the 11th to the 198th Infantry Brigade's control about August 1971.

Location	Service	Major Command
Duc Pho	Dec. 67 – Jan. 69	11th Infantry Brigade
Duc Pho	Feb. 69 – March 71	23d Infantry Division (AMERICAL)
Duc Pho/Dong Ha	April 71	23d Infantry Division (AMERICAL)
Duc Pho	May 71 – June 71	23d Infantry Division (AMERICAL)
Chu Lai/The Loi	July 71	23d Infantry Division (AMERICAL)
Chu Lai	Aug. 71 – Nov. 71	198th Infantry Brigade

1st Battalion, 5th Infantry (Mechanized Infantry)

Arrived Vietnam: 19 January 1966
Departed Vietnam: 30 April 1971
Previous Station: Hawaii

Authorized Strength	1966	1968	1970
Battalion	899	907	907

The 1st Battalion, 5th Infantry served with the 25th Infantry Division, becoming fully mechanized about August 1966 in Vietnam.

Location	Service	Major Command
Cu Chi	Jan. 66 – March 68	2d Brigade, 25th Infantry Division*
Cu Chi/Tay Ninh	April 68	2d Brigade, 25th Infantry Division
Cu Chi	May 68	2d Brigade, 25th Infantry Division
Cu Chi/Hoc Mon	June 68 – July 68	2d Brigade, 25th Infantry Division
Cu Chi	Aug. 68 – Jan. 70	2d Brigade, 25th Infantry Division
Cu Chi/Dau Tieng	Feb. 70	2d Brigade, 25th Infantry Division
Long Thanh/ Phuoc Hiep	March 70 – April 70	2d Brigade, 25th Infantry Division
Thien Ngon	May 70	2d Brigade, 25th Infantry Division
Tay Ninh	June 70	2d Brigade, 25th Infantry Division
Xuan Loc	July 70	2d Brigade, 25th Infantry Division
Xuan Loc/Xa Cam	Aug. 70 – Oct. 70	2d Brigade, 25th Infantry Division
Xuan Loc	Nov. 70 – Dec. 70	2d Brigade, 25th Infantry Division
Long Binh/Xuan Loc	Jan. 71 – April 71	2d Brigade, 25th Infantry Division

* Dismounted upon initial arrival in Vietnam.

1st Battalion, 6th Infantry (Light Infantry)

Arrived Vietnam: 22 October 1967
Departed Vietnam: 21 November 1971
Previous Station: Fort Hood
Authorized Strength: 920

The 1st Battalion, 6th Infantry ("The Regulars") served with the 198th Infantry Brigade (Light) and came under command of the

23d Infantry Division (AMERICAL) on 15 February 1969. On 1½ November 1971 the battalion became part of the 196th Infantry Brigade.

Location	Service	Major Command
Duc Pho	Oct. 67 – Nov. 67	198th Infantry Brigade
Chu Lai	Dec. 67 – Oct. 68	198th Infantry Brigade
Tam Ky	Nov. 68	198th Infantry Brigade
Chu Lai	Dec. 68 – Jan. 69	198th Infantry Brigade
Chu Lai	Feb. 69 – Nov. 69	23d Infantry Division (AMERICAL)
Chu Lai/Dong Le	Dec. 69 – March 70	23d Infantry Division (AMERICAL)
Chu Lai/Long Phu	April 70 – July 70	23d Infantry Division (AMERICAL)
Chu Lai/Trung Canh	Aug. 70	23d Infantry Division (AMERICAL)
Chu Lai/My Son	Sept. 70 – Oct. 70	23d Infantry Division (AMERICAL)
Chu Lai/Tri Binh	Nov. 70	23d Infantry Division (AMERICAL)
Chu Lai	Dec. 70 – Oct. 71	23d Infantry Division (AMERICAL)
Da Nang	Nov. 71	196th Infantry Brigade

3d Battalion, 7th Infantry (Light Infantry)

Arrived Vietnam: 28 December 1966
Departed Vietnam: 12 October 1970
Previous Station: Fort Benning
Authorized Strength: 920

The 3d Battalion, 7th Infantry ("Cottonbalers") served with the 199th Infantry Brigade (Light) in Vietnam.

Location	Service	Major Command
Song Be	Dec. 66 – Feb. 67	199th Infantry Brigade
Long Binh	March 67	199th Infantry Brigade
Bien Hoa	April 67 – June 67	199th Infantry Brigade
Long Binh/Cat Lai	July 67 – Sept. 67	199th Infantry Brigade
Long Binh/Phu My	Oct. 67 – Jan. 68	199th Infantry Brigade
Long Binh/Saigon	Feb. 68	199th Infantry Brigade
Gao Ho Nai/Bien Hoa	March 68	199th Infantry Brigade
Gao Ho Nai	April 68 – June 68	199th Infantry Brigade
Long Binh	July 68 – Oct. 68	199th Infantry Brigade
Long Binh/Saigon	Nov. 68 – June 69	199th Infantry Brigade
Long Binh/Courtenay	July 69 – Aug. 69	199th Infantry Brigade
Long Binh/Xuan Loc	Sept. 69 – July 70	199th Infantry Brigade
Long Binh/Gia Ray	Aug. 70 – Sept. 70	199th Infantry Brigade
Long Binh	Oct. 70	199th Infantry Brigade

1st Battalion, 8th Infantry (Infantry)

Arrived Vietnam: 4 October 1966
Departed Vietnam: 10 April 1970
Previous Station: Fort Lewis

Authorized Strength	1968	1970
Battalion	971	920

The 1st Battalion, 8th Infantry served with the 4th Infantry Division in Vietnam.

Location	Service	Major Command
Tuy Hoa	Oct. 66 – June 67	1st Brigade, 4th Infantry Division
Pleiku	July 67	1st Brigade, 4th Infantry Division
Tuy Hoa	Aug. 67	1st Brigade, 4th Infantry Division
Duc Co	Sept. 67 – Nov. 67	1st Brigade, 4th Infantry Division
Duc Co/Dak To	Dec. 67 – Feb. 68	1st Brigade, 4th Infantry Division
Dak To	March 68	1st Brigade, 4th Infantry Division
Pleiku/Dak To	April 68 – Dec. 68	1st Brigade, 4th Infantry Division
Pleiku/Suoi Doi	Jan. 69 – March 69	1st Brigade, 4th Infantry Division
Pleiku/Polei Kleng	April 69	1st Brigade, 4th Infantry Division
Pleiku/An Khe	May 69 – Nov. 69	1st Brigade, 4th Infantry Division
Pleiku/Ban Me Thuot	Dec. 69	1st Brigade, 4th Infantry Division
Pleiku/An Khe	Jan. 70	1st Brigade, 4th Infantry Division
An Khe	Feb. 70 – April 70	1st Brigade, 4th Infantry Division

2d Battalion, 8th Infantry (Mechanized Infantry)

Arrived Vietnam: 10 August 1966
Departed Vietnam: 7 December 1970
Previous Station: Fort Lewis
Authorized Strength: 907

The 2d Battalion, 8 Infantry was part of the 4th Infantry Division and was fully mechanized by March 1967 in Vietnam.

Location	Service	Major Command
Pleiku	Aug. 66 – Feb. 68	2d Brigade, 4th Infantry Division*
Dak To/Pleiku	March 68	2d Brigade, 4th Infantry Division
Pleiku/Plei Mong	April 68 – June 68	2d Brigade, 4th Infantry Division
Pleiku	July 68	2d Brigade, 4th Infantry Division
Pleiku/Ban Me Thuot	Aug. 68 – Nov. 68	2d Brigade, 4th Infantry Division
Pleiku/Kontum	Dec. 68	2d Brigade, 4th Infantry Division
Pleiku/Suoi Doi	Jan. 69	2d Brigade, 4th Infantry Division
Pleiku/Kontum	Feb. 69 – Oct. 69	2d Brigade, 4th Infantry Division
Pleiku/An Khe	Nov. 69 – Dec. 69	2d Brigade, 4th Infantry Division
An Khe	Jan. 70	2d Brigade, 4th Infantry Division
Pleiku	Feb. 70 – April 70	3d Brigade, 4th Infantry Division
Pleiku	May 70 – June 70	4th Infantry Division direct control
An Khe	July 70 – Dec. 70	4th Infantry Division direct control

* Dismounted upon initial arrival in Vietnam.

3d Battalion, 8th Infantry (Infantry)

Arrived Vietnam: 4 October 1966
Departed Vietnam: 7 December 1970
Previous Station: Fort Lewis

Authorized Strength	1968	1970
Battalion	971	920

The 3d Battalion, 8th Infantry was a component of the 4th Infantry Division.

Location	Service	Major Command
Tuy Hoa	Oct. 66 – June 67	1st Brigade, 4th Infantry Division
Pleiku	July 67	1st Brigade, 4th Infantry Division
Tuy Hoa	Aug. 67	1st Brigade, 4th Infantry Division
Duc Co	Sept. 67 – Nov. 67	1st Brigade, 4th Infantry Division
Duc Co/Dak To	Dec. 67 – Feb. 68	1st Brigade, 4th Infantry Division
Dak To	March 68	1st Brigade, 4th Infantry Division
Pleiku/Dak To	April 68 – Dec. 68	1st Brigade, 4th Infantry Division
Pleiku/Suoi Doi	Jan. 69 – March 69	1st Brigade, 4th Infantry Division
Pleiku/Polei Kleng	April 69	1st Brigade, 4th Infantry Division
Pleiku/Kontum	May 69 – Oct. 69	2d Brigade, 4th Infantry Division
Pleiku/An Khe	Nov. 69 – Dec. 69	2d Brigade, 4th Infantry Division
An Khe	Jan. 70	2d Brigade, 4th Infantry Division
An Khe	Feb. 70 – April 70	1st Brigade, 4th Infantry Division
Plei Djereng	May 70	1st Brigade, 4th Infantry Division
Plei Herel	June 70	1st Brigade, 4th Infantry Division
Kann Ack	July 70	1st Brigade, 4th Infantry Division
An Khe/Chanh Thuan	Aug. 70	1st Brigade, 4th Infantry Division
An Khe	Sept. 70 – Dec. 70	1st Brigade, 4th Infantry Division

4th Battalion, 9th Infantry (Infantry)

Arrived Vietnam: 29 April 1966
Departed Vietnam: 8 December 1970
Previous Station: Alaska via Hawaii*

Authorized Strength	1966	1968	1970
Battalion	829	971	920

The 4th Battalion, 9th Infantry ("Manchu") was part of the 25th Infantry Division in Vietnam.

Location	Service	Major Command
Cu Chi	April 66 – Feb. 68	1st Brigade, 25th Infantry Division

Location	Service	Major Command
Tay Ninh	March 68 – May 68	1st Brigade, 25th Infantry Division
Tay Ninh/Duc Hoa	June 68	1st Brigade, 25th Infantry Division
Tay Ninh	July 68 – April 70	1st Brigade, 25th Infantry Division
Thien Ngon	May 70	1st Brigade, 25th Infantry Division
Katum	June 70	1st Brigade, 25th Infantry Division
Tay Ninh	July 70	1st Brigade, 25th Infantry Division
Dau Tieng	Aug. 70	1st Brigade, 25th Infantry Division
Tri Tam	Sept. 70	1st Brigade, 25th Infantry Division
Dau Tieng	Oct. 70 – Dec. 70	1st Brigade, 25th Infantry Division

* Withdrawn from Alaska 22 January 1966 where it had been part of the 171st Infantry Brigade.

1st Battalion, 11th Infantry (Infantry)

Arrived Vietnam: 28 July 1968
Departed Vietnam: 5 August 1971
Previous Station: Fort Carson
Authorized Strength: 920

The 1st Battalion, 11 Infantry was part of the 1st Brigade Task Force of the 5th Infantry Division (Mechanized) in Vietnam.

Location	Service	Major Command
Cam Lo	July 68 – Oct. 68	1st Brigade, 5th Infantry Division (Mech)
Quang Tri/Dong Ha	Nov. 68	1st Brigade, 5th Infantry Division (Mech)
Quang Tri	Dec. 68 – March 71	1st Brigade, 5th Infantry Division (Mech)
Quang Tri/Khe Sanh	April 71	1st Brigade, 5th Infantry Division (Mech)
Quang Tri	May 71 – Aug. 71	1st Brigade, 5th Infantry Division (Mech)

1st Battalion, 12th Infantry (Infantry)

Arrived Vietnam: 9 August 1966
Departed Vietnam: 7 December 1970
Previous Station: Fort Lewis

Authorized Strength	1966	1968	1970
Battalion	789	971	920

The 1st Battalion, 12th Infantry was part of the 4th Infantry Division.

Location	Service	Major Command
Pleiku	Aug. 66 – Feb. 68	2d Brigade, 4th Infantry Division
Dak To/Pleiku	March 68	2d Brigade, 4th Infantry Division
Pleiku/Plei Mong	April 68 – June 68	2d Brigade, 4th Infantry Division
Pleiku	July 68	2d Brigade, 4th Infantry Division
Pleiku/Ban Me Thuot	Aug. 68 – Nov. 68	2d Brigade, 4th Infantry Division
Pleiku/Kontum	Dec. 68	2d Brigade, 4th Infantry Division
Pleiku/Suoi Doi	Jan. 69	2d Brigade, 4th Infantry Division
Pleiku/Kontum	Feb. 69 – Oct. 69	2d Brigade, 4th Infantry Division
Pleiku/An Khe	Nov. 69 – Dec. 69	2d Brigade, 4th Infantry Division
An Khe	Jan. 70 – March 70	2d Brigade, 4th Infantry Division
Ha Tien	April 70	2d Brigade, 4th Infantry Division
Pleiku	May 70 – June 70	4th Infantry Division direct control
An Khe	July 70 – Dec. 70	4th Infantry Division direct control

2d Battalion, 12th Infantry (Infantry)

Arrived Vietnam: 9 October 1966
Departed Vietnam: 16 April 1971
Previous Station: Fort Lewis

Authorized Strength	1968	1970
Battalion	971	920

The 2d Battalion, 12th Infantry entered Vietnam as a component of the 4th Infantry Division and on 1 August 1967 was transferred to the 25th Infantry Division.

Location	Service	Major Command
Bear Cat	Oct. 66 – Nov. 66	3d Brigade, 4th Infantry Division
Dau Tieng	Dec. 66 – June 67	3d Brigade, 4th Infantry Division
Pleiku	July 67	3d Brigade, 4th Infantry Division
Cu Chi/Tay Ninh	Aug. 67 – Feb. 68	3d Brigade, 25th Infantry Division
Dau Tieng/Hoc Mon	March 68	3d Brigade, 25th Infantry Division
Dau Tieng/Cu Chi	April 68 – June 68	3d Brigade, 25th Infantry Division
Dau Tieng/Hoc Mon	July 68	3d Brigade, 25th Infantry Division
Dau Tieng/Saigon	Aug. 68 – Oct. 68	3d Brigade, 25th Infantry Division
Dau Tieng	Nov. 68 – June 69	3d Brigade, 25th Infantry Division
Dau Tieng/Cu Chi	July 69	3d Brigade, 25th Infantry Division
Cu Chi/Bao Trai	Aug. 69 – Jan. 70	3d Brigade, 25th Infantry Division
Cu Chi/Dau Tieng	Feb. 70	2d Brigade, 25th Infantry Division
Long Thanh/ Phuoc Hiep	March 70 – April 70	2d Brigade, 25th Infantry Division
Thien Ngon	May 70	2d Brigade, 25th Infantry Division
Cambodia	June 70	2d Brigade, 25th Infantry Division
Xuan Loc	July 70	2d Brigade,

Xuan Loc/Xa Cam	Aug. 70 – Oct. 70	25th Infantry Division 2d Brigade,
		25th Infantry Division
Xuan Loc	Nov. 70 – Dec. 70	2d Brigade,
		25th Infantry Division
Long Binh	Jan. 71 – April 71	2d Brigade,
		25th Infantry Division

3d Battalion, 12th Infantry (Infantry)

Arrived Vietnam: 4 October 1966
Departed Vietnam: 7 December 1970
Previous Station: Fort Lewis

Authorized Strength	1968	1970
Battalion	971	920

The 3d Battalion, 12th Infantry served with the 4th Infantry Division in Vietnam.

Location	Service	Major Command
Tuy Hoa	Oct. 66 – June 67	1st Brigade,
		4th Infantry Division
Pleiku	July 67	1st Brigade,
		4th Infantry Division
Tuy Hoa	Aug. 67	1st Brigade,
		4th Infantry Division
Duc Co	Sept. 67 – Nov. 67	1st Brigade,
		4th Infantry Division
Duc Co/Dak To	Dec. 67 – Feb. 68	1st Brigade,
		4th Infantry Division
Dak To	March 68	1st Brigade,
		4th Infantry Division
Pleiku/Dak To	April 68 – Dec. 68	1st Brigade,
		4th Infantry Division
Pleiku/Suoi Doi	Jan. 69 – March 69	1st Brigade,
		4th Infantry Division
Pleiku/Polei Kleng	April 69	1st Brigade,
		4th Infantry Division
Pleiku/An Khe	May 69 – Nov. 69	1st Brigade,
		4th Infantry Division
Pleiku/Ban Me Thuot	Dec. 69	1st Brigade,
		4th Infantry Division
Pleiku/An Khe	Jan. 70	1st Brigade,
		4th Infantry Division
Pleiku	Feb. 70 – April 70	3d Brigade,
		4th Infantry Division
Pleiku	May 70 – June 70	4th Infantry Division direct control
An Khe	July 70 – Dec. 70	4th Infantry Division direct control

4th Battalion, 12th Infantry (Light Infantry)

Arrived Vietnam: 10 December 1966
Departed Vietnam: 12 October 1970
Previous Station: Fort Benning
Authorized Strength: 920

The 4th Battalion, 12th Infantry served with the 199th Infantry Brigade (Light).

Location	Service	Major Command
Song Be	Dec. 66 – Feb. 67	199th Infantry Brigade
Long Binh	March 67	199th Infantry Brigade

Bien Hoa	April 67 – June 67	199th Infantry Brigade
Long Binh/Cat Lai	July 67 – Sept. 67	199th Infantry Brigade
Long Binh/Phu My	Oct. 67 – Jan. 68	199th Infantry Brigade
Long Binh/Saigon	Feb. 68	199th Infantry Brigade
Gao Ho Nai/Bien Hoa	March 68	199th Infantry Brigade
Gao Ho Nai	April 68 – June 68	199th Infantry Brigade
Long Binh	July 68 – Oct. 68	199th Infantry Brigade
Long Binh/Saigon	Nov. 68 – June 69	199th Infantry Brigade
Long Binh/Courtenay	July 69 – Aug. 69	199th Infantry Brigade
Long Binh/Xuan Loc	Sept. 69 – July 70	199th Infantry Brigade
Long Binh/Gia Ray	Aug. 70 – Sept. 70	199th Infantry Brigade
Long Binh	Oct. 70	199th Infantry Brigade

5th Battalion, 12th Infantry (Light Infantry)

Arrived Vietnam: 7 April 1968
Departed Vietnam: 12 October 1970
Previous Station: Fort Lewis
Authorized Strength: 920

The 5th Battalion, 12th Infantry was activated 1 November 1967 and assigned to the 199th Infantry Brigade (Light) in 1968 to give the brigade a fourth maneuver battalion in Vietnam.

Location	Service	Major Command
Gao Ho Nai	April 68 – June 68	199th Infantry Brigade
Long Binh	July 68 – Oct. 68	199th Infantry Brigade
Long Binh/Saigon	Nov. 68 – June 69	199th Infantry Brigade
Long Binh/Courtenay	July 69 – Aug. 69	199th Infantry Brigade
Long Binh/Xuan Loc	Sept. 69 – July 70	199th Infantry Brigade*
Long Binh/Gia Ray	Aug. 70 – Sept. 70	199th Infantry Brigade
Long Binh	Oct. 70	199th Infantry Brigade

* Battalion participated in the Cambodian invasion in June 1970.

1st Battalion, 14th Infantry (Infantry)

Arrived Vietnam: 17 January 1966
Departed Vietnam: 8 December 1970
Previous Station: Hawaii

Authorized Strength	1966	1968	1970
Battalion	829	971	920

The 1st Battalion, 14th Infantry ("Golden Dragons") went to Vietnam with the 25th Infantry Division and on 1 August 1967 was transferred to the 4th Infantry Division.

Location	Service	Major Command
Pleiku	Jan. 66 – May 67	3d Brigade,
		25th Infantry Division
Duc Co	June 67	3d Brigade,
		25th Infantry Division
Pleiku/Duc Pho	July 67	3d Brigade,
		25th Infantry Division
Cu Chi/Tay Ninh	Aug. 67	3d Brigade,
		25th Infantry Division
Pleiku/Duc Pho	Sept. 67 – Jan. 68	3d Brigade,
		4th Infantry Division
Pleiku/Chu Lai	Feb. 68	3d Brigade,
		4th Infantry Division
Dak To/Bong Son	March 68	3d Brigade,
		4th Infantry Division
Pleiku/Bong Son/ Kontum	April 68	3d Brigade,
		4th Infantry Division

Pleiku/Kontum	May 68 – July 68	3d Brigade, 4th Infantry Division
Pleiku	Aug. 68 – Nov. 68	3d Brigade, 4th Infantry Division
Pleiku/Tuttle	Dec. 68	3d Brigade, 4th Infantry Division
Pleiku/Catecka	Jan. 69 – July 69	3d Brigade, 4th Infantry Division
Pleiku/Tuttle	Aug. 69 – Nov. 69	3d Brigade, 4th Infantry Division
Pleiku	Dec. 69 – Jan. 70	3d Brigade, 4th Infantry Division
An Khe	Feb. 70 – April 70	1st Brigade, 4th Infantry Division
Plei Djereng	May 70	1st Brigade, 4th Infantry Division
Plei Herel	June 70	1st Brigade, 4th Infantry Division
Kann Ack	July 70	1st Brigade, 4th Infantry Division
An Khe/ Chanh Thuan	Aug. 70	1st Brigade, 4th Infantry Division
An Khe	Sept. 70 – Dec. 70	1st Brigade, 4th Infantry Division

2d Battalion, 14th Infantry (Infantry)

Arrived Vietnam: 29 April 1966
Departed Vietnam: 8 December 1970
Previous Station: Hawaii

Authorized Strength	1966	1968	1970
Battalion	829	971	920

The 2d Battalion, 14th Infantry ("Golden Dragons") remained with the 25th Infantry Division throughout its service in Vietnam.

Location	Service	Major Command
Cu Chi	April 66 – Feb. 68	1st Brigade, 25th Infantry Division
Tay Ninh	March 68 – May 68	1st Brigade, 25th Infantry Division
Tay Ninh/Duc Hoa	June 68	1st Brigade, 25th Infantry Division
Tay Ninh	July 68 – Jan. 70	1st Brigade, 25th Infantry Division
Cu Chi/Bao Trai	Feb. 70 – April 70	3d Brigade, 25th Infantry Division
Cu Chi	May 70 – Dec. 70	3d Brigade, 25th Infantry Division

Company E, 14th Infantry (Rifle Security)

Arrived Vietnam: 30 June 1971
Departed Vietnam: 20 November 1972
Previous Station: Vietnam
Authorized Strength: 160

Company E, 14th Infantry ("Golden Dragons") was a separate rifle security company raised to guard Long Binh. The company was under the command of the U.S. Army Support Command, Saigon during its service in Vietnam.

1st Battalion, 16th Infantry (Mechanized Infantry)

Arrived Vietnam: 10 October 1965
Departed Vietnam: 7 April 1970
Previous Station: Fort Riley

Authorized Strength	1966	1968	1970
Battalion	829	971	920

The 1st Battalion, 16th Infantry was part of the 1st Infantry Division and was converted to a mechanized status around October 1968 from the assets of the 5th Battalion, 60th Infantry of the 9th Infantry Division.

Location	Service	Major Command
Bien Hoa	Oct. 65 – Nov. 65	1st Brigade, 1st Infantry Division*
Phuoc Vinh	Dec. 65 – Nov. 66	1st Brigade, 1st Infantry Division*
Lai Khe	Dec. 66 – May 67	3d Brigade, 1st Infantry Division*
Ben Cat	June 67	3d Brigade, 1st Infantry Division*
Lai Khe	July 67 – March 68	3d Brigade, 1st Infantry Division*
Lai Khe/Hoc Mon	April 68 – May 68	3d Brigade, 1st Infantry Division*
Lai Khe	June 68 – Sept. 68	3d Brigade, 1st Infantry Division*
My Tho	Oct. 68	3d Brigade, 9th Infantry Division
Lai Khe	Nov. 68 – Aug. 69	3d Brigade, 1st Infantry Division
Lai Khe/ Chon Thanh	Sept. 69	3d Brigade, 1st Infantry Division
Lai Khe/Ben Cat	Oct. 69 – Nov. 69	3d Brigade, 1st Infantry Division
Lai Khe	Dec. 69 – Jan. 70	3d Brigade, 1st Infantry Division
Bear Cat	Feb. 70	2d Brigade, 1st Infantry Division
Di An	March 70 – April 70	2d Brigade, 1st Infantry Division

* Dismounted during this time.

2d Battalion, 16th Infantry (Infantry)

Arrived Vietnam: 11 July 1965
Departed Vietnam: 8 April 1970
Previous Station: Fort Riley

Authorized Strength	1966	1968	1970
Battalion	829	971	920

The 2d Battalion, 16th Infantry served with the 1st Infantry Division in Vietnam.

Location	Service	Major Command
Qui Nhon/ Nha Trang	July 65 – Sept. 65	2d Brigade, 1st Infantry Division
Bien Hoa	Oct. 65 – Nov. 65	2d Brigade, 1st Infantry Division
Phu Loi	Dec. 65 – Feb. 66	2d Brigade, 1st Infantry Division
Bien Hoa	March 66 – Nov. 66	2d Brigade, 1st Infantry Division

Location	Service	Major Command
Di An	Dec. 66 – May 67	2d Brigade, 1st Infantry Division
Bien Hoa	June 67	2d Brigade, 1st Infantry Division
Di An/Lai Khe	July 67 – Feb. 68	2d Brigade, 1st Infantry Division
Di An	March 68 – May 69	2d Brigade, 1st Infantry Division
Di An/Binh Thoi	June 69	2d Brigade, 1st Infantry Division
Di An	July 69 – Aug. 69	2d Brigade, 1st Infantry Division
Di An/Cu Chi	Sept. 69	2d Brigade, 1st Infantry Division
Di An/Phu Cuong	Oct. 69 – Nov. 69	2d Brigade, 1st Infantry Division
Lai Khe/Di An	Dec. 69	2d Brigade, 1st Infantry Division
Bear Cat/ Thai Thien	Jan. 70	2d Brigade, 1st Infantry Division
Bear Cat	Feb. 70	2d Brigade, 1st Infantry Division
Di An	March 70 – April 70	2d Brigade, 1st Infantry Division

Company D, 17th Infantry (Rifle Security)

Arrived Vietnam: 30 June 1971
Departed Vietnam: 1 August 1972
Previous Station: Vietnam
Authorized Strength: 160

Company D, 17th Infantry was a rifle security company independently raised to guard the Cam Ranh Bay complex under the command of the U.S. Army Support Command, Cam Ranh Bay.

1st Battalion, 18th Infantry (Infantry)

Arrived Vietnam: 11 July 1965
Departed Vietnam: 8 April 1970
Previous Station: Fort Riley

Authorized Strength	1966	1968	1970
Battalion	829	971	920

The 1st Battalion, 18th Infantry was assigned to the 1st Infantry Division.

Location	Service	Major Command
Qui Nhon/ Nha Trang	July 65 – Sept. 65	2d Brigade, 1st Infantry Division
Bien Hoa	Oct. 65 – Nov. 65	2d Brigade, 1st Infantry Division
Phu Loi	Dec. 65 – Feb. 66	2d Brigade, 1st Infantry Division
Bien Hoa	March 66 – Nov. 66	2d Brigade, 1st Infantry Division
Di An	Dec. 66 – May 67	2d Brigade, 1st Infantry Division
Bien Hoa	June 67	2d Brigade, 1st Infantry Division

Location	Service	Major Command
Di An/Lai Khe	July 67 – Feb. 68	2d Brigade, 1st Infantry Division
Di An	March 68 – May 69	2d Brigade, 1st Infantry Division
Di An/Binh Thoi	June 69	2d Brigade, 1st Infantry Division
Di An	July 69 – Aug. 69	2d Brigade, 1st Infantry Division
Di An/Cu Chi	Sept. 69	2d Brigade, 1st Infantry Division
Di An/Phu Cuong	Oct. 69 – Nov. 69	2d Brigade, 1st Infantry Division
Lai Khe/Di An	Dec. 69	2d Brigade, 1st Infantry Division
Bear Cat/ Thai Thien	Jan. 70	2d Brigade, 1st Infantry Division
Di An	Feb. 70 – April 70	3d Brigade, 1st Infantry Division

2d Battalion, 18th Infantry (Infantry)

Arrived Vietnam: 11 July 1965
Departed Vietnam: 8 April 1970
Previous Station: Fort Riley

Authorized Strength	1966	1968	1970
Battalion	829	971	920

The 2d Battalion, 18th Infantry served with the 1st Infantry Division in Vietnam.

Location	Service	Major Command
Qui Nhon/ Nha Trang	July 65 – Sept. 65	2d Brigade, 1st Infantry Division
Bien Hoa	Oct. 65 – Nov. 65	2d Brigade, 1st Infantry Division
Phu Loi	Dec. 65 – Feb. 66	2d Brigade, 1st Infantry Division
Bien Hoa	March 66 – Nov. 66	2d Brigade, 1st Infantry Division
Di An	Dec. 66 – May 67	2d Brigade, 1st Infantry Division
Bien Hoa	June 67	2d Brigade, 1st Infantry Division
Di An/Lai Khe	July 67 – Feb. 68	2d Brigade, 1st Infantry Division
Di An	March 68 – May 69	2d Brigade, 1st Infantry Division
Di An/Binh Thoi	June 69	2d Brigade, 1st Infantry Division
Di An	July 69 – Aug. 69	2d Brigade, 1st Infantry Division
Di An/Cu Chi	Sept. 69	2d Brigade, 1st Infantry Division
Di An/Phu Cuong	Oct. 69 – Nov. 69	2d Brigade, 1st Infantry Division
Lai Khe/Di An	Dec. 69	2d Brigade, 1st Infantry Division
Bear Cat/ Thai Thien	Jan. 70	2d Brigade, 1st Infantry Division
Bear Cat	Feb. 70	2d Brigade, 1st Infantry Division
Di An	March 70 – April 70	2d Brigade, 1st Infantry Division

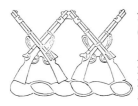

1st Battalion, 20th Infantry (Light Infantry)

Arrived Vietnam: 18 December 1967
Departed Vietnam: 30 November 1971
Previous Station: Hawaii
Authorized Strength: 920

The 1st Battalion, 20th Infantry ("Sykes' Regulars") served the 11th Infantry Brigade (Light), being transferred to the 23rd Infantry Division (AMERICAL) 15 February 1969.

Location	Service	Major Command
Duc Pho	Dec. 67 – Feb. 69	11th Infantry Brigade
Duc Pho	Feb. 69 – March 71	23d Infantry Division (AMERICAL)
Duc Pho/Dong Ha	April 71	23d Infantry Division (AMERICAL)
Duc Pho	May 71 – June 71	23d Infantry Division (AMERICAL)
Chu Lai/The Loi	July 71	23d Infantry Division (AMERICAL)
The Loi	Aug. 71 – Nov. 71	23d Infantry Division (AMERICAL)

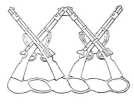

Company E, 20th Infantry (Long Range Patrol) (Rifle Security)

First Tour:
Arrived Vietnam: 25 September 1967
Departed Vietnam: 1 February 1969
Previous Station: Vietnam

Second Tour:
Arrived Vietnam: 30 June 1971
Departed Vietnam: 16 August 1972
Previous Station: Vietnam

Authorized Strength	1968	1971
Company	230	160

Company E, 20th Infantry ("Sykes' Regulars") served twice in Vietnam, first as a long-range reconnaissance patrol company serving with both I Field Force, Vietnam and the 4th Infantry Division, and later as a rifle security company providing convoy security for the 71st Transportation Battalion and installation defense at Long Binh under the U.S. Army Support Command, Saigon.

3d Battalion, 21st Infantry (Light Infantry)

Arrived Vietnam: 26 August 1966
Departed Vietnam: 23 August 1972
Previous Station: Fort Devens

Authorized Strength	1966	1968	1970
Battalion	778	920	920

The 3d Battalion, 21st Infantry ("Gimlet") was assigned to the 196th Infantry Brigade (Light), transferring on 15 February 1969 to the 23d Infantry Division (AMERICAL) with which it served until it returned to the separate 196th Infantry Brigade when the division departed Vietnam. The battalion became separate once the brigade left and was the last U.S. Army ground combat battalion to leave Vietnam.

Location	Service	Major Command
Tay Ninh	Aug. 66 – April 67	196th Infantry Brigade
Chu Lai	May 67 – Sept. 67	196th Infantry Brigade*
Chu Lai	Oct. 67 – Feb. 68	196th Infantry Brigade
Tam Ky	March 68 – April 68	196th Infantry Brigade
Phong Dien	May 68	196th Infantry Brigade
Hoi An	June 68 – July 68	196th Infantry Brigade
Chu Lai/Tam Ky	Aug. 68 – Nov. 68	196th Infantry Brigade
Chu Lai/Xuyen Tay	Dec. 68 – Jan. 69	196th Infantry Brigade
Chu Lai/Xuyen Tay	Feb. 69 – July 69	23d Infantry Division (AMERICAL)
Chu Lai/ Nuong Xuan	Aug. 69	23d Infantry Division (AMERICAL)
Chu Lai/Thang Binh	Sept. 69 – Dec. 69	23d Infantry Division (AMERICAL)
Chu Lai/ Tuang Dong	Jan. 70 – July 70	23d Infantry Division (AMERICAL)
Chu Lai/Tam Ky	Aug. 70	23d Infantry Division (AMERICAL)
Tam Ky	Sept. 70 – April 71	23d Infantry Division (AMERICAL)
Da Nang	May 71 – Nov. 71	23d Infantry Division (AMERICAL)
Da Nang	Dec. 71 – June 72	196th Infantry Brigade
Da Nang	July 72 – Aug. 72	Separate

* With duty in Task Force OREGON.

4th Battalion, 21st Infantry (Light Infantry)

Arrived Vietnam: 14 April 1968
Departed Vietnam: 28 June 1971
Previous Station: Hawaii
Authorized Strength: 920

The 4th Battalion, 21st Infantry ("Gimlet") was activated 1 November 1967 in Hawaii to serve as a fourth maneuver battalion of the 11th Infantry Brigade (Light). On 15 February 1969 the battalion officially became part of the 23d Infantry Division (AMERICAL).

Location	Service	Major Command
Duc Pho	April 68 – Jan. 69	11th Infantry Brigade
Duc Pho	Feb. 69 – March 71	23d Infantry Division (AMERICAL)
Duc Pho/Dong Ha	April 71	23d Infantry Division (AMERICAL)
Duc Pho	May 71 – June 71	23d Infantry Division (AMERICAL)

1st Battalion, 22d Infantry (Infantry)

Arrived Vietnam: 23 July 1966
Departed Vietnam: 30 January 1972
Previous Station: Fort Lewis

Authorized Strength	1966	1968	1970
Battalion	789	971	920

The 1st Battalion, 22d Infantry was part of the 4th Infantry Division. It was later attached to I Field Force, Vietnam in anticipation of the division's departure from Vietnam, finally becoming separate itself past April 1971.

Location	Service	Major Command
Pleiku	July 66 – Feb. 68	2d Brigade, 4th Infantry Division

Location	Service	Major Command
Dak To/Pleiku	March 68	2d Brigade, 4th Infantry Division
Pleiku/Plei Mong	April 68 – June 68	2d Brigade, 4th Infantry Division
Pleiku	July 68	2d Brigade, 4th Infantry Division
Pleiku/Ban Me Thuot	Aug. 68 – Nov. 68	2d Brigade, 4th Infantry Division
Pleiku/Kontum	Dec. 68	2d Brigade, 4th Infantry Division
Pleiku/Suoi Doi	Jan. 69	2d Brigade, 4th Infantry Division
Pleiku/Kontum	Feb. 69 – Oct. 69	2d Brigade, 4th Infantry Division
Pleiku/An Khe	Nov. 69 – Dec. 69	2d Brigade, 4th Infantry Division
An Khe	Jan. 70	2d Brigade, 4th Infantry Division
An Khe	Feb. 70 – April 70	1st Brigade, 4th Infantry Division
Plei Djereng	May 70	2d Brigade, 4th Infantry Division
An Khe	June 70 – Sept. 70	2d Brigade, 4th Infantry Division
Phu Nhieu	Oct. 70	2d Brigade, 4th Infantry Division
An Khe	Nov. 70	I Field Force, Vietnam
Tuy Hoa	Dec. 70	I Field Force, Vietnam
Tuy Hoa	Jan. 71 – Feb. 71	Military Assistance Command, Region 2
Tuy Hoa	March 71 – April 71	I Field Force, Vietnam
Tuy Hoa	May 71 – Jan. 72	U.S. Army Forces, Military Region 2

2d Battalion, 22d Infantry (Mechanized Infantry)

Arrived Vietnam: 9 October 1966
Departed Vietnam: 7 December 1970
Previous Station: Fort Lewis
Authorized Strength: 907

The 2d Battalion, 22d Infantry deployed to Vietnam as a fully mechanized infantry battalion, serving with the 4th Infantry Division until transferred officially to the 25th Infantry Division on 1 August 1967.

Location	Service	Major Command
Bear Cat	Oct. 66 – Nov. 66	3d Brigade, 4th Infantry Division
Dau Tieng	Dec. 66 – June 67	3d Brigade, 4th Infantry Division*
Pleiku	July 67	3d Brigade, 4th Infantry Division*
Cu Chi/Tay Ninh	Aug. 67 – Feb. 68	3d Brigade, 25th Infantry Division
Dau Tieng/ Hoc Mon	March 68	3d Brigade, 25th Infantry Division
Dau Tieng/ Cu Chi	April 68 – June 68	3d Brigade, 25th Infantry Division
Dau Tieng/ Hoc Mon	July 68	3d Brigade, 25th Infantry Division
Dau Tieng/ Saigon	Aug. 68 – Oct. 68	3d Brigade, 25th Infantry Division
Dau Tieng	Nov. 68 – June 69	3d Brigade, 25th Infantry Division
Dau Tieng/ Cu Chi	July 69	3d Brigade, 25th Infantry Division
Cu Chi/ Bao Trai	Aug. 69 – April 70	3d Brigade, 25th Infantry Division
Cu Chi	May 70 – Dec. 70	3d Brigade, 25th Infantry Division

* Battalion was under the operational control of the 25th Infantry Division during May – July 1967.

3d Battalion, 22d Infantry (Infantry)

Arrived Vietnam: 9 October 1966
Departed Vietnam: 20 April 1971
Previous Station: Fort Lewis

Authorized Strength	1968	1970
Battalion	971	920

The 3d Battalion, 22d Infantry was part of the 4th Infantry Division until officially transferred to the 25th Infantry Division on 1 August 1967.

Location	Service	Major Command
Bear Cat	Oct. 66 – Nov. 66	3d Brigade, 4th Infantry Division
Dau Tieng	Dec. 66 – June 67	3d Brigade, 4th Infantry Division
Pleiku	July 67	3d Brigade, 4th Infantry Division
Cu Chi/Tay Ninh	Aug. 67 – Feb. 68	3d Brigade, 25th Infantry Division
Dau Tieng/ Hoc Mon	March 68	3d Brigade, 25th Infantry Division
Dau Tieng/Cu Chi	April 68 – June 68	3d Brigade, 25th Infantry Division
Dau Tieng/ Hoc Mon	July 68	3d Brigade, 25th Infantry Division
Dau Tieng/Saigon	Aug. 68 – Oct. 68	3d Brigade, 25th Infantry Division
Dau Tieng	Nov. 68 – June 69	3d Brigade, 25th Infantry Division
Dau Tieng/Cu Chi	July 69	3d Brigade, 25th Infantry Division
Cu Chi/Bao Trai	Aug. 69 – Jan. 70	3d Brigade, 25th Infantry Division
Tay Ninh	Feb. 70 – April 70	1st Brigade, 25th Infantry Division
Thien Ngon	May 70	1st Brigade, 25th Infantry Division
Katum	June 70	1st Brigade, 25th Infantry Division
Tay Ninh	July 70	1st Brigade, 25th Infantry Division
Dau Tieng	Aug. 70	1st Brigade, 25th Infantry Division
Tri Tam	Sept. 70	1st Brigade, 25th Infantry Division
Dau Tieng	Oct. 70 – Nov. 70	1st Brigade, 25th Infantry Division
Xuan Loc	Dec. 70	2d Brigade, 25th Infantry Division
Xuan Loc/ Long Binh	Jan. 71 – April 71	2d Brigade, 25th Infantry Division

4th Battalion, 23d Infantry (Mechanized Infantry)

Arrived Vietnam: 29 April 1966
Departed Vietnam: 8 December 1970
Previous Station: Alaska via Hawaii*

Authorized Strength	1966	1968	1970
Battalion	920	907	907

The 4th Battalion, 23d Infantry was a component of the 25th Infantry Division, being reorganized as a fully mechanized battalion by January 1967.

Location	Service	Major Command
Cu Chi	April 66 – Feb. 68	1st Brigade, 25th Infantry Division*
Tay Ninh	March 68 – May 68	1st Brigade, 25th Infantry Division
Tay Ninh/Duc Hoa	June 68	1st Brigade, 25th Infantry Division
Tay Ninh	July 68 – April 70	1st Brigade, 25th Infantry Division
Thien Ngon	May 70	1st Brigade, 25th Infantry Division
Katum	June 70	1st Brigade, 25th Infantry Division
Tay Ninh	July 70	1st Brigade, 25th Infantry Division
Dau Tieng	Aug. 70	1st Brigade, 25th Infantry Division
Tri Tam	Sept. 70	1st Brigade, 25th Infantry Division
Dau Tieng	Oct. 70 – Dec. 70	1st Brigade, 25th Infantry Division

* Withdrawn from Alaska 22 January 1966 (where it had been part of the 172d Infantry Brigade). Dismounted upon initial arrival in Vietnam.

1st Battalion, 26th Infantry (Infantry)

Arrived Vietnam: 17 October 1965
Departed Vietnam: 7 April 1970
Previous Station: Fort Riley

Authorized Strength	1966	1968	1970
Battalion	829	971	920

The 1st Battalion, 26th Infantry was part of the 1st Infantry Division in Vietnam.

Location	Service	Major Command
Bien Hoa	Oct. 65 – Nov. 65	3d Brigade, 1st Infantry Division
Ben Cat	Dec. 65 – Jan. 66	3d Brigade, 1st Infantry Division
Lai Khe	Feb. 66 – Nov. 66	3d Brigade, 1st Infantry Division
Phuoc Vinh	Dec. 66 – June 67	1st Brigade, 1st Infantry Division
Phuoc Vinh/Lai Khe	July 67 – Feb. 68	1st Brigade, 1st Infantry Division
Quan Loi/An Loc	March 68 – May 68	1st Brigade, 1st Infantry Division
Quan Loi	June 68 – Oct. 68	1st Brigade, 1st Infantry Division
Quan Loi/Loc Ninh	Nov. 68	1st Brigade, 1st Infantry Division
Quan Loi/Lai Khe	Dec. 68 – March 69	1st Brigade, 1st Infantry Division
Quan Loi	April 69	1st Brigade, 1st Infantry Division
Quan Loi/Song Be	May 69 – June 69	1st Brigade, 1st Infantry Division
Quan Loi/ Dau Tieng	July 69 – Aug. 69	1st Brigade, 1st Infantry Division
Dau Tieng/Ben Cat	Sept. 69 – Nov. 69	1st Brigade, 1st Infantry Division
Phuoc Vinh	Dec. 69	1st Brigade, 1st Infantry Division
Dau Tieng	Jan. 70	1st Brigade, 1st Infantry Division
Di An	Feb. 70 – April 70	3d Brigade, 1st Infantry Division

1st Battalion, 27th Infantry (Infantry)

Arrived Vietnam: 19 January 1966
Departed Vietnam: 30 April 1971
Previous Station: Hawaii

Authorized Strength	1966	1968	1970
Battalion	829	971	920

The 1st Battalion, 27th Infantry ("The Wolfhounds") served with the 25th Infantry Division in Vietnam.

Location	Service	Major Command
Cu Chi	Jan. 66 – March 68	2d Brigade, 25th Infantry Division
Cu Chi/Tay Ninh	April 68	2d Brigade, 25th Infantry Division
Cu Chi	May 68	2d Brigade, 25th Infantry Division
Cu Chi/Hoc Mon	June 68 – July 68	2d Brigade, 25th Infantry Division
Cu Chi	Aug. 68 – Jan. 70	2d Brigade, 25th Infantry Division
Cu Chi/Bao Trai	Feb. 70 – April 70	3d Brigade, 25th Infantry Division
Cu Chi	May 70 – Nov. 70	3d Brigade, 25th Infantry Division
Xuan Loc	Dec. 70	2d Brigade, 25th Infantry Division
Long Binh/ Xuan Loc	Jan. 71 – April 71	2d Brigade, 25th Infantry Division

2d Battalion, 27th Infantry (Infantry)

Arrived Vietnam: 19 January 1966
Departed Vietnam: 8 December 1970
Previous Station: Hawaii

Authorized Strength	1966	1968	1970
Battalion	829	971	920

The 2d Battalion, 27th Infantry ("The Wolfhounds") served as part of the 25th Infantry Division in Vietnam.

Location	Service	Major Command
Cu Chi	Jan. 66 – March 68	2d Brigade, 25th Infantry Division

Location	Service	Major Command
Cu Chi/Tay Ninh	April 68	2d Brigade, 25th Infantry Division
Cu Chi	May 68	2d Brigade, 25th Infantry Division
Cu Chi/Hoc Mon	June 68 – July 68	2d Brigade, 25th Infantry Division
Cu Chi	Aug. 68 – Jan. 70	2d Brigade, 25th Infantry Division
Cu Chi/Dau Tieng	Feb. 70	2d Brigade, 25th Infantry Division
Long Thanh/ Phuoc Hiep	March 70 – April 70	2d Brigade, 25th Infantry Division
Thien Ngon	May 70	2d Brigade, 25th Infantry Division
Tay Ninh	June 70	2d Brigade, 25th Infantry Division
Xuan Loc	July 70	2d Brigade, 25th Infantry Division
Xuan Loc/Xa Cam	Aug. 70 – Oct. 70	2d Brigade, 25th Infantry Division
Xuan Loc	Nov. 70 – Dec. 70	2d Brigade, 25th Infantry Division

1st Battalion, 28th Infantry (Infantry)

Arrived Vietnam: 10 October 1965
Departed Vietnam: 8 April 1970
Previous Station: Fort Riley

Authorized Strength	1966	1968	1970
Battalion	829	971	920

The 1st Battalion, 28th Infantry ("Lions of Cantigny") served with the 1st Infantry Division in Vietnam.

Location	Service	Major Command
Bien Hoa	Oct. 65 – Nov. 65	1st Brigade, 1st Infantry Division
Phuoc Vinh	Dec. 65 – June 67	1st Brigade, 1st Infantry Division
Phuoc Vinh/Lai Khe	July 67 – Feb. 68	1st Brigade, 1st Infantry Division
Quan Loi/An Loc	March 68 – May 68	1st Brigade, 1st Infantry Division
Quan Loi	June 68 – Oct. 68	1st Brigade, 1st Infantry Division
Quan Loi/Loc Ninh	Nov. 68	1st Brigade, 1st Infantry Division
Quan Loi/Lai Khe	Dec. 68 – March 69	1st Brigade, 1st Infantry Division
Quan Loi	April 69	1st Brigade, 1st Infantry Division
Quan Loi/Song Be	May 69 – June 69	1st Brigade, 1st Infantry Division
Quan Loi/ Dau Tieng	July 69 – Aug. 69	1st Brigade, 1st Infantry Division
Dau Tieng/Ben Cat	Sept. 69 – Nov. 69	1st Brigade, 1st Infantry Division
Phuoc Vinh	Dec. 69	1st Brigade, 1st Infantry Division
Dau Tieng	Jan. 70 – Feb. 70	1st Brigade, 1st Infantry Division
Lai Khe	March 70	1st Brigade, 1st Infantry Division
Di An	April 70	1st Brigade, 1st Infantry Division

2d Battalion, 28th Infantry (Infantry)

Arrived Vietnam: 2 October 1965
Departed Vietnam: 8 April 1970
Previous Station: Fort Riley

Authorized Strength	1966	1968	1970
Battalion	829	971	920

The 2d Battalion, 28th Infantry ("Lions of Cantigny") was part of the 1st Infantry Division in Vietnam.

Location	Service	Major Command
Bien Hoa	Oct. 65 – Nov. 65	1st Brigade, 1st Infantry Division
Phuoc Vinh	Dec. 65 – Nov. 66	1st Brigade, 1st Infantry Division
Lai Khe	Dec. 66 – May 67	3d Brigade, 1st Infantry Division
Ben Cat	June 67	3d Brigade, 1st Infantry Division
Lai Khe	July 67 – March 68	3d Brigade, 1st Infantry Division
Lai Khe/Hoc Mon	April 68 – May 68	3d Brigade, 1st Infantry Division
Lai Khe	June 68 – Aug. 69	3d Brigade, 1st Infantry Division
Lai Khe/ Chon Thanh	Sept. 69	3d Brigade, 1st Infantry Division
Lai Khe/Ben Cat	Oct. 69 – Nov. 69	3d Brigade, 1st Infantry Division
Lai Khe	Dec. 69 – Jan. 70	3d Brigade, 1st Infantry Division
Dau Tieng	Feb. 70	1st Brigade, 1st Infantry Division
Lai Khe	March 70	1st Brigade, 1st Infantry Division
Di An	April 70	1st Brigade, 1st Infantry Division

4th Battalion, 31st Infantry (Light Infantry)

Arrived Vietnam: 26 August 1966
Departed Vietnam: 25 October 1971
Previous Station: Fort Devens

Authorized Strength	1966	1968	1970
Battalion	778	920	920

The 4th Battalion, 31st Infantry ("The Polar Bears") served as part of the 196th Infantry Brigade (Light) in Vietnam, being officially transferred to the 23rd Infantry Division (AMERICAL) on 15 February 1969.

Location	Service	Major Command
Tay Ninh	Aug. 66 – April 67	196th Infantry Brigade
Chu Lai	May 67 – Sept. 67	196th Infantry Brigade*
Chu Lai	Oct. 67 – Feb. 68	196th Infantry Brigade
Tam Ky	March 68 – April 68	196th Infantry Brigade
Phong Dien	May 68	196th Infantry Brigade
Hoi An	June 68 – July 68	196th Infantry Brigade
Chu Lai/Tam Ky	Aug. 68 – Nov. 68	196th Infantry Brigade
Chu Lai/Xuyen Tay	Dec. 68 – Jan. 69	196th Infantry Brigade
Chu Lai/Xuyen Tay	Feb. 69 – July 69	23d Infantry Division (AMERICAL)
Chu Lai/Nuong Xuan	Aug. 69	23d Infantry Division (AMERICAL)

Chu Lai/Thang Binh	Sept. 69 – Dec. 69	23d Infantry Division (AMERICAL)
Chu Lai/Tuang Dong	Jan. 70 – July 70	23d Infantry Division (AMERICAL)
Chu Lai/Tam Ky	Aug. 70	23d Infantry Division (AMERICAL)
Tam Ky	Sept. 70 – April 71	23d Infantry Division (AMERICAL)
Da Nang	May 71 – Oct. 71	23d Infantry Divison (AMERICAL)

* With duty in Task Force OREGON.

6th Battalion, 31st Infantry (Infantry)

Arrived Vietnam: 8 April 1968
Departed Vietnam: 12 October 1970
Previous Station: Fort Lewis
Authorized Strength: 920

The 6th Battalion, 31st Infantry ("The Polar Bears") was activated 1 November 1967 at Fort Lewis and joined the 9th Infantry Division in Vietnam as its last maneuver element.

Location	Service	Major Command
Binh Chanh	April 68 – June 68	3d Brigade, 9th Infantry Division
Bear Cat/Tan An	July 68	1st Brigade, 9th Infantry Division
Nha Be	Aug. 68 – Nov. 68	1st Brigade, 9th Infantry Division
Dong Tam/Cai Lay	Dec. 68 – March 69	1st Brigade, 9th Infantry Division
Ben Luc	April 69 – April 70	1st Brigade, 9th Infantry Division
Cambodia	May 70	1st Brigade, 9th Infantry Division
Can Giuoc	June 70 – Oct. 70	3d Brigade, 9th Infantry Division

1st Battalion, 35th Infantry (Infantry)

Arrived Vietnam: 17 January 1966
Departed Vietnam: 10 April 1970
Previous Station: Hawaii

Authorized Strength	1966	1968	1970
Battalion	829	971	920

The 1st Battalion, 35th Infantry ("The Cacti") served with the 25th Infantry Division before being transferred to the 4th Infantry Division on 1 August 1967.

Location	Service	Major Command
Pleiku	Jan. 66 – May 67	3d Brigade, 25th Infantry Division
Duc Pho	June 67	3d Brigade, 25th Infantry Division
Pleiku/Duc Pho	July 67	3d Brigade, 25th Infantry Division
Cu Chi/Tay Ninh	Aug. 67	3d Brigade, 25th Infantry Division
Pleiku/Duc Pho	Sept. 67 – Jan. 68	3d Brigade, 4th Infantry Division

Location	Service	Major Command
Pleiku/Chu Lai	Feb. 68	3d Brigade, 4th Infantry Division
Dak To/Bong Son	March 68	3d Brigade, 4th Infantry Division
Pleiku/Bong Son/ Kontum	April 68	3d Brigade, 4th Infantry Division
Pleiku/Kontum	May 68 – July 68	3d Brigade, 4th Infantry Division
Pleiku	Aug. 68 – Nov. 68	3d Brigade, 4th Infantry Division
Pleiku/Tuttle	Dec. 68	3d Brigade, 4th Infantry Division
Pleiku/Catecka	Jan. 69 – July 69	3d Brigade, 4th Infantry Division
Pleiku/Tuttle	Aug. 69 – Nov. 69	3d Brigade, 4th Infantry Division
Pleiku	Dec. 69 – Jan. 70	3d Brigade, 4th Infantry Division
An Khe	Feb. 70 – March 70	2d Brigade, 4th Infantry Division
Ha Tien	April 70	2d Brigade, 4th Infantry Division

2d Battalion, 35th Infantry (Infantry)

Arrived Vietnam: 17 January 1966
Departed Vietnam: 8 December 1970
Previous Station: Hawaii

Authorized Strength	1966	1968	1970
Battalion	829	971	920

The 2d Battalion, 35th Infantry ("The Cacti") was part of the 25th Infantry Division until transferred to the 4th Infantry Division officially on 1 August 1967.

Location	Service	Major Command
Pleiku	Jan. 66 – May 67	3d Brigade, 25th Infantry Division
Duc Pho	June 67	3d Brigade, 25th Infantry Division
Pleiku/Duc Pho	July 67	3d Brigade, 25th Infantry Division
Cu Chi/Tay Ninh	Aug. 67	3d Brigade, 25th Infantry Division
Pleiku/Duc Pho	Sept. 67 – Jan. 68	3d Brigade, 4th Infantry Division
Pleiku/Chu Lai	Feb. 68	3d Brigade, 4th Infantry Division
Dak To/Bong Son	March 68	3d Brigade, 4th Infantry Division
Pleiku/Bong Son/ Kontum	April 68	3d Brigade, 4th Infantry Division
Pleiku/Kontum	May 68 – July 68	3d Brigade, 4th Infantry Division
Pleiku	Aug. 68 – Nov. 68	3d Brigade, 4th Infantry Division
Pleiku/Tuttle	Dec. 68	3d Brigade, 4th Infantry Division
Pleiku/Catecka	Jan. 69 – July 69	3d Brigade, 4th Infantry Division
Pleiku/Tuttle	Aug. 69 – Nov. 69	3d Brigade, 4th Infantry Division
Pleiku	Dec. 69 – Jan. 70	3d Brigade, 4th Infantry Division
An Khe	Feb. 70 – March 70	2d Brigade,

Ha Tien	April 70	7th Infantry Division 2d Brigade, 4th Infantry Division
Plei Djereng	May 70	2d Brigade, 4th Infantry Division
An Khe	June 70 – Sept. 70	2d Brigade, 4th Infantry Division
Phu Nhieu	Oct. 70	2d Brigade, 4th Infantry Division
An Khe	Nov. 70 – Dec. 70	2d Brigade, 4th Infantry Division

2d Battalion, 39th Infantry (Infantry)

Arrived Vietnam: 3 January 1967
Departed Vietnam: 3 August 1969
Previous Station: Fort Riley
Authorized Strength: 818

The 2d Battalion, 39th Infantry ("AAA-O") served with the 9th Infantry Division.

Location	Service	Major Command
Bear Cat	Jan. 67 – Feb. 68	1st Brigade, 9th Infantry Division
Bear Cat/Dong Tam	March 68 – June 68	1st Brigade, 9th Infantry Division
Bear Cat/Tan An	July 68	1st Brigade, 9th Infantry Division
Tan An	Aug. 68 – Nov. 68	1st Brigade, 9th Infantry Division
Dong Tam/Cai Lay	Dec. 68 – March 69	1st Brigade, 9th Infantry Division
Dong Tam	April 69	1st Brigade, 9th Infantry Division
Dong Tam/Cai Lay	May 69 – Aug. 69	1st Brigade, 9th Infantry Division

3d Battalion, 39th Infantry (Infantry)

Arrived Vietnam: 1 January 1967
Departed Vietnam: 8 August 1969
Previous Station: Fort Riley
Authorized Strength: 818

The 3d Battalion, 39th Infantry ("AAA-O") served with the 9th Infantry Division.

Location	Service	Major Command
Rach Kien	Jan. 67 – Feb. 68	3d Brigade, 9th Infantry Division
Can Giuoc	March 68 – April 68	3d Brigade, 9th Infantry Division
Rach Kien	May 68 – July 68	3d Brigade, 9th Infantry Division
My Tho/Can Giuoc	Aug. 68 – Sept. 68	3d Brigade, 9th Infantry Division
My Tho	Oct. 68	3d Brigade, 9th Infantry Division
Dong Tam	Nov. 68	3d Brigade, 9th Infantry Division
Tan An	Dec. 68 – Feb. 69	3d Brigade, 9th Infantry Division
Dong Tam/Cai Lay	March 69	1st Brigade, 9th Infantry Division

| Dong Tam | April 69 | 1st Brigade, 9th Infantry Division |
| Dong Tam/Cai Lay | May 69 – Aug. 69 | 1st Brigade, 9th Infantry Division |

4th Battalion, 39th Infantry (Infantry)

Arrived Vietnam: 3 January 1967
Departed Vietnam: 30 July 1969
Previous Station: Fort Riley
Authorized Strength: 818

The 4th Battalion, 39th Infantry ("AAA-O") was part of the 9th Infantry Division.

Location	Service	Major Command
Bear Cat	Jan. 67 – Oct. 67	1st Brigade, 9th Infantry Division
Ban Me Thuot	Nov. 67 – Jan. 68	1st Brigade, 9th Infantry Division
Nha Be	Feb. 68 – July 68	3d Brigade, 9th Infantry Division
Nha Be	Aug. 68 – Oct. 68	3d Brigade, 9th Infantry Division
Binh Long	Nov. 68	3d Brigade, 9th Infantry Division
Binh Long	Dec. 68 – Feb. 69	1st Brigade, 9th Infantry Division
Dong Tam/Cai Lay	March 69	1st Brigade, 9th Infantry Division
Dong Tam	April 69	1st Brigade, 9th Infantry Division
Dong Tam/Cai Lay	May 69 – July 69	1st Brigade, 9th Infantry Division

1st Battalion, 46th Infantry (Light Infantry)

Arrived Vietnam: 22 October 1967
Departed Vietnam: 20 June 1972
Previous Station: Fort Hood
Authorized Strength: 920

The 1st Battalion, 46th Infantry ("The Professionals") served with the 198th Infantry Brigade (Light), being officially transferred to the 23d Infantry Division (AMERICAL) on 15 February 1969. In August 1971 the battalion joined the 196th Infantry Brigade which it served until it departed Vietnam.

Location	Service	Major Command
Duc Pho	Oct. 67 – Nov. 67	198th Infantry Brigade
Chu Lai	Dec. 67 – Oct. 68	198 Infantry Brigade
Tam Ky	Nov. 68	198th Infantry Brigade
Chu Lai	Dec. 68 – Jan. 69	198th Infantry Brigade
Chu Lai	Feb. 69 – Nov. 69	23d Infantry Division (AMERICAL)
Chu Lai/Dong Le	Dec. 69 – March 70	23d Infantry Division (AMERICAL)
Chu Lai/Long Phu	April 70 – July 70	23d Infantry Division (AMERICAL)
Chu Lai/Trung Canh	Aug. 70	23d Infantry Division (AMERICAL)
Chu Lai/My Son	Sept. 70 – Oct. 70	23d Infantry Division (AMERICAL)
Chu Lai/Tri Binh	Nov. 70	23d Infantry Division (AMERICAL)

Chu Lai	Dec. 70 – July 71	23d Infantry Division (AMERICAL)
Da Nang	Aug. 71 – June 72	196th Infantry Brigade

5th Battalion, 46th Infantry (Light Infantry)

Arrived Vietnam: 31 March 1968
Departed Vietnam: 21 May 1971
Previous Station: Fort Hood
Authorized Strength: 920

The 5th Battalion, 46th Infantry ("The Professionals") was activated 2 October 1967 at Fort Hood and joined the 198th Infantry Brigade (Light) as its fourth maneuver battalion, transferring officially to the 23d Infantry Division (AMERICAL) on 15 February 1969.

Location	Service	Major Command
Chu Lai	March 68 – Oct. 68	198th Infantry Brigade
Tam Ky	Nov. 68	198th Infantry Brigade
Chu Lai	Dec. 68 – Jan. 69	198th Infantry Brigade
Chu Lai	Feb. 69 – Nov. 69	23d Infantry Division (AMERICAL)
Chu Lai/Dong Le	Dec. 69 – March 70	23d Infantry Division (AMERICAL)
Chu Lai/Long Phu	April 70 – July 70	23d Infantry Division (AMERICAL)
Chu Lai/Trung Canh	Aug. 70	23d Infantry Division (AMERICAL)
Chu Lai/My Son	Sept. 70 – Oct. 70	23d Infantry Division (AMERICAL)
Chu Lai/Tri Banh	Nov. 70	23d Infantry Division (AMERICAL)
Chu Lai	Dec. 70 – May 71	23d Infantry Division (AMERICAL)

2d Battalion, 47th Infantry (Mechanized Infantry)

Arrived Vietnam: 30 January 1967
Departed Vietnam: 12 October 1970
Previous Station: Fort Riley
Authorized Strength: 907

The 2d Battalion, 47th Infantry deployed to Vietnam as a fully mechanized battalion with the 9th Infantry Division.

Location	Service	Major Command
Phu My	Jan. 67 – May 67	2d Brigade, 9th Infantry Division
Dong Tam	June 67 – Feb. 68	1st Brigade, 9th Infantry Division
Bear Cat	March 68	1st Brigade, 9th Infantry Division
Bear Cat	April 68 – May 68	1st Brigade, 9th Infantry Division
Bear Cat	June 68	2d Brigade, 9th Infantry Division
Bear Cat	July 68	2d Brigade, 9th Infantry Division
Binh Phuoc	Aug. 68 – April 70	3d Brigade, 9th Infantry Division
Cambodia	May 70 – June 70	3d Brigade, 9th Infantry Division
Binh Phuoc	July 70 – Oct. 70	3d Brigade, 9th Infantry Division

3d Battalion, 47th Infantry (Riverine Infantry)

Arrived Vietnam: 30 January 1967
Departed Vietnam: 18 July 1969
Previous Station: Fort Riley
Authorized Strength: 814

The 3d Battalion, 47th Infantry served as a component of the 9th Infantry Division's Mobile Riverine Force while in Vietnam.

Location	Service	Major Command
Phu My	Jan. 67 – May 67	2d Brigade, 9th Infantry Division*
Dong Tam	June 67 – Feb. 68	2d Brigade, 9th Infantry Division
Dong Tam	March 68	2d Brigade, 9th Infantry Division
Dong Tam/ Vinh Long	April 68 – May 68	2d Brigade, 9th Infantry Division
Dong Tam/ Mo Ca	June 68	2d Brigade, 9th Infantry Division
Dong Tam/ My Tho	July 68	2d Brigade, 9th Infantry Division
Dong Tam	Aug. 68 – Nov. 68	2d Brigade, 9th Infantry Division
Dong Tam/ Truc Giang	Dec. 68 – Jan. 69	2d Brigade, 9th Infantry Division
Dong Tam	Feb. 69 – April 69	2d Brigade, 9th Infantry Division
Truc Giang	May 69 – June 69	2d Brigade, 9th Infantry Division
Dong Tam	July 69	2d Brigade, 9th Infantry Division

* Battalion not afloat; housed in barracks ships during other periods.

4th Battalion, 47th Infantry (Riverine Infantry)

Arrived Vietnam: 30 January 1967
Departed Vietnam: 13 July 1969
Previous Station: Fort Riley
Authorized Strength: 814

The 4th Battalion, 47th Infantry served as a component of the 9th Infantry Division's Mobile Riverine Force in Vietnam.

Location	Service	Major Command
Phu My	Jan. 67 – May 67	2d Brigade, 9th Infantry Division*
Dong Tam	June 67 – Feb. 68	2d Brigade, 9th Infantry Division
Dong Tam/ Can Tho	March 68	2d Brigade, 9th Infantry Division
Dong Tam/ Vinh Long	April 68 – May 68	2d Brigade, 9th Infantry Division
Dong Tam/Mo Ca	June 68	2d Brigade, 9th Infantry Division
Dong Tam/ My Tho	July 68	2d Brigade, 9th Infantry Division
Dong Tam	Aug. 68 – Nov. 68	2d Brigade, 9th Infantry Division
Dong Tam/ Truc Giang	Dec. 68 – Jan. 69	2d Brigade, 9th Infantry Division

Dong Tam	Feb. 69 – April 69	2d Brigade, 9th Infantry Division
Truc Giang	May 69 – June 69	2d Brigade, 9th Infantry Division
Dong Tam	July 69	2d Brigade, 9th Infantry Division

* Battalion not afloat; housed in barracks ships during other periods.

1st Battalion, 50th Infantry (Mechanized Infantry)

Arrived Vietnam: 22 September 1967
Departed Vietnam: 13 December 1970
Previous Station: Fort Hood
Authorized Strength: 907

The 1st Battalion, 50th Infantry (Mechanized) was relieved from the 2d Armored Division at Fort Hood on 1 September 1967 and served in Vietnam under the U.S. Army, Pacific (USARPAC) command, where it served as a general reserve to various units.

Location	Service	Major Command
An Khe/Bong Son	Sept. 67 – Feb. 68	1st Cavalry Division
An Khe/Bong Son	March 68 – April 68	3d Brigade, 4th Infantry Division
An Khe/Bong Son	May 68 – Oct. 68	173d Airborne Brigade
An Khe	Nov. 68 – April 69	173d Airborne Brigade
Bong Son	May 69	173d Airborne Brigade
Phu My	June 69 – Sept. 69	173d Airborne Brigade
Phan Thiet	Oct. 69 – Sept. 70	Task Force South, I Field Force, Vietnam
Phan Thiet	Oct. 70 – Dec. 70	I Field Force, Vietnam

Company E, 50th Infantry (Long-Range Patrol)

Arrived Vietnam: 20 December 1967
Departed Vietnam: 1 February 1969
Previous Station: Vietnam
Authorized Strength: 118

Company E, 50th Infantry was raised as a separate long-range reconnaissance patrol company serving with the 9th Infantry Division in Vietnam.

Company F, 50th Infantry (Long-Range Patrol) (Rifle Security)

First Tour:
Arrived Vietnam: 20 December 1967
Departed Vietnam: 1 February 1969
Previous Station: Vietnam

Second Tour:
Arrived Vietnam: 30 June 1971
Departed Vietnam: 16 November 1972
Previous Station: Vietnam

Authorized Strength	1968	1971
Company	118	160

Company F, 50th Infantry served twice in Vietnam. It was initially raised as a long-range reconnaissance patrol company with the 25th Infantry Division, being replaced by Company F, 75th Infantry (Ranger). Company F, 50th Infantry was again raised as a rifle

security company guarding the Da Nang installation under the command of U.S. Army Support Command, Da Nang.

Company D, 51st Infantry (Rifle Security)

Arrived Vietnam: 29 November 1966
Departed Vietnam: 30 June 1972
Previous Station: Fort Lewis

Authorized Strength	1968	1970
Company	151	160

Company D, 51st Infantry was posted to highway security duty with the 97th Military Police Battalion at Phan Rang, later transferring to the 18th Military Police Brigade at Cam Ranh Bay. The U.S. Army Support Command, Cam Ranh Bay later assumed control of the separate company.

Company E, 51st Infantry (Long-Range Patrol)

Arrived Vietnam: 20 December 1967
Departed Vietnam: 1 February 1969
Previous Station: Vietnam
Authorized Strength: 118

Company E, 51st Infantry was a long-range reconnaissance patrol company serving the 23d Infantry Division (AMERICAL), later replaced by Company G, 75th Infantry (Ranger).

Company F, 51st Infantry (Long-Range Patrol)

Arrived Vietnam: 25 September 1967
Departed Vietnam: 26 December 1968
Previous Station: Vietnam
Authorized Strength: 230

Company F, 51st Infantry was a separate long-range reconnaissance patrol company serving with the 199th Infantry Brigade (Light) in Vietnam.

1st Battalion, 52d Infantry (Light Infantry)

Arrived Vietnam: 10 February 1968
Departed Vietnam: 1 November 1971
Previous Station: Fort Hood
Authorized Strength: 920

The 1st Battalion, 52d Infantry ("Ready Rifles") was part of the 198th Infantry Brigade (Light), becoming part of the 23d Infantry Division (AMERICAL) on 15 February 1969, and being transferred to the 11th Infantry Brigade in August 1971.

Location	Service	Major Command
Chu Lai	Feb. 68 – Oct. 68	198th Infantry Brigade
Tam Ky	Nov. 68	198th Infantry Brigade
Chu Lai	Dec. 68 – Jan. 69	198th Infantry Brigade
Chu Lai	Feb. 69 – Nov. 69	23d Infantry Division (AMERICAL)

Chu Lai/Dong Le	Dec. 69 – March 70	23d Infantry Division (AMERICAL)
Chu Lai/Long Phu	April 70 – July 70	23d Infantry Division (AMERICAL)
Chu Lai/ Trung Canh	Aug. 70	23d Infantry Division (AMERICAL)
Chu Lai/My Son	Sept. 70 – Oct. 70	23d Infantry Division (AMERICAL)
Chu Lai/Tri Binh	Nov. 70	23d Infantry Division (AMERICAL)
Chu Lai	Dec. 70 – July 71	23d Infantry Division (AMERICAL)
The Loi	Aug. 71 – Oct. 71	11th Infantry Brigade

Company C, 52d Infantry (Rifle Security)

Arrived Vietnam: 1 December 1966
Departed Vietnam: 15 August 1972
Previous Station: Fort Lewis

Authorized Strength	1968	1971
Company	151	137

Company C, 52d Infantry ("Ready Rifles") was a rifle security company posted to Saigon guard duty under the 716th Military Police Battalion and later the 18th Military Police Brigade during its service in Vietnam.

Company D, 52d Infantry (Rifle Security)

First Tour:
Arrived Vietnam: 26 November 1966
Departed Vietnam: 22 November 1969
Previous Station: Fort Lewis

Second Tour:
Arrived Vietnam: 30 June 1971
Departed Vietnam: 26 November 1972
Previous Station: Vietnam

Authorized Strength	1968	1971
Company	151	160

Company D, 52d Infantry ("Ready Rifles") was a separate rifle security company attached to the 95th Military Police Battalion at Long Binh. During its second tour in Vietnam it was posted to Qui Nhon security duty under the control of the U.S. Army Support Command, Qui Nhon.

Company E, 52d Infantry (Long-Range Patrol)

Arrived Vietnam: 20 December 1967
Departed Vietnam: 1 February 1969
Previous Station: Vietnam
Authorized Strength: 118

Company E, 52d Infantry ("Ready Rifles") served the 1st Cavalry Division as a separate long-range reconnaissance patrol company until replaced by Company H, 75th Infantry (Ranger).

Company F, 52d Infantry (Long-Range Patrol)

Arrived Vietnam: 20 December 1967
Departed Vietnam: 1 February 1969
Previous Station: Vietnam
Authorized Strength: 118

Comany F, 52d Infantry ("Ready Rifles") served the 1st Infantry Division as a separate long-range reconnaissance patrol company until replaced by Company I, 75th Infantry (Ranger).

Company C, 54th Infantry (Rife Security)

Arrived Vietnam: 29 November 1966
Departed Vietnam: 30 April 1972
Previous Station: Fort Lewis

Authorized Strength	1968	1970
Company	151	160

Company C, 54th Infantry was a separate rifle security company serving with the 97th Military Police Battalion at Tuy Hoa, later being transferred to Cha Rang under the U.S. Army Support Command, Cam Ranh Bay.

Company D, 58th Infantry (Rifle Security)

Arrived Vietnam: 29 November 1966
Departed Vietnam: 22 June 1972
Previous Station: Fort Lewis

Authorized Strength	1968	1971
Company	151	160

Company D, 58th Infantry ("The Patriots") was a rifle security company attached to the 93d Military Police Battalion at Phu Thang, being transferred in 1969 to the 18th Military Police Brigade control at Qui Nhon. It was later posted to Phu Tai under the U.S. Army Support Command, Cam Ranh Bay.

Company E, 58th Infantry (Long-Range Patrol)

Arrived Vietnam: 20 December 1967
Departed Vietnam: 1 February 1969
Previous Station: Vietnam
Authorized Strength: 118

Company E, 58th Infantry ("The Patriots") was raised as a separate long-range reconnaissance patrol company under the 4th Infantry Division, later being replaced by Company K, 75th Infantry (Ranger).

Company F, 58th Infantry (Long-Range Patrol)

Arrived Vietnam: 10 January 1968
Departed Vietnam: 1 February 1969
Previous Station: Vietnam
Authorized Strength: 118

Company F, 58th Infantry ("The Patriots") served the 101st Airborne Division (Airmobile) until it was replaced by Company L, 75th Infantry (Ranger).

2d Battalion, 60th Infantry (Infantry)

Arrived Vietnam: 20 December 1966
Departed Vietnam: 12 October 1970
Previous Station: Fort Riley
Authorized Strength: 818

The 2d Battalion, 60th Infantry was part of the 9th Infantry Division in Vietnam.

Location	Service	Major Command
Tan Tru	Dec. 66 – Oct. 67	3d Brigade, 9th Infantry Division
Ap Than Thuan	Nov. 67 – March 68	3d Brigade, 9th Infantry Division
My Phuoc Tuy	April 68 – Sept. 68	1st Brigade, 9th Infantry Division
Rach Kien	Oct. 68	1st Brigade, 9th Infantry Division
Tan Tru	Nov. 68	1st Brigade, 9th Infantry Division
Tan Tru	Dec. 68 – May 70	3d Brigade, 9th Infantry Division
Cambodia	June 70 – July 70	3d Brigade, 9th Infantry Division
Tan Tru	Aug. 70 – Oct. 70	3d Brigade, 9th Infantry Division

3d Battalion, 60th Infantry (Riverine Infantry)

Arrived Vietnam: 20 December 1966
Departed Vietnam: 8 July 1969
Previous Station: Fort Riley
Authorized Strength: 814

The 3d Battalion, 60th Infantry served as part of the 9th Infantry Division's Mobile Riverine Force in Vietnam.

Location	Service	Major Command
Bear Cat	Dec. 66 – Feb. 67	3d Brigade, 9th Infantry Division*
Dong Tam	March 67 – May 67	2d Brigade, 9th Infantry Division*
Dong Tam	June 67 – June 68	2d Brigade, 9th Infantry Division
Dong Tam/My Tho	July 68	2d Brigade, 9th Infantry Division
Mo Cay	Aug. 68 – Nov. 68	2d Brigade, 9th Infantry Division
Dong Tam/Truc Giang	Dec. 68 – Jan. 69	2d Brigade, 9th Infantry Division
Dong Tam	Feb. 69 – April 69	2d Brigade, 9th Infantry Division
Truc Giang	May 69 – June 69	2d Brigade, 9th Infantry Division
Dong Tam	July 69	2d Brigade, 9th Infantry Division*

* Battalion not afloat; housed in barracks ships during other periods. Battalion assumed mobile riverine force duty in December 1967.

5th Battalion, 60th Infantry (Mechanized Infantry)

Arrived Vietnam: 20 December 1966
Departed Vietnam: 12 October 1970
Previous Station: Fort Riley
Authorized Strength: 907

The 5th Battalion, 60th Infantry arrived in Vietnam fully mechanized with the 9th Infantry Division, but was reorganized as divisional infantry in September 1968 when it gave up its mechanized assets to the 1st Battalion, 16th Infantry of the 1st Infantry Division.

Location	Service	Major Command
Bear Cat	Dec. 66 – Jan. 67	3d Brigade, 9th Infantry Division
Binh Phuoc	Feb. 67 – May 67	3d Brigade, 9th Infantry Division
Binh Phuoc	June 67 – June 68	3d Brigade, 9th Infantry Division
Tan An/My Tho	July 68	3d Brigade, 9th Infantry Division
My Tho/Can Giuoc	Aug. 68 – Sept. 68	3d Brigade, 9th Infantry Division
Binh Phuoc	Oct. 68	3d Brigade, 9th Infantry Division*

Rach Kien	Nov. 68 — Dec. 69	3d Brigade, 9th Infantry Division*
Binh Phuoc	Jan. 70 – April 70	3d Brigade, 9th Infantry Division*
Cambodia	May 70 — June 70	3d Brigade, 9th Infantry Division*
Binh Phuoc	July 70 – Oct. 70	3d Brigade, 9th Infantry Division*

* Battalion dismounted during this period.

1st Battalion, 61st Infantry (Mechanized Infantry)

Arrived Vietnam: 27 July 1968
Departed Vietnam: 1 August 1971
Previous Station: Fort Carson
Authorized Strength: 907

The 1st Battalion, 61st Infantry (Mechanized) was part of the 1st Brigade Task Force of the 5th Infantry Division (Mechanized) in Vietnam.

Location	Service	Major Command
Cam Lo	July 68 – Oct. 68	1st Brigade, 5th Infantry Division (Mech)
Quang Tri/Dong Ha	Nov. 68	1st Brigade, 5th Infantry Division (Mech)
Quang Tri	Dec. 68 – March 71	1st Brigade, 5th Infantry Division (Mech)
Quang Tri/Khe Sanh	April 71	1st Brigade, 5th Infantry Division (Mech)
Quang Tri	May 71 – July 71	1st Brigade, 5th Infantry Division (Mech)

Companies C – I and K – P, 75th Infantry (Ranger)

The 75th Infantry ("Merrill's Marauders") was organized 1 January 1969 under the Combat Arms Regimental System (CARS) to provide a parent unit for the separate long-range reconnaissance patrol companies. That year the assets of the long-range patrol companies in Vietnam were transferred to the ranger companies of the 75th Infantry, continuing the tradition of the famed Merrill's Marauders of World War II — the 5307th Provisional Composite Unit which had been designated the 475th Infantry in August 1944 and redesignated as the 75th Infantry in 1954. Ranger companies in Vietnam were particularly elite.

Company	Strength*	Service	Command
Co C, 75th Inf	230	1 Feb. 69 – 25 Oct. 71	I Field Force, Vietnam

Company	Strength*	Service	Command
Co D, 75th Inf	198	20 Nov. 69 – 10 April 70	II Field Force, Vietnam
Co E, 75th Inf	118	1 Feb. 69 – 23 Aug. 69	9th Infantry Division
Co E, 75th Inf†	61	1 Oct. 69 – 12 Oct. 70	3d Brigade, 9th Infantry Division
Co F, 75th Inf	118	1 Feb. 69 – 15 March 71	25th Infantry Division
Co G, 75th Inf	118	1 Feb. 69 – 1 Oct. 71	23d Infantry Division (AMERICAL)
Co H, 75th Inf	198	1 Feb. 69 – 15 Aug. 72	1st Cavalry Division (Airmobile)
Co I, 75th Inf	118	1 Feb. 69 – 7 April 70	1st Infantry Division
Co K, 75th Inf	118	1 Feb. 69 – 10 Dec. 70	4th Infantry Division
Co L, 75th Inf	118	1 Feb. 69 – 26 Dec. 71	101st Airborne Division (AM)
Co M, 75th Inf	61	1 Feb. 69 – 12 Oct. 70	199th Infantry Brigade
Co N, 75th Inf	61	1 Feb. 69 – 25 Aug. 71	173d Airborne Brigade
Co O, 75th Inf	61	1 Feb. 69 – 20 Nov. 69	3d Brigade, 82d Airborne Division
Co P, 75th Inf	61	1 Feb. 69 – 31 Aug. 71	1st Brigade, 5th Infantry Division (Mech)

* Typical authorized strengths given, usually for the year 1970.

† Second tour in Vietnam.

Assets used to form Ranger Companies of the 75th Infantry in Vietnam:

Company	Assets Derived from
Co C, 75th Inf (Ranger)	Co E, 20th Inf (LRP)
Co D, 75th Inf (Ranger)	Co F, 51st Inf (LRP)
Co E, 75th Inf (Ranger)	Co E, 50th Inf (LRP)
Co F, 75th Inf (Ranger)	Co F, 50th Inf (LRP)
Co G, 75th Inf (Ranger)	Co E, 51st Inf (LRP)
Co H, 75th Inf (Ranger)	Co E, 52d Inf (LRP)
Co I, 75th Inf (Ranger)	Co F, 52d Inf (LRP)
Co K, 75th Inf (Ranger)	Co E, 58th Inf (LRP)
Co L, 75th Inf (Ranger)	Co F, 58th Inf (LRP)
Co M, 75th Inf (Ranger)	71st Inf Detachment (LRP)
Co N, 75th Inf (Ranger)	74th Inf Detachment (LRP)
Co O, 75th Inf (Ranger)	78th Inf Detachment (LRP)
Co P, 75th Inf (Ranger)	79th Inf Detachment (LRP)

Company C, 87th Infantry (Rifle Security)

Arrived Vietnam: 29 November 1966
Departed Vietnam: 26 November 1972
Previous Station: Fort Lewis

Authorized Strength	1968	1971
Company	151	160

Company C, 87th Infantry was a separate rifle security company attached to the 92d Military Police Battalion guarding Tan Son Nhut. It was later posted to Long Binh and there controlled by the U.S. Army Support Command, Saigon.

Company D, 87th Infantry (Rifle Security)

First Tour:
Arrived Vietnam: 1 December 1966
Departed Vietnam: 8 November 1969
Previous Station: Fort Lewis

Second Tour:
Arrived Vietnam: 30 June 1971
Departed Vietnam: 30 April 1972
Previous Station: Vietnam

Authorized Strength	1968	1971
Company	151	160

Company D, 87th Infantry was a separate rifle security company attached to the 95th Military Police Battalion at Long Binh, and on its second tour in Vietnam used by the 26th General Support Group to guard its installations at Tan My.

Company D, 151st Infantry (Long-Range Patrol)

Arrived Vietnam: 30 December 1968
Departed Vietnam: 20 November 1969
Previous Station: Greenfield, Indiana, via Fort Benning
Authorized Strength: 214

Company D, 151st Infantry, Indiana National Guard was the only National Guard infantry unit to serve in Vietnam. After extensive training at Fort Benning the company was sent to Vietnam where it was placed under the II Field Force, Vietnam and operated out of Long Binh. Upon the company's departure, Company D, 75th Infantry (Ranger) was raised to replace it. While in Vietnam this company wore the shoulder patch of its parent National Guard command, the 38th Infantry Division, which at the time was headquartered in Indianapolis, Indiana.

3d Battalion, 187th Infantry (Airmobile Infantry)

Arrived Vietnam: 16 December 1967
Departed Vietnam: 10 December 1971
Previous Station: Fort Campbell
Authorized Strength: 920

The 3d Battalion, 187th Infantry ("Rakkasans") served as part of the 101st Airborne Division (Airmobile) in Vietnam.

Location	Service	Major Command
Phuoc Vinh	Dec. 67 – May 68	3d Brigade, 101st Airborne Div
Phuoc Vinh/Dak To	June 68	3d Brigade, 101st Airborne Div
Phuoc Vinh/Cu Chi	July 68 – Sept. 68	3d Brigade, 101st Airborne Div
Phuoc Vinh/Long Binh	Oct. 68	3d Brigade, 101st Airborne Div (AM)
Bien Hoa/Phong Dien	Nov. 68 – June 69	3d Brigade, 101st Airborne Div (AM)
Bien Hoa/Ta Bat	July 69	3d Brigade, 101st Airborne Div (AM)
Berchtesgaden*	Aug. 69	3d Brigade, 101st Airborne Div (AM)
Bien Hoa/Ta Bat	Sept. 69	3d Brigade, 101st Airborne Div (AM)
Bien Hoa/Phong Dien	Oct. 69	3d Brigade, 101st Airborne Div (AM)
Bien Hoa/Mai Loc	Nov. 69	3d Brigade, 101st Airborne Div (AM)
Phong Dien	Dec. 69 – Aug. 70	3d Brigade, 101st Airborne Div (AM)
Hue/Phu Bai	Sept. 70 – Feb. 71	3d Brigade, 101st Airborne Div (AM)
Camp Carroll	March 71	3d Brigade, 101st Airborne Div (AM)
Camp Carroll	April 71	1st Brigade, 5th Infantry Div (Mech)
Hue/Phu Bai	May 71 – July 71	3d Brigade, 101st Airborne Div (AM)
Hue/Phu Bai	Aug. 71 – Oct. 71	U.S. Army Forces, Military Region 2
Hue/Phu Bai	Nov. 71 – Dec. 71	3d Brigade, 101st Airborne Div (AM)

* Fire Support Base.

1st Battalion, 327th Infantry (Airborne Infantry) (Airmobile Infantry)

Arrived Vietnam: 29 July 1965
Departed Vietnam: 20 January 1972
Previous Station: Fort Campbell

Authorized Strength	1966	1968	1970
Battalion	792	920	920

The 1st Battalion, 327th Infantry ("Bastogne Bulldogs") initially entered Vietnam as part of the 1st Brigade, 101st Airborne Division and was parachutist qualified. By 26 August 1968 the battalion was reorganized as purely airmobile infantry.

Location	Service	Major Command
Bien Hoa/Vung Tau	July 65 – Sept. 65	1st Brigade, 101st Airborne Div
Cam Ranh Bay	Oct. 65	1st Brigade, 101st Airborne Div
Ma Ca	Nov. 65	1st Brigade, 101st Airborne Div
Phan Rang	Dec. 65 – May 67	1st Brigade, 101st Airborne Div
Duc Pho	June 67	1st Brigade, 101st Airborne Div
Phan Rang/Duc Pho	July 67 – Nov. 67	1st Brigade, 101st Airborne Div
Phan Rang	Dec. 67	1st Brigade, 101st Airborne Div
Phan Rang/Song Be	Jan. 68	1st Brigade, 101st Airborne Div
Phan Rang/Bien Hoa	Feb. 68	1st Brigade, 101st Airborne Div
Phan Rang/Hue/ Phu Bai	March 68	1st Brigade, 101st Airborne Div
Phan Rang/Phu Bai	April 68	1st Brigade, 101st Airborne Div

Location	Service	Major Command
Phan Rang/Hue	May 68 – June 68	1st Brigade, 101st Airborne Div
Phan Rang/Phu Bai	July 68 – Oct. 68	1st Brigade, 101st Airborne Div
Bien Hoa/Phu Bai	Nov. 68 – April 69	1st Brigade, 101st Airborne Div (AM)
Bien Hoa/Gia Le	May 69	1st Brigade,101st Airborne Div (AM)
Bien Hoa/Tam Ky	June 69 – Aug. 69	1st Brigade, 101st Airborne Div (AM)
Bien Hoa/Gia Le	Sept. 69 – Nov. 69	1st Brigade, 101st Airborne Div (AM)
Hue/Phu Bai	Dec. 69 – Oct.71	1st Brigade, 101st Airborne Div (AM)
Hue/Phu Bai	Nov. 71 – Jan. 72	196th Infantry Brigade

2d Battalion, 327th Infantry
(Airborne Infantry)
(Airmobile Infantry)

Arrived Vietnam: 29 July 1965
Departed Vietnam: 21 April 1972
Previous Station: Fort Campbell

Authorized Strength	1966	1968	1970
Battalion	792	920	920

The 2d Battalion, 327th Infantry ("Bastogne Bulldogs") initially entered Vietnam as part of the 1st Brigade, 101st Airborne Division and was parachutist qualified. By 26 August 1968 the battalion was reorganized as purely airmobile infantry.

Location	Service	Major Command
Bien Hoa/Vung Tau	July 65 – Sept. 65	1st Brigade, 101st Airborne Div
Cam Ranh Bay	Oct. 65	1st Brigade, 101st Airborne Div
Ma Ca	Nov. 65	1st Brigade, 101st Airborne Div
Phan Rang	Dec. 65 – May 67	1st Brigade, 101st Airborne Div
Duc Pho	June 67	1st Brigade, 101st Airborne Div
Phan Rang/Duc Pho	July 67 – Nov. 67	1st Brigade, 101st Airborne Div
Phan Rang	Dec. 67	1st Brigade, 101st Airborne Div
Phan Rang/Song Be	Jan. 68	1st Brigade, 101st Airborne Div
Phan Rang/ Bien Hoa	Feb. 68	1st Brigade, 101st Airborne Div
Phan Rang/ Hue/Phu Bai	March 68	1st Brigade, 101st Airborne Div
Phan Rang/Phu Bai	April 68	1st Brigade, 101st Airborne Div
Phan Rang/Hue	May 68 – June 68	1st Brigade, 101st Airborne Div
Phan Rang/Phu Bai	July 68 – Oct. 68	1st Brigade, 101st Airborne Div
Bien Hoa/Phu Bai	Nov. 68 – April 69	1st Brigade, 101st Airborne Div (AM)
Bien Hoa/Gia Le	May 69	1st Brigade, 101st Airborne Div (AM)

Location	Service	Major Command
Bien Hoa/Tam Ky	June 69 – Aug. 69	1st Brigade, 101st Airborne Div (AM)
Bien Hoa/Gia Le	Sept. 69 – Nov. 69	1st Brigade, 101st Airborne Div (AM)
Hue/Phu Bai	Dec. 69 – Dec. 71	1st Brigade, 101st Airborne Div (AM)
Hue/Phu Bai	Jan. 72 – March 72	U.S. Army Support Command, Cam Ranh Bay
Hue/Phu Bai	April 72	U.S. Army Forces, Military Region 2

1st Battalion, 501st Infantry
(Airmobile Infantry)

Arrived Vietnam: 16 December 1967
Departed Vietnam: 4 February 1972
Previous Station: Fort Campbell
Authorized Strength: 920

The 1st Battalion, 501st Infantry served with the 101st Airborne Division (Airmobile) in Vietnam.

Location	Service	Major Command
Cu Chi	Dec. 67 – Jan. 68	2d Brigade, 101st Airborne Div
Cu Chi/Hue	Feb. 68	2d Brigade, 101st Airborne Div
Cu Chi/Quang Tri	March 68	2d Brigade, 101st Airborne Div
Cu Chi/Phu Bai	April 68 – Oct. 68	2d Brigade, 101st Airborne Div
Bien Hoa/Phu Bai	Nov. 68	2d Brigade, 101st Airborne Div (AM)
Bien Hoa/Van Xa	Dec. 68 – Nov. 69	2d Brigade, 101st Airborne Div (AM)
Van Xa	Dec. 69 – March 70	2d Brigade, 101st Airborne Div (AM)
Phu Bai	April 70 – Jan. 72	2d Brigade, 101st Airborne Div (AM)

2d Battalion, 501st Infantry
(Airmobile Infantry)

Arrived Vietnam: 16 December 1967
Departed Vietnam: 1 July 1972
Previous Station: Fort Campbell
Authorized Strength: 920

The 2d Battalion, 501st Infantry was part of the 101st Airborne Division (Airmobile) in Vietnam.

Location	Service	Major Command
Cu Chi	Dec. 67 – Jan. 68	2d Brigade, 101st Airborne Div
Cu Chi/Hue	Feb. 68	2d Brigade, 101st Airborne Div
Cu Chi/Quang Tri	March 68	2d Brigade, 101st Airborne Div

Cu Chi/Phu Bai	April 68 – Oct. 68	2d Brigade, 101st Airborne Div
Bien Hoa/Phu Bai	Nov. 68	2d Brigade,101st Airborne Div (AM)
Bien Hoa/Van Xa	Dec. 68 – Nov. 69	2d Brigade, 101st Airborne Div (AM)
Van Xa	Dec. 69 – March 70	2d Brigade, 101st Airborne Div (AM)
Phu Bai	April 70 – Oct. 71	2d Brigade, 101st Airborne Div (AM)
Phu Bai	Nov. 71	U.S. Army Forces, Military Region 2
Phu Bai	Dec. 71 – July 72	U.S. Army Support Command, Cam Ranh Bay

1st Battalion, 502d Infantry
(Airmobile Infantry)

Arrived Vietnam: 16 December 1967
Departed Vietnam: 8 February 1972
Previous Station: Fort Campbell
Authorized Strength: 920

The 1st Battalion, 501st Infantry served with the 101st Airborne Division (Airmobile) in Vietnam.

Location	Service	Major Command
Cu Chi	Dec. 67 – Jan. 68	2d Brigade, 101st Airborne Div
Cu Chi/Hue	Feb. 68	2d Brigade, 101st Airborne Div
Cu Chi/Quang Tri	March 68	2d Brigade, 101st Airborne Div
Cu Chi/Phu Bai	April 68 – Oct. 68	2d Brigade, 101st Airborne Div
Bien Hoa/Phu Bai	Nov. 68	2d Brigade, 101st Airborne Div (AM)
Bien Hoa/Van Xa	Dec. 68 – Nov. 69	2d Brigade, 101st Airborne Div (AM)
Van Xa	Dec. 69 – March 70	2d Brigade, 101st Airborne Div (AM)
Phu Bai	April 70 – Feb. 72	2d Brigade, 101st Airborne Div (AM)

2d Battalion, 502d Infantry
(Airborne Infantry)
(Airmobile Infantry)

Arrived Vietnam: 29 July 1965
Departed Vietnam: 19 January 1972
Previous Station: Fort Campbell

Authorized Strength	1966	1968	1970
Battalion	792	920	920

The 2d Battalion, 502d Infantry was part of the 1st Brigade, 101st Airborne Division and initially fully parachutist qualified, but by 26 August 1968 had been reorganized as airmobile infantry.

Location	Service	Major Command
Bien Hoa/Vung Tau	July 65 – Sept. 65	1st Brigade, 101st Airborne Division

Cam Ranh Bay	Oct. 65	1st Brigade, 101st Airborne Division
Ma Ca	Nov. 65	1st Brigade, 101st Airborne Division
Phan Rang	Dec. 65 – May 67	1st Brigade, 101st Airborne Division
Duc Pho	June 67	1st Brigade, 101st Airborne Division
Phan Rang/Duc Pho	July 67 – Nov. 67	1st Brigade, 101st Airborne Division
Phan Rang	Dec. 67	1st Brigade, 101st Airborne Div
Phan Rang/Song Be	Jan. 68	1st Brigade, 101st Airborne Div
Phan Rang/ Bien Hoa	Feb. 68	1st Brigade, 101st Airborne Div
Phan Rang/Hue/ Phu Bai	March 68	1st Brigade, 101st Airborne Div
Phan Rang/Phu Bai	April 68	1st Brigade, 101st Airborne Div
Phan Rang/Hue	May 68 – June 68	1st Brigade, 101st Airborne Div
Phan Rang/Phu Bai	July 68 – Oct. 68	1st Brigade, 101st Airborne Div
Bien Hoa/Phu Bai	Nov. 68 – April 69	1st Brigade, 101st Airborne Div (AM)
Bien Hoa/Gia Le	May 69	1st Brigade, 101st Airborne Div (AM)
Bien Hoa/Tam Ky	June 69 – Aug. 69	1st Brigade, 101st Airborne Div (AM)
Bien Hoa/Gia Le	Sept. 69 – Nov. 69	1st Brigade, 101st Airborne Div (AM)
Hue/Phu Bai	Dec. 69 – Jan. 72	1st Brigade, 101st Airborne Div (AM)

1st Battalion, 503d Infantry
(Airborne Infantry)

Arrived Vietnam: 31 May 1965
Departed Vietnam: 27 April 1971
Previous Station: Okinawa

Authorized Strength	1966	1968	1970
Battalion	821	920	920

The 1st Battalion, 503d Infantry (Airborne) ("The Rock Regiment") was one of the first U.S. ground maneuver combat elements in Vietnam. It was part of the 173d Airborne Brigade in Vietnam.

Location	Service	Major Command
Bien Hoa	May 65 – May 67	173d Airborne Brigade
Pleiku	June 67	173d Airborne Brigade
Bien Hoa/Dak To	July 67 – Sept. 67	173d Airborne Brigade
Bien Hoa/Tuy Hoa	Oct. 67	173d Airborne Brigade
An Khe/Tuy Hoa	Nov. 67	173d Airborne Brigade
An Khe/Dak To	Dec. 67 – Feb. 68	173d Airborne Brigade
An Khe/Kontum	March 68	173d Airborne Brigade
An Khe	April 68	173d Airborne Brigade
An Khe/Bong Son	May 68 – Nov. 69	173d Airborne Brigade
Bong Son	Dec. 69 – April 71	173d Airborne Brigade

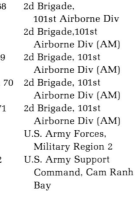

2d Battalion, 503d Infantry (Airborne Infantry)

Arrived Vietnam: 31 May 1965
Departed Vietnam: 30 July 1971
Previous Station: Okinawa

Authorized Strength	1966	1968	1970
Battalion	821	920	920

The 2d Battalion, 503d Infantry (Airborne) ("The Rock Regiment") was, along with the 1st Battalion, 503d Infantry (Airborne), one of the first U.S. Army ground combat maneuver elements to enter Vietnam. It served with the 173d Airborne Brigade, and had the distinction of being the only airborne infantry battalion to make a combat parachute assault during the war on 22 February 1967 into War Zone C of Tay Ninh Province (see U.S. Army Parachute Combat Assaults Vietnam Chart).

Location	Service	Major Command
Bien Hoa	May 65 – May 67	173d Airborne Brigade
Pleiku	June 67	173d Airborne Brigade
Bien Hoa/Dak To	July 67 – Sept. 67	173d Airborne Brigade
Bien Hoa/Tuy Hoa	Oct. 67	173d Airborne Brigade
An Khe/Tuy Hoa	Nov. 67	173d Airborne Brigade
An Khe/Dak To	Dec. 67 – Feb. 68	173d Airborne Brigade
An Khe/Kontum	March 68	173d Airborne Brigade
An Khe	April 68	173d Airborne Brigade
An Khe/Bong Son	May 68 – Nov. 69	173d Airborne Brigade
Bong Son	Dec. 69 – Nov. 70	173d Airborne Brigade
An Khe	Dec. 70 – March 71	173d Airborne Brigade
Bong Son	April 71 – June 71	173d Airborne Brigade
Bong Son	July 71	U.S. Army Support Command, Cam Ranh Bay

3d Battalion, 503d Infantry (Airborne Infantry)

Arrived Vietnam: 23 October 1967
Departed Vietnam: 5 August 1971
Previous Station: Fort Bragg
Authorized Strength: 920

The 3d Battalion, 503d Infantry (Airborne) ("The Rock Regiment") was raised to be the fourth maneuver element of the 173d Airborne Brigade, joining the brigade in Vietnam from Fort Bragg, where it had been activated 1 April 1967.

Location	Service	Major Command
Bien Hoa/Tuy Hoa	Oct. 67	173d Airborne Brigade
An Khe/Tuy Hoa	Nov. 67	173d Airborne Brigade
An Khe/Dak To	Dec. 67 – Feb. 68	173d Airborne Brigade
An Khe/Kontum	March 68	173d Airborne Brigade
An Khe	April 68	173d Airborne Brigade

An Khe/Bong Son	May 68 – Feb. 69	173d Airborne Brigade
An Khe/Bong Son	March 69 – Sept. 69	I Field Force, Vietnam
An Khe/Bong Son	Oct. 69 – Nov. 69	173d Airborne Brigade
Bong Son	Dec. 69 – Aug. 71	173d Airborne Brigade

4th Battalion, 503d Infantry (Airborne Infantry)

Arrived Vietnam: 25 June 1966
Departed Vietnam: 20 August 1971
Previous Station: Fort Campbell

Authorized Strength	1966	1968	1970
Battalion	792	920	920

The 4th Battalion, 503d Infantry (Airborne) ("The Rock Regiment") was activated at Fort Campbell on 1 April 1966 to provide a third maneuver element for the 173d Airborne Brigade. This role had been fulfilled by the 1st Battalion, Royal Australian Regiment, which served with the 173d Airborne Brigade in Vietnam from 25 May 1965 – 14 June 1966.

Location	Service	Major Command
Bien Hoa	June 66 – May 67	173d Airborne Brigade
Pleiku	June 67	173d Airborne Brigade
Bien Hoa/Dak To	July 67 – Sept. 67	173d Airborne Brigade
Bien Hoa/Tuy Hoa	Oct. 67	173d Airborne Brigade
An Khe/Tuy Hoa	Nov. 67	173d Airborne Brigade
An Khe/Dak To	Dec. 67 – Feb. 68	173d Airborne Brigade
An Khe/Kontum	March 68	173d Airborne Brigade
An Khe	April 68	173d Airborne Brigade
An Khe/Bong Son	May 68 – Nov. 69	173d Airborne Brigade
Bong Son	Dec. 69 – Aug. 71	173d Airborne Brigade

1st Battalion, 505th Infantry (Airborne Infantry)

Arrived Vietnam: 24 February 1968
Departed Vietnam: 11 December 1969
Previous Station: Fort Bragg
Authorized Strength: 920

The 1st Battalion, 505th Infantry (Airborne) ("Panthers") was part of the 3d Brigade Task Force of the 82d Airborne Division in Vietnam.

Location	Service	Major Command
Hue	Feb. 68 – April 68	3d Brigade, 82d Airborne Division
Hue/Phu Bai	May 68 – Aug. 68	3d Brigade, 82d Airborne Division
Phu Loi/Saigon	Sept. 68 – Dec. 69	3d Brigade, 82d Airborne Division

2d Battalion, 505th Infantry (Airborne Infantry)

Arrived Vietnam: 17 February 1968
Departed Vietnam: 11 December 1969
Previous Station: Fort Bragg
Authorized Strength: 920

The 2d Battalion, 505th Infantry (Airborne) ("Panthers") was a component of the 3d Brigade Task Force, 82d Airborne Division in Vietnam.

Location	Service	Major Command
Hue	Feb. 68 – April 68	3d Brigade, 82d Airborne Division
Hue/Phu Bai	May 68 – Aug. 68	3d Brigade, 82d Airborne Division
Phu Loi/Saigon	Sept. 68 – Dec. 69	3d Brigade, 82d Airborne Division

1st Battalion, 506th Infantry (Airmobile Infantry)

Arrived Vietnam: 16 December 1967
Departed Vietnam: 21 December 1971
Previous Station: Fort Campbell
Authorized Strength: 920

The 1st Battalion, 506th Infantry ("Currahee") was part of the 101st Airborne Division (Airmobile) in Vietnam.

Location	Service	Major Command
Phuoc Vinh	Dec. 67 – May 68	3d Brigade, 101st Airborne Div
Phuoc Vinh/Dak To	June 68	3d Brigade, 101st Airborne Div
Phuoc Vinh/Cu Chi	July 68 – Sept. 68	3d Brigade, 101st Airborne Div
Phuoc Vinh/ Long Binh	Oct. 68	3d Brigade, 101st Airborne Div (AM)
Bien Hoa/ Phong Dien	Nov. 68 – June 69	3d Brigade, 101st Airborne Div (AM)
Bien Hoa/Ta Bat	July 69	3d Brigade, 101st Airborne Div (AM)
Berchtesgaden*	Aug. 69	3d Brigade, 101st Airborne Div (AM)
Bien Hoa/Ta Bat	Sept. 69	3d Brigade, 101st Airborne Div (AM)
Bien Hoa/ Phong Dien	Oct. 69	3d Brigade, 101st Airborne Div (AM)
Bien Hoa/Mai Loc	Nov. 69	3d Brigade, 101st Airborne Div (AM)
Phong Dien	Dec. 69 – Aug. 70	3d Brigade, 101st Airborne Div (AM)
Hue/Phu Bai	Sept. 70 – Feb. 71	3d Brigade, 101st Airborne Div (AM)
Camp Carroll	March 71 – April 71	3d Brigade, 101st Airborne Div (AM)
Hue/Phu Bai	May 71 – Dec. 71	3d Brigade, 101st Airborne Div (AM)

*Fire Support Base.

2d Battalion, 506th Infantry (Airmobile Infantry)

Arrived Vietnam: 16 December 1967
Departed Vietnam: 14 December 1971
Previous Station: Fort Campbell
Authorized Strength: 920

The 2d Battalion, 506th Infantry ("Currahee") was part of the 101st Airborne Division (Airmobile) in Vietnam.

Location	Service	Major Command
Phuoc Vinh	Dec. 67 – May 68	3d Brigade, 101st Airborne Div
Phuoc Vinh/Dak To	June 68	3d Brigade, 101st Airborne Div

Location	Service	Major Command
Phuoc Vinh/Cu Chi	July 68 – Sept. 68	3d Brigade, 101st Airborne Div
Phuoc Vinh/ Long Binh	Oct. 68	3d Brigade, 101st Airborne Div (AM)
Bien Hoa/ Phong Dien	Nov. 68 – June 69	3d Brigade, 101st Airborne Div (AM)
Bien Hoa/Ta Bat	July 69	3d Brigade, 101st Airborne Div (AM)
Berchtesgaden*	Aug. 69	3d Brigade, 101st Airborne Div (AM)
Bien Hoa/Ta Bat	Sept. 69	3d Brigade, 101st Airborne Div (AM)
Bien Hoa/ Phong Dien	Oct. 69	3d Brigade, 101st Airborne Div (AM)
Bien Hoa/Mai Loc	Nov. 69	3d Brigade, 101st Airborne Div (AM)
Phong Dien	Dec. 69 – Aug. 70	3d Brigade, 101st Airborne Div (AM)
Hue/Phu Bai	Sept. 70 – Feb. 71	3d Brigade, 101st Airborne Div (AM)
Camp Carroll	March 71 – April 71	3d Brigade, 101st Airborne Div (AM)
Hue/Phu Bai	May 71 – Dec. 71	3d Brigade, 101st Airborne Div (AM)

*Fire Support Base.

3d Battalion, 506th Infantry (Airmobile Infantry)

Arrived Vietnam: 23 October 1967
Departed Vietnam: 15 May 1971
Previous Station: Fort Campbell
Authorized Strength: 920

The 3d Battalion, 506th Infantry ("Currahee") was part of the 101st Airborne Division (Airmobile) in Vietnam, seeing service with I Field Force, Vietnam and the 173d Airborne Brigade.

Location	Service	Major Command
Phan Rang/Duc Pho	Oct. 67 – Nov. 67	1st Brigade, 101st Airborne Div
Phan Rang	Dec. 67	1st Brigade, 101st Airborne Div
Phan Rang/Song Be	Jan. 68	1st Brigade, 101st Airborne Div
Phan Rang/Phan Thiet	Feb. 68	1st Brigade, 101st Airborne Div
Phan Rang/Phu Bai/ Hue	March 68	1st Brigade, 101st Airborne Div
Phan Rang/Phu Bai	April 68	1st Brigade, 101st Airborne Div
Phan Rang/Hue	May 68 – June 68	1st Brigade, 101st Airborne Div
Phan Rang/Phu Bai	July 68 – Oct. 68	1st Brigade, 101st Airborne Div
Bien Hoa/Phu Bai	Nov. 68 – April 69	I Field Force, Vietnam
Bien Hoa/Gia Le	May 69	I Field Force, Vietnam
Bien Hoa/Tam Ky	June 69 – Aug. 69	I Field Force, Vietnam
Bien Hoa/Gia Le	Sept. 69	I Field Force, Vietnam
Bien Hoa/Gia Le	Oct. 69 – Nov. 69	Task Force SOUTH, I Field Force, Vietnam
Hue/Phu Bai	Dec. 69 – Jan. 70	1st Brigade, 4th Infantry Division
Hue/Phu Bai	Feb. 70 – July 70	173d Airborne Brigade
Hue/Phu Bai	Aug. 70	I Field Force, Vietnam
Hue/Phu Bai	Sept. 70 – May 71	1st Brigade, 101st Airborne Div (AM)

1st Battalion, 508th Infantry
(Airborne Infantry)

Arrived Vietnam: 18 February 1968
Departed Vietnam: 11 December 1969
Previous Station: Fort Bragg
Authorized Strength: 920

The 1st Battalion, 508th Infantry (Airborne) was part of the 3d Brigade Task Force of the 82d Airborne Division in Vietnam.

Location	Service	Major Command
Hue	Feb. 68 – April 68	3d Brigade, 82d Airborne Div
Hue/Phu Bai	May 68 – Oct. 68	3d Brigade, 82d Airborne Div
Phu Loi/Saigon	Nov. 68 – Dec. 69	3d Brigade, 82d Airborne Div

Infantry Security Force
(Special Guard)

Arrived Vietnam: March 1965
Departed Vietnam: March 1973
Previous Station: Vietnam

Authorized Strength	1966	1968
Security Force	517	517

The U.S. Army Infantry Security Force was a battalion-sized TDA* organization infantry force under the direct control of the Military Assistance Command, Vietnam (MACV) and later of the Department of the Army. It served in multiple locations during the war and was composed of specially chosen soldiers.

* Table of Distribution and Allowances (see explanation under the section on General Army Structure).

INFANTRY SCOUT DOG & COMBAT TRACKER PLATOONS IN VIETNAM

Platoon	Type – Assignment	Vietnam Service	Typical Location	Authorized Strengths 1968	Authorized Strengths 1970
25th IN	Scout Dog – 1st Cav Div	18 June 66 – 27 March 71	Phuoc Vinh	21	31
33d IN	Scout Dog – 4th Inf Div	11 Oct. 66 – 10 Dec. 70	Pleiku	27	31
34th IN	Scout Dog – 1st Cav Div	18 Nov. 66 – 20 Aug. 72	Phuoc Vinh	27	31
35th IN	Scout Dog – 1st Inf Div	16 June 66 – 7 April 70	Di An	21	—
37th IN	Scout Dog – 3d Bde, 82d Abn Div and 1st Cav Div	29 Jan. 69 – 16 March 71	Phu Loi	28	31
38th IN	Scout Dog – 25th Inf Div	16 July 66 – 15 March 71	Cu Chi	21	31
39th IN	Scout Dog – 173d Abn Bde	25 July 66 – 21 July 71	An Khe	21	31
40th IN	Scout Dog – 25th and 4th Inf Divs	26 Aug. 66 – 1 Oct. 70	Pleiku	27	31
41st IN	Scout Dog – 1st Inf Div	27 Nov. 66 – 7 April 70	Di An	28	—
42d IN	Scout Dog – 101st Abn Div (AM)	Sept. 66 – 26 Dec. 71	Gia Le	27	31
43d IN	Scout Dog – 9th and 1st Inf Divs	19 Aug. 67 – 21 July 71	Dong Tam	28	31
44th IN	Scout Dog – 25th Inf Div	11 Jan. 67 – 10 Dec. 70	Dau Tieng	27	31
45th IN	Scout Dog – 9th Inf Div	19 Aug. 67 – 12 Oct. 70	Dong Tam	28	31
46th IN	Scout Dog – 11th Arm Cav (Rgt) and 25th Inf Div	24 Sept. 67 – 10 Dec. 70	Xuan Loc	28	31
47th IN	Scout Dog – 101st Abn Div (AM)	27 May 68 – 21 July 71	Gia Le	28	31
48th IN	Scout Dog – 196th Inf Bde	15 Jan. 67 – 30 March 72	Chu Lai	15	28
49th IN	Scout Dog – 199th Inf Bde	1 March 67 – 12 Oct. 70	Long Binh	27	28
50th IN	Scout Dog – 4th Inf Div	7 March 67 – 10 Dec. 70	Pleiku	27	28
57th IN	Scout Dog – 198th Inf Bde	17 Feb. 68 – 1 Oct. 71	Chu Lai	28	28
58th IN	Scout Dog – 101st Abn Div (AM)	20 Feb. 68 – 21 July 71	Gia Le	28	28
59th IN	Scout Dog – 11th Inf Bde	28 May 68 – 1 Oct. 71	Duc Pho	28	28
60th IN	Scout Dog – 25th Inf Div	22 April 69 – 20 Oct. 69	Cu Chi	—	—
61st IN	Combat Tracker – 1st Inf Div	15 Feb. 68 – 7 April 70	Lai Khe	23	—
62d IN	Combat Tracker – 1st Cav Div	15 Feb. 68 – 15 Aug. 72	Phuoc Vinh	23	23
63d IN	Combat Tracker – AMERICAL and 4th Inf Divs	15 Feb. 68 – 20 March 72	Chu Lai	23	41
64th IN	Combat Tracker – 4th and 9th Inf Divs	15 Feb. 68 – 10 Dec. 70	Pleiku	23	23
65th IN	Combat Tracker – 9th Inf Div	15 Feb. 68 – 15 July 69	Dong Tam	23	—
65th IN*	Combat Tracker – 3d Bde, 9th Inf Div	1 Oct. 69 – 12 Oct. 70	Tan An	—	10
66th IN	Combat Tracker – 25th Inf Div	15 Feb. 68 – 15 March 71	Cu Chi	23	23
75th IN	Combat Tracker – 11th Arm Cav (Rgt) 173d Abn Bde	15 Feb. 68 – 21 July 71	An Khe	10	10
76th IN	Combat Tracker – 173d Abn Bde and 199th Inf Bde	15 Feb. 68 – 12 Oct. 71	Long Binh	10	10
77th IN	Combat Tracker – USARV and 1st Bde, 5th Inf Div (Mech)	15 Feb. 68 – 21 July 71	Long Binh	10	10
557th IN	Combat Tracker – 101st Abn Div and AMERICAL Inf Div	15 Feb. 68 – 21 July 71	Gia Le	23	23

4th War Dog Company (Provisional) – 4th Infantry Division
34th War Dog Company (Provisional) – 3d Bde (separate), 1st Cavalry Division
USARV Dog Training Detachment – U.S. Army Vietnam

* Second tour in Vietnam.

INFANTRY LONG RANGE PATROL DETACHMENTS

Detachment	Major Command Served	Vietnam Service	Location	Authorized Strength
70th IN	11th Inf Bde	19 Dec. 67 – 15 Jan. 68	Duc Pho	61
71st IN	199th Inf Bde	20 Dec. 67 – 1 Feb. 69	Long Binh	61
74th IN	173d Abn Bde	20 Dec. 67 – 1 Feb. 69	An Khe	61
78th IN	U.S. Army Vietnam (USARV)	15 Dec. 68 – 1 Feb. 69	Long Binh	61
79th IN	U.S. Army Vietnam (USARV)	15 Dec. 68 – 1 Feb. 69	Long Binh	61

Selected Provisional Infantry Companies In Vietnam	Company	Formed
	II Field Force, Vietnam Long Range Patrol (Prov)	27 Dec. 68
	AMERICAL Aero Scout (Prov), 23d Infantry Division (AMERICAL)	1 Feb. 68
	Cam Ranh Bay Infantry (Prov)	12 April 72
	Long Binh Army Security Infantry Patrol (Prov)	15 Feb. 70
	Pathfinder, 1st Cavalry Division*	11 Sept. 65
	Saigon Port Security Infantry (Prov)	15 Feb. 70
	Qui Nhon Security Guard Infantry (Prov)	10 April 69
	Qui Nhon Support Command Guard Infantry (Prov)	4 March 67
	1st Qui Nhon Security Guard Infantry (Prov)	16 Feb. 70
	2d Qui Nhon Security Guard Infantry (Prov)	16 Feb. 70
	3d Qui Nhon Security Guard Infantry (Prov)	7 Feb. 70
	USARV Support Infantry (Prov)	28 Jan. 68

* Pathfinder Infantry consisted of teams dropped or air-landed at objectives to establish and operate navigational aids for guiding aircraft to the landing zones. While in Vietnam, every aviation group had its own Pathfinder platoons or detachments used for delivery into hostile territory for the purpose of determining the best approach and withdrawal lanes, landing zones, and sites for the heliborne forces. The 11th Aviation Group of the 1st Cavalry Division (Airmobile) expanded its organic Pathfinder element to the size of a provisional company; sometimes referred to as the 11th Pathfinder Company (Provisional). (See DA General Order 21, 1969.) All Pathfinder teams were elite infantry.

PROVISIONAL INFANTRY PLATOONS IN VIETNAM

Note: These were all formed for helicopter door gunner purposes in Hawaii, unless otherwise indicated. Parent units, however, were in Hawaii.

Provisional Platoon	Unit Origin	Date Formed	Notes
1st Machinegun	25th Inf Div	18 March 63	90 days temporary duty
2d Machinegun	25th Inf Div	18 March 63	90 days temporary duty
3d Machinegun	25th Inf Div	18 March 63	90 days temporary duty
4th Machinegun	25th Inf Div	18 March 63	90 days temporary duty
5th Machinegun	25th Inf Div	18 March 63	90 days temporary duty
1st Machinegun	1st Bn, 5th Inf	23 May 64	For temporary duty
1st Machinegun	1st Bn, 14th Inf	5 Sept. 64	For temporary duty
2d Machinegun	2d Bn, 27th Inf	23 May 64	For temporary duty
2d Machinegun	2d Bn, 14th Inf	5 Sept. 64	For temporary duty
3d Machinegun	3d Bn, 69th Arm	23 May 64	For temporary duty
3d Machinegun	1st Bn, 69th Arm	5 Sept. 64	For temporary duty
4th Machinegun	3d Sqdn, 4th Cav	23 May 64	For temporary duty
4th Machinegun	2d Bn, 27th Inf	5 Sept. 64	For temporary duty
5th Machinegun	65th En Bn	23 May 64	For temporary duty
5th Machinegun	1st Bn, 27th Inf	5 Sept. 64	For temporary duty
6th Machinegun	25th Inf Div Arty	23 May 64	For temporary duty
6th Machinegun	25th Inf Div Arty	5 Sept. 64	For temporary duty
7th Machinegun	2d Bn, 35th Inf	23 May 64	For temporary duty
7th Machinegun	1st Bn, 35th Inf	5 Sept. 64	For temporary duty
8th Machinegun	25th Inf Div Arty	23 May 64	For temporary duty
1st Machinegun	1st Bn, 35th Inf	10 Sept. 63	90 days temporary duty
1st Machinegun	1st Bn, 5th Inf	7 Dec. 63	90 days temporary duty
1st Machinegun	1st Bn, 14th Inf	6 March 64	90 days temporary duty
1st Machinegun	2d Bn, 35th Inf	10 May 64	Raised in Vietnam
1st Machinegun	1st Bn, 5th Inf	June – Sept. 64	90 days temporary duty
2d Machinegun	2d Bn, 35th Inf	10 Sept. 63	90 days temporary duty
2d Machinegun	2d Bn, 14th Inf	7 Dec. 63	90 days temporary duty
2d Machinegun	2d Bn, 35th Inf	6 March 64	90 days temporary duty
2d Machinegun	1st Bn, 14th Inf	10 May 64	Raised in Vietnam
3d Machinegun	25th Inf Div Arty	10 Sept. 63	90 days temporary duty
1st Aerial Gunner	1st Bn, 14th Inf	17 Feb. 65	Raised in Vietnam

2d Aerial Gunner	2d Bn, 14th Inf	17 Feb. 65	Raised in Vietnam
3d Aerial Gunner	1st Bn, 27th Inf	17 Feb. 65	Raised in Vietnam
4th Aerial Gunner	2d Bn, 27th Inf	17 Feb. 65	Raised in Vietnam
5th Aerial Gunner	1st Bn, 35th Inf	17 Feb. 65	Raised in Vietnam
6th Aerial Gunner	2d Bn, 35th Inf	17 Feb. 65	Raised in Vietnam
7th Aerial Gunner	3d Sqdn, 4th Cav	17 Feb. 65	Raised in Vietnam
8th Aerial Gunner	65th En Bn	17 Feb. 65	Raised in Vietnam
9th Aerial Gunner	1st Bn, 5th Inf	17 Feb. 65	Raised in Vietnam
10th Aerial Gunner	25th Inf Div Arty	17 Feb. 65	Raised in Vietnam
11th Aerial Gunner	25th Inf Div Arty	17 Feb. 65	Raised in Vietnam
12th Aerial Gunner	25th Inf Div Arty	17 Feb. 65	Raised in Vietnam
13th Aerial Gunner	25th Aviation Bn	17 Feb. 65	Raised in Vietnam
1st Aerial Gunner	1st Bn, 5th Inf	1 Dec. 64	For temporary duty
2d Aerial Gunner	1st Bn, 14th Inf	1 Dec. 64	For temporary duty
3d Aerial Gunner	2d Bn, 14th Inf	1 Dec. 64	For temporary duty
4th Aerial Gunner	1st Bn, 27th Inf	1 Dec. 64	For temporary duty
5th Aerial Gunner	2d Bn, 27th Inf	1 Dec. 64	For temporary duty
6th Aerial Gunner	1st Bn, 35th Inf	1 Dec. 64	For temporary duty
7th Aerial Gunner	2d Bn, 35th Inf	1 Dec. 64	For temporary duty
8th Aerial Gunner	3d Sqdn, 4th Cav	1 Dec. 64	For temporary duty
9th Aerial Gunner	65th En Bn	1 Dec. 64	For temporary duty
10th Aerial Gunner	25th Inf Div Arty	1 Dec. 64	For temporary duty
11th Aerial Gunner	25th Inf Div Arty	1 Dec. 64	For temporary duty
12th Aerial Gunner	25th Inf Div Arty	1 Dec. 64	For temporary duty
13th Aerial Gunner	25th Aviation Bn	1 Dec. 64	For temporary duty
1st Automatic Rifle	1st Bn, 14th Inf	10 Sept. 63	90 days temporary duty
2d Automatic Rifle	2d Bn, 27th Inf	7 Dec. 63	90 days temporary duty
3d Automatic Rifle	1st Bn, 35th Inf	6 March 64	90 days temporary duty
1st Automatic Rifle	25th Inf Div Arty	10 May 64	Raised in Vietnam
1st Automatic Rifle	2d Bn, 27th Inf	June – Sept. 64	90 days temporary duty
2d Automatic Rifle	1st Bn, 27th Inf	10 Sept. 63	90 days temporary duty
2d Automatic Rifle	65th En Bn	7 Dec. 63	90 days temporary duty
2d Automatic Rifle	25th Inf Div Arty	6 March 64	90 days temporary duty
2d Automatic Rifle	1st Bn, 35th Inf	10 May 64	Raised in Vietnam
2d Automatic Rifle	65th En Bn	June – Sept. 64	90 days temporary duty
3d Automatic Rifle	25th Inf Div Arty	7 Dec. 63	90 days temporary duty
3d Automatic Rifle	1st Bn, 27th Inf	6 March 64	90 days temporary duty
3d Automatic Rifle	1st Bn, 27th Inf	10 May 64	Raised in Vietnam
3d Automatic Rifle	25th Inf Div Arty	June – Sept. 64	90 days temporary duty
4th Automatic Rifle	25th Inf Div	10 May 64	Raised in Vietnam
5th Automatic Rifle	25th Inf Div	10 May 64	Raised in Vietnam
1st Door Gunner	1st Bn, 14th Inf	3 Sept. 64	90 days temporary duty
2d Door Gunner	2d Bn, 14th Inf	3 Sept. 64	90 days temporary duty
3d Door Gunner	1st Bn, 69th Arm	3 Sept. 64	90 days temporary duty
4th Door Gunner	2d Bn, 27th Inf	3 Sept. 64	90 days temporary duty
5th Door Gunner	1st Bn, 27th Inf	3 Sept. 64	90 days temporary duty
6th Door Gunner	25th Inf Div Arty	3 Sept. 64	90 days temporary duty
7th Door Gunner	1st Bn, 35th Inf	3 Sept. 64	90 days temporary duty

Combat
Support Units

Chapter 13

Engineers

U.S. Army Engineer Command, Vietnam

No Insignia
Authorized

Arrived Vietnam: 1 December 1966
(Provisional)
Discontinued: March 1968
Arrived Vietnam: 1 February 1970
(Non-provisional)
Departed Vietnam: 30 April 1972
Previous Station: Vietnam
Authorized Strength: HHC – 334 (1971)

Commanders*

Major General Robert R. Ploger	Dec. 66
Major General Charles M. Duke	Aug. 67
Major General William T. Bradley	May 68
Major General David S. Parker	July 68
Major General John A. B. Dillard†	Dec. 69
Brigadier General Robert M. Tarbox	May 70
Major General Charles C. Noble	June 70
Major General Robert P. Young	Aug. 71
Brigadier General James A. Johnson	April 72

* Includes USARV Engineer Command Staff; U.S. Army Engineer Construction Agency, Vietnam.

† Killed 12 May 1970 in helicopter crash.

The U.S. Army Engineer Command, Vietnam was first established as the Engineer Command, Vietnam (Provisional) in December 1966, utilizing the assets of the 921st Engineer Group. The Command was discontinued about March 1968 when it was consolidated with the U.S. Army Engineer Command Staff of USARV. At the same time, the U.S. Army Engineer Construction Agency, Vietnam (Provisional) was formed. The U.S. Army Engineer Construction Agency, Vietnam was created to direct and supervise both military and contractor efforts regarding property maintenance, base development, construction management and other facility engineering. The agency controlled the three district engineer offices at Qui Nhon, Cam Ranh Bay and Saigon, which in turn supervised the installation engineers at their bases throughout Vietnam. It was located at Long Binh and discontinued on 1 February 1970 to be used as a basis for raising the U.S. Army Engineer Command, Vietnam formed to provide command and control for non-divisional engineer units. On 30 April 1972 this Command was redesignated the U.S. Army Engineer Group, Vietnam. It was located at Long Binh.

Components of U.S. Army Engineer Command, Vietnam February 1970 – 30 April 1972

Headquarters & Headquarters Company, U.S. Army Engineer Command, Vietnam

Northern District Engineers, U.S. Army Engineer Command, Vietnam

Central District Engineers, U.S. Army Engineer Command, Vietnam

Southern District Engineers, U.S. Army Engineer Command, Vietnam

227th Engineer Detachment

18th Engineer Brigade

Arrived Vietnam: 20 September 1965
Departed Vietnam: 20 September 1971
Previous Station: Fort Bragg

Authorized Strength	1966	1968	1971
HHC	142	173	142

The 18th Engineer Brigade was formed 29 July 1921 as the 347th Engineers (General Service) in the Organized Reserves. It was ordered into active military service 6 May 1942 at Camp Claiborne, Louisiana, and redesignated the 347th Engineer General Service Regiment. For its service in Normandy, Northern France, the Rhineland, and Central Europe during World War II, the unit received the Meritorious Unit Commendation. After the war it was deactivated in Germany. Redesignated the 18th Engineer Brigade, it was reactivated at Fort Leonard Wood on 25 October 1954. On 26 March 1963 the brigade was again deactivated, but on 16 July 1965 was activated at Fort Bragg and prepared for deployment to Vietnam. An advance party of the brigade arrived in Vietnam 3 September 1965 and became operational two weeks later. It was originally in control of all U.S. Army engineer activities there until the U.S. Army Engineer Command, Vietnam (Provisional) was created in December 1966. At this point the 18th Engineer Brigade became responsible for engineer efforts in the I and II Corps Tactical Zones under I Field Force, Vietnam. It was located at Tan Son Nhut until 1 December 1966 when it was relocated to Dong Ba Thin.

20th Engineer Brigade

Arrived Vietnam: 3 August 1967
Departed Vietnam: 20 September 1971
Previous Station: Fort Bragg

Authorized Strength	1968	1971
HHC	173	142

The history of the 20th Engineer Brigade extends back to the American Civil War though the unit designations have changed many times since. It was originally constituted on 3 August 1861 (under a different title, however), and its ancestors fought in campaigns in the Civil War, the Spanish-American War, the Philippine Insurrection, the Mexican Expedition, and World Wars I and II. The brigade headquarters was reactivated 1 May 1967 and arrived in Vietnam later that year. It arrived to take over responsibility for engineer activities within the III and IV Corps Tactical Zones, as well as to render engineer support for II Field Force, Vietnam. It was located at Bien Hoa.

34th Engineer Group (Construction)

Arrived Vietnam: 21 March 1967
Departed Vietnam: 17 March 1972
Previous Station: Fort Lewis

Authorized Strength	1968	1970
HHC	111	111

The 34th Engineer Group (Construction) served under the Engineer Command, Vietnam (Provisional) commanding assigned and attached units which performed engineer planning and design functions required in support of field construction until August

1967 when it came under command of the 20th Engineer Brigade. Located first at Vung Tau, the group relocated to Bin Thuy in February 1969. The following engineer battalions served at one time or another under the group:

27th Engineer Battalion	36th Engineer Battalion
31st Engineer Battalion	69th Engineer Battalion
34th Engineer Battalion	86th Engineer Battalion
35th Engineer Battalion	93d Engineer Battalion

35th Engineer Group (Construction)

Arrived Vietnam: 9 June 1965
Departed Vietnam: 30 November 1971
Previous Station: Fort Polk

Authorized Strength	1966	1968	1970
HHC	98	111	111

The 35th Engineer Group (Construction) was part of the 18th Engineer Brigade, not only controlling its numerous engineer battalions and supporting engineer service units, but also designing, planning, and providing supervision for the construction and rehabilitation of communication routes, buildings and installations, forward cargo and tactical airfields, heliports, and other specialized facilities such as petroleum storage, railroads and port complexes. It was located at Phan Rang until April 1966 when it moved to Cam Ranh Bay. In July 1968 the brigade went to Qui Nhon but in December of that year moved back to Cam Ranh Bay where it remained until it departed Vietnam. The following engineer battalions served at one time or another under the group:

14th Engineer Battalion	116th Engineer Battalion
19th Engineer Battalion	169th Engineer Battalion
20th Engineer Battalion	554th Engineer Battalion
39th Engineer Battalion	577th Engineer Battalion
62d Engineer Battalion	589th Engineer Battalion
70th Engineer Battalion	815th Engineer Battalion
84th Engineer Battalion	864th Engineer Battalion
87th Engineer Battalion	

45th Engineer Group (Construction)

Arrived Vietnam: 8 June 1966
Departed Vietnam: 30 January 1972
Previous Station: Fort Bragg

Authorized Strength	1966	1968	1970
HHC	98	111	111

The 45th Engineer Group (Construction) was under the 18th Engineer Brigade throughout its service in Vietnam, planning and coordinating the activities of its assigned and attached units. These consisted of construction or other units engaged in field construction, rehabilitation or maintenance of facilities in support of U.S. Army or Air Force operations. The group arrived at Cam Ranh Bay and moved to Dong Ba Thin on 15 July 1966. It relocated to Tuy Hoa on 15 October 1966, moving to Qui Nhon that December. It moved north to the Phu Bai area in February 1968, where it assumed general construction support missions for the I Corps

Tactical Zone. The group then remained in the Da Nang area until departing Vietnam. The following engineer battalions served the group at one time or another:

14th Engineer Battalion	39th Engineer Battalion
19th Engineer Battalion	84th Engineer Battalion
20th Engineer Battalion	299th Engineer Battalion
27th Engineer Battalion	577th Engineer Battalion
35th Engineer Battalion	589th Engineer Battalion

79th Engineer Group (Construction)

Arrived Vietnam: 16 July 1966
Departed Vietnam: 15 December 1970
Previous Station: Fort Lewis

Authorized Strength	1966	1968	1970
HHC	94	111	111

The 79th Engineer Group was switched from the 18th Engineer Brigade, where it first served in Vietnam, to the Engineer Command (Provisional) in December 1966, and in the fall of 1967 received its final major command switch to the 20th Engineer Brigade. The group was located at Phan Rang where it assigned projects to its subordinate units, allocated troops, construction material and equipment, and supervised contract construction, contract labor, and indigenous personnel. In October 1966 the group relocated to Long Binh, where it stayed until its departure from Vietnam. The following engineer battalions served at one time or another under the group:

27th Engineer Battalion	93d Engineer Battalion
31st Engineer Battalion	168th Engineer Battalion
34th Engineer Battalion	554th Engineer Battalion
62d Engineer Battalion	588th Engineer Battalion
86th Engineer Battalion	

159th Engineer Group (Construction)

Arrived Vietnam: 30 October 1965
Departed Vietnam: 30 April 1972
Previous Station: Fort Bragg

Authorized Strength	1966	1968	1970
HHC	98	111	111

The 159th Engineer Group (Construction) served under the 18th Engineer Brigade until it was transferred to the Engineer Command (Provisional) in December 1966. After the arrival of the 20th Engineer Brigade in Vietnam, the group was transferred on 5 August, 1967 to that brigade's command. The group provided the overhead for command and control of three to five engineer battalions while possessing the capability to design, plan and supervise construction of routes of communication, cantonments, buildings, airfields, minimal petroleum storage facilities and minimal port facilities. The 159th Engineer Group was first located at Bien Hoa but in July 1966 was relocated to Long Binh where it remained for the duration of its service in Vietnam. The following engineer battalions served at one time or another under the group:

31st Engineer Battalion	168th Engineer Battalion
34th Engineer Battalion	169th Engineer Battalion
36th Engineer Battalion	554th Engineer Battalion
46th Engineer Battalion	588th Engineer Battalion
62d Engineer Battalion	815th Engineer Battalion
92d Engineer Battalion	

921st Engineer Group (Headquarters)

No Insignia Authorized

Arrived Vietnam: 1 October 1966
Departed Vietnam: 25 May 1968
Previous Station: Leonard Wood
Authorized Strength: HHC – 81 (1967)

The 921st Engineer Group never operated as a command organization in Vietnam. In December 1966 it furnished personnel to help build the U.S. Army Engineer Command, Vietnam (Provisional). First located at Tan Son Nhut, the group headquarters was moved in June 1967 to Bien Hoa and was posted next to Long Binh, where it was used merely as a basis for engineer personnel requisitions before being closed out in 1968.

937th Engineer Group (Combat)

Arrived Vietnam: 22 August 1965
Departed Vietnam: 20 September 1971
Previous Station: Fort Campbell

Authorized Strength	1966	1968	1970
HHC	116	120	116

The 937th Engineer Group (Combat) provided the overhead for three to six combat engineer battalions with command and control capabilities. The emphasis within the group headquarters rested with planning and coordinating combat support activities since the group was not authorized an engineer design section. It was part of the 18th Engineer Brigade, except for a short period in the fall of 1967 when it served the 20th Engineer Brigade. First serving at Qui Nhon, the group relocated to Pleiku in November 1966 and finally moved to Phu Tai on 10 March 1970, where it remained until it withdrew from Vietnam. The following engineer battalions served at one time or another with the group:

19th Engineer Battalion	84th Engineer Battalion
20th Engineer Battalion	116th Engineer Battalion
39th Engineer Battalion	299th Engineer Battalion
70th Engineer Battalion	815th Engineer Battalion

U.S. Army Engineer Group, Vietnam (Command)

No Insignia Authorized

Arrived Vietnam: 30 April 1972
Departed Vietnam: 28 March 1973
Previous Station: Vietnam
Location: Long Binh

The U.S. Army Engineer Group, Vietnam was formed using the assets of the U.S. Army Engineer Command, Vietnam at Long Binh. The 84th Engineer Battalion was directly assigned to this group. Other major components of the group were:

Engineer Distribution Activity, Vietnam
U.S. Army Engineer Group Facility, Saigon
U.S. Army Engineers, Military Region 1 (Da Nang)
U.S. Army Engineers, Military Region 2 (Pleiku)
U.S. Army Engineers, Military Region 3 (Long Binh)
U.S. Army Engineers, Military Region 4 (Can Tho)
U.S. Army Military Area Construction & Logistics
   Route Equipment Maintenance

1st Engineer Battalion (Divisional)

Arrived Vietnam: 28 November 1965
Departed Vietnam: 7 April 1970
Previous Station: Fort Riley

Authorized Strength	1966	1968
Battalion	936	972

The 1st Engineer Battalion was organic to the 1st Infantry Division, providing the division-level support required. This involved constructing and repairing bridges, roads and airfields as well as emplacing or removing obstacles and fortifications, dry-gap and float bridging, and fighting as infantry when required. It served with the division throughout its service in Vietnam though its companies were often scattered with the division's infantry and artillery units.

4th Engineer Battalion (Divisional)

Arrived Vietnam: 7 July 1966
Departed Vietnam: 15 December 1970
Previous Station: Fort Lewis

Authorized Strength	1966	1968	1970
Battalion	823	972	770

The 4th Engineer Battalion was part of the 4th Infantry Division and had the same responsibilities as those outlined for the 1st Engineer Battalion. The battalion was colocated with division headquarters though its subordinate companies were often detached to support the division's widespread brigades and battalions.

Company A, 7th Engineer Battalion (Brigade Support)

Arrived Vietnam: 30 July 1968
Departed Vietnam: 6 August 1971
Previous Station: Fort Carson
Authorized Strength: 256

Company A of the 7th Engineer Battalion was part of the 1st Brigade Task Force of the 5th Infantry Division (Mech). Its mission was to increase combat effectiveness of the brigade by providing engineer combat support as well as to undertake limited infantry combat missions when required. It served at Quang Tri in Vietnam.

8th Engineer Battalion (Divisional)

Arrived Vietnam: 19 November 1965
Departed Vietnam: 3 April 1971
Previous Station: Fort Benning

Authorized Strength	1966	1968	1971
Battalion	621	621	457

The 8th Engineer Battalion was part of the 1st Cavalry Division (Airmobile) and was lighter than a normal infantry division engineer battalion. It provided direct support to tactical elements in removal or emplacement of obstacles and fortifications, construction of bridges, fords, culverts, and airfield facilities, and fought as infantry when required. It specialized in rendering airmobile engineer equipment support. The battalion was often scattered, supporting the far-flung elements of the 1st Cavalry Division through its highly mobile pattern of warfare.

14th Engineer Battalion (Combat)

Arrived Vietnam: 19 October 1966
Departed Vietnam: 31 August 1971
Previous Station: Fort Bragg

Authorized Strength	1966	1968	1970
Battalion	794	812	812

The 14th Engineer Battalion (Combat) was equipped to perform forward area construction, obstacle preparation, demolition work and fighting as infantry. It provided all non-divisional engineer support in its area and served as a local construction agency for all projects, especially base construction, upgrading land lines of communication and airfield construction and rehabilitation. The battalion landed at Tuy Hoa but moved to the control of the 35th Engineer Group at Dong Ba Thin in November 1966 and Cam Ranh Bay in 1967. On 14 March 1968 it was transferred again to the 45th Engineer Group at Thon Me Thuy ("Wunder Beach"), Quang Tri, later at Gia Le and Da Nang.

15th Engineer Battalion (Divisional)

Arrived Vietnam: 19 October 1966
Departed Vietnam: 24 August 1969
Previous Station: Fort Riley

Authorized Strength	1966	1968
Battalion	980	972

The 15th Engineer Battalion was part of the 9th Infantry Division with the mission of providing the ordinary engineer support (see 1st Engineer Battalion). Additionally, C Company and other parts of the battalion became specialized in riverine operations required by the 2d Brigade's unique Vietnam mission. The battalion's elements were detached to various units of the division as needed. It also specialized in airmobile engineer support.

19th Engineer Battalion (Combat)

Arrived Vietnam: 2 September 1965
Departed Vietnam: 14 December 1970
Previous Station: Fort Meade

Authorized Strength	1966	1968	1970
Battalion	619	812	812

The 19th Engineer Battalion (Combat) was first posted to Qui Nhon with the 937th Engineer Group. It was equipped as a normal combat engineer battalion (see 14th Engineer Battalion) in Vietnam, though augmented to meet conditions there. In December 1966 it came under the command of the 45th Engineer Group and in July 1967 moved from Qui Nhon to Bong Son, where it engaged in road construction to Mo Duc. On 15 March 1968 it was placed under the 35th Engineer Group. In August 1969 the battalion was placed at Bao Loc under command of the 35th Engineer Group where it remained until it joined the 937th Engineer Group at Ban Me Thuot in 1970.

20th Engineer Battalion (Combat)

Arrived Vietnam: 1 January 1966
Departed Vietnam: 31 August 1971
Previous Station: Fort Devens

Authorized Strength	1966	1968	1970
Battalion	619	812	812

The 20th Engineer Battalion (Combat) was organized like the 14th Engineer Battalion and was a part of the 35th Engineer Group at Dong Ba Thin. It moved from Ninh Hoa to Ban Me Thuot on 5 October 1966 and on to Pleiku shortly after with the 45th Engineer Group. On 10 November 1966, it was placed under the 937th Engineer Group and stayed with this group until it was posted to the 35th Engineer Group at Cam Ranh Bay for departure from Vietnam.

26th Engineer Battalion (Divisional)

Arrived Vietnam: 8 December 1967
Departed Vietnam: 28 November 1971
Previous Station: Vietnam
Authorized Strength: 972

The 26th Engineer Battalion was part of the 23d Infantry Division (AMERICAL) and had the mission of a normal division engineer battalion (see 1st Engineer Battalion), serving the division at Chu Lai. It also specialized in airmobile engineer support.

27th Engineer Battalion (Combat)

Arrived Vietnam: 1 October 1966
Departed Vietnam: 31 January 1972
Previous Station: Fort Campbell
Authorized Strength: 812

The 27th Engineer Battalion (Combat) had the mission of a normal combat engineer battalion on Corps or Army level (see 14th Engineer Battalion). It arrived at Bien Hoa – Long Binh and on 15 November 1966 was located at Xuan Loc with the 79th Engineer Group, coming under the jurisdiction of the 34th Engineer Group on 20 April 1967. On 12 April 1968 it was transferred to the 45th Engineer Group at Gia Le and Camp Eagle in support of the 101st Airborne Division.

31st Engineer Battalion (Combat)

Arrived Vietnam: 24 March 1968
Departed Vietnam: 12 March 1972
Previous Station: Fort Bliss

Authorized Strength	1968	1970	1971
Battalion	812	794	659

The 31st Engineer Battalion (Combat) landed at Vung Tau and was initially part of the 34th Engineer Group at Xuan Loc and had capabilities similar to those of the 14th Engineer Battalion. On 1 July 1968 it was placed under the 159th Engineer Group and moved to Phuoc Vinh. The battalion was transferred to the 79th Engineer Group in June 1969 but returned to the 159th Engineer Group in December 1971 where it remained until leaving Vietnam. It was responsible for the III CTZ airmobile equipment support.

34th Engineer Battalion (Construction)

Arrived Vietnam: 2 May 1967
Departed Vietnam: 17 October 1971
Previous Station: Fort Stewart

Authorized Strength	1968	1970	1971
Battalion	899	905	674

The 34th Engineer Battalion (Construction) performed basic heavy construction tasks including construction of bases, structures, roads, airfields, bridges and pipelines, paving operations and construction of major facilities. It served at Bien Hoa as part of the 159th Engineer Group until 1 July 1967 when it was posted to Saigon with the 79th Engineer Group. In May 1968 it was relocated to Phu Loi and in December 1968 became part of the 159th Engineer Group there. In 1971 the battalion was placed under the jurisdiction of the 34th Engineer Group and posted to Vinh Long.

35th Engineer Battalion (Combat)

Arrived Vietnam: 3 November 1966
Departed Vietnam: 15 September 1970
Previous Station: Fort Lewis
Authorized Strength: 812

The 35th Engineer Battalion (Combat) had the same capabilities as the 14th Engineer Battalion. It was initially stationed at Bear Cat with the 45th Engineer Group and soon afterward moved to Qui Nhon, the group's headquarters. On 16 February 1968 it was moved to Da Nang. On 30 December 1968 it was transferred to the 34th Engineer Group, moving to Binh Thuy. The battalion remained with the latter group during the remainder of its service in Vietnam.

36th Engineer Battalion (Construction)

Arrived Vietnam: 1 September 1967
Departed Vietnam: 30 April 1972
Previous Station: Fort Irwin

Authorized Strength	1968	1970	1971
Battalion	899	905	899

The 36th Engineer Battalion (Construction) was capable of performing operations similar to those of the 34th Engineer Battalion. It served with the 34th Engineer Group at Vung Tau until moving to Vinh Long in February 1969. In 1971 the battalion was transferred to the 159th Engineer Group and relocated to Binh Thuy for departure from Vietnam in 1972.

39th Engineer Battalion (Combat)

Arrived Vietnam: 2 January 1966
Departed Vietnam: 18 April 1972
Previous Station: Fort Campbell

Authorized Strength	1966	1968	1970
Battalion	619	812	812

The 39th Engineer Battalion (Combat) had the same capabilities as the 14th Engineer Battalion. It was first assigned to the 937th

Engineer Group, then transferred to the 35th Engineer Group and moved to Cam Ranh Bay in March 1966. In July it went to the 45th Engineer Group and relocated to Tuy Hoa and Duc Pho. On 15 June 1967 it relocated to Chu Lai, where it was attached to the 23d Infantry Division. It remained until February 1972, and then was reassigned to Da Nang with the U.S. Army Engineer Command, Vietnam. It remained with the latter unit until it left Vietnam later that spring.

46th Engineer Battalion (Construction)

Arrived Vietnam: 18 September 1965
Departed Vietnam: 1 November 1971
Previous Station: Fort Polk

Authorized Strength	1966	1968	1970
Battalion	893	674	864

The 46th Engineer Battalion (Construction) was capable of performing heavy construction projects, such as base camps and cantonment areas. The battalion served with the 159th Engineer Group throughout its Vietnam service. Located initially at Bien Hoa, it moved to Long Binh in January 1966 and remained at that location until it departed Vietnam.

62d Engineer Battalion (Construction) (Land Clearing)

Arrived Vietnam: 27 August 1965
Departed Vietnam: 1 November 1971
Previous Station: Fort Leonard Wood

Authorized Strength	1966	1968	1970
Battalion	893	674	893

The 62d Engineer Battalion (Construction) had the same capabilities as the 34th Engineer Battalion. It was located at Phan Rang with the 35th Engineer Group, and from 28 November 1966 – 28 January 1967 transferred to Long Binh and on 10 December 1966 to the 159th Engineer Group. On 1 January 1969 it was restructured as a land clearing engineer battalion responsible for all such operations in the III CTZ. Remaining at that location, it came under the control of the 79th Engineer Group during the period June 1969 – November 1970 but returned to the 159th Engineer Group's command that December. It remained in this status until departing Vietnam.

65th Engineer Battalion (Divisional)

Arrived Vietnam: 17 January 1966
Departed Vietnam: 8 December 1970
Previous Station: Hawaii

Authorized Strength	1966	1968	1970
Battalion	932	972	972

The 65th Engineer Battalion was part of the 25th Infantry Division, having capabilities similar to those of the 1st Engineer Battalion. During its service in Vietnam it was primarily headquartered at Cu Chi, although the widespread divisional operations necessitated its fragmentation to provide proper engineer support to all divisional components.

69th Engineer Battalion (Construction)

Arrived Vietnam: 2 May 1967
Departed Vietnam: 17 November 1971
Previous Station: Fort Hood

Authorized Strength	1968	1970	1971
Battalion	674	905	899

The 69th Engineer Battalion (Construction) was assigned operational support, and road and base construction in the IV CTZ. It was initially posted to Vung Tau as a part of the 34th Engineer Group, moving to Can Tho in October 1967. The battalion remained subordinate to the group at that location during its remaining service in Vietnam.

70th Engineer Battalion (Combat)

Arrived Vietnam: 22 August 1965
Departed Vietnam: 21 November 1969
Previous Station: Fort Campbell

Authorized Strength	1966	1968
Battalion	619	812

The 70th Engineer Battalion (Combat) was stationed at An Khe until early 1967 when it moved to Qui Nhon with the 937th Engineer Group. On 10 October 1967 it was sent to Pleiku. In 1968 it was transferred to the 35th Engineer Group at Ban Me Thuot. The battalion was capable of the same responsibilities assigned to the 14th Engineer Battalion and engaged in major construction projects.

84th Engineer Battalion (Construction)

Arrived Vietnam: 11 June 1965
Departed Vietnam: 11 July 1972
Previous Station: Fort Ord

Authorized Strength	1966	1968	1970
Battalion	893	899	899

The 84th Engineer Battalion (Construction) had normal construction battalion capabilities (see 34th Engineer Battalion). It served at Qui Nhon, first with the 937th Engineer Group and after December 1966 with the 45th Engineer Group. On 15 March 1968 it was transferred to the 35th Engineer Group, returning to the 937th Engineer Group again in February 1969. In March 1971 the battalion went to the 45th Engineer Group and moved from Qui Nhon to Da Nang. The battalion came under the control of the U.S. Army Engineer Command after the 45th Engineer Group departed Vietnam. After the Command was reduced to the U.S. Army Engineer Group, Vietnam, the battalion served with it until it received orders deploying from Vietnam in July 1972.

86th Engineer Battalion (Combat)

Arrived Vietnam: 16 October 1966
Departed Vietnam: 15 August 1969
Previous Station: Fort Dix

Authorized Strength	1966	1968
Battalion	858	812

The 86th Engineer Battalion (Combat) was capable of normal combat engineer battalion functions (see 14th Engineer Battalion).

It initially served with the 79th Engineer Group at Phu Loi. From 10 – 20 April 1967 it was transferred to the 34th Engineer Group at Bear Cat. On 15 March 1968 it was sent to My Tho and assigned to the 45th Engineer Group, where it remained until leaving Vietnam.

87th Engineer Battalion (Construction)

Arrived Vietnam: 23 August 1965
Departed Vietnam: 1 March 1969
Previous Station: Fort Belvoir

Authorized Strength	1966	1968
Battalion	893	899

The 87th Engineer Battalion was capable of construction functions (see 34th Engineer Battalion) and served the 35th Engineer Group at Cam Ranh Bay, the 18th Engineer Brigade at Dong Ba Thin in 1968, and the 199th Infantry Brigade at Long Binh from February 1969 until departure. Its remaining assets were used to form the 687th Engineer Company in Vietnam.

92d Engineer Battalion (Construction)

Arrived Vietnam: 22 May 1967
Departed Vietnam: 3 May 1972
Previous Station: Fort Bragg

Authorized Strength	1968	1970	1971
Battalion	694	905	674

The 92d Engineer Battalion (Construction) constructed and rehabilitated roads, airfields, pipeline systems, structures and utilities. It was stationed at Long Binh under the 159th Engineer Group throughout its service in Vietnam.

93d Engineer Battalion (Construction)

Arrived Vietnam: 21 June 1967
Departed Vietnam: 31 July 1971
Previous Station: Fort Lewis

Authorized Strength	1968	1970	1971
Battalion	899	905	674

The 93d Engineer Battalion (Construction) was capable of construction-type missions similar to those of the 34th Engineer Battalion. It served initially under the 79th Engineer Group, transferring to the 34th Engineer Group in December 1967. The battalion was located at Bear Cat, and in January 1969 moved to Dong Tam, where it remained until posted to Binh Thuy in February 1971.

116th Engineer Battalion (Combat)

Arrived Vietnam: 14 September 1968
Departed Vietnam: 21 August 1969
Previous Station: Idaho Falls via
Fort Lewis
Authorized Strength: 812

The 116th Engineer Battalion (Combat), Idaho National Guard, was capable of missions similar to those of the 14th Engineer

Battalion. During its Vietnam service this battalion served at Bao Loc under the 35th Engineer Group.

168th Engineer Battalion (Combat)

Arrived Vietnam: 26 November 1965
Departed Vietnam: 9 April 1970
Previous Station: Fort Polk

Authorized Strength	1966	1968
Battalion	619	812

The 168th Engineer Battalion (Combat) had dual missions of combat engineer support and cantonment construction. First located at Di An with the 159th Engineer Group, the battalion was transferred to the 79th Engineer Group on 20 July 1966. The battalion moved to Lai Khe in February 1969.

169th Engineer Battalion (Construction)

Arrived Vietnam: 30 May 1966
Departed Vietnam: 29 April 1972
Previous Station: Fort Stewart via
Okinawa

Authorized Strength	1966	1968	1970
Battalion	893	899	899

The 169th Engineer Battalion (Construction) was responsible for construction around Saigon, Long Binh and Long Thanh. The battalion first served under the 35th Engineer Group but was transferred in July 1966 to the 159th Engineer Group at Long Binh, where it stayed for the remainder of its service in Vietnam.

299th Engineer Battalion (Combat)

Arrived Vietnam: 23 October 1965
Departed Vietnam: 17 November 1971
Previous Station: Fort Gordon

Authorized Strength	1966	1968	1970
Battalion	619	812	812

The 299th Engineer Battalion provided combat engineer support and performed construction tasks, such as base development. It landed at Cam Ranh Bay, moving to Tuy Hoa under the 937th Engineer Group, and was transferred to the 45th Engineer Group in the Phu Tai Valley. On 29 July 1966 the battalion returned to the 937th Engineer Group and was posted to Pleiku. It moved to Dak To in 1968. On 20 May 1969 it returned to Qui Nhon and on 14 February 1970 located to Phu Tai. It joined the 35th Engineer Group in June 1971.

Company C, 307th Engineer Battalion (Airborne Brigade Support)

Arrived Vietnam: 1 May 1968
Departed Vietnam: 11 December 1969
Previous Station: Fort Bragg
Authorized Strength: 165

Company C, 307th Engineer Battalion was part of the 3d Brigade Task Force of the 82d Airborne Division. The company provided forward combat engineer support.

326th Engineer Battalion (Divisional)

Arrived in Vietnam: January 1968
(except Co A)
Departed Vietnam: 17 January 1972
Previous Station: Fort Campbell

Authorized Strength	1966	1968	1970
Battalion	154*	621	621

* Company A only.

The 326th Engineer Battalion served as part of the 101st Airborne Division (Airmobile). Before the entire battalion arrived in early 1968, Company A (Airborne) had served with the division's 1st Brigade from July 1965, primarily at Phan Rang. The 326th was capable of the responsibilities assigned the divisional engineers of an airmobile division (see the 8th Engineer Battalion). The battalion itself was most often fragmented to lend support to the widespread combat elements of the division.

554th Engineer Battalion (Construction)

Arrived Vietnam: 14 April 1967
Departed Vietnam: 1 March 1972
Previous Station: Fort Knox

Authorized Strength	1968	1970
Battalion	899	899

The 554th Engineer Battalion (Construction) had capabilities similar to those of the 34th Engineer Battalion. It arrived at Cu Chi and was assigned to the 79th Engineer Group for most of its service in Vietnam. It transferred to the 35th Engineer Group in December 1970 and then to the 159th Engineer Group in June 1971. It was located to Lai Khe in October 1969. In 1971 it was posted to Bao Loc.

577th Engineer Battalion (Construction)

Arrived Vietnam: 31 July 1966
Departed Vietnam: 30 January 1972
Previous Station: Fort Benning

Authorized Strength	1966	1968	1971
Battalion	905	899	674

The 577th Engineer Battalion (Construction) had responsibilities of a construction battalion as listed under the 34th Engineer Battalion. It was sent to the 45th Engineer Group at Dong Ba Thin in October 1966 and later moved 9–19 November 1966 to Tuy Hoa. In December 1967 the battalion returned to 35th Engineer Group control while remaining at Tuy Hoa. On 1 May 1969 it moved to Dalat. The battalion was placed under the U.S. Army Engineer Command, Vietnam control in December 1971, and its assets were phased into Dillard Industries.

588th Engineer Battalion (Combat)

Arrived Vietnam: 2 November 1965
Departed Vietnam: 15 November 1970
Previous Station: Fort Lee

Authorized Strength	1966	1968	1970
Battalion	619	812	812

The 588th Engineer Battalion (Combat) had capabilities similar to those of the 14th Engineer Battalion. It was first stationed at Phu Loi with the 159th Engineer Group, moving to the 79th Engineer Group's control in July 1966 and on to Cu Chi. It relocated to Tay Ninh on 19 April 1967, where it remained until it moved back to Cu Chi in May 1970.

589th Engineer Battalion (Construction)

Arrived Vietnam: 29 April 1967
Departed Vietnam: 1 November 1971
Previous Station: Fort Hood

Authorized Strength	1968	1970
Battalion	899	905

The 589th Engineer Battalion (Construction) had the responsibilities given a construction battalion such as the 34th Engineer Battalion. It served with the 45th Engineer Group at Cha Rang, and transferred to the 35th Engineer Group in on 15 March 1968, later moving to Phan Rang. It remained at Phan Rang for the remainder of its Vietnam service.

815th Engineer Battalion (Construction)

Arrived Vietnam: 15 April 1967
Departed Vietnam: 30 January 1972
Previous Station: Fort Belvoir

Authorized Strength	1966	1968
Battalion	624	899

The 815th Engineer Battalion (Construction) was capable of the same type of assignments given the 34th Engineer Battalion. Part of the 937th Engineer Group stationed at Camp Holloway and Pleiku, it moved to the 35th Engineer Group at Bao Loc on 1 June 1970. It came under the command of the 159th Engineer Group just prior to the battalion's departure from Vietnam, and its assets were phased into Dillard Industries during 1971.

864th Engineer Battalion (Construction)

Arrived Vietnam: 9 June 1965
Departed Vietnam: 31 August 1971
Previous Station: Fort Wolters

Authorized Strength	1966	1968	1970
Battalion	893	674	899

The 864th Engineer Battalion (Construction) was used in heavy depot/complex construction. It served under the command of the 35th Engineer Group throughout its service in Vietnam, and was stationed at Cam Ranh Bay until 20 August 1967 when the battalion was moved to Nha Trang and finally located to Phan Thiet in June 1970.

ENGINEER COMPANIES IN VIETNAM

Company		Type	Previous Station	Vietnam Service	Typical Location	Authorized Strength 1966	1968	1970
6th	EN	Combat – 11th Inf Bde	Hawaii	31 Dec. 67 – 15 Jan. 68	Chu Lai	—	165	—
15th	EN	Light Equipment	Campbell	24 July 67 – 29 Aug. 71	Pleiku	—	186	186
15th	EN*	Equipment Maintenance	Vietnam	20 Dec. 71 – 20 March 72	Long Binh	—	—	—
41st	EN	Port Construction	Belvoir	2 Feb. 67 – 14 Dec. 70	Long Binh	—	225	225
43d	EN	Dump Truck	Bragg	12 Sept. 66 – 20 March 72	Long Binh	—	113	113
53d	EN†	Supply Point	Bragg	9 June 65 – 20 July 66	Cam Ranh Bay	59	—	—
54th	EN	Combat – 25th Inf Div	Vietnam	10 Feb. 71 – 14 April 71	Long Binh	—	—	165
59th	EN	Land Clearing	Vietnam	1 Jan. 69 – 26 Dec. 71	Quang Tri	—	—	132
60th	EN	Special Equipment Maint/later Land Clearing	Vietnam	26 Dec. 68 – 16 Jan. 72	Long Binh	—	—	132
66th	EN	Corps Topographic	Bragg	2 Sept. 66 – 20 March 72	Long Binh	—	130	141
67th	EN	Dump Truck	Campbell	17 Jan. 67 – 29 Jan. 72	Dong Tam	—	113	113
70th	EN	Dump Truck	Meade	4 June 67 – 1 Aug. 69	Long Binh	—	113	—
73d	EN	Construction Support	Belvoir	1 Oct. 66 – 16 Jan. 72	Qui Nhon	—	164	143
76th	EN	Direct Support Maintenance	Lee	8 June 66 – 6 July 66	Nha Trang	195	—	—
82d	EN	Water Supply Support	Riley	30 July 67 – 29 Jan. 72	Long Binh	—	109	110
87th	EN	Combat – 199th Inf Bde	Benning	12 Dec. 66 – 12 Oct. 70	Long Binh	—	165	165
100th	EN	Float Bridge	Belvoir	15 Oct. 66 – 26 Dec. 71	Long Binh	—	224	225
102d	EN	Construction Support	Bragg	30 Aug. 65 – 16 April 72	Pleiku	164	164	143
103d	EN	Construction Support	Wood	7 Feb. 66 – 20 March 72	Long Binh	164	164	164
104th	EN	Dump Truck	Meade	17 Jan. 67 – 1 Nov. 71	Cu Chi	—	113	113
111th	EN	Water Supply	Riley	30 July 67 – 5 Oct. 70	Da Nang	—	110	110
131st	EN ‡	Light Equipment	Belvoir	21 Sept. 68 – 4 Sept. 69	Ban Me Thuot	—	186	—
137th	EN	Light Equipment	Riley	25 May 67 – 16 Nov. 71	Qui Nhon	—	186	186
173d	EN	Combat Airborne – 173d Airborne Bde	Okinawa	7 May 65 – 16 July 71	An Khe	153	194	194
175th	EN	Combat – 196th Inf Bde	Devens	18 July 66 – 8 Dec. 67	Chu Lai	165	—	—
175th	EN *	Combat – 196th Inf Bde	Vietnam	31 May 72 – 29 June 72	Da Nang	—	—	—
178th	EN§	Supply	Lewis	16 March 66 – 20 July 66	Saigon	195	—	—
362d	EN	Light Equipment	Lee	2 Sept. 65 – 10 Dec. 70	Tay Ninh	186	186	186
497th	EN	Port Construction	Belvoir	23 Aug. 65 – 26 April 72	Cam Ranh Bay	227	225	225
500th	EN	Panel Bridge	Bragg	12 Dec. 66 – 30 April 71	Long Binh	—	126	126
501st	EN	Land Clearing	Vietnam	26 Dec. 68 – 8 April 70	Long Binh	—	—	199
501st	EN *	Combat – 1st Cav Div	Vietnam	30 June 71 – 14 Aug. 72	Bien Hoa	—	—	—
509th	EN	Panel Bridge	Riley	2 Sept. 65 – 29 Aug. 71	Pleiku	127	126	126
510th	EN	Maintenance	Benning	26 June 65 – 30 April 72	Pleiku	195	195	181
511th	EN	Panel Bridge	Campbell	2 Sept. 65 – 1 Jan. 72	Da Nang	127	126	126
513th	EN	Dump Truck	Wood	11 June 65 – 16 Jan. 72	Qui Nhon	108	113	113
517th	EN	Light Equipment	Campbell	24 July 67 – 14 Dec. 70	Da Nang	—	186	186
523d	EN	Port Construction	Belvoir	23 Feb. 67 – 29 Jan. 72	Vung Tau	—	225	225
538th	EN	Land Clearing	Vietnam	26 Dec. 68 – 26 Dec. 71	Nhon Co	—	—	132
544th	EN	Port Construction Support	Irwin	2 Sept. 67 – 20 March 72	Vung Tau	—	164	164
553d	EN	Float Bridge	Campbell	2 Sept. 65 – 29 Jan. 72	Phu Hiep	225	224	225
554th	EN	Float Bridge	Lewis	30 Sept. 66 – 8 Dec. 67	Chu Lai	225	—	—
555th	EN	Combat – 198th Inf Bde	Hood	31 Oct. 67 – 8 Dec. 67	Chu Lai	165‖	—	—
557th	EN	Light Equipment	Lewis	4 Nov. 65 – 1 April 72	Phuoc Vinh	186	186	186
569th	EN	Corps Topographic	Hood	15 Sept. 65 – 14 Feb. 70	Nha Trang	130	130	—
571st	EN	Combat – 9th Inf Div	Vietnam	1 Oct. 69 – 12 Oct. 70	Tan An	—	—	165
572d	EN	Light Equipment	Campbell	13 Jan. 66 – 22 March 71	Bao Loc	186	186	186
573d	EN	Float Bridge	Bragg	24 March 67 – 20 Dec. 68	Long Binh	—	224	—
574th	EN	Depot	Granite	28 Oct. 65 – 1 Dec. 66	Nha Trang	201	—	—
578th	EN#	Maintenance	Polk	24 Nov. 65 – 20 July 66	Pleiku	195	—	—
584th	EN	Light Equipment	Dix	11 June 65 – 1 April 72	Pleiku	186	186	186
585th	EN	Dump Truck	Belvoir	15 Sept. 66 – 29 Jan. 72	Pleiku	—	113	113
591st	EN	Light Equipment	Campbell	27 July 67 – 1 Jan. 72	Phu Bai	—	186	186
595th	EN	Light Equipment	Riley	24 March 67 – 14 Dec. 70	Dong Tam	—	186	186
610th	EN	Construction Support	Irwin	31 Aug. 67 – 20 March 72	Cam Ranh Bay	—	164	164
617th	EN	Panel Bridge	Lewis	4 Nov. 65 – 15 June 70	Long Binh	127	126	126
630th	EN	Light Equipment	Bliss	23 Oct. 65 – 28 Aug. 71	Pleiku	149	186	186
643d	EN	Pipeline Construction Support	Wood	1 Nov. 66 – 15 June 70	Cam Ranh Bay	—	178	—
687th	EN	Land Clearing	Vietnam	1 Jan. 69 – 10 Dec. 70	Cam Ranh Bay	—	—	132
697th	EN	Pipeline Construction Support	Wolters	26 – 28 Aug. 65 only**	Tan Son Nhut	—	—	—
919th	EN	Combat – 11th Arm Cav (Rgt)	Hood	5 Sept. 66 – 22 March 72	Long Giao	166	249	166
984th	EN	Land Clearing	Vietnam	1 Jan. 69 – 26 Dec. 71	Long Binh	—	—	132

In addition, there were numerous provisional engineer companies established on a temporary basis utilizing assets of existing engineer battalions or companies listed above.

* Second tour in Vietnam.

† 53d EN Company redesignated the 53d Supply Company 20 July 1966; see continuation of service under that designation.

‡ Vermont National Guard from Burlington, Vermont, via Ft. Belvoir.

§ 178th EN Company redesignated Supply Company 20 July 1966; see continuation of service under that designation.

‖ Strength of 1967.

578th EN Company redesignated Supply Company 20 July 1966; see continuation of service under that designation.

** The 697th EN Company was at Tan Son Nhut 26 – 28 August 1965 while being transshipped from California to Korat, Thailand, and thus carries campaign credit. See Appendix B for continuation of service.

Chapter 14

Military Police

18th Military Police Brigade

Arrived Vietnam: 8 September 1966
Departed Vietnam: 29 March 1973
Location: Saigon, Long Binh
Previous Station: Fort Meade

Authorized Strength	1966	1968	1971
HHC	55	80	219

Commanders

Colonel Thomas F. Guidera	June 66
Brigadier General Harley L. Moore, Jr.	July 67
Brigadier General Karl W. Gustafson	Nov. 67
Colonel W. N. Brandenburg	Aug. 68
Brigadier General Wallace K. Wittwer	Aug. 69
Brigadier General Paul M. Timmerberg	June 71
Colonel Harold I. Pitchford	June 72
Colonel Henry H. Gerecke*	Sept. 72

* Properly Commander of U.S. Army Military Police Group,
Vietnam (Provisional).

The 18th Military Police Brigade was established on 20 May 1966 and sent to Vietnam that fall. The brigade had the mission of commanding, coordinating and controlling the operations of military police groups, battalions and other assigned and attached units (including a river boat transportation company, the 458th) from the DMZ down to the middle of the Delta. The brigade was used in a combat support role in addition to its normal police function and provided convoy escorts, highway and bridge security, refugee and detainee evacuation and traffic control. The brigade also had control of a 22-square-mile area as its own tactical area of responsibility, including not only military operations, but civic action programs as well.

8th Military Police Group (Criminal Investigation)

Arrived Vietnam: 28 August 1968
Departed Vietnam: 1 July 1972
Location: Long Binh
Previous Station: Vietnam
Authorized Strength: HHD – 160

The 8th Military Police Group was established to provide planning, direction, and supervision for the criminal investigation work required by the U.S. Army in Vietnam. It was at Long Binh. In July 1972 it became the basis for the U.S. Army Criminal Investigation Center, Vietnam Field Office. A provisional Military Police Group (Criminal Investigation) had been first formed on 3 November 1966 in charge of all criminal investigative work in Vietnam except for metropolitan Saigon area.

16th Military Police Group

Arrived Vietnam: 11 September 1966
Departed Vietnam: 20 December 1970
Location: Nha Trang Sept. 66 – Sept. 70
Da Nang Oct. 70. – Dec. 71
Previous Station: Fort Meade
Authorized Strength: HHD – 38

The 16th Military Police Group provided command, control, staff planning and coordination for the military police units assigned and attached to it in the I and II Corps Tactical Zones of Vietnam. The 93d, 97th and 504th Military Police Battalions were under its control.

89th Military Police Group

Arrived Vietnam: 16 March 1966
Departed Vietnam: 20 December 1971
Location: Long Binh
Previous Station: Fort Benning

Authorized Strength	1966	1968	1970
HHD	37	38	38

The 89th Military Police Group provided command, control, staff planning and coordination for the military police units assigned and attached to it in the III and IV Corps Tactical Zones of Vietnam. The 92d, 95th, 716th and 720th Military Police Battalions were under its control.

92d Military Police Battalion

Arrived Vietnam: 11 April 1966
Departed Vietnam: 5 February 1970
Previous Station: Fort Bragg

Authorized Strength	1966	1968
HHD	20	27

The 92d Military Police Battalion deployed to Vietnam from Fort Bragg to provide command, control, staff planning, criminal investigation and supervision for organizational administration, training, operations and logistics of assigned or attached military police units. It was stationed at Tan Son Nhut rendering military police support for Saigon and was subordinate to the 89th Military Police Group.

93d Military Police Battalion

Arrived Vietnam: 30 August 1966
Departed Vietnam: 20 December 1971
Previous Station: Fort Sill

Authorized Strength	1966	1968	1970
HHD	20	27	26

The 93d Military Police Battalion was initially stationed at Qui Nhon. It moved to Phu Thanh in 1967 and in 1968 to Phu Bai (for capabilities, see 92d MP Battalion), rendering military police support in northern II Corps Tactical Zone of Vietnam under the 16th Military Police Group. On 29 March 1969 the battalion returned to Qui Nhon.

95th Military Police Battalion

Arrived Vietnam: 11 April 1966
Departed Vietnam: 13 April 1972
Previous Station: Fort Riley

Authorized Strength	1966	1968	1970
HHD	20	27	26

The 95th Military Police Battalion was stationed at Tan Son Nhut and after August 1966 at Long Binh (for capabilities, see 92d MP Battalion), rendering military police support in the III Corps Tactical Zone of Vietnam under the control of the 89th Military Police Group.

97th Military Police Battalion

Arrived Vietnam: 28 August 1966
Departed Vietnam: 26 April 1972
Previous Station: Fort Lewis

Authorized Strength	1968	1970
HHD	27	26

The 97th Military Police Battalion was located at Cam Ranh Bay (for capabilities, see 92d MP Battalion) providing military police support in southern II Corps Tactical Zone of Vietnam under the 16th Military Police Group. In April 1972 it went to Long Binh.

504th Military Police Battalion (Army)

Arrived Vietnam: 31 August 1965
Departed Vietnam: 31 July 1972
Previous Station: Fort Lewis

Authorized Strength	1966	1968	1970
Battalion	601	595	537

The 504th Military Police Battalion was sent to Vietnam to enforce military law, orders and regulations; to control traffic and stragglers, circulation of individuals, and protection of property; to handle prisoners of war; to operate checkpoints and route security; and to fight as infantry when required. The battalion was first located at Qui Nhon, in 1967 at Phu Thanh, in 1968 at Phu Bai, and moved on 13 August 1970 to Da Nang, rendering military police support in I Corps Tactical Zone under the 16th Military Police Group. In April 1972 it went to Long Binh.

716th Military Police Battalion (Army)

Arrived Vietnam: 24 March 1965
Departed Vietnam: 29 March 1973
Previous station: Fort Dix

Authorized Strength	1966	1968	1970
Battalion	602	595	537

The 716th Military Police Battalion was stationed at Saigon and Tan Son Nhut throughout its service in Vietnam (for capabilities, see 504th MP Battalion), providing military police support for the Saigon area. It was under the 89th Military Police Group.

720th Military Police Battalion (Army)

Arrived Vietnam: 19 October 1966
Departed Vietnam: 13 August 1972
Previous Station: Fort Hood

Authorized Strength	1968	1970
Battalion	595	537

The 720th Military Police Battalion was stationed initially at Long Binh in Vietnam (for unit capabilities, see 504th MP Battalion), rendering military police support for the III Corps Tactical Zone under the command of the 89th Military Police Group. In August 1970 the battalion relocated to Da Nang but in 1971 went back to Long Binh.

MILITARY POLICE COMPANIES IN VIETNAM

Company	Type	Previous Station	Vietnam Service	Typical Location	Authorized Strength 1966	1968	1970
1st MP	Divisional – 1st Inf Div	Riley	17 Oct. 65 – 15 April 70	Di An	189	189	—
4th MP	Divisional – 4th Inf Div	Lewis	8 Sept. 66 – 15 Dec. 70	Pleiku	—	189	189
9th MP	Divisional – 9th Inf Div	Riley	19 Dec. 66 – 25 Sept. 69	Dong Tam	—	189	—
23d MP	Divisional – AMERICAL Inf Div	Vietnam	8 Dec. 67 – 29 June 72	Chu Lai	—	126	189
25th MP	Divisional – 25th Inf Div	Hawaii	13 March 66 – 8 Dec. 70	Cu Chi	189	189	189
61st MP	Physical Security – 1st Sig Bde	Vietnam	1 March 70 – 19 March 73	Dalat	—	—	169
66th MP	Guard	Hood	23 Aug. 65 – 20 March 72	Phu Thanh	125	163	156
101st MP	Divisional – 101st Abn Div (AM)	Campbell	28 Dec. 67 – 16 Jan. 72	Gia Le	40*	156	189
127th MP	Corps/Army	Bragg	8 Jan. 67 – 30 Jan. 72	Qui Nhon	—	182	162
188th MP	Physical Security	Meade	31 July 66 – 20 March 72	Can Tho	159	182	162
194th MP	Physical Security	Vietnam	19 May 67 – 28 June 72	Long Binh	—	228	119
212th MP	Sentry Guard Dog	Vietnam	10 Jan. 66 – 8 Nov. 72	Long Binh	188	193	191
218th MP	Corps/Army	Bragg	18 Jan. 67 – 17 April 72	Nha Trang	—	182	162
272d MP	Airborne Corps – I FFV	Knox	4 Sept. 65 – 31 March 72	Nha Trang	182	181	182
284th MP	Confinement Facility	Hood	2 April 68 – 28 March 73	Long Binh	—	234	234
300th MP	Physical Facility	Benning	25 June 66 – 1 April 72	Tan Son Nhut	143	182	162
527th MP	Physical Facility	Lewis	7 Sept. 66 – 15 Oct. 68	Saigon	—	182	—
527th MP †	Confinement Facility	Vietnam	30 June 71 – 20 March 72	Da Nang	—	—	—
545th MP	Divisional – 1st Cav Div	Benning	28 July 65 – 29 April 71	Phuoc Vinh	156	156	156
552d MP	Corps – II FFV	Benning	1 Oct. 66 – 28 April 72	Long Binh	—	200	200
557th MP	Army Guard	Dix	5 Sept. 65 – 20 March 72	Long Binh	125	163	156
560th MP	Corps/Army	Hood	14 Sept. 62 – 28 March 73	Vung Tau	182	182	162
595th MP	Sentry Dog	Vietnam	2 Jan. 70 – 28 April 72	Da Nang	—	—	191
615th MP	Corps/Army	Hood	26 Aug. 65 – 28 March 73	Long Binh	182	182	162
630th MP	Escort Guard	Riley	23 Aug. 65 – 17 April 72	Cam Ranh Bay	142	182	162
981st MP	Sentry Dog	Carson	8 Dec. 67 – 17 April 72	Cam Ranh Bay	—	193	191

* One platoon only in country at the time.

† Second tour in Vietnam.

Chapter 15

Signal

1st Signal Brigade

Arrived Vietnam: 1 April 1966
Departed Vietnam: 7 November 1972
Previous Station: Fort Gordon

Authorized Strength	1966	1968	1970
HHC	259	245	258

Commanders

Brigadier General Robert D. Terry	April 66
Brigadier General M. Van Harlingen	Nov. 67
Brigadier General Thomas M. Rienzi	Feb. 69
Major General Hugh F. Foster	June 70
Brigadier General Wilburn C. Weaver	May 71
Brigadier General Charles R. Myer	June 72

The origins of the 1st Signal Brigade and the U.S. Army communications effort in Vietnam can be traced to the Strategic Communications Command Signal Brigade, Southeast Asia. Formed in April 1966, the 1st Signal Brigade arrived to assume command of all army communications-electronic resources in Vietnam as well as Thailand (U.S. Army operations in Thailand are considered in Appendix B). The brigade was not only in charge of planning, engineering, installing, operating and maintaining its extensive area communications system in those two countries, but also operated the Southeast Asian portion of the U.S. Army's worldwide strategic communications system. Scattered among more than 200 sites in Vietnam and Thailand, the brigade became the largest combat signal unit ever formed and controlled the most comprehensive military communications-electronics system in the history of warfare up to that point. The brigade was headquartered at Saigon and moved on 16 October 1967 to Long Binh.

USASTRATCOM, Southeast Asia

Arrived Vietnam: 1 March 1964
Departed Vietnam: 27 March 1973
Previous Station: Hawaii
Authorized Strength: HQ – 333 (1964)

The U.S. Army Strategic Communications Command (USASTRATCOM) managed the army's portion of the worldwide Defense Communications System (DCS), controlling and directing the telecommunications elements operating strategic radio, wire and cable facilities. Additionally, the command provided engineering and technical support of various assigned non-DCS communications. The first army signal elements were in South Vietnam as early as 1951, and in January 1962 the first troposcatter communications network was established, permitting long-range regional and global capabilities. In May 1965 the DCS mission in that area of the world was transferred from U.S. Army, Pacific (USARPAC) to USASTRATCOM, Southeast Asia. On 16 July 1965 USASTRATCOM, Vietnam was created. Previously the 2d Signal Group had handled part of the DCS mission as the major army signal headquarters in country, but on 19 August 1965 it was officially relieved of this global communications mission and USASTRATCOM, Vietnam assumed full responsibilities. On 4 July 1966, following the April arrival of the 1st Signal Brigade, USASTRATCOM shifted the combat theater signal burden to that brigade and created the Regional Communications Group, Vietnam (on 1 April 1968 adding USASTRATCOM to its title) to handle the DCS functions. This arrangement lasted until the 1st Signal Brigade departed Vietnam, and USASTRATCOM, Southeast Asia was reestablished on 5 November 1972. Stationed at Saigon, it controlled the army's signal missions until 27 March 1973.

U.S. Army Strategic Communications Command, Vietnam

Arrived Vietnam: 16 July 1965
Departed Vietnam: 22 July 1966
Location: Saigon
Previous Station: Vietnam
Authorized Strength: HHC – 357 (1966)

The U.S. Army Strategic Communications Command, Vietnam was formed in Saigon to command assigned and attached signal units; to formulate and implement signal plans, policies and procedures for the installation, operation, maintenance and management of the theater army communications system in Vietnam; and to furnish signal support for special-purpose communications systems. It later became the basis of the Regional Communications Group, Vietnam.

2d Signal Group

Arrived Vietnam: 3 June 1965
Departed Vietnam: 23 October 1971
Previous Station: Fort Bragg

Authorized Strength	1966	1968	1970
HHD	147	105	139

The 2d Signal Group directed the operations, training and administration of two to seven signal battalions to include logistical support and establish procedures for the communications system installed, operated and maintained by the group. The group was the major signal headquarters in Vietnam until mid-1966 when the 1st Signal Brigade arrived along with another signal group, the 21st. The 2d Signal Group was then responsible for communications in the III and IV Corps Tactical Zones. It was located at Tan Son Nhut until moved to Long Binh on 25 January 1967. The following signal battalions served at one time or another under the group:

36th Signal Battalion	52d Signal Battalion
39th Signal Battalion	54th Signal Battalion
40th Signal Battalion	69th Signal Battalion
41st Signal Battalion	86th Signal Battalion
44th Signal Battalion	972d Signal Battalion

12th Signal Group

Arrived Vietnam: 1 July 1969
Departed Vietnam: 27 February 1972
Previous Station: Vietnam

Authorized Strength	1969	1971
HHD	111	86

The 12th Signal Group was formed from assets of the I CTZ Signal Battalion (Provisional) and responsible for directing and coordinating the operations, training, administration and logistic support of assigned and attached units in the I Corps Tactical Zone. It relocated from Phu Bai to My Khe, Da Nang on 25 September 1970. The 37th and 63d Signal Battalions served with this group.

21st Signal Group

Arrived Vietnam: 9 June 1966
Departed Vietnam: 27 November 1971
Previous Station: Fort Bragg

Authorized Strength	1966	1968	1970
HHD	46	111	140

The 21st Signal Group was at Nha Trang and in charge of handling the command and coordination responsibilities for its assigned and attached signal units and communications in the II Corps Tactical Zone of Vietnam. The following signal battalions served at one time or another under the group's control:

37th Signal Battalion	73d Signal Battalion
41st Signal Battalion	307th Signal Battalion
43d Signal Battalion	459th Signal Battalion
63d Signal Battalion	509th Signal Battalion

160th Signal Group

Arrived Vietnam: 2 May 1967
Departed Vietnam: 2 June 1972
Previous Station: Fort Huachuca

Authorized Strength	1968	1970
HHD	118	116

The 160th Signal Group at Long Binh directed and coordinated the operations, training, administration and logistic support for the units responsible for communications in the Saigon – Long Binh area complex. The following signal organizations served the group at one time or another:

40th Signal Battalion	Saigon Signal Support Agency
44th Signal Battalion	Long Binh Signal Support Agency
60th Signal Battalion	Southeast Asia Signal School
69th Signal Battalion	

No Insignia Authorized

I Corps Tactical Zone Signal Group, Provisional

Arrived Vietnam: 8 September 1968
Departed Vietnam: 30 June 1969
Previous Station: Vietnam
Authorized Strength: 86

The I Corps Tactical Zone Signal Group was a provisional command established at Phu Bai to provide a temporary communications headquarters to control the expanding U.S. Army effort in that northern area. It was replaced by the 12th Signal Group on 1 July 1969.

Regional Communications Group, Vietnam

Arrived Vietnam: 4 July 1966
Departed Vietnam: 21 July 1972
Previous Station: Vietnam

Authorized Strength	1966	1968	1970
HHC	110	136	233

Unauthorized

The Regional Communications Group, Vietnam was formed at Saigon from the assets of the U.S. Army Strategic Command,

Vietnam. It provided the organizational structure and a nucleus of professional and technical communications-electronics and administrative personnel to staff a headquarters for support of an army component communications command in Vietnam. On 1 April 1968 the group was redesignated the U.S. Army Strategic Communications Regional Group, Vietnam. The following signal battalions served at one time or another under this group:

> 361st Signal Battalion
> 369th Signal Battalion
> USASTRATCOM Long Lines North Battalion
> USASTRATCOM Long Lines South Battalion
> Da Nang Signal Battalion (Provisional)
> Phu Lam Signal Battalion (Provisional)
> Nha Trang Signal Battalion (Provisional)

9th Signal Battalion (Divisional)

Arrived Vietnam: 19 December 1966
Departed Vietnam: 19 August 1969
Previous Station: Fort Riley
Authorized Strength: 641 (1968)

The 9th Signal Battalion had the mission of providing signal communications to include establishment and operation of a division area communications system of signal centers, wire and radio trunk and local lines, and radio/wire integration stations providing general and direct communications support for units in the division area. The battalion was part of the 9th Infantry Division in Vietnam and was headquartered with the division. However, its elements were often scattered to provide direct support to the separated divisional units.

13th Signal Battalion (Divisional)

Arrived Vietnam: 18 August 1965
Departed Vietnam: 29 April 1971
Previous Station: Fort Benning

Authorized Strength	1966	1968	1970
Battalion	352	352	256

The 13th Signal Battalion was part of the 1st Cavalry Division (Airmobile) in Vietnam and organized more lightly than a normal infantry division signal battalion. It was capable of planning and supervising communications, training and other signal activities to include installation, operation and maintenence of radio communications for the division elements as well as long-lines communications service to the division's far-flung elements. The battalion was responsible for the division area communications system.

36th Signal Battalion (Combat Area)

Arrived Vietnam: 28 November 1966
Departed Vietnam: 26 August 1971
Previous Station: Fort Bragg

Authorized Strength	1966	1968	1970
Battalion	845	675	754

The 36th Signal Battalion (Combat Area) was responsible for installing, operating and maintaining a base camp communica-

tions system and was also charged with communications in the III Corps Tactical Zone. Initially part of the 1st Signal Brigade, it was quickly transferred to the 2d Signal Group, and stationed at Long Binh until its departure from Vietnam.

37th Signal Battalion (Modified Support)

Arrived Vietnam: 20 October 1966*
Departed Vietnam: 28 June 1972
Previous Station: Vietnam

Authorized Strength	1966	1968	1970
Battalion	523	559	77 †

* Conflicting sources. 8 October 1966 by authority of 1st Signal Brigade; 1 August 1966 by unit card; above date from USASTRATCOM GO 53, 29 July 1966. However, its organic companies were not raised until 14 – 16 November 1966.

† HQ and HQ Detachment only.

The 37th Signal Battalion (Modified Support) provided an assigned segment of the area communications system in the I Corps Tactical Zone. In addition, it provided access to the system and signal center services—telephone, teletypewriter, data and facsimile—when appropriate for units in that area. It provided, on a 24-hour basis, numerous signal centers and related multichannel communications systems and terminal facilities. Located at Da Nang, the battalion was under the 21st Signal Group until March 1969 when it was placed under the command of the I Corps Tactical Zone Signal Group (Provisional), later replaced by the 12th Signal Group. After that group left Vietnam in February 1972, the battalion was placed under the U.S. Army Contract Management Agency, Vietnam (Provisional).

39th Signal Battalion (Support)

Arrived Vietnam: 23 March 1962
Departed Vietnam: 14 March 1973
Previous Station: Fort Gordon

Authorized Strength	1964	1966	1968
HHD	1,283 *	244	117

	1970	1972
	244	109

* Reinforced battalion.

The 39th Signal Battalion (Support) was originally responsible for all communications support in Vietnam under the command of the U.S. Army Support Group, Vietnam. In 1965 it was reduced to the normal capabilities of a support signal battalion (see 37th Signal Battalion). Under the 2d Signal Group it was responsible for service in the III and IV Corps Tactical Zones located at Tan Son Nhut. It was then placed in charge of the III Corps Tactical Zone service under the direct supervision of the 1st Signal Brigade in December 1971, moving to Vung Tau and then finally to Long Binh.

40th Signal Battalion (Construction)

Arrived Vietnam: 15 September 1966 *
Departed Vietnam: 28 June 1972
Previous Station: Fort Bragg

Authorized Strength	1968	1970
Battalion	688	652

* Main body of battalion arrived on 21 August 1966 but Company D (from Fort Polk) did not arrive until 15 September 1966.

The 40th Signal Battalion (Construction) was specifically charged with the installation of fixed-plant communications cable in Vietnam. It also performed rehabilitation of existing indigenous lead-covered cable, field cable, open wire circuits and other field cable tasks. It served with the 1st Signal Brigade before being placed under the 2d Signal Group on 22 August 1966 and then under the 160th Signal Group on 28 August 1967. The battalion was located at Long Binh, where it remained until it left Vietnam.

41st Signal Battalion (Combat Area)

Arrived Vietnam: 24 July 1965
Departed Vietnam: 27 February 1972
Previous Station: Fort Lewis

Authorized Strength	1966	1968	1970
Battalion	622	703	88 *

* HQ and HQ Company only.

The 41st Signal Battalion (Combat Area) was initially charged with communications in the I and II Corps Tactical Zones, later being limited to responsibility for the II Corps coastal area, specifically providing communications center, switchboard, radio and multi-channel communications facilities in the greater Qui Nhon vicinity. Based at Qui Nhon under the 2d Signal Group, the battalion was next transferred to the 21st Signal Group in 1966 and finally came under direct 1st Signal Brigade command in December 1971.

43d Signal Battalion (Modified Support)

Arrived Vietnam: 16 October 1966 *
Departed Vietnam: 30 May 1971
Previous Station: Vietnam

Authorized Strength	1966	1968	1970
Battalion		844	874	27 †

* Conflicting sources. Date used is by authority of USASTRATCOM GO 53, 29 July 1966; 1st Signal Brigade date is 10 October 1966; unit card date is given as 1 August 1966.

† HQ and HQ Detachment only.

The 43d Signal Battalion (Modified Support) was responsible for communications support in the II Corps Tactical Zone Highlands (for capabilities, see 37th Signal Battalion) and was located at Pleiku. The battalion served under the 21st Signal Group for the duration of its Vietnam service.

44th Signal Battalion (Modified Support)

Arrived Vietnam: 15 December 1966 *
Departed Vietnam: 2 June 1972
Previous Station: Vietnam

Authorized Strength	1966	1968	1970
Battalion	634	983	976

* Conflicting sources. USASTRATCOM authority chosen. Unit card claims 1 August 1966; 1st Signal Brigade GO 65 says 8 October 1966; activation ceremony held 22 December 1966, but reorganization of battalion not complete until 15 August 1967.

The 44th Signal Battalion (Modified Support) was charged with the III Corps Tactical Zone communications at Bien Hoa, including those of USARV headquarters, and was placed in command of the extensive Long Binh communications network in August 1967. It was located at Long Binh under the command of the 2d Signal Group until August 1967 when it came under the jurisdiction of the 160th Signal Group. On 1 March 1970 its assets were used to form the nucleus of the Signal Support Agency, Long Binh. Its five lettered companies became the bases of the Signal Support Agency and its Radio Company, Command Communications Center Company, Area Communications Center Company and its Telephone Operations Company. In May 1972 the 44th Signal Battalion was reformed at Phu Loi from the personnel of the Signal Support Agency, Long Binh.

52d Signal Battalion (Modified Support)

Arrived Vietnam: 8 October 1966 *
Departed Vietnam: 12 October 1971
Previous Station: Vietnam

Authorized Strength	1966	1968	1970
Battalion		894	909	460

* Conflicting sources. Unit card claims 1 August 1966.

The 52d Signal Battalion (Modified Support) was responsible for the communications in the IV Corps Tactical Zone and was stationed at Can Tho. The battalion served at that location under the command of the 2d Signal Group throughout its service in Vietnam.

53d Signal Battalion (Corps)

Arrived Vietnam: 4 June 1966
Departed Vietnam: 22 June 1971
Previous Station: Fort Hood

Authorized Strength	1966	1968	1970
Battalion	691	691	472

The 53d Signal Battalion (Corps) was responsible for providing signal communications for all echelons of the II Field Force, Vietnam headquarters. It was capable of installing, operating and maintaining multichannel communications facilities of major sub-

ordinate tactical units as well as to the II Field Force Vietnam Artillery. Among its modes were high frequency radio teletype, voice, communications center, switchboard, photo, FM radio-wire integration and the Military Affiliate Radio System (MARS). The battalion landed at Vung Tau and was airlifted to Bien Hoa. It then moved to Long Binh.

54th Signal Battalion (Corps)

Arrived Vietnam: 19 October 1965
Departed Vietnam: 16 February 1971
Previous Station: Fort Hood

Authorized Strength	1966	1968	1970
Battalion	717	726	731

The 54th Signal Battalion (Corps) served the communications requirements of the Field Force, Vietnam, later assuming responsibility for the communications within I Field Force, Vietnam upon its arrival (for capabilities, see 53d Signal Battalion). The battalion was stationed at Nha Trang.

60th Signal Battalion (Support)

No Insignia Authorized

Arrived Vietnam: 17 March 1972
Departed Vietnam: 28 June 1972
Previous Station: Vietnam
Authorized Strength: NA

The 60th Signal Battalion (Support) arrived in Vietnam to take over the functions of the Phu Lam Signal Support Agency (established in June 1967) which provided most of the assets for the battalion. It was stationed at Phu Lam under the 160th Signal Group.

63d Signal Battalion (Command Radio & Cable)

Arrived Vietnam: 28 March 1968
Departed Vietnam: 14 February 1972
Previous Station: Fort Riley

Authorized Strength	1968	1970
HHC	136	124

The 63d Signal Battalion (Command Radio and Cable) provided echelons of a corps-level headquarters and designated major subordinate units with a command multichannel communications system and RATT (radioteletypewriter) stations for operation in the corps radio nets. It provided radio wire integration stations for FM voice radio access to the corps HQ telephone distribution system and generally provided support to the corps communications system as required. The battalion served in the I Corps Tactical Zone under the newly formed I Corps Tactical Zone Signal Group (Provisional) and later the 21st Signal Group. It was created at Phu Bai from assets of the 459th Signal Battalion to render Provisional Corps, Vietnam both corps-level and post signal support.

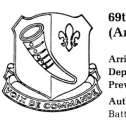

69th Signal Battalion (Army)

Arrived Vietnam: 2 November 1965
Departed Vietnam: 13 November 1972
Previous Station: Fort Eustis

Authorized Strength	1966	1968	1970
Battalion	1,449	986	?

The 69th Signal Battalion (Army) provided communications personnel and equipment for the operations post in Saigon-Long Binh as well as the other signal requirements of that complex. With the tremendous growth of the Military Assistance Command Vietnam (MACV) headquarters, the battalion was used solely in support of that command's signal needs. It was initially stationed at Tan Son Nhut under the 2d Signal Group but moved to the command of the 160th Signal Group in August 1967. In June 1970 its assets were used to help form the Signal Support Agency, Long Binh. In May 1972 the battalion moved to Saigon.

73d Signal Battalion (Support)

Arrived Vietnam: 31 July 1966
Departed Vietnam: 28 June 1972
Previous Station: Fort Bragg

Authorized Strength	1966	1968	1970
HHD	46	67	77

The 73d Signal Battalion (Support) was responsible for communications support in the II Corps Tactical Zone under the 21st Signal Group (for capabilities, see 86th Signal Battalion) until November 1971 when it was placed under the 1st Signal Brigade. It was stationed at Cam Ranh Bay throughout its Vietnam service.

82d Signal Battalion (Divisional)

Arrived Vietnam: 22 February 1968
(elements only)
Departed Vietnam: 11 December 1969
Previous Station: Fort Bragg
Authorized Strength: NA

The 82d Signal Battalion sent some elements to Vietnam along with the 3d Brigade Task Force of the 82d Airborne Division and was stationed at Phu Bai, where these elements became absorbed into the 58th Signal Company.

86th Signal Battalion (Support)

Arrived Vietnam: 1 September 1966
Departed Vietnam: 30 April 1971
Previous Station: Fort Bragg

Authorized Strength	1968	1970
HHD	67	77

The 86th Battalion directed and coordinated the operations of assigned signal units and provided the facilities with which the battalion commander controlled the battalion's assets. The battalion was responsible for communications support activities within the western III Corps Tactical Zone and was stationed at Cu Chi under the command of the 2d Signal Group throughout its service in Vietnam.

121st Signal Battalion (Divisional)

Arrived Vietnam: 10 October 1965
Departed Vietnam: 8 April 1970
Previous Station: Fort Riley

Authorized Strength	1966	1968
Battalion	617	641

The 121st Signal Battalion was part of the 1st Infantry Division (for its general capabilities, see 9th Signal Battalion). Its headquarters were colocated with the division, but the division's far-flung operations often entailed detaching the battalion's assets to accompany the division's separate elements in different locations.

124th Signal Battalion (Divisional)

Arrived Vietnam: 25 September 1966
Departed Vietnam: 7 December 1970
Previous Station: Fort Lewis

Authorized Strength	1966	1970
Battalion	641	605

The 124th Signal Battalion served the 4th Infantry Division (for capabilities see the 9th Signal Battalion) during its service in Vietnam. Its elements were scattered in support of the division's dispersed subordinate units.

125th Signal Battalion (Divisional)

Arrived Vietnam: 11 March 1966
Departed Vietnam: 8 December 1970
Previous Station: Hawaii

Authorized Strength	1966	1968	1970
Battalion	626	641	539

The 125th Signal Battalion was part of the 25th Infantry Division (for capabilities, see 9th Signal Battalion) and colocated with the division headquarters at Cu Chi. Its elements were sometimes called upon to provide signal support functions for division elements when they were moved to other locations.

307th Signal Battalion (Support)

No Insignia
Authorized

Arrived Vietnam: 1 March 1970
Departed Vietnam: 30 April 1971
Previous Station: Vietnam
Authorized Strength: HHD – 77

The 307th Signal Battalion (Support) was established at Cam Ranh Bay using the assets of the II Corps Tactical Zone Signal Battalion (Provisional). It was under the command of the 21st Signal Group.

361st Signal Battalion (Command Radio & Cable)

Arrived Vietnam: 15 June 1969
Departed Vietnam: 30 May 1971
Previous Station: Vietnam

Authorized Strength	1966	1971
Battalion	592	304

The 361st Signal Battalion (Command Radio & Cable) was formed in Vietnam using the assets of the USASTRATCOM Long Lines North Battalion. It operated and maintained a long haul communications system throughout the northern two-thirds of Vietnam. The battalion served at Cam Ranh Bay under the Regional Communications Group, Vietnam during its service in Vietnam.

369th Signal Battalion (Command Radio & Cable)

Arrived Vietnam: 15 June 1969
Departed Vietnam: 30 June 1971
Previous Station: Vietnam

Authorized Strength	1970	1971
Battalion	595	230*

The 369th Signal Battalion (Command Radio & Cable) was formed using the assets of the USASTRATCOM Long Lines South Battalion (for capabilities, see the 361st Signal Battalion). The battalion served the Regional Communications Group, Vietnam at Vung Tau.

* Company C only.

459th Signal Battalion (Combat Area)

Arrived Vietnam: 21 October 1966
Departed Vietnam: 30 November 1971
Previous Station: Fort Huachuca

Authorized Strength	1968	1970
Battalion	699	598

The 459th Signal Battalion (Combat Area) arrived at Phu Bai and moved to Nha Trang. It served the II Corps Tactical Zone and provided both area and base camp communications. The battalion was under control of the 21st Signal Group. On 29 January 1968 the battalion temporarily went to Phu Bai to lend assets to the 63d Signal Battalion. On 10 September 1968 it became responsible for Ban Me Thuot communications.

501st Signal Battalion (Divisional)

Arrived Vietnam: 24 December 1967
Departed Vietnam: 12 January 1972
Previous Station: Fort Campbell

Authorized Strength	1968	1970	1971
Battalion	352	500	399

The 501st Signal Battalion was part of the 101st Airborne Division (Airmobile) in Vietnam. Company B (Airborne) was serving the 1st Brigade of the division since July 1965, primarily at Phan Rang, by sending elements of the company to Vietnam. For capabilities of the battalion, see the 9th Signal Battalion. Due to the far-ranging nature of divisional operations, the battalion was often fragmented providing forward signal support to its scattered elements.

509th Signal Battalion (Support)

Arrived Vietnam: 15 September 1966
Departed Vietnam: 10 January 1968
Previous Station: Fort Huachuca
Authorized Strength: HHD – 53 (1967)

The 509th Signal Battalion first served at An Khe and in 1967 moved to Chu Lai. Its assets were used to form the personnel and equipment positions within the 523d Signal Battalion. The 509th Signal Battalion served under the command of the 21st Signal Group.

523d Signal Battalion (Divisional)

Arrived Vietnam: 10 January 1968
Departed Vietnam: 22 November 1971
Previous Station: Fort Huachuca

Authorized Strength	1968	1970
Battalion	490	641

The 523d Signal Battalion utilized assets of the 509th Signal Battalion to assist in providing a divisional signal battalion to the 23d Infantry Division (AMERICAL) (for capabilities, see 9th Signal Battalion). Its headquarters was colocated with the division at Chu Lai.

972d Signal Battalion (Supply and Maintenance) (Combat Area)

First Tour:
Arrived Vietnam: 3 September 1965
Departed Vietnam: 20 October 1967
Previous Station: Vietnam

Second Tour:
Arrived Vietnam: 28 October 1968
Departed Vietnam: 29 November 1969
Previous Station: Fort Lewis

Authorized Strength	1966	1968
HHD	115	127

The 972d Signal Battalion was first formed in Vietnam as part of the 1st Logistical Command operating the signal depots in Vietnam as well as signal supply and maintenance points. It provided semifixed general support and mobile fixed support for signal equipment. It came under command of the 1st Signal Brigade in April 1966 and then was transferred to the 2d Signal Group. It was then located at Qui Nhon. On its second Vietnam tour, the battalion provided contingency communications support throughout Vietnam while at Long Binh.

II Corps Tactical Zone Signal Battalion, Provisional

No Insignia Authorized

Arrived Vietnam: 1 October 1969 *
Departed Vietnam: 29 November 1969 *
Previous Station: Vietnam
Authorized Strength: Unknown

* Arrival and departure also put at 28 July 1969 and 1 March 1970 respectively.

The II Corps Tactical Zone Signal Battalion (Provisional) was formed to provide additional communications support to II CTZ area units experiencing unique logistical and control problems. It became the nucleus of the 307th Signal Battalion.

Da Nang Signal Battalion, Provisional

No Insignia Authorized

Arrived Vietnam: 24 June 1967
Departed Vietnam: September 1970
Previous Station: Vietnam

Authorized Strength	1966	1968	1970
Battalion	280*	276	213

* Facility.

The Da Nang Signal Battalion (Provisional) was formed from the assets of the U.S. Army Strategic Communications Facility, Da Nang, which had been established in August 1966. It served the Da Nang communications complex and in September 1970 was reduced to company size and redesignated as the U.S. Army Strategic Communications Facility, Da Nang.

Nha Trang Signal Battalion, Provisional

No Insignia Authorized

Arrived Vietnam: 24 June 1967
Departed Vietnam: September 1970
Previous Station: Vietnam

Authorized Strength	1966	1968
Battalion	526*	455

* Facility.

The Nha Trang Signal Battalion (Provisional) was formed from the assets of the U.S. Army Strategic Communications Facility, Nha Trang which had been established in November 1965. The battalion served the Regional Communications Group at Nha Trang and in September 1970 was reduced to company size and redesignated as the U.S. Army Strategic Facility, Nha Trang once more.

Phu Lam Signal Battalion, Provisional

Arrived Vietnam: 24 June 1967
Departed Vietnam: September 1970
Previous Station: Vietnam

Authorized Strength	1966	1968
Battalion	609*	543

Unauthorized

* Facility.

The Phu Lam Signal Battalion (Provisional) was formed from the assets of the U.S. Army Strategic Communications Facility, Phu

Lam, which had been established in November 1964. The battalion served the Regional Communications Group at Phu Lam and in September 1970 was folded to form the Phu Lam Signal Support Agency.

USASTRATCOM
Long Lines Battalion North

No Insignia
Authorized

Arrived Vietnam: 23 August 1966
Departed Vietnam: 15 June 1969
Previous Station: Vietnam

Authorized Strength	1966	1968
Battalion	192	789

The U.S. Army Strategic Communications (USASTRATCOM) Long Lines Battalion North was formed on a provisional basis in May 1966 to install, operate and maintain a multichannel system for the northern portion of the Vietnam communications system. It was also responsible for installing, operating and maintaining the battalion's signal control centers and sub-centers within this system. It served the Regional Communications Group at Pleiku. In June 1969 its assets were integrated into the 361st Signal Battalion.

USASTRATCOM
Long Lines Battalion South

No Insignia
Authorized

Arrived Vietnam: 23 August 1966
Departed Vietnam: 15 June 1969
Previous Station: Vietnam

Authorized Strength	1966	1968
Battalion	219	772

The U.S. Army Strategic Communications (USASTRATCOM) Long Lines Battalion South was established provisionally in May 1966 (for capabilities, see the USASTRATCOM Long Lines Battal-

ion North) at Vung Tau. It served the Regional Communications Group, Vietnam and in June 1969 provided assets for the 369th Signal Battalion.

Signal Support Agency,
Long Binh

No Insignia
Authorized

Arrived Vietnam: September 1970
Departed Vietnam: May 1972
Authorized Strength: HQ – 113 (1971)

The Signal Support Agency, Long Binh was established in Vietnam serving under the 160th Signal Group and later provided assets to the 44th Signal Battalion.

Signal Support Agency,
Phu Lam

No Insignia
Authorized

Arrived Vietnam: September 1970
Departed Vietnam: May 1972
Authorized Strength: HQ – 232 (1971)

The Signal Support Agency, Phu Lam was established in Vietnam serving under the 160th Signal Group and later provided assets to the 60th Signal Battalion.

Signal Support Agency,
Saigon

No Insignia
Authorized

Arrived Vietnam: September 1970
Departed Vietnam: May 1972
Authorized Strength: HQ – 108 (1971)

The Signal Support Agency, Saigon was established in Vietnam serving under the 160th Signal Group and later provided assets to the 69th Signal Battalion.

SIGNAL COMPANIES IN VIETNAM

Company		Type	Previous Station	Vietnam Service	Typical Location	Authorized Strength		
						1966	1968	1970
14th	SIG	Support	Vietnam	1 March 70 – 19 March 73	Da Nang	—	—	160
16th	SIG	Radio Operations and Hyperbolic Navigation	Vietnam	1 Dec. 67 – 1 April 69	Tan Son Nhut	—	?	—
54th	SIG	Forward Support Maintenance	Riley	29 Oct. 65 – 20 July 66	Tan Son Nhut	146	—	—
56th	SIG	Forward Support Maintenance	Lewis	9 July 65 – 20 July 66	Qui Nhon	146	—	—
56th	SIG †	Support – 3d Bde, 9th Inf Div	Vietnam	9 Oct. 69 – 12 Oct. 70	Tan An	—	—	106
57th	SIG	Communications Security Logistical Support	Vietnam	24 Feb. 69 – 1 April 70	Long Binh	—	—	?
58th	SIG	Airborne Forward Area Support –3d Bde, 82d Abn Div	Bragg	25 May 68 – 25 Nov. 69	Phu Loi	–	102	—
59th	SIG	Depot	Toby-hanna	4 Jan. 67 – 15 March 71	Long Binh	—	180	—
62d	SIG	Support	Vietnam	1 March 70 – 1 Sept. 71	Chu Lai	—	—	187
63d	SIG	Support	Vietnam	1 March 70 – 16 Jan. 72	Camp Evans	—	—	135
107th	SIG*	Support	Devens	21 Oct. 68 – 7 Oct. 69	Long Binh	—	350	—
128th	SIG	Depot	Toby-hanna	19 Sept. 65 – 30 April 72	Cam Ranh Bay	182	176	232
146th	SIG	Support	Vietnam	1 March 70 – 19 March 73	Pleiku	—	—	217
167th	SIG	Radio Relay	Gordon	21 Dec. 66 – 10 Dec. 70	Pleiku	—	308	302
173d SIG (Prov)		Airborne – 173d Abn Bde	Vietnam	18 July 67 – 19 Dec. 68(?)	Bien Hoa	—	?	—
175th	SIG	Support	Vietnam	1 March 70 – 1 Sept. 71	Kontum	—	—	119
178th	SIG	Support	Benning	5 May 62 – 1 Aug. 66	Da Nang	261	102	—

Unit		Type	Home Station	Dates	Location			
221st	SIG	Pictorial	Monmouth	3 May 67 – 29 Jan. 72	Long Binh	—	244	191
228th	SIG	Radio Relay VHF	Bragg	6 Sept. 65 – 16 Nov. 72	Nha Trang	170	170	170
232d	SIG	Support	Lewis	23 March 62 – 1 Aug. 66	Bien Hoa	270	172	94
232d	SIG†	Army Area	Vietnam	1 March 70 – 20 Dec. 71	Vung Chua Mtn	—	—	—
261st	SIG	Support	Hood	29 March 67 – 26 Feb. 72	Phu Hiep	—	350	350
267th	SIG	Cable Construction	Carson	27 Nov. 65 – 15 April 70	Long Binh	266	266	—
269th	SIG	Support	Vietnam	1 March 70 – 16 Jan. 72	Bien Hoa	—	—	145
270th	SIG	Combat Area	Bragg	31 Oct. 68 – 1 June 72	An Khe	—	172	130
275th	SIG	Support	Vietnam	1 March 70 – 30 June 71	Di An	—	—	206
278th	SIG	Support	Lewis	22 Aug. 66 – 1 Sept. 70	Pleiku	350	374	170
298th	SIG	Forward Area Communications –1st Bde, 5th Inf Div (Mech)	Vietnam	15 Aug. 68 – 30 July 71	Quang Tri	—	—	102
313th	SIG	Support – 199th Inf Bde	Benning	5 Nov. 68 – 12 Oct. 70	Long Binh	—	102	—
324th	SIG	Radio Relay VHF	Hood	25 Oct. 67 – 15 Nov. 69	Long Binh	—	308	—
327th	SIG	Tropospheric Radio Relay	Bragg	22 July 67 – 31 March 72	Long Binh	—	268	312
331st	SIG	Combat Area	Vietnam	1 March 70 – 26 Feb. 72	Long Binh	—	—	124
337th	SIG	Tropospheric Radio Relay	Bragg	29 Aug. 67 – 13 Feb. 72	Da Nang	—	260	260
362d	SIG	Long Lines Multichannel Troposcatter Radio Repair	Gordon	25 Aug. 62 – 28 June 72	Dalat	365	458	211
378th	SIG	Support	Benning	30 April 67 – Unknown	Unknown	—	?	—
504th	SIG	Army Area	Vietnam	1 March 70 – 6 Sept. 71	Phu Thanh	—	—	126
510th	SIG	Army Area	Vietnam	1 March 70 – 1 May 72	Cam Ranh Bay	—	—	90
518th	SIG	Tropospheric Radio Relay	Bragg	16 Dec. 65 – 20 Dec. 71	Nha Trang	287	287	288
525th	SIG	Command Operations	Vietnam	30 June 71 – 20 Aug. 72	Bien Hoa	—	—	147
532d	SIG	Automatic Secure Voice Comm	Vietnam	1 Oct. 68 – 1 March 70	Tan Son Nhut	—	—	154
532d	SIG †	Support – 2d Bde, 25th Inf Div	Vietnam	10 Feb. 71 – 25 April 71	Long Binh	—	—	—
534th	SIG	Airborne Forward Area Comm	Benning	5 June 66 – 20 July 66	An Khe	146	—	—
534th	SIG †	Support – 173d Abn Bde	Vietnam	20 Dec. 68 – 21 July 71	Bong Son	—	—	102
535th	SIG	Support	Vietnam	1 March 70 – 19 March 73	Duc Hoa	—	—	152
542d	SIG	Support	Vietnam	1 March 70 – 31 Aug. 71	Cam Ranh Bay	—	—	176
550th	SIG	Army Area	Vietnam	1 March 70 – 19 March 73	Bear Cat	—	—	126
556th	SIG	Support	Vietnam	1 March 70 – 26 Jan. 72	Dalat	—	—	161
578th	SIG	Cable Construction	Meade	31 Aug. 65 – 30 April 71	Qui Nhon	266	266	270
579th	SIG	Combat Area	Vietnam	1 March 70 – 30 April 71	Cu Chi	—	—	125
580th	SIG	Construction/ Telephone Operations	Bragg	4 Nov. 65 – 1 March 70	Long Binh	207	253	—
581st	SIG	Support	Vietnam	25 April 65 – 1 Aug. 66	Can Tho	244	—	—
586th	SIG	Support	Irwin	2 Sept. 65 – 15 Dec. 70	An Khe	277	304	172
587th	SIG	Support	Irwin	24 March 67 – 15 Dec. 70	Tay Ninh	—	350	145
587th	SIG †	Support – 196th Inf Bde	Vietnam	31 May 72 – 29 June 72	Da Nang	—	—	—
588th	SIG	Support	Irwin	3 May 67 – 31 Aug. 71	Quang Tri	—	350	157
589th	SIG	Support	Vietnam	1 March 70 – 26 Jan. 72	Cha Rang	—	—	168
593d	SIG	Signal Comm Center Operations/Telephone Operations	Gordon	9 July 65 – 1 March 70	Tan Son Nhut	216	369	—
595th	SIG	Support	Devens	27 May 66 – 30 April 71	Lai Khe	350	350	260
596th	SIG	Support	Huachuca	20 Feb. 68 – 1 April 72	Phu Bai	—	350	350
AVEL Central ‡		Avionics	Vietnam	1 Jan. 66 – 29 April 72	Phu Loi	—	?	—
AVEL Far North ‡		Avionics	Vietnam	20 Feb. 68 – 1 Dec. 69	Da Nang	—	?	—
AVEL North ‡		Avionics	Vietnam	1 Jan. 66 – 1 Dec. 69	Nha Trang	—	?	—
AVEL South ‡		Avionics	Vietnam	1 Jan. 66 – 1 December 69	Vung Tau	—	?	—
USASTRATCOM		Radio Company, Long Binh	Vietnam	1 March 70 – 16 June 72	Long Binh	—	?	—
USASTRATCOM		MACV Comm Center, Saigon §	Vietnam	1 March 70 – 10 March 73	Saigon	—	—	237
USASTRATCOM		Telephone Operations, Saigon	Vietnam	1 March 70 – 19 March 73	Saigon	—	—	?
Command SIG		Automatic Secure Voice Communications	Vietnam	1 March 70 – 19 March 73	Phu Lam	—	—	?

In addition there were numerous provisional signal companies established on a temporary basis to provide communications support by various levels of command, especially with regard to interior post facility networks.

* 107th Signal Company was Rhode Island National Guard from East Greenwich via Ft. Devens.

† Second tour in Vietnam.

‡ Provisional aviation electronics company.

§ Properly redesignated USASTRATCOM Telecommunications Facility, Saigon on 31 July 1972.

Service Units

Chapter 16

Support Commands and Groups

1st Logistical Command

Arrived Vietnam: 30 March 1965
Departed Vietnam: 7 December 1970
Location: Long Binh
Previous Station: Fort Hood

Authorized Strength	1966	1968
HHD	491	750

Commanders

Colonel Robert W. Duke	April 66
Major General Charles W. Eifler	Jan. 66
Major General Shelton E. Lollis	June 67
Major General Thomas H. Scott, Jr.	Aug. 67
Major General Joseph H. Heiser, Jr.	Aug. 68
Brigadier General Hugh A. Richeson	Aug. 69
Major General Walter J. Woolwine	Sept. 69

The 1st Logistical Command was activated at Fort McPherson, Georgia, on 20 September 1950 with 15 officers and 35 enlisted men. Its early years were spent at Fort McPherson and later at Fort Bragg. The command's varied responsibilities during this period included participation in logistical exercises and assisting in the testing and evaluation of new logistics doctrine and organization. In July 1958 the command was designated a major unit of the Strategic Army Corps; during the next three years it was responsible for administrative and logistical support to contingency forces of the corps. During the Berlin Crisis the command deployed to France and became a major unit of the Communications Zone, Europe. After nearly a year of service in Europe, the command returned to the U.S. and was posted to Fort Hood. As U.S. military involvement in Vietnam increased, an urgent need developed for immediate and responsive combat service support. By 1 April 1965 the 1st Logistical Command was established in Saigon to meet the challenge. Initially stationed in the capital, it

was responsible for all U.S. and Allied forces support south of Chu Lai since the I Corps Tactical Zone was at that time a U.S. Navy responsibility. The command possessed both a general and a special staff. It expanded its activities to control the major subordinate commands of U.S. Army Support Commands in Saigon, Cam Ranh Bay, Qui Nhon, Da Nang; the U.S. Army Inventory Control Center, Vietnam; as well as a host of separate elements such as the U.S. Army Procurement Agency, Vietnam. With the build-up of Army units in the I Corps Tactical Zone, the command established the Support Command, Da Nang in 1968, assuming responsibility for that area's support as well. On 26 June 1970 the 1st Logistical Command was consolidated with U.S. Army Vietnam. It departed Vietnam in this form and returned to the U.S., becoming the 1st Logistical Command once more at Fort Bragg.

Major Subordinate Components of 1st Logistical Command

58th Army Depot Headquarters & Headquarters Det	15 Dec. 66
504th Army Depot Headquarters & Headquarters Det	31 July 65
506th Army Depot Headquarters & Headquarters Det	31 July 65
32d Medical Depot (until 44th Med Bde assumed control)	4 Oct. 65
26th Support Group	18 Jan. 67
29th Support Group	2 Aug. 65
34th Support Group	24 Jan. 66
45th Support Group	27 Nov. 66
53d Support Group	9 March 67
54th Support Group	30 Nov. 66
80th Support Group	18 Jan. 67
593d Support Group	19 Nov. 66
U.S. Army Depot, Cam Ranh Bay (formerly 504th Army Depot)	1 Aug. 68
U.S. Army Depot, Da Nang	25 Feb. 68
U.S. Army Depot, Long Binh (formerly 506th Army Depot)	29 July 68

U.S. Army Depot, Qui Nhon (formerly 58th Army Depot)	1 Sept. 68
U.S. Army Logistical Command Security Force	4 Sept. 65
U.S. Army Marine Maintenance Activity	1 July 66
U.S. Army Mortuary, Da Nang	25 Aug. 67
U.S. Army Mortuary, Saigon	25 Nov. 69
U.S. Army Procurement Agency, Vietnam (USAPAV) *	10 May 66
U.S. Army Special Services Depot, Saigon	25 Nov. 69
U.S. Army Support Command, Saigon	10 Feb. 66
U.S. Army Support Command, Vung Tau	1 April 69
U.S. Army Support Command, Nha Trang	10 Feb. 66
U.S. Army Support Command, Cam Ranh Bay	16 May 66
U.S. Army Support Command, Da Nang	25 Feb. 68
U.S. Army Support Command, Qui Nhon	10 Feb. 66
U.S. Army Vietnam Headquarters Area Command, USARV	1 April 66
U.S. Army Vietnam Inventory Control Center †	9 Jan. 66

* Responsible for administering all civilian contracts and local outside purchases.

† First formed as the 14th Inventory Control Center, its HHC strength was 368 in 1967.

Unauthorized

U.S. Army Support Command, Cam Ranh Bay

Arrived Vietnam: 16 May 1966
Departed Vietnam: 29 June 1972
Previous Station: Vietnam

Authorized Strength	1966	1968	1970
Headquarters	125	358	1,300

On 1 May 1965 a detachment of one officer and six enlisted men arrived at Cam Ranh Bay to establish and operate a port. On 9 June 1965 the 35th Engineer Group arrived at Cam Ranh Bay and established the Cam Ranh Bay Logistical Area under the 1st Logistical Command. The Cam Ranh Bay Logistical Area was absorbed by the U.S. Army Support Command Nha Trang on 15 April 1966. Two weeks later the Cam Ranh Bay Sub Area Command, Cam Ranh Bay Depot and Cam Ranh Bay Port were organized under the support command as provisional subordinate units, the Nha Trang Support Command itself being converted into the U.S. Army Support Command Cam Ranh Bay on 16 May 1966. The new support command had the mission of providing logistical support and water terminal services to the U.S. Army forces in the southern half of the II Corps Tactical Zone as well as providing common-user supply support to the other U.S. and Allied military forces as directed. Organized with a single general support group, a depot, a marine maintenance activity, a terminal transportation command and a transportation motor group, it had assigned to it over 16,000 personnel and provided combat service support to approximately 72,000 troops at the height of its involvement in Vietnam.

U.S. Army Support Command, Cam Ranh Bay (Major Subordinate Elements)

Elements:	Assigned
Cam Ranh Bay Depot (formerly 504th Field Depot) *	Feb. 66
Cam Ranh Bay Port (Provisional)	June 66
Cam Ranh Bay Sub Area Command (Provisional)	June 66
Nha Trang – Tuy Hoa Sub Area Command (Provisional)	Feb. 68
U S. Army Marine Maintenance Activity †	Feb. 69
54th General Support Group	Oct. 66

124th Transportation Command (Terminal)	1967
500th Transportation Command (Motor Transport)	Jan. 69

Other Components:

GOCO Alaskan Barge and Transport Company Facility ‡
GOCO Center Navigation & Transportation
GOCO Equipment Vinnell Frequency Modulated (FM) Facility
GOCO Vinnell Corporation§
GOCO Vinnell Marine Repair Facility
Ordnance Proving Ground, Phu Thanh (Provisional)
U.S. Army Cam Ranh Bay Installation
U.S. Army Movement Control Center, 2d Traffic Region
U.S. Army Nha Trang Sub Area Command
U.S. Army Qui Nhon Sub Area Command
U.S. Army Phan Rang Sub Area Command
U.S. Army Rehabilitation Center, Cam Ranh Bay
U.S. Army Tuy Hoa Sub Area Command

* Redesignated U.S. Army Depot, Cam Ranh Bay on 3 June 1966, its headquarters numbered 226 in 1967. Inactivated 15 November 1971.

† Organized 1 July 1966. It had a strength of 496, was assigned 1 February 1969 and serviced 386 army vessels, from tugs to landing craft.

‡ Provided stevedore, trucking and intracoastal barge operations between Cam Ranh Bay and the entire South Vietnamese coast.

§ Constructed, operated and maintained high-voltage central power plants and other electrical systems (including T-2 tanker ships used as power sources) as well as stevedore support, beach and port clearance, and vessel maintenance support.

Unauthorized

U.S. Army Support Command, Da Nang

Arrived Vietnam: 25 February 1968
Departed Vietnam: 15 April 1972
Previous Station: Vietnam

Authorized Strength	1968	1970
Headquarters	231	857

In November 1967 the Commanding General of USARV advised the Commanding General of 1st Logistical Command that additional support units would be required in the northern I Corps Tactical Zone. This was because of: (1) the build-up of North Vietnamese Army troops along the DMZ and around Khe Sanh, (2) the build-up of U.S. forces in the area for planned counter offensive operations, (3) the restriction that the Hai Van Pass placed upon land resupply via Highway 1 into that area, and (4) the fact that the Naval Support Activity and the Forces Logistical Command of the U.S. Marines did not have the capability to support all of the additional Army units being deployed northward. Initially the Commanding General of the Qui Nhon Support Command conceived of a Forward Support Activity (FSA) to handle the situation, but planning was redirected toward establishment of an entirely new support command as a result of a 25 January 1968 planning conference between the 1st Logistical Command and MACV. On 21 February 1968 the Ad Hoc Planning Group, later to become members of the Support Command, Da Nang (Provisional), submitted a document that became the basis of the new command. Established at Da Nang to take advantage of the central location and the large deep water port there, the new command soon became responsible for all service support in the entire I Corps Tactical Zone to include supporting U.S. Army and Allied forces with logistical items and water terminal service. A complicated control structure evolved to coordinate with Navy and Marine support activities in the area. The support command had 9,300 personnel to provide combat service support to about 77,000 U.S. and Allied troops.

**U.S. Army Support Command, Da Nang
Major Subordinate Elements**

Elements:	Assigned
Da Nang Sub Area Command	Feb. 1968
Quang Tri Sub Area Command	April 1968
U.S. Army Field Depot, Da Nang *	Feb. 1968
26th General Support Group	Feb. 1968
80th General Support Group	Feb. 1968
159th Transportation Battalion (Terminal Service)	Feb. 1968

Other Components:

GOCO Fixed Field Maintenance Facility
GOCO Machine Shop, Da Nang
GOCO Philco-Ford Facility †
GOCO Tire Processing Facility
U.S. Army Da Nang Installation
U.S. Army Mortuary, Da Nang
U.S. Army Movement Control Center, 1st Traffic Region
U.S. Army Rehabilitation Center, Da Nang

* Established on 25 February 1968 with the mission of supplying Army peculiar items, this depot operated as a field depot of the Qui Nhon base depot. In March 1970 it was upgraded to a separate army depot. It was inactivated 1 April 1972.

† Trucking and labor contractor.

U.S. Army Support Command, Qui Nhon

Unauthorized

Arrived Vietnam: 6 November 1965 (Provisional)
10 February 1966 (Non-provisional)
Departed Vietnam: 30 April 1972
Previous Location: Vietnam

Authorized Strength	1966	1968	1970
Headquarters	123	358	334

Personnel from two units arriving in the summer of 1965, the 29th Quartermaster Group (later General Support Group) and the 5th Ordnance Battalion (later Maintenance Battalion), were utilized to provide the staff of the Qui Nhon Area (Provisional) on 10 August 1965. Its authorized strength was 101. On 1 December 1965 the Qui Nhon Support Area was redesignated as the U.S. Army Support Command, Qui Nhon (Provisional), the provisional qualifier being dropped 10 February 1966. The U.S. Army Support Command, Qui Nhon had the mission of providing logistical support and water terminal service to the U.S. and Allied forces in the northern half of II Corps Tactical Zone, as well as providing administrative support as directed. Prior to the formation of the U.S. Army Support Command, Da Nang on 25 February 1968, the support command responsibilities included limited combat service support for Army units in the I Corps Tactical Zone. It had an average of 19,500 personnel assigned to support approximately 95,000 U.S. and allied troops. It was subordinated to U.S. Army Support Command, Cam Ranh Bay on 17 May 1971 and subsequently redesignated as the Qui Nhon Sub Area Command.

U.S. Army Support Command, Qui Nhon (Major Subordinate Elements)

Element	Assigned
Pleiku Sub Area Command (formerly Pleiku Supply Point)	May 66
Qui Nhon Sub Area Command	Jan. 68
U.S. Army Depot, Qui Nhon (formerly 58th Field Depot)*	Dec. 66
5th Transportation Command (Terminal)	Oct. 66
8th Transportation Group (Motor Transport)	Oct. 66

45th General Support Group	Nov. 66
86th Maintenance Battalion (General Support)	Nov. 66
184th Ordnance Battalion (Ammunition)	Jan. 66
240th Quartermaster Battalion (Petroleum)	Jan. 67
593d General Support Group	Dec. 66

Other Components †

GOCO Class III Supply Facility
GOCO Class IV Supply Open Storage Facility
Ordnance Security Command, Phu Tai (Provisional)
Ordnance Proving Ground Command, Phu Thanh (Provisional)
U.S. Army Philco-Ford Equipment Pool
U.S. Army Philco-Ford Material Yard
U.S. Army Qui Nhon Transportation Terminal Unit

* Headquarters numbered 233 in 1967. The depot was redesignated as the Depot Qui Nhon 1 September 1968.

† The Han Jin Company of Korea was utilized for trucking and stevedore services in the Qui Nhon area.

U.S. Army Support Command, Saigon

Unauthorized

Arrived Vietnam: 10 April 1966
Departed Vietnam: 16 June 1972
Previous Station: Vietnam

Authorized Strength	1966	1968	1970
Headquarters	536	368	1,152

The U.S. Army Support Command, Saigon had its beginnings as the Saigon Logistical Area established by 1st Logistical Command on 7 August 1965. In September 1965 two separate elements were proposed, one establishing the U.S. Army Support Command, Saigon and one for a Saigon Administrative Area which was to provide Army staffing for support functions then performed by the U.S. Navy. In February 1966 U.S. Army, Pacific (USARPAC) directed that the two proposed elements be combined into the Saigon Support Command, but before reorganization was accomplished it was decided to place the former Navy functions under the newly established U.S. Army Headquarters Command, a part of USARV. Then USARV discontinued the U.S. Army Support Command, Vung Tau (which had been established 15 November 1965) on 1 June 1966 and consolidated its functions under the new U.S. Army Support Command, Saigon which had been formed out of the Saigon Logistical Area. The support command had the mission of providing logistical support and water terminal services to U.S. Army and allied forces in both the III and IV Corps Tactical Zones. It had an average of 33,000 personnel assigned to support approximately 235,000 U.S. and allied military troops. It relocated from Saigon to Long Binh on 7 September 1967.

U.S. Army Support Command, Saigon (Major Subordinate Elements)

Element	Assigned
U.S. Army Depot, Long Binh (formerly 506th Field Depot)*	July 65
U.S. Army Depot, Saigon †	June 66
Vung Tau Sub Area Command	May 66
3d Ordnance Battalion (Ammunition)	Nov. 65
4th Transportation Command (Terminal)	July 67
29th General Support Group	July 66
48th Transportation Group (Motor Transport)	May 66
64th Quartermaster Battalion (Petroleum)	April 66
79th Maintenance Battalion (General Support)	July 65
14th Inventory Control Center ‡	Jan. 66

Other Components §

GOCO Equipment Combat Readiness Evaluation & Preservation Facility

GOCO Equipment Field Maintenance Facility

GOCO Machine Shop, Cat Lai

GOCO Pacific Architects & Engineers Communication Vehicles Parts Facility ‖

GOCO Pacific Architects & Engineers Construction Yard ‖

GOCO Pacific Architects & Engineers High Voltage Facility ‖

GOCO Pacific Architects & Engineers Repair & Utilities Facility ‖

GOCO Tire Procurement/Replacement/Retread Facility

GOCO Vinnell Corporation element, Saigon

U.S. Army Mortuary, Saigon

U.S. Army Movement Control Center, 3d Traffic Region

U.S. Army Non-Appropriated Fund Agency

U.S. Army Special Services Depot

---

* Headquarters numbered 223 in 1967. Long Binh Depot formed 29 July 1968.

† Formerly Consolidated Supply & Maintenance Activity (CSA/CMA), Vietnam.

‡ Established 9 January 1966 and had authorized strength of 368.

§ The three major trucking contractors used in the Saigon area were Philco-Ford; Equipment, Inc.; and Do Thi Nuong.

‖ Pacific Architects and Engineers, Inc., were under contract for repairs and utilities support of the Army. From 1 May 1963 they furnished most facilities engineering support. The firm employed some 24,000 civilian personnel.

U.S. Army Support Command, Nha Trang

No Insignia Authorized

Arrived Vietnam: 15 November 1965 (Provisional) 10 February 1966 (Non-provisional)
Departed Vietnam: 1 July 1966
Authorized Strength: Unknown

The U.S. Army Support Command, Nha Trang was discontinued shortly after U.S. Army Support Command, Cam Ranh Bay was established.

U.S. Army Support Command, Vung Tau

No Insignia Authorized

First Tour:
Arrived Vietnam: 15 November 1965 (Provisional)
Departed Vietnam: 1 June 1966

Second Tour:
Arrived Vietnam: 1 April 1969
Departed Vietnam: 28 February 1970

The U.S. Army Support Command, Vung Tau was consolidated with the U.S. Army Support Command, Saigon but again raised as a separate command in 1969.

U.S. Army Support Command, Vietnam

See Major Command Section.

USARV/MACV Support Command

See Major Command Section.

U.S. Army MACV Support Command

Arrived Vietnam: 7 November 1972
Departed Vietnam: 28 March 1973
Authorized Strength: Unknown

The Military Assistance Command, Vietnam, Support Command was a final separate headquarters established to provide the remaining logistical support for the MACV forces which were hurriedly closing out of Vietnam.

Unauthorized

U.S. Army Delta Support Command

Arrived Vietnam: See narrative
Departed Vietnam: See narrative

The U.S. Army Delta Support Command, whose location was to be Can Tho, was never actually activated since the anticipated scale of tactical operations in the Delta area of IV CTZ never materialized. The IV Corps Tactical Zone was supported by the Vung Tau Support Command via sea and air, though a Can Tho Logistical Support Activity was established. This was often called the "Delta Support Command," even on its local emblem, but it was an unauthorized title.

15th Support Brigade

Arrived Vietnam: 29 November 1966
Departed Vietnam: 20 October 1967
Previous Station: Fort Hood

Authorized Strength	1966
HHC	204

The 15th Support Brigade was first activated at Fort Hood on 1 July 1966. It arrived in Vietnam with the mission of commanding, controlling and supervising assigned direct and general support groups and other designated units operating in its service area of responsibility. However, it was soon transferred from Long Binh to Chu Lai to provide a support command formation for Task Force Oregon. It was inactivated in Vietnam and its assets used to assist in forming the Support Command, 23d Infantry Division (AMERICAL), which was officially activated 8 December 1967.

26th General Support Group (Sub Area Command)

Arrived Vietnam: 18 January 1967
Departed Vietnam: 30 January 1972
Previous Station: Fort Lewis

Authorized Strength	1968	1970
HHC	103	91

The 26th General Support Group was stationed at Tuy Hoa, providing command and control, staff planning and technical supervision over a combination of units furnishing supply, maintenance and field service support as well as being the operational element of the Tuy Hoa Sub Area Command. In March 1968 it was transferred from Cam Ranh Bay to Quang Tri to assume support responsibility for the northern portion of I Corps Tactical Zone and later moved to Phu Bai. The group was under the U.S. Army Support Command, Da Nang. The group also planned for, coordinated and supervised rear area protection missions.

29th General Support Group (Logistical Area)

Arrived Vietnam: 2 August 1965
Departed Vietnam: 29 April 1972 *
Previous Station: Fort Hood

Authorized Strength	1966	1968	1970
HHC	92	92	74

* Conflicting sources. Unit card claims 30 November 1971, but group functioned in Vietnam until 29 April 1972.

The 29th General Support Group was a Quartermaster Group before 20 July 1966 when it was redesignated as a General Support Group, providing varied logistical support activities. It was stationed at Long Binh under the U.S. Army Support Command, Saigon and was responsible for supply and maintenance support for the III and IV Corps Tactical Zones.

34th General Support Group (Aviation Support)

Arrived Vietnam: 24 January 1966
Departed Vietnam: 30 November 1972
Previous Station: Vietnam

Authorized Strength	1966	1968	1970
HHC	145	143	138

The 34th General Support Group was specifically tailored to handle aviation supply and maintenance support in Vietnam and was stationed at Tan Son Nhut under the U.S. Army, Vietnam (USARV). A General Support Group (Aircraft Maintenance and Support) (Provisional) had been formed 18 December 1965 at Saigon, and the 34th GS Group took over its functions of supplying army aircraft repair parts, avionics, and aircraft armament. The group was heavily augmented by civilian contract maintenance personnel.

45th General Support Group (Sub Area Command)

Arrived Vietnam: 27 November 1966
Departed Vietnam: 15 December 1970
Previous Station: Fort Lee

Authorized Strength	1968	1970
HHC	103	91

The 45th General Support Group had the same capabilities as the 26th GS Group but handled the II Corps Tactical Zone Highlands supply and maintenance support under the U.S. Army Support Command, Qui Nhon, stationed at Pleiku. There the group assumed the duties of the Pleiku Sub Area Command, which included the normal housekeeping functions of running the post, camp and station.

53d General Support Group (Sub Area Command)

Arrived Vietnam: 9 March 1967
Departed Vietnam: 15 October 1969
Previous Station: Fort Bragg

Authorized Strength	1968
HHC	103

The 53d General Support Group had capabilities similar to those of the 26th GS Group but provided supply and maintenance support in III Corps Tactical Zone under the U.S. Army Support Command, Saigon, located at Vung Tau. It also had responsibility for the Vung Tau Sub Area Command and other logistical support activities at Dong Tam and Can Tho.

54th General Support Group (Sub Area Command)

Arrived Vietnam: 30 November 1966
Departed Vietnam: 29 April 1972
Previous Station: Fort Benning

Authorized Strength	1968	1972
HHC	103	87

The 54th General Support Group had capabilities similar to those of the 26th GS Group but provided supply and maintenance support in the southern portion of II Corps Tactical Zone, located at Nha Trang under the U.S. Army Support Command, Cam Ranh Bay. It was in charge of the Nha Trang Sub Area Command until 15 October 1969 when the group moved to Cam Ranh Bay. Its Nha Trang mission was taken over by the Nha Trang Logistical Support Activity.

80th General Support Group (Sub Area Command)

Arrived Vietnam: 18 January 1967
Departed Vietnam: 17 February 1972
Previous Station: Fort Bragg

Authorized Strength	1968	1970
HHC	103	84

The 80th General Support Group had capabilities similar to those of the 26th GS Group but rendered maintenance and supply support in the southern portion of the I Corps Tactical Zone. The group was stationed at Da Nang under the command of the U.S. Support Command, Da Nang. On 26 February 1968 the group was merged with the Da Nang Sub Area Command.

593d General Support Group (Sub Area Command)

Arrived Vietnam: 19 November 1966
Departed Vietnam: 2 April 1972
Previous Station: Granite City Army Depot

Authorized Strength	1968	1970
HHC	103	93

The 593d General Support Group had capabilities similar to those of the 26th GS Group but was responsible for maintenance and supply support in the northern portion of the II Corps Tactical Zone along the coast. The group was stationed at Qui Nhon under the U.S. Army Support Command, Qui Nhon. It was also responsible for the Qui Nhon Sub Area Command including all post, camp and station functions. HHD Qui Nhon installation was added to the group on 1 October 1969.

Unauthorized

U.S. Army Ryukyu Islands Support Group, Provisional

Arrived Vietnam: 5 February 1962
Departed Vietnam: 1 June 1962
Previous Station: Okinawa
Authorized Strength: 323 (1962)

The need for logistical support sharply increased when the first U.S. Army aviation units arrived in Vietnam in December 1961. Since no Army element then in Vietnam could provide this support, U.S. Army, Pacific (USARPAC) directed the 9th Logistic Command on Okinawa to send a logistic support team to Vietnam to set up a supply service between the newly arrived aviation units and the U.S. Army, Ryukyu Islands. On 17 December 1961 an 11-man team arrived, and this became the basis of the provisional group. This in turn eventually became the basis for the headquarters of the U.S. Army, Vietnam, since the U.S. Army Ryukyu Islands Support Group, Provisional, formed the nucleus of the U.S. Army Support Group, Vietnam which was in turn redesignated USARV.

U.S. Army Support Group, Vietnam

See Major Command Section.

Chapter 17

Adjutant General

22d Replacement Battalion

Arrived Vietnam: 31 August 1966
Departed Vietnam: 28 April 1972
Previous Station: Fort Lewis

Authorized Strength	1966	1968	1970
HHD	40	53	53

The 22d Replacement Battalion supervised and controlled processing, orientation, limited equipping, messing, billeting and transport of replacements and returnees for troop units within I and II Corps Tactical Zones. It was under U.S. Army, Vietnam (USARV) and located at Cam Ranh Bay.

1st Personnel Service Battalion, Provisional

No Insignia Authorized

Arrived Vietnam: 26 January 1968
Departed Vietnam: 1 July 1969
Previous Station: Vietnam
Authorized Strength: Unknown

The 1st Personnel Service Battalion was a provisional battalion created by the 1st Cavalry Division at An Khe.

90th Replacement Battalion

Arrived Vietnam: 30 August 1965
Departed Vietnam: 29 March 1973
Previous Station: Fort Benning

Authorized Strength	1966	1968	1970
HHD	40	53	114

The 90th Replacement Battalion received, controlled, oriented, billeted, messed and processed in-country replacements for onward movement as well as personnel scheduled to return to the United States. It was located under the U.S. Army, Vietnam (USARV) at Long Binh for the duration of its service in Vietnam.

ADJUTANT GENERAL COMPANIES IN VIETNAM (OFFICIALLY CLASSIFIED AG COMMENCING 1971)

Company	Type	Previous Station	Vietnam Service	Typical Location	Authorized Strength 1966	1968	1970
1st AG	Admin – 1st Inf Div	Riley	20 Oct. 65 – 15 April 70	Di An	370	545	—
4th AG	Admin – 4th Inf Div	Lewis	25 Sept. 66 – 7 Dec. 70	Pleiku	46*	545	—
9th AG	Admin – 9th Inf Div	Riley	30 Dec. 66 – 26 Aug. 69	Dong Tam	—	545	—
15th AG	Admin – 1st Cav Div	Benning	11 Sept. 65 – 29 April 71	An Khe	402	536	536
18th AG	Replacement	Bragg	30 Aug. 65 – 20 March 72	Long Binh	38	36	54
23d AG	Admin – AMERICAL Inf Div	Vietnam	8 Dec. 67 – 12 Nov. 71	Chu Lai	—	545	545
25th AG	Admin – 25th Inf Div	Hawaii	11 March 66 – 8 Dec. 70	Cu Chi	396	545	545
101st AG	Admin – 101st Abn Div	Campbell	18 Nov. 67 – 17 Jan. 72	Bien Hoa	101*	536	536
178th AG	Replacement	Hood	6 Sept. 65 – 26 March 73	Tan Son Nhut	27	27	64
222d AG	Personnel Service	Bragg	17 Jan. 67 – 6 Feb. 73	Long Binh	—	27	127
258th AG	Personnel Service	Hood	21 June 67 – 15 Feb. 69	Chu Lai	—	73	—
259th AG	Replacement	Hood	7 Sept. 66 – 22 June 72	Long Binh	—	27	44
381st AG	Replacement	Bragg	15 Jan. 67 – 30 April 72	Long Binh	—	27	27
400th AG	Personnel Service	Riley	26 April 68 – 1 Sept. 68	Da Nang	—	93	—
424th AG†	Personnel Service	Hood	21 Oct. 68 – 9 Oct. 69	Da Nang	—	117	—
507th AG	Replacement	Lewis	31 Aug. 66 – 20 March 72	Dong Ba Thinh	—	27	27
510th AG	Replacement	Benning	1 Aug. 66 – 30 April 72	Cam Ranh Bay	27	27	27
516th AG	Personnel Service	Benning	17 Nov. 66 – 29 Aug. 72	Da Nang	—	72	145
518th AG	Personnel Service	Dix	20 Oct. 66 – 18 March 73	Cam Ranh Bay	—	174	103
520th AG	Personnel Service	Lee	3 May 67 – 30 April 71	Long Binh	—	147	147
526th AG	Replacement	Dix	19 Sept. 65 – 31 Jan. 72	Cam Ranh Bay	27	36	36
527th AG	Personnel Service	Lewis	3 Nov. 66 – 28 March 73	Qui Nhon	—	174	74
537th AG	Personnel Service	Vietnam	20 July 66 – 30 April 72	Long Binh	219	174	169
544th AG	Replacement	Bragg	1 Sept. 66 – 31 Jan. 72	Dong Ba Thinh	—	27	27
589th AG	Personnel Service	Lee	24 March 68 – 20 Nov. 69	Qui Nhon	—	93	—

* Only a part of the company was present at the time.

† Missouri Army Reserve from Livonia via Ft. Hood.

Chapter 18

Composite Service

1st Supply & Transport Battalion (Divisional)

Arrived Vietnam: 10 September 1965
Departed Vietnam: 7 April 1970
Previous Station: Fort Riley

Authorized Strength	1966	1968
Battalion	464	485

The 1st Supply & Transport Battalion was part of the 1st Infantry Division rendering subsistence, clothing, POLs (petrol, oil, lubricants), construction, ammunition, personal demand items and major end items except for aircraft and communication security equipment. The battalion also provided and operated ground transportation required for unit distribution of the supply items.

6th Support Battalion (Infantry Brigade)

Arrived Vietnam: 19 December 1967
Departed Vietnam: 15 February 1969
Previous Station: Hawaii
Authorized Strength: 353 (1968)

The 6th Support Battalion was responsible for providing brigade-level supply, direct support and general support maintenance, medical service and miscellaneous services for all assigned or attached elements of the brigade. The battalion was organized with four lettered companies: A, administration; B, maintenance; C, supply and service; and D, medical, as well as a headquarters element. The battalion provided support for the 11th Infantry Brigade (Light) in Vietnam.

4th Supply & Transport Battalion (Divisional)

Arrived Vietnam: 15 September 1966
Departed Vietnam: 7 December 1970
Previous Station: Fort Lewis

Authorized Strength	1966	1968
Battalion	300	485

The 4th Supply & Transport Battalion served the 4th Infantry Division in Vietnam (for capabilities, see 1st Supply & Transport Battalion).

7th Support Battalion (Infantry Brigade)

Arrived Vietnam: 28 November 1966
Departed Vietnam: 12 October 1970
Previous Station: Fort Benning

Authorized Strength	1968	1970
Battalion	544	544

The 7th Support Battalion provided service to the 199th Infantry Brigade (Light) in Vietnam (for capabilities, see 6th Support Battalion).

8th Support Battalion (Infantry Brigade)

Arrived Vietnam: 22 September 1966
Departed Vietnam: 15 February 1969
Previous Station: Fort Devens

Authorized Strength	1966	1968
Battalion	451	348

The 8th Support Battalion served with the 196th Infantry Brigade (Light) in Vietnam (for capabilities, see 6th Support Battalion).

9th Support Battalion (Infantry Brigade)

Arrived Vietnam: 8 October 1967
Departed Vietnam: 15 February 1969
Previous Station: Fort Hood
Authorized Strength: 348 (1968)

The 9th Support Battalion served with the 198th Infantry Brigade (Light) in Vietnam (for capabilities, see 6th Support Battalion).

9th Supply & Transport Battalion (Divisional)

Arrived Vietnam: 16 December 1966
Departed Vietnam: 23 August 1969
Previous Station: Fort Riley
Authorized Strength: 485 (1968)

The 9th Supply & Transport Battalion provided support for the 9th Infantry Division in Vietnam (for capabilities, see 1st Supply & Transport Battalion).

15th Supply & Service Battalion (Divisional)

Arrived Vietnam: 28 July 1965
Departed Vietnam: 29 April 1971
Previous Station: Fort Benning

Authorized Strength	1966	1968	1970
Battalion	481	481	281

The 15th Supply & Service Battalion provided division-level combat supply and service support to include all classes of material, as well as even supplying a "firebase kit," complete with concertina wire, timbers, support steel culverts for hootches and thousands of sandbags. The battalion was part of the 1st Cavalry Division (Airmobile) in Vietnam.

23d Supply & Transport Battalion (Divisional)

Arrived Vietnam: 8 December 1967
Departed Vietnam: 25 November 1971
Previous Station: Vietnam

Authorized Strength	1968	1970
Battalion	447	485

The 23d Supply & Transport Battalion was part of the 23d Infantry Division (AMERICAL) in Vietnam (for capabilities, see 1st Supply & Transport Battalion).

25th Supply & Transport Battalion (Divisional)

Arrived Vietnam: 30 March 1966
Departed Vietnam: 14 October 1970
Previous Station: Hawaii

Authorized Strength	1966	1968
Battalion	485	485

The 25th Supply & Transport Battalion served as part of the 25th Infantry Division in Vietnam (for capabilities, see 1st Supply & Transport Battalion).

34th Supply & Service Battalion (Direct Support)

Arrived Vietnam: 25 August 1965
Departed Vietnam: 15 April 1971
Previous Station: Vietnam
Authorized Strength: HHC – 117

The 34th Supply & Service Battalion (Direct Support) was responsible for commanding, controlling and supervising the operations, employment and administration of assigned units providing direct logistical service support to nondivisional units. The battalion was quartermaster previous to July 1966. The battalion served at An Khe as the An Ke Sub Area Command under the U.S. Army Support Command, Qui Nhon. On 1 March 1968 it was relocated to Da Nang, where it came under the 80th General Support Group and U.S. Army Support Command, Da Nang. It assumed the mission of establishing and operating the army depot at Da Nang. In August 1970 the battalion made its final move to Tan Son Nhut under USARV.

75th Support Battalion (Mechanized Brigade)

Arrived Vietnam: 26 July 1968
Departed Vietnam: 31 August 1971
Previous Station: Fort Carson

Authorized Strength	1968	1970
Battalion	655	823

The 75th Support Battalion provided brigade-level combat service support consisting of supply, maintenance, transportation, medical, and personnel and administrative services and miscellaneous field service functions to all assigned and attached elements of the 1st Brigade Task Force, 5th Infantry Division (Mechanized) in Vietnam.

82d Support Battalion
(Airborne Brigade)

Arrived Vietnam: 25 May 1968
Departed Vietnam: 12 December 1969
Previous Station: Fort Bragg
Authorized Strength: 372 (1968)

The 82d Support Battalion provided brigade-level support and combat service consisting of supply, maintenance, medical service, airdrop equipment support, transportation, personnel administrative services and miscellaneous field service functions to the 3d Brigade Task Force, 82d Airborne Division in Vietnam.

88th Supply & Service Battalion
(Direct Support)

Arrived Vietnam: 18 September 1965
Departed Vietnam: 11 May 1972
Previous Station: Granite City Army Depot

Authorized Strength	1966	1968	1970
HHC	58	58	52

The 88th Supply & Service Battalion (Direct Support) had the mission of commanding and controlling direct support supply and service companies. It was stationed at Pleiku under the U.S. Army Support Command, Qui Nhon. It later served under the 45th General Support Group. It went to Tuy Hoa in early 1970 and was posted to Qui Nhon in 1971. Prior to July 1966 it had been an Engineer (Depot) Battalion. It provided all classes of supply and support in northern II Corps Tactical Zone.

91st Service Battalion
(Logistical Service)

Arrived Vietnam: 4 March 1969
Departed Vietnam: 27 March 1973
Previous Station: Vietnam
Authorized Strength: HHD – 28 (1971)

The 91st Service Battalion (Logistical Service) at Can Tho had the mission of providing command and control to include tactical and administrative supervision to assigned supply, support, maintenance, and other service units assigned or attached to it in the IV Corps Tactical Zone. On 15 October 1969 it went to Binh Thuy. In 1970 the 91st Service Battalion was relocated to Long Binh. It served the 29th General Support Group. Finally the battalion was relocated at Can Tho, where it became the DELTA Logistical Support Activity on 7 May 1972.

92d Service Battalion
(Logistical Service)

Arrived Vietnam: 20 October 1969
Departed Vietnam: 30 April 1972
Previous Station: Vietnam
Authorized Strength: HHD – 28 (1971)

The 92d Service Battalion (Logistical Service) was established to serve the I Corps Tactical Zone under the U.S. Support Command, Da Nang at Da Nang. It had the mission of providing command and control for assigned maintenance, supply and transport units.

94th Supply & Service Battalion
(Direct Support)

Arrived Vietnam: 1 December 1966
Departed Vietnam: 15 January 1968
Previous Station: Fort Lee
Authorized Strength: HHC – 117 (1967)

The 94th Supply & Service Battalion provided direct support supplies and services, except for those provided by the armywide services, to nondivisional units and was under the 53d General Support Group. It was located at Vung Tau and later at Chu Lai, where its assets were used to form the 23d Supply & Transport Battalion.

96th Supply & Service Battalion
(Direct Support)

Arrived Vietnam: 21 June 1966
Departed Vietnam: 1 September 1968
Previous Station: Fort Riley
Authorized Strength: HHC – 117

The 96th Supply & Service Battalion was at Cam Ranh Bay, where it supported the 504th Field Army Depot. It operated activities there to include depot warehouses, petroleum facilities, material handling equipment pool, vehicle park, engineer yard and cold storage facilities.

98th Supply & Service Battalion
(General Support)

Arrived Vietnam: 10 September 1965
Departed Vietnam: 1 September 1968
Previous Station: Fort Polk
Authorized Strength: HHC – 92

The 98th Supply & Service Battalion (General Support) was stationed at Qui Nhon under the U.S. Army Support Command, Qui Nhon. It was quartermaster until July 1966. It operated the Qui Nhon support command depot, where it provided the personnel, equipment and coordination for receipt, issue and storage of supplies there.

99th Support Battalion
(Infantry Brigade)

Arrived Vietnam: 1 October 1969
Departed Vietnam: 12 October 1970
Previous Station: Vietnam
Authorized Strength: 544 (1970)

The 99th Support Battalion serviced the 3d Brigade (separate) of the 9th Infantry Division after the rest of the division departed Vietnam (for capabilities, see 6th Support Battalion).

101st Support Battalion
(Airborne Brigade)

Arrived Vietnam: 29 July 1965
Departed Vietnam: 19 November 1967
Previous Station: Vietnam
Authorized Strength: 656 (1966)

Unauthorized

The 101st Support Battalion, at first only provisional, served the 1st Brigade (separate) of the 101st Airborne Division in Vietnam (for capabilities, see 82d Support Battalion).

173d Support Battalion (Airborne Brigade)

Arrived Vietnam: 6 May 1965
Departed Vietnam: 21 August 1971
Previous Station: Okinawa

Authorized Strength	1966	1968	1970
Battalion	674	704	704

The 173d Support Battalion provided service and support to the 173d Airborne Brigade in Vietnam (for capabilities, see 82d Support Battalion).

215th Support Battalion (Airmobile Brigade)

Arrived Vietnam: 30 June 1971
Departed Vietnam: 29 June 1972
Previous Station: Vietnam
Authorized Strength: 1,011 (1971)

Unauthorized

The 215th Support Battalion was part of the 3d Brigade (separate) of the 1st Cavalry Division (Airmobile) and provided separate brigade-level supply, field service, maintenance, and engineer and communications management.

225th Support Battalion (Infantry Brigade)

Arrived Vietnam: 10 February 1971
Departed Vietnam: 30 April 1971
Previous Station: Vietnam
Authorized Strength: 544

Unauthorized

The 225th Support Battalion served with the 2d Brigade (separate) of the 25th Infantry Division (for capabilities, see 6th Support Battalion).

264th Supply & Service Battalion (General Support)

Arrived Vietnam: 20 July 1966
Departed Vietnam: 1 September 1968
Previous Station: Vietnam
Authorized Strength: HHC – 89

The 264th Supply & Service Battalion (General Support) was stationed with the 506th Field Army Depot under the U.S. Army Support Command, Saigon.

266th Supply & Service Battalion (Direct Support)

Arrived Vietnam: 23 June 1966
Departed Vietnam: 14 March 1973
Previous Station: Fort Lewis

Authorized Strength	1966	1968	1970
HHC	117	117	85

The 266th Supply & Service Battalion (Direct Support) was stationed at Long Binh throughout its Vietnam service. It served

under the 29th General Support Group before coming under direct control of U.S. Army Support Command, Saigon. It served as a command and control center providing logistical service, convoy escort coordination, and coordination over movement of troops and cargo from Saigon and Vung Tau.

277th Supply & Service Battalion (Direct Support)

Arrived Vietnam: 20 July 1966
Departed Vietnam: 14 March 1973
Previous Station: Vietnam

Authorized Strength	1966	1968	1970
HHC	117	99	101

The 277th Supply & Service Battalion (Direct Support) was with the 506th Army Depot at Long Binh before moving in early 1969 to Tay Ninh with the 29th General Support Group, in August 1970 to Di An and then to the 80th General Support Group at Chu Lai. In November 1971 it moved to Da Nang as a long-range support battalion.

278th Supply & Service Battalion (General Support)

Arrived Vietnam: 18 November 1966
Departed Vietnam: 1 September 1968
Previous Station: Fort Lewis
Authorized Strength: HHC – 92 (1966)

The 278th Supply & Service Battalion (General Support) had various missions concerning depot storage operations and including industrial gas and air delivery responsibilities. The battalion served with the 504th Field Army Depot at Cam Ranh Bay during its service in Vietnam.

426th Supply & Service Battalion (Divisional)

Arrived Vietnam: 1 July 1968
Departed Vietnam: 30 January 1972
Previous Station: Vietnam
Authorized Strength: 481

The 426th Supply & Service Battalion was part of the 101st Airborne Division (Airmobile) in Vietnam (for capabilities, see 15th Supply & Service Battalion).

532d Supply & Service Battalion (Direct Support)

Arrived Vietnam: 1 October 1966
Departed Vietnam: 2 October 1968
Previous Station: Fort Campbell
Authorized Strength: HHC – 117 (1967)

The 532d Supply & Service Battalion (Direct Support) was under the U.S. Army Support Command, Cam Ranh Bay serving at Nha

Trang, Cam Ranh Bay and finally Tuy Hoa (for capabilities, see 88th Supply & Service Battalion).

558th Supply & Service Battalion (Direct Support)

No Insignia Authorized

Arrived Vietnam: 1 February 1968
Departed Vietnam: 16 March 1968
Previous Station: Vietnam
Authorized Strength: HHC – 85 (1968)

The 558th Supply & Service Battalion was organized at Cam Ranh Bay and sent a few weeks later to Korat, Thailand.

563d Supply & Service Battalion (Direct Support)

Arrived Vietnam: 29 April 1967
Departed Vietnam: 6 November 1968
Previous Station: Fort Lee
Authorized Strength: HHC – 117 (1968)

The 563d Supply & Service Battalion was located at Qui Nhon under U.S. Army Support Command, Qui Nhon during its service in Vietnam. It was assigned to the 58th Field Army Depot there.

567th Supply & Service Battalion (Direct Support)

Arrived Vietnam: 29 April 1967
Departed Vietnam: 20 October 1967
Previous Station: Fort Lee
Authorized Strength: HHC – 117 (1967)

The 567th Supply & Service Battalion arrived at Da Nang and was located to Tay Ninh under the U.S. Army Support Command, Qui Nhon, where it was inactivated to provide personnel and equipment for the Tay Ninh Logistical Support Activity.

PROVISIONAL SUPPORT AND SUPPLY/SERVICE BATTALIONS IN VIETNAM

The following is a representative listing of some of the more important provisional composite service battalions formed in Vietnam. In addition there were a myriad of others formed by large commands such as the USARV Provisional Aviation Support Battalion, by general support groups such as the 593d General Support Group Provisional Composite Service Battalion (15 December 1968 – 1 October 1969), and even forward support battalions of other battalions such as the 69th Maintenance Battalion's Provisional Support Battalion (19 September 1968 – 1 January 1970). Due to the transient nature and inflated titles of most of these units, which are not officially recognized and were often unauthorized, no attempt has been made to trace all of them.

1st Support Battalion, Provisional   1 June 66 – fall 1966
Formed to support the 1st Brigade, 25th Infantry Division at Cu Chi.

2d Support Battalion, Provisional   1 June 66 – Feb. 71
Formed to support the 2d Brigade, 25th Infantry Division at Cu Chi.

3d Support Battalion, Provisional   1 June 66 – Dec. 69
Formed to support the 3d Brigade, 25th Infantry Division at Cu Chi.

Cam Ranh Bay General Service Battalion, Provisional   June 65 – 1 July 66
Formed by the Cam Ranh Bay Logistical Area at Cam Ranh Bay.

Cam Ranh Bay Supply & Service Battalion, Provisional   1 Sept. 68 – 2 April 72
Formed by the U.S. Army Support Command, Cam Ranh Bay at Cam Ranh Bay.

Da Nang Supply & Service Battalion, Provisional   13 Dec. 71 – 1 Feb. 72
Formed by the U.S. Army Support Command, Da Nang at Da Nang.

Keystone Composite Service Battalion, Provisional   3 May 71 – 30 Nov. 72
Established at Da Nang to handle redeployment matters at that location.

Qui Nhon Supply & Service Battalion, Provisional   1 Dec. 70 – 30 April 72
Formed by the U.S. Army Support Command, Qui Nhon at Qui Nhon.

Vung Tau Supply & Service Battalion, Provisional   6 May 66 – 10 Dec. 66
Formed by the Vung Tau Sub Area Command at Vung Tau.

SUPPLY AND/OR SERVICE COMPANIES IN VIETNAM

Company	Type	Previous Station	Vietnam Service	Typical Location	Authorized Strength		
					1966	1968	1970
11th Supply*	Repair Parts General Support	Devens	11 July 65 – 1 Sept. 68	Saigon	191	191	—
19th Supply & Service †	Direct Support	Hood	3 June 65 – 1 May 72	Qui Nhon	270	270	284
21st Supply & Service	Direct Support	Campbell	13 Dec. 66 – 1 May 72	Phan Rang	—	233	233
31st Supply*	Heavy Material Supply General Support	Knox	23 Aug. 65 – 6 Nov. 68	Cam Ranh Bay	199	199	—
53d Supply ‡	General Support	Bragg	21 July 66 – 1 Sept. 68	Cam Ranh Bay	214	214	—
56th Supply	Heavy Material Supply General Support	Lee	24 Oct. 66 – 20 Sept. 71	Da Nang	—	199	199

59th Service †	Forward Field General Support	Bragg	30 Aug. 65 – 1 April 72	Cam Ranh Bay	297	297	268
74th Supply*	Repair Parts Forward General Support	Bliss	6 Sept. 65 – 15 April 71	Da Nang	198	198	198
75th Supply	Heavy Material Supply General Support	Carson	18 Sept. 66 – 6 Nov. 68	Long Binh	—	199	—
90th Supply	Heavy Material Supply General Support	Riley	18 Oct. 66 – 1 Oct. 70	Pleiku	—	199	136
126th Supply & Service §	Direct Support	Carson	18 Sept. 68 – 9 Aug. 69	Chu Lai	—	148	—
139th Supply	Heavy Material Supply General Support	Lewis	30 Sept. 66 – 6 Nov. 68	Long Binh	—	199	—
147th Service	Forward Field General Support	McClellan	28 April 67 – 20 Dec. 68	Cam Ranh Bay	—	305	—
148th Supply & Service †	Direct Support	Lewis	5 Sept. 65 – 13 March 73	Nha Trang	233	233	233
163d Supply	General Support	Vietnam	20 July 66 – 1 Sept. 68	Saigon	206	206	—
178th Supply ‖	Repair Parts General Support	Lewis	16 March 66 – 1 Sept. 68	Saigon	191	191	—
221st Supply	Direct Support	Vietnam	20 July 66 – 15 Jan. 68	Chu Lai	233	—	—
223d Supply & Service †	Direct Support	Bragg	30 Aug. 65 – 31 Aug. 71	Saigon	206	206	165
226th Supply & Service	Direct Support	Vietnam	20 July 66 – 26 Nov. 71	Tuy Hoa	233	233	233
228th Supply & Service	Direct Support	Vietnam	20 July 66 – 16 Feb. 73	Tay Ninh	233	233	233
229th Supply & Service	Direct Support	Vietnam	20 July 66 – 26 Dec. 71	Long Binh	233	233	233
243d Service	Forward Field General Support	Bragg	15 Dec. 66 – 14 Dec. 70	Pleiku	—	305	305
248th Supply	Repair Parts Forward General Support	Lewis	27 Sept. 66 – 1 Sept. 68	Qui Nhon	—	198	—
304th Supply & Service	Direct Support	Devens	29 Oct. 67 – 1 April 72	An Khe	—	233	223
305th Supply & Service	Direct Support	Vietnam	1 Feb. 68 – 11 March 68	Cam Ranh Bay #	—	148	—
334th Supply & Service	Direct Support	Vietnam	16 Oct. 69 – 27 March 73	Da Nang	—	—	148
423d Supply	Repair Parts Forward General Support	Lee	26 Sept. 66 – 1 Sept. 68	Cam Ranh Bay	—	198	—
452d Supply & Service**	General Support	Riley	29 Sept. 68 – 1 Aug. 69	Quang Tri	—	215	—
463d Supply	General Support	Vietnam	20 July 66 – 1 Sept. 68	Qui Nhon	253	253	—
483d Service	Forward Field General Support	Lee	1 Dec. 66 – 26 Dec. 71	Long Binh	—	305	305
490th Supply	General Support	Devens	6 Dec. 66 – 15 April 71	Vung Tau	—	214	214
501st Supply	Airborne Support – 101st Airborne Division	Campbell	19 Nov. 67 – 1 July 68	Bien Hoa	—	168	—
506th Supply & Service †	Direct Support	Riley	2 Nov. 65 – 30 June 72	Long Giao	233	233	284
539th Supply	Repair Parts Forward General Support	Meade	28 Sept. 66 – 1 Sept. 68	Cam Ranh Bay	—	198	—
540th Supply	Heavy Material Supply General Support	Lee	15 April 67 – 1 Sept. 68	Qui Nhon	—	199	—
548th Supply	General Support	Lee	30 Oct. 66 – 1 Sept. 68	Cam Ranh Bay	—	214	—
559th Supply	General Support	Lee	8 Nov. 66 – 1 Sept. 68	Long Binh	—	214	—
560th Supply	General Support	Lee	7 Nov. 66 – 14 Dec. 70	Da Nang	—	214	183
561st Supply	General Support	Lee	7 Nov. 66 – 10 Dec. 70	Pleiku	—	214	154
562d Supply	General Support	Lee	26 Jan. 67 – 1 Sept. 68	Qui Nhon	—	214	—
563d Supply	Heavy Material Supply General Support	Lee	23 Oct. 66 – 20 Dec. 68	Long Binh	—	199	—
569th Supply †	General Support	Lee	10 March 66 – 15 April 71	Saigon	206	145	?
570th Supply	Repair Parts Forward General Support	Carson	25 Sept. 66 – 20 Dec. 68	Long Binh	—	198	—
573d Supply & Service	Direct Support	Campbell	30 Aug. 66 – 1 May 72	Pleiku	196	233	196
574th Supply & Service †	Direct Support	Lee	9 March 66 – 15 Oct. 70	Dong Tam	207	207	207
575th Supply	Heavy Material Supply General Support	Lee	28 Sept. 66 – 1 Sept. 68	Cam Ranh Bay	—	199	—

Company	Type	Previous Station	Vietnam Service	Typical Location	1966	1968	1970
578th Supply ††	Heavy Material Supply General Support	Polk	21 July 66 – 1 Sept. 68	Qui Nhon	199	199	—
581st Supply	Heavy Material Supply General Support	Lee	29 Sept. 66 – 1 Sept. 68	Qui Nhon	—	199	—
624th Supply & Service †	Direct Support	Campbell	25 Aug. 65 – 21 Nov. 72	Long Binh	233	162	284
625th Supply & Service †	Direct Support	Campbell	2 Sept. 65 – 20 March 72	Quang Tri	266	266	284
629th Supply*	Repair Parts General Support	Lewis	2 Sept. 65 – 1 Sept. 68	Qui Nhon	275	275	—
758th Supply & Service	Direct Support	Riley	24 March 67 – 10 Dec. 70	Phu Loi	—	233	284
821st Supply	Heavy Material Supply General Support	Lewis	3 May 67 – 1 Sept. 68	Long Binh	—	199	—
855th Supply	General Support	Lee	28 Oct. 66 – 15 April 71	Da Nang	—	214	214
1002d Supply & Service ‡‡	Direct Support	Meade	20 Oct. 68 – Sept. 69	Phu Bai	—	244	—
1011th Supply & Service §§	Direct Support	Benning	23 Sept. 68 – 9 Aug. 69	Bear Cat	—	162	—
1018th Supply & Service ##	Direct Support	Lee	31 Oct. 68 – 16 Oct. 69	Da Nang	—	148	—

* Ordnance until 20 July 1966.

† Quartermaster until 20 July 1966.

‡ See 53d Engineer Company for earlier Vietnam service.

§ Illinois National Guard from Quincy via Ft. Carson.

‖ See also 178th Engineer Company.

En route to Thailand only.

** Minnesota Army Reserve from Worthington via Ft. Riley.

†† See 578th Engineer Company for earlier service.

‡‡ Ohio Army Reserve from Cleveland via Ft. Meade.

§§ Kansas Army Reserve from Independence via Ft. Benning.

New York Army Reserve from Schenectady via Ft. Lee.

COLLECTION, CLASSIFICATION AND SALVAGE COMPANIES IN VIETNAM

Company*	Type	Previous Station	Vietnam Service	Typical Location	Authorized Strength		
					1966	1968	1970
218th CS	Coll, Class & Salv	Vietnam	20 July 66 – 1 Sept. 68	Long Binh	91	91	—
241st CS	Coll, Class & Salv	Vietnam	15 April 72 – 30 June 72	Da Nang	—	—	—
526th CS †	Coll, Class & Salv	Riley	14 Dec. 65 – 1 Sept. 68	Qui Nhon	226	226	—
633d CS	Coll, Class & Salv	Hood	1 May 67 – 30 June 72	Cam Ranh Bay	—	91	91

CHEMICAL COMPANIES IN VIETNAM

Company	Type	Previous Station	Vietnam Service	Typical Location	Authorized Strength		
					1966	1968	1970
22d CHEM	Direct Support	Hood	31 May 66 – 20 July 66	Cam Ranh Bay	233	—	—

PROVISIONAL PROPERTY DISPOSAL OPERATIONS COMPANIES IN VIETNAM ‡

Company	Type	Previous Station	Vietnam Service	Typical Location	Authorized Strength		
					1966	1968	1970
Da Nang (Prov)	Property Disposal Opns	Vietnam	1 Dec. 69 – 1 June 70	Da Nang	—	—	?
Long Binh (Prov)	Property Disposal Opns	Vietnam	1 Dec. 69 – 1 May 72	Long Binh	—	—	?

* CS = Composite Service.

† Quartermaster until 20 July 1966.

‡ Property disposal operations were handled by the Property Disposal Office and later the Property Disposal Agency. Other such provisional companies at Cam Ranh Bay and elsewhere also existed.

Chapter 19

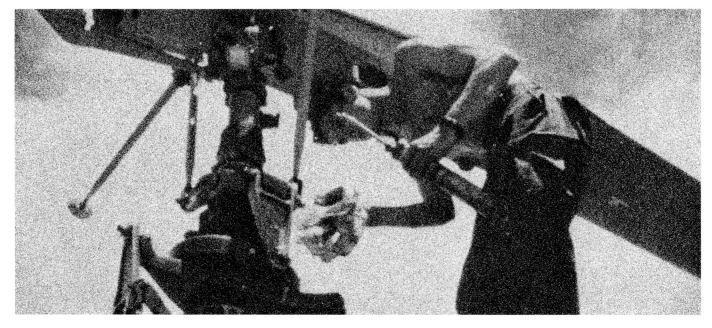

Maintenance

2d Maintenance Battalion (Direct Support)

Arrived Vietnam: 11 July 1965
Departed Vietnam: 30 April 1972
Previous Station: Fort Campbell

Authorized Strength	1966	1968	1970
HHC	288	288	277

The 2d Maintenance Battalion (Direct Support) provided direct support maintenance, field service and maintenance supply support for equipment of nondivisional units in the northern portion of I Corps Tactical Zone under the 26th General Support Group at Phu Bai after 20 September 1969. Previously the battalion was at Vung Tau under the 53d General Support Group supporting III Corps Tactical Zone. It was part of the Ordnance Corps prior to July 1966.

5th Maintenance Battalion (Direct Support)

Arrived Vietnam: 28 April 1965
Departed Vietnam: 30 April 1970
Previous Station: Fort Sill

Authorized Strength	1966	1968	1970
HHC	249	351	277

The 5th Maintenance Battalion (Direct Support) initially provided the nucleus of the U.S. Army Support Command, Qui Nhon upon arrival in Vietnam. It was at that time an Ordnance Battalion (changing designation in July 1966). The battalion handled direct support maintenance and repair parts supply to units in the Qui

Nhon – An Khe – Bong Son area. In 1968 the battalion was relocated to Phu Tai, where it became a component of the 593d General Support Group on 1 June 1968 (for capabilities, see the 2d Maintenance Battalion).

27th Maintenance Battalion (Divisional)

Arrived Vietnam: 15 September 1965
Departed Vietnam: 29 April 1971
Previous Station: Fort Benning

Authorized Strength	1966	1968	1970
Battalion	339	374	244

The 27th Maintenance Battalion was part of the 1st Cavalry Division (Airmobile) and provided direct support maintenance and repair parts supply service, except for medical, communication security, aircraft, and airdrop items, in support of the division.

62d Maintenance Battalion (Direct Support)

Arrived Vietnam: 7 January 1967
Departed Vietnam: 4 October 1972
Previous Station: Fort Bragg

Authorized Strength	1968	1970
HHC	351	233

The 62d Maintenance Battalion (Direct Support) served the U.S. Army Support Command, Qui Nhon at Pleiku during its service in Vietnam, coming under the 45th General Support Group's control

in February 1969. In 1971 it returned to Support Command jurisdiction and was posted to Qui Nhon on 5 March 1972 (for capabilities, see the 2d Maintenance Battalion).

63d Maintenance Battalion (Direct Support)

Arrived Vietnam: 29 May 1965
Departed Vietnam: 2 April 1972
Previous Station: Fort Lewis

Authorized Strength	1966	1968	1970
HHC	249	245	277

The 63d Maintenance Battalion (Direct Support) was stationed at Nha Trang under the 54th General Support Group. On 14 March 1968 the battalion moved north to Quang Tri and was attached to the 26th General Support Group. It was part of the Ordnance Corps before July 1966 (for capabilities, see the 2d Maintenance Battalion).

69th Maintenance Battalion (General Support)

Arrived Vietnam: 31 July 1966
Departed Vietnam: 11 May 1972
Previous Station: Fort Lewis

Authorized Strength	1966	1968	1970
HHD	52	52	52

The 69th Maintenance Battalion (General Support) provided command, tactical, administration, training, and technical operational supervision of attached functional general support maintenance units. The battalion was located at Cam Ranh Bay under the U.S. Support Command, Cam Ranh Bay during its service in Vietnam. It was assigned to the army depot there on 1 November 1968.

79th Maintenance Battalion (General Support)

Arrived Vietnam: 11 July 1965
Departed Vietnam: 26 February 1973
Previous Station: Fort Bliss

Authorized Strength	1966	1968	1971
HHD	52	52	40

The 79th Maintenance Battalion (General Support) was originally assigned as an ordnance battalion (it changed title in July 1966) at Tan Son Nhut. Attached to the 506th Field Depot, the battalion was assigned to the 29th General Support Group at Long Binh in September 1967. It was later reassigned to the 53d General Support Group on 1 April 1969 and after September directly to the U.S. Army Support Command, Saigon. It became the central working force for army withdrawal from both Military Regions 3 and 4, handling depot retrograde and equipment transfers.

86th Maintenance Battalion (General Support)

Arrived Vietnam: 23 November 1966
Departed Vietnam: 23 December 1971
Previous Station: Fort Devens

Authorized Strength	1968	1970
HHD	52	55

The 86th Maintenance Battalion (General Support) was deployed to the Cha Rang Valley upon arrival in Vietnam. It remained at that location throughout its service in Vietnam under the U.S. Army Support Command, Qui Nhon (for capabilities, see the 69th Maintenance Battalion).

185th Maintenance Battalion (Direct Support)

Arrived Vietnam: 2 August 1965
Departed Vietnam: 21 October 1972
Previous Station: Fort Hood

Authorized Strength	1966	1968	1970
HHC	249	249	265

The 185th Maintenance Battalion (Direct Support) was originally an ordnance battalion located at Long Binh under the 29th General Support Group, where it remained throughout the rest of its service in Vietnam. It provided supply and maintenance support to all nondivisional units in the Long Binh – Bien Hoa complex.

188th Maintenance Battalion (Direct Support)

Arrived Vietnam: 19 November 1966
Departed Vietnam: 8 December 1967
Previous Station: Fort Meade
Authorized Strength: HHC – 251 (1967)

The 188th Maintenance Battalion (Direct Support) was under the 29th General Support Group providing support at Long Giao and eastern III Corps Tactical Zone. Its assets were converted by the group into the 732d Maintenance Battalion formed in late 1967 when the 188th Maintenance Battalion moved to Chu Lai (for capabilities, see the 2d Maintenance Battalion).

227th Maintenance Battalion (General Support)

Arrived Vietnam: 31 July 1971
Departed Vietnam: December 1971
Previous Station: Fort Meade
Authorized Strength: HHD – 52 (1971)

The 227th Maintenance Battalion (General Support) was in Vietnam very briefly in late 1971 (for capabilities, see the 69th Maintenance Battalion).

513th Maintenance Battalion (Direct Support)

Arrived Vietnam: 18 October 1968
Departed Vietnam: 3 October 1969
Previous Station: Boston, MA via Fort Meade
Authorized Strength: HHC – 251 (1968)

The 513th Maintenance Battalion (Direct Support) was a Massachusetts Army Reserve unit that served at Phu Bai while in Vietnam. It provided direct support maintenance, supply and evacuation support in northern I Corps Tactical Zone.

610th Maintenance Battalion (Direct Support)

Arrived Vietnam: 2 December 1966
Departed Vietnam: 30 June 1971
Previous Station: Fort Lewis

Authorized Strength	1968	1970
HHC	249	221

The 610th Maintenance Battalion (Direct Support) served with the U.S. Army Support Command, Saigon at Phu Loi, coming under the control of the 29th General Support Group in 1969. It performed direct supply and maintenance support to nondivisonal units in its area, and back-up support to the 1st Infantry Division.

701st Maintenance Battalion (Divisional)

Arrived Vietnam: 20 October 1965
Departed Vietnam: 6 April 1970
Previous Station: Fort Riley

Authorized Strength	1966	1968
Battalion	762	854

The 701st Maintenance Battalion was part of the 1st Infantry Division in Vietnam. Due to the far-flung nature of divisional operations, the battalion's assets were often fragmented to provide the forward maintenance required for all units (for capabilities, see the 27th Maintenance Battalion).

704th Maintenance Battalion (Divisional)

Arrived Vietnam: 8 September 1966
Departed Vietnam: 7 December 1970
Previous Station: Fort Lewis

Authorized Strength	1966	1968	1970
Battalion	119*	854	751

* Maintenance forward support company only.

The 704th Maintenance Battalion was part of the 4th Infantry Division. The widely scattered divisional operations often meant the battalion was ordered to provide forward support at various locations for the different divisional elements (for capabilities, see the 27th Maintenance Battalion).

Company A, 705th Maintenance Battalion (Divisional)

Arrived Vietnam: 25 July 1968
Departed Vietnam: 27 April 1970
Previous Station: Fort Carson
Authorized Strength: 159 (1968)

Company A of the 705th Maintenance Battalion provided troops and assets to the 1st Brigade Task Force of the 5th Infantry Division (Mechanized) in Vietnam.

709th Maintenance Battalion (Divisional)

Arrived Vietnam: 26 January 1967
Departed Vietnam: 20 August 1969
Previous Station: Fort Riley
Authorized Strength: 854 (1968)

The 709th Maintenance Battalion was part of the 9th Infantry Division in Vietnam. Often its elements were sent to diverse forward locations to provide required maintenance for the scattered divisional units (for capabilities, see the 27th Maintenance Battalion).

723d Maintenance Battalion (Divisional)

Arrived Vietnam: 15 February 1969
Departed Vietnam: 24 November 1971
Previous Station: Vietnam

Authorized Strength	1969	1970
Battalion	298	854

The 723d Maintenance Battalion served with the 23d Infantry Division (AMERICAL) during its service in Vietnam.

725th Maintenance Battalion (Divisional)

Arrived Vietnam: 1 April 1966
Departed Vietnam: 14 October 1970
Previous Station: Hawaii

Authorized Strength	1966	1968	1970
Battalion	691	854	687

The 725th Maintenance Battalion was part of the 25th Infantry Division although it was often scattered to provide forward maintenance for far-flung divisional components (for capabilities, see the 27th Maintenance Battalion).

Company A, 782d Maintenance Battalion (Divisional)

Arrived Vietnam: 18 February 1968
Departed Vietnam: 1 May 1968
Previous Station: Fort Bragg
Authorized Strength: 159 (1968)

Company A of the 782d Maintenance Battalion was part of the 82d Airborne Division's 3d Brigade Task Force in Vietnam. Its assets went to the newly formed 82d Support Battalion.

801st Maintenance Battalion (Divisional)

Arrived Vietnam: 12 December 1967
Departed Vietnam: 30 January 1972
Previous Station: Fort Campbell

Authorized Strength	1966	1968	1970
Battalion	119*	339	337

* Company A only.

The 801st Maintenance Battalion was part of the 101st Airborne Division (Airmobile). Company A had provided assets to the separate 1st Brigade at Phan Rang since July 1965 (for capabilities, see the 27th Maintenance Battalion).

MAINTENANCE COMPANIES IN VIETNAM

Company	Type	Previous Station	Vietnam Service	Typical Location	Authorized Strength 1966	1968	1970
3d MAINT	Division Direct Support	Campbell	17 Jan. 67 – 10 April 70	Di An	—	175	—
5th MAINT	Light Equipment General Support	Hood	9 March 67 – 30 June 71	Long Binh	—	258	206
19th MAINT*	Light Equipment Direct Support	Ord	11 July 65 – 30 April 72	Long Binh	154	154	183
51st MAINT	Light Equipment Direct Support	Bliss	29 June 67 – 13 Aug. 70	Can Tho	—	154	—
61st MAINT	Heavy Equipment General Support	Knox	13 Dec. 66 – 1 Sept. 69	Long Binh	—	292	—
67th MAINT	Division Direct Support	Campbell	12 Dec. 67 – 6 Jan. 72	Phu Bai	—	130	180
79th MAINT	Light Equipment Direct Support	Vietnam	20 Oct. 69 – 30 April 72	Long Binh	—	—	183
85th MAINT*	Light Equipment Direct Support	Bliss	5 Sept. 65 – 31 Aug. 71	Da Nang	154	168	—
94th MAINT*	Division Direct Support	Lee	2 Nov. 65 – 15 March 72	Cu Chi	175	175	127
98th MAINT	Light Equipment General Support	Benning	13 Dec. 66 – 1 May 72	Qui Nhon	—	243	197
129th MAINT*	Main Support	Hood	15 Sept. 65 – 1 May 72	Nha Trang	221	216	216
135th MAINT	Heavy Equipment General Support	Campbell	20 Oct. 69 – 16 April 71	Cam Ranh Bay	—	291	183
136th MAINT*	Light Equipment Direct Support	Aberdeen	29 Oct. 65 – 1 May 72	Tuy Hoa	228	212	168
140th MAINT	Heavy Equipment General Support	Benning	25 June 66 – 20 Oct. 69	Long Binh	292	292	—
147th MAINT*	Light Equipment General Support	Benning	28 Aug. 65 – 30 April 72	Long Binh	182	190	190
149th MAINT*	Light Equipment Direct Support	Hood	27 Aug. 65 – 16 April 71	Pleiku	154	152	183
156th MAINT	Heavy Equipment General Support	Meade	23 Oct. 67 – 30 April 72	Da Nang	—	292	292
160th MAINT	Heavy Equipment General Support	Hood	26 Jan. 67 – 1 May 72	Qui Nhon	—	277	264
178th MAINT*	Division Direct Support	Bragg	15 Sept. 65 – 1 April 72	Quang Tri	175	175	180
237th MAINT †	Division Direct Support	Meade	22 Oct. 68 – 8 Oct. 69	Quang Tri	—	175	—
238th MAINT ‡	Division Direct Support	Hood	24 Oct. 68 – 21 Sept. 69	My Tho	—	175	—
263d MAINT	Light Equipment General Support Avionics	Vietnam	1 Dec. 69 – 1 April 72	Da Nang	—	—	163
317th MAINT	Light Equipment General Support Avionics	Vietnam	1 Dec. 69 – 1 April 72	Vung Tau	—	—	163
377th MAINT §	Light Equipment Direct Support	Riley	20 Nov. 68 – 5 Nov. 69	Cam Ranh Bay	—	154	—
378th MAINT	Main Support	Bragg	24 April 68 – 17 April 72	Long Binh	—	221	221
526th MAINT	Light Equipment Direct Support	Vietnam	1 Sept. 69 – 16 Nov. 72	Saigon	—	—	183
528th MAINT	Heavy Equipment General Support	Lewis	27 June 68 – March 69	Qui Nhon	—	292	—

528th MAINT‖	Light Equipment Direct Support	Vietnam	20 Oct. 69 – 30 April 72	Da Nang	—	—	183
536th MAINT*	Heavy Equipment General Support	Lewis	30 Oct. 65 – 20 Oct. 69	Tan Son Nhut	213	213	—
548th MAINT	Light Equipment Direct Support	Lewis	1 Sept. 66 – 30 June 71	Tay Ninh	—	154	183
549th MAINT	Light Equipment Direct Support	Benning	29 Oct. 67 – 22 June 72	Long Binh	—	154	183
551st MAINT	Light Equipment Direct Support	Campbell	2 Aug. 66 – 14 Dec. 69	Long Giao	—	154	—
552d MAINT	Light Equipment Direct Support	Riley	6 March 67 – 1 April 72	Qui Nhon	—	157	154
553d MAINT*	Heavy Equipment General Support	Riley	11 July 65 – 14 Dec. 69	Long Binh	213	213	—
554th MAINT*	Light Equipment General Support	Wood	29 April 65 – 20 Oct. 69	Qui Nhon	268	156	—
555th MAINT	Division Direct Support	Vietnam	8 Oct. 69 – 20 Sept. 71	Da Nang	—	—	175
557th MAINT	Light Equipment Direct Support	Carson	1 May 67 – 22 June 72	Cam Ranh Bay	—	154	183
560th MAINT	Light Equipment Direct Support	Meade	11 March 67 – 14 Dec. 70	Da Nang	—	156	183
578th MAINT*	Light Equipment General Support	Sheridan	4 Nov. 65 – 30 April 72	Phu Bai	182	203	206
588th MAINT	Division Direct Support	Lewis	20 Sept. 67 – 4 June 71	Chu Lai	—	175	180
590th MAINT	Division Direct Support	Lewis	20 Sept. 67 – 1 Oct. 70	Bear Cat	—	175	175
596th MAINT	Light Equipment Direct Support	Sheridan	7 March 68 – 30 Nov. 71	Quang Tri	—	154	183
604th MAINT	Equipment Processing	Eustis	15 June 69 – 30 June 72	Long Binh	—	—	185
614th MAINT	Light Equipment General Support Avionics	Vietnam	1 Dec. 69 – 15 Jan. 72	Nha Trang	—	—	163
618th MAINT*	Heavy Equipment General Support	Stewart	27 Aug. 65 – 20 Oct. 69	Qui Nhon	270	270	—
628th MAINT	Main Support	Vietnam	20 July 66 – 15 Oct. 68	Qui Nhon	221	221	—
632d MAINT	Heavy Equipment General Support	Bragg	2 Feb. 67 – 30 April 72	Long Binh	—	292	292
794th MAINT	Division Direct Support	Vietnam	1 Sept. 69 – 28 Nov. 71	Pleiku	—	—	180

Additionally, there were numerous provisional companies created to assist parent composite service battalions in forward areas.

* Ordnance until 20 July 1966.
† New York Army Reserve from New York City via Ft. Meade.
‡ Texas Army Reserve from San Antonio via Ft. Hood.
§ Wisconsin Army Reserve from Manitowoc via Ft. Riley.
‖ Second tour in Vietnam.

Chapter 20

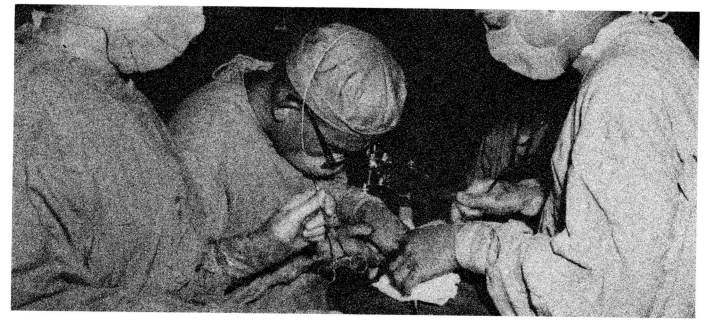

Medical

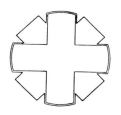

44th Medical Brigade

Arrived Vietnam: 24 April 1966
Operational Date: 1 May 1966
Departed Vietnam: 14 December 1970
Previous Station: Fort Sam Houston
Authorized Strength: HHD – 67

Commanders

Colonel James A. Wier	April 66
Colonel Ray L. Miller	June 66
Brigadier General Glenn J. Collines	Jan. 68
Brigadier General Spurgeon H. Neel, Jr.	Aug. 68
Brigadier General Hal B. Jennings, Jr.	Feb. 69
Colonel David E. Thomas	June 69

The 44th Medical Brigade was constituted in the Regular Army 30 December 1965 and then activated on New Year's Day 1966. It arrived in Vietnam to command the increased medical mission then controlled by the 1st Logistical Command. Initially the brigade was assigned to this command but in August 1967 was made an independent unit reporting directly to USARV. The brigade was initially established in a group of villas (Truong Quoc Dung) at Saigon and later moved to Long Binh. In December 1970 its assets were consolidated with the Surgeon General's Office, USARV, and redesignated the U.S. Army Medical Command, Vietnam. The following were the major elements of the brigade in Vietnam:

43d Medical Group	67th Medical Group
55th Medical Group	68th Medical Group
32d Medical Depot	

U.S. Army Medical Command, Vietnam, Provisional

No Insignia Authorized

Arrived Vietnam: 1 March 1970
Departed Vietnam: 30 April 1972
Previous Station: Vietnam
Authorized Strength: 164

The U.S. Army Medical Command was established when the 44th Medical Brigade headquarters assets and the Surgeon General's Office of USARV were consolidated at Long Binh. The command was later reduced to a group-level structure.

U.S. Army Health Services Group, Vietnam

No Insignia Authorized

Arrived Vietnam: 30 April 1972
Departed Vietnam: 28 March 1973
Previous Station: Vietnam
Authorized Strength: Unknown

The U.S. Army Health Services Group, Vietnam was established using the assets of the U.S. Army Medical Command, Vietnam during the final scale-down of the U.S. Army military involvement in Vietnam.

43d Medical Group

No Insignia
Authorized

Arrived Vietnam: 20 September 1965
Departed Vietnam: 7 February 1970
Previous Station: Fort Lewis

Authorized Strength	1966	1968
HHD	36	41

The 43d Medical Group provided command control and administrative supervision of its attached medical units which provided hospitalization, evacuation and area medical support at Nha Trang. It was operational 1 November 1965. On 15 June 1969 it assumed this responsibility for II Corps Tactical Zone.

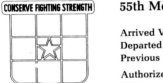

55th Medical Group

Arrived Vietnam: 11 June 1966
Departed Vietnam: 25 June 1970
Previous Station: Fort Bragg

Authorized Strength	1966	1968
HHD	36	41

The 55th Medical Group was stationed at Qui Nhon (for capabilities, see 43d Medical Group), becoming operational 1 July 1966. The group was phased out 15 June – 15 July 1969 and had been responsible for northern II CTZ.

67th Medical Group

Arrived Vietnam: 24 September 1967
Departed Vietnam: 30 January 1972
Previous Station: Fort Sam Houston

Authorized Strength	1968	1970
HHD	41	59

The 67th Medical Group was stationed at Bien Hoa (for capabilities, see 43d Medical Group), becoming operational 23 October 1967. In February 1968 the group moved to Da Nang to support XXIV Corps.

68th Medical Group

Arrived Vietnam: 7 February 1966
Departed Vietnam: 29 April 1972
Previous Station: Fort Meade

Authorized Strength	1966	1968	1970
HHD	36	41	59

The 68th Medical Group was stationed at Long Binh (for capabilities, see the 43d Medical Group) and became operational 1 March 1966. It had responsibilities in both III and IV Corps Tactical Zones.

1st Medical Battalion (Divisional)

Arrived Vietnam: 20 October 1965
Departed Vietnam: 9 April 1970
Previous Station: Fort Riley

Authorized Strength	1966	1968
Battalion	384	371

The 1st Medical Battalion was part of the 1st Infantry Division providing division-level service, including command and medical record administration, receiving, sorting, temporary medical and surgical treatment, emergency dental treatment and evacuation of patients from unit aid stations. Service also included furnishing unit-level medical service, transport of medical supplies and equipment, and providing medical supply support and limited maintenance.

4th Medical Battalion (Divisional)

Arrived Vietnam: 7 September 1966
Departed Vietnam: 7 December 1970
Previous Station: Fort Lewis

Authorized Strength	1966	1968	1970
Battalion	98*	371	366

* Company C only.

The 4th Medical Battalion was part of the 4th Infantry Division in Vietnam (for capabilities, see 1st Medical Battalion).

9th Medical Battalion (Divisional)

Arrived Vietnam: 4 January 1967
Departed Vietnam: 18 August 1969
Previous Station: Fort Riley
Authorized Strength: 371 (1968)

The 9th Medical Battalion was part of the 9th Infantry Division (for capabilities, see 1st Medical Battalion) in Vietnam.

15th Medical Battalion (Airmobile Division)

Arrived Vietnam: 28 July 1965
Departed Vietnam: 15 April 1971
Previous Station: Fort Benning

Authorized Strength	1966	1968	1971
Battalion	415	380	245

The 15th Medical Battalion was part of the 1st Cavalry Division, and in addition to normal divisional medical organization (see 1st Medical Battalion) had its own complement of 12 aeromedical evacuation helicopters.

23d Medical Battalion
(Divisional)

Arrived Vietnam: 8 December 1967
Departed Vietnam: 8 November 1971
Previous Station: Vietnam
Authorized Strength: 366 (1970)

The 23d Medical Battalion was part of the 23d Infantry Division (AMERICAL) in Vietnam (for capabilities, see 1st Medical Battalion). In 1968 it consisted of a Headquarters and Support Company numbering 132 men, reinforced by detachments.

25th Medical Battalion
(Divisional)

Arrived Vietnam: 30 March 1966
Departed Vietnam: 7 December 1970
Previous Station: Hawaii

Authorized Strength	1966	1968	1970
Battalion	396	371	277

The 25th Medical Battalion was part of the 25th Infantry Division (for capabilities, see 1st Medical Battalion) in Vietnam.

58th Medical Battalion
(Nondivisional)

Arrived Vietnam: 29 May 1965
Departed Vietnam: 25 May 1972
Previous Station: Fort Ord

Authorized Strength	1966	1968	1970
HHD	34	36	36

The 58th Medical Battalion provided command, control and planning for a medical battalion (nondivisional), including supply and organizational maintenance support. The battalion responsibilities included clearing and holding facilities and evacuation to hospital areas. It was stationed at Long Binh under the 68th Medical Group.

61st Medical Battalion
(Nondivisional)

Arrived Vietnam: 8 June 1966
Departed Vietnam: 17 February 1972
Previous Station: Fort Campbell
Authorized Strength: HHD – 36

The 61st Medical Battalion had the same capabilities as the 58th Medical Battalion and was stationed at Cam Ranh Bay and later Qui Nhon under the 43d Medical Group, later moving to Da Nang.

70th Medical Battalion
(Nondivisional)

Arrived Vietnam: 7 November 1965
Departed Vietnam: 2 February 1971
Previous Station: Fort Riley
Authorized Strength: HHD – 36

The 70th Medical Battalion was stationed with the 55th Medical Group effective 1 July 1966 at Phu Thanh (for capabilities, see 58th Medical Battalion).

74th Medical Battalion
(Nondivisional)

Arrived Vietnam: 4 June 1966
Departed Vietnam: 15 November 1969
Previous Station: Fort Polk
Authorized Strength: HHD – 36

The 74th Medical Battalion was stationed at Long Binh under the 67th Medical Group (for capabilities, see 58th Medical Battalion). It was redesignated a provisional "group" on 1 October 1967 and relocated to Chu Lai under the 55th Medical Group.

326th Medical Battalion
(Divisional)

Arrived Vietnam: 22 October 1967
Departed Vietnam: 23 December 1971
Previous Station: Fort Campbell

Authorized Strength	1966	1968
Battalion	76*	380

* Company D only.

The 326th Medical Battalion was part of the 101st Airborne Division (Airmobile). For capabilities, see 1st Medical Battalion. Company D (Airborne) arrived in Vietnam with the 1st Brigade (separate) at Phan Rang in July 1965.

2d Surgical Hospital
(Mobile Army)

Arrived Vietnam: 31 October 1965
Operational Date: 5 January 1966
Departed Vietnam: 10 March 1970
Previous Station: Fort Bragg

Authorized Strength	1966	1968
Hospital	119	119

The 2d Mobile Army Surgical Hospital (MASH) furnished resuscitative surgery and medical treatment necessary to prepare critically wounded or ill patients received from division medical elements for extended evacuation and had 35 beds in 1969. First located at Qui Nhon, it was established on 1 July 1966 under the 55th Medical Group at An Khe, where it stayed until moving to Chu Lai as part of Task Force OREGON in April 1967. It remained there until transferred to the 68th Medical Group and was sent to Lai Khe in 1968. It was located here in the vicinity of the 1st Infantry Division until departure from Vietnam.

3d Field Hospital

Arrived Vietnam: 26 April 1965
Operational Date: 11 May 1965
Departed Vietnam: 31 May 1972
Previous Station: Fort Lewis

Authorized Strength	1966	1968	1970
Hospital	62	62	222

The 3d Field Hospital was established at Tan Son Nhut to provide hospitalization to temporary personnel troop concentrations as required in the theater of operations and remained at that location under the 68th Medical Group for the duration of its service in Vietnam. Its assets were used to form the U.S. Army Saigon

Hospital. In 1969 it had a 292-bed capacity (including the 51st Field Hospital which was subordinated to it at that time).

3d Surgical Hospital (Mobile Army)*

Arrived Vietnam: 23 August 1965
Operational Date: 15 September 1965
Departed Vietnam: April 1972
Previous Station: Fort Meade

Authorized Strength	1966	1968	1970
Hospital	119	119	120

The 3d Mobile Army Surgical Hospital (MASH) initially served in the Bien Hoa – Long Binh vicinity but moved to Dong Tam in May 1967, where it was associated with the 9th Infantry Division while under the 68th Medical Group. It was posted to Binh Thuy on 5 September 1969 and was attached to the 29th Evacuation Hospital, which then operated as a station hospital. It had a 45-bed capacity in 1969 (for capabilities, see 2d Surgical Hospital).

* It received MUST equipment at Dong Tam in May 1967.

6th Convalescent Center

No Insignia
Authorized

Arrived Vietnam: 15 April 1966
Operational Date: 16 May 1966
Departed Vietnam: 30 October 1971
Previous Station: Fort Sam Houston

Authorized Strength	1966	1968	1970
Center	211	273	314

The 6th Convalescent Center provided facilities for the convalescent care and physical reconditioning of patients at Cam Ranh Bay and had 1,300 beds in 1969. It served under the 43d Medical Group until 1970 when it was placed under the 68th Medical Group.

7th Surgical Hospital (Mobile Army)

Arrived Vietnam: 4 June 1966
Operational Date: 1 August 1966
Departed Vietnam: 10 May 1969
Previous Station: Fort Jackson

Authorized Strength	1966	1968
Hospital	119	119

The 7th Mobile Army Surgical Hospital (MASH) served initially under the 68th Medical Group at Cu Chi, and moved to Long Giao on 23 April 1967, where it was associated with the 11th Armored Cavalry (Regiment). For capabilities, see 2d Surgical Hospital.

8th Field Hospital

Arrived in Vietnam: 10 April 1962
Operational Date: 18 April 1962
Departed Vietnam: August 1971
Previous Station: Fort Lewis

Authorized Strength	1964	1966	1968	1970
Hospital	148	86	208	39

The 8th Field Hospital was the first army hospital to be established in Vietnam, was located at Nha Trang and in 1965 attached to the 43d Medical Group. It moved to An Khe in September 1970

under the 68th Medical Group and in 1971 was at Tuy Hoa. The capacity of this hospital was 500 beds in 1969 (for capabilities, see 3d Field Hospital).

9th Field Hospital

No Insignia
Authorized

Arrived Vietnam: 14 July 1965
Operational Date: 20 July 1965
Departed Vietnam: September 1968
Previous Station: Fort Lewis

Authorized Strength	1966	1968
Hospital	60	60

The 9th Field Hospital was located at Nha Trang under the 43d Medical Group. In 1968 it was subordinated to the 8th Field Hospital but later its assets were merged with those of the 8th Field Hospital (for capabilities, see 3d Field Hospital).

12th Evacuation Hospital (Semi-Mobile)

Arrived Vietnam: 9 September 1966
Operational Date: 15 December 1966
Departed Vietnam: 15 December 1970
Previous Station: Fort Ord

Authorized Strength	1968	1970
Hospital	312	305

The 12th Semi-Mobile Evacuation Hospital provided hospitalization for all classes of patients as well as limited outpatient services in the immediate facility vicinity and prepared patients for evacuation to other medical facilities. The hospital was located at Cu Chi and associated with the 25th Infantry Division. It had 317 beds in 1969.

17th Field Hospital

Arrived Vietnam: 10 March 1966
Operational Date: 1 April 1966
Departed Vietnam: 1 August 1970
Previous Station: Fort Lewis

Authorized Strength	1966	1968
Hospital	90	90

The 17th Field Hospital served the Saigon – Cholon area under the 44th Medical Brigade. In the spring of 1968 it was moved to An Khe under the 55th Medical Group and in July 1969 transferred to Qui Nhon under the 43d Medical Group. It was transferred back to An Khe on 7 October 1969 and placed under the 67th Medical Group in 1970. It had an 80-bed capacity in 1969 (for capabilities, see 3d Field Hospital).

18th Surgical Hospital (Mobile Army)*

Arrived Vietnam: 18 June 1966
Operational Date: 1 July 1966
Departed Vietnam: 31 August 1971
Previous Station: Fort Gordon

Authorized Strength	1966	1968	1970
Hospital	119	119	132

The 18th Mobile Army Surgical Hospital (MASH) was initially stationed at Pleiku under the 55th Medical Group and was associated with the 4th Infantry Division. On 15 December 1967 it was at Lai Khe and in February 1968 was posted to Quang Tri in association with the 1st Brigade, 5th Infantry Division (Mechanized). In March 1969 it was sent to Camp Evans in the Gia Le vicinity but on 19 December 1969 the hospital moved to a fixed installation formerly occupied by the marines in the Quang Tri area. The hospital had a 70-bed capacity in 1969 (for capabilities, see 2d Surgical Hospital).

* This unit received MUST equipment 18 November 1967.

22d Surgical Hospital (Self-Contained, Transportable)

Arrived Vietnam: 27 December 1967
Operational Date: 11 March 1968
Departed Vietnam: 18 October 1969
Previous Station: Fort Sam Houston
Authorized Strength: 119 (1968)

The 22d Surgical Hospital Medical Unit, Self-Contained, Transportable (MUST) arrived at Long Binh and was moved on 30 January 1968 to the Phu Bai vicinity to render assistance to the 101st Airborne Division (Airmobile) while under the 45th Medical Group. It had an 80-bed capacity in 1969 (for capabilities, see 45th Surgical Hospital).

24th Evacuation Hospital (Semi-Mobile)

Arrived Vietnam: 10 July 1966
Operational Date: 9 January 1967
Departed Vietnam: 10 November 1972
Previous Station: Fort Sam Houston

Authorized Strength	1966	1968	1971
Hospital	313	312	303

The 24th Semi-Mobile Evacuation Hospital was located at Long Binh under the 68th Medical Group and had a 328-bed capacity in 1969 (for capabilities, see 12th Evacuation Hospital).

27th Surgical Hospital (Mobile Army)

Arrived Vietnam: 25 March 1968
Operational Date: 13 April 1968
Departed Vietnam: 16 June 1971
Previous Station: Fort Lewis

Authorized Strength	1968	1970
Hospital	168	166

The 27th Mobile Army Surgical Hospital (MASH) was located at Chu Lai under the 67th Medical Group where it was associated with the 23d Infantry Division (AMERICAL) and had a 110-bed capacity in 1969 (for capabilities, see 2d Surgical Hospital).

29th Evacuation Hospital (Semi-Mobile)

Arrived Vietnam: 20 May 1968
Operational Date: 24 August 1968
Departed Vietnam: 22 October 1969
Previous Station: Fort Devens
Authorized Strength: 313 (1968)

The 29th Semi-Mobile Evacuation Hospital was under the 68th Medical Group and provided medical support to the Can Tho – Binh Thuy area (for capabilities, see 12th Evacuation Hospital). It had 237 beds in 1969.

36th Evacuation Hospital (Semi-Mobile)

Arrived Vietnam: 7 March 1966
Operational Date: 30 March 1966
Departed Vietnam: 28 November 1969
Previous Station: Fort Meade

Authorized Strength	1966	1968
Hospital	313	312

The 36th Semi-Mobile Evacuation Hospital was located at Vung Tau under the 68th Medical Group and had a 400-bed capacity in 1969 (for capabilities, see 12th Evacuation Hospital).

45th Surgical Hospital (Self-Contained, Transportable)

Arrived Vietnam: 4 October 1966
Operational Date: 13 November 1966
Departed Vietnam: 24 October 1970
Previous Station: Fort Sam Houston

Authorized Strength	1968	1970
Hospital	122	123

The 45th Surgical Hospital was the first Medical Unit, Self-Contained, Transportable (MUST) hospital in Vietnam containing all hospital facilities, billets for medical personnel, mess halls and helipads which could be moved by 2½-ton trucks. Serving with the 68th Medical Group, it was located at Tay Ninh throughout its service in Vietnam and had a 40-bed capacity in 1969.

51st Field Hospital

No Insignia Authorized

Arrived Vietnam: 31 October 1965
Operational Date: 3 November 1965
Departed Vietnam: 30 June 1971
Previous Station: Fort Lewis

Authorized Strength	1966	1968
Hospital	156	156

The 51st Field Hospital was located at Tan Son Nhut and attached to and operated under the 3d Field Hospital, which see.

67th Evacuation Hospital (Semi-Mobile)

Arrived Vietnam: 7 March 1966
Operational Date: 5 October 1966
Departed Vietnam: 28 March 1973
Previous Station: Fort Carson

Authorized Strength	1966	1968	1970
Hospital	313	313	272

The 67th Semi-Mobile Evacuation Hospital was located at Qui Nhon under the 55th Medical Group. It was placed under the 43d Medical Group in mid-1969 and controlled by the 67th Medical Group after February 1970. In 1972 the hospital was moved to Pleiku and placed under control of the U.S. Army Health Services Group, Vietnam. In late 1972 it was still at Pleiku but subordinated to the U.S. Army Hospital, Saigon. It had 400 beds in 1969 (for capabilities, see 12th Evacuation Hospital).

71st Evacuation Hospital (Semi-Mobile)

Arrived Vietnam: 15 November 1966
Operational Date: 29 May 1967
Departed Vietnam: 15 December 1970
Previous Station: Fort Campbell

Authorized Strength	1968	1970
Hospital	312	305

The 71st Semi-Mobile Evacuation Hospital was stationed at Pleiku, where it served with the 4th Infantry Division. It was under the 43d Medical Group and had 400 beds in 1969 (for capabilities, see 12th Evacuation Hospital).

74th Field Hospital

Arrived Vietnam: 15 September 1968
Operational Date: 14 October 1968
Departed Vietnam: 14 August 1969
Previous Station: New York City via Fort Lee
Authorized Strength: 184 (1968)

The 74th Field Hospital was an Army Reserve hospital from New York. It served under the 68th Medical Group at Long Binh and had a 250-bed capacity in 1969 (for capabilities, see 3d Field Hospital).

85th Evacuation Hospital (Semi-Mobile)

No Insignia Authorized

Arrived Vietnam: 31 August 1965
Operational Date: 6 September 1965
Departed Vietnam: 9 December 1971
Previous Station: Fort Bliss

Authorized Strength	1966	1968	1970
Hospital	313	312	305

The 85th Semi-Mobile Evacuation Hospital was initially stationed at Qui Nhon under the control of the 43d Medical Group there. On 1 July 1966 it came under the control of the 55th Medical Group. In 1969 it was transferred to the 67th Medical Group at Phu Bai, where it remained until departing Vietnam. It had 133 beds in 1969 (for capabilities, see 12th Evacuation Hospital).

91st Evacuation Hospital (Semi-Mobile)

Arrived Vietnam: 3 December 1966
Operational Date: 15 March 1967
Departed Vietnam: 29 November 1971
Previous Station: Fort Polk

Authorized Strength	1968	1970
Hospital	312	305

The 91st Semi-Mobile Evacuation Hospital was initially located at Tuy Hoa under the 43d Medical Group, moving to the 67th Medical Group at Chu Lai on 1 July 1969, where it remained until leaving Vietnam. This hospital had a 325-bed capacity in 1969 (for capabilities, see 12th Evacuation Hospital).

93d Evacuation Hospital (Semi-Mobile)

Arrived Vietnam: 4 November 1965
Operational Date: 10 December 1965
Departed Vietnam: 29 April 1971
Previous Station: Fort Riley

Authorized Strength	1966	1968	1970
Hospital	313	312	304

The 93d Evacuation Hospital (Semi-Mobile) was initially at Long Binh and in 1966 was moved under the 68th Medical Group's control. The hospital had a 250-bed capacity in 1969.

95th Evacuation Hospital (Semi-Mobile)

Arrived Vietnam: 25 March 1968
Operational Date: 28 April 1968
Departed Vietnam: 28 March 1973
Previous Station: Fort Benning

Authorized Strength	1968	1970
Hospital	313	300

The 95th Semi-Mobile Evacuation Hospital was located at Da Nang under control of the 67th Medical Group. After that group left Vietnam it was placed under the U.S. Army Health Services Group, Vietnam but stayed at Da Nang. It had 320 beds in 1969 (for capabilities, see 12th Evacuation Hospital).

311th Field Hospital

Arrived Vietnam: 11 October 1968
Operational Date: 9 November 1968
Departed Vietnam: 8 August 1969
Previous Station: Sharonville, Ohio via Fort Leonard Wood
Authorized Strength: 184 (1968)

The 311th Field Hospital was an Army Reserve hospital from Ohio initially located at Qui Nhon, moving in early 1969 to Phu Thanh under the 55th Medical Group, where it remained until departing Vietnam. It had a 240-bed capacity in 1969 (for capabilities, see 3d Field Hospital).

Unauthorized

312th Evacuation Hospital (Semi-Mobile)

Arrived Vietnam: 6 September 1968
Operational Date: 10 October 1968
Departed Vietnam: 2 August 1969
Previous Station: Winston-Salem, North Carolina, via Fort Benning
Authorized Strength: 313 (1968)

The 312th Semi-Mobile Evacuation Hospital was an Army Reserve hospital from North Carolina. It served under the 67th Medical Group at Chu Lai and had a 325-bed capacity (for capabilities, see 12th Evacuation Hospital).

523d Field Hospital

No Insignia Authorized

Arrived Vietnam: 23 September 1965
Operational Date: 25 September 1965
Departed Vietnam: September 1968
Previous Station: Fort Lewis

Authorized Strength	1966	1968
Hospital	60	60

The 523d Field Hospital was located at Nha Trang but attached to and under the control of the 8th Field Hospital there.

U.S. Army Prisoner-of-War Hospital

No Insignia Authorized

Arrived Vietnam: 4 June 1966
Operational Date: 9 June 1967
Departed Vietnam: 31 December 1969
Previous Station: Vietnam
Authorized Strength: See narrative

The U.S. Army Prisoner-of-War Hospital was established at Long Binh. It was operated by the 74th Fied Hospital and after 1 August 1969 by the 24th Evacuation Hospital.

U.S. Army Hospital, Saigon

No Insignia Authorized

Arrived Vietnam: 31 May 1972
Operational Date: 31 May 1972
Departed Vietnam: 14 March 1973
Previous Station: Vietnam
Authorized Strength: Unknown

The U.S. Army Hospital, Saigon was established using assets of the 3d Field Hospital and served under the U.S. Army Health Services Group, Vietnam. In March 1973, upon close-out, it was converted into the Saigon Seventh-Day Adventist Hospital.

MEDICAL COMPANIES IN VIETNAM

Company	Type	Previous Station	Vietnam Service	Typical Location	Authorized Strength 1966	1968	1970
1st MED	Ambulance	Knox	23 Nov. 66 – 4 Feb. 70	Pleiku	—	97	—
37th MED	Separate Bde – 11th Arm Cav	Knox	7 Sept. 66 – 20 March 72	Long Giao	—	125	125
45th MED	Air Ambulance	Bragg	19 July 67 – 30 April 71	Long Binh	—	191	249
50th MED	Clearing	Benning	4 June 66 – 30 Oct. 71	Bear Cat	127	128	127
51st MED	Ambulance	Carson	7 Nov. 65 – 1 Oct. 70	Phu Thanh	98	97	84
418th MED	Ambulance	Bliss	21 June 66 – 30 April 71	Cam Ranh Bay	98	97	84
498th MED	Air Ambulance	Houston	16 Aug. 65 – 30 Aug. 71	An Son	183	191	167
520th MED	Clearing	Houston	26 March 68 – 26 Oct. 69	Chu Lai	—	81	—
542d MED	Clearing	Ord	27 Aug. 65 – 25 June 70	Phu Thanh	128	128	—
561st MED	Ambulance	Ord	23 Aug. 65 – 1 Oct. 70	Long Binh	98	97	84
563d MED	Clearing	Bragg	20 Sept. 66 – 25 June 70	Phu Bai	—	128	—
566th MED	Ambulance	Houston	26 March 68 – 30 April 72	Chu Lai	—	102	102
568th MED	Clearing	Campbell	1 Jan. 66 – 15 March 71	Cam Ranh Bay	128	128	107
584th MED	Ambulance	Bragg	15 Oct. 66 – 26 Dec. 71	Long Binh	—	97	98
616th MED	Clearing	Polk	18 Oct. 65 – 31 March 72	Phu Bai	128	128	128
658th MED	Team Area Control Headquarters	Houston	10 May 67 – 25 June 70	Long Binh	—	8	—
667th MED	Team Area Control Headquarters	Houston	10 May 67 – 25 June 70	Long Binh	—	8	—

Additionally, some other medical companies such as the USARV Patient Casual Company (organized 26 October 1966) were formed.

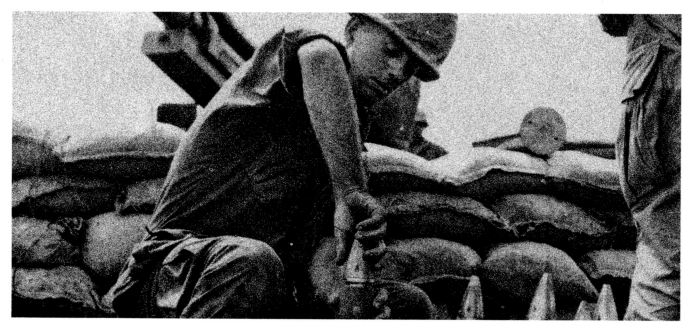

Chapter 21

Ordnance

Unauthorized

52d Ordnance Group (Ammunition)

Arrived Vietnam: 10 March 1966
Departed Vietnam: 20 October 1967
Previous Station: Fort Bragg
Authorized Strength: HHC – 72 (1966)

The 52d Ordnance Group was established to provide command and administrative, tactical and technical supervision over conventional and special ammunition and guided-missile support companies as well as to operate an EOD (explosive ordnance disposal) center, supervise the supply and maintenance of all ammunition stocks including special ammunition and missile items, and direct rear-area damage control and security activities. However, upon arrival the group was used as the nucleus of the Directorate of Ammunition at 1st Logistical Command, and ammunition units were not assigned or attached to the group's control. Instead, they were assigned to a general support group or field depot command or directly to army support commands in Vietnam as separate battalions. Thus, command and control of ammunition units in Vietnam was placed in the hands of ordnance battalion headquarters and headquarters companies and directors of ammunition at each of the area logistics commands.

60th Ordnance Group (Maintenance and Supply)

Arrived Vietnam: 6 September 1965
Departed Vietnam: 20 July 1966
Previous Station: Fort Lee
Authorized Strength: HHD – 54

The 60th Ordnance Group was deployed at Bien Hoa to provide command control, staff planning and supervision of from three to five ordnance maintenance and supply battalions. However, in mid-1966 these units were converted to composite service configurations, and the ordnance group was inactivated in Vietnam because its functions were then served by general support group headquarters.

3d Ordnance Battalion (Ammunition)

Arrived Vietnam: 4 November 1965
Departed Vietnam: 29 April 1972
Previous Station: Fort Bliss

Authorized Strength	1966	1968	1970
HHD		106	106	106

The 3d Ordnance Battalion (Ammunition) provided tactical, technical, and command and administrative supervision over operation of the Long Binh, Tan Son Nhut and Vung Tau ammunition supply depots and general ammunition services in both III and IV Corps Tactical Zones. It arrived at the Long Binh Ammunition Supply Depot and was part of the 29th General Support Group, transferring on 1 April 1969 to the 53d General Support Group.

184th Ordnance Battalion (Ammunition)

Arrived Vietnam: 31 December 1965
Departed Vietnam: 2 April 1972
Previous Station: Fort Sill

Authorized Strength	1966	1968	1970
HHD		106	106	104

The 184th Ordnance Battalion (Ammunition) was a conventional ammunition direct support battalion in control of the Qui Nhon Ammunition Base Depot in Vietnam.

191st Ordnance Battalion (Ammunition)

Arrived Vietnam: 30 September 1966
Departed Vietnam: 17 April 1972
Previous Station: Fort Sill

Authorized Strength	1968	1970
HHD	106	100

The 191st Ordnance Battalion (Ammunition) provided ammunition service support within the Cam Ranh Bay Ammunition Storage Depot.

336th Ordnance Battalion (Ammunition)

Arrived Vietnam: 28 September 1968
Departed Vietnam: 7 August 1969
Previous Station: Little Rock, Arkansas via Fort Carson
Authorized Strength: HHD – 124 (1968)

The 336th Ordnance Battalion (Ammunition) had the same capabilities as the 3d Ordnance Battalion and was placed in control of the Da Nang Ammunition Base Depot. The battalion was an Army Reserve unit from Arkansas.

No Insignia Authorized

528th Ordnance Battalion, Provisional

See 528th Quartermaster Battalion.

ORDNANCE COMPANIES IN VIETNAM

Company	Type	Previous Station	Vietnam Service	Typical Location	Authorized Strength 1966	1968	1970
33d ORD	Ammunition Direct/General Spt	Sill	1 Nov. 66 – 10 Dec. 70	Cam Ranh Bay	—	223	191
40th ORD	Ammunition Direct/General Spt	Rucker	17 Jan. 67 – 21 March 72	Da Nang	—	223	223
46th ORD	Ammunition Direct/General Spt	Vietnam	12 Nov. 68 – 30 June 71	Cam Ranh Bay	—	—	65
54th ORD	Ammunition Direct/General Spt	Knox	2 Nov. 65 – 30 March 72	Long Binh	240	223	240
59th ORD	Ammunition Direct/General Spt	Carson	12 Nov. 68 – 7 Jan. 69	Cam Ranh Bay	—	223	—
60th ORD	Ammunition Direct/General Spt	Bragg	19 Nov. 66 – 16 April 72	Long Binh	—	223	240
71st ORD	Ammunition Direct/General Spt	Sill	30 June 68 – 1 Jan. 72	Long Binh	—	223	223
148th ORD	Ammunition Direct/General Spt	Bragg	4 Nov. 65 – 30 June 71	Vung Tau	196	223	—
188th ORD	Ammunition Direct/General Spt	Bragg	27 Dec. 65 – 14 Dec. 70	Pleiku	240	223	220
295th ORD*	Ammunition Direct/General Spt	Carson	21 Oct. 68 – Sept. 69	Cat Lai	—	223	—
571st ORD	Ammunition Direct/General Spt	Campbell	26 June 68 – 20 March 72	Quang Tri	—	223	223
576th ORD	Ammunition Direct/General Spt	Lewis	13 Aug. 65 – 27 June 72	Long Binh	263	223	263
606th ORD	Ammunition Direct/General Spt	Dix	15 Sept. 65 – 31 Jan. 72	Cam Ranh Bay	196	223	196
611th ORD	Ammunition Direct/General Spt	Carson	4 Sept. 65 – 30 April 72	Cam Ranh Bay	245	223	240
630th ORD	Ammunition Direct/General Spt	Campbell	5 Nov. 65 – 31 Jan. 72	Phu Tai	240	223	240
661st ORD	Ammunition Direct/General Spt	Sill	24 Nov. 65 – 30 Nov. 71	Phu Tai	240	223	240
820th ORD	Ammunition Direct/General Spt	Benning	2 Sept. 65 – 14 Dec. 70	Phu Tai	240	223	218
826th ORD †	Ammunition Direct/General Spt	Knox	15 Oct. 68 – 2 Oct. 69	Long Binh	—	223	—

* Nebraska Army Reserve from Hastings via Ft. Carson.

† Wisconsin Army Reserve from Madison via Ft. Knox.

Chapter 22

Quartermaster

64th Quartermaster Battalion (Petroleum Operations)

Arrived Vietnam: 20 April 1966
Departed Vietnam: 8 April 1970
Previous Station: Fort Leonard Wood

Authorized Strength	1966	1968
HHC	67	67

The 64th Quartermaster Battalion (Petroleum Operations) provided command, administration, and technical and operational supervision for the operation and maintenance of a military petroleum distribution system and was assigned to the U.S. Army Support Command, Saigon. The assignment of this battalion headquarters consolidated all POL (petrol, oil, lubricants) units within the command under one headquarters. An additional duty of the battalion was as director of petroleum for the support command and for all petroleum depots in III CTZ. It was located at Long Binh.

240th Quartermaster Battalion (Petroleum Operations)

Arrived Vietnam: 13 January 1967
Departed Vietnam: 26 June 1971
Previous Station: Fort Lee

Authorized Strength	1968	1970
HHC	66	53

The 240th Quartermaster Battalion (Petroleum Operations) had the same capabilities as the 64th QM Battalion and was assigned to the 58th Field Depot at Qui Nhon. On 1 June 1968 the battalion was relieved of this duty and assigned directly to the U.S. Army

Support Command, Qui Nhon. It was stationed at Qui Nhon, Phu Tai and Din Dinh during its service in Vietnam.

259th Quartermaster Battalion (Petroleum Operations)

Arrived Vietnam: 30 September 1968
Departed Vietnam: 15 September 1969
Previous Station: Pleasant Grove, Utah, via Fort Wood
Authorized Strength: HHC – 91 (1968)

The 259th Quartermaster Battalion (Petroleum Operations) was an Army Reserve unit from Utah with the same general capabilities as the 64th QM Battalion. It was deployed to Da Nang and Phu Bai where it handled petroleum support for the U.S. Army Support Command, Da Nang.

262d Quartermaster Battalion (Petroleum Operations, Army)

Arrived Vietnam: 5 June 1967
Departed Vietnam: 13 August 1970
Previous Station: Fort Lee
Authorized Strength: HHC – 89 (1968)

The 262d Quartermaster Battalion (Petroleum Operations, Army) provided petroleum storage facilities and wholesale distribution of petroleum products for the U.S. Army Support Command, Cam Ranh Bay. It was stationed at Cam Ranh Bay, and was responsible for petroleum operations throughout the support command area. On 1 November 1968 it was attached to the Cam Ranh Bay depot.

528th Quartermaster Battalion (Petroleum Supply)

No Insignia
Authorized

Arrived Vietnam: 25 September 1969
Departed Vietnam: 15 April 1971
Previous Station: Vietnam
Authorized Strength: HHD – 60 (1970)

The 528th Quartermaster Battalion (Petroleum Supply) was formed to replace the 259th QM Battalion when it left Vietnam.

The 528th Battalion was stationed at Phu Bai and Da Nang to maintain control of attached petroleum and transportation (petroleum) companies. It was also assigned three ammunition companies and these often led the battalion to be known as an Ammunition Battalion or even the 528th Ordnance Battalion.

QUARTERMASTER COMPANIES IN VIETNAM

Company	Type	Previous Station	Vietnam Service	Typical Location	Authorized Strength 1966	1968	1970
101st QM (Prov)	Air Equipment Support	Campbell	29 July 65 – 16 Dec. 1967	Bien Hoa	95	217 (1967)	—
109th QM	Air Delivery	Campbell	12 Aug. 66 – 31 Jan. 72	Cam Ranh Bay	267	267	267
134th QM	Petroleum Supply	Wood	31 Aug. 65 – 15 March 72	Phu Tai	228	228	228
157th QM	Service	Polk	18 Sept. 65 – 1 Sept. 68	Qui Nhon	165	165	—
173d QM*	Petroleum Operations	Lee	30 Sept. 68 – 5 Aug. 69	Phu Bai	—	175	—
239th QM	Service	Lewis	28 Nov. 66 – 1 Sept. 68	Cam Ranh Bay	—	165	—
512th QM	Petroleum Supply and Petroleum Operations	Lee	19 Nov. 66 – 30 April 72	Long Binh	—	173	182
514th QM	Petroleum Supply and Petroleum Operations	Lee	23 Nov. 66 – 26 Dec. 71	Phu Tai	—	173	182
524th QM	Petroleum Depot and Petroleum Operations	Wood	20 July 65 – 1 May 72	Cam Ranh Bay	186	185	271
525th QM	Petroleum Depot	Lee	1 May 67 – 8 Nov. 72	Cam Ranh Bay	—	271	271
528th QM (Prov)	Petroleum Supply	Lee	14 April 67 – March 72	Saigon	—	228	228
623d QM	Air Equipment Repair Depot	Bragg	23 Aug. 66 – 20 Dec. 68	Cam Ranh Bay	149	149	—
647th QM	Field Depot and Petroleum Operations	Polk	16 Sept. 65 – 1 Oct. 70	An Khe	175	174	135
842d QM†	Petroleum Supply	Lee	14 Oct. 68 – 30 Sept. 69	Pleiku	—	237	—

* Mississippi Army Reserve from Greenwood, Mississippi via Ft. Lee.
† Kansas Army Reserve from Kansas City via Ft. Lee.

Chapter 23

Transportation

4th Transportation Command (Terminal)

No Insignia Authorized

Arrived Vietnam: 8 August 1965
Departed Vietnam: 26 June 1972
Previous Station: Fort Eustis

Authorized Strength	1966	1968	1970
Command HQ	664	661	141*

* HQ and HQ Company only.

The 4th Transportation Command was raised to command assigned and attached units engaged in the normal terminal command responsibilities, i.e., the transfer of personnel and cargo, establishing terminal operations, logistical over-the-shore operations and supporting amphibious operations. However, since the command was the first senior terminal command-and-control unit to arrive in Vietnam, it was given technical as well as operational control of all land and water transportation units assigned to the 1st Logistical Command. Included in this mission were the operation of the port complex at Saigon and the water terminals at Cam Ranh Bay, Nha Be, Qui Nhon, Phan Rang, Nha Trang and Vung Tau. It was further assigned to provide motor transport in support of port and beach clearance and tactical operations and to establish the Army Air Cargo Terminal at Tan Son Nhut. The command had an initial strength of 7,000 personnel. Upon establishment of the support commands at Cam Ranh Bay and Qui Nhon in early 1966, the original mission was changed to operation of the Saigon Port Complex, a sub-port at Vung Tau and various ammunition distribution sites. In early 1966 the 4th Transportation Command's assigned truck units

were reassigned. In July 1967 the command was officially assigned to the U.S. Army Support Command, Saigon. It took over operations at the U.S. Army Newport Terminal.

Unauthorized

5th Transportation Command (Terminal)

Arrived Vietnam: 1 October 1966
Departed Vietnam: 13 June 1972
Previous Station: Fort Story

Authorized Strength	1968	1970
HHC	139	135

The 5th Transportation Command (Terminal) had the same normal capabilities as the 4th Transportation Command. It assumed the duties of running the extensive Qui Nhon port and served under the U.S. Army Support Command, Qui Nhon. In May 1970 it was deployed to Da Nang.

124th Transportation Command (Terminal)

No Insignia Authorized

Arrived Vietnam: 1 October 1966
Departed Vietnam: 1 May 1972
Previous Station: Fort Eustis

Authorized Strength	1968	1971
HHC	139	108

The 124th Transportation Command (Terminal) had the same normal capabilities as the 4th Transportation Command. This command was responsible for operations at the port of Cam Ranh Bay under the U.S. Army Support Command, Cam Ranh Bay.

125th Transportation Command (Terminal)

No Insignia
Authorized

Arrived Vietnam: 4 October 1966
Departed Vietnam: 14 February 1970
Previous Station: Fort Eustis

Authorized Strength	1968
HHC	138

The 125th Transportation Command (Terminal) had the same normal capabilities as the 4th Transportation Command. It was posted to control transportation operations at Tan Son Nhut and adjacent Saigon terminal not covered by the 4th Transportation Command's jurisdiction and served under the U.S. Support Command, Saigon. It served in an advisory capacity to the Director of Ports, Vietnam until 30 April 1969.

863d Transportation Command, Provisional

No Insignia
Authorized

Arrived Vietnam: 15 April 1970
Departed Vietnam: 1 August 1970

The 863d Transportation Command (Provisional) was formed at Da Nang under the 26th General Support Group but was discontinued upon the arrival of the 5th Transportation Command. Its assets became the U.S. Army Port, Tan My (Provisional).

Cam Ranh Bay Transportation Command, Provisional

No Insignia
Authorized

Arrived Vietnam: 26 November 1967
Departed Vietnam: 1 January 1969
Previous Station: Vietnam
Authorized Strength: Unknown

The Cam Ranh Bay Transportation Command (Provisional) was established to provide command and control of all motor transportation units at Cam Ranh Bay by the U.S. Army Support Command, Cam Ranh Bay.

8th Transportation Group (Motor Transport)

Arrived Vietnam: 19 October 1966
Departed Vietnam: 28 April 1971
Previous Station: Fort Lewis
Authorized Strength: HHD – 59 (1968)

The 8th Transportation Group (Motor Transport) was capable of commanding, planning and supervising the activities of three to seven motor transport battalions. Signal and flight support augmentation provided additional long-range communications and control abilities and improved coordinated defense of the unit's area. The group was responsible for line haul motor transport operations in the northern portion of II Corps Tactical Zone and served with the U.S. Army Support Command, Qui Nhon. It was initially located at Qui Nhon, then moved to Da Nang in November 1970.

48th Transportation Group (Motor Transport)

Arrived Vietnam: 8 May 1966
Departed Vietnam: 13 June 1972*
Previous Station: Fort Eustis

Authorized Strength	1966	1968	1971
HHD		59	59	39

* On August 1970 group reduced to zero strength and spaces used for the DELTA Logistical Support Activity.

The 48th Transportation Group (Motor Transport) had the specific mission of carrying out motor transport operations in the III and IV Corps Tactical Zones, including line haul, local haul within the Long Binh post, port and beach operations, retrograde equipment transport, and driveaway operation at Newport Terminal. Serving under the U.S. Army Support Command, Saigon, it was variously located at Qui Nhon, Long Binh and Binh Thuy.

500th Transportation Group (Motor Transport)

Arrived Vietnam: 18 October 1966
Departed Vietnam: 15 October 1969
Previous Station: Fort Campbell
Authorized Strength: HHD – 59 (1968)

The 500th Transportation Group (Motor Transport) supported the logistical effort of U.S. Army Support Command, Cam Ranh Bay. The group was stationed at Cam Ranh Bay and had the specific mission of providing motor transport operations for the southern portion of II Corps Tactical Zone under the control of the U.S. Support Command, Cam Ranh Bay. On 1 May 1969 it was reorganized as Special Troops, Cam Ranh Bay and given responsibility over post and station functions.

507th Transportation Group (Traffic Management Agency, MACV)

Arrived Vietnam: 7 February 1966
Departed Vietnam: 14 December 1971
Previous Station: Fort Eustis

Authorized Strength	1966	1968	1971
HHC	287	401	323

The 507th Transportation Group (Movement Control) had the mission of planning and programming nontactical movements of personnel, material and supplies (except bulk POL—petrol, oil, lubricants) within the field army area, with the exception of those between general support/direct support groups and their supported units. It was also responsible for maintaining liaison with transportation elements of other component U.S. forces and with allied and South Vietnamese transportation agencies. The group provided a central organization and field offices required to manage planned movements. It was stationed at Tan Son Nhut and Saigon under the control of the U.S. Army Support Command, Saigon. On 9 March 1966 it was designated the Traffic Management Agency, MACV with the mission of transportation movement control and the management of the MACV common service-user transportation service in Vietnam.

1st Transportation Battalion (Aircraft Maintenance Depot, Seaborne)

Arrived Vietnam: 1 April 1966
Departed Vietnam: 31 October 1972
Previous Station: USNS *Corpus Christie Bay*

Authorized Strength	1966	1968	1970
Battalion	380	366	365

The 1st Transportation Battalion (Aircraft Maintenance Depot, Seaborne) was a unique augmentation of the U.S. Army helicopter maintenance capability. Based on a converted Navy seaplane tender, the USNS *Corpus Christie Bay,* the ship and battalion became a mobile maintenance facility staffed by civilian experts and a work force consisting of U.S. Army technicians. With its machine shops, technical library and relatively safe working area, the *Corpus Christie Bay* provided a maintenance back-up capability equivalent to a major rebuilding facility. The ship operated near combat areas, initially in the III Corps Tactical Zone and later at Cam Ranh Bay and other locations in II Corps. Through efforts such as these, the U.S. Army was able to maintain helicopters in numbers sufficient to meet the full range of combat operations. The battalion was under the control of the 34th General Support Group in Vietnam, where it served as limited depot support to the group as a whole.

5th Transportation Battalion (Aircraft Maintenance)

Arrived Vietnam: 1 July 1968
Departed Vietnam: 18 January 1972
Previous Station: Vietnam

Authorized Strength	1968	1971
Battalion	599	582

The 5th Transportation Battalion (Aircraft Maintenance) provided division-level aircraft maintenance to the 101st Airborne Division (Airmobile) in Vietnam.

6th Transportation Battalion (Motor Transport)

Arrived Vietnam: 13 August 1966
Departed Vietnam: 13 June 1972
Previous Station: Fort Eustis

Authorized Strength	1966	1968	1971
HHD	43	43	33

The 6th Transportation Battalion (Motor Transport) provided command and supervision of units engaged in all types of motor transport such as direct support of tactical units, traffic routing, depot and terminal operations, line hauls (military convoys) and through-put motor service in both III and IV Corps Tactical Zones. The battalion served as part of the 48th Transportation Group at Long Binh, later in 1971 coming under the control of the 4th Transportation Command and the U.S. Support Command, Saigon, but always headquartered at Long Binh.

7th Transportation Battalion (Motor Transport)

Arrived Vietnam: 2 August 1966
Departed Vietnam: 29 March 1972
Previous Station: Fort Campbell

Authorized Strength	1966	1968	1971
HHD	43	43	33

The 7th Transportation Battalion (Motor Transport) provided support to the 48th Transportation Group at Long Binh, later in 1971 coming under the control of the 4th Transportation Command and the U.S. Army Support Command, Saigon (for capabilities, see 6th Transportation Battalion).

10th Transportation Battalion (Terminal)

Arrived Vietnam: 19 September 1965
Departed Vietnam: 30 November 1971
Previous Station: Fort Story

Authorized Strength	1966	1968	1970
HHD	56	55	56

The 10th Transportation Battalion (Terminal) had the fourfold mission of (1) providing command, (2) administrating and supervising units of the type usually assigned and attached to transportation terminals and engaged in operation of logistical over-the-shore (LOTS) sites, (3) transferring of personnel and cargo from one mode of transportation to another at its water terminals, and (4) line haul operations. The battalion was stationed at the Cam Ranh Bay Terminal under the 124th Transportation Command during its service in Vietnam. On 21 July 1969 it assumed control of Phan Rang and Phan Thiet outports.

11th Transportation Battalion (Terminal)

Arrived Vietnam: 5 August 1965
Departed Vietnam: 12 February 1970
Previous Station: Fort Eustis

Authorized Strength	1966	1968
HHD	56	53

The 11th Transportation Battalion (Terminal) at Saigon had capabilities similar to those of the 10th Transportation Battalion. The battalion was moved in February 1967 to Cat Lai under the 4th Transportation Command of the U.S. Army Support Command, Saigon. It was initially responsible for the Saigon Army Terminal and Vung Tau port operations and, while at Cat Lai, ran the terminal there.

14th Transportation Battalion (Aircraft Maintenance Support)

Arrived Vietnam: 19 September 1965
Departed Vietnam: 29 April 1972
Previous Station: Atlanta Army Depot

Authorized Strength	1966	1968	1971
HHD	137	81	74

The 14th Transportation Battalion (Aircraft Maintenance Support) provided command, control, staff supervision and planning for subordinate transportation aircraft maintenance and supply companies. It provided direct, general and back-up aircraft; avionics; armament maintenance; and supply support to all aviation units in I and II CTZ. Later it only supported II CTZ aviation requirements. The battalion served under the 34th General Support Group at Nha Trang and after April 1971 at Tuy Hoa.

15th Transportation Battalion (Aircraft Maintenance)

Arrived Vietnam: 14 September 1965
Departed Vietnam: 27 April 1971
Previous Station: Fort Benning

Authorized Strength	1966	1968	1970
Battalion	1,428	1,428	600

The 15th Transportation Battalion (Aircraft Maintenance) was part of the 1st Cavalry Division (Airmobile) in Vietnam and was one of the largest in the army. The battalion's shops were equipped to handle any electrical, hydraulics or avionics problem. In mid-1969 the battalion underwent a massive reorganization and two companies were dropped; instead, separate maintenance detachments were assigned to each company-sized aviation unit within the division.

24th Transportation Battalion (Terminal)

Arrived Vietnam: 24 June 1966
Departed Vietnam: 23 May 1972
Previous Station: Fort Eustis

Authorized Strength	1966	1968	1970
HHD	58	58	58

The 24th Transportation Battalion (Terminal) directed activities of its assigned terminal and lighterage units at Vung Ro, Nha Trang, Phan Rang, Phan Thiet and Tuy Hoa. The battalion was located at Cam Ranh Bay under control of the 124th Transportation Command and U.S. Army Support Command, Cam Ranh Bay. On 15 May 1968 it assumed command of the Vung Ro outport and later was retailored to conduct line and local hauls throughout the southern II Corps Tactical Zone.

27th Transportation Battalion (Motor Transport)

Arrived Vietnam: 27 October 1965
Departed Vietnam: 10 May 1972
Previous Station: Fort Eustis

Authorized Strength	1966	1968	1970
HHD	45	45	45

The 27th Transportation Battalion (Motor Transport) had the same capabilities as the 6th Transportation Battalion. It was located initially at Qui Nhon but then moved to the control of the Qui Nhon Sub Area Command and was stationed at Phu Tai in October 1966 under the 8th Transportation Group, where it remained until departing Vietnam. It was responsible for northern II CTZ.

36th Transportation Battalion (Motor Transport)

Arrived Vietnam: 31 July 1966
Departed Vietnam: 13 August 1970
Previous Station: Fort Bragg
Authorized Strength: HHD – 43

The 36th Transportation Battalion (Motor Transport) had the same capabilities as the 6th Transportation Battalion. It served with the 500th Transportation Group and later with the U.S. Support Command, Cam Ranh Bay at Cam Ranh Bay.

39th Transportation Battalion (Motor Transport)

Arrived Vietnam: 31 July 1966
Departed Vietnam: 9 March 1972
Previous Station: Fort Benning

Authorized Strength	1966	1968	1970
HHD		43	43	45

The 39th Transportation Battalion (Motor Transport) had capabilities similar to those of the 6th Transportation Battalion. It was stationed at Cam Ranh Bay. On 28 November 1966 it went to Tuy Hoa and in late 1967 went to Phan Rang under the Phan Rang Sub Area Command. But on 2 May 1968 it moved north to Gia Le under the U.S. Army Support Command, Da Nang and later served with the 26th General Support Group there. In May 1969 it made its final move to Gia Le.

45th Transportation Battalion (Transport Aircraft)

No Insignia Authorized

Arrived Vietnam: 1 July 1962
Departed Vietnam: 24 September 1963
Previous Station: Fort Sill
Authorized Strength: HHD – 73

The 45th Transportation Battalion was deployed to provide command, control, staff planning and administrative supervision over the employment of several army transportation (CH-21) light helicopter companies and one aviation company composed of U-1A Otter aircraft. Besides the planning and supervisory duties, it also was responsible for overseeing maintenance, logistical and medical service for its assigned and attached units. Its assets were used to form the 145th Aviation Battalion.

Aircraft Company*	Type	Battalion Service/Remarks
8th Tr Co	Lt Hel	July 62 – June 63 See note
18th Avn Co	FWT	July 62 – Sept. 63 Transferred to 145th Avn Bn
33d Tr Co	Lt Hel	Sept. 62 – June 63 See note
57th Tr Co	Lt Hel	July 62 – June 63 See note

81st Tr Co	Lt Hel	July 62 – June 63
		See note
93d Tr Co	Lt Hel	July 62 – June 63
		See note

*See Transportation Company listing for complete Vietnam service of above listed transportation companies. On 25 June 1963 the assets of these transportation companies became the basis for the 117th, 118th, 119th, 120th and 121st Aviation Companies and their further Vietnam service can be traced in the Aviation Company section.

54th Transportation Battalion (Motor Transport)

Arrived Vietnam: 23 October 1966
Departed Vietnam: 13 August 1970
Previous Station: Fort Lewis
Authorized Strength: HHD – 41 (1968)

The 54th Transportation Battalion (Motor Transport) had capabilities similar to those of the 6th Transportation Battalion. The battalion served at Qui Nhon, where it was subordinate to the 8th Transportation Group. In February 1969 it was posted by the group to Cha Rang.

57th Transportation Battalion (Motor Transport)

Arrived Vietnam: 1 October 1966
Departed Vietnam: 24 October 1972
Previous Station: Fort Riley
Authorized Strength: HHD – 41

The 57th Transportation Battalion (Motor Transport) had capabilities similar to those of the 6th Transportation Battalion. The battalion served with the 500th Transportation Group at Cam Ranh Bay initially but was moved north to Quang Tri under the U.S. Army Support Command, Da Nang in March 1968 and later served with the 5th Transportation Command. In April 1969 it went to Chu Lai under the 80th General Support Group and to Da Nang in 1971.

58th Transportation Battalion (Aircraft Maintenance & Support)

Arrived Vietnam: 11 April 1966
Departed Vietnam: 29 April 1972
Previous Station: Fort Benning

Authorized Strength	1966	1968	1970
HHD	51	50	45

The 58th Transportation Battalion (Aircraft Maintenance & Support) was assigned as Aircraft Material Management Command (AMMC) on 15 April 1966 with the mission of providing the supply and maintenance function for all army aircraft in Vietnam. The battalion was located at Saigon until February 1968 when it was posted north to Da Nang, though it remained under the 34th General Support Group throughout its service in Vietnam. On 20 February 1968 the battalion ceased its role as AMMC and reverted to providing direct, back-up and general support maintenance for aircraft, armament and avionics equipment supply support in I Corps Tactical Zone.

71st Transportation Battalion (Terminal)

Arrived Vietnam: 7 September 1966
Departed Vietnam: 20 August 1972
Previous Station: Fort Story

Authorized Strength	1968	1971
HHD	58	37

The 71st Transportation Battalion (Terminal) had general capabilities similar to those of the 10th Transportation Battalion. The battalion served under the 4th Transportation Command and the U.S. Army Support Command, Saigon at Long Binh and at the Saigon – Newport complex during its service in Vietnam.

124th Transportation Battalion (Motor Transport)

Arrived Vietnam: 24 July 1967
Departed Vietnam: 16 May 1971
Previous Station: Fort Devens
Authorized Strength: HHD – 43

The 124th Transportation Battalion (Motor Transport) had capabilities generally similar to those of the 6th Transportation Battalion. The battalion was stationed in the Pleiku vicinity where it served under control of the 8th Transportation Group and the 4th Infantry Division. In August 1970 it moved to Cha Rang under the 8th Transportation Group.

159th Transportation Battalion (Terminal)

Arrived Vietnam: 10 August 1966
Departed Vietnam: 29 June 1971
Previous Station: Fort Eustis
Authorized Strength: HHD – 58

The 159th Transportation Battalion (Terminal) had responsibilities over lighterage and stevedore functions. The battalion served with the 5th Transportation Command at Qui Nhon and was assigned to the U.S. Army Support Command, Da Nang upon activation and posted to Vung Tau 1 April 1969. It transferred to Cat Lai after 7 January 1970 upon the phasedown of Vung Tau. It also served with the U.S. Army Support Command, Saigon during its service in Vietnam.

394th Transportation Battalion (Terminal)

Arrived Vietnam: 7 August 1965
Departed Vietnam: 26 November 1970
Previous Station: Fort Eustis

Authorized Strength	1966	1968
HHD	56	54

The 394th Transportation Battalion (Terminal) had the same general capabilities as the 10th Transportation Battalion. It served with the 5th Transportation Command at Qui Nhon during its service in Vietnam.

520th Transportation Battalion (Aircraft Maintenance & Support)

Arrived Vietnam: 24 March 1967
Departed Vietnam: 29 April 1972
Previous Station: Fort Benning

Authorized Strength	1968	1971
HHD	80	73

The 520th Transportation Battalion (Aircraft Maintenance & Support) was organized to provide army aircraft maintenance and supply support, aircraft recovery, aviation electronics and armament support requirements in the northern portion of III Corps Tactical Zone. The battalion was located at Phu Loi under the 34th General Support Group throughout its service in Vietnam.

765th Transportation Battalion (Aircraft Maintenance & Support)

Arrived Vietnam: 30 September 1965
Departed Vietnam: 29 April 1972
Previous Station: Vietnam

Authorized Strength	1966	1968	1971
HHD	67	81	74

The 765th Transportation Battalion (Aircraft Maintenance & Support) directed general, direct and back-up support in areas of airframe, engines, aircraft systems, armament and all navigation-

al and communications equipment for the southern portion of III CTZ and all of IV CTZ. The battalion was stationed at Vung Tau under the 34th General Support Group for the duration of its Vietnam service.

Unauthorized

Transportation Battalion Saigon, Provisional (Terminal Service & Boat Transport)

Arrived Vietnam: 25 May 1969
Departed Vietnam: 31 January 1970
Previous Station: Vietnam
Authorized Strength: Unknown

The Transportation Battalion, Saigon (Provisional) was a boat transport battalion serving under the U.S. Army Support Command, Saigon and the 4th Transportation Command. It operated the Saigon port, replacing the 125th Transportation Command.

Provisional Terminal Transportation Battalion

No Insignia
Authorized

Arrived Vietnam: 13 August 1971
Departed Vietnam: 28 November 1971
Previous Station: Vietnam
Authorized Strength: Unknown

The Provisional Terminal Transportation Battalion was formed by the U.S. Army to render assistance to the port of Da Nang during the latter half of 1971.

TRANSPORTATION COMPANIES IN VIETNAM

Company	Type	Previous Station	Vietnam Service	Typical Location	Authorized Strength		
					1966	1968	1970
2d TR	Composite Medium Truck (12-t)	Ord	31 Aug. 65 – 1 April 72	Phu Tai	186	183	186
5th TR	Heavy Boat	Eustis	20 Feb. 67 – 29 April 72	Vung Tau	—	171	171
8th TR	Light Helicopter (CH-21)	Bragg	11 Dec. 61 – 25 June 63	Qui Nhon	208 (Feb 63)		
9th TR	Airborne Car (Sedan)	Bragg	14 Aug. 66 – 28 April 72	Long Binh	107	107	107
10th TR	Medium Cargo Truck (12-t)	Eustis	6 Sept. 65 – 5 March 72	Long Binh	186	183	186
20th TR	Aircraft Direct Support	Campbell	3 May 67 – 15 March 71	Cu Chi	—	244	242
24th TR	Light Truck (2½-t)/ Medium Cargo Truck (12-t)	Bragg	31 Aug. 66 – 27 June 72	Cam Ranh Bay	174	183	183
31st TR	Medium Boat	Vietnam	6 Nov. 68 – 1 June 69	Dong Tam	—	181	—
33d TR	Light Helicopter (CH-21)	Ord	17 Sept. 62 – 25 June 63	Bien Hoa	194 (Feb 63)		
47th TR	Medium Petroleum Truck	Lee	1 Nov. 66 – 22 June 72	Long Binh	—	183	184
56th TR	Aircraft Direct Support	Lewis	16 Oct. 64 – 30 April 72	Tan Son Nhut	244	244	244
57th TR	Light Helicopter (CH-21)	Lewis	11 Dec. 61 – 25 June 63	Bear Cat	174 (Feb 63)		
57th TR*	Light Truck (5-t)	Devens	31 July 67 – 26 Dec. 71	Chu Lai	—	179	179
58th TR	Light Truck (2½-t)	Wood	27 Aug. 65 – 4 March 69	Phu Tai	174	175	—
61st TR	Medium Petroleum Truck	Eustis	31 Aug. 65 – 1 Nov. 69	Cam Ranh Bay	186	183	—
62d TR	Medium Cargo Truck (12-t)	Eustis	15 Sept. 65 – 29 April 72	Long Binh	184	183	184
63d TR	Light Truck (2½ and 5-t)	Eustis	27 Aug. 65 – 30 April 71	Phu Bai	174	179	179
64th TR	Medium Cargo Truck (12-t)	Bragg	4 Aug. 66 – 16 June 71	Pleiku	186	183	178
71st TR	Terminal Service	Eustis	27 Aug. 65 – 3 Feb. 68	Dong Ha	329	—	—
79th TR	Aircraft Direct Support	Hood	27 Aug. 65 – 30 April 72	Qui Nhon	244	244	244
81st TR	Light Helicopter (CH-21)	Hawaii	17 Sept. 62 – 25 June 63	Pleiku	200 (Feb 63)		
82d TR	Amphibious General Support	Story	3 Sept. 65 – 1 July 66	Cam Ranh Bay	185	—	—
86th TR	Medium Cargo Truck (12-t)	Campbell	12 Aug. 66 – 30 June 72	Long Binh	174	183	174
87th TR	Light Truck (2½-t)	Lewis	5 Oct. 66 – June 69	Long Binh	—	175	—
88th TR	Light Truck (2½-t)/ Medium Cargo Truck (12-t)	Hood	30 Aug. 66 – 1 May 72	Pleiku	174	183	178
93d TR	Light Helicopter (CH-21)	Devens	26 Jan. 62 – 25 June 63	Soc Trang	222 (Feb 63)		

97th TR	Heavy Boat	Eustis	31 May 65 – 2 March 72	Cam Ranh Bay	171	171	128
101st TR (Prov)	Motor Transport – 101st Abn Div	Vietnam	27 March 68 – Unknown	Gia Le	—	?	—
108th TR	Car (Sedan)	Vietnam	4 March 69 – 16 April 72	Phu Bai	—	—	75
110th TR	Depot	Eustis	4 Nov. 65 – 30 Sept. 72	Tan Son Nhut	116	233	195
116th TR	Terminal Service	Okinawa	16 Dec. 65 – 17 Feb. 69	Cam Ranh Bay	329	329	—
117th TR	Terminal Service	Eustis	4 Sept. 65 – 3 Feb. 68	Tuy Hoa	329	—	—
119th TR	Terminal Service	Eustis	31 Aug. 65 – 30 June 71	Vung Ro Bay	329	329	—
120th TR	Light Truck (2½-t)	Meade	25 June 65 – 16 Aug. 72	Can Tho	174	175	174
123d TR	Terminal Service	Eustis	30 May 65 – 20 Dec. 68	Cam Ranh Bay	329	329	—
124th TR	Terminal Service	Eustis	29 Nov. 65 – 15 March 71	Cat Lo	329	329	—
142d TR	Aircraft Maintenance Direct Spt	Campbell	23 Oct. 68 – 13 March 73	Phu Bai	—	244	241
151st TR	Light Truck (2½-t)	Campbell	2 Sept. 65 – June 69	Long Binh	174	175	—
154th TR	Terminal Service	Okinawa	1 Jan. 67 – 22 April 71	Long Binh	—	329	329
155th TR	Terminal Service	Story	4 June 65 – 27 June 72	Cam Ranh Bay	329	329	329
163d TR	Light Truck (2½-t)	Sill	12 Sept. 65 – 8 Dec. 67	Chu Lai	174	—	—
165th TR	Light Amphibious/ Aircraft Direct Support	Vietnam	25 Sept. 69 – 30 April 72	Phu Loi	—	—	241
172d TR †	Medium Cargo Truck	Lewis	11 Oct. 68 – 27 Sept. 69	Cam Ranh Bay	—	183	—
231st TR ‡	Medium Boat	Eustis	7 Sept. 68 – 25 Aug. 69	Vung Tau	—	183	—
233d TR	Heavy Truck (12-t)	Vietnam	20 Oct. 69 – 30 April 72	Long Binh	—	—	150
241st TR	Depot	Eustis	5 Feb. 66 – 4 June 71	Qui Nhon	116	233	159
261st TR	Light Truck (5-t)	Campbell	5 Oct. 66 – 15 Aug. 72	Long Binh	—	179	181
264th TR	Terminal Service	Eustis	16 Oct. 66 – 27 Nov. 72	Qui Nhon	—	329	329
285th TR	Terminal Service	Okinawa	16 Dec. 65 – 26 Nov. 70	Qui Nhon	329	329	329
297th TR	Car (Sedan)	Lewis	5 Oct. 66 – 20 March 72	Nha Trang	—	107	107
300th TR	Terminal Service	Eustis	10 Oct. 66 – 3 Feb. 68	Qui Nhon	—	329	—
303d TR	Aircraft Maintenance General Support	Benning	23 Sept. 68 – 4 Feb. 70	Long Thanh	—	253	—
319th TR §	Light Truck (5-t)	Lee	27 Sept. 68 – 13 Aug. 69	Long Binh	—	133	—
321st TR	Medium Cargo Truck (12-t)	Meade	26 Dec. 67 – 31 March 72	Long Binh	—	183	183
329th TR	Heavy Boat	Eustis	24 May 66 – 2 April 72	Da Nang	121	121	171
330th TR	Aircraft General Support	Travis AFB	22 April 63 – 30 April 72	Vung Tau	253	253	236
335th TR	Aircraft Direct Support	Bragg	1 Nov. 65 – 25 Nov. 71	Chu Lai	247	247	247
339th TR	Aircraft Direct Support	Riley	7 Feb. 62 – 1 July 68	Da Nang	244	—	—
344th TR	Light Amphibious (LARC)	Story	2 June 65 – 20 Oct. 67	Cam Ranh Bay	207	—	—
344th TR*	Aircraft Direct Support	Vietnam	31 Aug. 71 – 30 April 72	Tan Son Nhut	—	—	—
347th TR	Light Amphibious (LARC)	Story	30 May 65 – 10 Aug. 67	Cam Ranh Bay	207	—	—
352d TR	Light Truck (5-t)	Carson	8 Jan. 68 – 20 Oct. 69	Long Binh	—	179	—
357th TR ‖	Aircraft Maintenance Direct Support	Benning	15 Oct. 68 – 29 Sept. 69	Bien Hoa	—	265	—
359th TR	Medium Petroleum Truck	Riley	19 Oct. 66 – 1 May 72	Qui Nhon	—	183	184
360th TR	Medium Petroleum Truck	Riley	20 Oct. 66 – 10 May 72	Cam Ranh Bay	—	183	184
363d TR	Medium Cargo Truck (12-t)	Riley	30 Aug. 67 – 17 March 72	Dong Ha	—	183	183
368th TR	Terminal Service	Meade	21 Oct. 66 – 27 June 72	Long Binh	—	329	329
372d TR	Terminal Transfer	Vietnam	20 Dec. 68 – 21 June 72	Duc Pho	—	—	266
379th TR	Medium Reefer Truck (7½-t)	Vietnam	6 Nov. 68 – 29 June 72	Cam Ranh Bay	—	—	251
387th TR	Terminal Service	Eustis	11 Sept. 66 – 26 Nov. 70	Qui Nhon	—	329	329
388th TR	Aircraft Direct Support	Riley	9 March 67 – 13 March 73	Vung Tau	—	244	244
402d TR	Terminal Transfer	Campbell	6 Oct. 66 – 30 June 71	Long Binh	—	266	266
403d TR	Terminal Transfer	Bragg	17 Oct. 66 – 17 Feb. 72	Dong Ha	—	266	264
410th TR	Terminal Service	Benning	31 Aug. 66 – 3 Feb. 68	Cam Ranh Bay	329	—	—
435th TR (Prov)	Medium Cargo Truck (12-t)	Vietnam	28 Sept. 69 – unknown	Unknown	—	—	—
440th TR	Terminal Transfer	Vietnam	4 March 69 – 30 April 72	Can Tho	—	—	266
442d TR	Medium Cargo Truck (12-t)	Meade	23 Dec. 66 – 30 April 72	Cam Ranh Bay	—	183	184
444th TR	Light Truck (2½-t)/ Medium Cargo Truck (12-t)	Riley	28 Oct. 65 – 28 Nov. 71	Phu Tai	174	183	178
446th TR	Medium Cargo Truck (12-t)	Meade	19 Nov. 66 – 30 Sept. 72	Dong Ha	—	183	184
458th TR	River Patrol Boat	Story	13 Oct. 66 – 1 Sept. 71	Vung Tau	—	197	197
512th TR	Light Truck (5-t)	Campbell	23 Oct. 66 – 10 May 72	Qui Nhon	—	179	181
515th TR	Light Truck (2½- and 5-t)	Benning	14 July 65 – 20 March 72	Phu Bai	174	179	179
523d TR	Light Truck (5-t)	Campbell	23 Oct. 66 – 20 March 72	Qui Nhon	—	179	181
529th TR	Light Truck (2½-t)	Eustis	2 Jan. 67 – 4 March 69	Tuy Hoa	—	175	—
534th TR	Medium Cargo Truck (12-t)	Campbell	11 April 66 – 22 June 72	Long Binh	186	183	186
538th TR	Medium Petroleum Truck	Bragg	4 June 66 – 1 Jan. 72	Long Binh	184	183	184
539th TR	Aircraft General Maintenance Support	Cumberland	3 May 67 – 30 June 71	Phu Loi	—	254	236

Unit	Type	Station	Dates	Location			
540th TR	Aircraft Maintenance General Support	Atlanta	19 Sept. 65 – 30 April 71	Qui Nhon	256	289	236
541st TR	Light Truck (2½-t)	Bragg	2 Sept. 65 – 15 March 71	Pleiku	174	175	170
543d TR	Light Truck (2½-t)	Campbell	16 Oct. 66 – 10 Dec. 70	Long Binh	—	175	178
544th TR	Medium Boat	Okinawa	21 Jan. 66 – 20 March 72	Vung Tau	180	180	181
545th TR	Light Truck (5-t)	Campbell	18 Oct. 66 – 31 Jan. 72	Cam Ranh Bay	—	179	181
551st TR	Terminal Service	Eustis	11 Sept. 66 – 30 June 71	Long Binh	—	329	329
552d TR	Car (Sedan)	Lewis	10 March 66 – 31 July 72	Long Binh	130	130	130
556th TR	Medium Petroleum Truck	Lewis	16 Oct. 65 – 8 April 70	Long Binh	184	183	171
561st TR	Terminal Service	Eustis	23 Oct. 66 – 20 Dec. 68	Quang Tri	—	329	—
563d TR	Medium Cargo Truck (12-t)	Lewis	23 Oct. 66 – 30 Nov. 71	Pleiku	—	183	184
565th TR	Terminal Service	Eustis	25 June 65 – 4 March 69	Can Tho	329	329	—
566th TR	Medium Cargo Truck (12-t)	Meade	2 Jan. 67 – 31 Jan. 72	Cam Ranh Bay	—	183	184
567th TR	Terminal Service	Eustis	7 Sept. 66 – 16 April 72	Long Binh	—	329	329
572d TR	Medium Cargo Truck (12-t)	Meade	19 Nov. 66 – 24 March 73	Quang Tri	—	183	184
585th TR	Medium Cargo Truck (12-t)	Lewis	18 Oct. 66 – 22 June 72	Phu Bai	—	183	186
588th TR	Depot	Atlanta	2 Nov. 66 – 1 Sept. 68	Cam Ranh Bay	—	115	—
592d TR	Light Truck (5-t)	Campbell	18 Oct. 66 – 1 May 72	Cam Ranh Bay	—	179	181
597th TR	Medium Cargo Truck (12-t)	Eustis	23 July 65 – 1 May 72	Phu Tai	186	183	186
604th TR	Aircraft Direct Support	Campbell	7 March 66 – 13 March 73	Pleiku	247	247	247
605th TR	Aircraft Direct Support	Riley	8 March 66 – 1 May 72	Phu Loi	247	247	247
608th TR	Aircraft Direct Support	Bragg	23 July 67 – 30 April 72	Dong Ba Thinh	—	247	247
610th TR	Aircraft Maintenance General Support	Benning	1 Oct. 66 – 30 April 72	An Khe	—	289	306
611th TR	Aircraft Direct Support	Riley	5 Oct. 62 – 13 March 73	Vinh Long	244	244	244
630th TR#	Medium Cargo Truck	Meade	5 Sept. 68 – 2 Aug. 69	Phu Bai	—	183	—
666th TR	Light Truck (2½-t)	Benning	14 Aug. 67 – 4 Jan. 72	Cha Rang	—	175	175
669th TR	Light Truck (5-t)	Campbell	23 Oct. 66 – 15 March 71	Qui Nhon	—	179	174
670th TR	Medium Cargo Truck (12-t)	Hood	22 July 65 – 28 Oct. 71	Cam Ranh Bay	186	183	186
737th TR**	Medium Petroleum Truck	Lewis	18 Sept. 68 – 8 July 69	Quang Tri	—	183	—
805th TR	Light Truck (2½-t)/ Medium Truck (5-t)	Eustis	15 Oct. 66 – 20 March 72	Vung Tau	—	175	183
854th TR	Terminal Service	Story	12 Oct. 66 – 29 April 71	Qui Nhon	—	329	—
863d TR	Light Truck (2½-t)	Devens	12 Oct. 66 – 1 Aug. 70	Phu Bai	—	118	—
870th TR	Terminal Service	Story	18 Feb. 66 – 17 Feb. 72	Cam Ranh Bay	329	329	329
1097th TR	Medium Boat	Eustis	30 May 65 – 26 July 69	Dong Tam	181	246	—
1098th TR	Medium Boat	Eustis	30 May 65 – 17 Feb. 72	Qui Nhon	181	181	181
1099th TR	Medium Boat	Eustis	10 Nov. 65 – 28 Feb. 72	Cat Lai	181	181	181
"GOER" TR (Prov)	GOER Rough-terrain Cargo Carrier	Vietnam	1 Sept. 66 – 20 Oct. 69	Phuoc Vinh	—	?	—
Provisional Corps Transportation Company		Vietnam	3 April 68 – 4 March 69	Da Nang	—	?	—

Additionally, there were numerous provisional transportation companies formed on a temporary basis by support commands and composite service battalions.

* Second tour in Vietnam.

† Nebraska Army Reserve from Omaha via Ft. Lewis.

‡ Florida Army Reserve from St. Petersburg via Ft. Eustis.

§ Georgia Army Reserve from Augusta via Ft. Lee.

‖ Pennsylvania Army Reserve from Greencastle via Ft. Benning.

Pennsylvania Army Reserve from Washington via Ft. Meade.

** Washington Army Reserve from Yakima via Ft. Lewis.

Special
Warfare Units

Chapter 24

Army Security Agency

U.S. Army Security Agency Group, Vietnam*

Arrived Vietnam: 23 May 1961
(Provisional)
20 September 1961
(Nonprovisional)
Departed Vietnam: 7 March 1973
Previous Station: Vietnam

Authorized Strength	1964	1966	1968	1970
Headquarters	543	480	324	421

* See narrative for full details of evolution.

Since the U.S. Army Security Agency (USASA) command and control headquarters in Vietnam underwent numerous changes in numerical designation, they have all been grouped together under the title of the final headquarters in Vietnam. It should be remembered that all missions of this agency were highly classified during the war and secret cover designations (Radio Research Units) utilized in lieu of the actual unit designations on station lists and reports, rather than the true designations as given below. The 400th USASA Operations Unit (Provisional) was first organized at Saigon on 23 May 1961. This formation was soon replaced by an authorized formation, the 82d USASA Special Operations Unit, on 20 September 1961. This unit in turn was redesignated as the 53d USASA Special Operations Command on 1 November 1964. Less than two years later on 1 June 1966 this command was replaced by the 509th USASA Operations Group with a headquarters of 124 personnel (the 1966 strength given above is for the 53d USASA Command headquarters only). The group was finally redesignated as the USASA Group, Vietnam, on 15 December 1967. In March 1973 the USASA Group, Vietnam was discontinued. The headquarters of all these formations were located in Saigon.

8th U.S. Army Security Agency Field Station

No Insignia Authorized

Arrived Vietnam: 1 November 1964
Departed Vietnam: 26 February 1973
Previous Station: Vietnam

Authorized Strength	1966	1968	1970
Station	828	1,076	1,045

The 8th U.S. Army Security Agency Field Station was organized at Phu Bai and handled classified functions related to the safeguarding of the Army and its affiliated activities including signal security and electronic intelligence. It was redesignated as the U.S. Army Security Agency Field Station, Phu Bai on 15 December 1967 and relocated on 1 November 1972 (without a change in designation) to Da Nang, where it was discontinued in February 1973.

224th U.S. Army Security Agency Battalion (Aviation)

Arrived Vietnam: 1 June 1966
Departed Vietnam: 7 March 1973
Previous Station: Vietnam

Authorized Strength	1966	1968	1970
HHD	84	101	94

The 224th U.S. Army Security Agency Battalion was an aviation unit based at Tan Son Nhut and moved to Long Than North in August 1970. Five USASA aviation companies served with the battalion exclusively: the 1st (Special Aircraft) and the 138th, 144th, 146th and 156th (OV-1 Fixed Wing). Their exact terms of service can be found in the USASA company listings.

303d U.S. Army Security Agency Battalion

Arrived Vietnam: 8 May 1966
Departed Vietnam: 15 June 1971
Previous Station: Fort Wolters

Authorized Strength	1966	1968	1970
HHC	213	274	215

The 303d U.S. Army Security Agency Battalion's lettered companies were all redesignated—Company A became the 372d USASA Company, Company C became the 374th USASA Company and Company B did not serve in Vietnam. The battalion headquarters was located at Long Binh. All missions were classified during the Vietnam war.

313th U.S. Army Security Agency Battalion

Arrived Vietnam: March 1965
Departed Vietnam: 15 June 1971
Previous Station: Fort Bragg

Authorized Strength	1966	1968	1970
HHC	213	254	240

The 313th U.S. Army Security Agency Battalion's lettered companies were all redesignated—Company A became the 358th USASA Platoon (which served with the 3d Brigade, 82d Airborne Division at Phu Bai 24 June 1968 – 11 December 1969); Company B became the 337th USASA Company; and Company C became the 371st USASA Company. The battalion headquarters was located at Nha Trang. All missions were classified during the Vietnam war.

ARMY SECURITY AGENCY COMPANIES IN VIETNAM

Company	Type	Previous Station	Vietnam Service	Typical Location	1966	1968	1970
1st ASA	Aviation	Huachuca	3 July 67 – 30 April 72	Cam Ranh Bay	—	215	216
101st ASA*	Security	Vietnam	1 March 63 – 15 Dec. 67	Saigon	192	—	—
138th ASA	Aviation	Vietnam	1 June 66 – 1 March 73	Da Nang	192	237	261
144th ASA	Aviation	Vietnam	1 June 66 – July 72	Nha Trang	192	237	182
146th ASA	Aviation	Vietnam	1 June 66 – 17 Feb. 73	Tan Son Nhut	192	253	245
156th ASA	Aviation	Vietnam	1 June 66 – 20 April 72	Can Tho	167	170	162
175th ASA †	Operations	Vietnam	1 June 66 – 15 Dec. 67	Bien Hoa	124	—	—
265th ASA	Division Spt – 101st Abn Div	Campbell	25 Nov. 67 – 1 April 72	Gia Le	—	216	158
328th ASA	Division Spt – AMERICAL Inf Div	Vietnam	20 Nov. 68 – 30 June 72	Chu Lai	—	216	148
330th ASA	Operations	Wolters	20 Aug. 66 – 30 Sept. 71	Pleiku	353	403	433
335th ASA	Division Spt – 9th Inf Div	Riley	12 Jan. 67 – 5 April 71	Dong Tam	—	157	157
337th ASA	Division Spt – 1st Inf Div	Campbell	20 Oct. 65 – 15 April 70	Di An	168	157	—
371st ASA	Division Spt – 1st Cav Div	Benning	10 Sept. 65 – 30 April 71	An Khe	114	157	71
372d ASA	Division Spt – 25th Inf Div	Carson	29 Jan. 66 – 6 March 71	Cu Chi	168	157	157
374th ASA	Division Spt – 4th Inf Div	Lewis	16 Sept. 66 – 7 Dec. 70	Pleiku	—	157	157
USASA Security Company, Saigon ‡		Vietnam	15 Dec. 67 – 1 April 72	Saigon	—	192	213
USASA Operations Company, Saigon		Vietnam	15 Dec. 67 – 15 July 68	Bien Hoa	—	252	—
USASA Operations Company, Bien Hoa §		Vietnam	15 July 68 – 26 Feb. 73	Bien Hoa	—	252	398
USASA Operations Company, Can Tho		Vietnam	5 April 71 – 30 June 72	Can Tho	—	—	—
USASA Field Station, Pleiku		Vietnam	30 Sept. 71 – 1 Sept. 72	Nha Trang	—	—	—

* Organized 1 March 1963 as detachment, expanded to company; redesignated USASA Security Company, Saigon 15 December 1967.

† Organized at Saigon but moved to Bien Hoa on 3 July 1967; redesignated USASA Operations Company, Saigon 15 December 1967 at Bien Hoa.

‡ Was located at Long Binh (without change in designation) 30 March 1970 – 15 March 1971; moved back to Saigon on 16 March 1971.

§ USASA Operations Company, Bien Hoa was a redesignation of USASA Operations Company, Saigon, which had always been located at Bien Hoa. This in turn was properly redesignated USASA Field Station, Bien Hoa on 30 September 1971 and moved to Saigon without changing designation on 29 September 1972. It was discontinued at Saigon 26 February 1973, as noted above.

Chapter 25

Military Intelligence

135th Military Intelligence Group (Counterintelligence)

No Insignia Authorized

Arrived Vietnam: 1 September 1966
Departed Vietnam: 25 September 1969
Previous Station: Fort Bragg
Authorized Strength: HHC – 114 (1968)

The 135th Military Intelligence Group (Counterintelligence) was colocated with the South Vietnamese Security Service in Saigon and later Tan Son Nhut. The group performed specialized, long-range, counterintelligence special operations and interrogation functions. It provided MACV with centralized and specialized interrogation in support of counterespionage, countersabotage and countersubversion operations. Additionally, it conducted counterintelligence operations to prevent, detect or neutralize hostile espionage activities at their base of operations. The group was composed of personnel with special skills and foreign language abilities in support of the joint command. Its personnel could also engage in effective coordinated defense of the unit's installation.

149th Military Intelligence Group (Collection)

No Insignia Authorized

Arrived Vietnam: 18 November 1966
Departed Vietnam: 25 September 1969
Previous Station: Fort Bragg
Authorized Strength: HHC – 189 (1968)

The mission of the 149th Military Intelligence Group (Collection) was to command, control and support assigned military intelli-

gence units; provide interrogation and document translation support; plan, conduct and/or support intelligence collection operations; infiltrate trained personnel into specified areas and extract by air, land or sea; provide selective examination, evaluation and classification of captured enemy materiel; provide specialized, long-range, counterintelligence special operations and specialized interrogation in support of counterespionage, countersabotage and countersubversion missions; advise and assist the South Vietnamese in intelligence collection; provide liaison with other commands and agencies as required; and provide military intelligence staff advice and planning assistance. The group was located at Tan Son Nhut.

525th Military Intelligence Group (Command Support)

Arrived Vietnam: 28 November 1965
Departed Vietnam: 3 March 1973
Previous Station: Fort Bragg

Authorized Strength	1966	1968	1971
HHC	47	47	175

The 525th Military Intelligence Group (Command Support) provided command, minus operational control, for all units of the group, and limited administrative and logistic support to organic and attached units. It augmented the joint command staff and the office of the assistant chief of staff, security, plans and operations of MACV and the intelligence directorates of the area support groups. In essence, the group rendered overall control and personnel support for all U.S. Army intelligence-related activities in Vietnam. The group was located at Tan Son Nhut.

1st Military Intelligence Battalion (Air Reconnaissance Support)

Arrived Vietnam: 23 December 1965
Departed Vietnam: 19 April 1971
Previous Station: Fort Bragg

Authorized Strength	1966	1968	1971
Battalion	279	319	139

The mission of the 1st Military Intelligence Battalion (Air Reconnaissance Support) was to process, interpret, annotate, reproduce and deliver imagery obtained from tactical air force reconnaissance elements; provide air reconnaissance liaison officers; provide deployed operations parallel to any dispersion of the tactical air force reconnaissance wing; and disseminate all intelligence information obtained through imagery information and visual sightings by the tactical air force reconnaissance elements. It was located at Saigon.

519th Military Intelligence Battalion (Consolidated)

Arrived Vietnam: 25 October 1965
Departed Vietnam: 18 October 1972
Previous Station: Fort Bragg

Authorized Strength	1966	1968	1971
Battalion	1,695	1,910	214

The 519th Military Intelligence Battalion (Consolidated) was directly responsible for the U.S. Army Combined Intelligence Center, Vietnam; the Combined Document Exploitation Center, Vietnam; the Combined Military Interrogation Center, Vietnam; and the Combined Material Exploitation Center, Vietnam. It was located in Saigon.

PROVISIONAL MILITARY INTELLIGENCE BATTALIONS

1st Military Intelligence Battalion, Provisional
20 Nov. 67 – July 70
Established to control field collection efforts out of Da Nang under the 525th Military Intelligence Group.

2d Military Intelligence Battalion, Provisional
1 Dec. 67 – July 70
Established to control military intelligence efforts out of Nha Trang under the 525th Military Intelligence Group.

3d Military Intelligence Battalion, Provisional
1 Dec. 67 – July 70
Established to control field collection efforts out of Bien Hoa under the 525th Military Intelligence Group.

4th Military Intelligence Battalion, Provisional
1 Dec. 67 – July 70
Established to control military intelligence efforts from Can Tho under the 525th Military Intelligence Group.

5th Military Intelligence Battalion, Provisional
1 Dec. 67 – July 70
Established to control military intelligence operations from Saigon under the 525th Military Intelligence Group.

6th Military Intelligence Battalion, Provisional
1 Dec. 67 – fall 68
Established to control military intelligence efforts out of Tan Son Nhut.

U.S. Army Combat Intelligence Battalion, Vietnam
1 April 68 – 24 Sept. 68

MILITARY INTELLIGENCE COMPANIES IN VIETNAM

Company	Type	Previous Station	Vietnam Service	Typical Location	Authorized Strength		
					1966	1968	1970
1st MI*	Support – 1st Inf Div	Riley	20 Oct. 65 – 15 April 70	Di An	66	66	—
4th MI †	Support – 4th Inf Div	Lewis	8 Sept. 66 – 7 Dec. 70	Pleiku	—	62	80
9th MI †	Support – 9th Inf Div	Riley	29 Dec. 66 – 18 Aug. 69	Dong Tam	—	67	—
25th MI*	Support – 25th Inf Div	Hawaii	11 March 66 – 8 Dec. 70	Cu Chi	66	66	48
45th MI	Image Interpretation	Vietnam	21 Jan. 66 – 14 March 73	Saigon	85	85	461
101st MI*	Support – 101st Abn Div	Campbell	25 Nov. 67 – 17 Jan. 72	Gia Le	—	96	153
131st MI	Aerial Surveillance	Vietnam	1 July 71 – 22 Nov. 72	Phu Bai	—	—	313
184th MI	Collection	Bragg	4 Oct. 66 – 25 Sept. 69	Tan Son Nhut	—	70	—
185th MI	Image Interpretation	Bragg	1 Sept. 66 – 25 Sept. 69	Tan Son Nhut	—	75	—
191st MI*	Support – 1st Cav Div	Benning	15 Sept. 65 – 15 Aug. 72	Phuoc Vinh	66	66	39
635th MI*	Support – AMERICAL Inf Div	Hood	23 Oct. 67 – 31 March 72	Chu Lai	—	41	80

* Detachments which were redesignated as companies on 26 December 1969.

† Officially remained a detachment since the unit departed before 26 December 1969. Included in the above list for informational purposes.

Chapter 26

Civil Affairs and Psychological Operations

4th Psychological Operations Group

Arrived Vietnam: 1 December 1967
Departed Vietnam: 2 October 1971
Previous Station: Vietnam

Authorized Strength	1968	1970
HHC	175	270

The 4th Psychological Operations Group was based at Tan Son Nhut and charged with supplying psychological operations advice and support to the South Vietnamese Army, providing liaison and conducting field psychological mission command and administrative control over its assigned and attached units. Typical assignments included loudspeaker support, propaganda leaflet printing, radio and television production, mobile radio monitoring and research and analysis.

7th Psychological Operations Group

Arrived Vietnam: 20 October 1965*
Departed Vietnam: 1 December 1967*
Previous Station: Okinawa
Authorized Strength: Elements – 143

* Major elements only.

The 7th Psychological Operations Group was based on Okinawa 20 October 1965 – 29 June 1974. It conducted psychological operations in Vietnam until the 4th Psychological Operations Group

was established there. Elements continuously performed missions in Vietnam throughout the war.

6th Psychological Operations Battalion

Arrived Vietnam: 7 February 1966
Departed Vietnam: 30 June 1971
Previous Station: Fort Bragg

Authorized Strength	1966	1968
Headquarters Team	91	174

The 6th Psychological Operations Battalion was a command-and-control unit under USARV Special Troops and based at Tan Son Nhut until 1969 when it moved to Bien Hoa. It provided psychological operations support in the III Corps Tactical Zone.

7th Psychological Operations Battalion

Arrived Vietnam: 1 December 1967
Departed Vietnam: 21 December 1971
Previous Station: Vietnam
Authorized Strength: HQ Team – 174
(1968)

The 7th Psychological Operations Battalion was initially based at Nha Trang but moved in 1968 to Da Nang, providing psychological operations support to the I Corps Tactical Zone.

8th Psychological Operations Battalion

Arrived Vietnam: 1 December 1967
Departed Vietnam: 26 June 1971
Previous Station: Vietnam
Authorized Strength: HQ Team – 174
(1968)

The 8th Psychological Operations Battalion served the II Corps Tactical Zone at Nha Trang and later Pleiku, where it became closely associated with the 4th Infantry Division in 1968.

10th Psychological Operations Battalion

Arrived Vietnam: 1 December 1967
Departed Vietnam: 16 April 1971
Previous Station: Vietnam
Authorized Strength: HQ Team – 174
(1968)

The 10th Psychological Operations Battalion supplied psychological operations support in the IV Corps Tactical Zone and was located at Can Tho.

CIVIL AFFAIRS COMPANIES IN VIETNAM

Company	Type	Previous Station	Vietnam Service	Typical Location	1966	1968	1970
2d CA	Regional Support – II FFV	Gordon	6 Dec. 66 – 27 July 71	Long Binh	—	171	171
29th CA	Support	Gordon	24 May 66 – 26 Dec. 71	Da Nang	118	117	117
41st CA	Regional Support – I FFV	Gordon	26 Dec. 65 – 28 Feb. 70	Nha Trang	185	140	—

PSYCHOLOGICAL OPERATIONS COMPANIES IN VIETNAM

Company	Type	Previous Station	Vietnam Service	Typical Location	1966	1968	1970
19th	Advice and Support	Vietnam	19 Nov. 66 – 1 Jan. 68	Can Tho	60	—	—
244th	Tactical Propaganda	Vietnam	10 Feb. 66 – 1 Jan. 68	Nha Trang	60	—	—
245th	Tactical Propaganda	Vietnam	10 Feb. 66 – 1 Jan. 68	Pleiku	60	—	—
246th	Tactical Propaganda	Vietnam	10 Feb. 66 – 1 Jan. 68	Bien Hoa	60	—	—

Chapter 27

U.S. Army Special Forces

U.S. Army Special Forces, Vietnam, Provisional

Arrived Vietnam: September 1962
Departed Vietnam: September 1964
Previous Station: Vietnam
Authorized Strength: HHD – 98 (1963)*

Commanders

Colonel George C. Morton	Sept. 62
Colonel Theodore Leonard	Nov. 63

* Also had 576 U.S. Army Special Forces personnel in Vietnam
on temporary duty, giving a total 1963 strength of 674.

The U.S. Army Special Forces, Vietnam (Provisional) was formed at Saigon to control U.S. Army Special Forces activities in Vietnam as a Special Forces Operations Base (SFOB) and moved to Nha Trang in February 1963. The 1st U.S. Army Special Forces Group, formed in Japan on 24 June 1957, had been contributing personnel to Vietnam since that year when elements started training South Vietnamese at the Nha Trang Commando Center. When the U.S. Army Special Forces, Vietnam was created provisionally, its mission was to advise and assist the South Vietnamese government in the organization, training, equipping and employment of the Civilian Irregular Defense Group (CIDG) forces— with the first CIDG camp located near Ban Me Thuot in 1961. The provisional group depended on six-month temporary duty detachments from the 1st U.S. Army Special Forces Group on Okinawa as well as the 5th and 7th U.S. Army Special Forces Groups headquartered at Fort Bragg. On 1 July 1963 it was placed in complete charge of the CIDG program by the U.S. Operations Mission of the Central Intelligence Agency, which also turned over its border surveillance tasks to the group that October. The

network of fortified, strategically located camps, each with an airstrip, proved to be invaluable reconnaissance and fire support bases in the remote border areas, and soon the CIDG program was diverted from area development into combat operations. On 26 October 1963 responsibility for the Border Surveillance (BS) Program, which had started in June 1962, was also given to the group.

U.S. Army Special Forces, Vietnam, Provisional
October 1963

C-3	Nha Trang	A-234	Son Ha
B-7	Can Tho	A-311	Ha Tien
B-130	Pleiku	A-312	Bon Sar Pa
B-320	Da Nang	A-313	Dong Tre
B-410	Saigon	A-321	Plei Do Lim
A-21	Hiep Hoa	A-322	Plei Mrong
A-22	Loc Ninh	A-333	Buon Mi Ga
A-23	Tan Phu	A-413	Long Thanh
A-26	Long Phu	A-414	Dam Pau
A-27	An Long	A-431	Hiep Duc
A-30	Bughia	A-432	Buon Bang
A-31	Long Khanh	A-433	Ta Bat
A-33	Djirai	A-725	Gia Vuc
A-34	Nuoc Vang	A-726	Ta Rau
A-35	Tuc Trung	A-727	Khe Sanh
A-113	Song Mao	A-728	Tra My
A-121	Trang Sup	A-749	Dak Pek
A-131	Polei Krong	A-750	Chau Lang
A-212	Buon Yun	A-751	Plei Yt
A-214	An Diem	A-752	Chu Dron
A-232	Ban Don		

5th Special Forces Group (Airborne), 1st Special Forces

Arrived Vietnam: 1 October 1964
Departed Vietnam: 3 March 1971
Previous Station: Fort Bragg

Auth. Strength *	1964	1966	1968
HHC	208	219	383

* See 5th Special Forces Group Strengths in Vietnam 1967-70 section; also see Indigenous Troops under control of the 5th Special Forces in Vietnam 1967-70.

Commanders

Colonel John H. Spears	Aug. 64
Colonel William A. McKean	July 65
Colonel Francis J. Kelly	June 66
Colonel Jonathan F. Ladd	June 67
Colonel Harold R. Aaron	June 68
Colonel Robert B. Rheault	May 69
Colonel Alexander Lemberes	July 69
Colonel Michael D. Healy	Aug. 69

The 5th Special Forces Group (Airborne), 1st Special Forces arrived in Vietnam to take over and expand the activities of U.S. Army Special Forces, Vietnam (Provisional) and was located at Nha Trang. The primary change of tasks was the conventionalization of the Civilian Irregular Defense Group (CIDG) program as the area development emphasis was downgraded. CIDG forces were used in joint operations with Vietnamese army and other governmental units with mixed results since they lacked equipment and training in such tactics. New camps were established as a result of the higher priority given the border regions. This involved closing out numerous sites as new camps nearer the Laotian and Cambodian borders were built and manned. While much effort was devoted to retraining former CIDG troops, hamlet militias were discontinued and strike force personnel were raised to fulfill the border surveillance mission. The border defense/surveillance mission was based primarily on the fortified camps of the CIDG and their U.S. Special Forces advisors. Purposely located astride major supply and infiltration routes, these camps provided a valuable intelligence and surveillance function. Patrols operating from them inhibited enemy movement and upon contact could call in quantities of aerial firepower. As a consequence, the enemy sought to destroy or neutralize them with mixed results, usually unfavorable to the North Vietnamese and Viet Cong attackers because troop concentration and movement in the open allowed superior U.S. mobility and firepower to inflict substantial losses on exposed enemy units. However, to insure survival these camps had to be backed up by mobile South Vietnamese, U.S. and other allied forces. In 1966 the organization and employment of a multipurpose reaction force, at first known as the Mobile Guerrilla Force and later redesignated the Mobile Strike Force (see Mobile Strike Force Commands section), were refined. Composed initially of company-size groups of 150-200 personnel, the mobile guerrilla forces conducted sustained guerrilla operations against the enemy, employing guerrilla doctrine and using many techniques borrowed from the Viet Cong. Inserted clandestinely into an area of operations, these troops normally broke contact with their base and conducted mobile missions for periods as long as 45 days. To prevent compromising these units, resupply was also conducted clandestinely. These special operations were highly successful in penetrating isolated enemy bases, disrupting the enemy's lines of communication, attacking hidden logistical support bases and gathering intelligence. The U.S. Army and South Vietnamese Special Forces also created deep reconnaissance and reaction forces that operated throughout the country and beyond its borders in response to MACV directives. Striking into remote areas, these units gathered intelligence, conducted raids and interdicted the enemy's lines of communication. They attacked the enemy by calling in air strikes and directing artillery fire. Occasionally these units guided Mobile Strike Forces into contact with enemy troops. They also executed deception and photographic missions and performed post-strike assessments of bomb damage from air strikes. Other Special Forces activities included continuation of efforts in civic action and psychological operations, since in remote areas of South Vietnam they were frequently the only contact the local inhabitants had with the central government or the outside world. With minimum strength, the group and its CIDG personnel maintained a measure of control in vast areas that otherwise would have gone to the enemy by default. The group also brought some 45,000 fighting men and a proportionate population under government control or influence, all of whom might otherwise have been recruited or dominated by the enemy. An idea of the magnitude of civic action missions of the group can be gleaned from the fact that it set up 49,902 economic aid projects, 34,334 educational projects, 35,468 welfare projects and 10,959 medical projects. The U.S. Special Forces in Vietnam achieved a degree of success and professionalism only realizable by an elite, highly qualified and combat-proficient group of dedicated soldiers. U.S. Special Forces doctrine demanded that its members complete both parachute and 24- to 64-week-long Special Forces training programs with cross-training follow-up in a secondary specialty. This commando-style training placed a premium on independence, reliability and team loyalty which produced very skilled, albeit unconventional, personnel. The fragmented, independent operation of the group facilitated ad hoc attachments when and where required, and the flexibility of the 5th Special Forces Group structure allowed maximum response to mission adjustments. The role of the 5th Special Forces Group and its unique capabilities dominated the Vietnam battlefield in a manner impossible for larger conventional formations.

5th Special Forces Group (Airborne), 1st Special Forces Assigned and Attached Elements

Headquarters & Headquarters Company, 5th Special Forces Group, 1st Special Forces
Signal Company, 5th Special Forces Group, 1st Special Forces
Company A, 5th Special Forces Group, 1st Special Forces (C-3 Operations Detachment)
Company B, 5th Special Forces Group, 1st Special Forces (C-2 Operations Detachment)
Company C, 5th Special Forces Group, 1st Special Forces (C-1 Operations Detachment)
Company D, 5th Special Forces Group, 1st Special Forces (C-4 Operations Detachment)
Company E, 5th Special Forces Group, 1st Special Forces (C-5 Operations Detachment)
Joint Combined Coordination Detachment, 5th Special Forces Group, 1st Special Forces
B-50 (Project OMEGA), 5th Special Forces Group, 1st Special Forces
B-51, 5th Special Forces Group, 1st Special Forces
B-52 (Project DELTA), 5th Special Forces Group, 1st Special Forces
B-53, 5th Special Forces Group, 1st Special Forces
B-55 (5th Mobile Strike Force Command), 5th Special Forces Group, 1st Special Forces
B-56 (Project SIGMA), 5th Special Forces Group, 1st Special Forces
B-57, 5th Special Forces Group, 1st Special Forces (Project GAMMA)
MACV Recondo School, 5th Special Forces Group, 1st Special Forces
Special Operations Augmentation, Command and Control North
Special Operations Augmentation, Command and Control Central
Special Operations Augmentation, Command and Control South
Nha Trang Installation Defense Command
403d Army Security Agency Detachment (plus numerous signal, engineer and military intelligence detachments)

TRIBAL AND MINORITY GROUPS TRAINED BY U.S. SPECIAL FORCES IN VIETNAM

Group	Ethnology*	Estimated Population (in thousands)	CTZ	General Location	Jungle Fighting Rating†
Bahnar	Mon-Khmer Montagnard	80 – 200	II CTZ	Central Highlands	Effective
Bru	Mon-Khmer Montagnard	40 – 50	I CTZ	Western Quang Tri/Thuan Thien	Effective
Cao Dai	Politico-religious sect	2,000	II and IV CTZ	Mekong Delta/Tay Ninh	Effective
Cham	Malayo-Polynesian	45	III & IV CTZ	Chau Phu/Tay Ninh	Capable
Chinese	Mongoloid	1,200	III & IV CTZ	Cholon, along coast, etc.	Effective
Cua	Mon-Khmer Montagnard	15 – 20	I CTZ	Quang Nam/Quang Tin	Capable
Halang	Mon-Khmer Montagnard	30	II CTZ	Western Kontum, Cambodia, Laos	Capable
Hre	Mon-Khmer Montagnard	90 – 120	I & II CTZ	Binh Dinh/Quang Ngai	Superb
Hoa Hao	Hinayana Buddhist sect	50	IV CTZ	Western Mekong Delta	Effective
Hroi	Mon-Khmer Montagnard	10	II CTZ	Phu Yen/Phu Bon/lower Binh Dinh	Capable
Jarai	Malayo-Polynesian Montagnard	150	II CTZ	Central Highlands	Effective
Jeh	Mon-Khmer Montagnard	15	I & II CTZ	Western Laotian border	Capable
Katu	Mon-Khmer Montagnard	25	I CTZ	Northern plateau and mountains	Effective
Khmer ‡	Cambodian	400 – 600	III & IV CTZ	Mekong Delta/Cambodian border	Effective
Koho	Mon-Khmer Montagnard	90	II & III CTZ	Mountains from Saigon to Da Lat	Capable
Ma	Mon-Khmer Montagnard	22	II & III CTZ	Da Dung River region	Capable
Meo	Mongoloid/Caucasoid	2,600 – 8,000		Throughout Laos, mountains of Vietnam/China	Effective
M'nong	Mon-Khmer Montagnard	15 – 40	II CTZ	South and west of Ban Me Thuot	Effective
Muong	Mon-Khmer Montagnard	10	II CTZ	Pleiku and Ban Me Thuot	Capable
Nung	Mongoloid Thai/Chinese	15 §		North Vietnam, west South Vietnam, China	Superb
Raglai	Malayo-Polynesian Montagnard	40	II CTZ	West of Nha Trang and Phan Rang	Capable
Rengao	Mon-Khmer Montagnard	10	II CTZ	Kontum	Superb
Rhade	Malayo-Polynesian Montagnard	120	II CTZ	Darlac Plateau	Superb
Sedang	Mon-Khmer Montagnard	40 – 80	II CTZ	Kontum	Superb
Stieng	Mon-Khmer Montagnard	60	III CTZ	Phuoc Long/Binh Long	Effective

* The Mon-Khmer stock probably originated in the upper Mekong River valleys in Yunnan Province of south China.

† Raiding, scout, ambush, camp defense. The rating is general, of course. Most listed entities were hostile to the South Vietnamese government, but loyal to U.S. Army Special Forces commanders. Those indicated as effective could readily become transformed into excellent strike forces with proper training and leadership. Superb tribes saw extended offensive action under U.S. Army Special Forces control, while the Nungs were used for the most elite assignments.

‡ Includes the Khmer Kampuchea Kron (KKK) and the Khmer Serei (Free Cambodia), both underground Cambodian political factions.

§ South Vietnam only. There were about 300,000 Nungs in North Vietnam as well.

5th Special Forces Group Strengths in Vietnam 1964 – 70*

Component	Oct. 1964	Oct. 1965	Oct. 1966	Oct. 1967	Oct. 1968†	Oct. 1969†	Oct. 1970
Assigned U.S. Personnel	951	1,828	2,589	2,726	3,581	3,741	2,904
CIDG/Camp Strike Force	19,000	30,400	34,800	34,346	27,069	28,163	6,295
Regional Forces (RF/PF)	0	28,800	28,000	18,248	7,371	737	0
Mobile Strike Force	unverif.	1,800	3.200	5,733	7,032	9,326	1,804

Note: Detailed statistics on indigenous personnel strengths may be found for 1967-1979 in that section.

* Authorized strengths for a C-detachment was 24, for a B-detachment was 23, for an A-detachment (A-Team) was 12. The 5th Special Forces Group contained its own organic Signal Company (183 personnel), which is included in the above U.S. Personnel Assigned totals. When the group first deployed to Vietnam it was authorized at 1,297 men. This was raised to its peak authorized level of 3,480 by 1968. Note that teams on temporary duty, especially from the 1st Special Forces Group on Okinawa until mid-1965, served in Vietnam as a matter of course and are not reflected in the above strength tabulations.

† Does not include strengths for Company E, which was engaged in special operations. Often these fell under the auspices of MAC-SOC. For instance, during 1968, Project "Prairie Fire" (special operations in Laos) contained 598 U.S. Special Forces members not noted above, while Project "Flaming Arrow" had 198 assigned as augmentation. Additionally, the MACV Recondo School, run by 5th Special Forces Group, required 46 personnel. Appropriate authorized strengths for Projects "Sigma", "Omega" and "Delta" should be consulted in the Group narratives.

Company A,
5th Special Forces Group
C-3 Operations Detachment

Arrived Vietnam: November 1964
Departed Vietnam: 1 January 1971
Previous Station: Fort Bragg

Authorized Strength	1966	1968
Company and C-det	358	447

Company A, 5th Special Forces Group (Airborne), 1st Special Forces, was a Corps-level line Special Forces company commanded by a lieutenant-colonel. (In fact these "companies" would be redesignated after the Vietnam war by Department of the Army as proper battalions.) It was composed of an administrative detachment and a C detachment, or operations detachment. The company in turn controlled several B-detachments which were in command of the various A-detachments, mobile strike forces, etc. Specifically, Company A and its C-3 Operations Detachment were responsible for activities in the III Corps Tactical Zone (Military Region 3) with the administrative detachment located at Ho Ngoc Tau in Gia Dinh Province and the operations detachment posted to Bien Hoa. Full listings of the order of battle of Company A can be found in the III Corps Tactical Zone listings of indigenous personnel controlled as well as in the section on 5th Special Forces Group detachments. Company A was involved in combat operations and camps tasked with border defense and surveillance close to Cambodia. During the May 1970 offensive into Cambodia, elements from the company's A-detachments at Duc Hue and Tra Cu assaulted a Viet Cong training area and won the encounter, accounting for over one-third of all crew-served weapons captured during the May offensive.

Company B,
5th Special Forces Group
C-2 Operations Detachment

Arrived Vietnam: November 1964 *
Departed Vietnam: 15 January 1971
Previous Station: Fort Bragg

Authorized Strength	1966	1068
Company and C-det	359	447

* In Vietnam since October 1962 on a temporary basis.

Company B, 5th Special Forces Group (Airborne), 1st Special Forces, was a Corp-level Special Forces line company organized along the lines of Company A. The company was tasked with Special Forces responsibilities in the II Corps Tactical Zone (later Military Region 2) and located jointly with its C operations detachment at Pleiku. A full order of battle of this company can be found within the sections on indigenous personnel controlled and Special Forces detachments. Due to the rugged Highlands geography and close proximity to the Cambodian and lower Laotian border, the camps within Company B were often under fierce siege.

Company C,
5th Special Forces Group
C-1 Operations Detachment

Arrived Vietnam: November 1964*
Departed Vietnam: 1 November 1970
Previous Station: Fort Bragg

Authorized Strength	1966	1968
Co and C-Det	360	447

* In Vietnam since September 1962 on a temporary basis.

Company C, 5th Special Forces Group (Airborne), 1st Special Forces, was a Corps-level Special Forces line company organized along the lines of Company A. The company had charge of Special Forces activities in the I Corps Tactical Zone (later Military Region 1) and was colocated with its C-detachment at Da Nang. The full order of battle of this company can be found in the appropriate sections of the indigenous personnel controlled and Special Forces detachments. The heavy jungle, mountainous terrain and multitude of regular North Vietnamese Army contingents in the company's area of operations always placed their camps in particular jeopardy.

Company D,
5th Special Forces Group
C-4 Operations Detachment

Arrived Vietnam: November 1964
Departed Vietnam: 16 December 1970
Previous Station: Fort Bragg

Authorized Strength	1966	1968
Co and C-Det	361	447

Company D, 5th Special Forces Group (Airborne), 1st Special Forces, was a Corps-level Special Forces line company organized along the lines of Company A. The company (also known as the "Delta Company") was responsible for Special Forces activities in the IV Corps Tactical Zone (Military Region 4) and was colocated with its operations C-Detachment at Can Tho in the heart of the Delta region. A full order of battle of this company can be found in the relevant sections of indigenous personnel controlled and the Special Forces detachments. The flat Mekong Delta region of Vietnam gave rise to use of highly maneuverable fiberglass airboats fitted with 180-horsepower aircraft engines. Armed with a .30-caliber machinegun mounted up front and with a second man carrying an M79 grenade launcher, these airboats provided excellent mobility along the innumerable canals, rice paddies, and even across the dikes of the Delta. The terrain in the company's area of operations included the Seven Mountains near the Cambodian border which was the scene of some of the fiercest fighting of the war. Thus, the company's border camps close to Cambodia often came under attack. On 10 August 1969 Company D was placed under the operational control of 44th Special Tactical Zone.

Company E,
5th Special Forces Group
C-5 Operations Detachment

Arrived Vietnam: 31 March 1965
Departed Vietnam: 3 March 1971
Previous Station: Vietnam

Authorized Strength	1966	1968
Co and C-Det	198	216

Company E, 5th Special Forces Group (Airborne), 1st Special Forces was directly under the command of the group commander and utilized for special operations missions. It should be noted that many projects were usually under the operational control of either a Field Force/III Marine Amphibious Force Commander or

under MACV auspices. Both the company and its operations C-detachment were located at Ho Ngoc Tau in Gia Dinh Province. The typical order of battle of this company was as follows:

Detachment	Type	Location	Service
B-50	Project OMEGA	Ban Me Thuot	August 66 – June 72
B-51	Vietnamese Special Forces Training Center	Dong Ba Thin	April 64 – March 71
B-52	Project DELTA	Nha Trang	Nov. 64 – June 70
B-53	Special Missions Advisory Force	Long Thanh	Feb. 64 – Feb. 71
B-55	5th Mobile Strike Force Command	Nha Trang	Nov. 64 – Dec. 70
B-55 (Prov)	Liaison	Saigon	Sept. 62 – Feb. 71
B-56	Project SIGMA	Ho Ngoc Tau	Aug. 66 – May 71
B-57	Project GAMMA	Nha Trang	June 67 – March 70
A-501 *	Nha Trang Internal Security	Nha Trang	? – Dec. 64
A-502	Nha Trang Special Security	Thrung Dung	March 64 – Jan. 70
A-503	Nha Trang Mobile Strike Force	Dien Khanh	June 64 – Jan. 70

* Nung complement. Included only for informational purposes.

Special Operations Augmentation, 5th Special Forces Group (Airborne)

Arrived Vietnam: 24 January 1968
Departed Vietnam: 1 March 1971
Previous Location: Vietnam

Authorized Strength: 940*

* Ranged in number between 130-160 officers and 530-780 NCOs.

Special Operations Augmentation (SOA) was a cover designation to make it appear that selected special forces personnel were assigned to 5th Special Forces Group when, in fact, they were actually under secret orders posting them to MACV-SOG and engaged in highly classified clandestine operations.

B-50 Detachment Project OMEGA (Special Recon)

Arrived Vietnam: August 1966
Departed Vietnam: June 1972
Previous Location: Vietnam

Authorized Strength	U.S. Special Forces	South Vietnamese
Project OMEGA	127	894

Project OMEGA was an unconventional warfare operations project established by 5th Special Forces Group (Airborne), 1st Special Forces and formed August – October 1966 to increase the long-range reconnaissance and intelligence-gathering capability

of the group beyond that furnished by Project DELTA. It was composed of four (later eight) Roadrunner teams conducting long-distance reconnaissance over enemy trail networks and eight (later sixteen) reconnaissance teams conducting saturation patrols throughout specified reconnaissance zones. Backing up these elements were three commando companies used to exploit small unit contacts, to aid in the extraction of compromised teams and to perform reconnaissance-in-force missions. Personnel selected for such special warfare projects were taken from ethnic and religious minority groups who were qualified in parachutist, advanced infantry, and special unconventional warfare tactics and skills adapted to the environment of mainland Southeast Asia. It also had one camp defense company. On 1 September 1967 Project OMEGA was placed under MACV and operationally controlled by I Field Force, Vietnam and directly responsible to the field force commander. It was located at Ban Me Thuot and used Montagnard (Sedang, Jah, Rhade), Cham and Chinese ethnic minorities.

B-51 Detachment (Vietnamese Special Forces Training Center)

Arrived Vietnam: April 1964
Departed Vietnam: March 1971
Previous Location: Vietnam

Authorized Strength*	U.S. Special Forces	South Vietnamese
Training Ctr	28	760

* In 1968. There were 280 VNSF and 480 camp strike force members.

B-51 had the primary mission of advising and assisting the South Vietnamese training center at Dong Ba Thin in the training of the

Lac Luong Dac Biet (LLDB or Vietnamese Special Forces) and CIDG personnel. Advice and support were also rendered to the assigned camp strike force in combat operations training and local security. Joint operations were also conducted with Korean units. Courses included Tae Kwon Do (karate); U.S. basic airborne tactics; VNSF radio operator skills; city combat; MSF basic airborne and combat recon tactics; Vietnamese Navy infantry tactics; CIDG leadership and VNSF training. On 1 September 1968 B-51 moved the Mobile Strike Force Training Center to Hon Tre Island and from Dong Ba Thin to An Khe. The An Khe site was closed on 23 October 1969 and B-51 relocated again to Dong Ba Thin, then known as the National Training Center.

B-52 Detachment
Project DELTA
(Special Recon)

Arrived Vietnam: 15 May 1964
Departed Vietnam: 30 June 1970
Previous Location: Vietnam

Authorized Strength	U.S. Special Forces	South Vietnamese*
Project DELTA	93	1,208

* Includes 185 South Vietnamese Special Forces, 816 Rangers and 187 CIDG.

On 15 May 1964 Project DELTA (originally called Project LEAPING LENA) was initiated as a covert operation in Vietnam with one U.S. Special Forces A-Detachment training the CIDG and VNSF in the conduct of long-range reconnaissance patrols. By June 1965, 5th Special Forces Group assumed a more active role in Project DELTA and detachment B-52 was organized for command and control. Its missions encompassed location of enemy units, intelligence, bomb damage assessment, artillery/air strike coordination, hunter-killer missions, special purpose raids and conducting harassing and deception missions. It was organized into 12 reconnaissance teams, six (later 12) CIDG Roadrunner teams, one Nung camp security company and the 91st South Vietnamese Airborne Ranger Battalion (five companies) as a reaction and reinforcing unit. On 15 September 1966 Project DELTA was additionally ordered by MACV to train other U.S. Infantry in long-range patrol tactics. It had the capability of deploying into any corps tactical zone when so directed by the South Vietnamese Joint General Staff (JGS) and MACV. It was located at Nha Trang and used ethnic Chinese troops.

B-53 Detachment
(Special Missions
Advisory Force)

Arrived Vietnam: February 1964
Departed Vietnam: February 1971*
Previous Location: Vietnam

Authorized Strength †	U.S. Special Forces	South Vietnamese
Force	136	?

* Became the USARV Special Missions Advisory Group on 1 March 1971, which was not closed out until 19 April 1972.

B-53 was assigned to the Vietnamese airborne ranger training center which had been established in July 1961 at Long Thanh. B-53 was augmentation to MACV and its status was highly classified.

B-55 Detachment
(5th Mobile Strike Force
Command)

Arrived Vietnam: November 1964
Departed Vietnam: 30 December 1970
Previous Location: Vietnam
Authorized Strength: 2,570 (1968)

B-55 was the controlling detachment for the 5th Mobile Strike Force Command, which was the 5th Special Forces Group's countrywide reserve reaction force for Special Forces camps throughout the Republic of Vietnam. This force was officially created on 1 August 1965 as an expansion of the Nung security company originally established in 1964. Stationed at Nha Trang, the 5th Mobile Strike Force Command (MSFC) was composed of various ethnic minority groups: Rhade, Raglai, Koho and Cham, about 40% of whom were airborne qualified. Its headquarters was staffed by U.S. Special Forces and Chinese Nungs. It was organized into four 552-man battalions, one 135-man reconnaissance company and one 227-man headquarters and service company. Although the 5th MSFC was primarily intended for ready reaction missions, it also saw intense action in all four Corps Tactical Zones while engaged in battalion-size combat operations against enemy strongpoints in difficult or virtually inaccessible locations. Reinforcing missions were extended to non-Special Forces units as required, such as the 7 May 1970 combat assault on Nui Ek mountain to relieve an ARVN ranger regiment. The 5th MSFC was also capable of operating as a whole brigade, as demonstrated during the siege of Thuong Duc, when it spent three months in I CTZ as a combined force.

B-56 Detachment
Project SIGMA
(Special Recon)

Arrived Vietnam: August 1966
Departed Vietnam: 2 May 1971
Previous Location: Vietnam

Authorized Strength	U.S. Special Forces	South Vietnamese
Project SIGMA	127	894

Project SIGMA (B-56) was formed August–October 1966 as an unconventional warfare operations project by 5th Special Forces Group (Airborne), 1st Special Forces. It was similar in structure and capability to its companion, Project OMEGA. It contained eight reconnaissance teams, three commando companies and one camp defense company. On 1 November 1967 it was transferred to MACV control and provided long-range and intelligence-gathering capabilities directly to the II Field Force, Vietnam commander. It was located at Ho Ngoc Tau. B-56 used ethnic Cambodian and Chinese personnel.

B-57 Detachment
Project GAMMA
(Intelligence Collection)

Arrived Vietnam: June 1967
Departed Vietnam: 31 March 1970
Previous Location: Vietnam
Authorized Strength: 52

Project GAMMA (B-57) was established by 5th Special Forces Group (Airborne), 1st Special Forces as an information collection element to develop timely intelligence on NVA bases and infiltration into Cambodia and Cambodian support to the NVA and VC.

On 28 February 1968 B-57 relocated from Saigon to Nha Trang and on 1 April 1968 received the designation Project GAMMA. Its personnel operated at Duc Co and Duc Lap (II CTZ); Bu Dop, Loc Ninh, Thien Ngon, Tay Ninh and Duc Hue (III CTZ), and Moc Hoa and Chau Doc (IV CTZ).

5th Special Forces Group Mobile Strike Force Commands (Airborne)

MSFC*	Region of Responsibility	July 68 Strength	Organizational Remarks
5th MSFC †	Vietnam-wide	2,570 ‡	4 Bns, 1 Recon Co + HQ
1st MSFC	I CTZ (B-16)	1,463	2 Bns, 1 Recon Co, HHC
2d MSFC	II CTZ (B-20)	3,119	5 Bns, 1 Recon Co, HHC
3d MSFC	III CTZ (B-36)	2,015	3 Bns, 1 Recon Co, HHC
4th MSFC	IV CTZ (B-40)	2,199	3 Bns, 1 Airboat Co, 1 Recon Co, HHC

* Mobile Strike Force Commands (also known as MIKE Force).

† Also known as the Nha Trang Mobile Strike Force, or B-55 after its controlling detachment. Other MSFC command and control detachments are in parentheses after their respective CTZ region of responsibility.

‡ Authorized strength given only for 5th MSFC. Others have actual strengths given.

In June 1965 MACV approved the creation of a small reserve force for each 5th Special Forces Group company. Called Mobile Reaction Forces, these were formed that fall for multipurpose reaction. Each Mobile Strike Force Command (MSFC) had several 552-man battalions, one 135-man reconnaissance company and one 227-man headquarters and service company. The headquarters and service company was comprised of highly trained, airborne-qualified Chinese Nung or Cambodian personnel as well as elite Vietnamese CIDG members carefully selected and trained well beyond normal proficiency. Not only were these MSFC used for reserve and reinforcing elements to CIDG camps threatened or under attack, but also for conducting raids, ambushes and combat patrols. When initially organized in 1964, the first companies were placed under unilateral U.S. Special Forces command. At first, full use was not made of their capabilities as reaction and reconnaissance units. Instead, they were used as interior guards for the Corps Tactical Zone C-Detachments and the headquarters compound at Nha Trang. After June 1966, full use of the MSFC was made with excellent results. They were brought under joint U.S.-Vietnamese control in December 1966. The 5th MSFC was especially famous and saw intense combat in all four Corps Tactical Zones under the group commander's sole command.

In mid-1966 another concept for employing MIKE Forces evolved — the Mobile Guerrilla Force (MGF) concept. A mobile guerrilla task force consisted of one U.S. Special Forces A-Detachment for command and control, one 150-man mobile guerrilla company composed of MIKE Force personnel trained in guerrilla warfare, and one 34-man combat reconnaissance platoon. An MGF was capable of operating in remote regions formerly considered VC/NVA safe areas for periods of 30 to 60 days. Their missions included border surveillance, interdiction of enemy infiltration routes and the conduct of both reconnaissance and combat operations. The recon platoon would be deployed and then the MGF would be inserted to act on the new intelligence. These operations were called "Blackjack" operations and the first MGF operation, BLACKJACK 21, was conducted in southwest Kontum province on 13 October – 10 November 1966 after five weeks of planning and preparation. In mid-1967 integration of the MGF and MIKE Force began, and in October 1967 the two combined and officially became known as the Mobile Strike Force (MSF). The missions and capabilities of both were retained.

5TH SPECIAL FORCES GROUP (AIRBORNE), 1ST SPECIAL FORCES, ORDER OF BATTLE

December 1964

5th Special Forces Group Assigned Detachments

C-1	Da Nang	A-4	Bu Prang
C-2	Pleiku	A-5	Dak Pek
B-1	Dong Ba Thin	A-6	An Phu
B-2	Nha Trang	A-7	Vinh Gia
A-1	Plei Do Lim	A-8	Du Dop
A-2	Buon Me Ga	A-9	Minh Thanh
A-3	Ban Don		

Attachments From 1st Special Forces Group

B-130	Can Tho	A-312	Buon Brieng
B-210	Ban Me Thuot	A-313	Plei Me
B-320	Saigon	A-321	Vinh Loi

A-111	Nha Trang	A-322	Kham Duc
A-112	Gia Vuc	A-323	Khe Sanh
A-113	A Shau	A-324	Ta Ko
A-114	Suoi Da	A-331	Tinh Bien
A-131	Nha Trang	A-332	To Chau
A-132	Dong Ba Thin	A-333	Dak To
A-133	Polei Krong	A-334	Plei Mrong
A-211	Don Phuoc	A-411	Trang Sup
A-212	Long Thanh	A-412	Phuoc Vinh
A-213	An Long	A-413	Thu Duc
A-214	Plei Djereng	A-414	A Ro
A-221	Moc Hoa	A-422	Plei Ta Nangle
A-223	Bu Chia Map		
A-224	Duc Co	A-424	Moc Hoa
A-231	Kannack	A-431	Buon Beng
A-233	Dong Tre	A-432	Buon Beng
A-311	Pleiku	A-434	Loc Ninh

5TH SPECIAL FORCES GROUP (AIRBORNE)

October 1965

I Corps Tactical Zone

C-1		Da Nang	A-105	(formerly 121)	Kham Duc
A-101	(formerly 122)	Khe Sanh	A-106	(formerly 114)	Ba To
A-102*	(formerly 334)	A Shau	A-107		Tra Bong
A-103	(formerly 113)	Gia Vuc	A-113 †		Da Nang MIKE
A-104	(formerly 331)	Ha Thanh			

II Corps Tactical Zone

C-2		Pleiku	A-221	(formerly 112)	Kannack
A-219 ‡	(formerly 423)	Pleiku MIKE	A-224	(formerly 432)	Phu Tuc
A-212 †		Pleiku	A-222	(formerly 433)	Long Tre
A-211	(formerly 5)	Dak Pek	A-213 †		Van Canh
A-212	(formerly 333)	Plei Mrong	B-23	(formerly B-430)	Ban Me Thuot
A-213	(formerly 232)	Plei Djereng	A-232	(formerly 234)	Bao Loc
A-214	(formerly 3)	Plateau Gi	A-233	(formerly 2)	Buon Ea Yang
A-215	(formerly 132)	Duc Co	A-234	(formerly 124)	An Lac
A-216	(formerly 1)	Plei Do Lim	A-236		Lac Thien
A-217	(formerly 132)	Plei Me	A-321 †		Bong Son
A-322 †		Dak To	A-122 †		Tuy Phuoc
B-22		An Tuc	A-123		Binh Khe
B-22	(formerly A-121)	liaison, Quin Hon	A-223 †		Hoai An
A-112 †		Mai Linh			

III Corps Tactical Zone

C-3		Bien Hoa	A-322	(formerly 422)	Suoi Da
A-301	(formerly 314)	Ho Ngoc Tao	A-323	(formerly 111)	Trang Sup
A-302	(formerly 421)	Bien Hoa MIKE	B-33	(formerly B-11)	Hon Quan
			A-331	(formerly 314)	Loc Ninh
A-325B	(formerly 303)	Nui Ba Den	A-332	(formerly 332-A)	Minh Thanh
A-304	(formerly 235)	Tanh Linh	A-325A	(formerly 332-B)	Chon Thanh
B-31		Phuoc Vinh	B-34	(formerly B-21)	Song Be
A-311	(formerly 342)	Dong Xoai	A-341	(formerly 311)	Bu Dop
A-312	(formerly 321)	Cao Bien			
B-32	(formerly B-120)	Tay Ninh			

IV Corps Tactical Zone

C-4		Can Tho	A-422	(formerly 7)	Vinh Gia
B-41	(formerly B-410)	Moc Hoa	A-423	(formerly 134)	Tinh Bien
A-411	(formerly 412)	Binh Hung	A-424	(formerly 6)	An Phu
A-412	(formerly 313)	Dan Chu	A-425	(formerly 324)	An Long
A-413	(formerly 431)	Binh Thanh	A-426	(formerly B-230)	Xom Duong Dong
A-414	(formerly 424)	Moc Hoa	A-427 †		Tri Ton
A-415	(formerly 322)	Tuyen Nhon	A-428 †		Tan Chau
B-42	(formerly B-130)	Chau Duc	A-416 †	(formerly 221)	Ap Bac
A-421	(formerly 311)	Ha Tien			

Special Forces Operating Base (SFOB)

B-51	(formerly B-1)	Dong Ba Thin	A-521	(formerly 411)	Dong Ba Thin DELTA
B-52	(formerly B-220)	Nha Trang DELTA	A-502	(formerly 323)	Dien Khanh
			A-501	(formerly 218)	Trung Dung
B-53	(formerly A-412)	Long Thanh MACV			

* Overrun by enemy 11 March 1966.

† Temporary duty detachment.

‡ Temporarily at Duc Co.

5TH SPECIAL FORCES GROUP (AIRBORNE)
October 1966

I Corps Tactical Zone

C-1	Da Nang	A-104	Ha Thanh	A-108	Minh Long
A-101	Khe Sanh	A-105	Kham Duc	A-109	Thuong Duc
A-102	Tien Phuoc	A-106	Ba To	A-110	Da Nang
A-103	Gia Vuc	A-107	Tra Bong	A-113	Da Nang MIKE

II Corps Tactical Zone

C-2	Pleiku	B-23	Ban Me Thuot	B-24	Kontum
A-219	Pleiku MIKE	A-232	Tan Rai	A-241	Polei Kleng
B-22	Qui Nhon	A-233	Trang Phuc	A-242	Dak Pek
A-221	Cung Son	A-234	An Lac	A-243	Plateau Gi

A-222	Dong Tre	A-235	Nhon Co	A-244	Dak To
A-223	Van Canh	A-236	Lac Thien	A-245	Dak Seang
A-224	Phu Tuc	A-237	Luong Son	A-251	Plei Djereng
A-226	Mai Linh	A-238	Buon Blech	A-252	Plei Mrong
A-227	Bong Son	A-239	Duc Lap	A-253	Duc Co
A-228	Vinh Tranh			A-255	Plei Me

III Corps Tactical Zone

C-3	Bien Hoa	A-323	Trai Bi	A-342	Dong Xoai
A-301	Trang Sup	A-324	Nui Ba Den	A-343	Duc Phong
A-302	Bien Hoa	A-325	Bao Don	B-35	Hiep Hoa
	MIKE	A-326	Go Dau Ha	A-351	Hiep Hoa
B-31	Xuan Loc	B-33	Hon Quan	A-352	Hiep Hoa
A-311	Tanh Linh	A-331	Loc Ninh	A-353	Hiep Hoa
A-312	Xom Cat	A-332	Minh Thanh	A-354	Hiep Hoa
B-32	Tay Ninh	A-333	Chon Thanh	B-55	Saigon liaison
A-312	Ben Soi	B-34	Song Be	B-56	Ho Ngoc Tao
A-322	Suoi Da	A-341	Bu Dop		SIGMA

IV Corps Tactical Zone*

C-4	Can Tho	A-415	Tuyen Nhon	A-425	Thuong Thoi
B-41	Moc Hoa	A-416	Kinh Quan II	A-426	Phu Quoc Island
A-411	Binh Hung	B-42	Chau Doc	A-427	Phu Quoc Island
A-412	Cai Cai	A-421	Ha Tien	A-428	Tan Chau
A-413	Binh Thanh Thon	A-422	Vinh Gia †	A-429	Ba Xoai
A-414	Moc Hoa	A-423	Tinh Bien	A-430	Don Phuc MIKE
		A-424	Can Tho		

Special Forces Operating Base (SFOB)

B-50	Nha Trang	A-503	Nha Trang	B-51	Dong Ba Thin
	OMEGA				VNSF Tng Ctr
A-502	Trung Dung			B-52	Nha Trang DELTA

* Note that for cross reference with 1967-70 detachment order of battle, the numbers for IV Corps Tactical Zone were changed effective 1 June 1967 as follows:

† Note: A-422 withdrawn 30 June 1967 when Vinh Gia turned over to VNSF on 27 June 1967.

Location	Old #	New #
Don Phuc (MIKE)	A-430	A-401
To Chau	A-431	A-402
To Chau	A-432	A-403
Binh Hung	A-411	A-404
Ha Thien (new)	A-421	A-405
My Phuoc Tay	A-424	A-411
Kinh Quan II	A-416	A-412
Ba Xoai	A-429	A-421
Cai Cai	A-412	A-431
Thuong Thoi	A-425	A-432
My An	A-426	A-433
Phu Quoc	A-427	A-441
Phu Quoc	A-428	A-442

INDIGENOUS TROOPS UNDER CONTROL OF THE 5TH SPECIAL FORCES GROUP (AIRBORNE) I CORPS TACTICAL ZONE/MILITARY REGION 1 1967-70

Detachment & Mission		Camp/Opening Date		Oct. 1967	Oct. 1968	Oct. 1969	Oct. 1970	Disposition
C-1	Command & Control	Da Nang	Sept. 62	123	123	208	90	24 Nov. 70 Ranger
B-11	Command & Control	Chu Lai	Aug. 69	—	—	59	—	14 Nov. 70 closed
B-16	1st MSFC	Da Nang	Feb. 66	—	1,075 MIKE*	790 MIKE	—	14 Nov. 70 Ranger
A-101	CIDG/BS/SS	Lang Vei †	Dec. 66	328				7 Feb. 68 overrun
		Mai Loc	June 68		445	273	—	27 Aug. 70 closed
A-102	CIDG/BS	Tien Phuoc	Nov. 65	587+(739) ‡	538+(800)	494	422	31 Oct. 70 Ranger
A-103	CIDG	Gia Vuc	Feb. 62	487	485	515	460	31 Jan 69 to VNSF

				Oct. 1967	Oct. 1968	Oct. 1969	Oct. 1970	
A-104	CIDG/SS	Ha Thanh	April 65	502+(380)	498+(401)	467+(439)	415	31 Aug. 70 Ranger
A-105	CIDG/BS	Kham Duc	Sept. 63	256				12 May 68 closed
		Nong Son	June 68		213	281	392	31 Oct. 70 Ranger
A-106	CIDG/SS	Ba To	March 65	308+(319)	314+(273)	433	400	30 Sept. 70 Ranger
A-107	CIDG/SS	Tra Bong	March 65	358+(420)	374+(475)	510	486	31 Aug. 70 Ranger
A-108	CIDG/SS	Minh Long	March 66	430+(348)	399+(328)	455+(298)	386	30 Sept. 70 Ranger
A-109	CIDG/SS	Thuong Duc	March 66	519	359	311	424+ 177 MIKE	14 Nov. 70 Ranger
A-111	MIKE	Da Nang	March 67	125 MIKE	To VNSF			See A-111, II CTZ
A-113	MIKE	Da Nang	Aug. 65	445 MIKE	To VNSF			See A-113, II CTZ

* MIKE forces include mobile guerrilla units throughout tables.

† NVA attack penetrated and practically destroyed camp on 4 May 1967 before being ejected with heavy losses on both sides. On 7 February 68 NVA tanks accompanied by infantry overran the camp.

‡ First number indicates team's CIDG or CSF personnel; number in parentheses is strength of RF/PF assigned.

INDIGENOUS TROOPS UNDER CONTROL OF THE 5TH SPECIAL FORCES GROUP (AIRBORNE)
II CORPS TACTICAL ZONE/MILITARY REGION 2
1967 – 70

Detachment & Mission		Camp/Opening Date		Oct. 1967	Oct. 1968	Oct. 1969	Oct. 1970	Disposition
C-2	Command & Control	Pleiku	Oct. 62	123	232	125	—	31 Jan. 71 to Ranger
B-20*	2d MSFC	Pleiku	Nov. 67	—	1,593 MIKE	3,010 MIKE	—	31 May 70 to Ranger
B-22	Command & Control Liaison	Qui Nhon	Jan. 65	17	59	—	—	1 July 69 closed and moved to Chu Lai, becoming B-11
B-23	Command & Control MSF	Ban Me Thuot	Nov. 64	106	206+ 418 MIKE	104	60	31 Jan. 71 to Ranger
B-24	Command & Control MSF	Kontum	Jan. 66	111	146+ 164 MIKE	112	59	31 Jan. 71 to Ranger
A-204	MSF	Kontum	Unverified	—	—	—	567 MIKE	Unverified
A-217	MSF	Pleiku	Jan. 67	912 MIKE	—	—	—	In 1968 to B-20
A-218	MSF	Pleiku	Oct. 62	282 MIKE	—	—	—	In 1968 to B-20
A-219	MSF	Pleiku	Oct. 62	Unreported	—	—	—	In 1968 to B-20
A-221	CIDG/SS	Cung Son	Jan. 66	604 + (589)	527	—	—	31 March 69 to RF/PF
A-222	CIDG	Dong Tre	June 63	543	676	—	—	30 June 69 to RF/PF
A-223	CIDG/MSF	Van Canh	Aug. 65	433	—	—	—	10 Jan. 68 to RF/PF
		Qui Nhon	March 68		235 MIKE	—	—	June 1969 closed
A-224	CIDG/SS	Phu Tuc	April 65	468 + (433)	—	—	—	2 Aug. 68 to RF/PF
A-226	CIDG	Mai Linh	Sept. 65	614	—	—	—	Unverified
A-227	CIDG	Ha Tay	June 67	519	468	—	—	31 March 69 to RF/PF
A-228	CIDG/SS	Vinh Thanh	Nov. 65	515 + (138)	—	—	—	25 Dec. 67 to VNSF A-120
A-231	CIDG/BS	Tieu Atar	Dec. 67	—	398	479	414	30 Sept. 70 to Ranger
A-232	CIDG	Tan Rai	Jan. 66	383	215	—	—	31 March 69 to RF/PF
A-233	CIDG/BS	Trang Phuc	Sept. 66	766	451	556	399	30 Sept. 70 to Ranger
A-234	CIDG	An Lac	May 65	592	522	570	—	31 March 70 to RF/PF
A-235	CIDG/BS	Nhon Co	March 66	506	347	537	—	31 March 70 to RF/PF
A-236	CIDG/SS/BS	Lac Thien	May 65	525	—	—	—	30 Sept. 67 to RF/PF
		Bu Prang	Oct. 67	—	344	412	389	30 Nov. 70 to Ranger
A-237	CIDG	Luong Son	Jan. 66	570	—	—	—	3 Aug. 68 to RF/PF
A-238	CIDG	Buon Blech	July 66	643	528	—	—	30 June 69 to RF/PF
A-239	CIDG/BS	Duc Lap	Nov. 66	588	260	411	380	31 Dec. 70 to Ranger
A-241	CIDG/BS	Polei Kleng	March 66	390	272	356	403	31 Aug. 70 to Ranger
A-242	CIDG/BS	Dak Pek	Oct. 62	689	529	608	433	30 Nov. 70 to Ranger
A-243	CIDG	Plateau Gi	Jan. 65	444	277	—	—	15 Jan. 69 to VNSF A-111
A-244	CIDG/BS	Dak To	Aug. 65	549	—	—	—	15 May 68 to RF/PF
		Ben Hat	May 68		518	500	521	31 Dec. 70 to Ranger
A-245	CIDG/BS	Dak Seang	Aug. 66	480	289	405	342	30 Nov. 70 to Ranger
A-246	CIDG	Mang Buk	July 64	457	315	432	—	31 March 70 to RF/PF
A-251	CIDG/BS	Plei Djereng	Dec. 66	548	400	540	479	31 Oct. 70 to Ranger
A-252	CIDG	Plei Mrong	Feb. 62	474	—	—	—	1 May 67 to VNSF A-113
A-253	CIDG/BS	Duc Co	June 62	577	428	442	457	30 Sept. 70 to Ranger
A-254	CIDG	Plei Do Lim	April 62	Unreported	—	—	—	2 Aug. 68 to RF/PF
A-255	CIDG	Plei Me	Oct. 63	373	485	591	464	31 Oct. 70 to Ranger
A-111 (VNSF)	CSF	Plateau Gi	N/A	—	—	457	—	31 May 70 to RF/PF

			Oct. 1967	Oct. 1968	Oct. 1969	Oct. 1970	
A-113	(VNSF) CSF	Plei Mrong	N/A —	505	511	443	31 Oct. 70 to Ranger
A-120	(VNSF) CSF	Vinh Thanh	N/A —	525	—	—	30 June 69 to RF/PF

*B-20 detachment officially designated as 2d Mobile Strike Force Command control detachment for II CTZ in November 1967.

INDIGENOUS TROOPS UNDER CONTROL OF THE 5TH SPECIAL FORCES GROUP (AIRBORNE)
III CORPS TACTICAL ZONE/MILITARY REGION 3
1967 – 70

Detachment & Mission		Camp/Opening Date		Oct. 1967	Oct. 1968	Oct. 1969	Oct. 1970	Disposition
C-3	Command & Control	Bien Hoa	Nov. 64	68	203	100	99	31 Dec. 70 closed
B-32	Command & Control	Tay Ninh	Dec. 64	143 +(2,034)	202	100	90	30 Nov. 70 closed
B-33	Command & Control S/SS	Hon Quan	May 65	68+(864)	200	99	60	31 Dec. 70 closed
B-34	Command & Control S/SS	Song Be	May 65	98+(1,976)	200	98	—	31 May 70 closed
B-35	Command & Control	Duc Hoa	Dec. 66	104	—	—	—	closed Oct. 68
B-36*	3d MSFC	Long Hai	Sept. 67	—	457+ 1,948 MIKE	2,124 MIKE	500 MIKE	1 Jan. 71 closed
A-301	CIDG Training Center	Trang Sup	Feb. 63	285	386	530	510	30 Nov. 70 to Ranger
A-302	MSF	Bien Hoa	Nov. 64	1,049 MIKE	—	—	—	To B-36
A-303	MSF	Trang Sup	Feb. 67	—	—	—	—	To B-36
A-304	MSF	Trang Sup	Jan. 67	228 MIKE	—	—	—	To B-36
A-311	CIDG	Tanh Linh	April 65	319	—	—	—	31 Oct. 67 to RF/PF
A-321	CIDG/BS/SS	Ben Soi	March 65	511+(683)	—	—	—	In 1968 to VNSF A-136
A-322	CIDG/BS	Prek Klok	March 67	557				11 Dec. 67 closed
		Katum	Feb. 68		269	443	369	31 Oct. 70 to Ranger
A-323	CIDG/BS	Trai Bi	June 66	728				18 Dec. 67 closed
		Thien Ngon	Feb. 68		580	423	333	30 Sept. 70 to Ranger
A-324	Radio Relay	Nui Ba Den	Aug. 64	104	—	—	—	31 Oct. 70 closed
A-325	CIDG/BS	Duc Hue	Nov. 67	—	350	440	253	31 Oct. 70 to Ranger
A-326	CIDG/BS	Tra Cu	Jan. 67	—	330	505	334	31 Aug. 70 to Ranger
A-331	CIDG/SS/SS	Loc Ninh	Dec. 66	456+(386)	530	574	358	30 Sept. 70 to Ranger
A-332	CIDG	Minh Thanh	Dec. 63	562	301	375	—	30 April 70 to RF/PF
A-333	CIDG	Chi Linh	Jan. 67	290	344	394	—	15 Dec. 69 closed
A-334	CIDG/BS	Tong Le Chon	May 67	55	359	521	355	30 Nov. 70 to Ranger
A-341	CIDG/SS/BS	Bu Dop	Nov. 63	337+(382)	307	433	304	31 Dec. 70 to Ranger
A-342	CIDG/SS	Dong Xoai	May 65	444+(242)	309	392	—	31 Jan. 70 to RF/PF
A-343	CIDG/SS	Duc Phong	April 66	436+(277)	425	522	—	31 May 70 to RF/PF
A-344	CIDG	Bu Nard	April 67	286	357	250	—	30 April 70 to Ranger
A-351	CIDG/SS/BS	Hiep Hoa	April 66	477+(255)	—	—	—	Became A-325
A-352	CIDG/BS	Tra Cu	Jan. 67	276	—	—	—	Became A-329
A-353	CIDG/BS	Luong Hoa	May 67	343	—	—	—	Oct. 67 closed
A-136	(VNSF) CSF/BS	Ben Soi	March 65	—	599	623	386	31 Aug. 70 to Ranger

* B-36 was formed provisionally in August 1967 to fill the gap in tactical/strategic reconnaissance capabilities of II and III CTZ which would be created by the impending transfer of Projects OMEGA and SIGMA to MACV on 1 November 1967. Initially B-36 depended on U.S. Special Forces and CIDG forces as well as support from regular U.S. Army LRRP personnel from the III CTZ. However, after B-20 was established that November, B-36 became the command and control detachment for the 3d Mobile Strike Force Command only.

INDIGENOUS TROOPS UNDER CONTROL OF THE 5TH SPECIAL FORCES GROUP
IV CORPS TACTICAL ZONE/MILITARY REGION 4
1967 – 70

Detachment & Mission		Camp/Opening Date		Oct. 1967	Oct. 1968	Oct. 1969	Oct. 1970	Disposition
C-4	Command & Control	Can Tho	Jan. 63	185	170	194	80	16 Dec. 70 to Ranger
B-40*	4th MSFC	Can Tho	March 65	—	—	1,950 MIKE	—	31 May 70 to Ranger
B-41	Command & Control S/SS	Moc Hoa	Feb. 65	—	44+(1,838)	51	42	31 Oct. 70 to Ranger
B-42	Command & Control S/SS	Chau Doc	March 65	54+(1,962)	—	—	—	31 Aug. 68 B-42 inactivated
B-43	Command & Control S	Cao Lanh	Feb. 67	—	53+(408)			7 April 69 closed
		Chi Lang	April 69			53	119	8 Dec. 70 closed

B-44	Command & Control SS	Phu Quoc	Feb. 67	0+(538)	—	—	—	June 68 to RF/PF
A-401	MSF	Don Phuc	Jan. 66	422 MIKE	522 MIKE	To B-40	—	To B-40; 31 May 70 to RF/PF
A-402	MSF	To Chau	Feb. 67	78 MIKE				1968 closed
		Moc Hoa	1968		595 MIKE	To B-40	29+ 391 MIKE	31 Oct. 70 to Ranger
A-403	MSF	To Chau	March 67	110 MIKE	397 MIKE	To B-40	—	31 May 70 closed
A-404	CIDG/MSF	Binh Hung	Jan. 65	0+(131)				9 Nov. 67 closed
		Cao Lanh			86 MIKE	To B-40	15+ 169 MIKE	Unverified
A-405	CIDG/BS/SS	Ha Tien	April 65	514+(230)	—	—	—	24 Oct. 67 to RF/PF
A-411	CIDG	My Phuoc Tay	Feb. 67	759	525	574	—	30 March 70 to RF/PF
A-412	CIDG/BS/SS	Kinh Quan II	Oct. 65	627+(527)	528+(647)	—	—	15 Nov. 68 to VNSF
A-413	CIDG/BS/SS	Binh Than Thon	May 65	403+(532)	418+(388)	540	328	2 Nov. 70 to Ranger
A-414	CIDG/BS/SS	Moc Hoa	March 63	694+(592)				March 68 closed
		Thanh Tri	March 68		332	572	315	5 Sept. 70 to Ranger
A-415	CIDG/BS/SS	Tuyen Nhon	April 65	460+(201)	456 + (261)	541	302	2 Oct. 70 to Ranger
A-416	CIDG	My Dien II	Jan. 68	—	480	483	—	30 March 70 to RF/PF
A-421	CIDG/BS	Ba Xoai	May 66	468	803	895	457	30 Nov. 70 to Ranger
A-423	CIDG/BS/SS	Tinh Bien	April 64	840+(1,045)	—	—	—	30 Oct. 70 to RF/PF
A-431	CIDG/BS	Cai Cai	April 65	823	650	659	398	2 Oct. 70 to Ranger
A-432	CIDG/BS/SS	Thuong Thoi	May 66	604+(1,222)	496+(1,552)	519		Sept. 70 flooded, moved to Chi Lang; 30
		Chi Lang	Sept. 70				450	Nov. 70 to Ranger
A-433	CIDG/SS	My An/ My Da	March 67	555+(934)	790	618	—	31 Jan. 70 to RF/PF
A-441	CIDG	Phu Quoc	Feb. 65	521	—	—	—	March 68 to RF/PF
A-442	CIDG Training Center	Phu Quoc	Sept. 66	320				15 June 68 relocated
		To Chau	Feb. 68		212	490	379	5 Sept. 70 to Ranger
A-144	(VNSF) CSF	Kinh Quan II	Oct. 65	—	0	533	—	31 Jan. 70 to RF/PF
A-149	(VNSF) CSF/BS	Vinh Gia	Aug. 64	584	625	728	573	30 Nov. 70 to Ranger

* B-40 detachment moved to Can Tho as command and control headquarters of the 4th Mobile Strike Force Command in March 1968.

Chapter 28

MACV Special Operations

Unauthorized

MACV Studies & Observation Group (MACV-SOG)

Arrived Vietnam: 16 January 1964
Departed Vietnam: 30 April 1972
Previous Station: Vietnam

Authorized Strength*	1966	1968	1971	1972
Army Staff, MACV-SOG	101	215	239	166

* See narrative for actual overall operating strengths.

MACV-SOG was the joint service high command unconventional-warfare task force engaged in highly classified clandestine operations throughout Southeast Asia. It was given the title "Studies & Observation Group" as a cover. The joint staff was allegedly performing an analysis of the lessons learned to that point in the Vietnam war, but it was actually a special operations group with distinct command decision authority.

In 1958 the South Vietnamese government created a secret special service directly under their president, which was redesignated the Vietnamese Special Forces Command in 1963. Special operations were conducted by this branch. The U.S. Central Intelligence Agency (CIA) supported and financed the operations. In April 1964 the government of South Vietnam created the Special Exploitation Service to take over these operations, whereupon MACV-SOG was established to assume the CIA's job of assisting, advising and supporting the new organization in the conduct of highly classified sabotage and psychological and special operations in North and South Vietnam, Laos, Cambodia and southern China. MACV-SOG and the Special Exploitation Service (SES) were activated simultaneously. In September 1967 the South Viet-

namese renamed the SES the Strategic Technical Directorate. With the drawdown in U.S. personnel and operations, MACV-SOG was deactivated on 30 April 1972 and the Strategic Technical Directorate Assistance Team 158 was activated 1 May 1972 to take its place. This team was subsequently deactivated on 12 March 1973, and no other U.S. headquarters took its place.

Originally headquartered in Cholon, it moved to Saigon in 1966. However, its air assets (Air Studies Group) were based at Nha Trang and its navy assets (Maritime Studies Group) were based at Da Nang with its original Forward Operations Base (FOB 1). The Ground Studies Group launch sites were initially located at Hue – Phu Bai, Khe Sanh, Kham Duc and near Kontum. The MACV-SOG training center and airborne operations group were at Long Thanh. A Psychological Studies Group was located in Saigon with antenna stations at Hue and Tay Ninh.

MACV-SOG was assigned about 2,000 Americans, mostly U.S. Special Forces, and over 8,000 highly trained indigenous troops. It had its own air force (90th Special Operations Wing) comprised of a squadron of U.S. Air Force UH-1F "Green Hornet" helicopters, a squadron of U.S. Air Force C-130 aircraft, a covert C-123 aircraft squadron piloted and manned by Nationalist Chinese, as well as the South Vietnamese 219th H-34 helicopter squadron. The U.S. Navy resources included SEALs, Vietnamese Underwater Demolition Teams (UDT) and fast patrol boats. Ground forces included army military intelligence, psychological operations and some 70 ground RT mobile-launch teams. Later MACV-SOG reorganized its ground strike elements into three field commands; Command and Control South, Central and North (CCS, CCC and CCN). Details of ground force organization are found in those sections.

MACV-SOG had five primary responsibilities and the capability to undertake additional special missions as required. Primary responsibilities included: (1) Cross-border operations regularly conducted to disrupt the VC, Khmer Rouge, Pathet Lao and NVA in their own territories; (2) Keeping track of all imprisoned and missing Americans and conducting raids to assist and free them as part of the Escape and Evasion (E & E) mission for all captured U.S. personnel and downed airmen; (3) Training and dispatching agents into North Vietnam to run resistance movement operations; (4) "Black" psychological operations, such as establishing false (notional) NVA broadcasting stations inside North Vietnam; (4) "Gray" psychological operations as typified by the Hue – Phu Bai propaganda transmitter. MACV-SOG was also entrusted with specific tasks such as kidnapping, assassination, insertion of rigged mortar rounds into the enemy ammunition supply system (which were set to explode and destroy their crews upon use) and retrieval of sensitive documents and equipment if lost or captured through enemy action. MACV-SOG was often able to use the intelligence it gathered for its own internal purposes as well as for high command special activities.

Command and Control Central, MACV-SOG   (CCC)

No Insignia
Authorized

Arrived Vietnam: November 1967
Departed Vietnam: March 1971
Location: Kontum

Command and Control Central (CCC) was formed by MACV-SOG in late 1967 as an expansion of its Kontum Forward Operations Base (FOB) under the command of a lieutenant colonel. CCC had responsibility for classified unconventional warfare operations throughout the triborder regions of Laos, Cambodia and Vietnam. CCC was organized the same way as other MACV-SOG field commands, and its flexible composition permitted fluctuation in the number of subordinate elements depending on mission requirements. It had around 30 Spike Recon Teams (RT), Hatchet Forces, and four Search-Location-and-Annihilation Mission Companies (SLAM Companies A, B, C and D). RTs were composed of three U.S. special forces and nine indigenous personnel per team, the latter drawn from ethnic minority groups (see page 241) and selected for their intense loyalty and excellent jungle-fighting qualities. RTs were capable of diverse special assignments ranging from ambush and calling in air strikes to cache destruction and reconnoiter-and-attack, and were often shifted between MACV-SOG field commands as mission requirements demanded. Originally named after states, RTs later adopted names of Asian poisonous snakes and assorted designations once all state names had been exhausted. Hatchet Forces were composed of five U.S. special forces and thirty indigenous personnel and could perform larger missions as well as reinforce RTs. The four SLAM companies were assigned to exploit promising situations. Their platoons were also capable of independent action as needed. CCC folded in March 1971 when MACV-SOG's Task Force I Advisory Element was established at Da Nang.

Command and Control North, MACV-SOG   (CCN)

No Insignia
Authorized

Arrived Vietnam: November 1967
Departed Vietnam: March 1971
Location: Da Nang

Command and Control North (CCN) was formed by MACV-SOG in late 1967 as an expansion of its Da Nang Forward Operations Base (FOB) which included launch sites established as early as 1964 at Hue – Phu Bai, Khe Sanh and Kham Duc. CCN, always the largest of the three MACV-SOG field commands, was commanded by a lieutenant colonel. It was assigned conduct of classified special unconventional warfare missions into Laos and North Vietnam. CCN was organized along the lines of CCC and was composed of Spike recon teams (RT), Hatchet forces and lettered SLAM companies. Missions into North Vietnam were initiated as early as 1 February 1964 under Operation Plan 34A. Operations into Laos commenced in September 1965 as part of Operation SHINING BRASS, renamed PRAIRIE FIRE in 1968. By this time MACV-SOG had at its disposal two battalions of American-led Nung tribesmen as reaction forces capable of performing large combat missions. CCN often operated in conjunction with the CIA-trained Meo tribesmen of Gen. Vang Pao. In 1971 the Laotian operations were given the code name PHU DUNG, and in March of that year MACV-SOG created Task Force I Advisory Element to replace its three field commands. This task force was located at Da Nang.

Command and Control South, MACV-SOG   (CCS)

No Insignia
Authorized

Arrived Vietnam: November 1967
Departed Vietnam: March 1971
Location: Ban Me Thuot

Command and Control South (CCS) was a new field command created by MACV-SOG when permission was granted to conduct cross-border missions into Cambodia. Commanded by a major, CCS was the smallest of the MACV-SOG field commands and was engaged in classified special unconventional warfare missions inside VC-dominated South Vietnam and throughout Cambodia. Its organization was similar to that of CCC. It contained Spike recon teams (RT), Hatchet forces, and four SLAM companies. Cross-border operations had been conducted into northeastern Cambodia since May 1967 under Project DANIEL BOONE, later known as SALEM HOUSE. In 1971 the name was changed to THOT NOT. CCS folded in March 1971 when MACV-SOG created Task Force I Advisory Element at Da Nang.

U.S. Army Vietnam Individual Training Group (UITG)/ Forces Armée Nationale Khmer Training Command (FANK)

No Insignia
Authorized

Arrived Vietnam: 1 November 1970
Departed Vietnam: 30 December 1972
Previous Location: Vietnam
Authorized Strength: Unknown

The U.S. Field Training Group was established by U.S. Army, Vietnam and MACV. It included the USARV Individual Training Group composed of U.S. Special Forces instructors with the mission of training soldiers of the République Khymer (Cambodia). Training centers in South Vietnam were set up at Long Hai, Chi Lang, Dong Ba Thin and Phuoc Tuy. In May 1972 this group was renamed the FANK Training Command. This concept originated when B-36 entered Cambodia during the May 1970 invasion with its 3d Mobile Strike Force Command composed of Cambodian troops. After B-36 withdrew to Long Hai, these remained to become the Cambodian Palace Guards. Soon B-36 was ordered to train more Cambodians, and in January 1971 was converted into the nucleus of the Long Hai UITG Training Center. Similar training centers were established at Chi Lang and Dong Ba Thin and each instituted an intensive 15-week program whereby a Cambodian cadre and raw Cambodian recruits were transformed into combat-ready light infantry battalions. Each center processed four to five such battalions at any given time, staggered at two-week intervals in which everything from basic rifle marksmanship to combined unit tactics was taught.

U.S. Army Vietnam Individual Training Group	24 Feb. 71 – 14 May 72
FANK Training Command, Army Advisory Group Vietnam (AAGV)	15 May 72 – 30 Nov. 72
Long Hai Training Battalion	24 Feb. 71 – 30 Nov. 72
Chi Lang Training Battalion	24 Feb. 71 – 1 Sept. 71
Phuoc Tuy Training Battalion	1 Sept. 71 – 30 Nov. 72
Dong Ba Thin Training Battalion	24 Feb. 71 – 30 Nov. 72

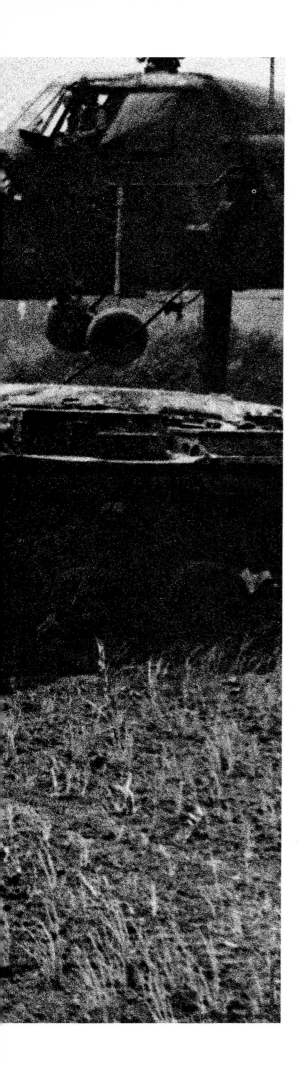

Other
U.S. Services

Chapter 29

U.S. Air Force and U.S. Navy Construction

U.S. AIR FORCE CONSTRUCTION AND COMBAT SECURITY FORCES IN VIETNAM

Combat Security Police Squadrons, each composed of 21 officers and 538 airmen, were introduced in Vietnam by the U.S. Air Force as a response to VC and NVA attacks on USAF air bases during the 1968 Tet battles.

Unit	Vietnam Service
821st Combat Security Police Squadron	April 68 – Aug. 68
821st Combat Security Police Squadron*	Aug. 69 – Feb. 71
822d Combat Security Police Squadron	Aug. 68 – March 69
823d Combat Security Police Squadron	March 69 – Aug. 69
1041st USAF Police Squadron (Test)†	Jan. 67 – July 67

* Second tour in Vietnam. Squadron had a reduced strength of 250 commencing January 1970.

† Strength about 200.

RED HORSE (Rapid Engineer Deployable Heavy Operational Repair Squadron, Engineering) units were introduced in Vietnam during 1966. These civil engineering squadrons had a complement of 15 officers and 385 enlisted men. They were unique among military engineer units in that each employed between 600 – 1,000 Vietnamese workers, which greatly expanded their construction capability. Prior to RED HORSE deployments, the Air Force had relied on 60-man PRIME BEEF (Prime Base Engineer Emergency Force) teams drawn from base maintenance units in the United States. Such teams, however, had been supplemented with up to 300 local civilian workers.

There was also one RED HORSE Squadron in Thailand (566th Civil Engineering Squadron, Heavy Repair) located primarily at U-Tapao (Sattahip) which arrived in July 1966 and by departure in August 1969 employed over 3,000 Thais.

Unit	Vietnam Service
554th Civil Engineering Squadron, Heavy Repair	Jan. 66 – June 72 Phan Rang
555th Civil Engineering Squadron, Heavy Repair	Feb. 66 – March 70 Cam Ranh Bay
819th Civil Engineering Squadron, Heavy Repair	Aug. 66 – Feb. 70 Phu Cat
820th Civil Engineering Squadron, Heavy Repair	Oct. 66 – Feb. 69 Tuy Hoa
823d Civil Engineering Squadron Heavy Repair	Oct. 66 – Aug. 71 Bien Hoa

U.S. NAVY CONSTRUCTION FORCES IN VIETNAM

Although most of the construction in Vietnam was done by civilian contractors, military engineer force personnel from all the services — Navy Seabees, Marines, Army and Air Force — carried out a significant portion. As early as 1954, Seabees from Amphibious Construction Battalion 1 were building refugee camps in Vietnam, and from 1962 through 1965 Seabees were building U.S. Army Special Forces camps. Naval Mobile Construction

Battalions, each with a complement of 24 officers and 738 men, began landing at Da Nang in May and June of 1965. Primarily engaged in the I Corps region, Navy Seabees were used to build waterfront facilities, cantonments, storage areas, ammunition dumps, roads and bridges. They were based at Da Nang, Chu Lai, Hue – Phu Bai, Dong Tam and Quang Tri.

Units	Arrived Vietnam	Departed Vietnam	Number of Teams*
3d Naval Construction Brigade	1 June 66	9 Nov. 71	N/A
30th Naval Construction Regiment	10 May 65	8 Dec. 69	N/A
32d Naval Construction Regiment	1 Aug. 67	1 May 71	N/A
Amphibious Construction Battalion 1	April 64	May 65	— †
Naval Mobile Construction Battalion 1	8 March 66	22 March 70	7
Naval Mobile Construction Battalion 3	28 May 65	23 April 71	12
Naval Mobile Construction Battalion 4	9 Dec. 65	2 Dec. 69	7
Naval Mobile Construction Battalion 5	25 Sept. 65	7 Nov. 71	14
Naval Mobile Construction Battalion 6	21 May 66	7 April 68	5
Naval Mobile Construction Battalion 7	13 April 66	23 June 70	8
Naval Mobile Construction Battalion 8	11 Sept. 65	22 Nov. 69	5
Naval Mobile Construction Battalion 9	27 June 65	29 May 68	9
Naval Mobile Construction Battalion 10	7 May 65	16 Sept. 70	16
Naval Mobile Construction Battalion 11	3 Feb. 66	18 Nov. 69	6
Naval Mobile Construction Battalion 12 (Reserve)	21 Sept. 68	21 April 69	— †
Naval Mobile Construction Battalion 22 (Reserve)	13 Aug. 68	5 March 69	— †
Naval Mobile Construction Battalion 40	14 Aug. 66	21 July 69	4
Naval Mobile Construction Battalion 53	18 Jan. 68	4 Nov. 69	1
Naval Mobile Construction Battalion 58	29 Oct. 66	10 Oct. 69	4
Naval Mobile Construction Battalion 62	8 Dec. 66	13 Nov. 70	6
Naval Mobile Construction Battalion 71	10 April 67	18 Nov. 68	7
Naval Mobile Construction Battalion 74	5 June 67	12 April 71	6
Naval Mobile Construction Battalion 121	2 Aug. 67	20 July 70	4
Naval Mobile Construction Battalion 128	24 Oct. 67	18 Aug. 69	2
Naval Mobile Construction Battalion 133	10 Feb. 67	16 Jan. 70	6

* This represents the number of Seabee teams deployed to Vietnam from each battalion. Note that each battalion's effort varied widely. Eight-to-ten-month-long team deployments appear to have been the rule. Dates indicate when the unit first entered Vietnam and when it departed Vietnam for the last time. Times of subordinate team tours in Vietnam would fluctuate greatly within the time frame of its parent battalion.

† Represents HQ utilization only.

Chapter 30

Marine Corps

U.S. MARINE CORPS IN VIETNAM

MAJOR MARINE HEADQUARTERS IN VIETNAM	Arrived Vietnam	Departed Vietnam
9th Marine Amphibious Brigade	**8 March 1965**	**6 May 1965**

The 9th Marine Expeditionary Brigade, later redesignated the 9th Marine Amphibious Brigade because the word "Expeditionary" recalled memories of the French colonial forces, was sent to Vietnam from Okinawa and posted to Da Nang to provide security for the Da Nang Air Base. The brigade consisted of two Battalion Landing Teams (BLT) composed of the 3d Battalion, 9th Marines and 1st Battalion, 3d Marines.

III Marine Amphibious Force	**7 May 1965**	**14 April 1971**

The III Marine Amphibious Force was formed in Vietnam to command the Marine units which had been committed in the I Corps Tactical Zone. The U.S. Marines had been sent to meet the immediate enemy threat in the area, to post elite troops next to the North Vietnamese border and to take advantage of their unique ability to supply themselves "over the beach" without major logistical facilities developed at ports and airfields. The III Marine Amphibious Force acted as a corps-level headquarters over all U.S. Marine and Army units within the I Corps area. In February 1968 MACV Forward Headquarters was established in I CTZ to facilitate control over the increasing number of major army units deploying into the area. Although army units were present, this headquarters (later the XXIV Corps) came under III Marine Amphibious Force command.

1st Marine Division	**February 1966**	**April 1971**

The 1st Marine Division controlled primarily the 1st, 5th and 7th Marine Regiments as well as the 26th and 27th Marine Regiments attached from the 5th Marine Division. It was stationed at Chu Lai until November 1966 when the division headquarters relocated to the Da Nang area where it remained. Division operations are discussed in the operational section of this work.

3d Marine Division	**6 May 1965**	**30 November 1969**

The 3d Marine Division was primarily in command of the 3d, 4th and 9th Marine Regiments in Vietnam. It was located initially at Da Nang but moved into the Hue area in October 1966. In March 1968 the division relocated to Quang Tri and in June moved to Dong Ha, where it remained until November 1969 when it was posted back to Da Nang for redeployment from Vietnam.

U.S. MARINE CORPS NON-DIVISIONAL AND SUB-DIVISIONAL GROUND UNITS IN VIETNAM

Marine Infantry

Unit	Location	Arrived Vietnam	Departed Vietnam
1st Marine Regiment	Chu Lai (Jan. 66) Da Nang (June 66) Quang Tri (Oct. 67) Hue (Feb. 68) Khe Sanh (April 68) Gio Linh (Aug. 68) Da Nang (Sept. 68)	January 1966	May 1971
1st Battalion	—	August 1965	May 1971
2d Battalion	—	November 1965	May 1971
3d Battalion	—	January 1966	May 1971
3d Marine Regiment	Da Nang (April 65) Hue (Dec. 66) Dong Ha (May 67) Camp Carroll (Jan. 68) Dong Ha (Feb. 68) Cam Lo (Aug. 68) Dong Ha (Dec. 68) Khe Sanh (June 69)	April 1965	September 1969
1st Battalion	—	March 1965	October 1969
2d Battalion	—	April 1965	November 1969
3d Battalion	—	May 1965	October 1969
4th Marine Regiment	Hue (May 65) Phong Dien (Jan. 68) Camp Carroll (Feb. 68) Khe Sanh (July 68) Cam Lo (Dec. 68)	May 1965	November 1969
1st Battalion	—	May 1965	November 1969
2d Battalion	—	May 1965	November 1969
3d Battalion	—	April 1965	October 1969
5th Marine Regiment	Chu Lai (May 66) Da Nang (June 67) Hoi An (Jan. 68) Hue (Feb. 68) Phu Loc (March 68) Da Nang (Aug. 68)	May 1966	April 1971
1st Battalion	—	May 1966	April 1971
2d Battalion	—	April 1966	March 1971
3d Battalion	—	May 1966	March 1971
7th Marine Regiment	Chu Lai (Aug. 65) Da Nang (May 67)	August 1965	October 1970
1st Battalion	—	August 1965	September 1970
2d Battalion	—	August 1965	October 1970
3d Battalion	—	September 1965	October 1970

9th Marine Regiment	Da Nang (July 65)	July 1965	August 1969
	Dong Ha (May 67)		
	Con Thien (Feb. 68)		
	Cam Lo (May 68)		
	Khe Sanh (Nov. 68)		
	Cam Lo (Feb. 69)		
1st Battalion	—	June 1965	July 1969
2d Battalion	—	July 1965	August 1969
3d Battalion	—	March 1965	August 1969
26th Marine Regiment	Da Nang (April 67)	April 1967	March 1970
	Dong Ha (June 67)		
	Khe Sanh (Dec. 67)		
	Hoi An (May 68)		
	Phu Loc (Aug. 68)		
	Da Nang (Nov. 68)		
1st Battalion	—	September 1966	March 1970
2d Battalion	—	August 1966	March 1970
3d Battalion	—	August 1966	March 1970
27th Marine Regiment	Da Nang (Feb. 68)	February 1968	September 1968
1st Battalion	—	February 1968	September 1968
2d Battalion	—	February 1968	September 1968
3d Battalion	—	February 1968	September 1968

Armor

1st Tank Battalion	March 1966	March 1970
3d Tank Battalion	July 1965	October 1969
1st Amphibian Tractor Battalion	July 1965	July 1969
3d Amphibian Tractor Battalion	March 1966	January 1970
1st Armored Amphibian Company	November 1966	July 1969

Reconnaissance

1st Reconnaissance Battalion	March 1966	March 1971
3d Reconnaissance Battalion	May 1965	November 1969
1st Force Recon Company	October 1965	April 1971
3d Force Recon Company	April 1967	August 1970

Artillery

1st Field Artillery Group	November 1966	July 1969
11th Marine Artillery Regiment	February 1966	March 1971
1st Battalion, 11th Marines	January 1966	May 1971
2d Battalion, 11th Marines	May 1966	March 1971
3d Battalion, 11th Marines	August 1965	October 1970
4th Battalion, 11th Marines	February 1966	October 1970
12th Marine Artillery Regiment	July 1965	November 1969
1st Battalion, 12th Marines	April 1965	September 1969
2d Battalion, 12th Marines	July 1965	August 1969
3d Battalion, 12th Marines	May 1965	November 1969
4th Battalion, 12th Marines	July 1965	November 1969
1st Battalion, 13th Marines	July 1967	March 1970
2d Battalion, 13th Marines	February 1968	September 1968

Antitank

1st Antitank Battalion	March 1966	December 1967
3d Antitank Battalion	July 1965	December 1967

Other Artillery

1st 8-inch Howitzer Battery	July 1965	September 1970
3d 8-inch Howitzer Battery	March 1966	June 1971
1st 155mm Gun Battery	March 1966	October 1970
3d 155mm Gun Battery	August 1965	September 1970
5th 155mm Gun Battery (SP)	July 1967	March 1970
1st Searchlight Battery	July 1967	July 1969
1st Air-Naval Gun Liaison Co	December 1965	May 1971

Engineer

1st Engineer Battalion	January 1966	March 1971
3d Engineer Battalion	July 1965	October 1969
7th Engineer Battalion	August 1965	December 1970
9th Engineer Battalion	June 1966	August 1970
11th Engineer Battalion	November 1966	November 1969
1st Bridge Company	August 1965	August 1970
3d Bridge Company	October 1966	October 1969

Radio

1st Radio Battalion	February 1967	April 1971
5th Radio Battalion	November 1965	October 1970
7th Radio Battalion	July 1966	June 1971

Medical

1st Medical Battalion	March 1966	April 1970
3d Medical Battalion	June 1965	November 1969
1st Hospital Company	March 1966	February 1970

MP

1st Military Police Battalion	May 1966	June 1971
3d Military Police Battalion	May 1967	August 1970

Force Service

1st Force Service Regiment	February 1967	April 1971
Headquarters & Service Battalion*	February 1967	April 1971
Supply Battalion*	February 1967	April 1971
Maintenance Battalion*	February 1967	April 1971

Motor Transport

1st Motor Transport Battalion	April 1966	April 1971
3d Motor Transport Battalion	June 1965	July 1969
7th Motor Transport Battalion	March 1966	February 1970
9th Motor Transport Battalion	July 1965	November 1969
11th Motor Transport Battalion	December 1966	April 1971

Service

1st Service Battalion	March 1966	September 1970
3d Service Battalion	June 1965	October 1969
1st Supply Battalion	March 1966	April 1971
1st Shore Party Battalion	January 1966	March 1970
3d Shore Party Battalion	April 1965	November 1969
7th Separate Bulk Fuel Company	December 1966	March 1970

Combined Action

1st Combined Action Battalion	October 1967	September 1970
2d Combined Action Battalion	October 1967	May 1971
3d Combined Action Battalion	October 1967	September 1970
4th Combined Action Battalion	July 1968	July 1970

* Element of 1st Force Service Regiment, III Marine Amphibious Force, Vietnam.

9th Marine Amphibious Brigade

Arrived Vietnam: 1 April 1972
Departed Vietnam: 31 July 1972
Authorized Strength: 893*

* Marines actually present in South Vietnam only.

On 30 March 1972 the North Vietnamese Army crossed the DMZ in strength and the U.S. Marine Corps, by virtue of its sea-basing and amphibious capability, maintained a force off the coast of Vietnam ready for immediate commitment to combat. Although Marine air and ground units had been engaged in Southeast Asia until June 1971, their reemployment drew attention to quick Marine response to crises. Amphibious Ready Group Alpha with the 31st Marine Amphibious Unit containing some 1,700 troops and Amphibious Ready Group Bravo with Battalion Landing Team (BLT) Bravo (1st Battalion, 9th Marines) arrived on 2 April. The 9th Marine Amphibious Brigade commanding general assumed control 9 April 1972.

The missions included possible evacuation of U.S. personnel and cargo from Military Region 1, forcible entry into NVA-held territory of either North or South Vietnam and operations in support of allied forces. The assault force increased in strength as additional lift became available, and by 28 April 1972 the brigade had 5,200 men and 50 helicopters. Maximum response posture was achieved in late May when four of the six BLTs were at sea. The 2d Battalion, 4th Marines was assigned a 72-hour air contingency mission at Okinawa and the 3d Battalion, 9th Marines furnished security elements for Bien Hoa and Nam Phong air bases.

Ground elements included:

Regimental Landing Team 4 (4th Marine Regiment)
9th Marine Regiment

Allies

Chapter 31

Australia and New Zealand

Australian Army Training Team, Vietnam (AATTV)

Arrived Vietnam: 31 July 1962
Departed Vietnam: 18 December 1972

Australia's first military contribution to the Vietnam conflict was a small team of army officer and warrant officer advisors who arrived in mid-1962. Those advisors (originally 30) joined with U.S. advisory teams training South Vietnamese forces primarily in the northern provinces. Over the years this Australian Army Training Team, Vietnam (AATTV) grew to over 100 officers and warrant officers who were employed with operational units of the Army of the Republic of Vietnam and the VNSF. As such, they often led South Vietnamese troops as well as trained them. They earned four Victoria Crosses, the highest gallantry award for members of the British Commonwealth armies, during the course of the Vietnam conflict.

Headquarters, Australian Army Force, Vietnam (HQ, AAFV)

Arrived Vietnam: 25 May 1965
Departed Vietnam: 2 May 1966
Location: Saigon

Following a decision of the Australian government to increase its assistance to the Republic of Vietnam, the 1st Battalion of the Royal Australian Regiment (RAR), together with a logistics support company, arrived in Vietnam May – June 1965 (see Australian Army Order of Battle). Supporting artillery, armored personnel carriers, engineers and light aircraft arrived in September 1965. The operational element comprised 1,300 men and was

located at Bien Hoa as part of the U.S. 173d Airborne Brigade. Many of their operations were conducted in War Zone D. HQ, AAFV was located in Saigon and the AATTV remained deployed with the U.S. advisory teams. The 1st Battalion, RAR, completed its tour of duty and returned to Australia in June 1966. At that time there was a substantial increase in Australia's commitment, and the battalion group was replaced by a task force organization with its own logistical support. At the same time, HQ, AAFV was upgraded to a joint Australian headquarters with naval and air force representation to be called Headquarters, Australian Forces, Vietnam (HQ, AFV).

Headquarters, Australian Forces, Vietnam (HQ, AFV)

Arrived Vietnam: 3 May 1966
Departed Vietnam: 15 March 1972
Location: Saigon

When command of the HQ, AFV was upgraded, this headquarters was established to replace it. The deputy commander of HQ, AFV was the Royal Australian Air Force Commodore, who in addition to being Forces Deputy Commander also retained his position as air commodore and commander of the Royal Australian Air Force in South Vietnam.

Headquarters, 1st Australian Task Force (ATF)

Arrived Vietnam: 1 April 1966
Departed Vietnam: 12 March 1972
Location: Nui Dat

During 1966, due to increased Australian army strength, the two major ground units were called the 1st Australian Task Force and the 1st Australian Logistic Support Group. The principal infantry units first serving this formation were the 5th and 6th Battalions of the Royal Australian Regiment (see Australian Army Order of Battle) and the 3d Special Air Service Squadron. The artillery contained two Australian batteries and one New Zealand battery. The task force was given its own tactical area of responsibility in Phuoc Tuy Province southeast of Saigon, and the task force headquarters was established at a rubber plantation at Nui Dat just north of the provincial capital of Baria, about 35 miles southeast of Saigon. The task force was withdrawn from Vietnam in stages during 1971, and apart from small detachments necessary to provide security during this withdrawal phase, all combat troops and members of supporting arms were effectively returned to Australia by late December 1971.

Australian Army Assistance Group, Vietnam   (AAAGV)

Arrived Vietnam: 6 March 1972
Departed Vietnam: 31 January 1973
Location: Saigon

The Australian Army Assistance Group, Vietnam (AAAGV) was established following the withdrawal of combat elements from Vietnam. Its role was to provide training and advisory assistance to both South Vietnamese and Cambodian troops, especially in Phuoc Tuy province. Composed of 23 officers and 120 other ranks, the headquarters (including a guard and escort detachment with signals) located in Saigon, and the Australian Army Training Team, Vietnam (AATTV) located in Phuoc Tuy province.

AUSTRALIAN ARMY ORDER OF BATTLE IN VIETNAM

Unit	Length of Service	
	From	To
1st Battalion, Royal Australian Regiment	25 May 1965	14 June 1966
	19 Jan. 1968	28 Feb. 1969
2d Battalion, Royal Australian Regiment	2 March 1967	18 June 1968
	28 April 1970	4 June 1971
3d Battalion, Royal Australian Regiment	12 Dec. 1967	5 Dec. 1968
	12 Feb. 1971	19 Oct. 1971
4th Battalion, Royal Australian Regiment	29 Jan. 1968	30 May 1969
	1 May 1971	12 March 1972
5th Battalion, Royal Australian Regiment	1 April 1966	5 July 1967
	28 Jan. 1969	5 March 1970
6th Battalion, Royal Australian Regiment	1 April 1966	5 July 1967
	7 May 1969	28 May 1970
7th Battalion, Royal Australian Regiment	2 March 1967	26 April 1968
	10 Feb. 1970	10 March 1971
8th Battalion, Royal Australian Regiment	18 Nov. 1969	12 Nov. 1970
9th Battalion, Royal Australian Regiment	5 Nov. 1968	5 Dec. 1969
1st Armored Personnel Carrier Troop (became part of 1st APC Squadron)	14 Sept. 1965	31 March 1966
1st Armored Personnel Carrier (APC) Squadron (redesignated A Squadron, 3d Cavalry Regiment)	1 April 1966	15 Jan. 1967
A Squadron, 3d Cavalry Regiment	16 Jan. 1967	12 May 1969
	7 Jan. 1971	12 March 1972
B Squadron, 3d Cavalry Regiment	13 May 1969	6 Jan. 1971
A Squadron, 1st Armored Regiment	23 Dec. 1969	16 Dec. 1970
B Squadron, 1st Armored Regiment	11 Feb. 1969	22 Dec. 1969
C Squadron, 1st Armored Regiment	29 Jan. 1968	10 Feb. 1969
	17 Dec. 1970	30 Sept. 1971
104th Field Artillery Battery	5 May 1971	20 Dec. 1971
105th Field Artillery Battery, 4th Field Regiment	14 Sept. 1965	31 March 1966
1st Field Artillery Regiment (minus one battery) (complete)	1 April 1966	5 July 1967
	25 Feb. 1969	10 May 1970
4th Field Artillery Regiment (minus one battery) (complete)	2 March 1967	28 May 1968
	24 Feb. 1970	18 March 1971
12th Field Artillery Regiment (minus one battery) (complete)	29 Jan. 1968	11 March 1969
	27 Jan. 1971	20 Dec. 1971
3d Field Troop, 1st Field Squadron	14 Sept. 1965	31 March 1966
1st Field Squadron (minus one Troop) (complete)	1 April 1966	30 Nov. 1967
	1 Dec. 1967	18 Nov. 1971

1st Special Air Service Squadron (minus one troop)*	2 March 1967	18 Feb. 1968
	3 Feb. 1970	18 Feb. 1971
2d Special Air Service Squadron (minus one troop)*	29 Jan. 1968	4 March 1969
	18 Feb. 1971	15 Oct. 1971
3d Special Air Service Squadron (minus one troop)*	1 April 1966	5 July 1967
	3 Feb. 1969	20 Feb. 1970
21st Engineer Support Troop, 1st ATF	1 April 1966	9 Dec. 1971
1st Australian Civil Affairs Unit, AFV	2 March 1967	25 Nov. 1971
103d Signal Squadron, 1st ATF	1 April 1966	5 July 1967
104th Signal Squadron, 1st ATF	2 March 1967	15 Dec. 1971
110th Signal Squadron, AFV (headquarters only)	2 March 1967	20 Nov. 1967
(complete; see below)	21 Nov. 1967	12 March 1972
503d Signal Troop (absorbed into 110th Sig Sqdn)	2 March 1967	20 Nov. 1967
506th Signal Troop	1 April 1966	5 July 1967
520th Signal Troop	1 April 1966	5 July 1967
527th Signal Troop	14 Sept. 1965	5 July 1967
532d Signal Troop (absorbed into 110th Sig Sqdn)	2 March 1967	20 Nov. 1967
547th Signal Troop	2 March 1967	23 Dec. 1971
552d Signal Troop	1 April 1966	5 July 1967
557th Signal Troop (absorbed into 110th Sig Sqdn)	2 March 1967	20 Nov. 1967
561st Signal Troop (absorbed into 110th Sig Sqdn)	2 March 1967	20 Nov. 1967
581st Signal Troop	1 April 1966	5 July 1967
704th Signal Troop (absorbed into 110th Sig Sqdn)	2 March 1967	20 Nov. 1967
709th Signal Troop (absorbed into 110th Sig Sqdn)	25 May 1965	20 Nov. 1967
Headquarters, 145th Signal Squadron	1 April 1966	5 July 1967
Australian Logistics Support Company	25 May 1965	31 March 1966
1st Australian Logistics Support Group	1 April 1966	16 Oct. 1971
55th Engineer Workshop and Park Squadron		
(elements)	1 April 1966	14 June 1971
(complete)	15 June 1971	12 March 1972
17th Construction Squadron (minus one troop)	1 April 1966	1 March 1967
(complete)	2 March 1967	12 Feb. 1972
26th Royal Australian Army Service — Company	8 Jan. 1968	30 June 1971
1st Royal Australian Army Service — Company	1 April 1966	5 July 1967
5th Royal Australian Army Service — Company	2 March 1967	12 March 1972
176th AD Company	1 June 1967	18 Nov. 1971
1st Australian Field Hospital	13 Nov. 1967	14 Dec. 1971

* The Special Air Service (SAS) comprised elite commando formations. In December 1969 the 3d SAS Squadron conducted an operational parachute descent in eastern Phuoc Tuy Province; the first operational parachute descent by Australian soldiers since the assault on Nadzab, New Guinea, in 1943.

New Zealand "V" Force

Arrived Vietnam: 21 July 1965
Departed Vietnam: June 1972*
(residual force)

* The first rifle company was withdrawn November 1970; the artillery battery, March 1971 and the "V" rifle company, at the end of 1971.

New Zealand's first significant military contribution to the Vietnam conflict was the sending of the 161st Battery, New Zealand Artillery, to support the Australian forces with the U.S. 173d Airborne Brigade in Phuoc Tuy Province. The New Zealand Battalion of the 28th Commonwealth Brigade was in Malaysia at the time and could not be spared for Vietnam duty, but a rifle company of the Royal New Zealand Infantry Regiment was provided from the battalion on a rotational basis to Vietnam. This "V" company first arrived in South Vietnam on 11 May 1967 and a "W" company followed on 17 December 1967, so that two companies of New Zealand infantry were present to form an ANZAC (Australian – New Zealand Army Corps) Battalion with the third element from Australia. Additionally, a platoon of the elite New Zealand Special Air Service (SAS) commandos joined to provide a reconnaissance patrol capability.

"V" Force Order of Battle:

161st Artillery Battery (105mm), Royal New Zealand Artillery
"V" Rifle Company, Royal New Zealand Infantry
"W" Rifle Company, Royal New Zealand Infantry
Number 4 Troop, Royal New Zealand Special Air Service (SAS)
Administrative Element
Logistical Support Element

Chapter 32

Philippines and Thailand

1st Philippine Civic Action Group, Vietnam (PHILCAG)

Arrived Vietnam: 14 September 1966
Departed Vietnam: 13 December 1969*
Location: Tay Ninh

* Rear element departed 15 January 1970.

The 1st Philippine Civic Action Group, Vietnam (PHILCAG) arrived in September 1966 and was located to the Thanh Dien Forest region of Tay Ninh Province. It was concerned with pacification in the area as well as defense of its base camp at Tay Ninh. In September 1968 the PHILCAG commenced withdrawal to the Philippines through reduction in personnel and on 1 December 1969 began actual redeployment. Upon its departure the U.S. 25th Infantry Division took over the PHILCAG's former base camp.

PHILCAG Order of Battle:

Philippine Infantry Security Battalion
Philippine Field Artillery Battalion (105mm)
Construction Engineer Battalion
Medical & Dental Battalion
Logistical Support Company
Headquarters & Service Company

Royal Thai Army Regiment

Arrived Vietnam: 19 September 1967
Departed Vietnam: 15 August 1968
Location: Bear Cat

The Royal Thai Army Volunteer Force initially sent to South Vietnam was the "Queen's Cobras," an elite infantry regiment stationed at Bear Cat in conjunction with the U.S. 9th Infantry Division. This regiment was rotated back to Thailand when the Royal Thai Army Expeditionary Division arrived.

Royal Thai Army Expeditionary Division

Arrived Vietnam: 25 February 1969
Departed Vietnam: 31 August 1971*

* Reduced to brigade strength; see Royal Thai Army Volunteer Force.

The Royal Thai Army Expeditionary Division ("Black Panthers") arrived in increments and served at Bear Cat. The first troops arrived in the latter part of July 1968, followed by divisional headquarters, the 2d Brigade and two artillery battalions which were in Vietnam on 9 January 1969. The 3d Brigade then arrived 5 July – 5 August 1969 and replaced the 1st Brigade, which rotated back to Thailand as the 3d Brigade arrived in Vietnam. Around August 1970 the "Black Panthers" Division was redesignated the Royal Thai Army Volunteer Force, a title it retained throughout subsequent phase-downs.

Royal Thai Army Expeditionary Division Order of Battle:

1st Royal Thai Army Brigade
 1st, 2d, 3d Infantry Battalions

2d Royal Thai Army Brigade
 1st, 2d, 3d Infantry Battalions

3d Royal Thai Army Brigade
 1st, 2d, 3d Infantry Battalions

Division Artillery
   1st Artillery Battalion (155mm)
   1st Artillery Battalion (105mm)
   2d Artillery Battalion (105mm)
   3d Artillery Battalion (105mm)

1st Armored Cavalry Squadron
Combat Engineer Battalion
Signal Battalion

1st Long Range Reconnaissance Troop
Military Police Company
Division Headquarters
Aviation Company

Royal Thai Army
Volunteer Force

Arrived Vietnam: 1 September 1971*
Departed Vietnam: March 1972

* As brigade-sized element.

The Royal Thai Army Volunteer Force (RTAVF) had been in existence since August 1970 when the Royal Thai Army Expeditionary Division ("Black Panthers") was renamed. However, when its 1st Brigade redeployed to Thailand at the end of August 1971, the RTAVF lost all divisional connotation. The RTAVF was headquartered at Saigon and maintained its base camp at Bear Cat. The 2d Brigade, the major combat element of the RTAVF, redeployed back in stages in early 1972. The 1st Battalion departed 4 February 1972, the 2d Battalion departed 25 January 1972 and the 3d Battalion departed 15 January 1972.

Royal Thai Army Volunteer Force
Order of Battle:

2d Royal Thai Army Brigade
   1st, 2d, 3d Infantry Battalions

Brigade Artillery
   1st Artillery Battalion (155mm)
   1st Artillery Battalion (105mm)
   2d Artillery Battalion (105mm)

Combat Engineer Battalion (partial)
Signal Battalion (partial)
Aviation Company
Military Police Company
Force Headquarters

Chapter 33

Republic of Korea

Republic of Korea Forces Vietnam Field Command

Arrived Vietnam: August 1966
Departed Vietnam: 17 March 1973
Location: Nha Trang

The first Republic of Korea military forces to enter South Vietnam were in the form of a Survey (liaison) Team which departed for Vietnam on 19 August 1964. On 25 February 1965 the advance element of a Korean "Dove" unit arrived and was located at Bien Hoa. This unit consisted of an engineer battalion, a transport company, a Marine engineer company, a security battalion, a service unit, a control group and a mobile hospital. The main body arrived 16 March. During the period September – November 1965, the Republic of Korea rapidly reinforced its assets with the crack Capital Division ("Tigers") — less one regimental combat team — and the 2d Marine Corps Brigade ("Blue Dragons") along with supporting elements. In April 1966 Korea sent in another division, the 9th Infantry Division ("White Horse"). In 1967 another Marine battalion landed with additional support forces. After the 9th Infantry Division arrived, Korea established a corps headquarters, the Field Command, close to I Field Force of the U.S. Army at Nha Trang. Though the 2d Korean Marine Brigade departed Vietnam between December 1971 and February 1972, the bulk of the Korean forces in Vietnam did not commence withdrawal until 31 January 1973. The last Republic of Korea units were out of South Vietnam by 23 March 1973.

Republic of Korea Capital Division

Arrived Vietnam: 29 September 1965
Departed Vietnam: 10 March 1973
Location: Qui Nhon

The Republic of Korea Capital Division headquarters ("Tigers") deployed to South Vietnam on 29 September 1965. The Cavalry Regiment arrived 14 October 1965, the 1st Infantry Regiment, on 29 October 1965, and the 26th Infantry Regiment, on 16 April 1966. The division was posted to the Qui Nhon – Binh Khe area of Binh Dinh Province, where it remained throughout its service in Vietnam.

Capital Division Order of Battle:

Headquarters and Headquarters Company

The Cavalry Regiment	3 infantry battalions
1st Infantry Regiment	3 infantry battalions
26th Infantry Regiment	3 infantry battalions

Headquarters and Headquarters Battery, Division Artillery

10th Field Artillery Battalion (105mm)
60th Field Artillery Battalion (105mm)
61st Field Artillery Battalion (105mm)
628th Field Artillery Battalion (155mm)

Capital Division Engineer Battalion
Capital Division Armor Company

Capital Division Reconnaissance Company
Capital Division Signal Company
Capital Division Military Police Company
Capital Division Medical Company
Capital Division Ordnance Company
Capital Division Quartermaster Company
Capital Division Replacement Company
Capital Division Aviation Section

Republic of Korea
9th Infantry Division

Arrived Vietnam: 27 September 1966
Departed Vietnam: 16 March 1973
Location: Ninh Hoa

The Republic of Korea's 9th Infantry Division ("White Horse") arrived at Ninh Hoa during the period 5 September – 8 October 1966 and was stationed along the length of Highway 1 around Ninh Hoa. The headquarters remained in that city. The 28th Infantry Regiment arrived 7 September 1966, the 29th Infantry Regiment arrived 27 September 1966 and the 30th Infantry Regiment arrived at Cam Ranh Bay 9 October 1966.

9th Infantry Division Order of Battle:

Headquarters and Headquarters Company

28th Infantry Regiment	3 infantry battalions
29th Infantry Regiment	3 infantry battalions
30th Infantry Regiment	3 infantry battalions

Headquarters and Headquarters Battery, Division Artillery

30th Field Artillery Battalion (105mm)
51st Field Artillery Battalion (105mm)
52d Field Artillery Battalion (105mm)
966th Field Artillery Battalion (155mm)

Division Engineer Battalion
Division Armor Company
Division Reconnaissance Company
Division Signal Company
Division Military Police Company
Division Medical Company
Division Ordnance Company
Division Quartermaster Company
Division Replacement Company
Division Aviation Section

Republic of Korea
2d Marine Corps Brigade

Arrived Vietnam: 19 October 1965
Departed Vietnam: February 1972
Locations: Cam Ranh Bay, Tuy Hoa, Phu Bai, Hoi An

The Republic of Korea's 2d Marine Corps Brigade ("Blue Dragons") was sent to South Vietnam during September 1965, joining a Marine engineer company that had been in the country since March. In 1967 another Marine infantry battalion joined the brigade. The 1st and 2d Battalions of the brigade departed Vietnam in December 1971, the 3d Battalion departed in January 1972 and the 5th Battalion departed in February 1972. The brigade assumed responsibility for the Cam Linh Peninsula – Dong Ba Thin area. On 29 August 1966 the brigade moved to the I CTZ and operated in the Hoi An vicinity.

1st Marine Battalion, 2d Republic of Korea Marine Brigade
2d Marine Battalion, 2d Republic of Korea Marine Brigade
3d Marine Battalion, 2d Republic of Korea Marine Brigade
5th Marine Battalion, 2d Republic of Korea Marine Brigade

OTHER REPUBLIC OF KOREA FORCES IN VIETNAM

COMMANDS:	100th Logistical Command
Groups:	Construction Support Group
	1st Logistical Support Group
	2d Logistical Support Group
Army elements:	Army Intelligence Unit
	Army Security Corps
BATTALIONS:	
Service:	Headquarters & Service Battalion
	100th Logistical Command
Engineer:	127th Engineer Battalion
Transportation:	237th, 239th Transportation Battalions
Signal:	5th Signal Battalion
Hospitals:	102d, 106th Evacuation Hospitals
	201st Mobile Army Surgical Hospital
COMPANIES:	
Infantry:	51st Rifle, 101st Infantry Companies
Engineer:	1st, 2d Engineer Companies
	Facilities Engineering Company
	100th Logistical Command
Ordnance:	10th, 26th Ordnance Companies
Ammunition:	53d, 102d Ammunition Companies
Quartermaster:	257th, 258th Quartermaster Companies
Military Police:	26th Military Police Company
Aviation:	11th Aviation Company
Psychological Operations:	Psychological Operations Company
Transportation:	801st Transportation Company

Chapter 34

Vietnam

THE REPUBLIC OF VIETNAM ARMED FORCES ON THE EVE OF THE U.S. WITHDRAWAL, DECEMBER 1972

Division	Location	Corps	Infantry Regiments
1st Infantry Division	Hue	I	1st, 3d, 51st, 54th
2d Infantry Division	Quang Ngai	I	4th, 5th, 6th
3d Infantry Division*	Quang Tri	I	2d, 56th, 57th
5th Infantry Division	Lai Khe	III	7th, 8th, 9th
7th Infantry Division	Dong Tam	IV	10th, 11th, 12th
9th Infantry Division	Rach Gia	IV	14th, 15th, 16th
18th Infantry Division	Xuan Loc	III	43d, 48th, 52d
21st Infantry Division	Bac Lieu	IV	31st, 32d, 33d
22d Infantry Division	Bai Gi	II	40th, 42d, 47th
23d Infantry Division	Ban Me Thuot	II	41st, 44th, 45th, 53d
25th Infantry Division	Duc Hoa	III	46th, 49th, 50th
			Airborne Brigades
Parachutist Division	Saigon	†	1st, 2d, 3d + 7th Ranger Group
			Marine Brigades
Marine Division	Saigon	†	147th, 258th, 369th

Corps/Command		Subordinate Elements
I Corps	Da Nang	1st Ranger Group, 1st Armor Brigade
II Corps	Pleiku	2d Ranger Group, 2d Armor Brigade
III Corps	Bien Hoa	81st Ranger Group (battalion), 3d Armor Brigade
IV Corps	Can Tho	—
44th Special Tactical Zone	Chi Long	4th Ranger Group, 4th Armor Brigade, 41st and 42d Ranger Border Defense Groups
3d Ranger Command	Bien Hoa	3d Ranger Group, 5th Ranger Group, 6th Ranger Group

* Activated 1 October 1971.

† General reserve.

REPUBLIC OF VIETNAM ARMED FORCES BATTALIONS, DECEMBER 1972

Type	Total	Battalion Types
Armored Cavalry Squadrons	18	11 divisional + seven separate
Infantry Battalions	124	115 regimental + nine airborne
Marine Battalions	9	nine marine regimental
Ranger Battalions	55	22 ranger + 33 ranger border defense
Artillery Battalions (105mm)*	44	33 divisional + eight separate + three airborne
Artillery Battalions (155mm)	15	11 divisional + four separate
Artillery Battalions (175mm)	5	five separate
Artillery Battalions – Air Defense	4	four 40mm and .50-cal machinegun
Engineer Battalions	40	23 combat + 17 construction
Signal Battalions	16	13 combat + three support
Military Police Battalions	12	12 military police

* In addition there were 176 howitzer platoons (105mm) of two guns each.

Combat Strengths:	108,675	Regular
	376,946	Regional/Popular Forces
	14,365	Border Rangers
	499,986	Total reported combat strength

NORTH VIETNAMESE/VIET CONG ORDER OF BATTLE ON THE EVE OF THE U.S. WITHDRAWAL, DECEMBER 1972

Present in South Vietnam:

Major Command	Regiments*
1st NVA Infantry Division	44th Sapper, 52d NVA, 101-D NVA
2d NVA Infantry Division	1st NVA, 52d VC, *141st NVA*
3d NVA Infantry Division	2d NVA, 12th NVA, 21st NVA
5th Viet Cong Division	E-6 NVA, 174th NVA, 205th NVA, 275th NVA
7th NVA Infantry Division	*141st NVA, 165th NVA, 209th NVA*
9th Viet Cong Division	95-C NVA, *271st NVA*, 272d NVA
304th NVA Infantry Division	9th NVA, 24-B NVA, *66th NVA*
308th NVA Infantry Division	36th NVA, 88th NVA, 102d NVA
312th NVA Infantry Division	*141st NVA, 165th NVA, 209th NVA*
320th NVA Infantry Division	48th NVA, 64th NVA
320-B NVA Infantry Division	48-B NVA, 64-B NVA
324-B NVA Infantry Division	29th NVA, 803d NVA, 812th NVA
325th NVA Infantry Division	18th NVA, *95th NVA, 101st NVA*
711th NVA Infantry Division	3d NVA, 38th NVA, 270th NVA
B-3 Front (Central Highlands)	28th NVA, *66th NVA*, 95-B NVA, 40th NVA-Artillery
B-5 Front (DMZ)	27-B NVA, 31st NVA, 246th NVA, 270-B NVA, 38th NVA-Artillery, 84th NVA-Artillery
Military Region 3 (Delta)	D-1 VC, D-2 VC, D-3 VC, 18-B NVA, *95th NVA*
Military Region 2	DT-1 VC, 86th NVA
Military Region 7	33d NVA, 274th VC, 74th NVA-Artillery(?)
Military Region Tri-Thien-Hue	4th NVA(?), 5th NVA, 6th NVA
Independent Regiments	24th NVA, *101st NVA, 271st NVA*

Combat Strengths:	89,834	NVA regular
	20,000	NVA filters in VC units
	30,332	Viet Cong
	140,166	Total estimated combat strength (in SVN)

Unit Strengths: 309 maneuver battalions (sapper, infantry, security, reconnaissance)

* Duplications of numerical unit designations result from the NVA tendency to regenerate units which have suffered heavy losses in combat, such as the famous 95th NVA — the first NVA regiment to enter South Vietnam in December 1964. These have been italicized.

Photo Section:

Army Aircraft, Weapons, Vessels and Vehicles

SELECTED U.S. ARMY INFANTRY WEAPONS: SMALL ARMS*

Weapon	Model	Weight (Pounds)	Method of Feed	Operation	Sustained Rate of Fire [†] (Rounds/Min)	Effective Range (Meters)	Muzzle Velocity	Length
Pistol, .45-cal automatic	M1911A1	2.5	7-round magazine	Short recoil	35	50	830 ft/sec	8⅝"
Submachinegun, .45-cal	M3A1	9	30-round magazine	Blow-back auto	40 – 60	100	920 ft/sec	22.8" (stock retracted)
Submachinegun, 5.56mm commando	XM177E2	7.1	20-round magazine	Gas semi-auto	12 – 15	460	3,000 ft/sec	28" (butt telescoped)
Rifle, .30-cal	M1	9.5	8-round clip	Gas semi-auto	8 – 10	460	2,805 ft/sec	43.6"
Carbine, .30-cal	M2	5.5	30-round magazine	Gas semi or auto	40 – 60	250	1,970 ft/sec	35.5"
Rifle, 7.62mm	M14	9.3	20-round magazine	Gas semi or auto	20	460	2,800 ft/sec	44.1"
Rifle, 5.56mm	M16A1	7.6	20-and 30-round magazines	Gas semi or auto	12 – 15	460	3,250 ft/sec	39"
40mm Grenade launcher on rifle	M203 on M16	11	Single shot (launcher)	Single-shot	3 – 5 (M203)	350 [‡]	—	15⅝" (launcher only)
Grenade launcher, 40mm	M79	6.2	Break-open	Single-shot	5 – 7	350 [‡]	250 ft/sec	29"
Machinegun, .30-cal	M1919A6	33	Metallic link belt	Short recoil auto	75	1,100	2,800 ft/sec	32.5"
Machinegun, .50-cal	M2	126	Metallic link belt	Short recoil auto	40	1,825	2,930 ft/sec	66"
Machinegun, 7.62mm	M60	23	Disintegrating link belt	Gas auto	100	1,100	2,800 ft/sec	43.5"

*Does not consider the large number of commercially produced revolvers, shotguns, rifles and submachineguns also used.

[†] The rate at which a weapon can fire indefinitely without seriously overheating.

[‡] With an effective casualty radius against standing targets at 25 meters; against prone targets, 5 meters.

SELECTED U.S. ARMY INFANTRY WEAPONS

Weapon	Model	Weight (Pounds)	Method of Feed	Operation	Maximum Effective Range (Meters)	Effective Casualty Radius (Meters)	Size
Flamethrower, portable	M2A1-7	42.5	Manual	Fuel propelled by gas	20 unthickened 45 thickened	N/A	N/A
Recoilless rifle with spotting .50-cal gun	M40A1 (106mm)	460	Breech-loaded	Air-cooled recoilless	700-1,000	14	134" length
66mm light antitank weapon (LAW)*	M72	5.2	Single shot and discard	Rocket	325	N/A	35" (extended length)
60mm mortar	M19	45.2	Muzzle-loaded	Drop fire, manual	2,000	15 x 10	32.25" length
81mm mortar	M29	132	Muzzle-loaded	Drop fire, manual	3,650	25 x 20	3'9½" length
4.2" mortar	M30	672	Muzzle-loaded	Drop fire, manual	5,500	40 x 15	60" length
Antipersonnel weapon (Claymore)	M18A1	3.5	none	Controlled electric detonation or uncontrolled trip-wire operation	50 50	Directional fragmentation 60° sector with radius of 50	—
Incendiary burster in Phougas barrel	M4	2.25 (burster only)	none	Blasting cap device or fuse, etc.	5-gallon container=35 55-gallon container=85		Depends on container
Hand grenade, delay fragmentation	M33/M67	14 oz.	none	Throw	40	15	2.5" diameter
Hand grenade, delay fragmentation	M26/M61	1.7	none	Throw	40	15	2.25" diameter
Hand grenade, impact fragmentation	M59/M68	14 oz.	none	Throw	40	15	2.5" diameter
Hand grenade, offensive	Mk3A2	15.6 oz.	none	Throw	35	25	5.3" cylindrical
Hand grenade, riot †	M7	17 oz.	none	Throw	35	20 – 60 sec	5.7" cylindrical
Hand grenade, smoke ‡	M8 – White/ M18 – Colored	24 oz.	none	Throw	25	90 – 150 sec smoke	5.7" cylindrical

* Used in Vietnam against bunkers.

† Contained CS gas with a powerful lachrymal effect irritating to upper respiratory passages causing difficulty in breathing, nausea and vomiting.

‡ Other types of hand grenades include colored-smoke, white phosphorus and incendiary. A wide variety of shapes was used.

CHARACTERISTICS OF U.S. ARMY ARTILLERY WEAPONS USED IN VIETNAM

Weapons	On Carriage Traverse Mils	Range (Meters)	Weight (Pounds)	Time to Emplace (Minutes)	Max Rate of Fire First 3 Minutes	Sustained Rate of Fire Per Minute	No. of Weapons Per Unit	Prime Mover	Ammunition Types	Ammunition Fuses*	Ammunition Weight HE Proj Pounds	Effective Area Covered by Impact Burst in Meters Depth	Width	Radius	Rds/Wpn in Battalion Basic Load
105mm how, towed M101A1	809	11,000	4,980	3	30	3	18 per bn	Helicopter 2½-t trk	HE HEAT HEP-T	Q D VT	Fused proj- 33 lbs	20	20	175	200
105mm how, towed M102	6,400	11,500	3,017	4	30	3	18 per bn	Helicopter ¾-t trk	Smoke Illum Leaflet	TI CP	Complete round-	20	30	175	190
105mm how, SP M108	6,400	11,500	46,221	1	30	3	18 per bn	SP	Gas Anti-pers Flechette		42 lbs	20	30	175	200
155mm how, towed M114A1	866	14,600	12,950	5	12	1	18 per bn	5-t trk Helicopter	HE Illum Smoke	Q D VT	Fused Proj- 95 lbs	30	50	360	150
155mm how, SP M109	6,400	14,600	52,461	1	12	1	18 per bn	SP	Gas	TI CP	Complete round- 104 lbs	30	50	360	275
8-inch how, SP M110	1,066	16,800	58,500	2	4.5	0.5	12 per bn	SP	HE Spotting Gas	Q D VT TI CP	Fused Proj- 200 lbs	30	80	470	100
175mm gun SP M107	1,066	32,700	62,100	3	4.5	0.5	12 per bn	SP	HE	Q D VT	Fused proj- 147 lbs Complete round- 202 lbs	35	95	520	114
40mm gun AW SP M42	6,400	1,650† 3,500-5,000‡	48,000	1	240 RPM	N/A	64 per bn	SP	HE	PD Tracer	Entire round- 2 lbs	N/A	N/A	N/A	720
.50-cal MG M55	6,400	1,825	3,000	1	1,800-2,000	N/A	96 per bn	2½-t trk	Ball armor-piercing tracer	N/A	N/A	N/A	N/A	N/A	10,000
Vulcan XM741	6,400	3,000	26,000;SP 3,000, Towed	1	3,000 RPM† 1,000 RPM‡	N/A	32 per bn	SP	Ball armor-piercing tracer	N/A	N/A	N/A	N/A	N/A	2,000

* Fuses:
Q—Quick
D—Delay
VT—Variable time
TI—Time
CP—Concrete piercing
† Air defense role
‡ Ground role

CHARACTERISTICS OF U.S. ARMY MISSILES USED IN VIETNAM

System	Range (Meters)	Weight (Pounds)	Number of Launchers Per Unit	Fuel	Guidance	Type Warhead
HAWK Air Defense Missile	26,000 m at 38,000 ft altitude	1,295	24 per bn	Solid	Homing	HE

ARMY HELICOPTER ARMAMENT SUBSYSTEMS USED IN VIETNAM

Weapons Subsystem	Mounted On
M2* Dual machinegun subsystem, 7.62mm M60C MG	OH-13, OH-23
XM3 Armament subsystem, 2.75" rocket launcher, 48-tube	UH-1B/C
M5* Armament subsystem, 40mm M75 grenade launcher	UH-1B/C
M6* Armament subsystem, Quad 7.62mm M60C MG	UH-1B/C
XM8 Armament subsystem, 40mm M75 grenade launcher	OH-6
XM9 SUU-7 bomblet dispenser	UH-1B/C
XM12 Armament pod, aircraft 20mm automatic gun, M61	
XM13 Armament pod, aircraft 40mm grenade launcher	
XM14 Armament pod, aircraft .50-cal MG	
XM16 Armament subsystem, four 7.62mm M60C MG, two 2.75" seven-tube launchers	UH-1B/C
XM18 Armament pod, 7.62mm high-rate XM134 MG	AH-1G
XM19 Armament pod, twin 7.62mm M60C MG	
M21* Armament subsystem, 7.62mm high-rate XM134 MG; 2.75" rocket launcher, XM158	UH-1B/C
M22 Antitank guided missile subsystem XAGM-22B	UH-1B/C
M23 Armament subsystem, 7.62mm M60D MG	UH-1D
XM24 Armament subsystem, 7.62mm M60D MG	CH-47A
XM25 Armament pod, aircraft 20mm automatic gun	
XM26 Armament subsystem, TOW missile	UH-1B/C, AH-1G
XM27 Armament subsystem, 7.62mm high-rate XM134 MG	OH-6A
XM28 Armament subsystem, two 7.62mm XM134 MG, two 40mm M75 grenade launchers, or one XM134 and one turret-mounted M75	AH-1G
XM29 Armament subsystem, one 7.62mm M60D MG	UH-1B/C
XM30 Armament subsystem, 30mm automatic gun XM140	AH-1G
XM31 Armament subsystem, 20mm M24A1 automatic gun	UH-1B/C
XM32 Armament subsystem, four .50-cal M2 or 7.62mm M60D MG's (two per side)	CH-47
XM33 Armament subsystem, .50-cal M2 or 7.62mm M60D MG	CH-47
XM34 Armament subsystem, dual 20mm M24A1 guns	CH-47
XM36 Mine dispenser for helicopter	UH-1B/C
XM47 Mine dispersing system. Aircraft: Two XM3 Anti-personnel mine dispensers for the XM27 antipersonnel mine.	UH-1B/C

* These subsystems were acceptable standard armament subsystems.

CHARACTERISTICS OF SELECTED U.S. ARMY HELICOPTERS USED IN VIETNAM

A. Helicopter	Unit	OH-6A	OH-13H	OH-58A	UH-1B	UH-1C	UH-1D	UH-1H	AH-1G	CH-34C	CH-47A	CH-47B	CH-47C	CH-54A	CH-54B
B. Name		Observation Cayuse (Loach)	Observation Sioux	Armed Observation Kiowa	Utility Huey	Utility Huey	Utility Huey	Utility Huey	Attack Cobra	Cargo Choctaw	Cargo Chinook	Cargo Chinook	Cargo Chinook	Cargo Tarhe	Cargo Tarhe
C. Crew (200 Lbs Ea)	Ea	2	1	2	2-4	2-4	2-4	2-4	2	2	3	3	3	3	3
D. Dimensions															
(1) Length — fuselage	Ft & In	23'6"	31'4¾"	32'3½"	42'8½"	42'8"	41'11¼"	41'11¼"	44'5¼"	46'9"	31'0"	51'0"	51'0"	70'3"	70'3"
(2) Length — blades unloaded	Ft & In	30'3¾"	41'4¾"	40'11¾"	53'0"	53'0"	57'1"	57'1"	52'11¾"	65'10"	98'3¼"	98'11"	99'0"	83'5"	88'5"
(3) Length — blades folded	Ft & In	23'0"	NA	32'3½"	NA	NA	NA	NA	NA	37'0"	51'0"	51'0"	51'0"	77'6"	77'6"
(4) Width — blades folded	Ft & In	NA	NA	NA	NA	NA	NA	NA	NA	13'0"	12'5"	12'5"	12'5"	21'10"	21'10"
(5) Width — tread	Ft & In	6'9¼"	7'6"	6'3½"	8'4¾"	8'4½"	8'6½"	8'6½"	7'4"	12'0"	11'11"	10'6"	10'6"	19'9"	19'9"
(6) Height extreme	Ft & In	8'6"	9'5½"	9'6½"	14'8½"	14'9"	14'5½"	14'5½"	11'7"	15'11"	18'6½"	18'7"	18'7"	25'5"	25'5"
(7) Diameter main rotor	Ft & In	26'4"	35'1½"	35'4"	44'0"	44'0"	48'0"	48'0"	44'0"	56'0"	59'1¼"	60'0"	60'0"	72'0"	72'2"
(8) Diameter tail rotor	Ft & In	4'3"	5'10¼"	2'3¼"	8'6"	8'6"	8'6"	8'6"	8'6"	9'6"	51'2"	52'0"	52'0"	16'0"	16'0"
E. Cargo Door															
(1) Dimensions — width/height	In	NA	NA	NA	48/48	48/48	74.5/48	74.5/48	NA	53/48	90/78	90/78	90/78	Pod – 114/92	Pod – 114/92
(2) Location — side of fuselage	In	NA	NA	NA	Both	Both	Both	Both	NA	Right	Rear	Rear	Rear	Pod – Rear	Pod – Rear
F. Cargo Compartment															
(1) Height of floor above ground	In	NA	NA	NA	27	27	32	32	NA	34	30	30	30	Pod – 18	Pod – 18
(2) Length, usable	In	NA	NA	NA	48	48	92	92	NA	161	362½	362½	362½	Pod – 329	Pod – 329
(3) Width, floor	In	NA	NA	NA	80½	80½	96	96	NA	60	90	90	90	Pod – 104	Pod – 104
(4) Height (clear of obstructions)	In	NA	NA	NA	48	48	49	49	NA	70	78	78	78	Pod – 78	Pod – 78
(5) Cargo space, optimum	Cu Ft	NA	NA	NA	140	140	220	220	NA	405	1,487	1,487	1,487	Pod – 1,599	Pod – 1,599
G. External Cargo															
(1) Maximum recommended external load	Lbs	NA	NA	NA	3,675	4,000	4,000	4,000	NA	4,000	14,916	20,000	20,000	20,000	25,000
(2) Rescue hoist capacity	Lbs	NA	NA	NA	600	600	600	600	NA	600	600	600	600	NA	NA
(3) Winch capacity	Lbs	NA	NA	NA	NA	NA	NA	NA	NA	NA	3,000	3,000	3,000	15,000	25,000
H. Passenger Capacity															
(1) Troop seats (240 lbs per man*)	Ea	2	2	2	6	6	11	11	0	18	33	33	33	Pod – 45	Pod – 45
(2) Litters	Ea	0	2	0	3	3	6	6	0	8	24	24	24	Pod – 24	Pod – 24
I. Operational Characteristics															
(1) Maximum allowable gross weight	Lbs	2,400	2,450	3,000	8,500	9,500	9,500	9,500	9,500	12,068	33,000	40,000	46,000	42,000	47,000
(2) Basic weight	Lbs	1,163	1,850	1,700	4,600	4,830	4,939	4,900	8,404	7,800	18,084	19,194	19,772	20,650	21,000
(3) Useful load	Lbs	1,237	600	1,300	3,900	4,670	4,561	4,100	1,096	4,268	14,916	20,806	26,228	21,350	26,000
(4) Internal fuel capacity	Lbs/Gal	400/61.5	250/41.5	475/73	1,075/163	1,575/242	1,450/224	1,450/224	1,605/247	1,572/262	4,036/621	4,036/621	7,353/1,131	8,800/1,353	8,775/1,350
(5) Normal cruising speed	Knots	100	70	100	90	110	110	110	120	100	110	120	120	95	80
(6) Endurance of cruising speed	Hrs + Min	2 + 30	1 + 30	2 + 10	1 + 30	1 + 55	1 + 50	1 + 55	1 + 50	2 + 20	1 + 30	1 + 0	2 + 0	1 + 50	1 + 40
(7) Grade of fuel	Oct	JP-4/5	80/87	JP-4	JP-4	JP-4	JP-4	JP-4/5	JP-4	115/145	JP-4	JP-4	JP-4	JP-4	JP-4
(8) Fuel consumption per hour	Lbs/Gal	130/20	120/20	180/28	528/81	657/101	618/95	605/93	630/105	630/105	1,980/305	2,620/400	3,000/462	3,614/556	3,990/613

* Allows for full equipment and weapons.

CHARACTERISTICS OF SELECTED U.S. ARMY AIRPLANES USED IN VIETNAM*

	Unit	O-1A	O-1E	O-1F	O-1G	OV-1A	OV-1B	OV-1C	U-1A	U-6A	U-8D	U-8F	U-21A	CV-2B
A. Airplane		Observation	Observation	Observation	Observation	Observation	Observation	Observation	Utility	Utility	Utility	Utility	Utility	Cargo
B. Name		Bird Dog	Bird Dog	Bird Dog	Bird Dog	Mohawk	Mohawk	Mohawk	Otter	Beaver	Seminole	Seminole	Ute	Caribou
C. Crew (200 Lbs Ea)	Ea	1	1	1	1	2	2	2	1	1	1	1	2	3
D. Dimensions														
(1) Length — fuselage	Ft & In	25'0"	25'9½"	25'9½"	25'9½"	41'1½"	43'11½"	41'1½"	41'10"	30'5"	31'6½"	33'4"	35'6"	72'7"
(2) Width — tread	Ft & In	7'6½"	7'6½"	7'6½"	7'6½"	9'2"	9'2"	9'2"	11'2"	10'2½"	12'9"	12'9"	12'9"	23'2"
(3) Height— extreme	Ft & In	9'2½"	9'2"	7'6"	9'2"	12'8"	12'8"	12'8"	12'7"	10'5"	11'6½"	14'2"	14'2½"	31'9"
(4) Wing span	Ft & In	36'0"	36'0"	36'0"	36'0"	42'0"	48'0"	48'0"						
E. Cargo Door									58'0"	48'0"	45'3½"	45'10½"	45'10½"	95'7½"
(1) Dimensions — width/height	In	45/33	45/33	45/33	45/33	NA	NA	NA	44.5/45	40/40	26.5/26.75	50.5/26.5	53.5/51.5	73½"x74"
(2) Location — side of fuselage	In	Right	Right	Right	Right	NA	NA	NA	Left	Both	Right	Left	Left	Rear
F. Cargo Compartment														
(1) Height of floor above ground	In	NA	NA	NA	NA	NA	NA	NA	46½	46	48	48	54	45.6"
(2) Length, usable	In	59	59	59	59	NA	NA	NA	44	92	86	110½	150	345"
(3) Width, floor	In	26	26	26	26	NA	NA	NA	51½	48	54	55	55	81"
(4) Height (clear of obstructions)	In	29	29	29	29	NA	NA	NA	56½	51	53	55	57	75"
(5) Cargo space, optimum	Cu Ft	25	25	25	25	NA	NA	NA	70	110	115	128	272	1,150"
G. External Cargo														
Maximum recommended external load	Lbs	500	500	500	500	4,000	4,000	4,000	NA	1,000	NA	NA	NA	1,500†
H. Passenger Capacity														
(1) Troop seats (240 lbs per man)‡	Ea	1	1	1	1	0	0	0	10	5	5	5	6	32
(2) Litters	Ea	1	1	1	1	NA	NA	NA	8	5	NA	NA	7	14 + 8 20 + 2
I. Operational Characteristics														
(1) Maximum allowable gross wt	Lbs	2,100	2,400	2,195	2,400	15,020	16,643	15,302	8,000	5,100	7,300	7,700	9,650	28,500
(2) Basic weight	Lbs	1,542	1,618	1,707	1,618	9,781	11,217	10,379	4,900	3,310	4,978	5,282	5,500	18,576
(3) Useful load	Lbs	558	782	488	782	5,239	5,426	4,923	3,100	1,790	2,322	2,418	4,100	9,924
(4) Internal fuel capacity	Lbs/Gal	252/42	246/41	246/41	246/41	1,901/292½	1,930/297	1,930/297	1,280/213	828/138	1,380/230	1,380/230	2,405/370	4,968/828
(5) Normal cruising speed	Knots	86	86	86	86	200	200	200	104	105	155	160	164	150
(6) Endurance at cruising speed	Hrs + Min	4 + 0	4 + 0	4 + 0	4 + 0	1 + 15	1 + 15	1 + 15	6 + 35	6 + 0	6 + 0	6 + 0	4 + 30	6 + 30
(7) Grade of fuel	Octane	80/87	80/87	80/87	80/87 or 115/145	JP-4	JP-4	JP-4	115/145	115/145	115/145	115/145	JP-4/5	115/145
(8) Fuel consumption per hour	Lbs/Gal	54/9	54/9	54/9	54/9	1,105/170	1,105/170	1,105/170	180/30	132/22	204/34	204/34	500/83	660/110

* All data computed at standard conditions at sea level. † Cargo Loading Winch Capacity ‡ Allows for full equipment and weapons.

CHARACTERISTICS OF SELECTED U.S. ARMY VEHICLES USED IN VIETNAM

Nomenclature	Gross Vehicle Weight	Height (Inches)	Width (Inches)	Length (Inches)	Crew	Fuel	Max Speed (mph)	Cruising Range (miles)	Fording w/o Kit (Inches)	Fording Depth w/Kit (Inches)	Vertical Obstacle (Inches)	Span (Inches)	Main Armament	Secondary Armament	Basic Load (Rounds)	Effective Range § (Meters)
Armored recon vehicle M551	33,460	116	110	248	4	Diesel	43	373		Unlimited	33	84	152mm Gun	1x.50-MG 1x7.62mm-MG	20	3,000
Carrier, cargo 6-ton M548	28,190	105½	105¾	226½	1	Diesel	38	300		Unlimited	24	66	—	—	—	—
Carrier, comd and recon M114A1	15,276	84⅞	91¾	175¾	3	Gas	36	300		Unlimited	18	60	1x.50 MG	2x7.62mm-MG	1,000	1,825
Carrier, comd and recon M114A1E1	15,678	84⅞	91¾	175¾	3	Gas	36	300		Unlimited	18	60	1x.50 MG	2x7.62mm-MG	1,000	1,825
Carrier, comd post M577A1	24,750	101	106	191½	1	Diesel	35	300		Unlimited	24	66	None	None	—	—
Carrier, mortar 81mm M125A1	24,527	86½	106	191½	6	Diesel	40	300		Unlimited	24	66	81mm Mortar	Kit B ‖	114	3,650
Carrier, mortar 107mm M106A1	26,147	86½	112¾	194	6	Diesel	40	300		Unlimited	24	66	4.2" Mortar	Kit B ‖	88	5,500
Carrier, personnel M113	22,900	86½	106	191½	1	Gas	40	200		Unlimited	24	66	12.7mm MG	1x7.62mm-MG	2,000	1,825
Carrier, personnel M113A1 ACAV #	24,238	86½	106	191½	1	Diesel	40	300		Unlimited	24	66	Kit A**	Kit A	2,000	1,825
Launcher for AVLB M60A1 tk chassis	83,000	124½	144	340½	2	Diesel	30	310	48	None	36	102	—	—	—	—
Tk, combat 90mm M48A3 †	104,000	122	143	271	4	Diesel	30	310	48	96	36	102	90mm Gun	1x.50-MG 1x.30-MG	64	4,400
XM-706 commando vehicle (V-100)	16,250	96	89	224	4	Diesel	62	600	—	—	24	—	2x.30-MG‡ in turret	None	1,000	1,100
M56 antitank gun	15,500	81	101½	179⅜	4	Gas	28	140	42	610	30	—	90mm Gun	None	29	4,600
Tk, recovery vehicle light M578	54,000	130½	124	250¼	3	Diesel	37	450	42	None	40	93	1x.50 MG	—	500	1,825
Tk, recovery vehicle med M88	110,000	123½	135	325½	4	Gas	31	222	64	102	42	103	1x.50 MG	—	500	1,825
Trk, amb ¼-ton M718	3,560	76 3/10	71	143	1	Gas	65	300	21	48			—	—	—	—
Trk, amb 1¼-ton M792	10,200	90 4/5	84	226 3/5	1	Diesel	55	400	30	Unlimited	18		—	—	—	—
Trk, cargo 1¼-ton M561	10,200	90 4/5	84	226 3/5	1	Diesel	55	400	30	Unlimited	18		—	—	—	—
Trk, cargo 1¼-ton M715	3,300*	95	85	220¾	1	Gas	60	220	30	60			—	—	—	—
Trk, cargo 2½-ton M35A2 w/o winch	13,425	112	96	264¼	1	Multi	56	350	30	72			—	—	—	—
Trk, cargo 2½-ton M35A2 w/winch	13,920*	112	96	278½	1	Multi	56	350	30	72			—	—	—	—
Trk, cargo 5-ton 6x6 M54A2 w/winch	20,535*	116	97	314¼	1	Multi	54	400	30	78			—	—	—	—
Trk, cargo 5-ton 8x8 M656	36,150	108	96	299	1	Multi	50	272		Unlimited			—	—	—	—
Trk, cargo 8-ton 4x4 M520	40,780	134	108	384	2	Diesel	30	300		Unlimited	33		—	—	—	—
Trk, tank fuel servicing 2500-Gal 4x4 M559	45,470	134	108	391	2	Diesel	30	300		Unlimited	33		—	—	—	—
Trk, utility ¼-ton M151 Series	3,600	71	64	132 7/10	1	Gas	65	300	21	48			—	—	—	—
Trk, wrecker 5-ton 6x6 M816	36,100	114	98	356	2	Diesel	52	350	30	78			—	—	—	—
Trk, wrecker 10-ton 4x4 M553	47,300	134	108	401	2	Diesel	30	300		Unlimited	33		—	—	—	—
Vehicle, combat engineer M728	115,000	128 1/5	146	350 4/5	4	Diesel	30	280	48	162	30	99	165mm Demolition Gun	1x.50 MG 1x7.62mm MG	30	1,000

* Net weight.
† Also modified by U.S. Marines for flamethrower use. This variant had a range of 100-250 meters.
‡ Armament could vary since some were open-topped (without turret) and had 7.62mm machinegun(s) attached.
§ Armor-defeating ranges not considered; only effective ranges against "other" targets such as bunkers and fortified positions. In addition the 152mm gun could fire a very lethal canister round for use against bamboo thickets with a range of 274 meters.
‖ Kit B = hatch armor, shield for .50-cal machinegun.
ACAV = armored cavalry assault vehicle. Sometimes modified Kit A with 40mm grenade launchers, 106mm and 57mm recoilless rifles or Hughes grenade launcher.
** Kit A = hatch armor, shielded, .50-cal machinegun, 2 elbow-pintle mounted with gun shields for mounting 7.62mm M60 machineguns on both sides.

CHARACTERISTICS OF SELECTED U.S. ARMY HELICOPTERS AND AIRPLANES USED IN VIETNAM

DEFINITIONS:

MAXIMUM ALLOWABLE GROSS WEIGHT: The maximum allowed total weight of the aircraft prior to takeoff; the *basic weight* of the aircraft plus the crew, personnel equipment, special devices, passengers/cargo, and usable fuel and oil. This is limited by structure, power available, or landing load.

BASIC WEIGHT: The empty weight of an aircraft in its basic configuration, including all appointments, integral equipment, instrumentation, and trapped fuel and oil, but excluding passengers, cargo, crew, and fuel and oil.

USEFUL LOAD: The load-carrying capability of an aircraft. It includes the payload, crew and usable fuel and oil required for the mission; that is, the difference between *maximum allowable gross weight* and the *basic weight* as defined above. Thus, a reduction of the fuel load will reduce the *endurance* and increase the *payload.* Full oil is required for all missions.

PAYLOAD: The useful load less the crew, full oil, and the required fuel for the mission.

NORMAL CRUISING SPEED: The air speed which an aircraft can normally be expected to maintain at some standard power setting below rated military power. This speed will vary with altitude.

ENDURANCE AT CRUISING SPEED: The time that an aircraft can remain airborne at normal cruising speed with fuel aboard without using the required fuel reserve. The data listed under *Operational Characteristics* is computed utilizing full fuel minus a 30-minute reserve, except for turboprop, which requires a 20-minute reserve.

U.S. ARMY AIRCRAFT FUEL IDENTIFICATION

80/87	91/96	100/130	115/145	JP-4
Red	Blue	Green	Purple	Clear

Fixed-wing Aircraft

1

CV-2 CARIBOU was an all-weather utility transport which saw heavy use in Vietnam. Its design was suited to the short takeoff and landing necessary for forward battlefield resupply. First delivered in 1959, it had a length of 74', a basic weight of 20,000 lbs. and a payload of 5,000 lbs. Tan Son Nhut, March 1966.

2

U-8F SEMINOLE aircraft was used for transport of personnel. First delivered in 1956, it had a length of 33'4'', a basic weight of 5,381 lbs. and a payload of 830 lbs.

3

U-1 OTTER was a utility aircraft used for light cargo and passenger service. First delivered in 1950, it had a length of 41'10'', a basic weight of 4,900 lbs. and a payload of 1,398 lbs. 54th Aviation Company, Vung Tau, May 1968.

4

OV-1B MOHAWK was fitted for electronic surveillance using side-looking airborne radar (SLAR). There were 107 MOHAWKS in Vietnam by 1 July 1969. 1st Cavalry Division, An Khe, 1967.

5

U-21 UTE was a twin-turboprop utility plane first procured in September 1967 as an off-the-shelf version of the commercial Beechcraft model. Used for command purposes, it had a length of 35', a basic weight of 5,250 lbs. and a payload of 1,600 lbs.

6

O-1 BIRD DOG (formerly the L-19) was a reconnaissance and observation plane. First delivered in 1950, it had a length of 25', a basic weight of 1,542 lbs. and a payload of 100 lbs. Pictured here is one from the 199th Aviation Company. Mekong Delta, October 1969.

7

OV-1A reconnaissance rocket-firing aircraft. The OV-1 MOHAWK was first delivered in 1961, had a length of 41'1'', a basic weight of 9,781 lbs. and a payload of 341 lbs. 73d Aviation Company, Vung Tau, June 1967.

8

U-6 BEAVER was a utility aircraft first delivered in 1951. It had a length of 30'5'', a basic weight of 3,100 lbs. and a payload of 930 lbs. 74th Aviation Company, Phu Loi, May 1968.

Helicopters

1

UH-1B HUEY entered service in March 1964 and was used as a transport craft as well as an aerial weapons platform. Length was 52'11", basic weight was 4,600 lbs. and payload was 2,704 lbs.

2

OH-13S SIOUX was a scout helicopter used for visual observation and target acquisition. First delivered in 1956, it had a length of 43'3", a basic weight of 1,715 lbs. and a payload of 400 lbs. 1st Squadron, 9th Cavalry, An Lo Valley, September 1967.

3

AH-1G HUEY COBRA helicopter being refueled shows the slender silhouette this craft presented. By July 1969 441 COBRAs were in Vietnam. 101st Airborne Division, October 1969.

4

UH-1A HUEY was used for transport of personnel as well as supplies and equipment. First delivered in 1959, it had a length of 52'10", a basic weight of 4,020 lbs. and a payload of 2,175 lbs.

5

OH-23 RAVEN was a light observation helicopter used for reconnaissance and medical evacuation. First delivered in 1955, it had a length of 40'8", a basic weight of 1,821 lbs. and a payload of 851 lbs.

6

UH-19D CHICKASAW was a utility helicopter used for transport of cargo and up to ten troops. First delivered in 1953, it had a length of 62'3", a basic weight of 5,650 lbs. and a payload of 844 lbs.

7

UH-1D HUEY was a larger tactical transport helicopter capable of carrying 11 troops as well as flying a myriad of other support missions. First delivered in 1963, it had a length of 57'1", a basic weight of 4,900 lbs. and a payload of 3,116 lbs. Phan Thiet, 1967.

8

CH-37B MOHAVE seen hovering over a downed CH-21C SHAWNEE helicopter in 1964 as a hoisting sling is hooked up. First delivered in 1956, it had a length of 88', a basic weight of 21,500 lbs. and a payload of 5,300 lbs.

9

UH-1C HUEY was used to transport troops and supplies, evacuate wounded and support ground troops. First delivered in June 1965, it had a length of 53', a basic weight of 4,830 lbs. and a payload of 4,500 lbs.

10

UH-1E HUEY was a Marine assault support and rescue helicopter first delivered in March 1963 with the same basic airframe as the B and C models, but with a hoist housing on the cabin roof.

1

AH-1G HUEY COBRA provided escort reconnaissance and direct fire support. First delivered in 1967, it had a length of 52′11″, a basic weight of 5,783 lbs. and a payload of 1,993 lbs. Helicopter pictured here was used by Troop D, 3d Squadron, 4th Cavalry (25th Infantry Division).

2

CH-21C SHAWNEE transported cargo, equipment and personnel. First delivered in 1962, it had a length of 86′4″, a basic weight of 8,900 lbs. and a payload of 1,920 lbs. It could carry up to 20 troops. Seen here is a craft of the 57th Transportation Company in Vietnam, February 1963.

3

UH-1H HUEY, featuring a more powerful engine which was introduced in 1967, was in other respects the same as the UH-1D. By April 1969 some 2,202 UH-series helicopters were serving the army in Vietnam.

4

UH-1F HUEY was used by the U.S. Air Force. It was similar to the UH-1B but had a General Electric T58-3 turbine engine, an exhaust pipe and longer blades. Seen over Vietnam.

5

UH-1M HUEY was a modification employing the INFANT remote and direct view image intensifier surveillance system. This craft is seen with the 11th Aviation Group at Phu Loi, September 1970.

6

CH-34C CHOCTAW transported cargo and personnel. First delivered in 1955, it had a length of 65′10″, a basic weight of 7,800 lbs. and a payload of 2,175 lbs. It could carry up to 18 soldiers. Seen here with Marines in Vietnam, April 1964.

1

CH-54 SKY CRANE was designed so that it could carry virtually all of its payload externally. Using its hoist mechanism, the TARHE could lift a great variety of external loads weighing up to ten tons. Here it carries a detachable personnel pod. Vinh Long, November 1968.

2

OH-58A KIOWA was used for command and control, observation and transportation. First delivered in 1969, it had a length of 32′3″, a basic weight of 1,583 lbs. and a payload of 760 lbs. This craft is from the 1st Signal Brigade in Vietnam, April 1970.

3

CH-54 SKY CRANE (TARHE) was used to move heavy outsized loads and recover downed aircraft. It often used detachable pods. First delivered in 1966, it had a length of 88′5″, a basic weight of 20,700 lbs. and a payload of 15,400 lbs.

4

OH-6A CAYUSE ("Loach") was a light observation helicopter (LOH) first delivered in 1966. It had a length of 30′3″, a basic weight of 1,157 lbs. and a payload of 930 lbs. By April 1969 the army had 635 in Vietnam. Vung Tau, April 1969.

5

CH-47A CHINOOK transported cargo, equipment, artillery pieces and up to 33 troops. First delivered in 1961, it had a length of 98′3″, a basic weight of 18,500 lbs. and a payload of 10,114 lbs. In May 1969 311 were in Vietnam with the army. Vietnam, October 1969.

6

CH-47A CHINOOK armed with M5 grenade subsystem, 2.75″ rocket pods, two M60 7.62mm machineguns, as well as M24A1 20mm machineguns. CHINOOK models A, B and C were used in Vietnam.

7

Airmobile Surgical Center pod was sling-loaded under the CH-54 SKY CRANE for transport to forward battle areas. Large enough to hold 14 people and support four operations at the same time, it weighed 4,000 lbs. and was 30′ long. Vietnam, February 1966.

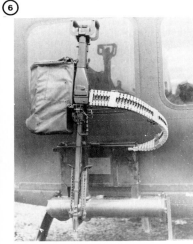

Helicopter Armament

1

Typical AH-1G COBRA shown armed with a bow-mounted XM28 armament subsystem with 40mm M75 grenade launcher/XM134 minigun, as well as wing-mounted XM18 7.62mm high-rate machineguns and 2.75'' rocket pods. Vung Tau, September 1970.

2

The M21 armament subsystem featured 7.62mm XM134 high-rate miniguns combined with XM158 2.75'' seven-tube rocket launchers and was very successful in combat. This was mounted on UH-1B or 1C HUEY helicopters.

3

Typical armed HUEY ''hog'' was outfitted with M5 bow-mounted 40mm grenade launcher as well as an XM3 48-tube 2.75'' rocket pod system and two M60 machineguns suspended by bungi straps which could be fired by the crew chief and door gunner. Company A, 501st Aviation Battalion, Bien Hoa, October 1965.

4

A .50-cal. machinegun could be incorporated into the ''Firefly'' system mounted on a UH-1D HUEY. This system consisted of a battery of landing lights to facilitate night target detection. Vietnam, August 1969.

5

The XM31 armament subsystem consisted of dual 20mm M24A1 automatic guns installed in pods on each side of the HUEY helicopter as a response to enemy .50-cal. machineguns. Bien Hoa, April 1966.

6

The M23 armament subsystem consisted of a 7.62mm M60D machinegun mounted beside the cargo door, usually on a UH-1D HUEY helicopter. Tan Son Nhut, August 1969.

7

The XM134 7.62mm minigun fired six barrels at 6,000 rounds per minute. It is seen here on a Sagami mount on a UH-1B HUEY. Phu Loi, August 1969.

8

Typical rocket armament subsystem pictured here is the XM3, which had two 24-tube 2.75'' folding-fin aerial rocket launcher pods. The UH-1B and UH-1C helicopters could use this direct-fire area weapon.

9

The XM16 armament system consisted of four 7.62mm M60C machineguns plus two 2.75'' seven-tube launchers. This combination proved well suited to a wide range of operational missions. It was used on UH-1B and 1C HUEY model helicopters.

Artillery and Mortars

1

M30 4.2″ mortar weighed 672 lbs. and had a maximum range of 5,650 meters. Its barrel was a rifled tube 60″ long. Phu Loi, October 1969.

2

M109 155mm self-propelled howitzers had a range of 14,600 meters and were the largest direct-support artillery weapons. The army had 108 of these in Vietnam in January 1968. 1st Battalion, 27th Artiller, Phu Loi, July 1968.

3

M107 175mm gun was an excellent self-propelled artillery piece with a maximum range of 32,600 meters and a crew of five. By 1969 the army had some 152 of these in Vietnam. 6th Battalion, 14th Artillery, Vietnam, late 1966.

4

M110 8″ self-propelled howitzer was a fine weapon with a range of 16,800 meters requiring a five-man crew. 8th Battalion, 6th Artillery, Lai Khe, April 1966.

5

M114A1 155mm howitzer had a range of 14,600 meters requiring an 11-man crew. Overall length was 24′, and it weighed 12,700 lbs. 101st Airborne Division, Mai Loc, October 1969.

6

M102 105mm howitzer was an improved light towed weapon with a range of 11,500 meters. This one is being fired by paratroopers of the 2d Battalion, 320th Artillery (101st Airborne Division) in 1967.

7

Artillerymen of the 1st Battalion, 92d Artillery prepare to fire their M114A1 155mm howitzer near Dak To.

8

M29 81mm mortar had a range of 3,500 meters. This picture of the 69th Signal Battalion shows the typical mortar emplacement in action. Dalat, October 1967.

9

M55 quad .50-cal. machinegun system featured a combination of four M2 heavy Browning machineguns on a semi-armored gun mount, often truck mounted in Vietnam. Maximum range was 7,275 yards. Battery G, 65th Artillery on Route 9 between Khe Sanh and Dong Ha, July 1967.

1

M102 105mm howitzer is being fired by 9th Infantry Division artillerymen from a 7,300-lb. aluminum air-portable platform designed for rapid emplacement via helicopter in boggy or inundated terrain. Vietnam, 1968.

2

M108 105mm light, self-propelled howitzer had a range of 11,500 meters. This one is from the 1st Battalion, 40th Artillery. Demilitarized Zone (DMZ), 1967.

3

Typical 105mm howitzer field artillery position. They were circular with ammunition racks around the sandbagged emplacement. The fighting bunker is seen with door open, but most troops preferred sleeping outside on folding cots and air mattresses. 2d Battalion, 13th Artillery, Phu Loi, April 1966.

4

The M101A1 105mm howitzer was an older weapon used throughout the war in Vietnam. It had a range of 11,000 meters. Vietnam, 1968.

5

HAWK was a surface-to-air missile capable of searching out and destroying enemy aircraft traveling at supersonic speeds at altitudes of 100–38,000 feet. Quang Trang (northeast of Saigon), July 1967.

6

AN/MPQ 4 counter-mortar radar set antenna group is leveled on a fishnet-factory roof in Saigon. 2d Battalion, 40th Artillery, Saigon, July 1968.

7

M19 60mm mortar had been phased out of active army inventory but was used by the Marines, and many still found their way into army units where their lightweight portability was favored. Vietnam, May 1965.

Infantry Weapons and Radios

1

XM148 40mm grenade launcher mounted on M16A1 rifle was an early attempt to link the rifle point fire and M79 launcher area fire in a single weapon. 2d Battalion, 502d Infantry (101st Airborne Division), Quang Ngai Province, September 1967.

2

M203 40mm semiautomatic grenade launcher mounted on M16A1 rifle. It could fire three M79 grenades in succession and enabled the combined weapon to have both area and point fire. However, the M79 grenade launcher's performance was judged to be superior to the M203's.

3

Typical example of a 12-gauge shotgun, this one fitted with an M1905 bayonet. The army used several different makes of shotguns in Vietnam, principally Remington, Winchester and Stevens commercial models.

4

M79 40mm grenade launcher gave the infantryman in Vietnam a light, compact weapon to cover the area between the longest reach of a hand grenade and the shortest range of a mortar.

5

XM177E2 5.56mm submachinegun known as the Colt Commando (or CAR 15) was a shorter and handier version of the M16 rifle. It had an 11½" barrel, telescoping stock, stronger flash hider and revised handguard.

6

M16 5.56mm rifle was the most widely used personal weapon in Vietnam. Modified by the army to the M16E1 in 1966 and in 1967 to the M16A1, it was the military version of the AR15 originally developed by Armalite and manufactured by Colt. It was an excellent jungle-fighting weapon and the army had 230,000 in Vietnam by July 1969.

7

M60 7.62mm machinegun was a light, general-purpose weapon with a rotating locking bolt firing 600 rounds a minute. It had an air-cooled barrel with integral gas system which could be replaced in seconds. This one is being fired by a Thai soldier from the Queen's Cobra Regiment.

8

The M79 was a percussion-type single-shot grenade launcher which fired its 40mm round as far as 400 meters. Easy to handle, it became a standard favorite in Vietnam. Here, a four-man fire team blasts enemy village defenses in the Duc Pho area (2d Battalion, 35th Infantry), September 1967.

9

XM174 40mm automatic grenade launcher had a 12-round magazine and was a very accurate and versatile weapon. It was designed by the Aerojet Ordnance and Manufacturing Company.

299

RIFLE, 7.62 mm
SNIPER XM21

1

M40A1 106mm recoilless rifle with M8C .50-cal. spotting rifle (which used a shorter cartridge than the M2 .50-cal. machinegun) mounted on M151 utility truck. This weapon was used in an antipersonnel role when firing high-explosive plastic with tracer ammunition.

2

XM177E2 Colt Commando submachinegun was designed as a survival weapon but proved so useful in close-quarter combat that U.S. Army Special Forces and other special formations were often issued this submachinegun.

3

M14 7.62mm rifle was designed for selective semiautomatic or automatic fire. Although M14 production ceased in 1964, many of the army units arriving early in Vietnam were equipped with them. 1st Infantry Division, Bien Hoa, October 1965.

4

XM21 7.62mm sniper rifle with Redfield three-power to nine-power rangefinder scope. This was the standard army sniping rifle during the Vietnam war.

5

XM21 sniper rifle with bipod and silencer. The noise suppressor fitted at the muzzle reduced the velocity of the emerging gases to below that of sound (without affecting bullet velocity).

6

Colt Commander 9mm general officers model pistol was issued permanently to all army generals during the Vietnam war. Various other 9mm pistol models were carried by some U.S. Army Special Forces soldiers as well.

7

M119A1 .45-cal. automatic pistol was the standard army sidearm in Vietnam. It had great stopping power and dependability under harsh tropical combat conditions.

8

M16A1 rifle fitted with the AN/PVS-2 "Starlight Scope," a lightweight night-vision image intensifier used for visual observation and aimed fire at night while allowing its user security from detection. It had a range of 300–400 meters and provided four-power magnification.

9

HB, M2 .50 cal. machinegun on M3 tripod. The Browning machinegun was used extensively in Vietnam and again proven as one of the most successful guns of all time.

1

Phougas Barrel was filled with jellied gasoline which, when detonated, would throw burning napalm inside perimeter wire. The explosive-incendiary-illumination fire drum was fired remotely using an electrical circuit, the range and lateral dispersion hinging on size and angle of the container. Vietnam, October 1968.

2

Close combat in Vietnam saw little use of the bayonet. Instead, jungle-clearing tools such as the axe and machete were called upon. 1st Battalion, 2d Infantry (1st Infantry Division), north of Phuoc Vinh, 1967.

3

AN/PRS 3 metallic mine detector is used by soldiers of the 199th Infantry Brigade, probing and sweeping to inspect a trail near Saigon. The detector alerted its user to metallic objects buried in the ground. The bayonet was used to unearth the metallic mine.

4

E8 35mm 16-tube CS (tear gas) expendable launcher. Light and portable, it fired 16 riot-control agent canisters in each of four volleys, producing a rapid build-up of a large chemical cloud (each tube holding four 35mm canisters) and was used for perimeter defense. 9th Infantry Division, Dong Tam, November 1968.

5

E8 35mm 16-tube CS (tear gas) expendable launcher. Top view.

6

AN/TVS 2 "Starlight Scope" was a surveillance, target acquisition, and night-observation weapon sight adaptable to the 106mm recoilless rifle or the .50 cal. M2 machinegun, as illustrated here. 9th Infantry Division, Dong Tam, April 1968.

7

M2A17 portable flamethrower was a 42½-lb. weapon which saw considerable service. This paratrooper of the 1st Battalion, 508th Infantry, with soaked towels draped to ward off heat, uses one near Trung Lap, June 1969.

8

M18A1 antipersonnel (Claymore) mine threw out 700 steel balls ahead of it in an arc of about 60 degrees. Lethal range was about 50 meters. Here a "mousetrap" pull-release device is used to detonate the charge in ambush.

9

Smith & Wesson .38-cal. revolver with a 2″ barrel (also issued with a 4″ barrel) was issued to army aviation personnel. Its open-faced design exposed the working parts to foreign matter, and its shock power was weak.

10

M2 .50-cal. machinegun shown in action on a typical vehicle mount. Troop E, 17th Cavalry (173d Airborne Brigade), February 1969.

11

The M60 machinegun could be fired from the hip as this asbestos-gloved soldier proves. The M60 was very popular with the troops. 2d Battalion, 1st Infantry (196th Infantry Brigade), Tay Ninh, September 1966.

12

Armed jeep with M134 7.62mm minigun adapted to ground vehicle use (required power provided by jeep batteries) and a Honeywell hand-cranked 40mm grenade launcher. Note sandbags for driver protection as well as XM177E2 submachinegun and M79 grenade launcher. 13th Aviation Battalion, Can Tho, March 1968.

1

AN/PRC25 radio was a transistorized FM receiver-transmitter that provided two-way communications in platoons and companies. The manpacked radio provided 920 channels and is being used here by a company commander in the 2d Battalion, 27th Infantry (25th Infantry Division), Xuan To Truong, June 1968.

2

AN/PRR9 (helmet-mounted receiver) and AN/PRT4 (hand-held transmitter) provided radio communications over a distance of one mile between the platoon leader and squad leaders. 2d Battalion, 8th Infantry (4th Infantry Division), June 1968.

3

AN/PRC10 FM radio had a range of 5–8 kilometers, weighed 26 lbs. and contained 170 channels. It was later replaced by the AN/PRC25. 1st Battalion, 27th Infantry (25th Infantry Division), Cu Chi, May 1966.

4

URC-10 was an emergency radio used by Special Forces and long-range reconnaissance patrol forces in Vietnam. Here a communications check is made by a member of Company E, 50th Infantry (9th Infantry Division), July 1968.

5

The M72 high-explosive antitank (HEAT) 66mm rocket known as the LAW (light antitank weapon) was used for all purposes in Vietnam, especially for bunker suppression. The launcher was discarded after firing. Against troops it was as lethal as the hand grenade.

6

The 3.5-inch M20 rocket launcher had an effective range of 825 meters against area targets. This picture, taken during training in Virginia in 1964, shows soldiers of the 1st Battalion, 3d Infantry in action.

7

The M67 90mm recoilless rifle had an effective range of between 450 and 800 meters. Though designed primarily as an anti-tank weapon, the M67 saw extensive service against fortifications in Vietnam and was often mounted on vehicles in a support role.

Fighting Vehicles

1

M56 self-propelled antitank (SPAT) gun had a 90mm gun, but crew exposure to snipers soon terminated its usefulness. Company D, 16th Armor (173d Airborne Brigade), 1965.

2

The M113A1 APC fitted with the ACAV armament kit featuring shielded machineguns fords a river in Phu Yen Province. The speed of the M113 was 40–42 mph on land and 3½ mph in water. By January 1968 some 2,134 M113-series vehicles were used by the army in Vietnam.

3

M113 firefighting vehicle distributes foam at the Long Binh Fire Department. The M113 hull proved readily adaptable to a host of field modifications. Long Binh, June 1971.

4

XM706 security vehicle (V100) modified with a turret-mounted XM182 grenade launcher. It was further modified in Vietnam by the addition of a pedestal machinegun mount in front for the driver's use topside if needed.

5

XM706 security vehicle (V100) typically fitted with revolving turret housing twin .30-cal. machineguns was used by the military police for convoy escort in Vietnam. 560th MP Company, March 1970.

6

M551 armored reconnaissance assault vehicle, SHERIDAN, had a primary 152mm gun with coaxial 7.62mm machinegun and a shielded .50-cal. machinegun on the commander's hatch. 1st Squadron, 1st Cavalry, Tam Ky, March 1970.

7

A 40mm M42 of the 5th Battalion, 2d Artillery. These vehicles were gathered from Reserve and National Guard units and proved extremely popular and efficient ground support weapons despite their official "obsolescence." Vietnam, 1967.

1

M557A1 command post carrier was a standard M113-series variant. It was modified for a mobile command post by adding a higher hull to make room for tables and radios inside. 1st Brigade, 5th Infantry Division, Khe Sanh, June 1969.

2

M578 light armored recovery vehicle from the 11th Armored Cavalry in the Vietnam Highlands. Armed with a single .50-cal. machinegun, it had a speed of 37 mph.

3

M48A3 tank modified by the addition of a hydraulic bulldozer blade and an E8 35mm 16-tube CS (tear gas) expendable launcher on top of its xenon searchlight over the main 90mm gun. 1st Infantry Division, Phuoc Vinh, February 1969.

4

M48A3 tank heavily sandbagged after a B-40 rocket-propelled grenade (RPG) had hit its turret. The tank had been hit by seven B-40 RPGs, which killed two of its crew. 3d Squadron, 4th Cavalry (25th Infantry Division), July 1968.

5

M132 self-propelled flamethrower had a cupola containing an M108 flamegun and an M73 7.62mm machinegun. It carried 200 gallons of fuel for the flamegun which had an effective range of 150 yards. 3d Squadron, 11th Armored Cavalry, Long Binh, September 1966.

6

M113A1 marginal terrain bridge ("porta-bridge") resulted from field requests and was only issued in Vietnam, where its 30-foot spanning capacity proved very popular. 3d Squadron, 4th Cavalry, August 1969.

7

M113A1 escort vehicle was fitted with the M134 7.62mm minigun on a General Electric factory-produced mount and served with the XM163 Vulcan in Vietnam. Phu Loi, December 1968.

8

The M113-series armored personnel carriers (APC) were used widely by the army in Vietnam both as troop carriers and, with the addition of ACAV kits, as assault vehicles. This one is fitted with an early "Okinawa"-pattern gun shield draped with smoke grenades and is being used as a mobile command post. 1st Infantry Division, Lai Khe, January 1968.

9

XM163 Vulcan was a modified 20mm M161A1 automatic six-barrel gun mounted on an XM741 hull (a modified M113 chassis). While designed as a low-altitude air defense weapon, it was used against ground targets in Vietnam and had only dummy radar mounted. Phu Loi, December 1968.

10

M125A1 self-propelled 81mm mortar was also a standard M113-series variant. Here the mortar can be seen through the rear of the vehicle. 2d Squadron, 1st Cavalry, Vietnam, December 1968.

1

M88 armored recovery vehicle with gunshield added. It had a crew of four and a speed of 30 mph. 3d Squadron, 11th Armored Cavalry, Phu Loi, September 1968.

2

M113A1 support APC has placed an M67 90mm recoilless rifle behind the commander's shield and has moved the M2 .50-cal. machinegun over to the side replacing the standard M60 machinegun. An interesting modification seen in heavy action at the "Y" Bridge in Saigon, May 1968, with the 9th Infantry Division.

3

M106A1 self-propelled 107mm (4.2") mortar was a standard M113-series variant. The mortar base and stand are carried externally so that its mortar can also be fired away from the vehicle itself. Lam Son, 3d Squadron, 11th Armored Cavalry, September 1968.

4

M113 APC converted to a command vehicle by the U.S. senior advisor to the ARVN 1st Armored Cavalry Regiment with the addition of armored helicopter seats. Lam Son, August 1968.

5

This Ford Lynx II scout car was previously used by Canadians, then Malaysians, and finally by the ARVN before being reconditioned (re-engined from a M3781 truck and painted yellow) by the 1st Squadron, 4th Cavalry for U.S. Army convoy duty. Di An, July 1968.

6

M113A1 diesel APC became a mainstay of army ground mobility throughout Vietnam. This one has survived a solid 90 percent hit from a B-40 rocket-propelled grenade (RPG), the hole and splatter rings still very visible. Phu Coung Bridge over Saigon River, July 1968.

7

M48A3 main battle tank had a 90mm gun with coaxial 7.62mm machinegun, cupola-mounted .50-cal. machinegun, and infrared fire-control equipment and xenon searchlight. Spare tracks on turret afford extra protection. The army had some 370 M48 tanks in Vietnam by July 1969.

Cargo and Utility Vehicles

1

Caterpillar 4x4 tractor with 25-ton trailer, carrying an HD6M engineer tractor (dozer).

2

Semi-trailer, 5,000-gallon fuel, M131-series, was typical of those used by medium petroleum truck companies in Vietnam. This particular model has two 2,500-gallon compartments and is being filled with JP-4 aviation fuel. 47th Transportation Company, Long Binh.

3

Wrecker, 5-ton, 6x6 M543A2.

4

Wrecker, 5-ton, 6x6 M246-series equipped with fifth wheel for towing trailers. This one is removing the main rotor hub assembly from a UH-1C helicopter. Bear Cat, June 1968.

5

Asphalt distributor (800-gallon capacity) on an M61 chassis. This vehicle from the 169th Engineer Battalion is spreading peneprime liquid asphalt, a very thin asphalt which provided a waterproof, semi-hard surface with a minimum amount of time and effort. Long Binh, December 1966.

6

GOER wrecker, 10-ton 4x4 M553 was a large-tire, rough-terrain vehicle built by Caterpillar. It was especially useful during the monsoon season. This early model had headlamps mounted horizontally rather than vertically. Pleiku, July 1967.

7

Semi-trailer, van supply, 12-ton M129A1 used by the 69th Maintenance Battalion for small machinery storage. Cam Ranh Bay, October 1967.

8

Truck, 5-ton, 6x6 M52-series tractor with semi-trailer, 12-ton M127-series, distributing barbed wire for perimeter defense. 57th Transportation Company, Vietnam, March 1968.

9

Hugh tractor with 25-ton engineer equipment lowboy trailer.

1

Fuel tank truck, 1,200-gallon, 2½-ton, 6x6 M49A2C pilot model.

2

Cargo truck, 1¼-ton, 4x4 M715 (Kaiser-Jeep).

3

Gama Goat cargo truck, 1¼-ton articulated 6x6 M561.

4

Expansible van truck, 2½-ton, 6x6 M292A1, had sides which moved out about two feet on each side.

5

Shop van truck, 2½-ton, 6x6 M109A2.

6

Cargo truck, 2½-ton, 6x6 M35 loaded with empty pallets backs up to a CH-47 helicopter. An Khe, December 1965.

7

Water distributor, 1,000-gallon, on 5-ton, 6x6 M61 chassis refills water drums at a shower point. 864th Engineer Battalion, Cam Ranh Bay, August 1965.

8

Cargo truck, 2½-ton, 6x6 M35 loaded with combat-weary soldiers of the 1st Battalion, 7th Cavalry (1st Cavalry Division). This is a typically worn vehicle which obviously saw much service in Vietnam. July 1971.

9

Electronic container van truck, 2½-ton, 6x6 M35 with signal shelter in bed.

1

Bus, 40-passenger (Isuzu). This is typical of several types purchased by the army from Japanese firms and used in Vietnam. 90th Replacement Battalion at Long Binh, February 1970.

2

Rough terrain forklift, 6,000-lb. diesel (Chrysler). The army had 590 rough terrain forklifts in Vietnam by July 1969.

3

Sedan car (1970 Ford Falcon) and utility truck, ¼-ton, 4x4 M151-series in Vietnam.

4

Convoy security utility truck, ¼-ton, 4x4 M151-series, modified by adding improvised armor shielding and two .30-cal. machineguns for duty along Highway 19. Vietnam, June 1970.

5

XM571 1-ton payload utility articulated vehicle (Canadair). 3d Squadron, 4th Cavalry at Long Binh, January 1969.

6

Radio vehicle, ¾-ton, 4x4 M43B1 ambulance conversion, used as a MARS-station relay with the 9th Infantry Division in Vietnam.

7

Cargo truck, ¾-ton, 4x4 M37B1 with S-318/G signal shelter housing an AN/GRC 142 radioteletypewriter (RTT) set. 501st Signal Battalion, Camp Eagle, July 1968.

8

CONEX transporter, 16-ton, 6x6 cross-country XM8002 (Barries & Reinicke). 597th Transportation Company, Vietnam, November 1968.

9

Rough terrain forklift, 10,000-lb. (Pettibone-Mulliken) lifting a CONEX container. Saigon, September 1967.

10

Forklift, 10,000-lb. H100 (Hyster) lifting a CONEX container in Vietnam, October 1967.

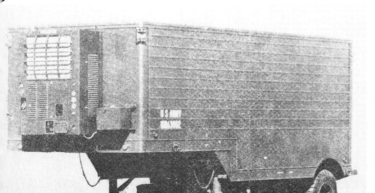

1

M548 6-ton ammunition carrier with 1,500-lb. capacity hoist, used for artillery resupply. 1st battalion, 27th Artillery, Phu Loi, July 1968.

2

Truck, 10-ton, 6x6 M123 tractor with semi-trailer, 45-ton M15A1 carrying two M113 armored personnel carriers, in Vietnam.

3

Truck, 5-ton, 6x6 M52A1 diesel tractor with semi-trailer, 12-ton M127-series, carrying two 175mm gun tubes. The army had 3,299 5-ton tractors and 1,715 5-ton cargo trucks in Vietnam by July 1969.

4

Cargo truck, 2½-ton, 6x6 M35 converted into a wrecker. This was a Vietnam field modification.

5

XM45E1 armored flamethrower servicing unit was attached to a lightly armored M548 and provided additional fuel to the M132 flamethrower vehicle. 2d Squadron, 11th Armored Cavalry, near Phuoc Vinh, January 1969.

6

Reconnaissance utility truck, ¼-ton, 4x4 M151A1 with pedestal-mounted M60 7.62mm machinegun in Vietnam.

7

Utility truck, ¼-ton, 4x4 M151A2.

8

Light weapons carrier, ½-ton, 4x4 M274 Mechanical Mule.

9

Refrigerated trailer, 7½-ton, two-wheeled, was typical of those used by medium reefer truck companies in Vietnam.

1

GOER cargo carrier, 8-ton, 4x4 M520 with a material handling crane.

2

M548 6-ton liquid transporter. While this one carries fuel, a variety of tanks placed in its bed could carry water or lubricants. North of Phuoc Vinh, January 1969.

3

Stake bed truck, 1½-ton, 4x2 D500 commercial model (Dodge).

4

Tunnel clearing truck, ¾-ton, 4x4 M37B1, equipped with CS-gas-dispensing blower unit and water pumps for flooding or draining used in antitunnel work. Northeast of Ben Cat, November 1968.

5

M548 6-ton cargo carrier with air compressor. North of Phuoc Vinh, February 1969.

6

Armed escort truck, ¾-ton, 4x4 M37B1, modified by adding improvised steel armor siding and a pedestal machinegun with shield in Vietnam.

7

Military police utility truck, ¼-ton, 4x4 M151A1, modified by adding armor sides, flooring and seats. 716th Military Police Battalion in Vietnam.

8

Illumination utility truck, ¼-ton, 4x4 M151A1, modified by adding a 23-inch xenon searchlight in the rear in Vietnam.

Engineer Vehicles and Equipment

1

LeTourneau tree crusher being assembled — here its 25-ton knife-edged wheels are being bolted on. A 475-hp. diesel engine with electric motors in each wheel propelled the massive machine, which on firm ground could clear ten acres of woodland in one hour. Long Binh, July 1967.

2

Transphibian tactical tree crusher was a 100-ton tracked tanklike vehicle built by R. G. LeTourneau, Inc. It could fell large trees and cut moderate-sized timber into sticks which were then pressed into the ground. Vietnam, August 1967.

3

Crane Carrier Company Model 20TA chassis with Quickway M202 crane loads a dump truck, 5-ton, 6x6 M51A2. 34th Engineer Group, Vung Tau, September 1967.

4

Caterpillar 4x4 wheeled tractor, Model 830 MB Scraper engaged in construction of a supply storage area, dumps dirt prior to surfacing. 169th Engineer Battalion, Long Binh, December 1966.

5

Caterpillar Model 12 heavy road grader preparing a new airfield surface. The grader had front- and rear-wheel steering and power to all four wheels and was essential for maintenance and crowning of roads, digging ditches and grading of airstrips. Bao Loc, 62d Engineer Battalion, December 1966.

6

Caterpillar D7E tractor (dozer) — full-tracked, low speed, medium drawbar pull — grades a road. Dozers were used in quarry work, road construction and large-scale ground clearance projects. The army had 1,417 bulldozers in Vietnam by 1 July 1969. 4th Engineer Battalion, An Khe, March 1970.

7

Heavy duty crane loads blasted rock onto a dump truck — 5-ton, 6x6 M51-series — at a gravel pit for transport to a rock crusher. 864th Engineer Battalion, Cam Ranh Bay, August 1965.

1

Lorain front-end loader and dump truck, 5-ton, 6x6 M51. The army had 2,105 5-ton dumptrucks in Vietnam by July 1969. Phan Rang, April 1965.

2

Parsons ditching machine Model 624VL was an entrencher capable of digging a trench two feet wide and six feet deep in a matter of minutes. 4th Engineer Battalion, Vietnam, March 1970.

3

Rock crusher machine in operation at Cam Ranh Bay by the 864th Engineer Battalion. To the right is a loader, scoop-type, 2½-cubic-yard, Michigan Model 175A-M and to the left is an M51-series, 5-ton, 6x6 dump truck. August 1965.

4

P & H Model M315T 15-ton, 6x6 crane is used to drive pilings for a new bridge. Phu Loc, March 1968.

5

Allis Chalmers 645M scoop loader, 2½-cubic-yard, operates beside a highway in Vietnam. 27th Engineer Battalion, August 1969.

6

Rex cement mixer is used to pour concrete for a building surface. 69th Engineer Battalion, Can Tho, March 1970.

7

Asphalt spreader is being used to surface the Binh Minh Bypass by the 69th Engineer Battalion, March 1970.

8

Dump truck, 2½-ton, 6x6 M342A2, prepares area for future buildings of the 84th Engineer Battalion, 199th Infantry Brigade, Long Binh.

⑥

1

Class 30 assault trackway being laid by the 5-ton, 6x6 M139 truck. Designed to aid wheeled and rubber-padded vehicles in crossing areas of low bearing capacity and poor traction, it was available only to army units in Vietnam.

2

M60 armored vehicle launched bridge was powered by a Continental diesel engine and could span water obstacles by bridging up to 60 feet which could support a maximum of 60 tons. 1st Engineer Battalion, Phu Loi, July 1968.

3

Rough terrain 5-ton, 4x4 Hanson crane Model H446A (chassis built by FWD) unloads a float raft from an engineer bridge truck, 5-ton, 6x6, on M139 chassis, which used oversized tires. 20th Engineer Brigade, Vietnam.

4

M728 combat engineer vehicle provided armor support for forward engineer tasks. Its 165mm demolition gun had an indirect firing range of 4,870 meters, and its beam and winch had a 17,500-lb. hoisting capability and 25,000-lb. winching capacity. Phu Loi, September 1968.

5

20-ton, 4x4 rough terrain crane, American Hoist & Derrick Model 2380, combined unique cross-country mobility with its own earth-moving capability. 617th Engineer Company, Long Binh, December 1968.

6

Dump truck, ¾-ton, 4x4 XM708 based on the M37 Dodge vehicle in Vietnam.

7

The Rome Plow was a military standard D7E tractor equipped with a heavy-duty protective cab and a special tree-cutting blade manufactured by the Rome Company of Rome, Georgia. The potency of the Rome Plow made it synonymous with land clearing. North of Phuoc Vinh, February 1969.

Vessels

1

Barracks ships, such as the USS *Mercer* (APB-39), seen with an ammi barge and several armored troop carriers and assault support boats, housed riverine soldiers of the 9th Infantry Division.

2

U.S. Army Beach Discharge Lighter *LTC U.D. Page* was operated by the 124th Transportation Command. Cam Ranh Bay, March 1970.

3

Landing craft, mechanized (LCM) was used by the army for lighterage and harbor service as well as limited intercoastal and inland waterway operations. The army had 153 of these in Vietnam by July 1969. Vung Tau, August 1969.

4

A BARC (barge amphibious resupply cargo), a 60-ton amphibious lighter later known as the LARC LX, from the 159th Transportation Battalion. Sa Huynh, August 1967.

5

River patrol boat Mark II, a fiberglass-hull craft, operated by the 458th Transportation Company. Vung Tau Harbor, January 1969.

6

Navy armored troop carrier (ATC) could carry 40 soldiers of the army mobile riverine force. Other navy riverine craft included assault support boats, command and control boats, and monitors.

7

A LARC V (five-ton lighter amphibious resupply Cargo) of the 334th Transportation Company in Vietnam. June 1965.

8

Landing craft, utility (LCU) of the 97th Transportation Company carries soldiers of the 1st Logistical Command ashore from the transport *Gen. J.C. Breckinridge*. Vung Tau, July 1965.

1

USNS *Corpus Christie Bay* was an aircraft repair ship (helicopter) operated by the Military Sea Transportation Service and used as the base of the 1st Transportation Battalion. Anchored off Vung Tau, July 1970.

2

Ski boat of the 1st Engineer Battalion, 1st Infantry Division, moves up the Saigon River testing engines and equipment prior to an operation. December 1969.

3

Airboats carried a crew of two and up to five soldiers. Capable of 41.7 knots per hour, they were armed with a .30-cal. machinegun. This craft is operated by 5th Special Forces Group's Team A-404 in the Delta.

4

Motorized RB-15 (15-man rubber boat) is used as an assault boat for paratroopers of the 173d Airborne Brigade as they jump to shore along the Song Be River in War Zone D.

5

RB-3 (three-man rubber boat) is used to pull equipment across a canal by soldiers of the 1st Battalion, 27th Infantry, 25th Infantry Division in Vietnam. May 1968.

6

The air cushion vehicle (ACV) was a modified Bell Aerosystem commercial craft capable of traveling on a cushion of air more than four feet thick at a speed of 75 knots. The airboat platoon of the 3d Brigade, 9th Infantry Division (later 39th Cavalry Platoon) used them. October 1968.

7

River patrol boat Mark I was adapted from a commercial design and especially suited for shallow-water operations. These were used by both army and navy units. Saigon River, October 1969.

8

An armored troop carrier (ATC) converted to facilitate aerial evacuation of wounded troops by adding a light steel helicopter platform. Such adaptations were essential to the 9th Infantry Division's riverine operations.

9

U.S. Army 100-ton floating crane mounted on a barge. Saigon River, September 1967.

APPENDIX A:

Army Deployments and Stations During the Vietnam Conflict

STRENGTHS OF ALLIED MILITARY FORCES IN SOUTH VIETNAM*

Country	End 1964	End 1965	End 1966	End 1967	End 1968	End 1969	End 1970	End 1971	End 1972
Australia	200	1,560	4,530	6,820	7,660	7,670	6,800	2,000	130
Korea	200	20,620	25,570	47,830	50,000	48,870	48,540	45,700	36,790
New Zealand	30	120	160	530	520	550	440	100	50
Philippines	20	70	2,060	2,020	1,580	190	70	50	50
South Vietnam†	514,000	643,000	735,900	798,800	820,000	897,000	968,000	1,046,250	1,048,000
Thailand	—	20	240	2,200	6,000	11,570	11,570	6,000	40
United States	23,310	184,310	385,300	485,600	536,000	484,330	335,790	158,120	24,000

* Countries providing nonmilitary personnel are not listed. An average of 30 Republic of China and 10 Spanish advisors served throughout this period as well.

† Includes the Army, Navy, Marines, Air Force, Regional and Popular Forces, but does not include paramilitary formations such as National Police, CIDG, "Armed Combat Youth," etc.

SUMMARY OF DEPLOYMENTS AND REDEPLOYMENTS OF U.S. ARMY COMBAT AND COMBAT SUPPORT UNITS IN VIETNAM*

Units	Prior July 1965	July-Dec. 1965	Jan.-June 1966	July-Dec. 1966	Jan.-June 1967	July-Dec. 1967	Jan.-June 1968	July-Dec. 1968	Jan.-June 1969	July-Dec. 1969	Jan.-June 1970	July-Dec. 1970	Jan.-June 1971	July-Dec. 1971	Jan.-June 1972	July-Dec. 1972	Total
Divisions	0	2	1	1	1	2	0	0	0	−1	−1	−2	−1	−1	−1	0	7
Brigades/Arm Cav Regts †	1	7	3	8	1	4	1	1	0	−3	−4	−6	−4	−6	−3	0	26
Infantry Battalions	2	20	10	22	3	15	7	2	0	−9	−11	−20	−13	−16	−11	−1	81
Tank Bn/Cavalry Sqdns	0	1	2	6	0	2	0	1	0	0	−2	−3	−2	−3	−2	0	12
105mm T Arty Battalions	1	10	3	9	3	4	2	0	−1	−4	−7	−7	−4	−6	−3	0	32
105mm SP Arty Battalions	0	0	1	1	0	0	0	0	0	−1	−1	0	0	0	0	0	2
155mm T Arty Battalions	0	1	0	1	2	0	2	1	−1	0	0	0	−1	−4	−1	0	7
155mm SP Arty Battalions	0	0	1	0	1	0	0	2	0	1	−1	−1	−2	−1	0	0	5
155mm/8″ Arty Battalions	0	1	1	1	1	0	0	1	0	−1	−1	−1	−1	−1	0	0	5
175mm/8″ Arty Battalions‡	0	4	0	2	2	3	0	0	0	0	1	−2	−1	−8	−1	0	12
Aer Rocket Arty Battalions	0	1	0	0	0	0	0	1	0	0	0	0	−1	0	−1	0	2
Missile, AWSP Battalions	0	2	0	2	1	0	0	−1	0	−1	0	0	−1	−2	0	0	5
Engr Combat Battalions	0	7	3	6	0	2	1	1	0	−4	−2	−5	−2	−5	−2	0	20
Engr Constr Battalions	2	4	0	1	7	1	0	0	−1	0	0	0	−1	−10	−3	0	15
Signal Battalions	1	6	2	12	5	−1	1	2	0	−1	−4	−2	−5	−5	−9	−2	31
Aviation Companies and Air Cavalry Troops	16	35	11	11	17	29	8	7	8	−2	−5	−22	−13	−32	−28	−40	142

* Based primarily on Dept. of Defense Army Activities Report: Southeast Asia, 12 April 1972, p. 10. Though updated and with additions, may not totally agree with calculations made from actual unit service as stand-down dates sometimes used for redeployment purposes above.

† Includes the divisional brigades.

‡ Previous to the first half of 1969 these battalions were either 8″ SP or 175mm SP battalions; there were three 175mm and five 8″ SP battalions. In early 1969 all were converted into dual 175mm/8″ SP artillery battalions.

THE U.S. ARMY WITHDRAWAL FROM VIETNAM

Increment	Time Frame	Major Unit(s) Involved	Army Reduction	Total U.S. Reduction*	Army Strength at Completion of Increment*
I	1 July 69 – 31 Aug. 69	9th Infantry Division (–) [†]	15,712	25,000	352,400
II	18 Sept. 69 – 15 Dec. 69	3d Brigade, 82d Airborne Division	14,092	40,500	338,300
III	1 Feb. 70 – 15 April 70	1st Infantry Division 3d Brigade, 4th Infantry Division	29,396	50,000	308,900
IV	1 July 70 – 15 Oct. 70	3d Brigade, 9th Infantry Division 199th Light Infantry Brigade	15,932	50,000	292,900
V	16 Oct. 70 – 31 Dec. 70	4th Infantry Division (–) 25th Infantry Division (–)	38,054	40,000	254,800
VI	1 Jan. 71 – 30 April 71	1st Cavalry Division (–) 11th Armored Cavalry Regiment (–) 2d Brigade, 25th Infantry Division	41,848	60,000	213,000
VII	1 May 71 – 30 June 71	One Air Cavalry Squadron Three infantry battalions	15,030	29,300	198,000
VIII	1 July 71 – 1 Sept. 71	173d Airborne Brigade	21,769	28,700	176,200
IX	1 Sept. 71 – 30 Nov. 71	AMERICAL Division (–) 11th Infantry Brigade 198th Infantry Brigade	35,000	42,000	141,200
X	1 Dec. 71 – 31 Jan. 72	101st Airborne Division (Airmobile) (–)	36,718	45,000	104,500
XI	1 Feb. 72 – 30 April 72	Two cavalry squadrons Five infantry battalions Four air cavalry squadrons	58,096	70,000	46,400
XII	1 May 72 – 30 June 72	3d Brigade, 1st Cavalry Division 196th Infantry Brigade Four infantry battalions	14,552	20,000	31,900
XIII	1 July 72 – 31 Aug. 72	Two infantry battalions	8,484	10,000	23,400
XIV	1 Sept. 72 – 30 Nov. 72	Miscellaneous units	7,282	12,000	16,100

* Approximate figures.

[†] (–) Indicates only partial withdrawal of this unit.

U.S. ARMY DIVISION AND SEPARATE BRIGADE/REGIMENT GLOBAL SERVICE DURING THE VIETNAM CONFLICT, 1965 – 73*

DIVISIONS	Activation†	Inactivation‡	Notes and Primary Locations
1st Armored Division	P	—	May 71 replaced 4th Armored Division in Germany
2d Armored Division	P	—	Fort Hood
3d Armored Division	P	—	Germany
4th Armored Division	P	10 May 71	Replaced by 1st Armored Division from Fort Hood
1st Cavalry Division (Airmobile)	P	—	May 71 replaced 1st Armored Division at Fort Hood when returned from Vietnam
1st Infantry Division	P	—	April 70 replaced 24th Infantry Division at Fort Riley and Germany
2d Infantry Division	P	—	Korea
3d Infantry Division (Mechanized)	P	—	Germany
4th Infantry Division	P	—	Dec. 70 replaced 5th Infantry Division at Fort Carson
5th Infantry Division (Mechanized)	P	15 Dec. 70	Replaced by 4th Infantry Division returning from Vietnam
6th Infantry Division	24 Nov. 67	25 July 68	Fort Campbell/Hawaii
7th Infantry Division	P	2 April 71	Reactivated 21 Oct. 74 at Fort Ord; previously in Korea
8th Infantry Division (Mechanized)	P	—	Germany
9th Infantry Division	1 Feb. 66	25 Sept. 69	Reactivated 21 April 72 at Fort Lewis
11th Air Assault Division	P	1 July 65	Raised 5 Feb. 63 merely as a test unit and never actually intended to be a deployable division. Fort Benning
23d Infantry Division	25 Sept. 67	29 Nov. 71	Vietnam
24th Infantry Division (Mechanized)	P	15 April 70	Replaced by 1st Infantry Division returning from Vietnam
25th Infantry Division	P	—	Vietnam and Hawaii
82d Airborne Division	P	—	Fort Bragg
101st Airborne Division (Airmobile) §	P	—	Fort Campbell and Vietnam
BRIGADES			
11th Infantry Brigade (Light)	1 July 66	30 Nov. 71	Vietnam
171st Infantry Brigade (Mechanized)	P	13 Nov. 72	Alaska
172d Infantry Brigade (Mechanized)	P	—	Alaska
173d Airborne Brigade	P	14 Jan. 72	Vietnam
193d Infantry Brigade	P	—	Canal Zone
194th Armored Brigade	P	—	Fort Knox
196th Infantry Brigade (Light)	10 Sept. 65	30 June 72	Vietnam
197th Infantry Brigade	P	—	Fort Benning
198th Infantry Brigade (Light)	10 May 67	30 Nov. 71	Vietnam
199th Infantry Brigade (Light)	1 June 66	30 Oct. 70	Vietnam
ARMORED CAVALRY REGIMENTS			
2d Armored Cavalry	P	—	Germany
3d Armored Cavalry	P	—	Germany and Fort Lewis
6th Armored Cavalry	23 March 67	21 June 73 ‖	Fort Meade
11th Armored Cavalry	P	—	May 72 replaced 14th Armored Cavalry (Regiment) in Germany
14th Armored Cavalry	P	17 May 72	Replaced by 11th Armored Cavalry returning from Vietnam

* See Chart of Active United States Army on April 8, 1968, pages 340-43, for typical location and interior organization of these units.

† "P" signifies unit had been activated prior to 1965.

‡ "—" signifies unit was continuously active during time frame of this table.

§ Designated Airmobile officially 1 July 1968; transformation not completed until March 1969.

‖ The 6th Armored Cavalry (Regiment) was inactivated less 1st Squadron on 31 March 1971, and its 1st Squadron was inactivated on 21 June 1973. On 22 June 1973 the 6th Armored Cavalry was reduced to zero strength and reorganized as a parent regiment under the Combat Arms Regimental System (CARS).

THE 1st SPECIAL FORCES DURING THE VIETNAM WAR*

Unit	Activated [†]	Location	Area of Operations
1st Special Forces Group (Airborne)	4 Oct. 1960	Okinawa	Asia
3d Special Forces Group (Airborne)	10 March 1964	Fort Bragg	Africa
5th Special Forces Group (Airborne)	21 Sept. 1961	Vietnam	SouthEast Asia
6th Special Forces Group (Airborne)	Dec. 1963	Fort Bragg	Middle East
7th Special Forces Group (Airborne)	20 May 1960	Fort Bragg	Global Reserve
8th Special Forces Group (Airborne)	1 April 1963	Canal Zone	Latin America
10th Special Forces Group (Airborne)	20 March 1961	Germany	Europe
46th Special Forces Company (Airborne) [‡]	15 April 1967	Thailand	Thailand and adjacent areas

* In addition, the following Special Forces Groups were on reserve during this time frame: 2d, 9th, 11th, 12th, 13th, 17th and 24th.

[†] The most recent activation prior to the Vietnam war is used and in most cases represents the date the group and its organic elements were activated.

[‡] Company D, 1st Special Forces Group, 1st Special Forces arrived in Thailand in October 1966. The 46th Special Forces Company, 1st Special Forces was constituted and activated in Thailand on 15 April 1967 using the personnel and equipment formerly of Company D, 1st Special Forces Group.

SELECTED ARMY UNITS AVAILABLE FOR VIETNAM BUT NEVER SENT*

Unit	Authorized Strength	Station	Activation	Notes
5th Infantry Division (Mechanized) (–) [†]		Fort Carson, CO		
1st Battalion, 10th Infantry (Mechanized)	899		P	
2d Battalion, 10th Infantry (Mechanized)	899		P	
3d Battalion, 10th Infantry (Mechanized)	899		May 67	
2d Battalion, 11th Infantry (Mechanized)	899		P	
3d Battalion, 11th Infantry (Mechanized)	899		May 67	
2d Battalion, 61st Infantry (Mechanized)	899		P	
3d Battalion, 77th Armor	571		P	
4th Squadron, 12th Cavalry (–)	599		P	
1st Battalion, 19th Artillery (155mm SP)	458		P	
1st Battalion, 29th Artillery (155mm SP)	458		P	
6th Battalion, 20th Artillery (155mm/8" SP)	592		P	
7th Engineer Battalion (–)	611		P	
5th Signal Battalion	518		P	
82d Airborne Division (–) [†]		Fort Bragg, NC		
1st Battalion, 325th Infantry (Airborne)	792		P	
2d Battalion, 325th Infantry (Airborne)	792		P	
3d Battalion, 325th Infantry (Airborne)	792		P	
1st Battalion, 504th Infantry (Airborne)	792		P	
2d Battalion, 504th Infantry (Airborne)	792		P	
2d Battalion, 508th Infantry (Airborne)	792		P	
1st Squadron, 17th Cavalry (–)	589		P	
1st Battalion, 319th Artillery (105mm T)	468		P	
1st Battalion, 320th Artillery (105mm T)	468		P	
307th Engineer Battalion (Airborne) (–)	576		P	
82d Signal Battalion (Airborne) (–)	528		P	

	Authorized Strength	Station	Activation	Notes
6th Infantry Division		Ft. Campbell, KY (except if marked Hawaii)		
4th Battalion, 1st Infantry	762		Nov. 67	
5th Battalion, 1st Infantry	762		Nov. 67	
6th Battalion, 1st Infantry	762		Nov. 67	
5th Battalion, 3d Infantry	762		Nov. 67	
6th Battalion, 3d Infantry	762		Nov. 67	
7th Battalion, 3d Infantry	762		Nov. 67	
2d Battalion, 20th Infantry	762	Hawaii	Nov. 67	
3d Battalion, 20th Infantry	762	Hawaii	Nov. 67	
6th Battalion, 20th Infantry	762	Hawaii	Nov. 67	
4th Squadron, 9th Cavalry	818		Nov. 67	
6th Battalion, 1st Artillery (105mm T)	475		Nov. 67	
5th Battalion, 3d Artillery (105mm T)	475		Nov. 67	
6th Battalion, 78th Artillery (105mm T)	475	Hawaii	Nov. 67	
1st Battalion, 80th Artillery (155mm/8" SP)	612		Nov. 67	
96th Engineer Battalion	890		Nov. 67	
6th Signal Battalion	575		Nov. 67	
29th Infantry Brigade, Hawaii N.G.		Schofield Barracks, HI		Ordered to active duty 13 May 68
1st Battalion, 299th Infantry	841		—	
2d Battalion, 299th Infantry	841		—	
100th Battalion, 442d Infantry	841		—	
1st Battalion, 487th Artillery (105mm T)	508		—	
40th Aviation Company	135		—	
Troop E, 19th Cavalry	170		—	
227th Engineer Company	217		—	
69th Infantry Brigade, Kansas N.G.		Fort Carson, CO		Ordered to active duty 13 May 68
2d Battalion, 133d Infantry (Mechanized)	911		—	
1st Battalion, 137th Infantry	841		—	
2d Battalion, 137th Infantry	841		—	
2d Battalion, 130th Artillery (105mm T)	508		—	
169th Aviation Company	135		—	
Troop E, 114th Cavalry	170		—	
160th Engineer Company	217		—	
6th Armored Cavalry (Regiment)		Fort Meade, MD		
1st Squadron, 6th Armored Cavalry	1,002		March 67	
2d Squadron, 6th Armored Cavalry	1,002		March 67	
3d Squadron, 6th Armored Cavalry	1,002		March 67	
Artillery Battalions				
4th Battalion, 14th Artillery (105mm T)	516	Sill	Aug. 66	Sch Spt
8th Battalion, 12th Artillery (155mm T)	554	Bragg	Feb. 68	
6th Battalion, 16th Artillery (155mm T)	554	Sill	P	Sch Spt
2d Battalion, 31st Artillery (155mm T)	554	Sill	P	Sch Spt
1st Battalion, 211th Artillery (155mm T)	554	Benning	—	MA N.G.
8th Battalion, 17th Artillery (155mm SP)	506	Campbell	Aug. 67	
3d Battalion, 73d Artillery (155mm SP)	506	Irwin	Jan. 67	
6th Battalion, 82d Artillery (155mm SP)	506	Bragg	June 67	
9th Battalion, 1st Artillery (8" SP)	549	Carson	Aug. 67	
2d Battalion, 36th Artillery (8" SP)	549	Sill	P	Sch Spt
4th Battalion, 39th Artillery (8" SP)	549	Bragg	March 67	
4th Battalion, 73d Artillery (8" SP)	549	Bragg	Feb. 67	
4th Battalion, 80th Artillery (8" SP)	549	Carson	March 67	

2d Battalion, 84th Artillery (8" SP)	549	Carson	May 67	
4th Battalion, 84th Artillery (8" SP)	549	Carson	Feb. 67	
4th Battalion, 94th Artillery (8" SP)	549	Irwin	Aug. 67	
6th Battalion, 8th Artillery (175mm SP)	522	Carson	March 67	
4th Battalion, 28th Artillery (175mm SP)	522	Sill	Jan. 66	Sch Spt
8th Battalion, 7th Artillery (HAWK Missile)	669	Bliss	P	
4th Battalion, 56th Artillery (HAWK Missile)	669	Bliss	May 67	
Battery E, 333d Artillery (Searchlight)	151	Sill		Sched to RVN July 67
Battery F, 333d Artillery (Searchlight)	151	Sill		Sched to RVN July 67

Armor Battalions ‡

6th Battalion, 32d Armor	599	Knox	June 66	Sch Spt
1st Battalion, 63d Armor (1st Inf Div)	571	Riley	P	
4th Battalion, 68th Armor (82d Abn Div)	598	Knox	P	
Company E, 15th Armor (Light Tank Security)	129	Hood	—	Sched to RVN Aug. 67
Company F, 15th Armor (Light Tank Security)	129	Hood	—	Sched to RVN Aug. 67

Engineer Battalions

5th Engineer Battalion (Combat)	794	Leonard Wood	Sept. 66
18th Engineer Battalion (Combat)	794	Devens	Oct. 67
47th Engineer Battalion (Combat) (Abn)	695	Bragg	Feb. 67
51st Engineer Battalion (Combat)	794	Campbell	Oct. 67
613th Engineer Battalion (Combat)	794	Carson	Sept. 67
818th Engineer Battalion (Combat)	794	Benning	Feb. 68
43d Engineer Battalion (Construction)	905	Benning	April 66
52d Engineer Battalion (Construction)	905	Carson	Feb. 68
63d Engineer Battalion (Construction)	905	Hood	July 66
75th Engineer Battalion (Construction)	905	Meade	July 66
339th Engineer Battalion (Construction)	905	Lewis	March 66
575th Engineer Battalion (Construction)	905	Stewart	May 66
748th Engineer Battalion (Construction)	905	Knox	March 68
808th Engineer Battalion (Construction)	905	Alaska	April 68

Signal Battalions

50th Signal Battalion (Airborne Corps)	769	Bragg	P
57th Signal Battalion (Corps)	691	Hood	June 66
58th Signal Battalion (Cable Construction)	647	Lewis	April 67
67th Signal Battalion (Combat Area)	815	Riley	April 67
78th Signal Battalion (Combat Area)	815	Lewis	July 66
426th Signal Battalion (Combat Area)	815	Bragg	April 67

Air Cavalry Squadron

8th Squadron, 1st Cavalry	770	Knox	Aug. 67

Armored Cavalry Squadron

1st Squadron, 18th Cavalry, CA N.G.	931	Lewis	Ordered to active duty 13 May 68	Sched to RVN Nov. 68

* The 1st and 2d Armored Divisions at Fort Hood could also have been assigned to other units. A "P" signifies the unit was raised previous to 30 June 1965 and thus before the Vietnam build-up. Activation is meant only to signify the unit's most recent activation during the Vietnam era and is not to be understood as a lineage factor. A (–) signifies that part of a given element served in Vietnam during the conflict.

† Both the 5th Infantry Division and the 82d Airborne Division had deployed a brigade to Vietnam. In July 1968 the 82d Airborne Division activated a fourth brigade to replace the one sent overseas, consisting of the 4th Battalion, 325th Infantry; 3d Battalion, 504th Infantry; and the 3d Battalion, 505th Infantry. Likewise in November 1969 the 5th Infantry Division raised a new brigade consisting of the 5th Battalion, 10th Infantry; 5th Battalion, 11th Infantry; and the 3d Battalion, 61st Infantry. Both added brigades were seriously understrength and only intended to temporarily "round out" the stateside divisions until their Vietnam-based units rejoined them. They are not listed above because the added battalions were never intended for Vietnam duty.

‡ All armored battalions deployed to Vietnam were to have been refitted with the diesel-powered M48A3's instead of the gasoline-powered M48A2C tanks. There was a chronic shortage of these vehicles, however.

The Active United States Army Worldwide in April 1968 — By Major Command and Location

The following two charts, pages 340-43, show the location of every U.S. Army infantry, armor, cavalry, engineer, aviation and artillery battalion on April 8, 1968. Some lettered companies and batteries are also illustrated. The first chart is divided by Major Commands and the second by location for those units not assigned to such a command. For separate company-sized aviation units, see the chart below.

At this date several units were engaged in riot combat in the United States. The U.S. city is specifically named in the chart in each case. It should be remembered, of course, that large contingents of National Guard troops and other army units (such as Military Police) were also present in those riot areas.

The 24th Infantry Division (Mechanized) was in the process of deploying to the United States. The units shown as en route arrived as follows: Infantry — 1/19 (21 May), 2/21 (8 April), 1/34 (26 April), 2/34 (13 May); Armor — 5/32 (5 April), 2/70 (22 April); Cavalry — 2/9(–) (24 May); Artillery — 2/7 (12 April), 1/13 (16 May), 3/11 (9 May); Engineers — 3(–) (2 April). The 3d Armored Cavalry (Regiment) was also returning to Fort Lewis but at this time only the 2/3 Cavalry was en route and scheduled to arrive in the United States 13 May. The 29th Infantry Brigade (Hawaii National Guard) actually closed its mobilization station at Schofield Barracks on 13 May, and the 69th Infantry Brigade (Kansas National Guard) closed its mobilization station 23 May 1968. Similarly, the 1st Battalion of the 211th Artillery (Massachusetts National Guard) closed into Fort Benning on 20 May.

Reference should be made to the Major Command segment of the overview to track exact post compositions in any given location. Many vital posts engaged in conducting infantry training are not reflected here because Infantry Training Center battalions are not considered maneuver infantry battalions. However, note that the infantry companies at Fort Ord were part of Army Combat Developments Command's Infantry Experimentation Battalion.

INVENTORY OF ARMY AVIATION UNITS WORLDWIDE, MAY 1968

Aviation Unit	U.S.	Vietnam	Other Areas	Total
Division/Brigade/Squadron Units:				
Air Cavalry Troop	11	17	7	35
Aviation Company (General Support)	1	7	2	10
Aviation Company (Airmobile Light)	1	6	2	9
Aviation Company (Assault Helicopter)(AM Div)	—	6	—	6
Aviation Artillery Battery (Aerial Weapons)(AM Div)	—	4	—	4
Aviation Company (Assault Support Helicopter)(AM Div)	—	3	—	3
Aviation Company (Aerial Weapons)(AM Div)	—	2	—	2
Aviation Company (Separate Brigade)	1	—	1	2
Aviation Detachment, Berlin Brigade	—	—	1	1
Non-divisional Units:				
Aviation Company (Airmobile Light)	3	38	3	44
Aviation Company (Surveillance)*	1	20	1	22
Aviation Company (Medium Helicopter) †	3	13	3	19
Aviation Company (Army & Corps)	1	2	6	9
Medical Company (Air Ambulance) ‡	1	2	2	5
Aviation Company (Heavy Helicopter)	1	3	—	4
Aviation Company (Fixed Wing)	—	2	1	3
Aviation Company (Armed Escort)	—	2	—	2

* Three types of surveillance units included: OV-1, O-1 (Light) and U-6/U-8 aircraft.

† Includes the Advance Weapons Support Command (AWSCOM) Aviation Detachment.

‡ Does not include air ambulance detachments.

Major Command	Location	Infantry*	Armor
1st Armored Div	Fort Hood	5/6 (M), 2/46 (M), 4/46 (M) Chicago, 2/52 (M) Chicago	1/13 Chicago, 2/13, 1/81, 2/81
1st Cavalry Div	Camp Evans	1/5 Cav, 2/5 Cav, 1/7 Cav, 2/7 Cav, 5/7 Cav, 1/8 Cav, 2/8 Cav, 1/12 Cav, 2/12 Cav, E/52	
1st Infantry Div	Lai Khe	1/2, 2/2 (M), 1/16, 2/16, 1/18, 2/18, 1/26, 1/28, 2/28, F/52	
2d Armored Div	Fort Hood	7/6 (M), 1/41 (M), 2/41 (M), 2/50 (M)	1/66, 2/66, 1/67, 2/67
2d Infantry Div	Tonggu Ri	1/9, 2/9 (M), 1/23 (M), 2/23 (M), 3/23, 1/38, 2/38	1/72, 2/72
3d Armored Div	Frankfurt	1/36 (M), 2/36 (M), 3/36 (M), 1/48 (M), 2/48 (M)	1/32, 2/32, 3/32, 1/33, 2/33, 3/33
3d Infantry Div	Wurzburg	1/4 (M), 1/7 (M), 1/15 (M), 2/15 (M), 1/30 (M), 2/30 (M)	1/64, 2/64, 3/64, 4/64
4th Armored Div	Goppingen	1/51, 2/51, 3/51, 1/54, 2/54	1/35, 3/35, 4/35, 1/37, 2/37, 3/37
4th Infantry Div	Pleiku	1/8, 2/8 (M), 3/8, 1/12, 3/12, 1/14, 1/22, 1/35, 2/35, E/58	1/69
5th Infantry Div Elements en route to	Fort Carson Vietnam	1/10, 2/10 Chicago, 3/10 (M) Chicago, 2/11 (M), 3/11 (M), 2/61 1/11, 1/61 (M)	3/77 1/77
6th Infantry Div	Fort Campbell Hawaii	4/1, 5/1, 6/1, 5/3, 6/3, 7/3 2/20, 3/20, 6/20	
7th Infantry Div	Dopsu-dong	1/17 (M), 2/17 (M), 1/31, 2/31, 1/32, 2/32, 3/32	1/73
8th Infantry Div	Bad-Kreuznach	1/13, 2/13, 1/39, 1/87, 1/509 (Abn/M), 2/509 (Abn/M)	1/68, 2/68, 3/68, 5/68
9th Infantry Div	Bear Cat	6/31, 2/39, 3/39, 4/39, 2/47 (M), 3/47, 4/47, 2/60, 3/60, 5/60 (M), E/50	
23d Infantry Div	Chu Lai	2/1, 3/1, 4/3, 1/6, 1/20, 3/21, 4/21, 4/31, 1/46, 5/46, 1/52, E/51	
24th Infantry Div Elements en route to	Augsburg Fort Riley	3/19 (M), 1/21 (M) 1/19 (M), 2/21 (M), 1/34 (M), 2/34 (M)	1/70, 3/70 5/32, 2/70
25th Infantry Div	Cu Chi	1/5 (M), 4/9, 2/12, 2/14, 2/22 (M), 3/22, 4/23 (M), 1/27, 2/27, F/50	2/34
82d Airborne Div	Fort Bragg Gia Le	1/325 (Abn) D.C., 2/325 (Abn) D.C., 3/325 (Abn) D.C., 1/504 (Abn) D.C., 2/504 (Abn) D.C., 2/508 (Abn) D.C. 1/505 (Abn), 2/505 (Abn), 1/508 (Abn)	4/68 (at Fort Knox)
101st Airborne Div	Hue–Phu Bai	3/187, 1/327 (Abn), 2/327 (Abn), 1/501, 2/501, 1/502, 2/502 (Abn), 1/506, 2/506, 3/506, F/58	
2d Armored Cav Regt	Nürnberg		
3d Armored Cav Regt	Baumholder		
6th Armored Cav Regt	Fort Meade		
11th Armored Cav Regt	Xuan Loc		
14th Armored Cav Regt	Fulda		
11th Infantry Bde	(Part of 23d Infantry Div)		
171st Infantry Bde	Fort Wainwright (AK)	6/9, 1/47 (M)	A/40
172d Infantry Bde	Fort Richardson (AK)	5/23, 1/60 (M)	D/40
173d Airborne Bde	Bong Son	1/503 (Abn), 2/503 (Abn), 3/503 (Abn), 4/503 (Abn)	D/16
193d Infantry Bde	Canal Zone	4/10, 4/20, 3/508	
194th Armored Bde	Fort Knox	4/54 (M)	5/33, 4/37
196th Infantry Bde	(Part of 23d Infantry Div)		
197th Infantry Bde	Fort Benning	1/29 Baltimore, 5/31, 1/58 (M) Baltimore, E/21	4/69
198th Infantry Bde	(Part of 23d Infantry Div)		
199th Infantry Bde	Long Binh	2/3, 3/7, 4/12, 5/12, F/51	
BERLIN Bde	Berlin	2/6, 3/6, 4/18	F/40
29th Infantry Bde (HI NG)	Hawaii	1/299, 2/299, 100/442	
69th Infantry Bde (KS NG)	Fort Carson	1/137, 2/137, 2/133 (M)	

* (M)=Mechanized, (Abn) = parachutist-qualified airborne infantry

† Artillery is 105mm unless otherwise specified.

Cavalry	Engineer	Artillery †	Aviation
1/1 Vietnam, 3/1 Chicago	16	3/2 (HJ), 4/3, 1/6, 3/19, 1/73, (155/8")	
1/9	8	2/19, 2/20 (ARA), 1/21, 1/30 (155), 1/77, E/82 (Avn)	227, 228, 229
1/4	1	1/5, 8/6 (155/8"), 1/7, 6/15, 2/33	1
2/1 Vietnam, 6/1	17	1/3, 5/14, 1/16 (HJ), 1/78, 6/92 (155/8")	
4/7	2	1/12 (HJ), 1/15, 7/17, 5/38, 6/37 (155/8")	2
3/12	23	2/3, 2/6, 2/27 (155), 6/40, 2/73 (155/8")	
3/7	10	1/9 (HJ), 1/10 (Mxd), 2/39, 2/41 (Mxd), 3/76 (Mxd)	
2/4	24	2/14, 2/16 (HJ), 1/22, 2/78, 1/94 (8")	
1/10	4	2/9, 5/16 (155), 6/29, 4/42	4
4/12	7 Chicago	1/19, 6/20 (155/8"), 6/21 (HJ), 1/29 5/4	
4/9	96	6/1, 5/3, 1/80 (155) 6/78	6
2/10	13	2/8, 1/31, (HJ), 4/76 (Mxd), 1/79 (Mxd), 6/80 (Mxd)	7
3/8	12	1/2 (155), 7/16, 1/28 (HJ), 5/81, 5/83	
3/5	15	2/4, 1/11, 3/34, 1/84 (155)	9
E/1, F/8, F/17, H/17	26	6/11, 1/14, 3/16 (155), 3/18 (175), 3/82	123
2/9	3	1/34 (HJ), 1/35 2/7 (155), 1/13 (155), 3/11 (155/8")	
3/4	65	1/8, 7/11, 3/13 (155), 2/77, 6/77	25
1/17	307 (Abn)	1/319 D.C., 1/320 D.C.	82
		2/321	
2/17	326	2/11 (155), 2/319, 2/320, 1/321	101
1/2, 2/2, 3/2			
1/3, 3/3, 2/3 (en route to Fort Lewis)			
1/6 D.C., 2/6 D.C., 3/6 D.C.			
1/11, 2/11, 3/11			
1/14, 2/14, 3/14			
		2/15	
		1/37	
E/17		3/319 (Abn)	
		B/22	
D/10		3/3	
		2/10 (Mxd)	
D/17		2/40	
		C/94	
E/19		1/487	
E/114		2/130	

Location	Infantry (Sep)	Armor	Cavalry	Combat Engineer	Construction Engineer	Missile Artillery
Vietnam	E/20 Pleiku 1/50 (Mech) Bong Son D/51 Phan Rang C/52 Saigon D/52 Long Binh C/54 Tuy Hoa D/58 Qui Nhon C/87 Tan Son Nhut D/87 Long Binh		7/1 Di-An 3/17 Tay Ninh 7/17 Pleiku	14 Thon Me Thuy 19 Bong Son 20 Pleiku 27 Bien Hoa 31 Xuan Loc 35 Da Nang 39 Chu Lai 70 Pleiku 168 Di An 299 Pleiku 588 Tay Ninh	34 Phu Loi 36 Vung Tau 46 Long Binh 62 Long Binh 69 Can Tho 84 Qui Nhon 86 Bear Cat 87 Cam Ranh Bay 92 Long Binh 93 Bear Cat 169 Long Binh 554 Cu Chi 577 Phu Hiep 589 An Khe 815 Pleiku 864 Nha Trang	6/56 (Ha) Long Binh 6/71 (Ha) Cam Ranh Bay
Korea			11 Uijongbu		44 Waegwan 76 Kimpo Air Base 802 Pyong-Taek	7/2 (Ha) Toksan-Ni 7/5 (Ha) Chunchon 1/42 (HJ) Chunchon 4/44 (He) Pyong Taek 6/44 (Ha) Kwang Chun 2/71 (Ha) Uijongbu 3/81 (NH) Koyang Gok
Thailand					538 Korat 809 Phanom Sarakam	
Okinawa						8/1 (Ha), 8/3 (Ha), 1/57 (LJ), 2/61 (NH), 1/65 (NH)
Italy					64 (Topo) Livorno	5/30 (SG) Vicenza
Hawaii					29 (Topo)	2/21 (HJ)
Canal Zone						4/517 (Ha)
Alaska					808 Wainwright 813 Richardson	4/43 (He) Richardson 2/562 (He) Wainwright
Germany	D/17 Frankfurt C/58 Nellingen			9 Aschaffenburg 54 Wildflecken 78 Neu Ulm 82 Bamberg 237 Heilbronn 317 Eschborn 547 Darmstadt	79 Neu Ulm 83 Heilbronn 94 Nellingen 97 Pimasens 249 Karlsruhe 293 Baumholder 656 (Topo) Schwetzingen	5/1 (He) Weisbaden 6/61 (Ha) Landshut 4/6 (He) Spangdahlem 6/62 (Ha) Aschaffenburg 5/6 (He) Baumholder 1/67 (He) Wertheim 3/7 (Ha) Schweinfurt 1/68 (SG) Schwaebisch 3/21 (HJ) Kitzingen 3/71 (He) Stuttgart 1/32 (HJ) Hanau 5/73 (SG) Schwaebisch 1/33 (HJ) Ansbach 5/77 (SG) Babenhausen 4/41 (Pe) Schwaebisch 3/79 (HJ) Giessen 6/52 (Ha) Wurzburg 3/80 (SG) Darmstadt 2/56 (He) Pirmasens 1/81 (Pe) Wackernheim 4/57 (Ha) Ansbach 3/84 (Pe) Neckarsulm 6/59 (Ha) Hanau 6/517 (Ha) Giessen 6/60 (Ha) Grafenwohr 6/562 (Ha) Butzbach
Continental United States:						
Fort Belvoir				91 D.C.	30 (Topo)	
Fort Benning	D/151 (IN NG)			818	43	
Fort Bliss						8/7 (Ha), 4/56 (Ha), 5/57 (Ha), 6/57 (Ha), 6/61 (Ha), 4/62 (NH), 1/65 (NH), 1/333 (NH)
Fort Bragg				47 Baltimore		
Fort Campbell			C/7/17	51		
Fort Carson				613	52	
Fort Chaffee						
Fort Devens				18		
Fort Hood					63	
Fort Irwin						
Fort Knox		6/32	8/1, I/17		748	
Fort Lewis			1/18 (Ca NG)	116 (ID NG)	339	1/20 (HJ)
Fort Meade			6/6		75	
Fort Meyer	1/3 ("Old Guard") D.C.					
Fort Ord	D/41, E/41, F/41 G/41 (M) H/41 (M)	D/73	E/9			
Fort Riley		1/63			83, 97	3/28 (HJ), 5/32 (HJ)
Fort Rucker	E/30				603, 548 (fm Ft. Bragg)	
Fort Sill	4/30	B/40				1/18 (LJ) 2/30 (HJ), 3/32 (HJ) 3/38 (SG), 2/44 (Pe), 2/79 (Pe)
Fort Stewart	E/54				575	
Fort Leonard Wood				5		
West Point Mil Res	1/1 (USMA)		4/1 (USMA)	21 (USMA)		
Fort Monroe						

Automatic Weapon, Self-Propelled	175mm Artillery	8" Artillery	155mm Artillery	105mm Artillery	Target Acquisition Artillery	Aviation
5/2 Long Binh	8/4 Dong Ha	7/8 Bien Hoa	1/27 Dau Tieng	3/6 Pleiku	8/25 Long Binh	Capital Tan Son Nhut
1/44 Dong Ha	6/14 Pleiku	7/15 Phu Cat	2/35 Xuan Loc	7/9 Bear Cat	8/26 Qui Nhon	10 Dong Ba Thin
4/60 Qui Nhon	5/22 An Khe	6/27 Quan Loi	5/42 Bear Cat	2/13 Phu Loi		11 Phu Loi
	2/32 Tay Ninh	6/32 Tuy Hoa	6/84 An Khe	7/13 Phu Cat		13 Can Tho
E/41 (MG) Qui Nhon	2/94 Dong Ha	1/83 Phu Bai	1/92 Pleiku	2/17 An Khe		14 Chu Lai
G/55 (MG) Chu Lai				5/27 Phu Hiep		52 Pleiku
G/65 (MG) Dong Ha				6/33 Quang Tri		58 Long Binh
D/71 (MG) Long Binh				1/40 Dong Ha		145 Bien Hoa
						210 Long Thanh
						212 Da Nang
						214 Bear Cat
						222 Vung Tau
						223 Qui Nhon
						224 Saigon
						268 Phu Hiep
						269 Tay Ninh
						307 Soc Trang
						308 Hue–Phu Bai
	6/12 Uijongbu	1/17 Masa Ri			1/25 Uijongbu	
		2/76 Chongong-Ni				
						19 Richardson
						USARAL Richardson
	6/9 Giessen	3/17 Nurnberg	2/5 Babenhausen		2/25 Mohringen	
	6/10 Bamberg	2/18 Rothwestern	(Battery B only)		1/26 Darmstadt	16 Nellingen
		3/35 Wertheim	4/18 Hanau			18 Hanau
		1/36 Neu Ulm	2/28 Ansbach			
		3/37 Dachau	2/34 Nurnberg			
		1/75 Bamberg				
		2/75 Hanau				
		2/83 Budingen				
		2/92 Giessen				
			1/211 (Mass NG)	7/18		
3/62						
G/68 (MG)						
		4/39 Baltimore	8/12		2/26	
		4/73 Baltimore	6/82			
			3/197 (N.H. NG)			
		8/17				
	6/8	9/1, 4/80				20
		2/84, 4/84				
	4/28 (fm Ft. Sill)					
			2/138 (Ky NG)			55
	6/75	4/94	3/73			
		2/18	4/18, 2/34			Prov Avn Bn
			2/37, 1/82			22
			E/78			
						21
				H/18		53
	8/17	2/36	6/16	2/1	3/25	
			3/30	2/2	3/26	
			2/31	4/14		
			G/75			267
			1/1 (USMA)			
						100

APPENDIX B:

The U.S. Army in Thailand During the Vietnam Conflict

The United States Army build-up in Thailand can be traced to the establishment of the U.S. Military Assistance Command, Thailand on 15 May 1962. Early that year a combined U.S. task force was deployed to Thailand on a military exercise which included a Marine Battalion Landing Team (BLT), the 1st Battle Group, 27th Infantry* (25th Infantry Division) and supporting elements under a detachment of the 9th Logistical Command. They were joined by an army aviation company composed of Caribou aircraft on 10 July 1962. In late August the 1st Battle Group, 35th Infantry* (25th Infantry Division) replaced the 1st Battle Group, 27th Infantry. However, this task force was withdrawn November 1962 after the situation in Laos stabilized. In the meantime, several U.S. Army units had been sent to Thailand on a permanent basis and by November 1966 the U.S. Army Support Command, Thailand, was established. This Appendix provides a listing of the army units stationed in Thailand, since they fulfilled direct or indirect support functions related to the Vietnam conflict to the extent that most received Vietnam service credit in recognition of their supporting role.

* These battle groups were redesignated battalions by DA as follows:

1st Battle Group, 27th Infantry	26 August 1963
1st Battle Group, 35th Infantry	12 August 1963

Major U.S. Army Commands in Thailand

Deputy Chief, Joint U.S. Military Assistance Group
Joint U.S. Military Advisory Group, Thailand
Joint U.S. Military Advisory Group, Thailand, Support Group, Provisional
Joint U.S. Military Advisory Group, Thailand, Support Group A
U.S. Army Bangkok Area Command, Provisional
U.S. Army Depot, Thailand, Provisional (later 501st Field Depot)
U.S. Army Sattahip Area Command, Provisional
U.S. Army Special Troops, Bangkok
U.S. Army Special Troops, Korat
U.S. Army Special Troops, Sattahip
U.S. Army Support Command, Thailand

SELECTED U.S. ARMY UNITS STATIONED IN THAILAND DURING THE VIETNAM CONFLICT

U.S. Army Unit	Type	Thailand Service	Typical Location	Authorized 1968 Strength
256th AG Co	Personnel Service	28 Dec. 67 – 25 June 71	Korat	73
44th EN Group, HHD	Construction	May 62 – 1 Jan. 70	Korat	97
538th EN Battalion	Construction	14 July 65 – 15 June 70	Korat	893
809th EN Battalion	Construction	24 March 62 – 3 Feb. 71	Phanom Sarakam	905
16th EN Company	Dump Truck	2 Aug. 67 – 20 Feb. 71	Sakhon Nakhon	112
54th EN Company	Construction Support	20 Dec. 68 – 15 June 70	Sakhon Nakhon	164
91st EN Company	Dump Truck	7 Aug. 67 – 15 June 70	Kanchanaburi	112
561st EN Company	Construction	10 Aug. 63 – 15 June 70	Kanchanaburi	265
593d EN Company	Construction	6 June 63 – 1 Aug. 63	Korat	—
697th EN Company	Pipeline Construction Support	29 Aug. 65 – 1 Dec. 69	Korat	178
738th EN Company	Supply Point	2 March 63 – 15 July 65	Korat	—
9th Logistical Command, HHD	Logistics Support	April 63 – 12 June 70	Korat, Sattahip	226
7th MAINT Battalion	Direct Support	15 July 65 – 25 June 71	Korat	229
57th MAINT Company*	Direct Support	1 April 63 – 20 Feb. 71	Korat	139
562d MAINT Company	Light Direct Support	13 Jan. 67 – 25 June 71	Sattahip	154
556th MAINT Company	Light Direct Support	7 Feb. 68 – 1 July 69	Kanchanaburi	154
597th MAINT Company †	Direct Support	9 May 66 – 1 Sept. 69	Korat	139
133d MED Group, HHD	Medical Support	1 Jan. 68 – 10 Nov. 70	Korat	41

428th MED Battalion, HHD	Medical Support	1 June 66 – 1 Jan. 68	Korat	36
21st MED Depot	Medical Depot	15 March 67 – 15 May 70	Korat	39
5th MED Hospital	Field Hospital	9 May 66 – 10 Nov. 70	Bangkok	112
31st MED Hospital	Field Hospital	1 June 62 – 15 May 70	Korat	94
40th MP Battalion, HHD	Military Police Support	18 March 67 – 30 Dec. 70	Korat	21
13th MP Company	Separate	24 Jan. 69 – 29 March 73	Korat	—
219th MP Company	Physical Security	20 Nov. 66 – 25 June 71	Korat	159
281st MP Company	Security Guard	11 Nov. 66 – 31 Oct. 75	Sattahip	123
41st ORD Company	Direct Ammunition Support	6 March 66 – 1 Sept. 66	Korat	—
599th ORD Company	Ammunition Direct/ General Support	7 May 67 – 25 June 71	Sattahip	97
93d Psychological Operations Company	Special Warfare	23 June 67 – 30 June 74	Bangkok	43
596th QM Company	Petroleum Depot	27 June 66 – 20 Dec. 68	Sattahip	207
29th SIG Group, HHD	Signal Support	12 Sept. 66 – 30 June 71	Bangkok	183
Bangkok SIG Battalion, Provisional	Support	Unknown – 14 July 69	Bangkok	359
USASTRATCOM SIG Battalion, Provisional	Long Lines Communications	Unknown – 14 July 69	Udorn-Ubon	261
302d SIG Battalion, HHD	Support	14 July 69 – 30 June 71	Bangkok	—
325th SIG Battalion, HHD	Support	14 July 69 – 31 Dec. 70	Bangkok	—
379th SIG Battalion, HHD	Support	25 Aug. 63 – 30 June 71	Sattahip	129
442d SIG Battalion	Support – Long Lines	6 Nov. 67 – 30 June 71	Korat	377
55th SIG Company	Support	1 July 65 – 1 July 69	Korat	204
167th SIG Company	Radio Relay VHF	May 62 – 6 May 63	Bangkok	—
207th SIG Company	Tropospheric	15 April 63 – 1 July 69	Korat	329
324th SIG Company	Tropospheric	30 June 71 – 1 Jan. 72	Sattahip	—
334th SIG Company	Support	6 Nov. 67 – 1 July 69	Bangkok	117
347th SIG Company	Support	6 Nov. 67 – 1 July 69	Bangkok	117
558th Supply & Service Bn	General Support	17 March 68 – 1 July 69	Kanchanaburi	56
305th Supply & Service Co	Direct Support	12 March 68 – 15 April 69	Kanchanaburi	169
331st Supply & Service Co	Forward Repair Parts	15 July 65 – 20 Dec. 68	Korat	172
511th Supply Company	General Support	5 Jan. 67 – 20 Dec. 68	Korat	216
558th Supply & Service Co*	Heavy Material Support	15 July 65 – 20 Dec. 68	Korat	158
590th Supply & Service Co ‡	Direct Support	30 Sept. 63 – 20 Dec. 68	Korat	169
499th TR Battalion, HHD	Terminal	25 Oct. 66 – 20 Dec. 68	Sattahip	58
519th TR Battalion, HHD	Motor Transport	16 Dec. 66 – 20 Feb. 71	Korat	41
53d TR Company	Medium Truck	10 April 67 – 30 Dec. 70	Sattahip	87
165th TR Company	Light Amphibious Vehicle (LARC)	26 April 67 – 1 Nov. 68	Sattahip	207
229th TR Company	Terminal Service	30 April 67 – 20 Dec. 68	Sattahip	113
233d TR Company	Terminal Service	11 Nov. 66 – 20 Dec. 68	Sattahip	113
260th TR Company	Medium Petrol Truck	15 Dec. 66 – 31 Oct. 75	Sattahip	87
291st TR Company	Medium Cargo Truck	28 Feb. 67 – 20 Feb. 71	Korat	87
313th TR Company	Medium Reefer Truck	24 Nov. 66 – 31 March 72	Bangkok	102
505th TR Company	Medium Truck	12 Nov. 66 – 30 Dec. 70	Sattahip	87
569th TR Company	Medium Truck	1 Dec. 67 – 1 April 70	Khon Kaen	183
501st U.S. Army Depot	Field Depot	18 March 67 – 20 Dec. 68	Korat	194
7th U.S. ASA Unit	Field Station §	15 May 62 – 30 June 71	Bangkok	792
11th U.S. ASA Unit	Special Reconnaissance	1 Aug. 62 – 1 Sept. 69	Bangkok	16
46th U.S. Army Special Forces Company (Airborne) ‖	Special Warfare	Oct. 66 – April 74	Lopburi	369

* Previously Ordnance until 20 July 1966.

† Previously Engineer until 1 September 1966.

‡ Quartermaster until 20 July 1966.

§ Includes the 83d U.S. Army Security Agency Special Operations Unit.

‖ In October 1966 Company D, 1st Special Forces Group (Airborne), 1st Special Forces, which was organized on 15 April 1966 at Fort Bragg, arrived in Thailand. The 46th Special Forces Company, 1st Special Forces was activated 15 April 1967 in Thailand using assets of that Company D, 1st Special Forces Group. In 1968 the 46th Special Forces Company (Airborne) was headquartered at Lopburi and had three subordinate B-Detachments at Muang Sakon Nakhon, at Pakchong and at Ban Kachon. On 31 March 1972 its assets were used to form HHD, 3d Battalion, 1st Special Forces Group (Airborne), 1st Special Forces. However, for security reasons it was known locally simply as U.S. Army Special Forces, Thailand.

APPENDIX C:
U.S. Casualties

U.S. MILITARY LOSSES IN SOUTHEAST ASIA*

Hostile Action:	Army	Navy	Coast Guard	Marines	Air Force	Total
Killed	25,341	1,093	4	11,490	504	38,432
Died of wounds	3,521 [†]	145	1	1,454	48	5,169
Presumed dead	1,806	266	0	67	735	2,874
Died in captivity	34	18	0	8	23	83
Nonhostile						
Died, noncombat cause	4,901	569	2	1,377	340	7,189
Illness	1,422	60	0	307	122	1,911
While missing but from nonhostile cause	870	279	0	0	141	1,290
Missing						
Missing, unaccounted for	155	59	0	41	407	662
Captured, unaccounted for	11	18	0	2	2	33
Totals						
Hostile deaths [‡]	30,702	1,522	5	13,019	1,310	46,558
Nonhostile deaths [‡]	7,193	908	2	1,684	603	10,390

* Period is from 1 January 1961 – 31 December 1976. Information current as of 31 December 1976.

[†] A total of 208,576 army personnel were wounded in action.

[‡] Total hostile and nonhostile deaths do not include the categories above of *Missing* or *Captured, unaccounted for*.

U.S. MILITARY AIR LOSSES IN SOUTHEAST ASIA

Air Deaths In Southeast Asia*

Type Personnel	Army	Navy	Coast Guard	Marines	Air Force	Total
Fixed-wing pilots	40/52	174/86	0	64/20	569/79	847/237 = 1,084
Fixed-wing air crew	13/23	89/97	0	43/13	468/144	613/277 = 890
Fixed-wing passengers	39/210	7/39	0	67/18	33/72	146/339 = 485
Helicopter pilots	564/362	12/5	1/0	74/30	17/4	668/401 = 1,069
Helicopter air crew	1,155/850	42/18	0	217/118	57/8	1,471/994 = 2,465
Helicopter passengers	682/734	20/39	0	158/101	14/7	874/881 = 1,755

* Period covered is 1 January 1961 – 31 December 1976. Figures to left of slash indicate killed in action; figures to right of slash indicate nonhostile deaths incurred in air accidents, etc.

Helicopter Sorties (in thousands)

This information is provided to show air traffic density for comparison with losses incurred in the other tables.

Helicopter Type Sortie	1961–65	1966	1967	1968	1969	1970	1971	Total
Attack Sorties	—	332	627	862	915	799	417	3,952
Assault Sorties	—	672	1,151	1,687	1,826	1,467	744	7,547
Cargo Sorties	—	289	546	819	798	690	406	3,548
Other Sorties	—	1,700	3,112	4,050	4,902	4,608	2,646	21,098
Total	N/A	2,993	5,516	7,418	8,441	7,564	4,213	36,145
Helicopter Losses*								
North Vietnam	3	1	4	2	—	—	—	10
South Vietnam	106	123	260	495	459	393	230	2,066
Other Locations and Nonhostile Losses†	166	197	400	511	589	419	284	2,566
Total	275	321	664	1,008	1,048	812	514	4,642

SOURCE: Comptroller, Office of The Secretary of Defense, in *Air War in Indochina*, Tables 6 and SS-10, pp. 267-72, 283.

* Helicopter losses appear to be based on helicopters shot down or crashed. In fact, some of these aircraft were recovered, repaired, and returned to service, unlike most downed fix-wing aircraft.

† "Other Locations" includes losses to hostile fire in Laos through 1969 in addition to nonhostile losses in Vietnam.

OFFICER LOSSES IN SOUTHEAST ASIA BY RANK

Period covered is 1 January 1961 – 31 December 1976. Figures to left of slash indicate killed in action; figures to right of slash indicate nonhostile deaths.

Rank*	Army	Navy	Coast Guard	Marines	Air Force	Total	
General – *Admiral*	0/0	0/0	–/–	0/0	0/0	0/0	
Lt. General – *Vice Admiral*	0/0	0/0	–/–	0/0	0/0	0/0	
Major General – *Rear Admiral*	2/0	0/0	0/0	1/0	1/1	4/1 =	5
Brig. General – *Commodore*	2/3	0/1	0/0	0/0	1/0	3/4 =	7
Colonel – *Captain*	8/9	12/1	0/0	1/3	52/3	73/16 =	89
Lt. Colonel – *Commander*	61/50	48/23	0/0	17/6	69/21	195/100 =	295
Major – *Lt. Commander*	142/86	80/43	0/0	51/15	223/56	496/200 =	696
Captain – *Lieutenant*	748/261	84/70	1/0	163/39	450/82	1,446/452 =	1,898
First Lt. – *Lt. Junior Grade*	1,222/246	81/70	1/1	246/57	157/54	1,707/428 =	2,135
Second Lt. – *Ensign*	463/33	9/8	0/0	266/18	7/1	745/60 =	805
Chief Warrant Officer W-4	0/4	0/0	0/0	1/1	0/4	1/9 =	10
Chief Warrant Officer W-3	14/15	0/0	0/0	2/0	0/0	16/15 =	31
Chief Warrant Officer W-2	136/141	0/0	0/0	7/0	0/0	143/141 =	284
Warrant Officer W-1	554/350	2/2	0/0	3/3	0/0	559/355 =	914

* First rank given is for Army/Marine/Air Force; second rank (italicized) is for Navy. Warrant Officer ranks are identical for all services.

ENLISTED LOSSES IN SOUTHEAST ASIA BY RANK

Period covered is from 1 January 1961 – 31 December 1976. Figures to left of slash indicate killed in action; figures to right of slash indicate nonhostile deaths incurred by accident, illness, etc.

Enlisted Pay Grade	Army	Navy	Coast Guard	Marines	Air Force	Total		
E-9	20/21	1/3	0/0	11/6	9/5	41/35	=	76
E-8	123/62	5/6	0/0	17/13	8/10	153/91	=	244
E-7	712/239	29/34	1/0	88/19	20/32	850/324	=	1,174
E-6	1,697/436	99/83	1/0	255/38	57/57	2,109/614	=	2,723
E-5	4,123/1,000	202/120	0/1	610/108	99/97	5,034/1,326	=	6,360
E-4	9,252/2,242	434/179	0/0	2,031/275	103/97	11,820/2,793	=	14,613
E-3	11,041/1,762	414/219	1/0	3,848/491	51/80	15,355/2,552	=	17,907
E-2	295/178	21/44	0/0	5,089/526	3/3	5,408/751	=	6,159
E-1	87/55	1/2	0/0	312/66	0/0	400/123	=	523

U.S. ARMY LOSSES BY CAUSE IN SOUTHEAST ASIA*

Cause of death	Hostile	Nonhostile	Total
Aircraft loss over sea	10	49	59
Aircraft loss over ground	2,484	2,182	4,666
Vehicle loss or crash	28	864	892
Gunshot or small-arms fire	12,389	—	12,389
Artillery or rocket explosion	2,362	—	2,362
Bomb explosion	37	—	37
Grenade or mine explosion	4,103	—	4,103
Multiple fragmentation wounds	7,364	—	7,364
Misadventure	834	—	834
Drowned or suffocated	143	634	777
Burns	352	97	449
Illness (not malaria or hepatitis)	—	362	362
Malaria	—	75	75
Hepatitis	—	17	17
Heart attack	—	175	175
Stroke	—	33	33
Suicide	—	354	354
Accidental self-destruction	—	680	680
Intentional homicide	—	199	199
Accidental homicide	—	552	552
Other accident	—	834	834
Other causes	458	53	511
Unknown	138	33	171
Total	30,702	7,193	37,895

* Covers period 1 January 1961 – 31 December 1976.

U.S. ARMY LOSSES BY STATE AND TERRITORY

Covers period 1 January 1961 – 31 December 1976. Figures to left of slash indicate killed in action; figures to right of slash indicate nonhostile deaths.

State	Losses	State	Losses
Alabama	683/159	New Hampshire	105/24
Alaska	29/14	New Jersey	752/169
Arizona	310/80	New Mexico	201/55
Arkansas	318/79	New York	2,166/482
California	2,941/659	North Carolina	947/220
Colorado	296/80	North Dakota	110/24
Connecticut	285/59	Ohio	1,548/374
Delaware	73/8	Oklahoma	558/113
District of Columbia	114/42	Oregon	334/83
Florida	1,015/265	Pennsylvania	1,490/371
Georgia	904/222	Rhode Island	114/22
Hawaii	172/42	South Carolina	529/121
Idaho	101/38	South Dakota	101/33
Illinois	1,509/347	Tennessee	730/156
Indiana	814/169	Texas	1,754/423
Iowa	447/86	Utah	192/51
Kansas	315/71	Vermont	55/13
Kentucky	618/145	Virginia	672/193
Louisiana	453/118	Washington	522/139
Maine	169/45	West Virginia	400/97
Maryland	517/122	Wisconsin	636/124
Massachusetts	557/151	Wyoming	70/13
Michigan	1,550/295	Canal Zone	2/0
Minnesota	602/105	Guam	47/11
Mississippi	385/102	American Samoa	1/0
Missouri	758/188	U.S. Virgin Islands	11/3
Montana	127/41	Puerto Rico	254/67
Nebraska	210/50	Other	59/15
Nevada	70/15		

APPENDIX D:

U.S. Army Medal of Honor Recipients

U.S. ARMY MEDAL OF HONOR RECIPIENTS, VIETNAM

Name	Rank	Date of Act	Major Unit
William E. Adams*	Major	25 May 71	1st Aviation Brigade
Lewis Albanese*	Private First Class	1 Dec. 66	1st Cavalry Division
Webster Anderson	Staff Sergeant	15 Oct. 67	101st Airborne Division
Eugene Ashley, Jr.*	Sergeant First Class	7 Feb. 68	5th Special Forces Group
John P. Baca*	Specialist 4	10 Feb. 70	1st Cavalry Division
Nicky D. Bacon	Staff Sergeant	26 Aug. 68	AMERICAL Division
John F. Baker, Jr.	Private First Class	5 Nov. 66	25th Infantry Division
John A. Barnes III*	Private First Class	12 Nov. 67	173d Airborne Brigade
Gary B. Beikirch	Sergeant	1 April 70	5th Special Forces Group
Ted Belcher*	Sergeant	19 Nov. 66	25th Infantry Division
Leslie A. Bellrichard*	Private First Class	20 May 67	4th Infantry Division
Roy Benavidez	Staff Sergeant	2 May 68	5th Special Forces Group
Thomas W. Bennett*	Corporal	11 Feb. 69	4th Infantry Division
Michael R. Blanchfield*	Specialist 4	3 July 69	173d Airborne Brigade
James L. Bondsteel	Staff Sergeant	24 May 69	1st Infantry Division
Hammett L. Bowen, Jr.*	Staff Sergeant	27 June 69	25th Infantry Division
Patrick Henry Brady	Major	6 Jan. 68	44th Medical Brigade
William M. Bryant*	Sergeant First Class	24 March 69	5th Special Forces Group
Paul W. Bucha	Captain	19 March 68	101st Airborne Division
Brian L. Buker*	Sergeant	5 April 70	5th Special Forces Group
Jon R. Cavaiani	Staff Sergeant	5 June 71	Vietnam Training Advisory Group
Michael J. Crescenz*	Corporal	20 Nov. 68	AMERICAL Division
Nicholas J. Cutinha*	Specialist 4	2 March 68	25th Infantry Division
Larry G. Dahl*	Specialist 4	23 Feb. 71	27th Transportation Battalion
Sammy L. Davis	Private First Class	18 Nov. 67	9th Infantry Division
Edward A. Devore, Jr.*	Specialist 4	17 March 68	9th Infantry Division
Drew D. Dix	Staff Sergeant	1 Feb. 68	IV Corps Advisory Group
Stephen H. Doane*	First Lieutenant	25 March 69	25th Infantry Division
David C. Dolby	Specialist 4	21 May 66	1st Cavalry Division
Hugh C. Donlon	Captain	6 July 64	U.S. Special Forces, Vietnam
Kern W. Dunagan	Captain	13 May 69	AMERICAL Division
Harold B. Durham, Jr.*	Second Lieutenant	17 Oct. 67	1st Infantry Division
Glenn H. English, Jr.*	Staff Sergeant	7 Sept. 70	173d Airborne Brigade
Donald W. Evans, Jr.*	Specialist 4	27 Jan. 67	4th Infantry Division
Rodney J. Evans*	Sergeant	18 July 69	1st Cavalry Division
Frederick E. Ferguson	Chief Warrant Officer	31 Jan. 68	1st Cavalry Division
Daniel Fernandez*	Specialist 4	18 Feb. 66	25th Infantry Division
Michael J. Fitzmaurice	Specialist 4	23 March 71	101st Airborne Division
Charles C. Fleek*	Sergeant	27 May 67	25th Infantry Division
Robert F. Foley	Captain	5 Nov. 66	25th Infantry Division
Michael F. Folland*	Corporal	3 July 69	199th Infantry Brigade
Douglas B. Fournet*	First Lieutenant	4 May 68	1st Cavalry Division
James W. Fous*	Private First Class	14 May 68	9th Infantry Division
Frank R. Fratellenico*	Corporal	19 Aug. 70	101st Airborne Division
Harold A. Fritz	First Lieutenant	11 Jan. 69	11th Armored Cavalry Regiment
James A. Gardner*	First Lieutenant	7 Feb. 66	101st Airborne Division
John G. Gertsch*	Staff Sergeant	19 July 69	101st Airborne Division
Bruce A. Grandstaff*	Platoon Sergeant	18 May 67	4th Infantry Division
Joseph X. Grant*	First Lieutenant	13 Nov. 66	25th Infantry Division

Peter M. Guenette*	Specialist 4	18 May 68	101st Airborne Division
Loren D. Hagen*	First Lieutenant	7 Aug. 71	U.S.A. Vietnam Training Advisory Group
Charles C. Hagemeister	Specialist 4	20 March 67	1st Cavalry Division
Robert W. Hartsock*	Staff Sergeant	23 Feb. 69	25th Infantry Division
Carmel B. Harvey, Jr.*	Specialist 4	21 June 67	1st Cavalry Division
Frank A. Herda	Private First Class	29 June 68	101st Airborne Division
Robert J. Hibbs*	Second Lieutenant	5 March 66	1st Infantry Division
John N. Holcomb*	Sergeant	3 Dec. 68	1st Cavalry Division
Joe R. Hooper	Sergeant	21 Feb. 68	101st Airborne Division
Charles E. Hosking, Jr.*	Master Sergeant	21 March 67	5th Special Forces Group
Robert L. Howard	First Lieutenant	30 Dec. 68	MACV-SOG†
George A. Ingalls*	Specialist 4	16 April 67	1st Cavalry Division
Jack H. Jacobs	First Lieutenant	9 March 68	Military Assistance Command, Vietnam
Don J. Jenkins	Private First Class	6 Jan. 69	9th Infantry Division
Delbert O. Jennings	Staff Sergeant	27 Dec. 66	1st Cavalry Division
Lawrence Joel	Specialist 5	8 Nov. 65	173d Airborne Brigade
Dwight H. Johnson*	Specialist 5	15 Jan. 68	4th Infantry Division
Donald R. Johnston*	Specialist 4	21 March 69	1st Cavalry Division
Stephen E. Karopczyc*	First Lieutenant	12 March 67	25th Infantry Division
Terry T. Kawamura*	Corporal	20 March 69	173d Airborne Brigade
Kenneth M. Kays	Private First Class	7 May 70	101st Airborne Division
John J. Kedenburg*	Specialist 5	13 June 68	MACV-SOG†
Leonard B. Keller	Sergeant	2 May 67	9th Infantry Division
Thomas J. Kinsman	Private First Class	6 Feb. 68	9th Infantry Division
Joseph G. La Pointe, Jr.*	Specialist 4	2 June 69	101st Airborne Division
Paul R. Lambers	Sergeant	20 Aug. 68	25th Infantry Division
George C. Lang	Specialist 4	22 Feb. 69	9th Infantry Division
Garfield M. Langhorn*	Private First Class	15 Jan. 69	1st Aviation Brigade
Billy L. Lauffer*	Private First Class	21 Sept. 66	1st Cavalry Division
Robert D. Law*	Specialist 4	22 Feb. 69	1st Infantry Division
Milton A. Lee*	Private First Class	26 April 68	101st Airborne Division
Robert R. Leisy*	Second Lieutenant	2 Dec. 69	1st Cavalry Division
Peter C. Lemon	Specialist 4	1 April 70	1st Cavalry Division
Matthew Leonard*	Platoon Sergeant	28 Feb. 67	1st Infantry Division
Angelo J. Liteky	Chaplain (Captain)	6 Dec. 67	199th Infantry Brigade
Gary L. Littrell	Sergeant First Class	8 April 70	II Corps Advisory Group
Donald R. Long*	Sergeant	30 June 66	1st Infantry Division
Carlos J. Lozada*	Private First Class	20 Nov. 67	173d Airborne Brigade
Andre C. Lucas*	Lieutenant Colonel	23 July 70	101st Airborne Division
Allen J. Lynch	Specialist 4	15 Dec. 67	1st Cavalry Division
Walter J. Marm, Jr.	Second Lieutenant	14 Nov. 65	1st Cavalry Division
Finnis D. McCleery	Platoon Sergeant	14 May 68	AMERICAL Division
Phill G. McDonald*	Private First Class	7 June 68	4th Infantry Division
Ray McKibben*	Sergeant	6 Dec. 68	1st Aviation Brigade
Thomas J. McMahon*	Specialist 4	19 March 69	AMERICAL Division
David H. McNerney	First Sergeant	22 March 67	4th Infantry Division
Edgar L. McWethy, Jr.*	Specialist 5	21 June 67	1st Cavalry Division
Don L. Michael*	Specialist 4	8 April 67	173d Airborne Brigade
Franklin D. Miller	Staff Sergeant	5 Jan. 70	MACV-SOG†
Gary L. Miller*	First Lieutenant	16 Feb. 69	1st Infantry Division
Frankie Z. Molnar*	Staff Sergeant	20 May 67	4th Infantry Division
James H. Monroe*	Private First Class	16 Feb. 67	1st Cavalry Division
Charles B. Morris	Sergeant	29 June 66	173d Airborne Brigade
Robert C. Murray*	Staff Sergeant	7 June 70	AMERICAL Division
David P. Nash*	Private First Class	29 Dec. 68	9th Infantry Division
Michael J. Novosel	Chief Warrant Officer	2 Oct. 69	44th Medical Brigade
Milton L. Olive*	Private First Class	22 Oct. 65	173d Airborne Brigade
Kenneth L. Olson*	Specialist 4	13 May 68	199th Infantry Brigade
Robert M. Patterson	Sergeant	6 May 68	101st Airborne Division
Richard A. Penry	Sergeant	31 Jan. 70	199th Infantry Brigade
Danny J. Petersen*	Specialist 4	9 Jan. 70	25th Infantry Division
Larry S. Pierce*	Sergeant	20 Sept. 65	173d Airborne Brigade
Riley L. Pitts*	Captain	31 Oct. 67	25th Infantry Division
William D. Port*	Private First Class	12 Jan. 68	1st Cavalry Division
Robert L. Poxon*	First Lieutenant	2 June 69	1st Cavalry Division
Robert J. Pruden*	Staff Sergeant	29 Nov. 69	AMERICAL Division
Laszlo Rabel*	Staff Sergeant	13 Nov. 68	173d Airborne Brigade
Ronald E. Ray	First Lieutenant	19 June 66	25th Infantry Division
Anund C. Roark*	Sergeant	16 May 68	4th Infantry Division

Gordon R. Roberts	Specialist 4	11 July 69	101st Airborne Division
James W. Robinson*	Sergeant	11 April 66	1st Infantry Division
Louis R. Rocco	Sergeant First Class	24 May 70	Military Assistance Command, Vietnam
Charles C. Rogers	Lieutenant Colonel	1 Nov. 68	1st Infantry Division
Euripides Rubio*	Captain	8 Nov. 66	1st Infantry Division
Hector Santiago-Colon*	Specialist 4	28 June 68	1st Cavalry Division
Rupert L. Sargent*	First Lieutenant	15 March 67	25th Infantry Division
Clarence E. Sasser	Private First Class	10 Jan. 68	9th Infantry Division
William W. Seay*	Sergeant	25 Aug. 68	48th Transportation Group
Daniel J. Shea*	Private First Class	14 May 69	AMERICAL Division
Clifford C. Sims*	Staff Sergeant	21 Feb. 68	101st Airborne Division
George K. Sisler*	First Lieutenant	7 Feb. 67	MACV-SOG†
Donald S. Skidgel*	Sergeant	14 Sept. 69	1st Cavalry Division
Elmelindo R. Smith*	Staff Sergeant	16 Feb. 67	4th Infantry Division
James M. Sprayberry	First Lieutenant	25 April 68	1st Cavalry Division
Russell A. Steindam*	First Lieutenant	1 Feb. 70	25th Infantry Division
Jimmy G. Stewart*	Staff Sergeant	18 May 66	1st Cavalry Division
Lester R. Stone, Jr.*	Sergeant	3 March 69	AMERICAL Division
Mitchell W. Stout*	Sergeant	12 March 70	1st Battalion, 44th Artillery
Robert F. Stryker*	Specialist 4	7 Nov. 67	1st Infantry Division
Kenneth E. Stumpf	Specialist 4	25 April 67	25th Infantry Division
James A. Taylor	First Lieutenant	9 Nov. 67	AMERICAL Division
Brian M. Thacker	First Lieutenant	31 March 71	1st Battalion, 92d Artillery
John E. Warren, Jr.*	First Lieutenant	14 Jan. 69	25th Infantry Division
Charles J. Watters*	Chaplain (Major)	19 Nov. 67	173d Airborne Brigade
Dale E. Wayrynen*	Specialist 4	18 May 67	101st Airborne Division
Gary G. Wetzel	Private First Class	8 Jan. 68	1st Aviation Brigade
Jerry W. Wickam*	Corporal	6 Jan. 66	11th Armored Cavalry Regiment
Louis E. Willett*	Private First Class	15 Feb. 67	4th Infantry Division
Charles Q. Williams	Second Lieutenant	10 June 65	5th Special Forces Group
David F. Winder*	Private First Class	13 May 70	AMERICAL Division
Raymond R. Wright	Specialist 4	2 May 67	9th Infantry Division
Maximo Yabes*	First Sergeant	26 Feb. 67	25th Infantry Division
Rodney J. T. Yano	Sergeant First Class	1 Jan. 69	11th Armored Cavalry Regiment
Gordon D. Yntema*	Sergeant	18 Jan. 68	5th Special Forces Group
Marvin R. Young*	Staff Sergeant	21 Aug. 68	25th Infantry Division
Fred W. Zabitosky	Staff Sergeant	19 Feb. 68	MACV-SOG†

* Awarded posthumously.

† On cover orders to 5th Special Forces but actually assigned to MACV-SOG (see narrative for Special Operations Augmentation, 5th Special Forces Group, page 243).

Medals of Honor awarded by conflict period (Army only):

Civil War	1,199
Indian Campaigns	419
Spanish-American War	30
Philippine Insurrection	70
Boxer Rebellion 1900	4
Mexican Campaign 1911	1
World War I	95
World War II	294
Korean War	78
Vietnam	155

APPENDIX E:

U.S. Army Military Terms, Acronyms, Abbreviations and Troop Slang Used in Vietnam and Index to Stations Cited in the Text

Abn   Airborne (paratrooper or parachutist-qualified)

Admin   Administration

AG   Adjutant General

AHC   Assault helicopter company

A-I-K   Assistance in kind, to mean money or funds

Airborne   Personnel or equipment dropped by parachute

Air mattress   Nickname for the 3d Brigade of the 82d Airborne Division. A play on "airborne," which was a title of distinction.

Airmobile   Personnel or equipment inserted by helicopter

AK-47   Assault rifle used by the enemy

All-Afro   Nickname for the 3d Brigade of the 82d Airborne Division derived from the double AA on the divisional shoulder patch officially signifying "All American."

Alpha bravo   Phonetic alphabetization for ambush.

AM or AMBL   Airmobile (troops carried by helicopter)

AMERICAL   23d Infantry Division

AML   Airmobile Light

A-O   Area of operations

Ap   Vietnamese word meaning hamlet

APC   Armored personnel carrier, of which a variety of models existed

Ap Doi Moi   "New Life" hamlet

Ap Tan Sin   A secure hamlet

AR   Army Reserve

ARA   Aerial rocket artillery

Arc Light   A B-52 bomber strike

ARLO   Army liaison officer

Arm   Armored

Arty   Artillery

ARVN   (Arvin) The South Vietnamese Army (Army of the Republic of Vietnam)

ASAP   (A-sap) As soon as possible. To do something with utmost urgency

ASA   Army Security Agency

ASH   Assault support helicopter

ATC   Air traffic control

ATFV or ATFG   Australian Task Force, Vietnam

Avn   Aviation

AWC   Aerial weapons company

Base area   Section of terrain including installations, defensive fortifications or other physical structures used by the enemy.

Base camp   A semipermanent administrative and logistical center for a given unit, usually within that unit's tactical areas of responsibility (TAOR). Depending on its mission, the unit may operate in, out of or totally away from its base camp. Base camps normally contain all or part of a given unit's service support elements.

Baseball   Baseball-shaped grenade about $2\,{}^1/_2$" in diameter used for delay fragmentation (M67), impact fragmentation (M68) and riot control (CN1, etc.).

BC   Body count. Tally of enemy dead on a given battlefield.

Bde   Brigade

Beans   Any meal, chow

Beehive   Artillery rounds filled with hundreds of small metal darts

Believer   Any dead soldier, but particularly a dead enemy soldier

Berm, berm line   Hedgerow or foliated built-up area which compartmentalizes rice paddies; a rise in the ground such as dikes; a dirt parapet around fortifications.

Bird dog   A light fixed-wing observation aircraft, but in particular the Army O-1A or E planes.

Big shotgun   106mm recoilless rifle using antipersonnel canister ammunition

Big stuff   Artillery fire support or Air Force ordnance

Black hats   Amiable term for Pathfinders. Pathfinder teams were dropped or air-landed at an objective to establish a landing zone, or air-delivered into enemy territory for purposes of determining best approach and withdrawal lanes, landing zones and sites for heliborne forces.

Black Magic   Nickname for the M16A1 rifle

Bladder   A heavy-duty, rubberized collapsible drum for POL (petroleum, oil and lubricant) items ranging from 2,000 – 50,000 gallons.

Bladder bird   A C-123 or C-130 aircraft equipped with rubberized collapsible drum and 350-g.p.m. pumps. Also called "Cow" or "Flying Cow."

Blade time   Used when referring to available helicopter support. Units were generally allocated a specific amount of "blade time" daily for command and control and logistical support.

Blanket Division   Nickname for the 1st Cavalry Division derived from the large size of its shoulder patch.

Blivet   A 250- or 500-gallon rubberized fabric collapsible drum (see bladder).

Bluper   Nickname for an M-79 grenade launcher

Bloody One   Nickname for the 1st Infantry Division derived from its red numeral "1" on an olive drab patch. Also known as "Big Dead One."

Bn   Battalion

Boondocks, boonies, bush   Terms used for the jungle, or any remote area away from a base camp or city. Sometimes used to refer to any area in Vietnam.

Bring smoke Place intense artillery fire or Air Force ordnance on an enemy position.

BS Border surveillance

Bubble Nickname for the small two-man OH-13 "Sioux" helicopter

Buddy system Placing South Vietnamese units under U.S. sponsorship for on-the-job training. Also used when a U.S. soldier newly arrived in Vietnam was paired up with an experienced soldier.

Bushmasters Any elite unit skilled in jungle operations such as Special Forces, long-range reconnaissance patrols, ambush patrols, sniper patrols or ranger companies. A Bushmaster operation was a saturation patrol usually conducted by a company or platoon concentrating on night ambush.

Butcher Brigade Nickname given the 11th Infantry Brigade after exposure of Lieutenant William L. Calley's actions at My Lai.

Butterfly Patrolling on multiple axes in frequently changing patterns. Often used as a technique of advance through unknown terrain.

C's C-rations or combat rations. Canned army meals for field use.

CA Civil Affairs or combat assault

CAC Corps aviation company

C and S Cordon and search. Operation to seal off and search an area or village.

CAP Capital Division (Republic of Korea)

Caribou The CV-2 twin-engine cargo airplane used by the army until turned over to the Air Force in December 1966.

CARS Combat Arms Regimental System

CAS (Cass) Saigon Office of the Central Intelligence Agency

CAT (Cat) Combat artist team or civil action team

Cat Caterpillar tractor

Caterpillar Administrative or logistical convoy on a normally secure road

Cav Cavalry

Cbt Combat

CBU Cluster bomb unit

Charlie, Charles, Chuck Viet Cong. Short form of "Victor Charlie," the official phonetic initialing of V.C. "Mr. Charles" was used derisively in order to render proper "respect" to the enemy. Since the term came to mean the enemy in general, it was often used also to signify the North Vietnamese troops, though strictly speaking this was incorrect.

Charlie rats Army combat rations (C-rations). Double meaning since "Charlie" was both the phonetic alphabetization of the "C" in C-rations and used to signify the enemy or enemy activity.

Checkerboard sweep A specific technique employed dividing a fixed area into blocks, into one of which a ground element is inserted while mechanized/armor elements operate around the periphery to completely saturate the area and deny enemy escape.

Checkmate Security roadblock

Chem Chemical

Cherry New replacement

Chicom (Cheye-com) Chinese communist; applied to weapons manufactured in China.

Chieu Hoi (Choo Hoy) The "open arms" program promising clemency and financial aid to guerrillas who stopped fighting and returned to live under South Vietnamese government authority. Since many of these men later served as scouts for the U.S. Army, the word also meant former enemy soldiers now serving U.S. units. Often enemy soldiers would shout this just prior to surrender to gain favorable treatment.

Chinook The CH-47 cargo helicopter. Also called "Shit-hook" or "Hook."

Chogie, cut a chogie To move out quickly. A Korean term brought to Vietnam by U.S. soldiers who had served in Korea.

Chopper Helicopter

Chops Chief of Operations

CIA Central Intelligence Agency or simply "The Agency" or "The Company." Also Captured in Action.

CIDG (Sidgee) Civilian Irregular Defense Group. Special Forces-trained native village and tribal security/reaction forces. Some were of elite commando quality while others were of marginal combat use.

CINCPAC Commander-in-Chief, Pacific

Civic action A combination of MEDCAPS (medical civic action programs), ICAPS (intelligence civic action programs) and other civil affairs activities.

Claymore A popular fan-shaped antipersonnel land mine which, when detonated, propelled small steel cubes in a 60° fan-shaped pattern.

Close air support Air action against hostile targets that are close to friendly forces requiring detailed integration of each air mission with the fire and movement of those forces.

Cloverleaf A method of patrolling in which subordinate elements move out from a central area and "loop" back to the vicinity of the main advance's direction or starting point. Used as a technique of advance by units in unknown terrain.

CO Commanding officer

Co Company

Cobra The AH-1G attack helicopter

Combat sky spot Radar-controlled air strike

Comm Communications

Commo Communications or signal capacity, personnel or equipment.

Company lift Number of helicopters in flight with the assault elements of a rifle company in one lift.

Cong Shortened form of Viet Cong

Const Construction

CONUS Continental United States

CORDS Civil Operations and Rural Development Support

COSVN Communist Office of South Vietnam

Counterguerrilla warfare Operations conducted by armed forces, paramilitary forces or nonmilitary forces of a government against insurgents.

Counterintelligence Aspect of intelligence activity devoted to destroying the effectiveness of hostile foreign intelligence activities; protection of information against espionage, individuals against subversion, and installations and material against sabotage.

Cow C-123 or C-130 aircraft equipped with a rubberized collapsible drum and 350-g.p.m. pumps. Also called "Bladder Bird," "Flying Cow."

CPO Civilian Personnel Office

CRB Cam Ranh Bay

CRID (Crid) Republic of Korea Capital Infantry Division, affectionately called the "Tiger" Division by the Americans.

Crispie critter Enemy soldier killed through burning to death. Any severely burned soldier.

Crunchies Infantrymen. Also "Ground Pounders" and "Grunts."

CS Composite Service. Also riot control gas agent, such as a CS-grenade, used widely to clear out enemy tunnel works.

CSF Camp strike force

CSMO Close-station march order. Prepare to move equipment.

C Spt Combat Support

CTZ Corps Tactical Zones. I CTZ ("i Corps") was the northern military region of South Vietnam, II CTZ was the central military region of South Vietnam, III CTZ was the military region surrounding Saigon, and IV CTZ was the Delta southern military region of South Vietnam.

Cu Chi National Guard Nickname of the 25th Infantry Division because the division headquarters and the majority of its elements were stationed at Cu Chi throughout the war.

Dai-uy (Die-wee) Captain. Could also mean "man-in-charge," village chief

Dead space Area which cannot be covered by fire or observation due to the nature of the terrain

DECCA Low-level radio navigational aid chain installed and maintained by the army but rarely used because of nonacceptance by the Air Force and mistrust by senior army officers.

Deep serious In the worst possible position, such as nearly overrun.

Defcon Defensive contact artillery fire. Plotted primarily at night by artillery forward observers "ringing the perimeter with steel."

Delta Tango Phonetic alphabetization of DT, meaning Defensive Target(s)

Dentcap Dental civic action program or mission

DePuy foxhole Defensive position insuring interlocking defensive fire named after Major General William E. DePuy, commanding the 1st Infantry Division in Vietnam in 1966.

DEROS (Dee-ros) Date eligible for return from overseas. The date a person's tour in Vietnam was estimated to end.

Desoto Destroyer naval patrols off Vietnam

Det Detachment

Detainee Indigenous personnel taken into custody

Det-cord Detonating cord used for explosives

Dime nickel A 105mm howitzer

Div Division

DMS boot Direct molded-sole jungle boot

DMZ The demilitarized zone once separating North and South Vietnam at the 17th parallel.

DNG Da Nang

Doc Affectionate title given to the enlisted medical aidman

DOD Department of Defense

Dong Vietnamese monetary unit; one piaster

Double force Buddy operations by combined U.S. and ARVN forces

Doubtfuls Indigenous personnel who after screening and records check cannot be categorized as either Viet Cong or civil offenders. Also can mean suspect personnel spotted from ground or aircraft.

Doughnut dollies Red Cross girls

Doughnut six Chief of Red Cross girls. Six was the customary military number of a commander on any level when using the radio.

Dozer-infantry Team of tank-dozers, bulldozers, Rome plows and infantry which use jungle-busting techniques to press into difficult terrain.

The Drag Squad behind the main maneuver element to insure rear safety

DRAC Delta Regional Assistance Command

Dragon ship AC-47 aircraft fitted out with Gatling-type machineguns and illum-flares. Also called Puff, Puff the Magic Dragon, Spooky.

Drum Metal container for fuel

Dud Any explosive that fails to detonate when activated.

Duster Nickname of the M42 tracked vehicle mounting twin 40mm antiaircraft guns used as ground support in Vietnam.

Dust-off Nickname for a medical evacuation helicopter or mission

DX Direct exchange of equipment for repair and replacement

DZ Drop zone in airborne operations

Eagle flight Airmobile force used to temporarily secure either a key piece of ground or on air or ground alert to perform rapid reaction missions.

ECM Electronic countermeasures, such as jamming and deception

Eidal laundry Laundry unit with single trailer, mounted, with canvas cover.

Electric strawberry Nickname for the 25th Infantry Division gleaned from the division's shoulder patch representing "Tropic Lightning."

Eleven bush Infantryman; derived from the military occupational specialty code 11B.

Embassy ceiling price Specific rental limitation for various types of real estate in Vietnam.

En Engineer

ENGR CMD/COM Engineer Command

ENI Enemy-initiated incident

E-Nine, E-9 A sergeant major, the highest enlisted rank

ENSURE Expedited nonstandard urgent requirement for equipment.

Errand boy Daily scheduled courier flight; also called Pony Express

Escort Armed helicopter escort

Extraction Voluntary or involuntary withdrawal by air of troops from any operational area via helicopter.

FAC (Fack) Forward air controllers attached to ground units to coordinate air strikes.

FAL-FAR Pro-U.S. Royal Armed Forces of Laos

Fatikees Nickname for jungle fatigues

FFM Flight facilities, mobile

FFV Field Force, Vietnam

Field of fire Area that a weapon or group of weapons can cover effectively with fire from a given position.

Fireballing Concentration of large amounts of artillery fire in an area; also used to mean vehicles moving rapidly.

Fire base Artillery firing position often secured by infantry

Fire fight Skirmish between opposing units

Firefly Helicopter team consisting of one helicopter equipped with a searchlight or arc lamps and two gunships; also called a lightning bug.

Fire support base A semifixed artillery base established to increase indirect fire coverage of an area and provide security for the firing unit.

Fix   To prevent the enemy from withdrawing from one area for use elsewhere.

Flaming dart   Bombing operations in reprisal for attacks on U.S. forces in Vietnam

Flare ship   Any aircraft used primarily to drop illumination flares

Flower power   Nickname for the 9th Infantry Division gleaned from the Octofoil design on the division shoulder patch.

Flying cow   C-123 or C-130 aircraft equipped with rubberized collapsible drum and 350-g.p.m. pump. Also called Cow, Bladder Bird.

Flying crane   The CH-54 heavy helicopter

FNG   Most common name for newly arrived person in Vietnam; literally a "Fuckin' new guy."

FOB   Forward operating base. A combined command post and logistical base established in the field, usually by a battalion but also widely used by Special Forces organizations.

Foo-gas   See Phougas

Forest penetrator   Device lowered and raised by cable from a helicopter and used for extracting a person from heavy jungle.

Forward support area   A fixed or semifixed area utilized as a forward logistical base as differentiated from a more permanent base camp.

Four corners   Specifically the town of Di An where the 1st Infantry Division was stationed, but generally expanded to mean any small town near a U.S. military base.

FRAC   First Regional Assistance Command

Frag   To kill or attempt to kill one's own officers or sergeants, usually with a fragmentation grenade; also the common term for any grenade.

Freak   Short term used for radio frequency

Free fire zone   Any area in which permission was not required prior to firing on targets.

FRI   (Fry) Friendly initiated incident

Funky fourth   Nickname of the 4th Infantry Division

FUO   Fever of undetermined origin

FWMAF   Free World Military Assistance Forces; used to mean any allies of South Vietnam.

FWT   Fixed-wing transport

FWU   Fixed-wing utility

Gen   General

Ghost   Take off; take it easy in a unit; do nothing; being absent; shirking duty.

Ghost time   Free time; time off duty

GOCO   Government-owned, contractor-operated

Go-go ship   Heavily armed CH-47 helicopter

Gooney bird   Nickname for the utility C-47 aircraft.

Gravel   Type of mine

Green   Used to signify "safe," such as a Green LZ (safe landing zone).

Green Berets   Universal nickname for the elite Special Forces of the U.S. Army; highly skilled and trained sergeants and officers who were awarded the green beret as their headgear and as a mark of distinction. This term applied only to Special Forces troops themselves, who reminded users that "they weren't hats."

Ground pounder   Infantryman

Grunt   Most popular nickname for an infantryman in Vietnam; supposedly derived from sound one made when lifting up his rucksack.

GS   General Support

Guerrilla   Armed combat element of a resistance movement organized on a military or paramilitary basis.

Guerrilla warfare   Military operations conducted in enemy-held or hostile territory by irregular, predominantly indigenous forces.

Gun jeep or truck   Armored vehicle equipped with machineguns.

Gung ho   Hard charging, very enthusiastic

Gunney   Marine gunnery sergeant

Gunship   An armed helicopter

Gypsy operation   Frequent displacement of small unit bases

Ha   HAWK missile

Hardspot   Mounted ambush by a tank element

Hasty defense   Defense normally organized while in contact with the enemy and under pressure.

Hawks   Nickname for the battalion reconnaissance platoon

HE   High explosive, such as HE artillery rounds

He   HERCULES missile

Heavy arty   B-52 bombing strikes

Heavy gun team   Three armed helicopters operating together.

Heavy stuff   Heavy artillery such as 8-inch or 175mm cannon, but also meaning fire support from the battleship *New Jersey*.

Heliborne   Aloft in a helicopter

Helix   Air force spotter

Herringbone   Tactical formation used by mechanized and armor units during halts (or during ambush), when the unit is moving in column. The armored vehicles turn alternately to the sides of the road in such a manner as to orient their main armament and heaviest armor obliquely to the flanks.

HH   Heavy helicopter

HHB   Headquarters and Headquarters Battery

HHC   Headquarters and Headquarters Company

HHD   Headquarters and Headquarters Detachment

HHT   Headquarters and Headquarters Troop

H & I   Harassing and interdictory fire by artillery

High angle hell   Mortar fire

HJ   HONEST JOHN missile

Hog flight   Helicopter(s) mounting the 40mm cannon M5 nose-mounted armament subsystem for direct fire weapon support.

Hoi Chanh   One who rallied under the Chieu Hoi program

Honcho   Individual in charge; also meaning to supervise.

Hook   Nickname for the CH-47 Chinook helicopter

Hootch   House or living quarters or a native hut

Horse pill   The chloroquine primaquine malaria prophylaxis tablet taken weekly by U.S. personnel in Vietnam.

Hot   Dangerous, such as Hot LZ (where aircraft are receiving enemy fire).

Hotel Alpha   Phonetic alphabetization of HA meaning haul ass, move immediately, get out at once.

Hotel Echo   Phonetic alphabetization of HE, high-explosive artillery or mortar rounds.

HQ   Headquarters

Huey   Popular nickname for the UH-series helicopters

Hug   To close with the enemy or to be pinned down in close quarters with the enemy.

Hump   Rotation of 25 percent or more of a unit within a 30-day period; also called "rotational hump." It also meant to carry or march.

Illum   To illuminate, as with flares or searchlights.

Impact award   An award for valorous action presented by a high-ranking officer, usually the day after an action.

In, Inf Infantry

Incoming Receiving enemy mortar or rocket fire

Infusion A program for transfer of personnel within or between commands to reduce rotational hump.

Insertion Helicopter placement of combat troops in an operational area, usually secret.

Insurgency Condition resulting from a revolt or insurrection against a constituted government which falls short of being a civil war.

Intelligence & Interdiction (I & I) Generally refers to planned night artillery fire aimed at suspected enemy locations, disturbing their sleep, curtailing their movement and lowering their morale through threat of losses. See H & I.

Internal defense Full range of measures taken by a government and its allies to stay in power.

In the field In any forward combat area or any area outside of a town or base camp.

INTSUM (Entsum) Intelligence Summary

IP Instructor pilot

IR Infra-red or Intelligence Reports

Irregulars Armed individuals and groups who are not members of the regular armed forces, police or other internal security forces.

Jacob's Ladder A rope ladder dropped by a Chinook helicopter and used to climb down through difficult foliage or onto terrain too rough to land on.

Jolly Green Giant Heavily armed Air Force C-47 aircraft supporting troops or an Air Force HH-53 heavy rescue helicopter.

Jump CP A temporary command post established for a brief operation or for a main command post displacement, normally including only those personnel and equipment necessary to control the immediate operation.

Jumping Junkies Derisive nickname for paratroopers or parachutist-qualified troops

Jungle-busting Using a tank or armored vehicle to cut trails through the jungle or other heavy vegetation.

KANZUS (Kanzus) Korean, Australian, New Zealand, and U.S. combined force

Keystone, Keystoning KEYSTONE was the operational codeword for the series of retrograde increments by which the U.S. Army was withdrawn from Vietnam. These were divided into Keystone Eagle, Cardinal, Bluejay, Robin, Oriole, Mallard, Owl, etc. and spanned the period July 1969 – November 1972. A host of terms arose connected with this word, such as "Keystoned" (as a unit turned in its equipment and moved to port, etc.) and "Keystoning" (as a support unit effected a unit's transfer of equipment and retrograde movement).

K-Fifty Chinese Communist 7.62mm submachinegun

KHA Killed in Hostile Action. Since the United States was not engaged in a "declared war," the use of the official term "KIA (Killed in Action)" was not authorized by Department of Defense. KIA came to mean enemy dead.

Killer team Marine mobile ambush team

Kit Carson Scout Name given an ex-VC/NVA soldier employed by U.S. units as a scout.

KKK Khmer Kampuchea Krom, a pro-U.S. Cambodian exile group.

Klick Short for kilometer

Laager Positioning of helicopters in a secure forward area so that weapons systems may be used in defense. Also all-around night defensive position established by mechanized vehicles.

Land tail That part of an air-transported unit not committed to combat by air but which joins the unit via land movement.

LAW (Law) M72 light antitank weapon. An expendable rocket launcher which could be carried as a round of ammunition and was popular with infantrymen who fired it against bunkers and fortifications.

LBJ Ranch (L-B-J) Long Binh Jail. Actually the Long Binh Stockade. The last word was changed to jail to pun on the initials of President Lyndon Baines Johnson.

Leapfrog Form of movement in which supporting elements are moved successively through or by one another.

Lifer Career soldier

Lift A single helicopter trip carrying cargo from a loading area to a landing zone

Lightning bug Helicopter equipped with searchlights. Also called "firefly."

Line haul Long-distance military truck convoys. Also called Long Haul.

Little Appalachia Nickname for the Division headquarters of the 1st Infantry Division, derived from the poor living conditions in some parts of the Appalachian Mountains in the United States.

LJ LITTLE JOHN missile

LOH (Loach) A light observation helicopter, notably the OH-6A.

Local force Viet Cong combat unit subordinate to a district or province headquarters.

LOCC (Lock) Logistical Operations Control Center

LOG Logistical command

Log bird Logistical resupply helicopter

Log run Aerial logistical resupply mission

Long green line Column of infantry advancing through jungle terrain

LP Listening post forward of a defensive perimeter

LRP or LRRP (Lurp) Long-range reconnaissance patrol

Lt Hel Light Helicopter

Luc Luong Dac Biet (LLDB) South Vietnamese Special Forces

Lurps Long-range reconnaissance patrol members. Also, an experimental lightweight food packet consisting of a dehydrated meal and named after the soldiers it was most often issued to.

LZ A landing zone

MAAG Military Assistance Advisory Group

MAB Marine Amphibious Brigade

MAC-SOG Military Assistance Command Studies & Observation Group

MACV (Mac-vee) Military Assistance Command, Vietnam. The senior U.S. military headquarters in Vietnam.

Mad minute Concentrated fire of all weapons for a brief period of time at optimum rate, usually set at favorite attacking times of the enemy and used to upset their attack schedule. Also called "Mike-mike."

MAF Marine Amphibious Force

Main Force Viet Cong and North Vietnamese military units.

Maint Maintenance

Marching fire Fire delivered by infantry in an assault, especially with automatic rifles and machineguns fired from the hip or rapidly firing rifles from the shoulder while advancing.

MARS (Mars) Military Affiliate Radio System. Radio transmissions linking the United States civilians with soldiers calling from Vietnam through use of Signal Corps apparatus and volunteer amateur radio operators stateside.

Maverick A government vehicle stolen or misused

MASH Mobile Army Surgical Hospital

MAW Marine Air Wing

Mech Mechanized infantry

Med Medical

MEDCAP (Med-cap) Medical civic action program

Medevac   Medical evacuation by helicopter. Also called "Dust-off."

Meeting engagement   Collision between two advancing forces, neither of which is fully deployed for battle

Metal test   Detection process used on Viet Cong suspects

MG   Machinegun

MGF   Mobile guerrilla force, composed of highly trained indigenous personnel commanded by U.S. Special Forces, who operated as a guerrilla force in Viet Cong-controlled areas.

MH   Medium helicopter

MI   Military intelligence

Midnight requisition   Unauthorized material procurement at the local troop level

Mighty Mite   Blower used to force smoke and tear gas throughout tunnel systems.

Mike Force, MSF   Special Forces Mobile Strike Force composed of indigenous personnel and used as a reaction or reinforcing unit.

Mike-mike   Phonetic alphabetization of "mad minute" and used interchangeably. Also used for millimeter, such as "twenty mike-mike."

Mission ready   Any equipment, but especially helicopters, completely capable of performing assigned missions.

Moonshine   A flare-carrying aircraft

MOOSE   (moose) Move out of Saigon expeditiously. Refers to displacement of units.

MOOT   (moot) Move out of town. Program to reduce concentrations of troops in city areas.

Mort   Mortar

MP   Military Police

MR   Military Region

MSFC   Mobile Strike Force Command

MTOE   Modified Table of Organization and Equipment

Mxd   Mixed artillery of 105mm/155mm types

Nap-of-the-earth   Flight as close to the earth's surface as vegetation and obstacles will permit and following the contours of the earth.

Native sport   Hunting for Viet Cong

NDP   Night defensive position

Net   Short for radio network

Neutralize   To render an enemy force, installation, action, operation or the like ineffective by military action.

Next   Soldier due for rotation to United States in a few days; also "Short."

NG   National Guard

NH   NIKE-HERCULES missile

No-doze mission   Airborne broadcast of psychological operations tapes of appeals, music and propaganda during the hours of darkness.

No Fire Zone   An area in which the employment of all military fire must be cleared by the appropriate authority.

NORS   (Nors) Not operationally ready — reason, supply

No sweat   With little effort or no trouble

Number One   The best, prime

Number Ten   The worst. "Number ten-thou" meant the very worst.

Number Sixty   The M60 machinegun

Nuoc-man   A pungent Vietnamese concentrated fish-sauce used to flavor rice.

Nungs   Chinese tribal troops from the highlands of North Vietnam which provided special troops to the U.S. Special Forces.

NVA   The North Vietnamese Army

NZ   New Zealand

OJT   On-the-job training

One-buck   Code designation for units held in readiness in the United States for deployment to Vietnam on 48-hour notice.

One-oh-worst   Derisive nickname for the 101st Airborne Division (Airmobile) based on its numerical designation.

On station   Armed helicopter flight in position to support a ground commander

Opcon   Under operational control of another unit

Opns   Operations

Ord   Ordnance

Oscar Papa, OP   Phonetic alphabetization for outpost

Out-country   That part of Southeast Asia conflict outside South Vietnam (i.e., Laos and North Vietnam, sometimes Thailand, Cambodia and China)

P or PROV   Provisional

P's   Piasters, a Vietnamese monetary unit. See also piaster.

P-38   Can opener for canned C-rations

Paramilitary   Forces or groups distinct from the country's armed forces but resembling them in organization, equipment, training or mission.

Pattern activity   Detailed plotting on maps of enemy activity obtained from a variety of sources over an extended period of time.

PAVN   (Pavin) People's Army of Vietnam. The North Vietnamese Army, also NVA

PCS   Permanent change of station

PE   PERSHING missile

Penny nickel nickel   The 155mm howitzer

Pentagon East   The Military Assistance Command, Vietnam headquarters complex at Tan Son Nhut air base.

Pentomic   (Penta=five, tomic=from atomic) Organizational concept designed for possible nuclear conflict using five divisional elements instead of formerly standard three regiments.

Perim   Perimeter surrounding a fire base or position or even base camp

Phil CAG   Philippine Civic Action Group

Phougas   Drums of jellied gasoline fired defensively as a fixed-fire weapon. Also spelled foo-gas.

Piaster   South Vietnamese currency, 100 of which equaled roughly 85¢ in 1966 and $1.15 by 1970.

Piss tube   A mortar

Pods   Rubberized 500-gallon containers

Point man   Lead soldier in a unit cutting a path through dense vegetation if needed and constantly exposed to the danger of tripping booby traps or being the first in contact with the enemy.

Poison ivy   Nickname for the 4th Infantry Division derived from both the design of its shoulder patch and its official title of the Ivy Division.

Pony soldiers   Members of a long-range patrol; also any soldier in the 1st Cavalry Division

Prep   Preparation or pre-strike by air force, artillery or armed helicopter fire placed on an LZ or objective prior to attack or landing.

Prick   Nickname for the PRC-25 lightweight infantry field radio

Psychedelic cookie   Nickname for the 9th Infantry Division derived from the Octofoil design of its shoulder patch.

Psy-ops   Psychological operations. Planned use of propaganda to influence enemy thinking.

Puff the Magic Dragon, Puff   A C-47 up-gunned air force support aircraft. Also called dragon ship.

Puking buzzards   Derisive term for the 101st Airborne Division gleaned from the design of the screaming eagle on its shoulder patch.

Punji stake Razor sharp bamboo stake sometimes coated with poison or feces and usually hidden under water, along trails, at ambush sites or in elaborately concealed man-pits.

PZ Pickup zone for helicopter loading and troop assembly. Also, a pickup point for helicopter extraction of ground patrol.

QNH Qui Nhon

QM Quartermaster

R & R Rest-and-recreation vacation taken during one's one-year tour in Vietnam. Out-of-country R & R was at Bangkok, Hawaii, Tokyo, Australia, Hong Kong, Manila, Penang, Taipei, Kuala Lampur or Singapore. In-country R & R locations were at Vung Tau or China Beach.

RA Regular Army

RAC Reconnaissance Airplane Company

Rallier Individual who voluntarily surrenders to the South Vietnamese.

Ramp alert Fully armed aircraft on the ground at a base or forward strip ready for takeoff in about fifteen minutes.

Ranch hand Operations to conduct defoliation and anticrop activities.

RCT Regimental Combat Team

RD Revolutionary Development

Recon Reconnaissance

Recon-by-fire A method of reconnaissance in which fire is placed on suspected enemy positions to cause the enemy to disclose his presence by movement or return fire.

Reconnaissance in Force (RIF) A very broadly used term describing military sweeps aimed at finding the enemy. Variations in connotation make the term imprecise.

Red ball System for expediting procurement of repair parts.

Red haze Reconnaissance flight to detect heat emissions from the ground.

Redleg Nickname for an artilleryman

Red LZ Landing zone under hostile fire. See also Hot.

Regt, Rgt Regiment(s)

Rehab Rehabilitate; recuperate

Retrograde Any movement, voluntary or involuntary, to the rear

Rev-dev Troop nickname for revolutionary development programs

RF/PF Regional and Popular Forces of South Vietnam

RFZ Restrictive fire zone

RNZ Royal New Zealand

ROAD Reorganization Objective Army Divisions

Roadrunner Road-clearing operation with mission of catching local guerrillas by surprise. Also, a Special Forces trail-watch team.

Rock 'n' roll To put M16A1 rifle on full automatic fire

Rocket belt Encircling zone around friendly locality from which enemy large-caliber (122mm, 140mm, etc.) rocket attacks could be launched.

ROKs (Rocks) Republic of Korea soldiers and marines

Rolling thunder The sustained bombing of North Vietnam taken from the operation's code name.

Rome plow Specially mounted bulldozer blade used in forest or jungle clearing and heavy-duty land clearing.

RON (Ron) Remain overnight position. Known also as "NL" for night location.

RPG Russian-manufactured antitank grenade launcher

RR Either recoilless rifle or radio relay

RTAVF Royal Thai Army Volunteer Force

RTAVR Royal Thai Army Volunteer Regiment

RTO Radio telephone operator who carried the "lightweight" infantry field radio.

Ruck, Rucksack Backpack issued to infantry in Vietnam

Ruff-puffs South Vietnamese Regional Forces and Popular Forces (RF/PF); paramilitary forces usually of squad or platoon size recruited and utilized within a hamlet, village or district.

Rules of Engagement A directive or regulation which provided specific rules for the conduct of the air and surface battles in Vietnam applicable to the U.S. and allied forces, restricting their ability to combat the enemy. (Specifically, MACV Directive 525-13. Subordinate units issued the instructions as regulations.)

RVN Republic of Vietnam. South Vietnam

S Sector Advisory Role

S & T Supply & Transport

SAC Surveillance Aircraft Company

Saigon tea An "alcoholic" beverage consisting primarily of Coca-Cola.

Saigon warrior Derisive term for troops stationed in Saigon

Salty dog A "battle loss item" lost as a result of enemy action

Same same The same as; to do likewise

Sappers North Vietnamese Army or Viet Cong demolition assault pioneers

Scared Horse Nickname for the 11th Armored Cavalry Regiment, derived from the design on its shoulder patch displaying a rearing horse.

Sch School/Demonstration

Science fiction Nickname for the U.S. Army Special Forces

Scoutships OH-13 or OH-23 helicopters used for surveillance or reconnaissance.

Screaming Chickens Nickname for the 101st Airborne Division derived from the eagle emblem of the divisional shoulder patch as well as a disparagement of the division motto "Screaming Eagles."

Seabees Naval construction engineers. Derived from C.B. — navy construction battalion.

SEAL Highly qualified navy special-warfare force members.

Seal bins 500-gallon rubberized containers

Search and clear Offensive military operations to sweep through areas with the mission of locating, driving out or destroying the enemy.

Search and destroy Offensive operations designed to seek out and destroy enemy forces, headquarters and supply installations with emphasis on destruction rather than establishment of government control. Also called "Zippo missions."

SEATO (Seatoe) Southeast Asia Treaty Organization

Sector A South Vietnamese province

Self-help Construction work done by a unit for its own benefit involving the issue of material to the troop unit though engineer personnel may supervise the work.

SEP Separate

SF U.S. Army Special Forces. Also called "Green Berets."

SG SERGEANT missile

SGN Saigon

Shadow AC-119 with three miniguns used for aerial fire support.

Shake 'n' bake Sergeant who earned his rank quickly through NCO schools or other means with little time overall in the service.

Short, shortimer Individual with little time remaining in Vietnam. See also "Next."

Short rounds Rounds of ammunition or bombs falling short of the target. Also the inadvertent or accidental delivery of ordnance, sometimes resulting in death or injury to friendly forces or noncombatants.

Shotgun, shotgunner   Armed guard on or in a vehicle who watches for enemy activity and returns fire if attacked; a bodyguard; a door gunner on a helicopter.

Sky pilot   Nickname for an army chaplain

Sig   Signal

Skyspot   Radar controlled bombing

Slapflare   Hand-held flare resembling a paper towel cylinder with a cap on the bottom.

Slick   Helicopter used to lift troops or cargo with only protective armaments systems.

Smokey Bear   C-47 aircraft used to drop illuminating flares or a helicopter-mounted smoke generator.

Sneaky Petes   U.S. Army Special Forces; rangers; long-range recon elements.

Snoop 'n' poop   Marine search and destroy offensive mission

SOP   Standard operating procedure. A set of instructions covering intended responses to certain fixed features of activity or circumstances.

Sorry goat   Report of a unit location

Sortie   One aircraft making one takeoff and landing to conduct the mission for which it was scheduled.

Special operations   Military operations requiring specialized or elite forces

Special warfare   All military and paramilitary measures and activities related to unconventional warfare, psychological operations and counterinsurgency operations.

Specified Strike Zone   Area designated for a specific period of time in which targets may be attacked on a commander's intiative; very rare unless no civilian and friendly forces are in the vicinity of such a zone.

Spectre   AC-130 with miniguns, Vulcan machineguns and 105mm howitzer on board

Sperm   Marine light observation helicopter

Spider hole   Viet Cong guerrilla foxhole, often connected to a tunnel network

Spook   Civilian intelligence agent

Spooky   AC-47 aircraft with Gatling guns and illumination flares

Spray   To open fire, usually on automatic

SPT   Support

Sqdn   Squadron

SRAC   Second Regional Assistance Command

SRAG   Second Regional Assistance Group

SS   Subsector advisory role

Stability operation   An internal defense operation to restore order in the face of irregular forms of violence.

Stage   To process troops in a specified area that are in transit from one locality to another.

Stand-down   Period of rest and refitting; cessation of all operational activity except that necessary for security. Also used to mean preparation for final deployment of a unit back to the U.S.; "stack arms" also used in this context.

Starlight   Night reconnaissance or surveillance mission employing a light-intensifier scope.

Starlight scope   An image intensifier using reflected light from the stars or moon to identify targets.

Stopper   Prearranged barrier of fire immediately available to impede enemy movement across a defensive line or area.

Strac   Ready in the best possible condition. Derived from STRAC (Strategic Army Command, where units were kept at peak readiness in the United States itself).

Strip alert   Fully armed aircraft on the ground at a base or

forward strip ready to take off within five minutes.

STZ   Special Tactical Zone

Sugar reports   Mail from home or specifically from a girlfriend at home

Surv   Surveillance Aircraft

Surv L   Surveillance Light Aircraft

SVC   Service

Tac air   Tactical air support

Tac CP   Tactical command post

Tac E   Tactical emergency

Tac wire   Tactical wire entanglements used to break up enemy attack formations and hold him in areas covered by intense defensive fires.

Tail-end Charlie   Last man in a given file

Talk-quick   Nickname for a secure voice communications system

Tank farm   Group of storage tanks

TAOR   Tactical area of operational responsibility with mission of key installation defense; reaction missions necessary for the security of the area and support of pacification activities as required.

TBO   Aviation jargon for "time before overhaul"

TDA   Table of Distribution and Allowances

Tet   Vietnamese Lunar New Year Holiday period. The enemy Tet offensive of 1968 and on a lower scale, 1969, gave this a special military significance.

TF   Task Force

The Herd   Affectionate nickname of the 173d Airborne Brigade, a crack paratrooper force that was the first major army combat unit sent into Vietnam.

The Line   On the line meant being on duty with an infantry unit in the field.

The Pill   See "Horse pill"

Thump-gun   Nickname for the M-79 40mm grenade launcher, a popular squad weapon. Also any 40mm grenade launcher (on aircraft, etc.) var. "Thumper."

Thunder road   Vietnam's Highway 13

Thunder run   Movement of armored columns up and down a road or trail with the vehicles firing alternately to each side.

Tigers   Battalion patrol and ambush element

Tiger suits   Multicolor striped camouflage jungle fatigues

TL   Vietnamese provincial route

TOE   Table of Organization and Equipment

Top   First Sergeant of a company. Also known as the First Shirt.

Topo   Topographic Base Engineers

TOT   Time on target; an artillery term meaning artillery rounds from different batteries dropped onto a target simultaneously.

Tp   Troop

Tr   Transportation

TRAC   Third Regional Assistance Command

Tri-border   Area west of Dak To, South Vietnam, at the convergence of the Cambodian, Laotian and South Vietnamese borders.

Tunnel rat   A U.S. soldier, generally of small build, who searched enemy tunnel systems armed with a flashlight, .45 cal pistol and earplugs. Sometimes they used cap- or head-mounted lamps, small throat or head-mounted microphones, telephones with wire and revolvers with silencers as well.

Turtle   One's replacement, so named because it seemed like forever until he arrived.

Unconventional warfare   Guerrilla warfare conducted within hostile areas by predominantly indigenous personnel, usually supported and sometimes directed by a foreign power.

unkwn   Unknown or information unavailable

USAECV   U.S. Army Engineer Command,Vietnam

USARMYFMR   U.S. Army Forces Military Region

USARPAC   U.S. Army, Pacific

USARV   (Uze-ar-vee) U.S. Army, Vietnam

USASA   U. S. Army Security Agency

USASTRATCOM   U.S. Army Strategic Communications Command

USMA   United States Military Academy

Utilities   Marine slang for their combat fatigues

UTT   Utility Tactical Transport

VC   Viet Cong

VHF   Variable high frequency

Vic   Vicinity

Victor Charlie   Phonetic alphabetization of V.C. and the popular name for the Viet Cong

VNSF   South Vietnamese Special Forces

Waste   To kill or destroy

Wheel jockies   Truck drivers on convoy or line-haul operations.

Whiskey Papa, Willie Peter, W-P   Phonetic alphabetization for white phosphorus mortar or artillery rounds and grenades. See also "Willie Peter" and "W-H."

Whistler   Artillery fuse deliberately set to scare troops up front.

Widow-maker   Nickname for the M16 rifle

Willie Peter   Popular nickname for white phosphorus mortar or artillery rounds or grenades. See "Whiskey Papa."

W-P   White phosphorus mortar/artillery rounds or grenades

XO   Executive officer second in command to the senior officer

Yards   Montagnard soldiers usually trained, equipped and led by the U.S. Army Special Forces.

Zap   To shoot at and hit, wound, kill or destroy.

Zippo   Flamethrower

Zippo mission   A search-and-destroy mission

INDEX TO STATIONS CITED IN THE TEXT*

Station	Full Title of Post	Major Activity at Location
Aberdeen	Aberdeen Proving Ground (Maryland)	U.S. Army Test & Evaluation Command
Atlanta	Atlanta Army Depot (Georgia)	Depot
Belvoir	Fort Belvoir (Virginia)	U.S. Army Engineer Center
Benning	Fort Benning (Georgia)	U.S. Army Infantry Center
Bliss	Fort Bliss (Texas)	U.S. Army Air Defense Center
Bragg	Fort Bragg (North Carolina)	XVIII Airborne Corps and John F. Kennedy Center for Military Assistance (U.S. Army Special Forces)
Campbell	Fort Campbell (Kentucky)	U.S. Army Training Center
Carson	Fort Carson (Colorado)	5th Infantry Division
Detrick	Fort Detrick (Maryland)	USASTRATCOM East Coast Telecommunications Center
Devens	Fort Devens (Massachusetts)	U.S. Army Security Agency Training Center and School
Dix	Fort Dix (New Jersey)	U.S. Army Training Center
Dugwood	Dugwood Proving Ground (Utah)	U.S. Army Chemical/Biological Proving Ground
Eustis	Fort Eustis (Virginia)	U.S. Army Transportation School
Gordon	Fort Gordon (Georgia)	U.S. Army Training Center, U.S. Army Military Police School
Granite	Granite City Depot (Illinois)	Depot
Holabird	Fort Holabird (Maryland)	U.S. Army Intelligence Corps Command
Hood	Fort Hood (Texas)	III Corps
Houston	Fort Sam Houston (Texas)	Brooke Army Medical Center and Fourth U.S. Army
Huachuca	Fort Huachuca (Arizona)	U.S. Army Strategic Communications Command, Electronic Warfare School
Irwin	Fort Irwin (California)	U.S. Army and Desert Training Center
Jackson	Fort Jackson (South Carolina)	U.S. Army Training Center
Knox	Fort Knox (Kentucky)	U.S. Army Training Center, Armor School
Lee	Fort Lee (Virginia)	U.S. Army Quartermaster Center
Lewis	Fort Lewis (Washington)	U.S. Army Training Center
McClellan	Fort McClellan (Alabama)	U.S. Army Training Center
McPherson	Fort McPherson (Georgia)	Third U.S. Army
Meade	Fort George C. Meade (Maryland)	First U.S. Army
Monmouth	Fort Monmouth (New Jersey)	U.S. Army Electronics Command, Signal Center
Monroe	Fort Monroe (Virginia)	Continental Army Command (CONARC)
Ord	Fort Ord (California)	U.S. Army Training Center
Polk	Fort Polk (Louisiana)	U.S. Army Training Center
Riley	Fort Riley (Kansas)	U.S. Army Training Center
Rucker	Fort Rucker (Alabama)	U.S. Army Aviation Center and School
Sheridan	Fort Sheridan (Illinois)	Fifth U.S. Army
Sill	Fort Sill (Oklahoma)	U.S. Army Field Artillery Center
Stewart	Fort Stewart (Georgia)	U.S. Army Flight Training Center
Story	Fort Story (Virginia)	Amphibious Engineers
Tobyhanna	Tobyhanna Army Depot (Pennsylvania)	Depot
Wolters	Fort Wolters (Texas)	U.S. Army Primary Helicopter Center
Wood	Fort Leonard Wood (Missouri)	U.S. Army Training Center

* Information reflects data for 1969, the height of the conflict.

APPENDIX F:

Map Locations of Major Allied Combat Elements in South Vietnam, 1965-73

Cambodia

NOTE: Effective 21 Jul 70 MR 5 and MR 6 were combined into one Military Region (MR 5)

Laos

Phong Saly

Muang Luong
Nam Tha
Houa Khong
• Muong Sai
MR 1
Luang Prabang
Pak Beng • • Luang Prabang
Sayaboury

• Samneua
Houa Phan
MR 2

• Muong Soui
Xiangkhoang
Plaine Des Jarres
MR 5
Borikhane
Vientiane
• Paksane
Vientiane

Nape •
Khammouane
MR 3
• Mahaxay

Tchepone •
Savannakhet
Savannakhet

Vapikham Thong
MR 4
• Saravane
Saravane

Pakse •
Champassak
Se-done
Attopeu
• Attopeu

Sithandone

0   100
Statute Miles
0   100
Kilometers

Vietnam

I CTZ
(MR1)

II CTZ
(MR2)

III CTZ
(MR3)

IV CTZ
(MR4)

Quang
Tri

Hue

Thua
Thien

Da Nang

Quang Nam

Chu Lai

Quang Tin

Quang Ngai

Kontum

Binh Dinh

An Khe

Qui Nhon

Pleiku

Pleiku

Phu
Bon

Phu
Yen

Darlac

Khanh
Hoa

Nha Trang

Quang
Duc

Tuyen
Duc

Ninh
Thuan

Cam Ranh Bay

Lam Dong

Phuoc
Long

Binh
Thuan

Binh
Long

Long
Khanh

Tay
Ninh

Binh Tuy

Binh
Duong

Bien
Hoa

Saigon

Hau
Nghia

Kien
Tuong

Long
An

Gia
Dinh

Phuoc Tuy

Chau
Doc

Kien
Phong

Dinh
Tuong

Go
Cong

An
Giang

Sa
Dec

Kien
Hoa

Can
Tho

Vinh
Long

Kien
Giang

Phong
Dinh

Vinh
Binh

Chuong
Thien

Sa
Xuyen

Sac Lieu

An
Xuyen

Scale 1:1.250.000

0   40   80   100 Kilometers

0   40   80   100 Statute Miles

NOTE: CTZ renamed as MR in July 1970.

364

The following maps (pages 366 – 385), while basically reflecting standard military symbolization used by the U.S. Army during the Vietnam era, contain certain important modifications made in the interest of clarity. Careful study of the following data, even by the experienced military reader, is suggested.

The military symbols are composed of a box containing the symbol applicable to its type or function, a size indicator on top of the box, a brigade/regimental number or CARS combination to the left of the box, and the division identification (if applicable) always to the right of the box. Unless the CARS combination is present or a battalion size indicator on top, every box equals one brigade or brigade-equivalent unit (usually three-four battalions).

	Engineer
	Infantry
	Ranger
	Marine
	Mechanized Infantry
	Special Forces

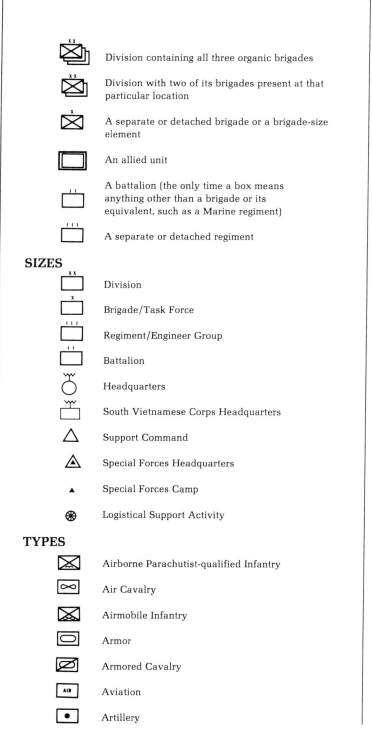

Division containing all three organic brigades

Division with two of its brigades present at that particular location

A separate or detached brigade or a brigade-size element

An allied unit

A battalion (the only time a box means anything other than a brigade or its equivalent, such as a Marine regiment)

A separate or detached regiment

SIZES

Division

Brigade/Task Force

Regiment/Engineer Group

Battalion

Headquarters

South Vietnamese Corps Headquarters

Support Command

Special Forces Headquarters

Special Forces Camp

Logistical Support Activity

TYPES

Airborne Parachutist-qualified Infantry

Air Cavalry

Airmobile Infantry

Armor

Armored Cavalry

Aviation

Artillery

CARS Number Combination

2/1   A number combination with a slash represents the battalion number followed by the traditional parent regimental number.

SAMPLES

1C   1st Cavalry Division (with all three of its brigades)

3   3d Marine Division (with two of its regiments)

3   25   3d Brigade of the 25th Infantry Division

9   3   9th Marine Regiment of the 3d Marine Division

173   173d Airborne Brigade

2   2d Marine Brigade, Republic of Korea

2/34   4   2d Battalion, 34th Armor of the 4th Division

1/1   1st Squadron, 1st Armored Cavalry (separate)

3/17   3d Squadron, 17th Air Cavalry (separate)

1   AIR   1st Aviation Brigade

ABBREVIATIONS USED IN THE MAPS

ATF	Australian Task Force
C	Cavalry
CAP	Republic of Korea CAPITAL Division
DRAC	Delta Regional Assistance Command
FFV	Field Force, Vietnam
FRAC	First Regional Assistance Command
MAF	Marine Amphibious Force
QC	Queen's COBRAS (Thailand)
RTA	Royal Thai Army Force
SRAC/SRAG	Second Regional Assistance Command/Group
STZ	Special Tactical Zone
TFS	Task Force SOUTH
TRAC	Third Regional Assistance Command

LOCATIONS OF MAJOR U.S. AND ALLIED COMBAT UNITS IN VIETNAM (EXCEPT ARVN)
December 1965

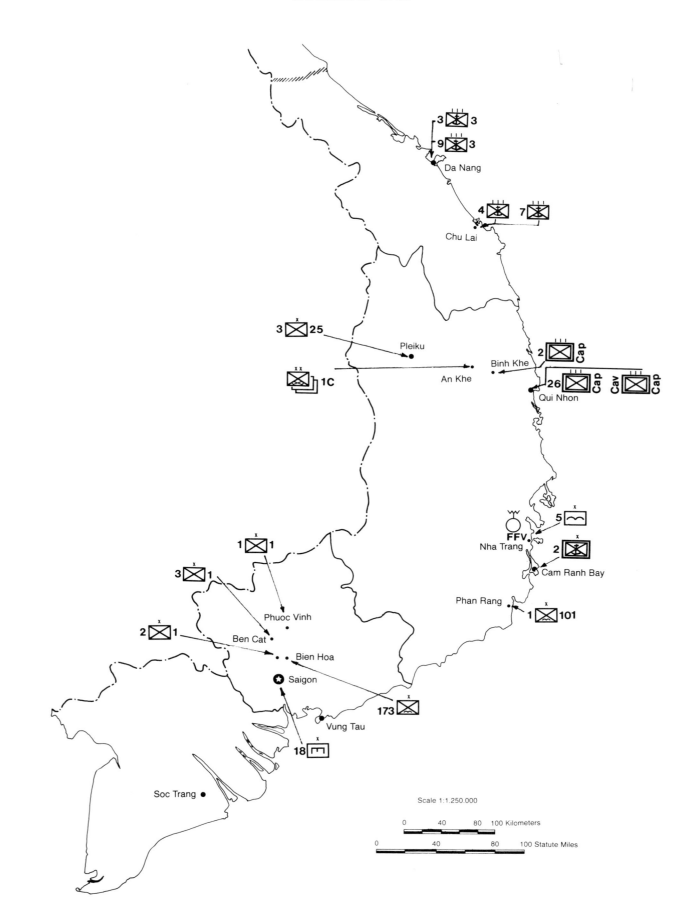

LOCATIONS OF MAJOR U.S. AND ALLIED COMBAT UNITS IN VIETNAM (EXCEPT ARVN)
June 1966

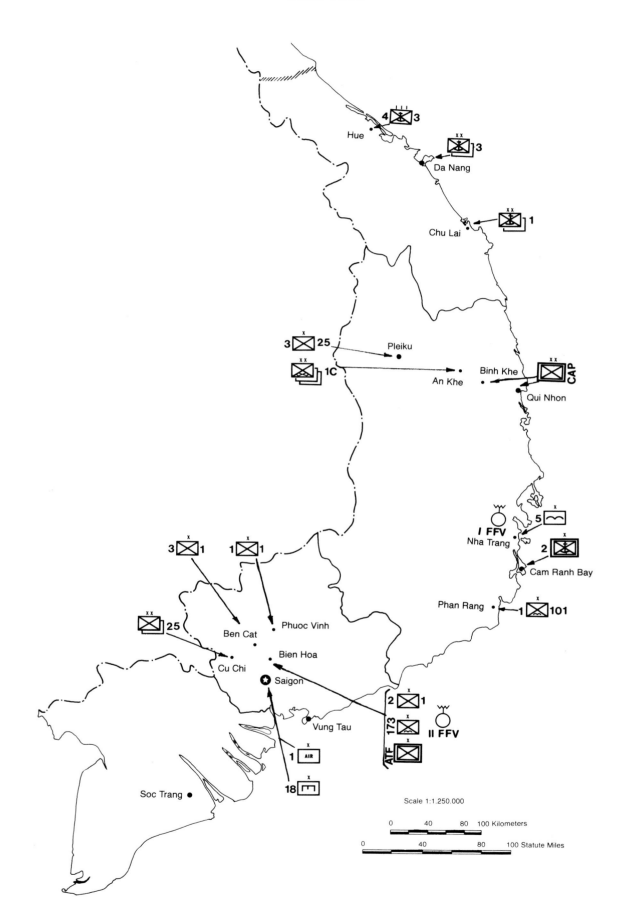

LOCATIONS OF MAJOR U.S. AND ALLIED COMBAT UNITS IN VIETNAM (EXCEPT ARVN)
December 1966

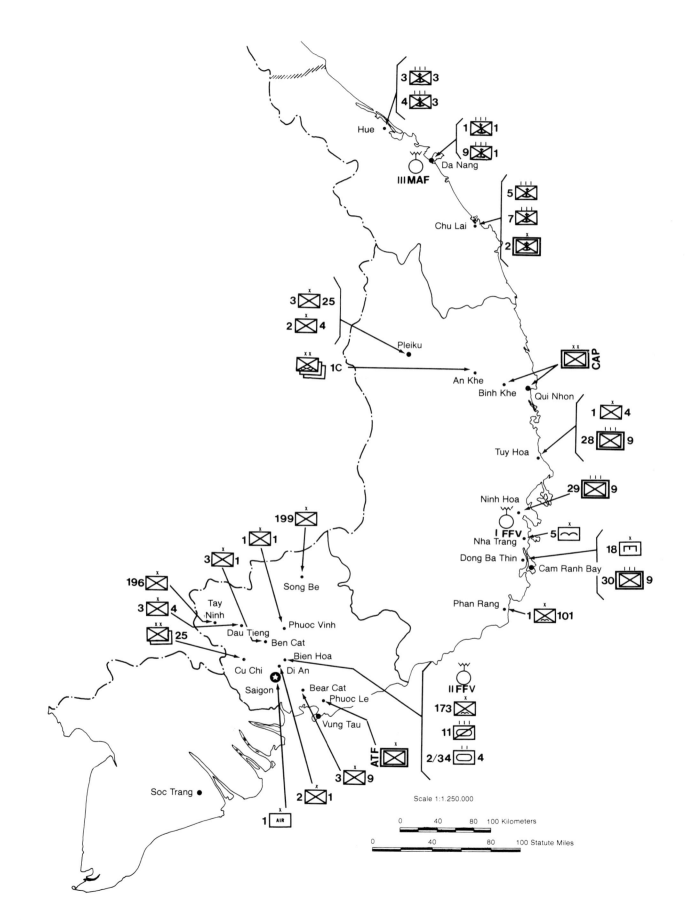

LOCATIONS OF MAJOR U.S. AND ALLIED COMBAT UNITS IN VIETNAM (EXCEPT ARVN)
June 1967

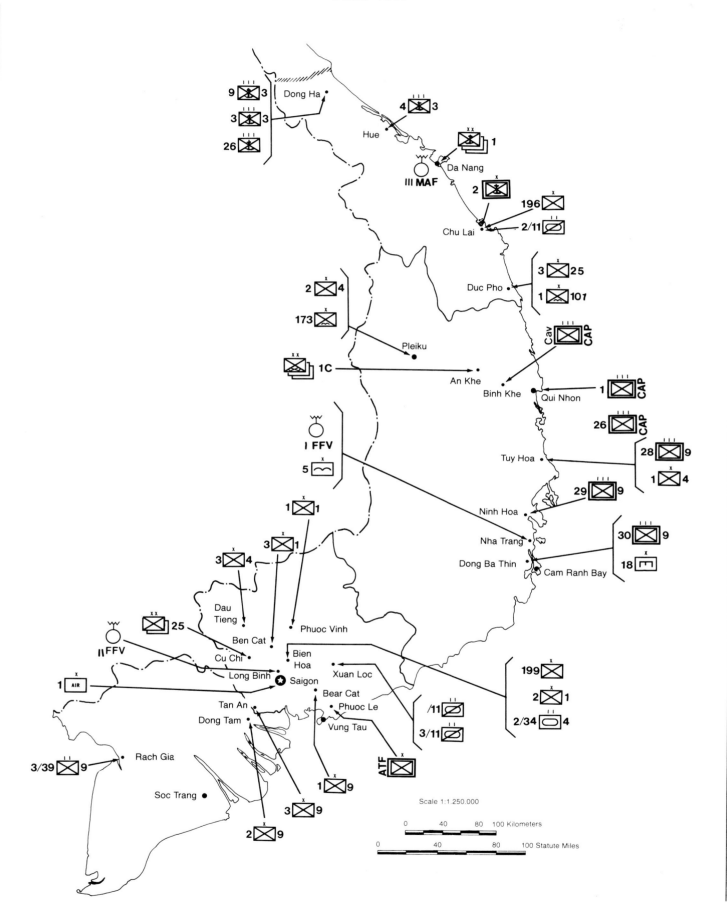

Scale 1:1.250.000

LOCATIONS OF MAJOR U.S. AND ALLIED COMBAT UNITS IN VIETNAM (EXCEPT ARVN)
December 1967

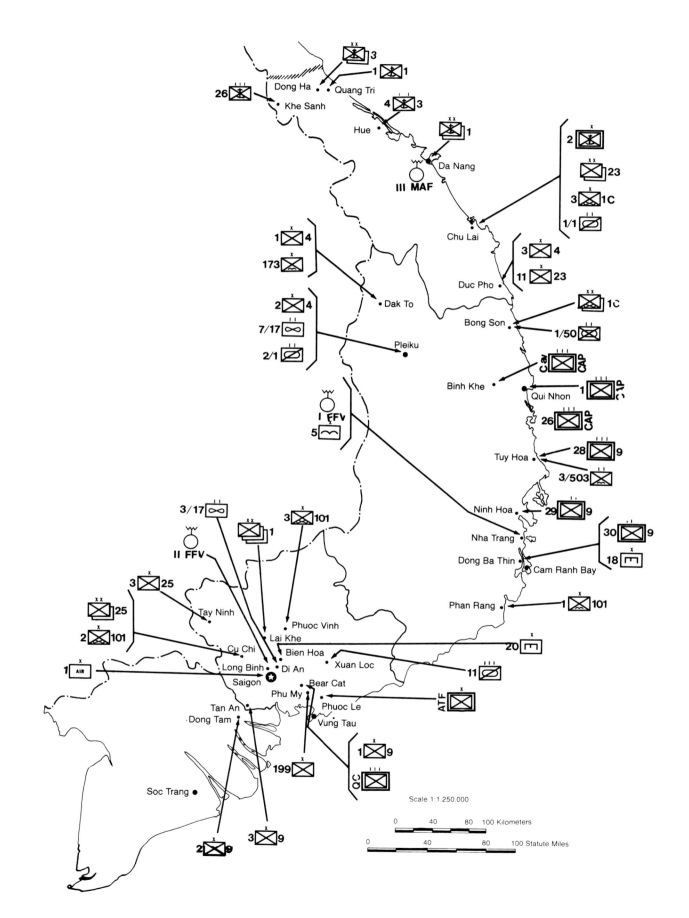

LOCATIONS OF MAJOR U.S. AND ALLIED COMBAT UNITS IN VIETNAM (EXCEPT ARVN)
February 1968

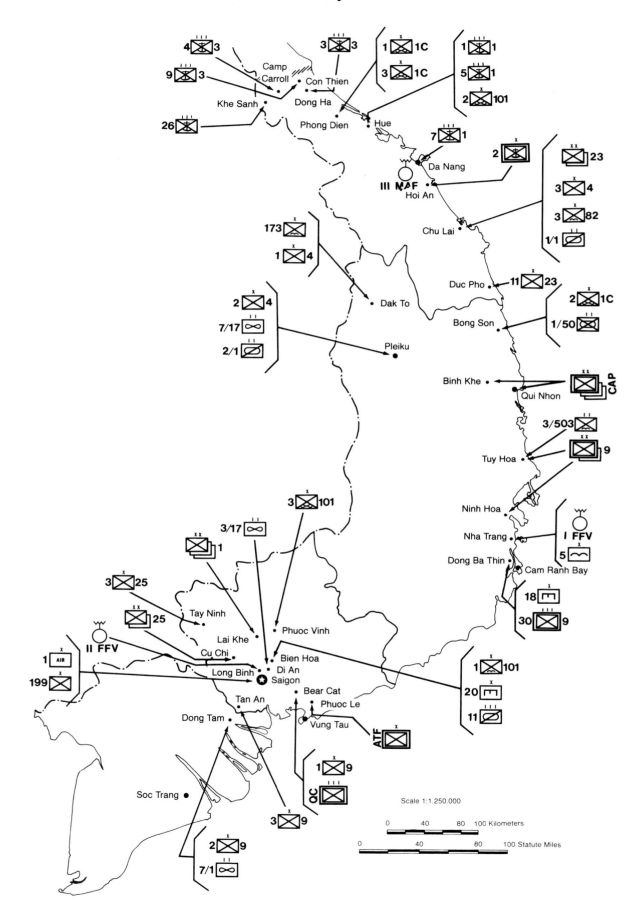

LOCATIONS OF MAJOR U.S. AND ALLIED COMBAT UNITS IN VIETNAM (EXCEPT ARVN)
June 1968

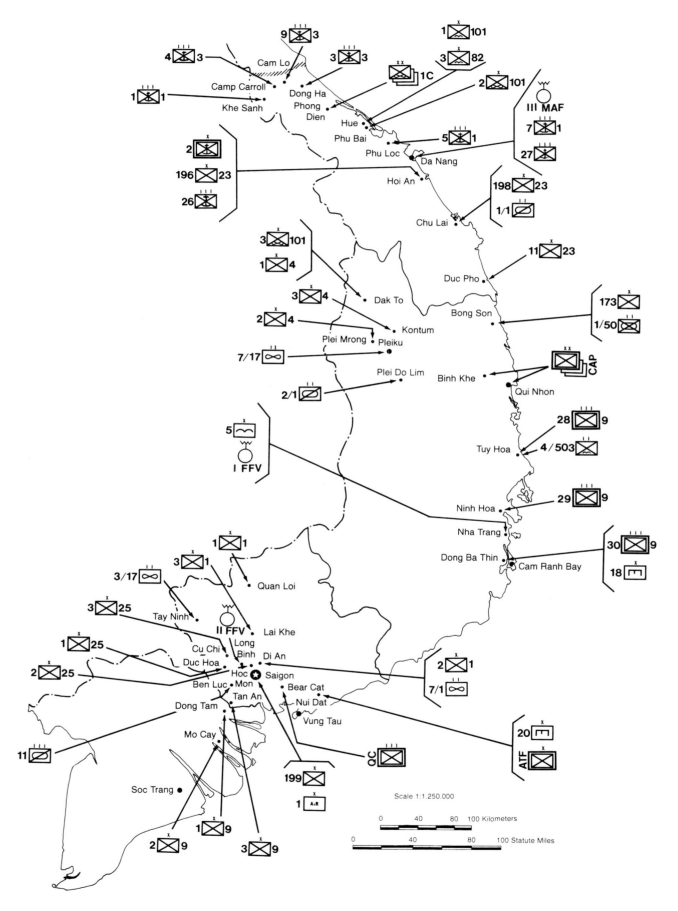

Scale 1:1.250.000

| | 0 | 40 | 80 | 100 Kilometers |

| | 0 | 40 | 80 | 100 Statute Miles |

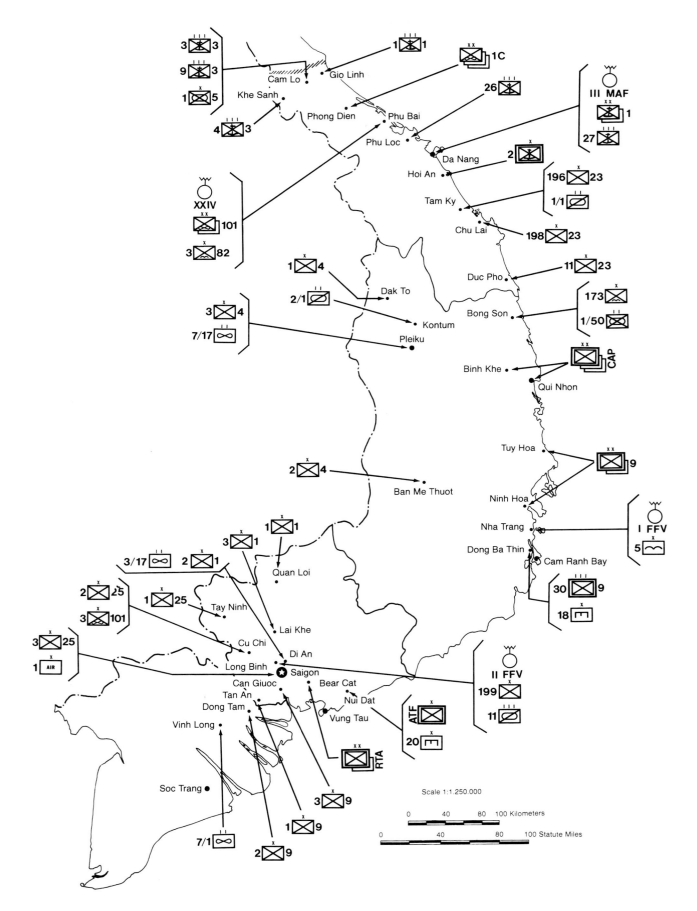

LOCATIONS OF MAJOR U.S. AND ALLIED COMBAT UNITS IN VIETNAM (EXCEPT ARVN)
December 1968

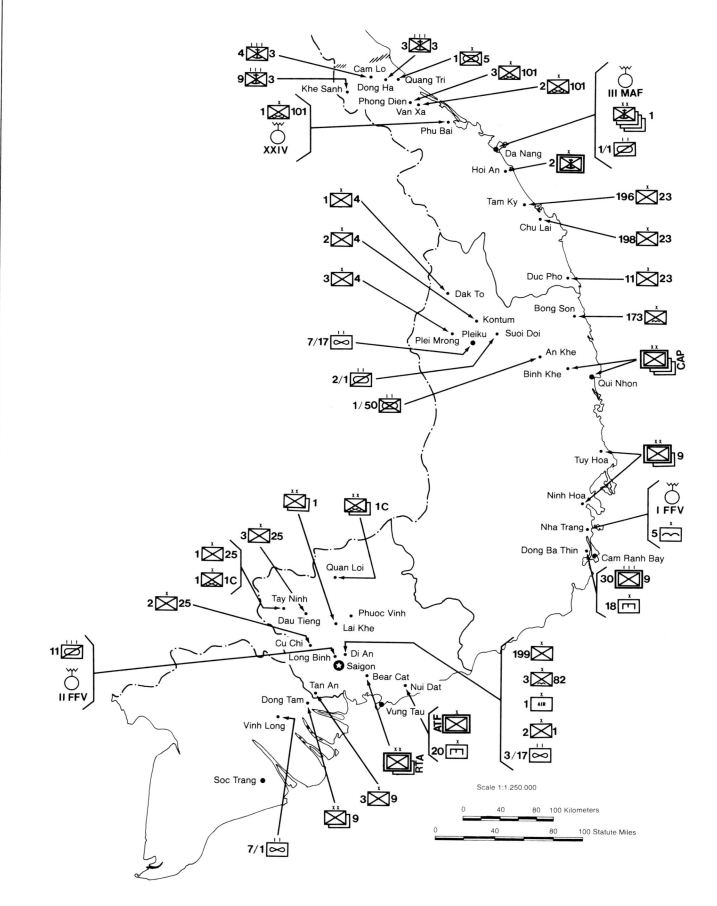

LOCATIONS OF MAJOR U.S. AND ALLIED COMBAT UNITS IN VIETNAM (EXCEPT ARVN)
June 1969

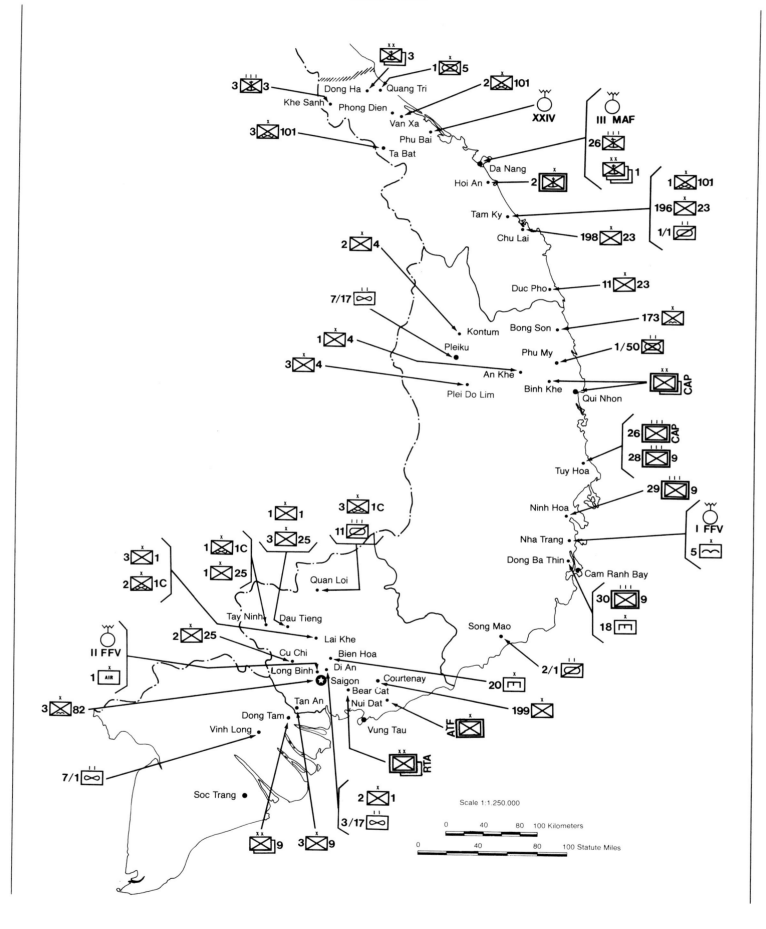

Scale 1:1.250.000

0   40   80   100 Kilometers

0   40   80   100 Statute Miles

LOCATIONS OF MAJOR U.S. AND ALLIED COMBAT UNITS IN VIETNAM (EXCEPT ARVN)
December 1969

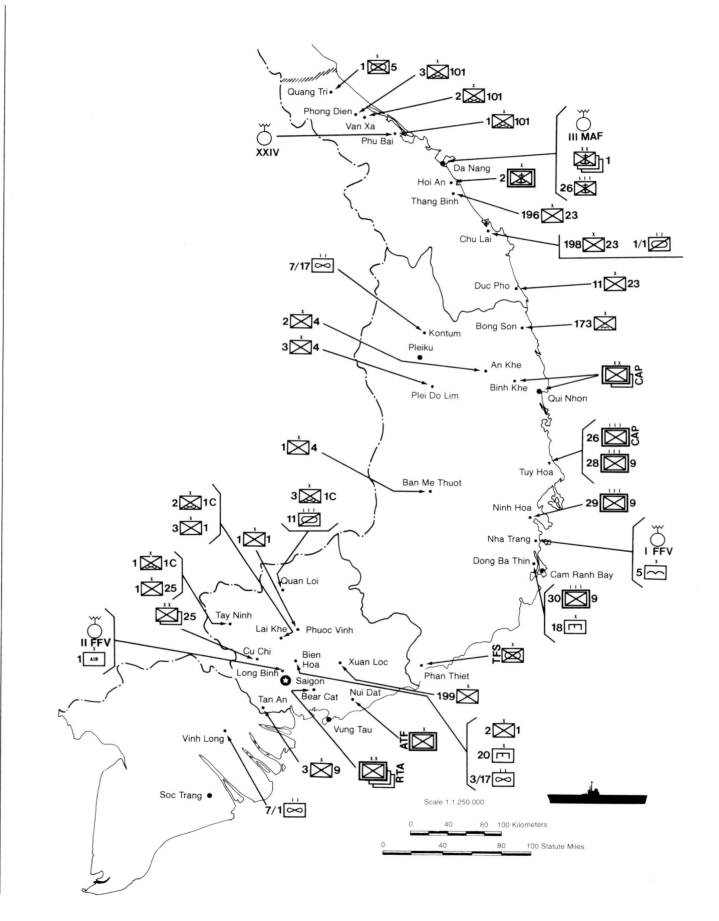

LOCATIONS OF MAJOR U.S. AND ALLIED COMBAT UNITS IN VIETNAM (EXCEPT ARVN)
June 1970

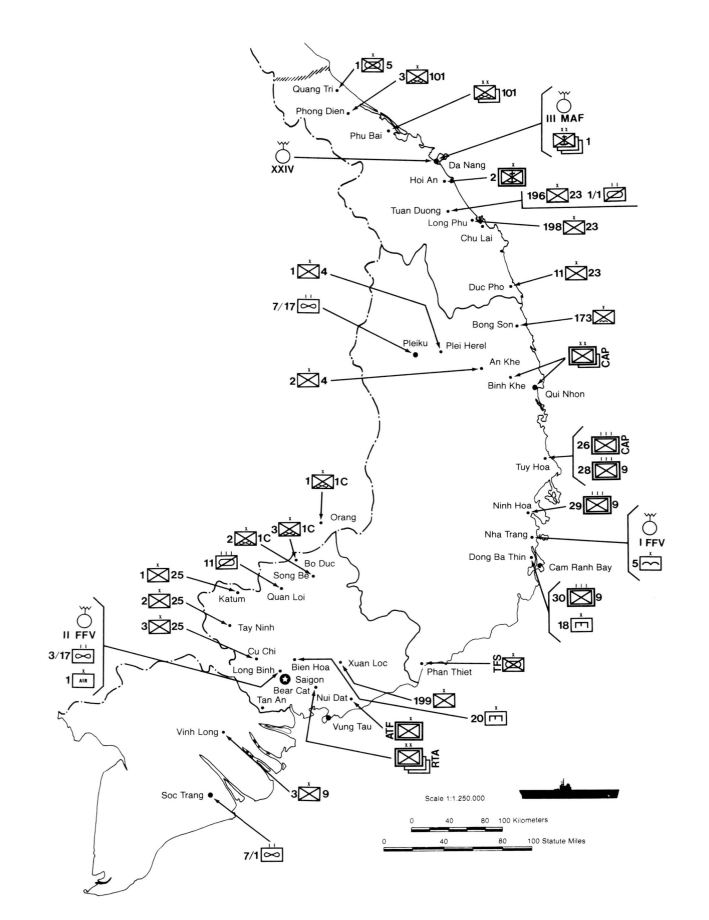

LOCATIONS OF MAJOR U.S. AND ALLIED COMBAT UNITS IN VIETNAM (EXCEPT ARVN)
December 1970

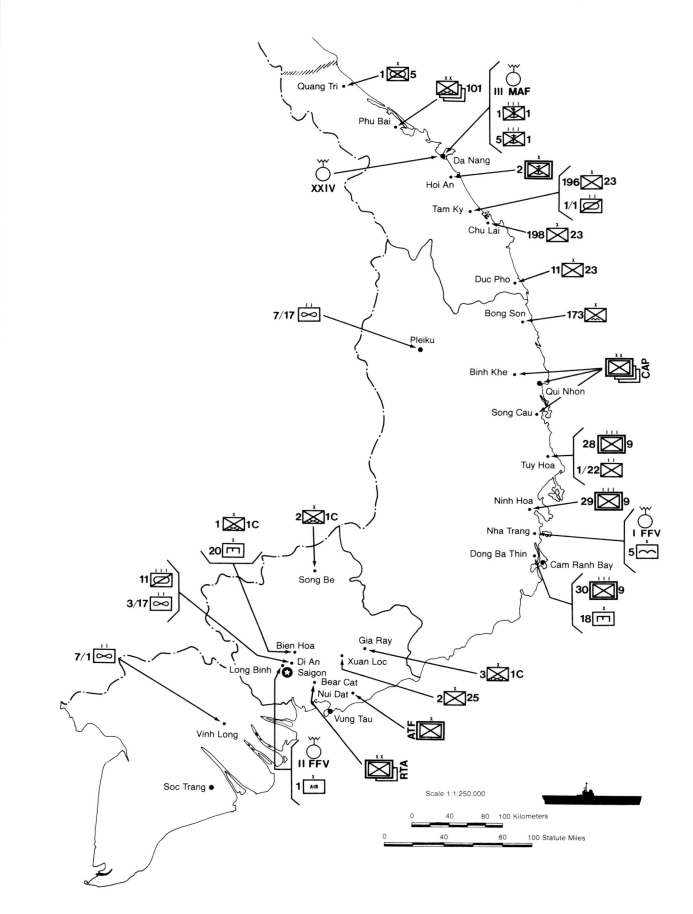

LOCATIONS OF MAJOR U.S. AND ALLIED COMBAT UNITS IN VIETNAM (EXCEPT ARVN)
June 1971

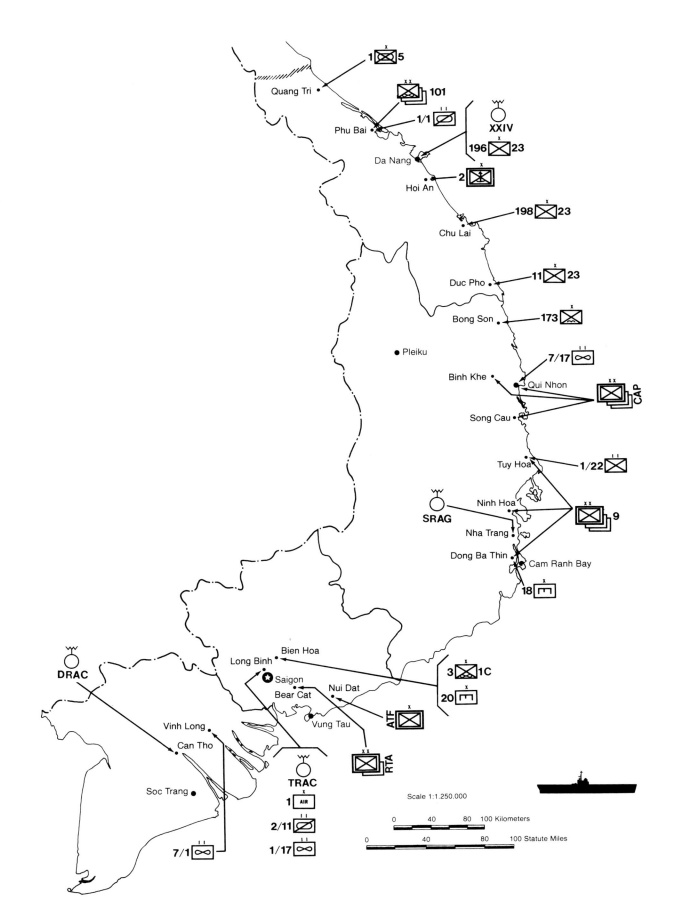

LOCATIONS OF MAJOR U.S. AND ALLIED COMBAT UNITS IN VIETNAM (EXCEPT ARVN)
December 1971

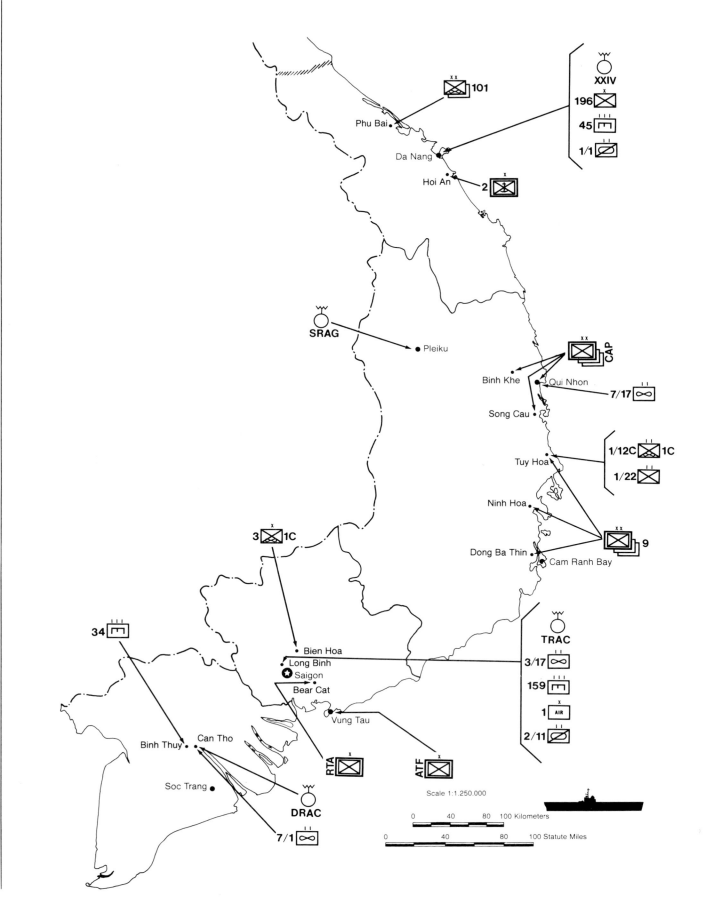

LOCATIONS OF MAJOR U.S. AND ALLIED COMBAT UNITS IN VIETNAM (EXCEPT ARVN)
June 1972

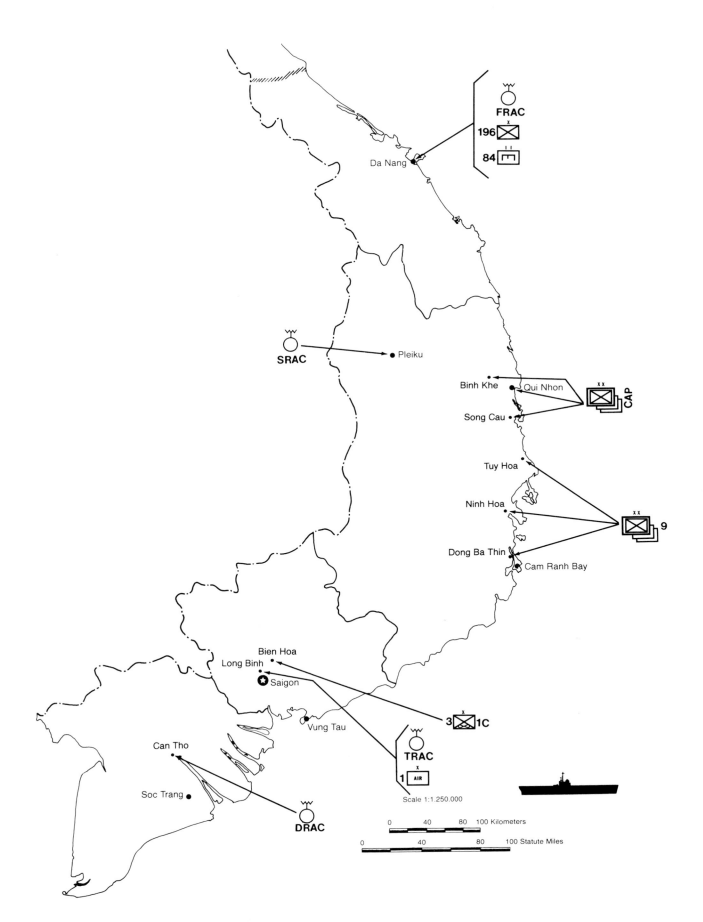

Scale 1:1.250.000

0   40   80   100 Kilometers

0   40   80   100 Statute Miles

LOCATIONS OF MAJOR ALLIED COMBAT UNITS IN VIETNAM
December 1972
All units are ARVN unless double boxed (Korean) or labeled U.S.A.

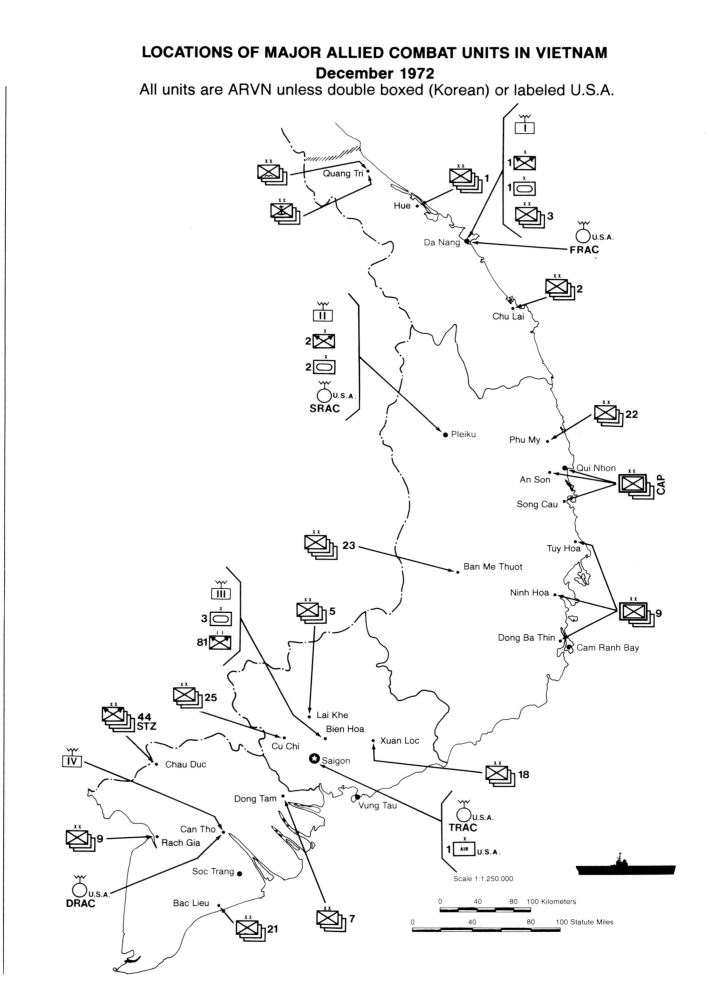

PORTS, LAND LINES OF COMMUNICATIONS AND MAJOR LOGISTICAL COMMANDS IN VIETNAM

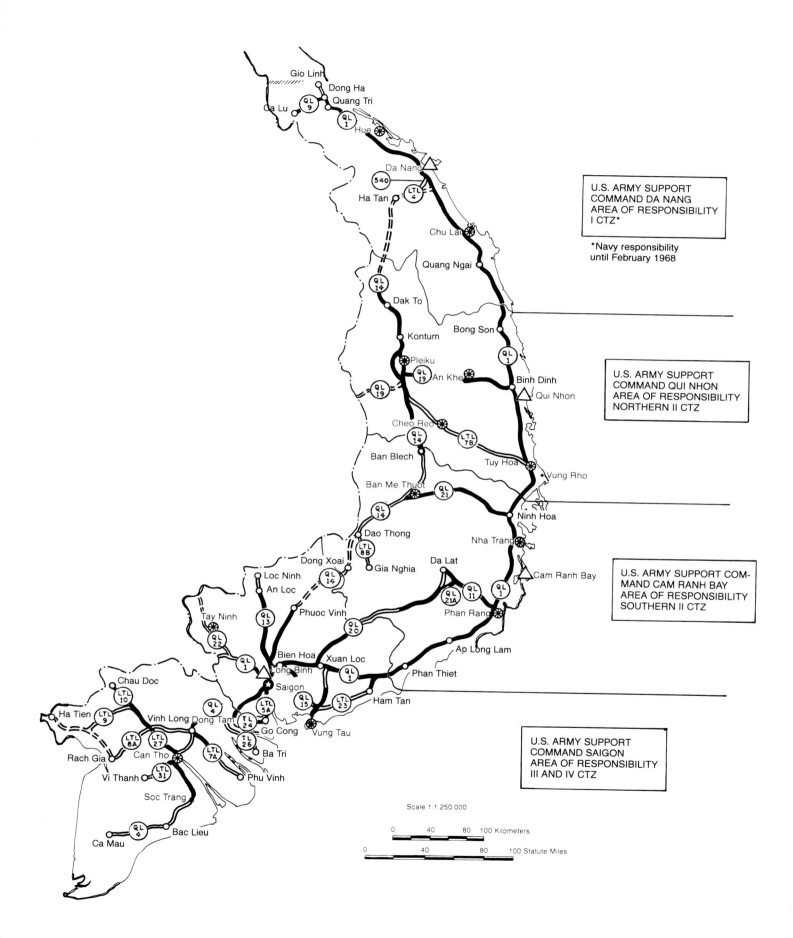

U.S. ARMY SUPPORT
COMMAND DA NANG
AREA OF RESPONSIBILITY
I CTZ*

*Navy responsibility
until February 1968

U.S. ARMY SUPPORT
COMMAND QUI NHON
AREA OF RESPONSIBILITY
NORTHERN II CTZ

U.S. ARMY SUPPORT COM-
MAND CAM RANH BAY
AREA OF RESPONSIBILITY
SOUTHERN II CTZ

U.S. ARMY SUPPORT
COMMAND SAIGON
AREA OF RESPONSIBILITY
III AND IV CTZ

Scale 1:1.250.000

0   40   80   100 Kilometers

0   40   80   100 Statute Miles

LOCATIONS OF U.S. ARMY SPECIAL FORCES CAMPS IN VIETNAM, 1964-70

Da Nang

Pleiku

Qui Nhon

Ban Me Thuot

Nha Trang

Cam Ranh Bay

Ho Ngoc Tau

Saigon

Vung Tau

Can Tho

Soc Trang

Scale 1:1.250.000

| 0 | 40 | 80 | 100 Kilometers |

| 0 | 40 | 80 | 100 Statute Miles |

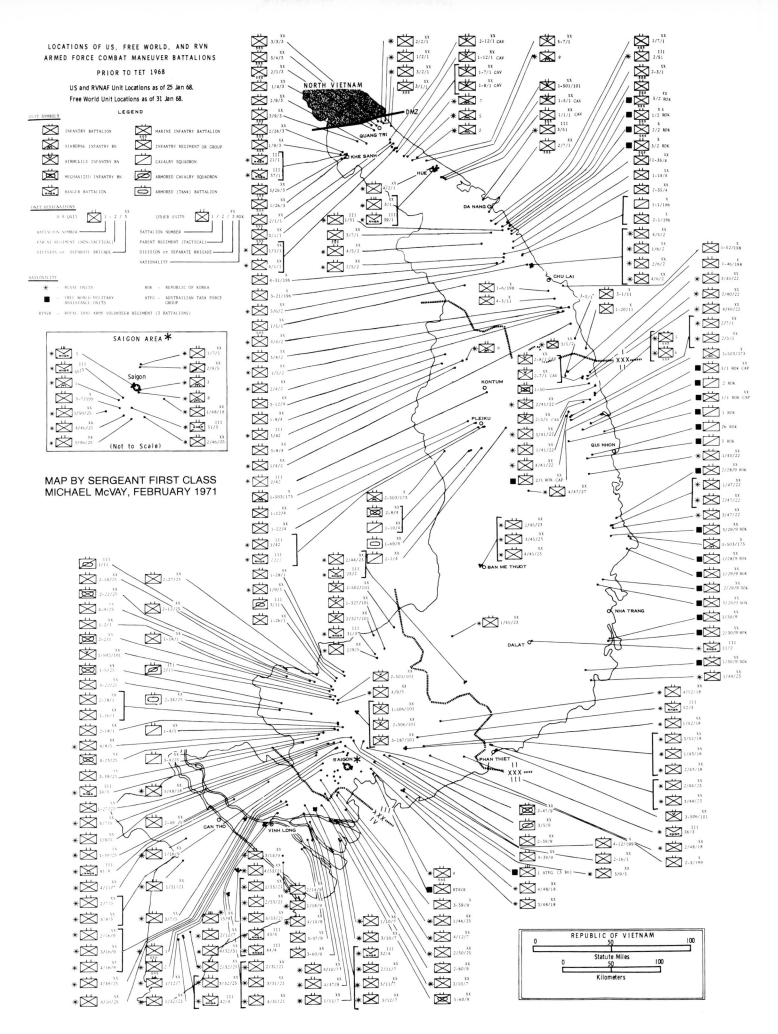

LOCATIONS OF US, FREE WORLD, AND RVN
ARMED FORCE COMBAT MANEUVER BATTALIONS
PRIOR TO TET 1968

US and RVNAF Unit Locations as of 25 Jan 68.
Free World Unit Locations as of 31 Jan 68.

MAP BY SERGEANT FIRST CLASS
MICHAEL McVAY, FEBRUARY 1971

Photographic Credits

1. U.S. Army, CC27754.
3. U.S. Army, CC045355.
8. Don North.
15. Department of the Army.
47. U.S. Army, SC646411.
57. Army News Features.
59. Army News Features.
66. Army News Features.
69. Army News Features.
71. U.S. Army, SC639044.
87. U.S. Army, SC647334.
91. Army News Features.
93. Army News Features.
95. Army News Features.
109. U.S. Army, SC622388.
124. U.S. Army, CC39777.
136. Army News Features.
165. Army News Features.
167. Army News Features.
176. Army News Features.
179. U.S. Army, CC058331.
189. Author's Collection.
191. U.S. Army, CC060646.
197. U.S. Army, CC080631.
199. U.S. Army, SC656677.
206. U.S. Army, CC70790.
211. Army News Features.
218. Army News Features.
220. U.S. Army, CC36252.
222. Army News Features.
231. Army News Features.
233. U.S. Army, CC055958.
235. Army News Features.
237. Army News Features.
239. U.S. Army, CC044006.
251. U.S. Army, CC073919.
255. U.S. Marine Corps, A184966.
257. U.S. Navy, K77009.
259. U.S. Marine Corps, A186282.
265. U.S. Army, CC32266.
267. Army News Features.
270. Author's Collection.
272. U.S. Army, SC630276.
274. U.S. Army, SC604594.
284. #1, U.S. Army.
    #2, U.S. Army, 614299.
    #3, U.S. Army, 048889.
    #4, U.S. Army.
285. #5, U.S. Army, 75561.
    #6, U.S. Army, 061617.
    #7, U.S. Army, 040830.
    #8, U.S. Army, 49564.
286. #1, Bell Helicopter.
    #2, U.S. Army, 043032.
    #3, U.S. Army, 65043.
    #4, Bell Helicopter.
    #5, U.S. Army, 037707.
    #6, U.S. Army, 22925.
    #7, U.S. Army, 637955.
287. #8, U.S. Army, 611612.
    #9, Bell Helicopter.
    #10, Bell Helicopter.
288. #1, Author's Collection.
    #2, U.S. Army, 022326.
289. #3, Bell Helicopter.
    #4, Bell Helicopter.
    #5, U.S. Army, 073215.
    #6, U.S. Marine Corps, A329571.
290. #1, U.S. Army, 052731.
    #2, U.S. Army, 067804.
    #3, Army News Features.
291. #4, U.S. Army, 056223.
    #5, U.S. Army, 655988.
    #6, Army News Features.
    #7, Army News Features.

292. #1, U.S. Army, 074027.
    #2, U.S. Army Aviation School.
    #3, U.S. Army, 624623.
    #4, U.S. Army, 061949.
293. #5, U.S. Army, 034151.
    #6, U.S. Army, 061952.
    #7, U.S. Army, 061965.
    #8, U.S. Army Aviation School.
    #9, U.S. Army Aviation School.
294. #1, U.S. Army, 063220.
    #2, Jim Loop.
    #3, Army News Features.
    #4, U.S. Army.
    #5, U.S. Army, 654047.
    #6, U.S. Army, 646233.
295. #7, Army News Features.
    #8, U.S. Army, 654225.
    #9, U.S. Army, 041943.
296. #1, Army News Features.
    #2, Army News Features.
    #3, U.S. Army.
    #4, U.S. Army, 647597.
    #5, U.S. Army, 041613.
297. #6, U.S. Army, 050428.
    #7, U.S. Marine Corps, A184243.
298. #1, U.S. Army, 43120.
    #2, Author's Collection.
    #3, Rock Island Arsenal.
    #4, Author's Collection.
    #5, Author's Collection.
299. #6, Army News Features.
    #7, Author's Collection.
    #8, U.S. Army, 43085.
    #9, Rock Island Arsenal.
300. #1, Jim Loop.
    #2, UPI.
    #3, Army News Features.
    #4, Rock Island Arsenal.
    #5, Rock Island Arsenal.
301. #6, Rock Island Arsenal.
    #7, Author's Collection.
    #8, U.S. Army, 85321.
    #9, Author's Collection.
302. #1, U.S. Army, 064225.
    #2, U.S. Army, 642376.
    #3, Army News Features.
    #4, U.S. Army, 052813.
    #5, U.S. Army, 052816.
    #6, U.S. Army, 049157.
    #7, U.S. Army, 651795.
    #8, U.S. Army, 641538.
    #9, Rock Island Arsenal.
    #10, U.S. Army, 056401.
303. #11, U.S. Army, 633797.
    #12, U.S. Army, 048196.
304. #1, U.S. Army, 49436.
    #2, U.S. Army, 049700.
    #3, U.S. Army, 630523.
    #4, U.S. Army, 049753.
305. #5, Army News Features.
    #6, U.S. Army, 026609.
    #7, U.S. Army, 029055.
306. #1, Army News Features.
    #2, Army News Features.
    #3, U.S. Army, 077397.
    #4, U.S. Army, 989322.
307. #5, U.S. Army, 066486.
    #6, U.S. Army, 656674.
    #7, U.S. Army, 637374.
308. #1, U.S. Army, 650965.
    #2, Army News Features.
    #3, Jim Loop.
    #4, Jim Loop.
    #5, U.S. Army, 634543.
    #6, U.S. Army, 059817.
    #7, Jim Loop.
309. #8, U.S. Army, 45606.
    #9, Jim Loop.
    #10, U.S. Army, 054434.
310. #1, Jim Loop.
    #2, U.S. Army, 646407.
    #3, Jim Loop.
311. #4, Jim Loop.
    #5, Jim Loop.
    #6, Jim Loop.
    #7, Jim Loop.
312. #1, Fred Crismon.

#2, Army News Features.
    #3, U.S. Army, 046761.
    #4, U.S. Army, 049412.
    #5, U.S. Army, 037628.
313. #6, U.S. Army, 041243.
    #7, U.S. Army, 044008.
    #8, U.S. Army, 048856.
    #9, Fred Crismon.
314. #1, Aberdeen Proving Ground.
    #2, Aberdeen Proving Ground.
    #3, Aberdeen Proving Ground.
    #4, Aberdeen Proving Ground.
    #5, Aberdeen Proving Ground.
315. #6, U.S. Army, 032894.
    #7, U.S. Army, 031770.
    #8, Author's Collection.
    #9, Aberdeen Proving Ground.
316. #1, U.S. Army, 064740.
    #2, Aberdeen Proving Ground.
    #3, U.S. Army, 086947.
    #4, U.S. Army, 069923.
    #5, U.S. Army, 054417.
    #6, Army News Features.
    #7, U.S. Army, 049744.
317. #8, U.S. Army, 052623.
    #9, U.S. Army, 043603.
    #10, U.S. Army, 043985.
318. #1, Jim Loop.
    #2, Jim Loop.
    #3, Jim Loop.
    #4, Jim Loop.
    #5, Jim Loop.
319. #6, Jim Loop.
    #7, Fred Crismon.
    #8, Fred Crismon.
    #9, Fred Crismon.
320. #1, Fred Crismon.
    #2, Jim Loop.
    #3, Fred Crismon.
    #4, Jim Loop.
321. #5, Jim Loop.
    #6, Jim Loop.
    #7, Jim Loop.
    #8, Jim Loop.
322. #1, U.S. Army, 066474.
    #2, U.S. Army, 042588.
    #3, U.S. Army, 043493.
323. #4, U.S. Army, 037625.
    #5, U.S. Army, 038189.
    #6, U.S. Army, 066029.
    #7, U.S. Army, 03457.
324. #1, U.S. Army, 032029.
    #2, U.S. Army, 066031.
    #3, U.S. Army, 031751.
    #4, U.S. Navy, K45861.
    #5, U.S. Army, 060108.
325. #6, U.S. Army, 074010.
    #7, U.S. Army, 0740718.
    #8, Army News Features.
326. #1, Fred Crismon.
    #2, Jim Loop.
    #3, Author's Collection.
    #4, Jim Loop.
327. #5, U.S. Army, 054905.
    #6, Jim Loop.
    #7, Jim Loop.
328. #1, U.S. Navy.
    #2, U.S. Army, 065554.
    #3, U.S. Army, 062885.
    #4, U.S. Army, 042822.
    #5, U.S. Army, 060874.
329. #6, U.S. Navy.
    #7, U.S. Army, 030764.
    #8, U.S. Army, 031463.
330. #1, U.S. Army, 073714.
    #2, U.S. Army, 063423.
    #3, Author's Collection.
    #4, Army News Features.
    #5, U.S. Army, 485023.
    #6, U.S. Army, 51894.
331. #7, U.S. Army, 653094.
    #8, Army News Features.
    #9, U.S. Army, 044111.

Dust Jacket
Back flap, U.S.News & World Report.
Back, UPI/Jeff Taylor.

Sources

I. Published Sources

While the bulk of this book's information was extracted from original unit records, several published books also proved quite useful. Foremost were the specialized Vietnam Studies, a series of monographs printed by the Department of the Army to fill the gap before official histories were written. Written by major commanders either during the war or shortly thereafter, these volumes are marked by their unevenness and uniform slimness. Because most of the actual writing was done during the war years, much information was deleted due to classification restrictions. However, some of these volumes were truly excellent and comprehensive within the confines of the space allowed, and they materially added to the researcher's data base. The author found the following most useful in the preparation of this volume:

Dunn, Lt. Gen. Carroll H. 1972. *Base Development in South Vietnam, 1965-1970.* Vietnam Studies. Washington, D.C.: Department of the Army.

Eckhardt, Maj. Gen. George S. 1974. *Command and Control, 1950-1969.* Vietnam Studies. Washington, D.C.: Department of the Army.

Fulton, Maj. Gen. William B. 1973. *Riverine Operations, 1966-1969.* Vietnam Studies. Washington, D.C.: Department of the Army.

Heiser, Lt. Gen. Joseph M., Jr. 1974. *Logistic Support.* Vietnam Studies. Washington, D.C.: Department of the Army.

Kelly, Col. Francis J. 1973. *U.S. Army Special Forces, 1961-1971.* Vietnam Studies. Washington, D.C.: Department of the Army.

Larson, Lt. Gen. Stanley R. and Brig. Gen. James L. Collins, Jr. 1975. *Allied Participation in Vietnam.* Vietnam Studies. Washington, D.C.: Department of the Army.

Ott, Maj. Gen. David Ewing. 1975. *Field Artillery, 1954-1973.* Vietnam Studies. Washington, D.C. : Department of the Army.

Ploger, Maj. Gen. Robert. 1974. *U.S. Army Engineers, 1965-1970.* Vietnam Studies. Washington, D.C.: Department of the Army.

Starry, Gen. Donn A. 1978. *Mounted Combat in Vietnam.* Vietnam Studies. Washington, D.C.: Department of the Army.

Tolson, Lt. Gen. John J. 1973. *Airmobility, 1961-1971.* Vietnam Studies. Washington, D.C.: Department of the Army.

It should be noted that several other volumes of the Vietnam Studies were designed to assist the army in developing future operational concepts while at the same time contributing to the historical record. Especially significant in this limited area were:

Ewell, Lt. Gen. Julian J. and Maj. Gen. Ira A. Hunt, Jr. 1974. *Sharpening the Combat Edge: The Use of Analysis to Reinforce Military Judgment.* Vietnam Studies. Washington, D.C.: Department of the Army.

Hay, Lt. Gen. John H., Jr. 1974. *Tactical and Materiel Innovations.* Vietnam Studies. Washington, D.C.: Department of the Army.

The most valuable single historical document available in this field remains the *Report on the War in Vietnam (as of June 1968)* by

Adm. U.S.G. Sharp and Gen. William C. Westmoreland, 1968 (Washington, D.C.: U.S. Government Printing Office). This is a 347-page soft-cover interim history covering operations in South Vietnam and bombing activity over North Vietnam from January 1964 – June 1968. Although brief and with the army's section limited to Part II, it proved eminently useful despite its date and inherent incompleteness.

The army's military effort in Vietnam in general has been rounded out by the addition of three good postwar books: *A Soldier Reports* by Gen. William C. Westmoreland (New York: Doubleday & Company, 1976) is largely devoted to the war in Vietnam from Westmoreland's perspective. *Summons of the Trumpet* by Brig. Gen. Dave Richard Palmer (San Rafael, California: Presidio Press, 1978) is a perceptive overview of the military's war in Vietnam. Its value is enhanced by a complete section on sources which provides the reader with a handy appraisal of most of the general books on Vietnam to date. While first appearing to be an illustrated history with a lot of gloss, *The Vietnam War,* edited by Ray Bonds (New York: Crown Publishers, 1979), transcends a purely photographic format with a highly informative and well-researched narrative written by recognized military experts. Not only is an objective history presented, but data on almost every aspect of U.S. operations and weaponry in the Vietnam conflict are given. While providing a graphic visual and factual understanding of the military campaign, it lacks hard Order of Battle data and unfortunately has no references to sources.

The Army Lineage Series (Office of the Chief of Military History, U.S. Army) does not address Vietnam specifically but was of considerable use in unit background material. These volumes are lineage-oriented and do not contain information on exact dates of Vietnam service, commanders, etc. Unfortunately, only two were applicable and available to this author's research:

Mahon, John K. and Romana Danysh. *Infantry.* [Revised and enlarged edition.] Part 1. *Regular Army.* Washington, D.C.: Office of the Chief of Military History, U.S. Army, 1972. (Army lineage series.) xvi, 938 pages.

Stubbs, Mary L. and Stanley R. Connor. *Armor-cavalry.* Part 1. *Regular Army and Army Reserve.* Washington, D.C.: Office of the Chief of Military History, U.S. Army, 1969. (Army lineage series.) xi, 477 pages.

It can only be hoped that this excellent series will eventually cover all army formations.

Infantry in Vietnam, edited by Lt. Col. Albert N. Garland (Fort Benning, Ga., Infantry Magazine, 1967), a book designed to describe combat experiences and assist fellow officers, remains an unsurpassed treatise on ground tactics in the war despite its early date of publication.

The five-volume *Pentagon Papers* (The Senator Gravel Edition, Boston: Beacon Press, 1971) has a number of pages devoted to force strength projections and recommendations for Vietnam. Because it contains much then-classified material, it is one of the few published sources to detail how some major U.S. Army components were scheduled to Vietnam and it was relied upon heavily for such information.

Unit Scrapbook (Washington, D.C.: Office of the Chief of Information, U.S. Army Command Information Unit) is a series of reprinted newspaper articles collected from various editions, generally between 1966 and 1969, for each of the major tactical units in Vietnam. Extra copies are now nonexistent.

Many Army Regulations and Field Manuals (AR and FM) were utilized to provide unit mission statements and tactical material. Of special significance were the extracts of tables of organization and equipment found in the three-part FM 101-10 *Staff Officers' Field Manual* issued and updated throughout the war. These, of course, were intended to provide general troop planning data only and specific units in Vietnam were often modified and structured differently.

Probably the most valuable army publications pertaining to the organization and weapons status peculiar to units operating in Vietnam were the numerous condensed data booklets put out by each army branch school during the period. These were generated for internal education purposes but those secured were invariably of great value. The U.S. Army Infantry School (Fort Benning, Georgia) printed the following handbooks for officer training purposes: *Airmobility Handbook – 1968, Engineer Handbook – 1970* and the *Artillery Handbook ST 7 – 163.*

Limited and usually restricted special published reports such as the excellent *MACOV* (Mechanized and Armor Combat Operations in Vietnam) by USARV (March 1967) were utilized where found — most commonly now within the original Vietnam records (see Unpublished Sources). An excellent guide to elite insignia worn in Vietnam is the 44-page soft-cover booklet by Cecil B. Symth, Jr., *Special Forces in Southeast Asia* (ARV-CAT, Glendale, California, 1978).

Of considerably less value was Department of the Army Pamphlet 672-3, *Unit Citation and Campaign Participation Credit Register – Vietnam Conflict,* a listing so marred by errors and replete with omissions that it must be avoided as an unreliable reference.

Published unit histories were generally written on an annual basis by most large units and some smaller ones, usually in a yearbook format, in Asia (often Japan) by Public Information Officers and their staffs. While no complete list exists of all those published, the following list provides a partial reference:

1st Cavalry Division

The Air Cavalry Division. An authorized publication of the 1st Cavalry Division, published for the benefit of division members serving in Vietnam. Published by the 1st Cavalry Division, 1969.

"Airmobile Division." *Military Review,* August 1965, p. 97.

"The Airmobile Division Joins Up." *Army,* August 1965, pp. 12-18.

Albright, John, John A. Cash and Allan W. Sandstrum. 1970. *Seven Firefights in Vietnam.* Washington, D.C.: U.S. Government Printing Office.

Brand, William F. "Airmobile Firepower — Hallmark of the 1st Cavalry Division," *US Army Aviation Digest,* March 1967, pp. 18-23.

Coleman, J. D. 1969. *Memories of the First Team in Vietnam.* Information Office, 1st Cavalry Division.

Cowan, Sidney C. "Ride a Slick Ship. (16 Nov. 65 Battle of Ia Drang Valley)," *US Army Aviation Digest,* June 1966, pp. 23-25.

"1st Cavalry Division (Airmobile) Created." *Army Information Digest,* August 1965, pp. 32-37.

Harris, Lt. Michael M. "First Team Moves South." *Army,* May 1969, pp. 43-48.

Hoffman, Fred S. "The Airmobile Division: Trial by Combat." *National Guardsman,* October 1965, pp. 2-6.

Hymoff, Edward. 1967. *The First Air Cavalry Division, Vietnam.* New York: M. W. Lads Publishing Co.

Kinnard, Maj. Gen. Harry W. O. "Activation to Combat in 90 Days." *Army Information Digest,* April 1966, pp. 24-31.

"Battlefield Mobility of New 1st Air Cavalry Division." *NATO's Fifteen Nations,* April – May 1966, p. 38.

———. "A Victory in the Ia Drang: The Triumph of a Concept. The 1st Air Cavalry Division in Battle." *Army,* September 1967, pp. 71-91.

"PUC to 1st Cavalry Division (Airmobile)." *Army Digest,* November 1967, inside back cover.

Sharp, Adm. U. S. G. and Gen. W. C. Westmoreland. 1968. *Report on the War in Vietnam (as of 30 June 1968).* Washington, D.C.: U.S. Government Printing Office.

Spore, John B. "The Airmobile Division: Lean, Fast and Flexible." *AF/SD International,* September 1965, p. 21.

Tolson, Lt. Gen. John J. III. "Pegasus," *Army.* December 1971, pp. 10-19. [Operation Pegasus/Lam Son 207A was the code name given to the fifteen days of air assault operations that ended the battle of Khe Sanh.]

1st Infantry Division

First Engineer Battalion, 1st Infantry Division 1967-1968. 1st Engineer Battalion, 1st Infantry Division.

Geist, 1st Lt. William. *The First Infantry Division in Vietnam 1969, Volume III: A Pictorial History.* 1st Infantry Division.

In Vietnam. Oct 1965 – Mar 1967. "Always First." A Pictorial History of the 1st Infantry Division. 1967. No publisher shown.

Vietnam, The First Year. A Pictorial History of the 2d Brigade, 1st Infantry Division. c. 1966. Tokyo: Dai Nippon Printing Co., Ltd.

4th Infantry Division

Albright, John, John A. Cash and Allan W. Sandstrum. 1970. *Seven Firefights in Vietnam.* Washington, D.C.: U.S. Government Printing Office.

Hardy, Lee. "The Fighting Fourth (Infantry Division)." *Army Digest.* August 1967, pp. 50-53.

"The History of the Famous Fourth Infantry Division." Mimeographed. 1969. Prepared by the 29th Military History Detachment.

Hymoff, Edward. *The Fourth Infantry Division in Vietnam.* New York: M. W. Lads Publishing Co.

Marshall, S. L. A. 1968. *West to Cambodia.* New York: Cowles Education Corp.

Sharp, Adm. U. S. G. and Gen. W. C. Westmoreland. 1968. *Report on the War in Vietnam (as of 30 June 1968).* Washington, D.C.: U.S. Government Printing Office.

9th Infantry Division

"Army to Add New Division." *Journal of the Armed Forces.* 30 October 1965, p. 103.

Carden, 1st Lt. Peter B. *3d Brigade, 9th Infantry Division Vietnam 1970 Orientation Brochure.* An unpublished booklet released by the 3d Brigade, 9th Infantry Division.

Endsley, Mark C. "9th Infantry Division Activated—." *Army Information Digest,* March 1966, pp. 6-11.

Fulton, Maj. Gen. William B. 1973. *Riverine Operations, 1966-1969.* Vietnam Studies. Washington, D.C.: Department of the Army.

Kutscheid, 1st Lt. Timothy, ed. *9th Infantry Division Vietnam 1968: Combat Art.* An unpublished booklet released by the 9th Infantry Division Information Office.

Reysen, Capt. Frank, ed. *9th Infantry Division 1918-1968.* A 44-page orientation booklet released by the 9th Infantry Information Office.

Sharp, Adm. U. S. G. and Gen. W. C. Westmoreland. 1968. *Report on the War in Vietnam (as of 30 June 1968)*. Washington, D.C.: U.S. Government Printing Office.

23d Infantry Division (AMERICAL)

Kelsey, Pfc. Mike, ed. *The AMERICAL*. An unpublished booklet released by the AMERICAL Div. Information Office, May 1968.

25th Infantry Division

Clark, Capt. Michael H., ed. *Tropic Lightning Vietnam: 1 October 1967 to 1 October 1968*. 25th Infantry Division.

Combat Art of the 25th Infantry Division. 3 volumes. c. 1968. Tokyo: Dai Nippon Printing Co., Ltd.

Marshall, S. L. A. *The River and the Gauntlet*. 1953. New York: William Morrow and Co.

———. *West to Cambodia*. 1968. New York: Cowles Education Corp.

McKeand, Lt. Patrick J., ed. *Tropic Lightning, 25th Infantry Division: 1 October 1941 – 1 October 1966*. 1966. Doraville, Ga.: Albert Love Enterprises, Inc., Division of McCall Corp.

Rottmann, 1st Lt. Larry. *The 25th Infantry Division in Vietnam 1966-1967*. 1968. Doraville, Ga.: Albert Love Enterprises, Inc., Division of McCall Corp.

Sharp, Adm. U. S. G. and Gen. W. C. Westmoreland. 1968. *Report on the War in Vietnam (as of 30 June 1968)*. Washington, D.C.: U.S. Government Printing Office.

Tropic Lightning. A History of the 25th Infantry Division. 25th Infantry Division. 1970.

"The 25th's 25th ... in Combat" *Tropic Lightning. 1 October 1940 – 1 October 1966*. 1966. 25th Infantry Division. Doraville, Georgia: Albert Love Publishing Co.

Zavyalov, Lt. Col. V. "Tropical Lightning (25th Infantry Division) Impotent." *Soviet Military Review*, No. 11. (November 1968), pp. 50-53.

82d Airborne Division

Porter, Capt. William R. and Capt. Thomas M. Fairfull. *The History of the 3d Brigade, 82d Airborne Division (February 1968 to March 1969)*. 3d Brigade, 82d Airborne Division, printed in Tokyo by Image Public Relations.

101st Airborne Division

Benton, Lt. Lewis E., ed. *History of the 101st Airborne Division 1942-1968*. An unpublished booklet released by the 101st Airborne Division Information Office.

Conner, Judson. "DRF (Division Ready Force) of 101st Airborne Division—Dynamic Deterrent." *Army Information Digest*, March 1965, pp. 38-41.

Dines, Capt. Allen J. *101st Airborne 1969 Vietnam*. An unpublished booklet released by the 101st Airborne Division Information Office.

Horvath, Maj. Richard L. *101st Airborne 1968 Vietnam*. An unpublished booklet released by the 101st Airborne Division Information Office.

McKenzie, Fred. 1968. *The Men of Bastogne*. New York: David McKay Co.

101st Airborne. 1968. Vietnam. 1969. Tokyo: Dai Nippon Printing Co., Ltd.

101st Airborne Division, 1968-1969. 1969. 101st Airborne Division.

Pearson, Willard. "Find 'Em, Fix 'Em, Finish 'Em." *Army Digest*, December 1966, pp. 15-21.

Rapport, Leonard. 1965. *Rendezvous with Destiny: A History of the 101st Airborne Division*. Greenville, Texas: 101st Airborne Division Assoc.

Sharp, Adm. U. S. G. and Gen. W. C. Westmoreland. 1968. *Report on the War in Vietnam (as of 30 June 1968)*. Washington, D.C.: U.S. Government Printing Office.

Miscellaneous Units

Anderson, CW2 James D., ed. *The Jagged Sword: A History of the 1st Signal Brigade, Vietnam – Thailand*. 1st Signal Brigade.

Barrow, Sgt. Gerald D., ed. *Company F, 51st Infantry, Airborne Long Range Patrol*. Company F, 51st Infantry. September 1967.

Bowers, 1st Lt. James R. *Redcatcher 199th Infantry Brigade Vietnam*. 199th Infantry Brigade Information Office.

Jett, Lt. Michael J. *Pictorial History of the 145th Combat Aviation Battalion "First in Vietnam": Volume II (June 1967-May 1968)*. 145th Combat Aviation Battalion Public Information Office. Tokyo: Dai Nippon Printing Co., Ltd.

Jones, SFC. Robert E. *Redcatcher Yearbook*. 199th Infantry Brigade Information Office. May 1969.

1969 The Year of Quiet Valor: Historical Summary, XXIV Corps. 31st Military History Detachment. June 1970.

Russill, Lt. George A. and Lt. James B. Channon. *The First Three Years: A Pictorial History of the 173d Airborne Brigade*. 173d Airborne Brigade. Tokyo: Dai Nippon Printing Co., Ltd.

Vaughan, Maj. W. Jr., *23rd Artillery Group Vietnam*. 23d Artillery Group. April 1969.

White, WO Jerry E. and WO Eric W. Gibson. 1965. *History of the 114th Aviation Company*. 114th Aviation Company.

II. Unpublished Sources

The majority of material for this book was compiled from original documents of the period.

The Unit Historical Data Branch, The Adjutant General Center, maintains the unit data cards (AGAZ Form 373) for selected TOE and TDA organizations covered in this volume. These unit cards contain essential data such as all stations (post if in the U.S., country if outside the U.S.), dates of assignment and abbreviated organizational notes — usually the TOE or TDA number. Unit awards (which this book does not cover since almost every unit in Vietnam was decorated in some manner to keep up morale) are entered on this card as well. These cards are classified in accordance with regulation and become declassified according to schedules contained therein. These cards are available on microfilm with entries through 1972.

The Organizational History Branch, U.S. Army Center of Military History, keeps historical reference files for all TOE units, but these are primarily concerned with unit lineage and awards. They contain little, if any, raw historical data such as dates in or out of Vietnam, commanders, etc. Unit redesignations, though covered by cross-indexing, also hamper convenient research of this source. Additionally, files are not maintained for either TDA or provisional units. Nevertheless, this proved to be a very useful source of general Vietnam credits which then could be tracked further in the actual unit records for details.

Department of the Army General Orders, 1961 – 1973, maintained throughout the U.S. at post level, announced awards and campaign credits for units. However, numerical misprints and other errors, as well as an absolute requirement to cross-check entries with subsequent changes (if posted), limited their usefulness.

The *U.S. Army Directory and Station List of the United States* (Washington, D.C.: United States Army, The Office of the Adjutant General) was issued bimonthly during this time frame. It is classified secret until downgraded by general declassification procedures. Arranged both by unit sequence and area of assignment, the listings contain title, limited description, place of assignment (often merely "Vietnam") and APO number. The reliability of these lists was limited by their dependence on computerized input, so that numerical errors were repeated indefinitely and some organizations weren't even picked up as serving in Vietnam. Often units that were programmed for Vietnam but never actually arrived there were picked up as being "in-country" and thus were carried for extended periods until the entries were corrected.

Strength of the Army, a monthly summarization by Headquarters, Department of the Army, Office of the Adjutant General, USA Data Services and Administrative Systems Command (Washington, D.C.) was consulted for the years 1961 – 1973.

The Reference File, Tables of Organization and Equipment (TOE), maintained by the Center of Military History, were also used. It must be remembered that each generic unit had its own TOE and most units in Vietnam operated under modification of the standard G and E series. All TOE series are indexed in DA Pamphlet 20-21.

The material used in this book came mostly out of the Vietnam-era retired operational records housed in the Washington National Records Center, Suitland, Maryland, by the General Archives, Division, National Archives and Records Service. Of these, the following record groups were used:

Record Group 338 (Vietnam War: MACV/USARV records)
Record Group 319 (Center of Military History)

Access to Vietnam-era records is obtained by contacting The Adjutant General Center Access and Release Branch (DAAG-AMR-S), Washington, D.C. These records contain the annual historical summaries, operational reports, and "Lessons Learned" analysis documents. The principal records used within these record groups are outlined below.

"Quarterly Operational Reports: Lessons Learned" (ORLL) were generally prepared by military history detachments in the field and other commands and cover major commands down to brigade level. The information includes missions, operations and organizational changes.

To supplement this basic information, the records groups also contain staff journals, files of major command general orders, combat operational interview reports, monthly summarizations and senior commander debriefing reports.

Of particular interest to this Order of Battle were the USARV Circular Number 210-2 (Installations) and USASCV Circular Number 210-1 (Station List). These periodic listings had the purpose of providing accurate and current information concerning the next higher headquarters, geographic location and servicing APO of activities down to and including company size and other selected units of the commands. These were essentially far more accurate than the published army-level lists, but still suffered from glaring locational errors as listings unfortunately depended on subordinate unit input for updating purposes. These were compiled masterfully by John Henry Hatcher, PhD, in the DA publication "United States Army Combat Units of the War in the Republic of Vietnam, 1966 – 1973, a Preliminary List (1 April 1979)."

One Department of Defense report issued on a monthly basis that provided much information was the *Army Build-up Progress Report,* which in 1969 changed its title to the *Army Activities Report: SE Asia.* (Both came under the Reports Control Symbol CSOCS-74 and are classifed subject to general declassification schedules). These contained a wealth of diverse statistics, including commanding officers of major units and good order-of-battle documentation. Weapons and troop status are also discussed in detail. For example, aircraft maintenance was usually highlighted with a myriad of charts and tables. This report, initiated in 1965, was discontinued in 1972.

Another extremely useful source was the *DEPSTAR* (Deploy-ment Status Army Units – Southeast Asia), a quarterly computerized report programmed to give the Joint Chiefs of Staff a detailed appraisal of army forces in Vietnam. Because of the sensitive nature of this report, it was usually painstakingly checked before issuance. Information contained therein included JCS requisition numbers, current planned close dates of units, unit descriptions and TOE identifications, *CTSTR* (current in-country authorized strengths), actual close dates and stations prior to Vietnam scheduling or entry. This report is also classified.

Other sources used in this research included the major command annual historical summaries, especially those for USARV, MACV, the 5th Special Forces Group (Airborne), USARPAC and CINCPAC. A paper prepared by the Military History Branch, Secretary Joint Staff, MACV, on 29 September 1972, "Chronology of Events Pertaining to US Involvement in the War in Vietnam and Southeast Asia," was also used.

Personnel records are not located at Suitland. They are in the National Personnel Records Center at St. Louis, Missouri. Key items of historical value are the daily morning reports (DA Form 1) showing the exact location of the reporting unit on a day-by-day basis by geographic location and grid map coordinates, casualties, changes of key personnel, effective strength and major events. Individual personnel records are restricted by the 1974 Privacy Act.

Information on the U.S. Marines came from *Marine Corps Bulletin 5750* (WestPac Deployment Charts for Marine Corps Units) and from further correspondence with the Headquarters, U.S. Marine Corps as noted in the acknowledgments.

U.S. Navy Seabee activity information was gleaned from the U.S. Pacific Fleet Detachment, Republic of Vietnam, Commander Naval Construction Battalions *Completion Report* covering the years 1963 – 1972 and the *NAVFAC Command History, 1965 – 1974.*

Foreign allies were found to be well documented within the U.S. military record groups, especially MACV and USARV histories. However, details on the Royal Australian Army were obtained from the Historical Studies and Information Section, Department of Defense (Army Office), in Canberra, Australia. The Military Historical Section of the Australian War Memorial (Canberra City) was also helpful.

Information for the listing of Medal of Honor recipients was taken from the 14 February 1979 edition of *Medal of Honor Recipients, 1863 – 1978* by the Committee on Veterans Affairs, U.S. Senate and updated by correspondence with the Army Awards and Decorations Branch in Arlington, Virginia.

Finally, casualty extracts were taken from a series of papers compiled by the Chief of Casualty Services Division, Department of the Army Adjutant General and put out by the OASD (Comptroller), Directorate of Information Operations.

Index